Global Population Health and Well-Being in the 21st Century

George R. Lueddeke, BA, OTC, MEd, PhD, is an educational advisor in higher and medical education residing in Southampton, UK Originally from Canada, he worked in both northern and southern communities as a teacher, educational developer, researcher, and national program consultant across a wide range of disciplines and professions. In the U.K., he has held posts such as founding director of Bradford University's Centre for Educational Development and senior lecturer in medical education at Southampton University's Faculty of Medicine. He was also a consultant education adviser on quality assurance with the Kent, Surrey and Sussex Postgraduate (KSS) Deanery in London.

Publishing widely on educational transformation, innovation, and leadership, his latest book, *Transforming Medical Education for the 21st Century: Megatrends, Priorities and Change,* now also translated into complex Chinese, complements and builds on the seminal *Lancet* Commission global report "Health Professionals for a New Century: Transforming Education to Strengthen Health Systems in an Interdependent World."

Invitations he has received as a keynote speaker/presenter include, among others, the UK General Medical Council (GMC, London); Universitas 21 UN Millennium Development Goal Workshops (UNMDG, Dublin); the Association of Schools of Public Health in the European Region (ASPHER, Brussels, Maastricht); the American Medical Association (AMA, Chicago); the Public Health Association of South Africa (PHASA, Polokwane); the European Public Health Association (EUPHA, Glasgow); the Catharina Pijls Lecture for the Annual Maastricht Symposium on Global and European Health (Maastricht University); the World Mental Health Association (WMHA, Athens); and the Faculty of Nursing (Chiang Mai University, Thailand) international conference on "Optimizing Healthcare Quality: Teamwork in Education, Research, and Practice."

He lives in the New Forest, England, with his wife Jill and family members.

Global Population Health and Well-Being in the 21st Century

Toward New Paradigms, Policy, and Practice

George R. Lueddeke, PhD

SPRINGER PUBLISHING COMPANY

NEW YORK

Springer Publishing Company, LLC
11 West 42nd Street
New York, NY 10036
www.springerpub.com

Acquisitions Editor: Sheri W. Sussman
Production Editor: Michael O'Connor
Composition: Exeter Premedia Services Private Ltd.

ISBN: 978-0-8261-2767-9
e-book ISBN: 978-0-8261-2768-6

Online ancillary materials are available for download from www.springerpub.com/lueddeke

Research Tools: 978-0-8261-3202-4
Learning Objectives: 978-0-8261-3203-1

15 16 17 18 19 / 5 4 3 2 1

The author and the publisher of this Work have made every effort to use sources believed to be reliable to provide information that is accurate and compatible with the standards generally accepted at the time of publication. The author and publisher shall not be liable for any special, consequential, or exemplary damages resulting, in whole or in part, from the readers' use of, or reliance on, the information contained in this book. The publisher has no responsibility for the persistence or accuracy of URLs for external or third-party Internet websites referred to in this publication and does not guarantee that any content on such websites is, or will remain, accurate or appropriate.

Library of Congress Cataloging-in-Publication Data
Lueddeke, George R., author.
Global population health and well-being in the 21st century : toward new paradigms, policy, and practice / George R. Lueddeke.
    p. ; cm.
Includes bibliographical references and index.
ISBN 978-0-8261-2767-9
I. Title.
[DNLM: 1. Global Health.   2. Public Health.   3. Health Policy.   4. Public Health Practice.   WA 100]
RA441
362.1–dc23
2015010164

Printed in the United States of America by Bradford & Bigelow.

For Ulrich Laaser and Vesna Bjegovic- Mikanovic—their leadership; book contributors—their time and commitment; and my spouse, Jill, family members, friends, and colleagues—their encouragement. Thank you.

Never doubt that a small group of thoughtful,
committed citizens can change the world.
Indeed, it is the only thing that ever has.

Margaret Mead (1901–1978)
Anthropologist

Contents

Foreword

This is a remarkable, much-needed book that fills a significant gap in the health and social care literature in the early decades of the 21st century—public, global, clinical, and ecological. It is powerful, ambitious, comprehensive, and sweeping at the same time that it is visionary, focused, and deep. Its power and passion are about the potential of population health and well-being optimally applied around the globe to help in creating a world that is healthier, safer, more just, and more sustainable.

The book is written for a wide-ranging readership. One of the main reasons for this broad audience is that striving toward planetary and population health and well-being must be one of the top priorities of this century. This work affirms this stance.

WHY NOW?

The world is facing an "ingenuity gap." After thousands of years of human evolution, we seem to have arrived at a turning point, where the problems we face—social, political, and economic—seem greater than our capacity to resolve them, where, as one example, the technology we possess could advance civilization or, in an instant, make us extinct.

The chapters of this far-reaching, evidence-based, highly readable, and authoritative work put into stark contrast the differences between the "have" and "have-not" countries, while reminding us of our global interconnections. In the West and North, we now realize more than ever before in human history that although an epidemic may be thousands of miles from where we live, it is also only a plane ride away. Fundamentally, George R. Lueddeke alerts us to the growing recognition that, of the 7.2 billion people on the planet, only about one fifth reap the benefits of the modern world. Thus, there is an increasing urgency of grappling, as examples, with health and income inequality, along with access to food, water, and sanitation for billions of people, many of whom live in extreme poverty and in fear.

And while developing countries have special, urgent needs, so do middle- and high-income nations that also have serious challenges—stemming arguably in some measure from modernity, fragile economies, and uncertainties about the future, including the consequences of climate change; pandemics of noncommunicable conditions and diseases, like obesity, diabetes, heart disease, and cancer; and infectious diseases, including emerging ones.

TOWARD THE "WORLD WE WANT"

Substantive consideration is given to the United Nations (UN) Millennium Development Goals (MDGs) and post-2015 Sustainable Development Goals (SDGs), along with the World Bank's priorities to 2030. A hallmark of these discussions is the recommendation for the UN and other decision makers to adopt an integrated, Sustainable Development Goals framework. The framework could facilitate, the author posits, the movement toward universal health care (UHC), which is inclusive, unifies services, and delivers them in a comprehensive, integrated way based on primary health care. WHO Director-General Margaret Chan has identified UHC as "the" most important public health priority.

Current health statistics highlight that many public health measures, based largely on 20th-century assumptions about health and well-being, have had limited success. Dr. Lueddeke traces the reasons for slow progress, including the constraints of conventional health care measures and the need to reconcile health-funding expenditures. Most of these expenditures are presently allocated to acute illnesses with hospital dominance, while most deaths (close to 70%) and morbidities worldwide now are caused by noncommunicable diseases (many, diseases of affluence) and chronic illnesses, related to a large degree to an aging population—both, however, likely best treated in family or community contexts. The way forward, he asserts, is to create and adopt a new vision of public health, one that embraces, among other elements, the recognition of the impact of social determinants of health and the need for interprofessional health care approaches, applying "fifth" wave (complex, adaptive) thinking, while working closely with "struggling" communities and addressing inequities in health. It is through these transformations that we will create effective, sustainable public health interventions that promote wellness instead of sickness, hope instead of despair, and connectedness and collaboration instead of competition.

The author emphasizes the need to shift toward a holistic view of public health, not separate from health and primary care, built on sustainable partnerships that are grounded in a recognition of "One Health." The One Health concept and approach advocate two fundamental truths: that the environment and animal and human health are inextricably interconnected and that all actions have consequences. A biopsychosocial, ecological model is the appropriate foundation because it takes into account the many health and nonhealth influences on health, including those that are volitional and those that are outside one's control, and those that are changeable and those that are immutable.

The myriad challenges facing us demand a dramatic change in how we prepare our health and social care workforce. The author's vision and practical guidance are consistent with recommendations of the seminal *Lancet* Commission report that emphasizes improving "the performance of health systems by adapting core professional competencies to specific contexts while drawing on global knowledge." Transformative learning and interdependence in education call for major shifts in the educational process, including, inter alia, moving "from fact memorization to searching . . . adopting competency-driven approaches to instructional design and adapting these to rapidly changing local conditions drawing on global resources," promoting active and collaborative learning (versus learning in silos), as well as taking full advantage of new digital technologies. Our education must be lifelong and not sequestered into a small window in one's lifetime. The implications for faculty and educational development are considerable, but need to be robustly pursued to make a fundamental difference to local, national, and global health and well-being in this decade and beyond.

A FINAL COMMENT

The vision of public health contained in this volume has many strengths. Particularly noteworthy is a timely recognition of the One Health concept, which highlights that the health of humans is intimately connected to the health of animals and the environment; another forte is about individuals *and* populations, a shift in thinking about public health—and a good one. For too long, public health was framed as focused on communities without attention to individuals. There is no contradiction here. What are populations but people? We are all in this together!

Barbara K. Rimer, DrPH, Dean
Alumni Distinguished Professor
UNC Gillings School of Global Public Health
Chapel Hill, North Carolina, United States

Preface

The history of modern *Homo sapiens*—us!—is short, although our tiny, fragile planet is billions of years old—about 4.56 billion years to be more exact—and the universe is even older, estimated at 13.8 billion years, expanding from "an unimaginably hot, dense point a billionth of the size of a nuclear particle" (1). While we have been evolving for millions of years, the journey of modern *Homo sapiens* (Latin for "wise man") dates to about 200,000 years ago in East Africa, then spilling out into the rest of the world, and culminating in our becoming "anatomically human" at least 100,000 years ago and more "behaviourally human" perhaps 40,000 to 50,000 years ago. However, in line with the European archaeological record, it is "only over the last 20,000 years," that "we consistently see the usual archaeological signatures of behavioural modernity: broad-range foraging; environmental management; technological innovation; and obvious symbolic culture" (2).

The story of more scientific approaches to caring for the sick is even more punctuated. Indeed, it was not until the 1940s—roughly 70 years ago—that we were able to treat infections with antibiotics. Since that time—especially in the last 60 years or so—our technological progress has been immense.

In the past few decades, we have seen many changes triggered, to a large extent, by the genomic revolution, including pharmacogenomics, nutrigenomics, molecular diagnostics, regenerative medicine, and designer vaccines, to name several areas (3,4). In addition, there have been enormous changes in communications and data management technology, thereby offering new opportunities for data collection, analysis, and dissemination, as well as advancing distance medicine.

Regrettably, however, throughout history—and continuing to this day—the same cannot be said for our social or humanitarian advances, despite a global framework enshrined in the 1948 "Universal Declaration of Human Rights" (5) and subsequent covenants (6).

More specifically, while we have been able to map the human genome and make huge strides in life expectancy—mostly in the more developed nations—and medicine generally, we fall short when it comes to realizing the "well-being," psychological, economic, social, and physical, or simply "life satisfaction," of most of the planet's population, now exceeding over 7.3 billion people. Globally, there are a few rich, but far too many are still living in poverty—economic, social, and aspirational—and in fear.

We seem to be facing what some writers have called an "ingenuity gap," that is, the incapacity of tackling many of the global problems relating to health inequities and inequalities, many of which appear to be the result of "unequal distribution of power, money and resources" (7). Other health risks stem from modern lifestyles or "modernity," bolstered by "prevailing norms and practices" that can "exert illegitimate or undemocratic influence in global health processes" (7). In fact, it may be argued that current health epidemics—for example, obesity and associated diseases; environmental threats, such as climate change; and ongoing "people" conflicts, often resulting from self-interest, corruption, differing ideologies, lust for power, and control—may seriously hamper the long-term survival of our—and perhaps other—species. Indeed, we might expect that images of the vast cosmos and classics like Carl Sagan's *The Pale Blue Dot: A Vision of the Human Future in Space* (8) would put everything into perspective for most decision makers but, bafflingly, they do not.

Taken together, it seems timely to reflect on the state of the human condition and consider options that call for a change in mindset with regard to improving and sustaining the health and well-being of the planet and its people.

Public or population health, which is at the core of societal wellness and cuts across all fields of human endeavor—energy, agriculture, urban planning, and transportation, to name but a few sectors—arguably needs to be at the forefront of essential global transformations in order to help people to stay healthy and to protect them from threats to their health.

This book builds on *Transforming Medical Education for the 21st Century: Megatrends, Priorities and Change* (9), which complements the findings of the global *Lancet* Commission report on transforming education for health professionals (10). The Commission report has been a catalyst—not unlike the groundbreaking Abraham Flexner medical education report in 1910 (11)—for stimulating efforts to advance the education and training of health professionals worldwide. Most recently, *The Lancet* report contributed to the WHO guidelines for transforming and scaling up the education of health professionals (12).

With its focus on public/population/global health, the book draws on current literature as well as the knowledge and experience of experts from around the world. It has seven broad aims:

- To raise awareness about and inform the discussion on contemporary challenges related to population health and well-being
- To suggest ways of tackling some of the unprecedented global health issues
- To assist in positioning public health globally "as a force for social change" (13) and a catalyst for the development of a new "worldview"
- To share insights from individuals and practitioners across the globe in terms of health concerns or priorities and strategies for responding to these now and in the years ahead
- To advocate better understanding of the complex interdependence of natural, socioeconomic, and political systems at local, national, regional, and global levels

- To help transform public and global health education and learning in line with changing societal needs through the application of innovative pedagogical approaches and the provision of contemporary research tools and learning resources (see online ancillary materials "Public Health Research Tools and Learning Resources" and "Educational Objectives")
- To help raise awareness of and support for the implementation of the UN Sustainable Development Goals (SDGs) (2016–2030)

In the light of these aims, the book's primary audience includes public and global health academics and students, health professionals, health services managers, and policy makers across social, economic, and political sectors from developed, developing, and underdeveloped nations and regions. It is also meant for staff involved with national and international population health and humanitarian initiatives and individuals from non-governmental and community-based organizations. Its wide-ranging content—addressing, inter alia, problems caused by "modernity," namely the obesity epidemic, aging society, urbanization, mental health, poverty, social intolerances—could also help to inform the public at large.

Note: Online ancillary materials "Public Health Research Tools and Learning Resources" and "Educational Objectives" are available for download from www .springerpub.com/lueddeke

REFERENCES

1. Bhattacharjee Y. Cosmic dawn. *National Geographic.* 2014;225(4):77–85. http://www.nationalgeographic.com/cosmic-dawn/. Accessed June 20, 2014.
2. Sterelny K. From hominins to humans: How sapiens became behaviourally modern. *Philos Trans R Soc ond B Biol Sci.* 2011;366(1566):809–822. http://rstb.royalsocietypublishing.org/content/366/1566/809.full. Accessed October 20, 2013.
3. Schimpff SC. *The future of medicine: Megatrends in healthcare that will improve your quality of life.* Nashville, TN: Thomas Nelson; 2007.
4. Brücher B, Lyman G, van Hillegersbery R, et al. Imagine a world without cancer. *BMC Cancer.* 2014;14:186. http://www.biomedcentral.com/content/pdf/1471-2407-14-186.pdf
5. UN General Assembly. *The universal declaration of human rights.* Paris: United Nations; 1948. http://www.un.org/en/documents/udhr/. Accessed May 13, 2013.
6. United Nations Human Rights. *International covenant on civil and political rights.* New York, NY: United Nations, 1966. http://www.ohchr.org/en/professionalinterest/pages/ccpr.aspx. Accessed May 18, 2013.
7. Commission on Social Determinants of Health. *Closing the gap in a generation: Health equity through action on the social determinants of health. Final report of the Commission on Social Determinants of Health.* Geneva: World Health Organization; 2008.
8. Sagan C. *The pale blue dot: A vision of the human future in space.* 1st ed. New York, NY: Ballantine Books; 1997.
9. Lueddeke G. *Transforming medical education for the 21 century: Megatrends, priorities and change.* London: Radcliffe Publishing; 2012.
10. Frenk J, Chen L, Bhutta ZA, et al. Health professions for a new century: Transforming education to strengthen health systems in an interdependent world. *The Lancet.* 2010;376(9756):1923–1958.

11. Bonner TN. *Iconoclast: Abraham Flexner and a life in learning.* Baltimore, MD: The Johns Hopkins University Press; 2002.

12. World Health Organization. *Transformative education for health professionals.* http://whoeducationguidelines.org/. Accessed March 16, 2014.

13. Joy B. *Why the future doesn't need us.* http://archive.wired.com/wired/archive/8.04/joy.html. Accessed December 20, 2011.

Acknowledgments

My sincere gratitude is extended to Professor of Medicine Ulrich Laaser, past president of the World Federation of Public Health Associations (WFPHA), for encouraging and contributing to this work. His dedication and the commitment of Professor Vesna Bjegovic-Mikanovic, president of ASPHER, have been exceptional and much appreciated.

I am indebted to Professor Barbara Rimer, dean of the University of North Carolina (UNC) Gillings Global School of Public Health in the United States for writing the Foreword to this publication.

The enthusiasm and guidance (and patience) of my editor, Sheri W. Sussman, and Alina Yurova, associate editor, along with their colleagues at Springer Publishing Company, have been facilitative in turning multifaceted ideas and images on population health and well-being into a readable volume. I also thank Katrina Lueddeke for her valuable support throughout the writing of the manuscript.

Many people have contributed to the development of this work, including those who helped develop the book's structure and content, reviewed chapters or sections, and supplied text for some of the chapters (also acknowledged in respective chapters):

Deborah Allen (USA), Russell Ampofo (UK), Leonel Arguello (Nicaragua), Rebecca Bagette (USA), Lamine Bal (USA), Meredith Barrett (USA), Francisco Becerra-Posada (Mexico), David Benton (Switzerland), Peter Berman (USA), Janine Bezuidenhoud (South Africa), Tom Bigg (Australia), Tewabech Bishaw (South Africa), Colin Bloom (USA), Nicole Bodnar (Canada), Brea Bondi-Boyd (Cuba), Carmel Bouclaous (Lebanon), Helmut Brand (Netherlands), Kevin Buckett (Australia), Maxine Builder (USA), Gro Bundland (Norway), Genc Burazeri (Netherlands), James Campbell (UK), Sara Carr (UK), Lincoln Chen (USA), Sadia Chowdhury (Bangaldesh), Jonathan Chung (USA), Michael Coplan (USA), Loren Cordain (USA), Marcus Cueta (Peru), Patricia Cuff (USA), Ron de Have (USA), Courtney Dusenbury (USA), Gilles Dussault (Portugal), Timothy Evans (USA), Sharon Fonn (South Africa), Jennifer Foskett (USA), Elizabeth French (USA), Julio Frenk (USA), Luiz Augusto Galvão (Mexico), Niloy Ganguly (India), Karen Gardner (USA), Bill Genat (Australia), Tobias Gerber (Germany), Annette Gerritsen (South Africa), Rita Giacaman (Palestine), Andrew Giambrove (USA), Karen Goodwin (UK), David Gordon (UK), Lawrence Gostin (USA), David Griggs (Australia), Fiona Hack (Canada), Alex Hakuzimana (Belgium), Sophie Hall (UK), Phil Hanlon (UK), Joerg

Heldmann (Germany), Ann Hemingway (UK), Stephen Hendricks (South Africa), Zsuzsa Horvath (Denmark), Markéta Houšková (Czechoslovakia), Amanda Howe (UK), Lesley Hughes (UK), Samer Jabbour (Lebanon), Hans Jacobs (Germany), Peter Jacobson (USA), Hilliard Jason (USA), Jonathan Jay (USA), Laura Kahn (USA), Bruce Kaplan (USA), Rajendra Karkee (Nepal), Sylvia Karpagam (India), Sharada Keats (UK), Patrick Kelley (USA), Janko Kersnik (Slovenia), Ilona Kickbusch (Switzerland), Keeley Knowles (UK), Jeffrey Koplan (USA), Glenn Laverack (Denmark), Pamela Lee (USA), Ingrid Leijs (Netherlands), Sanna Leppamaki (Finland), Joann Lindenmayer (USA), Stefan Lindgren (Sweden), Bjorn Lombors (Denmark), Christina LoNigro (USA), Akiko Maeda (Switzerland), Garth Manning (Thailand), Jose Martin-Moreno (Spain), Zoltan Massay-Kosubes (Hungary), Roland Mathiasson (Denmark), Natalie Mayet (South Africa), Yata Mboup-Kande (USA), Richard McLellan (Switzerland), Catherine Michaud (USA), Christina Mills (Canada), Robert Moodie (Australia), Julia Moorman (South Africa), Laura Morlock (USA), Devaki Nambian (India), Shan Naidoo (South Africa), Anders Nattestad (USA), David Nelson (USA), André-Jacques Neusy (Belgium), Terry Nolan (Australia), Anders Nordstrom (Norway), Joanna Nurse (UK), Onora O'Neill (UK), Gorik Ooms (Belgium), Robert Otok (Belgium), Gerald Paccione (USA), Dineke Paget (Netherlands), Claudia Pagliari (UK), Pinaki Panigrahi (India), Mark Pearson (Switzerland), Puska Pekka (Finland), Nicki Pender (UK), Donna Petersen (USA), Melody Petersen (USA), Ole Peterson (Norway), Meng Qingyue (China), Simon Rabkin (Canada), Julie Rafferty (USA), Sisodia Rajendra (USA), Sabina Rashid (Bangladesh), Srinath Reddy (India), Helena Ribeiro (Brazil), Javier Rivera (Belgium), Breiman Roberts (USA), Niels Rygaard (Denmark), Wendy Santis (USA), Rolf Sattler (Canada), Flavia Senkenbuge (South Africa), Ruchira Sharma (India), Gaudenz Silberschmidt (Switzerland), Ian Smith (Switzerland), Christine Sow (USA), Roger Strasser (Canada), Cheryl Stroud (USA), Charles Surjadi (Indonesia), Julia Tainijoki-Seyer (Switzerland), Fraser Tennant (UK), Ellen 'tHoen (Netherlands), Ted Tulchinsky (Israel), Jon Thomas (USA), Jeff Waage (UK), Joanne Walker (Australia), David Waltner-Toews (Canada), Erica Wheeler (Switzerland), Steve Wiggins (UK), Suzanne Wingate (USA), Amanda Yohn (USA), Sanjay Zodpey (India).

I am also extremely thankful to contributors of the organizational profiles: Appendix A1, "Profiles of Leading Global, Regional, and National Health Organizations" (page 356); and Appendix A2, "Profiles of Leading Schools/Institutes of Public Health" (page 428).

I also express my personal gratitude to those engaged in developing brief descriptions for Appendix B (pages 453–458): "Think Tank on Global Health, Governance, and Education."

Moreover, the writing teams from the Netherlands, the United States, and Brazil, who developed the accompanying digital education supplement for the book entitled *Facilitator's Guide to Educational Objectives and Public Health Research Tools & Learning Resources* are heartily thanked for their commitment and support: Professors Barbara Rimer and Suzanne Babich, UNC Gillings School of Global Public Health, United States; Professor Katarzyna Czabanowska and Dr. Daniela Popa, School of Public Health and Primary Care, Maastricht University, The Netherlands; Dr. Eliudi

Eliakimu, Ministry of Social Welfare, Tanzania; Professors Helena Ribeiro and Gabriela Marques di Giulio, School of Public Health, University of São Paulo; Dr. Bruce Kaplan and Dr. Laura Kahn, global One Health Initiative (USA); Dr. Cheryl Stroud, executive director, and Dr. Deeanna Burleson, associate executive director, U.S. One Health Commission.

For providing copyright permission to reproduce images or cite text, appreciation is extended to the following organizations:

WHO; Worldmapper SASI Group (University of Sheffield) and Mark Newman (University of Michigan); UN Population Division; United Nations Human Settlements Programme (UN-Habitat); National Geographic; National Climate Assessment, U.S. Global Change Research Program; NOAA National Climatic Data Center; Overseas Development Institute; UN Food and Agricultural Organization; UN Women; UNICEF; Centers for Disease Control and Prevention; Ipsos; Organisation for Economic Co-operation and Development (OECD); *British Medical Journal (BMJ)*; World Bank; MiniWatts Marketing Group; *The Telegraph*; Gapminder; World Economic Forum; Northern Ontario School of Medicine; National Health Service (NHS); Care Pathways; Centres for Medicare & Medicaid Services; Universitas 21; Independent Research Forum; Springer Publishing; *The Lancet* Commission; *The Times*; World Public Health Nutrition Association; SOS Children's Villages; Institute of Sustainable Development; The King's Fund; Albert Einstein College of Medicine; Harvard School of Public Health; One Health Initiative; *Frontiers in Ecology*; Worldometers; Public Health Canada; Association of Schools of Public Health in the European Region; Public Health Foundation of India; Faculty of Public Health (England); Johns Hopkins Bloomington School of Public Health; Council on Linkages; Josiah Macy Jr. Foundation; *MEDICC Review*; The Taskforce for Global Health; WFPHA; Global Health Workforce Alliance; World Wildlife Fund; and National Aeronautics and Space Administration (NASA).

Appreciation is extended to the following for their permission to reference the work of these organizations listed in Appendix C:

The Medical Education Partnership Initiative (MEPI): Dr. Robert Glass, Director; Kathleen Stover, Staff Assistant; and Ann Puderbaugh, Communications Director at the Fogarty International Center at the U.S. National Institutes of Health.

Global Forum on Innovation in Health Professional Education: Dr. Patrick Kelley, Director, Boards on Global Health and African Science Academy Development, and Patricia Cuff, Senior Program Officer, Institute of Medicine.

The Training for Health Equity Network (THEnet): Professor Andre-Jacques Neusy, CEO, and Bjorg Palsdottir, MPA Executive Director, co-founder of THEnet.

Introduction: Inspiring a New Vision

Several years ago, William Joy, American computer scientist, showed considerable foresight when he said, "if we could agree, as a species, what we wanted, where we are headed, and why, then we would make our future much less dangerous—then we might understand what we can and should relinquish" (1).

Realizing his vision seems to be even more remote today—but at the same time more urgent—when we are faced with "life threatening problems common to all of us, such as global warming, global divides (demographic, economic and social inequity) and global security" (2). In their paper, "Threats to Global Health and Opportunities for Change: A New Global Health," Professors Ulrich Laaser and Leon Epstein insist that "these concerns are closely interconnected . . . all too often resulting in poverty and hunger, and impeding the health of entire populations." A major step forward in this century, they contend, depends on departing "from the Old Thinking of the 20th century still concerned with diplomatic, economic and military power play and to face real challenges," including "unchecked demographic growth, poverty, the burden of disease, and violent conflicts."

While there is evidence globally for positive health outcomes, including progress in supporting women's and children's health, poverty alleviation, and HIV antiretroviral therapy (3), the present trajectory on which we are traveling is cause for concern and reflection. World Health Organization (WHO) Secretary-General Dr. Chan affirmed the fragility of life across the globe at a recent World Health Assembly in Geneva:

> We are living in deeply troubled times. These are times of financial insecurity, food insecurity, job insecurity, political insecurity, a changing climate, and a degraded environment that is asked to support more than it can bear. These are times of armed conflict, hostile threats among nations, acts of terrorism and mass violence, and violence against women and children. Large numbers of people are living on edge, fearing for their lives. Insecurity and conflict mar several parts of the world, endangering the health of large populations.

In the introduction to a 75th anniversary paper on the Welch–Rose report (1915), demanding the need for training of public health workers in the United States, Professor Alfred Summer, then dean of the Johns Hopkins University School of Hygiene and Public Health (now The Bloomberg School of Public Health), observed that the report "remains refreshingly current" (4). Moreover, he concluded that two issues remain unresolved: "the distinction between 'maintenance of health' and 'cure of disease,'" while the second relates to "our widespread failure to gain understanding of (and support for) what Public Health 'professionals' do."

Viewed historically, medical researchers (5) have concluded that public health was "sidelined 'as a lower priority'" in the 20th century, as attention focused from poor living conditions and major epidemics in the 19th century (especially in the 1850s)—including outbreaks of cholera, dysentery, tuberculosis, typhoid fever, influenza, yellow fever, malaria, and smallpox—to clinical medicine" (6) and "national provision of national health insurance or national health services" (5). Although these diseases are still a matter of considerable urgency for policy makers, especially in the developing, underdeveloped, or poor nations, throughout the 20th century, in richer countries, "strategic vaccination campaigns," antibiotics, and other antimicrobial medicines along with technological advances "virtually eliminated diseases that previously were common" (5).

Dr. Francisco Becerra, assistant director of the Pan American Health Organization/World Health Organization (PAHO/WHO), opines that achieving these aims, as was the case "in the Region of the Americas, which has poor and rich countries, and the first to achieve polio and other vaccine preventable diseases," is "a matter of having a good strategy, political will and funds." Furthermore, he asserts "we need to learn lessons from both positive and negative experiences and replicate those that hold the greatest potential" (7).

The overarching premise of this book is quite straightforward—although the proposed changes are not: In terms of enhancing global health and well-being, it is argued that we need to learn to think and act differently in the richer, middle-income, and poorer countries. Realizing what is at stake requires greater awareness of public health issues facing us in this century, new conceptualizations of public health and others' roles and responsibilities, and more aligned and creative approaches to education and training (8,9), underpinned, fundamentally, by "improved global governance across all sectors" (10).

This view is reinforced in this book's transnational epilogue on "Global Health, Governance, and Education." The importance of intersectionality in addressing public health issues is also informed by the contributors to this book. As one example, Dr. Eliudi Eliakimu, who is with the Ministry of Health and Social Welfare in Tanzania, reminds us that much more attention must be given to taking "a human rights-based approach to global health, in particular in matters relating to security, disasters and emergencies," and the "human impact of war and conflicts generally" (11). The crucial need for interdisciplinarity in dealing with today's complex and increasingly uncertain health and social issues is very much at the heart of *The Lancet*–University of Oslo Commission on Global Governance for Health report (10), cited previously. According to Professor Ole Petter Ottersen, Rector of Oslo University, who chaired the commission, the commissioners were "overwhelmed by the need to bring into the picture expertise from so widely different arenas as law, economics, political science, and cultural and political history" (12). Moreover, "all of these disciplines," he notes, "had to be drawn upon for us to better understand how the post-war development of supranational governance mechanisms has failed to appropriately take into account the need for health equity." In addition, Professor Ottersen observes, "this realization had a strong impact on our reflections upon contemporary educational systems, where the leaders of tomorrow will have to grapple with this complexity." Above all, he says,

> they will have to recognize the human face behind the graphs that measure economic development of nations—in crises and in times of austerity. They will have to identify the sad impacts on health of conflicts or irregular migration. In brief: they will have to see the full picture—the entanglement of health with policies in all other sectors. It is this coupling between social, environmental and economic sustainability that we have to bring to the fore in the post 2015 agenda. (12)

The Commission's longer term aspiration, which resonates meaningfully with Chapter 7.0, "Toward a New Worldview," is "an expression of a shared vision, an emerging global social norm: that the global economic system should serve a global population of healthy people in sustainable societies, within the boundaries of nature" (10).

Reaching this universal ideal in this century will not be an easy road to tread and requires, as two examples, rethinking of "social resources" and reducing global "inequalities in daily living conditions" (10). In this regard, one of the most serious challenges facing public health worldwide is responding to the threats posed by the exponential rise of noncommunicable diseases (NCDs) or conditions—for example, obesity and diabetes, cardiovascular diseases, and cancers—and chronic illnesses due to an aging population along with high consumption of sugar, fatty food, and salt. While communicable diseases are still a major problem in poor nations, NCDs are emerging as the main causes of death globally, along with unsustainable costs, estimated "over the next 20 years," at "more than US$30 trillion, representing 48 percent of global GDP in 2010, and pushing millions of people below the poverty line" (13).

Of these, on being elected president of the World Heart Federation in 2013, Professor K. Srinath Reddy concludes:

> Cardiovascular diseases are collectively the leading cause of death across the world and are increasing at an alarming rate in low- and middle-income countries. This global threat requires a global thrust to counter and contain it. Efforts are needed to protect populations from acquiring heart disease and to provide timely, effective and affordable care to individuals who have developed disease. The ambit of heart health must extend from the hub of global policy to the throb of a person's pulse. From tobacco control to promotion of healthy diets and physical activity, national and global policies must encourage and enable people to practice healthy habits. Health services should enable risk reduction and cost-effective management of disease at all levels of health care. The World Heart Federation will catalyse these policies at the global level and assist national efforts through capacity building and collaborative research. (14)

Finding effective and sustainable responses to these health and social care concerns ("wicked" problems, as they have been called) is proving difficult as many are created by modernity or are population-based, are "highly resistant to resolution with many interdependencies and are often multi-causal in origin" (15). However, according to WHO Director-General Dr. Chan, "getting people to lead healthy lifestyles and adopt healthy behaviors faces opposition from forces that are not so friendly. Not at all" (16). For Dr. Chan, it is clear that "efforts to prevent noncommunicable diseases go against the business interests of powerful economic operators . . . one of the biggest challenges facing health promotion." In today's world, she contends, "it is not just Big Tobacco anymore. Public health must also contend with Big Food, Big Soda, and Big Alcohol. All of these industries fear regulation, and protect themselves by using the same tactics."

Without question, a vital dimension in moving forward with regard to global health issues lies, as both Professor Ottersen and Professor Reddy point out, with the involvement of multisectoral partners, exemplified, for example, by the Health Literacy Study-Asia (HLS-Asia) project (17).

Patterned after a similar international study, the European Health Literacy Survey (HLS-EU) (18), the project, coordinated by Professor Peter Chang, dean of the International Office of Taipei Medical University, has been carried out between 2013 and 2015 across more than 15 countries in Asia: Brunei, Cambodia, India, Indonesia, Japan, Kazakhstan, Laos, Malaysia, Myanmar, Pakistan, Singapore, South Korea, Taiwan, Thailand, and Vietnam (19).

The project aims to measure health literacy levels across Asia and to provide an overview of the health literacy status in Asia. More particularly,

> the study involves close collaboration between universities, research institutions and ministries across Asia. Not only will the current state of health literacy in identified countries be evaluated but the health services and healthcare deliveries will be compared. Social and cultural determinants as well as measures to enhance the health service capacities in each country will also be considered. (19)

The results will likely impact on the structure and provision of future health care services across Asia. Dr. Chan asserts that transformations in how we deliver health care services call "for nothing less than a radical change in mindset, a fundamental rethinking of the way health systems deliver services and maintain good health outcomes" (30).

This restructuring also necessitates changing societal expectations of health care delivery systems; integration and streamlining of hospital specialization and services; transferring considerably more care and resources into the community; placing more personal responsibility on individuals for their own health and wellness; and improving coordination as well as communication between health and social care support (8).

In essence, while recognizing the urgent need to tackle global health inequities through political action and strengthening global governance processes (9,10), it is also becoming apparent that there is a parallel issue that needs surfacing.

The case being put forward in this book is that governments, regulators, associations, health professionals, or practitioners need to consider making a basic paradigm shift, that is, espousing a global social norm that moves away from a disease-driven or curative model of health care (provision of a "sickness" service), largely underpinned by 20th century biomedical assumptions about illness, to one that is population-centered, community-driven, and advocates disease or illness prevention and health promotion (provision of a "wellness" service) through the adoption of a biopsychosocial model of health (21). Interestingly, the need to transition (or return) to a more holistic care model is rooted historically in the deeper philosophies of healing and caring of individuals promoted more than 2,500 years ago by Hippocrates and other ancient Greek physicians! Although improving governance is justifiably vital across the globe, valuing, respecting, and providing for the physical, social, and emotional needs of all people must be the centerpiece of this quest.

To realize this transformation, public health professionals may need to increasingly bolster their collaboration with struggling communities and, in particular, primary care practitioners (22), ideally guided by the Adelaide Declaration and the "Health in All Policies" (HiAP) (23) approach, discussed in Chapter 5.0, to pave the way in making these core transitions in developed, emerging, and developing economies.

Considered collectively, systemic developments in public health will demand a radical reconceptualization and restructuring of professional public and clinical health education curricula (8,9). Innovations for health professions education include:

- Aligning education outcomes with the changing needs of the health/social care systems
- Evolving new models of public/clinical health education, including the integration of interprofessional learning
- Incorporating new educational and information technologies with a view to improving safety and efficiency
- Developing "the next generation of leaders and innovators in Health Professionals' Education" (24)

These educational innovations are made all the more urgent as, according to Dr. George Thibault, president of the Josiah Macy Jr. Foundation, an organization in the United States dedicated to improving the health of the public, "we will not have enduring healthcare delivery reform without changes in the preparation of health professionals" (24).

Today in an interconnected and interdependent world, where the former "describes the nature of health threats and effects" and the latter "refers to the distribution of power, responsibility, and capacity to respond" (25), "we need a shift in awareness towards the idea of building global public goods," or as German philosopher Immanuel Kant posited in the 18th century "man must develop this tendency towards *the good*" (26). This reconceptualization or reorientation "can help us reap the huge potential benefits of globalization while at the same time containing the risks and vulnerabilities that come with it. The main question is one of taking responsibility, of using our democracies to promote change" (27).

Professor John Ashton, president of the Faculty of Public Health in the United Kingdom, advises that an essential requisite for public health is "to get the values right and to build strong capacity for public health leadership to pursue a national, regional and global vision" (28,29). This vision can be augmented by incorporating the notion of "reciprocal maintenance" allied to sustainability. In other words, fundamentally, "public health is about how well we are able to lead our lives" —that is, at all societal levels we need to "look after the things that look after us, whether that is the earth that sustains us, security, prosperity, freedom or personal relationships."

Surely, a "global public good" that goes beyond self-interest, craving for power, or social fragmentation and is founded on "a shared commitment to health . . . as a human right based on a recognition of our common humanity" (25), deserves to be placed at the top of all transnational agendas. The survival of our planet and our species may depend on it.

Dr. Richard Horton, editor-in-chief of *The Lancet*, alleges that a key "determinant of sustainability is the *strength of our civilizations*—their solidarity and wealth, their degrees of inequality and corruption, their susceptibility to conflict, and the quality of their deliberative institutions." In terms of ongoing discussions relating to the United Nations post-2015 Sustainable Development Goals (SDGs) agenda, he maintains that "unless we embrace and measure the full meaning of sustainability, the SDGs will fail. None of us, and certainly not our children, can afford that failure" (30).

This century may be the last that we have to rebalance or harmonize global threats and inequities, in particular addressing climate change and the unsustainability of only a fifth of the world's population reaping the benefits of the world's dwindling resources and basic goods—health, education, peace, and security, to name but a few.

Our key challenge is to build an enduring future, which necessitates moving away from a societal stance that conceptualizes "the world as a place made especially for humans and a place without limits: our task is to subdue and exploit the earth" to a new worldview, which is "compatible not only with our needs as human beings" but also "an outer world that is compatible with the needs of our ecosystem" (15).

The One Health philosophy—discussed later in this book—embraces the need for this fundamental shift and provides a complex and difficult path to the much-needed global transformation in thinking and acting that needs to take place in this century. In essence, the approach, according to Dr. Joann Lindenmayer, chair of the U.S. One Health Commission Board of Directors, focuses on

> the shared health (the overlap) of people, animals and the environment, whether that be for prevention of control of infectious, including zoonotic disease, but also chronic disease, the built environment, antimicrobial resistance, violence/welfare, and many other areas that involve all three "healths." (31)

"That application of the definition," she emphasizes, "is inclusive of not only public health professionals, but also physicians, veterinarians, environmental health specialists and experts in the social sciences."

Finally, perhaps it is through the innocent yet determined eyes of the younger generation that we may come closest to safeguarding the "strength of our civilizations" (30), including "hope and change for reconciliation" among the myriad divergent voices and cultures that inhabit our planet. This prospect was affirmed not long ago in Belfast, Northern Ireland. Here a young teenage girl, who had just won an essay contest, spoke from the heart, not harnessed by years of conditioning, to an audience where U.S. President Obama and other G8 summit world leaders were present.

> I just realised everyone is the same as me; peace is something we need to achieve in Northern Ireland . . . it is achievable and I just want to live in a society where we are safe and can be friends with everybody and there are no divisions. That's what I want so I decided I would try to write something about that. (32)

REFERENCES

1. Joy B. *Why the future doesn't need us.* http://archive.wired.com/wired/archive/8.04/joy.html. Accessed December 20, 2011.
2. Laaser U, Epstein L. Threats to global health and opportunities for change: A new global health. *Public Health Reviews.* 2010;32:54–89.
3. Chan M. *Who director-general addresses the sixty-sixth World Health Assembly.* http://www.who .int/dg/speeches/2013/world_health_assembly_20130520/en/. Accessed November 15, 2013.
4. Fee E. *The Welch–Rose Report: Blueprint for public health education. In: The Welch–Rose Report: A public health classic, a publication by the Delta Omega Alpha Chapter to mark the 75th anniversary of the founding of the Johns Hopkins University School of Hygiene and Public Health, 19161992.* Baltimore, MD: Delta Omega Honorary Public Health Society; 1992:1–42.
5. Tulchinsky TH, Varavikova EA. What is the "New Public Health?" Public Health Reviews 2010;32(1):25–53.
6. Centers for Disease Control and Prevention. *Achievements in public health, 1900-1999: Control of infectious diseases.* http://www.cdc.gov/mmwr/preview/mmwrhtml/mm4829a1.htm. Accessed June 30, 2010.
7. Becerra F. Assistant Director, Pan American Health Organization (PAHO). Personal communication. December 27, 2013.
8. Lueddeke G. *Transforming medical education for the 21 century: Megatrends, priorities and change.* London: Radcliffe Publishing; 2012.
9. Frenk J, Chen L, Bhutta ZA, et al. Health professions for a new century: Transforming education to strengthen health systems in an interdependent world. *The Lancet.* 2010;376(9756):1923–1958.
10. Ottersen P, Frenk J, Horton R. *The Lancet*-University of Oslo Commission on Global Governance for Health, in collaboration with the Harvard Global Health Institute. *The Lancet.* 2011;378(9803): 1612–1613.
11. Eliakimu E. Principal Medical Officer, Ministry of Health & Social Welfare, Tanzania. Personal communication. April 4, 2014.
12. Ottersen OP. Rector of the University of Oslo. Personal communication. April 4, 2014.
13. Horton R. Global burden of diseases 2010: Understanding disease, injury, and risk. *The Lancet* 2012;380(9859):2053–2054.
14. World Heart Federation. *World Heart Federation appoints Prof. K. Srinath Reddy as president 2013-2015.* http://www.world-heart-federation.org/press/releases/detail/article/world-heart-federation-appoints-prof-k-srinath-as-president-2013-2015/. Accessed March 15, 2014.
15. Hanlon P, Carlisle S, Hannah M, Reilly D, Lyon A. Making the case for a 'fifth wave' in public health. *Public Health.* 2011;125(1):30–36.
16. WHO. *WHO director-general addresses health promotion conference.* http://www.who.int/dg/speeches/2013/health_promotion_20130610/en/. Accessed October 28, 2014.
17. Asian Health Literacy Association (AHLA). *Health literacy study-Asia (HLS-Asia).* http://ahls-asia.org/hls-asia.php?h_id=1#btn. Accessed April 17, 2014.

18. CAPHRI School for Public Health and Primary Care. *Health literacy (HLS-EU).* http://www.maastrichtuniversity.nl/web/Institutes/FHML/CAPHRI/DepartmentsCAPHRI/InternationalHealth/ResearchINTHEALTH/Projects/HealthLiteracyHLSEU.htm. Accessed January 12, 2014.

19. Asian Health Literacy Association (AHLA). Global Health Literacy Newsletter. http://www.ahla-asia.org/epaperShow.php?epaper_id=38. Accessed August 25, 2015.

20. Chan M. *WHO director-general addresses conference on health systems.* http://www.who.int/dg/speeches/2012/qualitycare_20120430/en/. Accessed November 15, 2013.

21. Engel GL. The need for a new medical model: A challenge for biomedicine. *Science.* 1977;196(4286):129–136.

22. Institute of Medicine. *Primary care and public health. Exploring integration to improve population health.* Washington, DC: The National Academies Press; 2012.

23. WHO and Government of South Australia. *Adelaide statement on health in all policies: Moving towards a shared governance for health and well-being.* Report from the International Meeting on Health in All Policies, Adelaide; 15-19 April, 2010.

24. Thibault GE. Innovations in medical education: Aligning education with the needs of the public. Paper presented at: the American Medical Association 'Accelerating Change in Medical Education' Conference; October 3–5, 2013; Chicago, IL. http://www.ama-assn.org/sub/accelerating-change/pdf/thibault.pdf. Accessed November 19, 2013.

25. Frenk J, Gómez-Dantés O, Moon S. From sovereignty to solidarity: A renewed concept of global health for an era of complex interdependence. *The Lancet.* 2014;383(9911):94–97.

26. Kant I. *On education (Ueber paedagogik).* Churton A, trans. Boston, MA: D.C. Heath and Co; 1900.

27. Brundtland GH. Public health challenges in a globalizing world. *Eur J Public Health.* 2005;15(1):3–5. http://eurpub.oxfordjournals.org/content/15/1/3.full.pdf+html. Accessed November 16, 2014.

28. Ashton J. President of the UK faculty of public health. Personal communication. Apr 18, 2014.

29. Czabanowska K, Rethmeier KA, Lueddeke G, et al. Public health in the 21st century: Working differently means leading and learning differently. *Eur J Public Health.* 2014;24(2):1–6.

30. Horton R. Offline: Why the Sustainable Development Goals will fail. *The Lancet.* 2014;383(9936):2196. http://www.thelancet.com/journals/lancet/article/PIIS0140-6736%2814%2961046-1/fulltext?rss=yes. Accessed June 29, 2014.

31. Lindenmayer J. Chair One health commission (U.S.). Personal communication. October 26, 2014.

32. Alexander, H. Girl, 16, whose vision of peace stole G8 limelight. *The Daily Telegraph.* June 17, 2013. http://www.telegraph.co.uk/news/uknews/northernireland/10126273/Girl-16-whose-vision-of-peace-stole-G8-limelight.html. Accessed July 15, 2013.

Global Population Health and Well-Being in the 21st Century

1.0

A Snapshot of Public and Population Health Through the Ages

1.1 DEFINING AND CONTEXTUALIZING PUBLIC AND POPULATION HEALTH

Views on the meaning of "public health" vary considerably. Professor C. E. A. Winslow, an American bacteriologist, public health expert, and founder of the School of Public Health (1915)—and the person instrumental in establishing the School of Nursing! at Yale University—was "a seminal figure in public health, not only in his own country, the United States, but in the wider Western world" (1). In 1820, he defined "public health" as "the science and art of preventing disease, prolonging life and promoting health and efficiency through organized community effort." While his definition has been in use for close to 200 years, it has serious limitations when applied to the concept of "health" in the modern world, discussed further in Chapter 6.0, as have the terms "public" and "population" health.

"Population health" seeks to distinguish between the "individual-level focus of traditional clinical and preventive medicine" and the improvement of "the health of an entire human population" (2). Although WHO defined "health" as "a state of complete physical, mental, and social well-being" more than 60 years ago (3), historically, "public health" focused solely on physical health and communicable diseases, particularly maternal and child health, throughout much of the 20th/21st centuries (4). Today much more attention is being paid to noncommunicable diseases and mental conditions such as depression, toxic substances, and reducing "health inequities or disparities among different population groups due to, among other factors, the social determinants of health," highlighted in Chapter 2.0.

In addition, "the full spectrum" of population health now encompasses health care systems, traditional public health, and social policy. While "health" is being redefined, the concept of "population" is also undergoing change from "geographic communities" to global, networked, and social communities underpinned by the Internet. Although health issues have been scrutinized by well-intentioned boards, institutes, and commissions, success in responding to these through workable strategies is proving difficult.

As one example, in the report by the U.S. Board on Health Promotion and Disease Prevention/Institute of Medicine, *The Future of the Public's Health in the 21st Century* (5), the "guiding vision of *Healthy People 2010*, the health agenda for the nation," the authors make a number of recommendations. Their proposals highlight the importance of paying greater attention to multiple determinants of health, public health infrastructure, intersectoral partnerships, accountability, evidence-based practice, and communications within the public sector system. While these proposals were timely and highly commendable, the health of the U.S. population as well as that of many other societies has, arguably, deteriorated since 2003, judging by increases in noncommunicable diseases, such as obesity, diabetes mellitus type 2, and cardiovascular diseases. Their finding that "the public health workforce must have appropriate education and training to perform its role" may be particularly relevant and a factor in the status quo, especially in the light of a working hypothesis or possibility that, given funding imbalances described in Chapter 2.0, "a majority of governmental public health workers" still "have insufficient training in public health," thereby making it difficult to ensure that "essential public health services are competently delivered" (5).

Reflecting on historical perspectives, Professor Julio Frenk, now dean of Harvard's School of Public Health, in an earlier article (6) voiced the concern that public health was "experiencing a severe identity crisis, as well as a crisis of organization and accomplishment." Moreover, citing an Institute of Medicine report in the late 1980s (7), he noted that public health "as a profession, as a government activity, and as a commitment of society is neither clearly defined, adequately supported, nor fully understood." While there have been many achievements in the 20th and early 21st centuries, some outlined later in this chapter, fundamental issues relating to the "intellectual tradition"—conceptual base, production base, reproduction base, and utilisation base" (6)—of public health remain. However, perspectives on the rising importance of public health in the developed and developing worlds and its emerging roles appear to be coming into sharper focus as we journey through the uncertainties and ambiguities of this century.

Modern public health emerged in response to the conditions that resulted from industrialization and the subsequent rise in infectious diseases. However, the majority of today's health and well-being problems and issues now originate within society, with increasing emphasis on "improving conditions where people spend their lives outside of healthcare settings" (8) and with the growing need that "public health's broad mission of ensuring healthy communities requires interactions among a number of health-influencing actors, such as communities, businesses, the media, governmental public health, and the health delivery system" (9).

Over the past few decades, international and national bodies have refined concepts of "public health," defined needs and strategies, evolved professional competences, established accreditation bodies, and strengthened education and training, as well as initiating research and development programs. Further details on the types of priority projects in which these—and other health organizations—are engaged are discussed in later chapters of this book.

1.2 THE NEW PUBLIC HEALTH

A continuing challenge that cuts across these organizations, and advocated at the Alma-Ata International Conference in 1978 (10), which "identified primary health care as the key to the attainment of the goal of Health for All," relates to strengthening intersectoral and multidimensional approaches to health and socioeconomic development. In retrospect, it seems regrettable that a number of governments, agencies, and individuals felt that Alma-Ata's declaration of primary health care and the goal of "Health for All in the Year 2000" were "unrealistic" and "unattainable." Those who opposed implementation of the declaration were able to argue successfully that the focus should be "on achieving tangible results instead of promoting change" (11). An alternative plan involved "reducing Alma-Ata's idealism to a practical set of technical interventions that could be implemented and measured more easily, focusing on an alternative concept to that articulated at Alma-Ata—'Selective Primary Health Care'—which was built on the notion of pragmatic, low-cost interventions that were limited in scope and easy to monitor and evaluate." Backed by the United Nations Children's Fund (UNICEF), Selective Primary Health Care "was soon operationalized under the acronym *GOBI* (Growth monitoring to fight malnutrition in children, Oral rehydration techniques to defeat diarrheal diseases, Breastfeeding to protect children, and Immunizations)," (11) and, while very important, there was a missed opportunity to do "much more for many more," the driving spirit of the new public health (NPH).

Despite this setback, Professors Judith Green and Ron Labonté, recognizing the need for a broader, multidimensional or socioecological view of health, observe in their book, *Critical Perspectives in Public Health* (12), that "by the 1980s public health was already branding itself as the new public health in the UK and elsewhere." As one example, they reference the work of Professors John Ashton and Howard Seymour, who were "calling for a turn towards the social and economic 'upstream' determinants of health, and away from the dominance of therapeutic, curative medicine" (13). Similarly, in Australia, they mention the efforts of Professor Fran Baum (14), whose renewed "concern for the social determinants of health as well as social justice, healthy public policy" along with "a globalizing vision that took account of international inequalities," informed the WHO *Ottawa Charter for Health Promotion* (15). The charter, inter alia, addressed "health as a goal for which disease reduction was simply just one of the many means of achievement." Other fundamental conditions and resources for health identified in the charter included peace, shelter, education, food, income, a stable ecosystem, sustainable resources, social justice, and equity.

With a view to revitalizing and contextualizing public health within the larger health community in the 1990s, Julio Frenk, then working for the National Institute of Public Health in Mexico and Harvard University's Center for Population Studies, succinctly summarized the fundamentals governing the NPH (6):

> The modern conception of public health goes beyond fragmentary dichotomies, such as personal versus environmental services, preventive versus curative activities, and public versus private responsibilities. Instead of lending itself to these dichotomies, the new public health addresses the systematic efforts to identify health needs and organize

comprehensive services with a well defined population base. It thus encompasses the information required for characterizing the conditions of the population and the mobilization of resources necessary for responding to such conditions. In this sense, the essence of public health is the health of the public.

Therefore, it includes "the organization of personnel and facilities to provide all health services required for the promotion of health, prevention of disease, diagnosis and treatment of illness, and physical, social and vocational rehabilitation" (16). Public health encompasses the more narrow concept of medical care, but not in its technical and interpersonal aspects as applied to individuals in clinical situations, but rather in its organizational dimension as related to well-defined groups of providers and users.

In the last few years, many factors have contributed to setting the stage for accelerating change in health care generally, and public health in particular, especially the urgent need to focus on the prevention of disease, "the pillar of public health's work" (17). Issues that have come to the fore and are endangering national budgets, discussed further in Chapter 2.0, include the rapid rise of noncommunicable diseases, the urgent need for community (vs. hospital-dominated) interventions, a shrinking workforce, inadequate investment in health education and information technology, and the need to think more globally in terms of health inequities and the social determinants of health (18).

To pave the way, there appears to be growing understanding that "disease prevention and the organization of personal care services," as Professor Frenk emphasizes, are "interlinked and interdependent with health promotion and social conditions" and that public health has to widen its scope to address "such contemporary health issues as are concerned with equitable access to health services, the environment, political governance and social and economic development" (19). This theme also underpins the position paper of the Association of Schools of Public Health (ASPHER) in response to the new European health policy, *Health 2020* (20). Author Dr. Anders Foldspang and ASPHER director Robert Otok hold that "individually-oriented health work also constitutes part of the public health toolbox. As do, for example, health promotion mass campaigns, disease and disaster prevention, urban planning, management and financing of health systems, etc." (20).

Indeed, the charge that "public health, as practice and academic endeavour, has traditionally been at the margins of both health policy and the academy, and the public health movement has had to position itself throughout its history as both new and radical" (12) requires reconsideration, as its place in society now needs to be seen as central to enabling current and future population health and well-being.

Radical changes are needed globally in the light of evidence that calls for not only rebalancing of infrastructure but also, and more importantly, reducing inequities and inequalities at population levels.

An important NPH attribute is that it is action oriented, and as physicians Theodore Tulchinsky and Elena Varavikova observe in their seminal article (19), one of NPH's key challenges is "with finding a blueprint to address many of the burning issues of our time, but also with identifying implementable strategies in the endeavour to solve these problems" and that "responsibility and accountability" rest not only with governments "but also involves self care by the individual and the community."

This global reorientation in public health, say the authors, may be particularly problematic "in many countries that have placed priority of funding on hospitals and tertiary care, while health needs and primary care remain weak and underfunded." This schism has been further eroded through "the longstanding separation in administrative, funding, and training between public health and personal healthcare [which] has hindered development of effective personal care and population health." This gap also "has both day-to-day and long-term consequences" as "managers and public health professionals need to have a common cultural orientation, language, and base of learnin" (19).

In the last century, public health as well as health and social care generally have moved on considerably, particularly in the richer nations, and it may be useful to look back how far we have actually traveled, reminded by Winston Churchill's insight that "the farther backward you can look, the farther forward you can see." It is with his reflection in mind that the following "snapshot" of the sociohistorical record in medicine and health care was written.

1.3   HISTORICAL DIMENSIONS OF PUBLIC HEALTH: A SYNOPSIS

Early Medicine to Medicine in the 1700s

Viewed historically, public and individual health were interdependent as "early medicine in China, Ayurvedic medicine in India (400 BCE), Hippocrates in Greece (460–377 BCE), and Galen (129–199 CE) in Rome" shared the belief that "season, diet, the winds and lifestyle for individual people's health" influenced personal health and quality of life (21).

Hippocrates, known as "the father of medicine" and, according to some, "the first epidemiologist" is also credited with "the idea of collecting and analyzing data." Believing "that diseases were caused naturally and not because of superstition and gods," he concluded that "disease was a consequence of local conditions, which had to be favorable for a particular disease to occur," thereby establishing "the concept of collecting data on place, natural environment and people for determination of illness" (22).

Moreover, Hippocrates began to define "illnesses as acute (short duration) or chronic (long lasting)," and coined the terms "endemic" (for diseases usually found in some places but not in others; steady state) and "epidemic" (for diseases that are seen at some times but not others; abrupt change in incidence).

His book, *On Airs, Waters, and Places* (23,24)—written more than 2,500 years ago!— reflects his meticulous attention to detail in diagnosing health conditions of his day:

> The men are subject to attacks of dysentery, diarrhea, hepialus, chronic fevers in winter, of epinyctis, frequently, and of hemorrhoids about the anus. Pleurisies, peripneumonies, ardent fevers, and whatever diseases are reckoned acute, do not often occur, for such diseases are not apt to prevail where the bowels are loose. Ophthalmies occur of a humid character, but not of a serious nature, and of short duration, unless they attack epidemically from the change of the seasons. And when they pass their fiftieth year, defluxions supervening from the brain, render them paralytic when exposed suddenly to strokes of the sun, or to cold. These diseases are endemic to them, and, moreover, if any epidemic disease connected with the change of the seasons, prevail, they are also liable to it. (24)

During the so-called Dark Ages (ca. 500 CE–1000 CE), medicine advanced very little in Europe and actually took a backward step (25–27), unlike in the Arab world, as one example, where individuals such as the Persian Avicenna (Ibn Sina) (980–1037), sometimes called the "Father of Modern Medicine," wrote the 14-volume *The Canon of Medicine*.

While detailed diagnoses were done in ancient Egypt (ca. 2600 BCE–332 BCE), Greece (ca. 500 BCE–300 CE), and Rome (ca. 146 BCE–374 CE), effective treatments for most diseases or illnesses were nonexistent, even after about 3,000 years of medical practice and public health interventions, including improved sanitation practiced by the Romans. It is not surprising then that nothing could be done to counter the effects of the first major global pandemic, likely originating from China: the Bubonic Plague, also known as "The Plague of Justinian." The plague occurred in the 6th and 7th centuries, killing as many as 40% of the population of Constantinople, capital of the Eastern Roman Empire (Byzantine Empire), and spread to central and south Asia, North Africa, and Arabia, wiping out half of Europe's population, including as far north as Denmark and Ireland (25–27).

A recurrence of the Bubonic Plague, or Black Death, was caused and spread by a bacillus—*Yersinia pestis*—carried in the guts of fleas on black rats or other rodents. One of the most devastating viral pandemics in human history, the disease ravaged Europe from 1348 to 1350 and reinforced the limitations or futility of public health interventions, as doctors simply wore bird masks to protect themselves from the disease.

> The outbreak has shattered communities. Families have been set against each other—the well rejecting the sick. Essential services have collapsed; law and order, with so many administrators struck down, barely exist in some areas. A sense of panic pervades Europe and everyone, it appears, is struggling only for his own survival. Properties stand empty, deserted by desperate owners; the sick die alone, for even the most devoted doctors cannot save them: corpses are simply dumped in the street or buried in mass graves. Some depraved creatures, themselves already infected, break into houses and threaten to contaminate all within unless bribed to leave. Agriculture is at a standstill. Crops wither in the fields; cattle wander untended. Doctors do what they can, but the plague seems irresistible. Even the most expert physicians can do little more than help strengthen people's resolve and build morale. (28)

Black Death—so-called because "symptoms produced a blackening of the skin around the swellings"—killed about 200 million people in Europe and may have reduced the world population from an estimated 450 million down to 250 to 275 million by the year 1400. Major social and economic changes followed, with "higher value being placed on labour. In England the Peasants Revolt followed in 1381. Farming changed and the wool industry boomed. People became disillusioned with the church and its power and influence went into decline. This ultimately resulted in the English reformation." (25).

The Middle Ages (ca. 1000–1450 CE) witnessed a shift from Greek and Roman values regarding personal hygiene and physical fitness. As medicine was dominated by religion—cure the soul, not the body—the physical body became much less important than religion (25–27). The Renaissance (ca. 1450–1650) was essentially a rebirth of Greek and Roman ideas and a time when physicians became medical humanists, beginning to rely increasingly on "curiosity and invention," epitomized by Leonardo da Vinci (1452–1519; 25–27).

In his book *Natural and Political Observations Made Upon the Bills of Mortality* (1662), John Graunt (1620–1674), an amateur scientist living in London, was the first to "quantify the patterns of disease and to understand that numerical data on a population could be used to study the cause of disease." Graunt was also "the first to estimate the population of London and to count the number of deaths from specific causes," an idea first formulated by Girolamo Fracastoro (1478–1553), an Italian doctor, who proposed that "very small, unseeable, particles that cause disease were alive," contradicting Galen's miasma theory. However, it took another 300 years or so before Fracastoro's theory could be confirmed, and at least 200 years from the 16th century before Edward Jenner, an English scientist, developed the first vaccine against smallpox, using the much less virulent cowpox virus (25–27).

Medicine From the 1800s to the Present Day

In the 1800s, North American and European countries were characterized by rapid industrialization, urbanization, and unsanitary living conditions; this period was similar to the situation in many developing nations today, such as those known as the BRICS countries—Brazil, Russia, India, China, and South Africa. Collectively, these developments led to the establishment of public health departments, the "great sanitary awakening" (29,30) on both continents, and "a move toward humanitarian ideals." The roots for public health were firmly established when policy makers began to make a connection between poverty and disease, water supply and sewage removal, and monitoring "community health status."

In her retrospective on the Welch-Rose report, Professor Fee at Johns Hopkins University gave a particularly clear portrayal of life in the United States at this time before sanitation measures were introduced (31).

> The population moving from the land to the rapidly growing cities competed for living space with the flow of immigrants from western, southern, and eastern Europe; families crowded into tenement housing, back alleys, and damp basement apartments, supplied with communal privies and polluted water sources. City streets were heaped with garbage, including dead and decaying animals, and the waste products of small manufactories; factories produced their own noise, smells, smoke, and industrial wastes to add to the dirt and confusion of the new industrial order. Children died young of diarrheal and respiratory diseases, diphtheria, whooping cough, smallpox, and typhoid fever. Tuberculosis and other infectious diseases killed young adults and further impoverished families already struggling for survival. City health departments, especially in the eastern port cities, faced overwhelming social and health problems.

Jacob Riis, who emigrated to the United States from Denmark in 1870, wrote *How the Other Half Lives* (1890), providing "a factual, first-hand account of poverty in 19th century New York" (32). It is difficult to imagine but, as he noted, "There are numerous examples of tenement-houses in which are lodged several hundred people that have a pro rata allotment of ground area scarcely equivalent to two square yards upon the city lot." It was estimated that "the tenement houses in East Side Manhattan were once the most densely populated district in the world, not excluding China," as they were "packed at the rate of 290,000 to the square mile." In these crowded conditions, diseases such as "Cholera, Typhus fever, and Smallpox" were rampant with "scores of children dying before their 5th birthday."

The New York Bureau of Vital Statistics commented that solely due to "suffocation in the foul air of an unventilated apartment . . . there are annually cut off from the population by disease and death enough humans to people a city, and enough human labour to sustain it." The stifling air in the warmest of months was the cause of many cases of suffocation and ill health, particularly among young children. Riis's work in public health, which led to the birth of the Board of Health and other reforms, not only demonstrates "the importance of awareness" but also "shows how we each have a moral obligation to recognize the plight of the poor and that real lasting change is achievable."

As a nation that was quickly becoming industrialized, Britain suffered along similar lines as "in the 1830s and 1840s three contagious diseases had swept across the country: from 1831 to 1833 there were two influenza epidemics, and the first-ever outbreak of cholera in Britain, which alone killed 52,000; from 1836 to 1842 there were epidemics of influenza, typhus, typhoid, and cholera again, especially Asiatic cholera which spread quickly among the waterways." An inspection in 1849 of London houses found that "up to one third of the houses had major hygiene problems," many stemming from contaminated water from the Thames (33).

Roy Porter, in his seminal book *The Greatest Benefit to Mankind* (25), paints a vivid picture of industrial life in Britain, which echoes the squalor in the United States in the 19th century.

> For millions, entire lives—albeit often very short ones—were passed in new industrial cities of dreadful night with an all too typical socio-pathology: foul housing, often in flooded cellars, gross overcrowding, atmospheric and water-supply pollution, overflowing cesspools, contaminated pumps; poverty, hunger, fatigue and abjection everywhere. Such conditions, comparable to today's Third World shanty towns or refugee camps, bred rampant sickness of every kind. Appalling neo-natal, infant and child mortality accompanied the abomination of child labour in mines and factories; life expectations were exceedingly low—often under twenty years among the working classes—and everywhere sickness precipitated family breakdown, pauperisation and social crisis. The squalor of the slums was exposed time and again by social reformers, novelists, newsmen, and clergymen appalled to find hell at the heart of civilization.

In 1849, an important contribution was made by Dr. John Snow (1813–1858), an anesthesiologist and recognized by many as the "Father of Modern Epidemiology" (34). Seeking to find the cause of cholera outbreaks, "he mapped cholera cases in London and identified the source of the outbreak as the public water pump on Broad Street (now Broadwick Street)." Using a dot map, he illustrated the cluster of cholera cases around the pump. His account "is a good illustration of collection, analysis, interpretation, and dissemination of data leading to public health intervention."

On proceeding to the spot, I found that nearly all the deaths had taken place within a short distance of the [Broad Street] pump. There were only ten deaths in houses situated decidedly nearer to another street-pump. In five of these cases the families of the deceased persons informed me that they always sent to the pump in Broad Street, as they preferred the water to that of the pumps which were nearer. In three other cases, the deceased were children who went to school near the pump in Broad Street. . . . With regard to the deaths occurring in the locality belonging to the pump, there were 61 instances in which I was informed that the deceased persons used to drink the pump water from Broad Street, either constantly or occasionally. The result of the inquiry, then, is that there has been no particular outbreak or prevalence of cholera in this part of London except among the persons who were in the habit of drinking the water of the above-mentioned pump well. I had an interview with the Board of Guardians of St James's parish, on the evening of Thursday, 7th September, and represented the above circumstances to them. In consequence of what I said, the handle of the pump was removed on the following day. (34)

In both North America and Europe, generally "it was recognised early on that poor sanitation was at the heart of disease transmission, long before it was known why." Edwin Chadwick's *Inquiry Into the Sanitary Conditions of the Labouring Population of Great Britain* (1842) and, a few years later, Lemuel Shattuck's *Report of the Sanitary Commission of Massachusetts* (1850) represented major milestones in detailing how filth contributed to the spread of disease, thereby informing directions and policies set by boards of health (25–27).

Although it became evident that poor sanitation and hygiene were at the root of many illnesses, more progress in identifying the causes of diseases was being made on the continent; as one example, in 1847, the Prussian province of Silesia was struck by a typhoid epidemic (35). Recognizing the seriousness of the problem, the Minister of Education appointed Rudolf Virchow (1821–1902), a cellular pathologist, aged 26, to investigate. But rather than poring over statistical information, Virchow decided to live with miners and their families over a 3-week period.

In his paper "Report on the Typhus Epidemic in Upper Silesia" (36), which "has since become a classical work in social medicine" (12), he named typhoid, dysentery, measles, and tuberculosis "artificial" as "their prevalence was due to poor housing, working conditions, diet and a lack of sanitation among the coal miners" (36). For Virchow, what needed to be done was obvious: "we must begin to promote the advancement of the entire population and to stimulate general common effort. A population will never achieve full education, freedom and prosperity as a gift from the outside" (36).

Other short-term measures he wanted to introduce included forming "a committee of lay people and professionals to monitor the spread of typhoid and other diseases and organise agricultural cooperatives to ensure people had sufficient food to eat" (37). But, "his long-term solutions were more radical—improved occupational health and safety, better wages, decreased working hours, and strong regional and local government." Further, he "argued for progressive tax reform, removing the burden from the working poor and placing it on the 'plutocracy, which drew large amounts from the Upper Silesian mines, [and] did not recognise the Upper Silesians as human beings, but only as tools'" (37). Moreover, "he advocated democratic forms of industrial development, and even suggested hiring temporarily unemployed miners to build roadways, making it easier to transport fresh produce during the winter."

In the end, going beyond government expectations in criticizing "the economics of industrial capitalism" cost him his job. Later collaborating with Salomon Neumann (1819–1908; 38), a physician to the poor and statistician, they advanced "the notion that the aetiology of many diseases has a social component." This deduction was a master stroke in German public health, in particular the idea that "major improvements to the health of the public could only be made if housing, sanitary, and working conditions were improved for the majority of the population" (36). Based on his successful career as "anthropologist, pathologist, prehistorian, biologist, writer, editor, and politician, and known for his advancement of public health," Virchow is regarded as one of the most influential physicians in the 19th century.

Across the Channel in the 1860s, due to increasing awareness that contaminated water in London caused many to become ill, "the first great metropolitan sewage system was begun, with huge pipes to carry away the city's effluent in embankments all along the Thames, treatment plants and outfall sewers"; this project was completed in the 1870s. The last big epidemic was in 1866, although "France did not pass laws for main-drainage system for another fifty years," and both Dresden and Hamburg suffered typhoid and cholera outbreaks in the 1890s (34).

Arguably the greatest figure in medical microbiology, the French chemist and microbiologist Louis Pasteur (1822–1895) confirmed in 1862 that germs rather than miasma theory (bad air) caused many diseases (25–27). In 1883, Robert Koch (1843–1910), a German doctor considered the founder of modern bacteriology, identified the vibrio that causes cholera and discovered the tuberculosis bacterium. Whereas Koch advocated public health interventions, Pasteur's approach favored the development of vaccines and set the stage for "the biomedical model of disease" that has dominated medical thinking and "the microbiological revolution" ever since.

In short, "this model focuses on pathological processes, and on understanding, diagnosing, and treating the physical and biological aspects of disease. The goal of treatment is to restore the patient's physiological integrity and function" (38). The germ theory made it possible to "differentiate between diseases that had previously been thought of as one, and diagnosis improved: diphtheria could now be told apart from scarlet fever or croup, syphilis from gonorrhea, typhoid from typhus . . . but once the patient's illness was defined the lack of cure was still an insuperable problem" (34).

For many in the 19th century living in confined and unsanitary environments, "the best solution to illness was to prevent" (34). In the more advanced nations, such as Britain and Germany, there was growing consensus "on how this was to be done: a child should lead an orderly, well-regulated daily life, simple in every element."

However, although these aspirations were commendable, the treatment of most conditions—many imagined (34)—was mostly more risky than the problem in the first place. Unable to distinguish between cause and effect of an illness, the public often made assumptions that actually made situations worse rather than better. As one example, when babies fretted before their new teeth began to grow, worried parents decided that "milk no longer agrees with the child," so they stopped the milk and instead fed the infants unsuitable food, upsetting "their digestion" and giving "drugs, most of which contained opium, and, not unnaturally, the babies died in convulsions" (34).

As the latter case demonstrates, health care support was equally deficient well into the 19th century. Nursing was about to change, however, largely due to the dedication of Florence Nightingale (1820–1910), who became known for her efforts—along with 30 other nurses—in caring for troops in the Crimean War in the 1850s (39). She is often referred to as the "Lady With the Lamp," and has been called the Founder of Modern Nursing, who, to her credit and influence, was also a "compassionate statistician."

The thinking and interventions—along with medicine generally and the concept and practices of public health specifically—evolved very slowly over the centuries. Perhaps, unsurprisingly, it was not until the early to mid-20th century, with foundations laid in the period between 1750 and 1830, that progress of any significance was made in areas such as sanitation across Europe and North America. Germany, which, as mentioned, pursued the notion of "social medicine triggered to a large extent by the typhus epidemic in Upper Silesia" (37), also became the first nation to establish some form of universal health care and social insurance (later national insurance) in 1883 (40).

Two main reasons for these social reforms in Europe in the late 19th and early 20th centuries were "income stabilization and protection against the wage loss of sickness rather than payment for medical expenses, which came later." Another factor for introducing these programs was their potential in "buying political allegiance of the workers" (40).

Another breakthrough in medical research was the discovery by Paul Ehrlich (1854–1915) of the first antibiotic or first antibacterial drug in modern medicine, salvarsan, "arsenic compound 606," to treat syphilis. Ehrlich also coined the term "magic bullet" in 1909 (25–27). In 1935, the drug prontosil, the first of the sulfa drugs to treat streptococcal infections (e.g., puerperal fever), was discovered. As many infections resisted sulfa drugs, penicillin, a substance from living mold, came into wider use, followed in 1948 by tetracycline, which proved effective for most infections (25–27).

At the turn of the 20th century, all that doctors could bring on home visits was "a good bedside manner and a dose of something soothing (or even nasty)," thereby reassuring "the patient that something was being done, that the disease was not being ignored" (41). Indeed, a typical physician's bag was usually full of narcotics, analgesics, and antipyretics—cocaine hydrochlorate, a sedative sleeping potion, strychnine nitrate, morphine sulfate, quinine, nitroglycerine, digitalis, and prescriptive whiskey. In addition, his bag contained instruments such as a stethoscope, forceps, sutures, needles, bandages, and knives, to name several (25–27).

> Before the end of the 19th century, medicines were concocted with a mixture of empiricism and prayer. Trial and error, inherited lore, or mystical theories were the basis of the world's pharmacopoeias. The technology of making drugs was crude at best: Tinctures, poultices, soups, and teas were made with water- or alcohol-based extracts of freshly ground or dried herbs or animal products such as bone, fat, or even pearls, and sometimes from minerals best left in the ground—mercury among the favored. The difference between a poison and a medicine was a hazy differentiation at best: In the 16th century, Paracelsus declared that the only difference between a medicine and a poison was in the dose. All medicines were toxic. It was cure or kill. (42)

Taken together, these interventions were usually dangerous, "yielding little or no results and often killing the patient with a different affliction than the original ailment" (42). Common practices well into the 19th century included "leeching (or bloodletting), purgation, poor liquid diets, and cold water dousing." It seems curious that "even after newer, more effective methods of medical treatment had been introduced, many of the physicians, surgeons, and apothecaries hesitated to use them. Fearing the loss of their reputations, they hung on to superstitious beliefs, doubting the effectiveness of such advances, and were basically unwilling to try something new" (42).

Professor David Wootton in *Bad Medicine: Doctors Doing Harm Since Hippocrates* comments, "To ask why doctors didn't do better makes little sense," as "they did what they did in a world that was not of their making." On the other hand, he argues that "it makes perfect sense to ask why doctors for centuries imagined that their therapies worked when they didn't" (42).

1.4 THE WELCH-ROSE REPORT (1915)

Unlike European and Asian countries, organized public health was nonexistent in the United States for much of the 19th century. However, "increasing urbanization . . . and the growth of mechanization and factories, with their attendant health and safety risks" made the need for improving public health a high priority, especially "in the absence of good sanitation practices" (43).

At the beginning of the 20th century, American physicians preferred the German approach to public health and were drawn to Robert Koch's bacteriology, which essentially became "the foundation of modern medicine" (25–27). The scientific basis of public health was also embraced by Professor William Welch, a pathologist, who had been named the first dean of Johns Hopkins medical school in 1883. In 1915, Professor Welch and Wickliffe Rose, an original trustee of the Rockefeller Foundation, published the Welch-Rose report (32) "that outlined a system of public health education in the US, initially targeted at control of infectious diseases—a system that was university-based, research intensive and independent of medical schools." It must be said, however, that Rose favored practical public health training, after the British model, and the establishment of a "national system of public health training with central national schools acting as the focus for a network of state schools."

In 1916, Welch became the first dean of America's first public health school. Other schools of public health quickly followed—Harvard, Columbia, and Michigan, to name a few.

The report had far-reaching consequences: First, it raised awareness about the urgency of more coordinated public health interventions and in many ways paralleled "the Flexner Report that had proposed a systematic approach to medical education in the wake of concerns about proliferating numbers of medical schools of dubious quality" (44). Second, it has been viewed as "legitimizing the rift between medicine's laboratory investigations of the mechanics of disease and public health's non-clinical concern with environmental and social influences on health and wellness" (44). Third, while both models have made substantial contributions on many fronts and coexist globally today, they seem to be equally stymied when it comes to addressing many of today's population health problems (45).

1.5   MILESTONES IN THE 20TH AND EARLY 21ST CENTURIES

In their book, *Milestones in Public Health: Accomplishments in Public Health Over the Last 100 Years* (46), the authors, supported by expert reviewers, identified, as summarized in Box 1.1, 10 milestones in public health. The list is similar to one produced by The U.S. Centers for Disease Control and Prevention (CDC) produced a similar list (47) but added family planning, fluoridation of drinking water, and tobacco as a health hazard. A subsequent CDC report (48) for 2000 to 2010 included many of the same categories but added prevention of childhood lead poisoning, improved public health preparedness and response, and sanitation.

Similarly, the *British Medical Journal* (*BMJ*) published a commemorative supplementary edition on the occasion of its first publication in 1840 (49). Out of 70 submissions, 15 made it to the final list, compiled by a panel of editors and advisers "to stir debate and elicit reflection." The final listing (Box 1.2) was grouped under 11 headings.

"More than 11,300 readers of the *BMJ* chose the introduction of clean water and sewage disposal—'the sanitary revolution'—as the most important medical milestone." Antibiotics came a close second (50).

Dr. Jeffrey Koplan, director of the Emory Global Health Institute, who contributed extensively to the supplementary *BMJ* edition, observed: "One common feature of all these milestones is that their existence and significance were likely unforeseen when the *BMJ* was established in 1840, but they have all had a major effect on the length and quality of life" (49).

Also of note is that all milestones in Boxes 1.1 and 1.2 are attributable to advances in public health. However, most achievements focus on the physical state of individuals, not on the inner self—emotions, personal well-being, or milestones in addressing mental disorders such as anxiety or depression, aside from the use of chlorpromazine to treat various psychoses.

This is what makes the achievements listed by the Canadian Public Health Association in 2010 unique (51). While supporting nine of the CDC milestones, two additional "population-centered" milestones were recognized in Canada: "acting on

BOX 1.1

Milestones in Public Health (United States)

- *Vaccines and the eradication of smallpox*
- *Automotive safety*
- *Environmental health*
- *Infectious disease control*
- *Cancer*
- *Cardiovascular disease*
- *Safer and healthier foods*
- *Advances in maternal and child health*
- *Oral health*
- *Addictions*

BOX 1.2

Milestones in Public Health (United Kingdom)

- *Diagnostic*—Imaging
- *Therapeutic Advances*—Anesthesia, antibiotics, oral rehydration
- *Therapy*—Chlorpromazine
- *Preventive measures*—The pill, vaccines, sanitation
- *Theories*—Germ theory
- *Technology*—Computers
- *Basic scientific discoveries*—Structure of DNA
- *Epidemiological discoveries*—Risks of smoking medicine
- *Medical science*—Evidence-based medicine
- *Major disciplines of bioscience*—Immunology
- *Laboratory technique*—Tissue culture

the social determinants of health" and the development of "universal programs for income maintenance, social welfare services and health care services."

Weighing the "relative contributions of biomedical science and public health," Dr. Koplan concedes that while "biomedical science has won more Nobel prizes, public health has had a greater role in reducing morbidity and mortality and improving our quality of life." "Of course, each approach contributes to the other," he concedes (49).

However, future breakthroughs will not come easily. Dr. Fiona Godlee, editor-in-chief of the *BMJ* and the commemorative supplementary edition, reminds us about today's economic realities (49), while a research study on the art and science of healing admonishes the imbalances that currently exist between the two.

Dr. Godlee highlights that scientific discoveries rely on expensive "infrastructure that supports applied as well as basic research, encourages the systematic implementation of what we already know, nurtures young talent by creating career structures in research, and encourages commercial investment while protecting against the erosive influence of vested interest." At a time of severe austerity, finding funds to sustain costly large-scale research trials will come under considerable pressure.

Second, while clinicians and scientists have made significant contributions in the 20th century, such as systems biology and evidence-based medicine, progress has come at a steep price: "a growing imbalance between the art and science of healing as greater reliance is being given to the technical side of medicine rather than human intervention" (52).

A study by the authors of the monograph *21st Century Medicine: A New Model for Medical Education and Practice* found that "clinicians are no longer taught how to integrate the science and the art of medicine—indeed, the art of medicine has all but disappeared as a subject of teaching" (52). Further, the researchers conclude, "From the evidence-based medicine perspective, all you really need to do is gather data, focus the data toward securing the diagnosis, and then research the evidence about the best molecule (Rx) or procedure to treat that diagnosis."

This scientific reductionist approach—the "acute care model"—to population health runs counter to the types of health services most people actually do require in the early decades of this century: not "technicians, who are able to deliver care in less and less time (often for less and less money)" but professionals who make the overall well-being of the individual their first concern and who recognize "the opportunity to better impact the all-important social determinants of health" (46).

REFERENCES

1. Winslow CE. The untilled fields of public health. *Science.* 1920;51(1306):23–33. https://archive .org/details/cihm_90880. Accessed June 20, 2014.
2. University of Wisconsin (School of Medicine and Public Health). What is population health and public health? http://www.pophealth.wisc.edu/prospective-students/pophealth-publichealth. Accessed September 20, 2013.
3. Frankish CJ, Green LW, Ratner PA, Chomik T, Larsen C. Health impact assessment as a tool for health promotion and population health. *WHO Reg Publ Eur Ser.* 2001;92:405–437.
4. Riegelman R, Kirkwood B. Principles of population health. In: *Public Health 101: Healthy people– Healthy populations.* London: Jones and Bartlett Publishing International; 2010.
5. Institute of Medicine. *The future of the public's health in the 21st century.* Washington, DC: The National Academies Press; 2003.
6. Frenk J. The new public health. *Annu Rev Public Health.* 1993;14:468–490.
7. Institute of Medicine. *The future of public health.* Washington, DC: National Academy Press; 1988.
8. Institute of Medicine. *The future of the public's health in the 21st century.* Washington, DC: The National Academies Press; 2002.
9. Institute of Medicine. *Primary care and public health. Exploring integration to improve population health.* Washington, DC: The National Academies; 2012.
10. World Health Organization. WHO called to return to the Declaration of Alma-Ata. http://www .who.int/social_determinants/tools/multimedia/alma_ata/en/. Accessed January 10, 2011.
11. Brown T, Cueto M, Fee E. The World Health Organization and the transition from "international" to "global" public health. *Am J Public Health.* 2006;96(1):62–72.
12. Green J, Labonté R. *Critical perspectives in public health.* Oxon: Routledge; 2007.
13. Ashton J, Seymour H. *The new public health: The Liverpool experience.* Maidenhead, Berkshire: Oxford University Press; 1988.
14. Baum FE. *The new public health.* 3rd ed. South Melbourne: Oxford University Press; 2003.
15. World Health Organization. The Ottawa charter for health promotion. http://www.who.int/ healthpromotion/conferences/previous/ottawa/en/. Accessed February 27, 1998.
16. Terris M. The distinction between public health and community/social/preventive medicine. *J Public Health Policy.* 1985;6(4):435–439.
17. Department of Health. *Healthy lives, healthy people: Improving outcomes and supporting transparency. A public health outcomes framework for England, 2013–2016.* London: Department of Health. https://www.rcpsych.ac.uk/pdf/The%20Public%20Health%20Outcomes%20Framework.pdf. Accessed July 13, 2014.
18. World Health Organization. *Health 2020:* The European policy for health and well-being. http:// www.euro.who.int/en/health-topics/health-policy/health-2020-the-european-policy-for-health-and-well-being. Accessed April 14, 2014.
19. Tulchinsky TH, Varavikova EA. What is the "New Public Health"? *Public Health Reviews.* 2010;32(1):25–53.

20. Foldspang A, Otok R. *ASPHER's position paper concerning: The new European policy for health—Health 2020 and the European action plan for strengthening public health capacities and services.* Belgium: ASPHER. http://www.aspher.org/foto/EB032014/ASPHER_Position_Paper_RE_Health2020 .pdf. Accessed April 20, 2012.

21. Kate K. *History of medicine: Early civilizations. Prehistoric times to 500 C.E.* New York, NY: Infobase Publishing; 2009. http://www.scribd.com/doc/26657174/The-History-of-Medicine-2009#scribd. Accessed January 20, 2010.

22. Wear A. *Medicine in society. Historical essays.* Cambridge: Cambridge University Press; 1998.

23. Choi BC. The past, present, and future of public health surveillance. *Scientifica.* 2012;2012. http:// www.hindawi.com/journals/scientifica/2012/875253/. Accessed August 23, 2013.

24. Hippocrates. *On airs, waters, and places* (written 400 BCE, Francis Adams, trans, 1796–1861). http://classics.mit.edu/Hippocrates/airwatpl.html. Accessed August 24, 2013.

25. Porter R. *The greatest benefit to mankind: A medical history of humanity from antiquity to the present.* 2nd ed. London: Fontana Press; 1997.

26. Duffin J. *History of medicine: A scandalously short introduction.* Toronto: University of Toronto Press; 2004.

27. Lueddeke G. *Physicians through the ages: From bad to good medicine?* (lecture series). Southampton: University of Southampton; 2009.

28. Alchin LK. *Lords and ladies.* http://www.lordsandladies.org/copyright.htm. Accessed February 25, 2013.

29. Secretariat of Indian Academy of Public Health. Background paper on public health. http:// www.iphaonline.org/academy/concept-papers/pdf/background_paper_developed_by_the_ secretariat_of_ipha.pdf. Accessed September 25, 2013.

30. Supercourse. *Epidemiology, the Internet and Global Health.* http://www.pitt.edu/~super1/index .htm. Accessed November 28, 2010.

31. Fee E. The Welch-Rose Report: Blueprint for public health education. In: *The Welch-Rose Report: A public health classic, a publication by the Delta Omega Alpha Chapter to mark the 75th anniversary of the founding of the Johns Hopkins University School of Hygiene and Public Health, 1916-1992.* Baltimore, MD: Delta Omega Honorary Public Health Society; 1992:1–42.

32. Riis J. *How the other half lives.* New York, NY: Charles Scribner's Sons; 1890. http://www.bartleby. com/208/1.html. Accessed July 15, 2012.

33. Flanders J. *The Victorian house.* London: HarperCollins Publishers; 2003.

34. Snow J. *On the mode of communication of cholera.* London: Churchill; 1855. http://www.ph.ucla. edu/epi/snow/snowbook2.html. Accessed August 20, 2013.

35. Brown T, Fee E. Rudolf Carl Virchow. Medical scientist, social reformer, role model. *Am J Public Health.* 2006;96(12):2104–2105. http://www.ncbi.nlm.nih.gov/pmc/articles/PMC1698150/. Accessed August 28, 2013.

36. Virchow RC. Report on the typhus epidemic in Upper Silesia. *Am J Public Health.* 2006;96(12):2102–2105. http://www.ncbi.nlm.nih.gov/pmc/articles/PMC1698167/. Accessed August 28, 2013.

37. Green J, Labonté R. Preface. In: Green J, Labonté R, eds. *Critical perspectives in public health.* Oxon: Routledge; 2007:xiii–xiv.

38. The Association of Faculties of Medicine of Canada (AFMC). Primer on Population Health. http://www.afmc.ca/pdf/AFMC-Primer-on-Population-Health-2013-08-14.pdf. Accessed June 20, 2012.

39. Florence Nightingale. Biography. http://www.biography.com/people/florence-nightingale -9423539. Accessed July 19, 2013.

40. Palmer K. *A brief history: Universal healthcare efforts in the US.* Chicago, IL: Physicians for a National Health Program. http://www.pnhp.org/facts/a-brief-history-universal-health-care-efforts-in-the-us. Accessed January 9, 2013.

41. Anon. *Student paper on 19th-century medicine.* http://www-personal.umd.umich.edu/~jonsmith /19cmed.html. Accessed October 10, 2009.

42. Wootton D. *Bad medicine: Doctors doing harm since Hippocrates*. Oxford: Oxford University Press; 2007.

43. Rosenstock L, Helsing K, Rimer BK. Public health education in the United States: Then and now. *Public Health Reviews*. 2011;33(1):39–65. http://publichealthreviews.eu/upload/pdf_files/9/Rosenstock.pdf. Accessed February 17, 2014.

44. Patel K, Rushefsky ME. *The politics of public health in the United States*. New York, NY: M E Sharpe Inc; 2004.

45. Jabbour S, Giacaman R, Khawaja M, Nuwayhid I, Yamout R. *Public health in the Arab world*. Cambridge: Cambridge University Press; 2012.

46. Association of Schools of Public Health. *Milestones in public health: Accomplishments in public health over the last 100 years*. New York, NY: Pfizer Global Pharmaceuticals. http://www.soph.uab.edu/isoph/pfizer/Milestones.pdf. Accessed May 15, 2013.

47. Centers for Disease Control and Prevention. Ten great public health achievements in the 20th century 1900–1999. http://www.cdc.gov/about/history/tengpha.htm. Accessed May 26, 2013.

48. Centers for Disease Control and Prevention. Ten great public health achievements—United States, 2001–2010. *Morbidity and Mortality Weekly Report (MMWR)*. 2011;60(19):619–623. http://www.cdc.gov/mmwr/preview/mmwrhtml/mm6019a5.htm. Accessed August 20, 2013.

49. BMJ. *Medical milestones. Celebrating key advances since 1840*. London: BMJ Publishing Group; 2007. http://www.bmj.com/content/suppl/2007/01/18/334.suppl_1.DC2/milestones.pdf. Accessed May 25, 2013.

50. Ferriman A. *BMJ* readers choose the "sanitary revolution" as greatest medical advance since 1840. *BMJ*. 2007;334(7585):111–117. http://www.ncbi.nlm.nih.gov/pmc/articles/PMC1779856/. Accessed November 17, 2013.

51. Canadian Public Health Association. History of public health. http://resources.cpha.ca/CPHA/ThisIsPublicHealth/landing.php?l=E. Accessed March 10, 2013.

52. Jones DS, Hofmann L, Quinn S. *21st century medicine: A new model for medical education and practice*. Gig Harbor, WA: Institute for Functional Medicine; 2010. http://www.faim.org/guestwriters/ifmexecutivesummary.html. Accessed October 15, 2013.

2.0

Contemporary Challenges in Public Health

2.1 CHILDREN'S LIVES "AT A GLANCE": SPOTLIGHT ON SIX NATIONS

In a brief but insightful report entitled "Kids These Days: A Portrait of Childhood Around the World" (1), British journalist Adam Lusher "looks at the lives of young people in six very different nations."

Beginning with The Netherlands, he notes that children's life expectancy at birth is about 80; they get plenty of "treats" and are not given homework until the age of 10. It may not be a coincidence that, according to a UNICEF survey, Dutch children, "treated as mini-adults," are "the happiest in the world."

Unsurprisingly, this lifestyle contrasts considerably with children living in India, where life expectancy is around 65; children are taught by volunteers and the percentage "of five to 14-year-olds engaged in child labour" is about 12. More than a third fail to complete primary school, while 5 out of 10 children in high-income families are obese and are rarely seen on the streets, but they are usually accompanied by their *ayah* (nanny).

Life is worse in the Democratic Republic of Congo (DRC), with a life expectancy of only 48 and with approximately 170 children out of 1,000 dying before their fifth birthday. At least 42% "of five to 14-year-olds . . . are engaged in child labour," making it difficult to reconcile with an education policy that makes education free and compulsory until 16. Begging and theft triggered by poverty are dealt with ruthlessly.

Life expectancy in Saudi Arabia is 74, but life is still hard, especially in terms of youth justice and male–female relationships. Chinese children on average can live to about 73, but life is particularly difficult for those living in China's poverty-stricken rural communities. Children "start the day at 7 a.m.—by saluting the flag—and finish at 8.30 p.m., after three hours of supervised homework," thereby remaining "one of the most pressurized" school systems in the world.

Children in the United Kingdom, as in most other developed nations, can expect to live to 80 or more—although this figure may be reduced by lifestyle factors discussed later in this chapter. Collectively, they have "a total of £7.3 billion worth of goods in their bedrooms" (with the annual spend per child, £270, being the highest in Europe). While children from the DRC spend no time on the Internet, the lives of British children are consumed by it. They also are, according to Adam Lusher, "among the most brand-conscious in the world," perhaps reflecting the values of the 21st century that are likely shared by many other "modern" societies (1).

Few, however, can imagine the horrors brought on the lives of children and others by the world conflicts, in particular the plight of those in refugee camps, such as Zaatari, with over 120,000 Syrian people. António Guterres, the United Nations (UN) High Commissioner for Refugees, has described the Syrian conflict—now topping over 2 million refugees—as "the great tragedy of this century—a disgraceful humanitarian calamity with suffering and displacement unparalleled in recent history" (2).

Michelle Dockery—of TV's *Downton Abbey* fame—visited a Syrian refugee camp on behalf of Oxfam (3). During this visit, something that became clear to her quickly was that "many of the refugees had come from a life not dissimilar to ours—with jobs homes and families—but the war had robbed them of the life they knew and loved." She also realized "that what all these children needed was attention and expressions of affections and love. They were sad, bewildered and lonely. They missed their friends, their teachers, their homes." And, as journalist Margarette Driscoll reports, "while primary school pupils in Britain draw flowers, trees and rainbows, children sitting in a chilly, mud-spattered tent in Iraq after escaping the war in Syria create vivid depictions of people being shot at by helicopters and tanks or blown up in streets" (4). However, the resilience of the human spirit is humbling. When asked by a teacher "what they wanted to be when they grew up," students to whom Ms. Dockery spoke answered "clearly, and with pride: 'A pharmacist', 'A doctor', 'A teacher', 'A farmer'."

The profiles of these children's lives may make us search for answers as to why many who have life advantages and many more who are denied life choices and opportunities are both facing threats to their health and well-being.

2.2 GLOBAL PUBLIC HEALTH: REFLECTIONS ON THE "BIG" PICTURE

There are more than 7.3 billion people on the planet. Of those, approximately 15% live in developed countries. The remaining 85% live in either developing or underdeveloped nations, with many surviving on less than US$2 a day (roughly 2.4 billion people), and, "according to UNICEF, 22,000 children die each day due to poverty." And they "die quietly in some of the poorest villages on earth, far removed from the scrutiny and the conscience of the world" (5). Surely, knowing what we know, we cannot go on as if we are still in the 20th century.

The children's profiles highlight a recurring theme that weaves throughout the WHO-commissioned report, *Closing the Gap in a Generation: Health Equity Through Action on the Social Determinants of Health* (6). As illustrated in Figure 2.1, the authors conclude that the "high burden of illness" in poor countries "arises in large part because of the conditions in which people are born, grow, live, work, and age and the consequences of poor social policy."

Global inequities continue unabated. As examples, "many of the 300 million indigenous people face discrimination, which hinders them from meeting their daily needs and voicing their claims" (7). Moreover, "girls and women face barriers to access education and secure employment compared with boys and men, and women worldwide still face inequalities with respect to reproductive and sexual health rights" (8).

And, it is not just in the developing world that these injustices prevail. According to George Soros, financier and chair of the Open Society Foundations, the plight of the 11 million Roma (primarily from Bulgaria and Romania) living in Europe, who suffer from discrimination and from segregated housing and schooling, is particularly troubling (9). Continuing to migrate across Europe, the "divide is physical, not just mental" and as "Europe's largest ethnic minority," Mr. Soros highlights, "the greatest divide between the Roma and majority populations is not one of culture or lifestyle— as is so often portrayed by the media—but poverty and inequality." As with other disaffected groups, the main issue "is a matter of human rights and basic values, and it is vital to peace and cohesion in societies across Europe," and, by extension, across the globe, where, indicative of Figure 2.1, the inequities in "living and working conditions" at all societal levels appear to be widening.

The WHO Commission's main aspiration relates to "closing the gap in a generation." Their recipe for enabling action—integral to the Millennium Development Goals (MDGs) outlined in Chapter 4.0—includes improving "the conditions of daily life" and tackling "the inequitable distribution of power, money, and resources"; it also includes steps to measure and understand "the problem and assess the impact of action." Achieving these ends will not be easy, as global health issues, "which should have been easy to solve" (5), and many shown in Box 2.1 remain alarming in the beginning decades of this century.

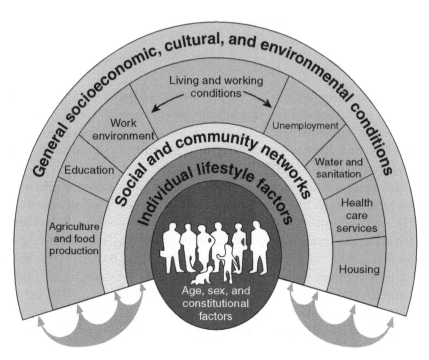

FIGURE 2.1 The socioeconomic, cultural, and environmental conditions of health and well-being.

Source: Dahlgren and Whitehead, Tackling Inequalities in Health: An Agenda for Action (1993;10).

BOX 2.1

Global Health Statistics

- One billion people lack access to health care systems.
- 36 million deaths each year are caused by noncommunicable diseases, such as cardiovascular disease (CVD), cancer, diabetes, and chronic lung diseases.
- CVDs are the number one group of conditions causing death globally. An estimated 17.5 million people died from CVDs in 2005, representing 30% of all global deaths. Over 80% of CVD deaths occur in low- and middle-income countries.
- Over 7.5 million children under the age of 5 die from malnutrition and mostly preventable diseases each year.
- In 2008, some 6.7 million people died of infectious diseases alone, far more than the number killed in the natural or man-made catastrophes that make the headlines.
- AIDS/HIV has spread rapidly. The UNAIDS estimate for 2008 is that there are roughly 33.4 million people living with HIV.
- Tuberculosis kills 1.7 million people each year, with 9.4 million new cases a year.
- 1.6 million people still die from pneumococcal diseases every year, making it the number one vaccine-preventable cause of death worldwide. More than half of the victims are children.
- Malaria causes some 225 million acute illnesses and over 780,000 deaths annually.

Source: A. Shah, Poverty Facts and Stats (5).

Nor, as we have seen with reference to children's lives in Britain, are these health issues restricted to the developing or underdeveloped nations. For example, the *CDC Health Disparities and Inequalities Report* (11) records that "striking disparities in noncompletion of high school and poverty exist within the U.S. adult population; no improvement was realized between 2005 and 2009."

In Britain, a recent study suggests that "social mobility has gone into reverse with middle class youngsters increasingly threatened with lower living standards than their parents" (12). Across Europe, the debt spiral continues unabated, with the economic crisis across the south deepening and youth unemployment in Greece standing at around 63%; 56% in Spain; and close to 40% in Italy, Cyprus, and Portugal (13). These socioeconomic factors impinge acutely on "living and working conditions," identified in Figure 2.1, and gravely on individual health and well-being. In the United States, the number of homeless is growing—approximately 53,800 in Los Angeles alone—"as the gulf between rich and poor reaches levels not seen since the Gilded Age of the late 19th century" (14).

In a keynote address at the 63rd World Health Assembly in Geneva, the Norwegian Minister of Foreign Affairs Jonas Gahr Store reminded delegates that "the largest inequalities today are found within countries rather than between countries" (15), and that "talking about rich and poor countries gives little meaning." Moreover, he declared that "the largest number of people living in absolute poverty is now to be found in middle-income countries," thereby creating "serious challenges in terms of equity and stability."

According to the Global Burden of Disease 2010 study (GBD 2010; 16) involving 50 countries and published in *The Lancet*, significant improvements have been made in reducing communicable diseases, leading generally to longer life expectancy. In particular, there has been a decline in childhood infectious diseases, especially a decrease in "diarrhoeal disease, lower respiratory infection, neonatal disorder, measles and tetanus" and under-five mortality (except in sub-Saharan Africa). Although there has been better control of HIV and preventive measures against malaria, death rates have increased considerably: "HIV/Aids increased from 300,000 in 1990 to 1.5 million in 2010 (peaking at 1.7 million in 2006) and malaria mortality rose by an estimated 19.9% over 20 years to 1.17 million deaths in 2010. TB killed 1.2 million people that year."

The GBD 2010 study confirms that huge discrepancies remain between rich and poor countries, and some of the following indicators could conceivably help to reinforce awareness of the challenges that face the global community generally and public health particularly.

Figures 2.2 and 2.3, in terms of territory size (infographs), show the proportion of all physicians (17) and nurses (18) who work in that territory across 12 global regions. Figure 2.2 shows that 50% of physicians are concentrated in territories with less than a fifth of the world's population. Those whose burden of disease is the greatest are served by only 2% of the world's physicians—about 9 million globally (7).

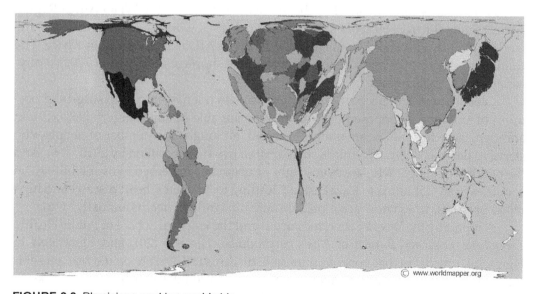

FIGURE 2.2 Physicians working worldwide.

Source: Worldmapper.org. © Copyright SASI Group (University of Sheffield) and Mark Newman (University of Michigan). Reproduced under Creative Commons license https://creativecommons.org/licenses/by-nc-nd/3.0.

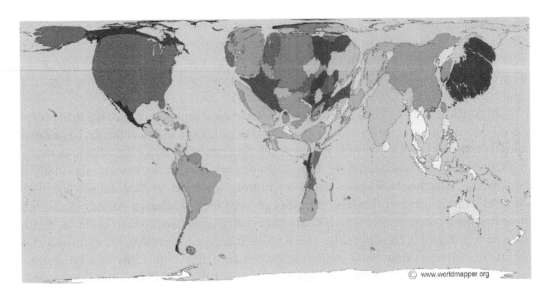

FIGURE 2.3 Nurses working worldwide.

Source: Worldmapper.org. © Copyright SASI Group (University of Sheffield) and Mark Newman (University of Michigan). Reproduced under Creative Commons license https://creativecommons.org/licenses/by-nc-nd/3.0.

Figures 2.2 and 2.3 clearly demonstrate that Africa with over 1 billion people remains utterly underresourced.

The continent comprises some 11% of the world population, yet it accounts for 25% of the global burden of disease and hosts just 4% of the global health workforce to address this. There are urgent health needs in the region.

Of the 20 countries with the highest maternal mortality rates in the world, 19 are in Africa; 11 of the 15 countries with the highest incidence of tuberculosis are in Africa; malaria is endemic in 42 of the 46 member states of the WHO Africa Region and accounts for over 90% of estimated clinical cases worldwide. Two-thirds of the world's people with HIV live in Africa and 72% of AIDS deaths occur in Africa. The continent faces an extreme human health resource shortage estimated at 720,000 physicians and 670,000 nurses.

Globally, 2 billion people—most in Africa—do not have access to surgical procedures of any kind as opposed to 4 billion who are able to have surgery (96%; 19). In addition, close to a billion are undernourished, although "the number of people who starve to death is down two-thirds since 1990 to less than a million by 2010" (16). And the number of people who are overweight or obese has increased to over a billion "in countries from Columbia to Kazakhstan," leading to "diabetes, heart disease, and high blood pressure, which now accounts for some nine million deaths annually" (16).

A report by the World Economic Forum and the Harvard School of Public Health, *The Global Economic Burden of Non-Communicable Diseases* (20), and illustrated in Figure 2.4, concludes that noncommunicable diseases (NCDs) are on the rise, presenting "a direct threat to health financing schemes in all countries, rich and poor alike."

NCDs claim "63% of all deaths," and "are currently the world's main killer" (20). Deaths from NCDs "rose by just under 8 million between 1990 and 2010. Cancer

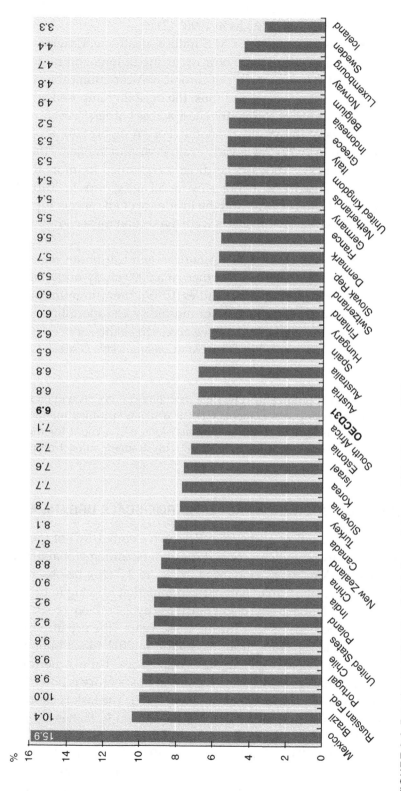

FIGURE 2.4 Prevalence estimates of diabetes, adults aged 20–79 years, 2011.

Note: The data cover both type 1 and type 2 diabetes. Data are age standardized to the World Standard Population.
Source: OECD, *Health at Glance, 2013: OECD Indicators*, OECD Publishing. http://dx.doi.org/10.1787/health_glance-2013-en (24).

killed 8 million people in 2010 (a 38% rise since 1990). Heart disease and strokes killed 12.9 million people worldwide in 2010—accounting for one in four deaths. Diabetes killed 1.3 million people, twice as many as in 1990" (21).

In total, NCD deaths accounted for 34.5 million deaths worldwide in 2010. It is estimated that 80% of these deaths are now occurring in low- and middle-income countries. Moreover, "half of those who die of chronic non-communicable diseases are in the prime of their productive years, and thus, the disability imposed and the lives lost are also endangering industry competitiveness across borders" (16).

Echoing the findings of the World Economic Forum report (20), a panel in the United Arab Emirates (UAE; 22) reviewed, evaluated, and ranked "the top four main public health issues: 1) Cardiovascular disease accounted for more than 25% of deaths in 2010; 2) Injury caused 17% of mortality for all age groups in 2010; 3) Cancer accounted for 10% of all deaths in 2010, and the incidence of all cancers is projected to double by 2020; and 4) Respiratory disorders were the second most common non-fatal condition in 2010."

Similar results are found in the Latin American and Caribbean region with an estimated population of 580,000 million. Further, in a 2009 study undertaken by the U.S. Center for Strategic and International Studies (CSIS), "noncommunicable chronic diseases are emerging as a significant cause of morbidity and mortality. . . . At least 125 million of the region's residents do not have access to health services" (23).

Authors of *The Global Economic Burden of Non-Communicable Diseases* (20) emphasize that

> the evidence gathered is compelling. Over the next 20 years, NCDs will cost more than US$ 30 trillion, representing 48% of global GDP in 2010, and pushing millions of people below the poverty line. Mental health conditions alone will account for the loss of an additional US$ 16.1 trillion over this time span, with dramatic impact on productivity and quality of life.

2.3 POPULATION GROWTH: IMPACT OF LARGE-SCALE URBANIZATION

Thomas Kemper, scientific officer at the Joint Research Centre (JRC) of the European Commission in Ispra, Italy, provides a context for understanding global urbanization in the 21st century (25). Already, as evidenced in Figure 2.5 (26), he observes, of the world's 7.3 billion people, "more than half of the population is living in urban areas." By 2050, "the world population is expected to increase by 2.3 billion—to 9.3 billion."

Most threatening, perhaps, is that during these years "the urban population is projected to gain 2.6 billion, passing from 3.6 billion in 2011 to 6.3 billion in 2050" (25), mostly in the less developed regions like Asia, Africa, Latin America, and the Caribbean. The major challenge facing these regions in this century is how "to manage the development of urban areas in a sustainable way" (27). The task is enormous.

As two examples, escalating urbanization in China and India has led to eroding social conditions, which will likely be exacerbated in the coming decades. Population predictions indicate that India will add a further 497 million people to its urban population by 2050; China, 341 million; Nigeria, 200 million; and the United States, 100 million (26). This fast and unplanned growth will, without question, have a

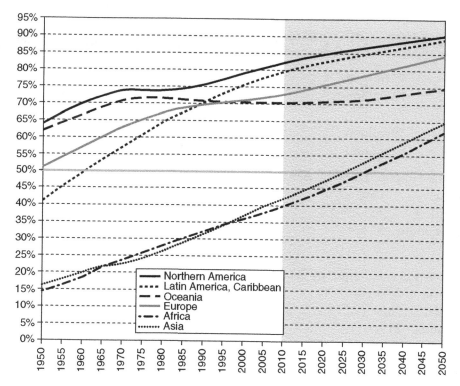

FIGURE 2.5 Urban population by major geographical area (in per cent of total population).
Source: United Nations Department of Economic and Social Affairs, *World Urbanization Prospects, the 2011 Revision* (26).

significant impact on the health and well-being of the planet and populations. On the other hand, Western Europe's population is expected to decrease considerably in the next 30 years—by as much as 25%—given the low birth rates, which is a major factor responsible for population decreases among several European nations (Box 2.2; 28)

Africa's population reached 1 billion in 2009 and joined India and China as the third region of the world to reach this threshold. It is expected to grow by more than 500 million people in the next 17 years and a further 500 million by 2050, with 60% of its population living in cities, compared to 1950 when the continent had fewer than 500,000 urban dwellers (27). By 2100, estimates are that Africa's population will be between 9 and 13 billion. Growth of Africa's largest cities is shown in Figure 2.6.

The World Bank predicts that

as the coastal cities of Africa and Asia expand, many of their poorest residents are being pushed to the edges of livable land and into the most dangerous zones for climate change. Their informal settlements cling to riverbanks and cluster in low-lying areas with poor drainage, few public services, and no protection from storm surges, sea-level rise, and flooding.

These communities—the poor in coastal cities and on low-lying islands—are among the world's most vulnerable to climate change and the least able to marshal the resources to adapt, a new report finds. They face a world where climate change will increasingly threaten the food supplies of sub-Saharan Africa and the farm fields and water resources of South Asia and South East Asia within the next three decades, while extreme weather puts their homes and lives at risk. (29)

BOX 2.2

Population of Major European Countries by 2060

UK   77 million
France   72 million
Germany   71 million
Italy   59 million
Spain   52 million

Increases in population by 2060:
Cyprus   66%
Ireland   53%
Luxembourg   52%
UK   25%

Decreases in population by 2060:
Bulgaria   28%
Latvia   26%
Lithuania   24%
Romania   21%

Gurgaon, India's new model city, represents another major crisis in the making. Just 20 years ago, it was "a sleepy town—little more than a village—surrounded by miles of open farmland" (30). Now, the city with a population of about 17,000,000, swelling at a rate of around 1 million per year, is illustrative of problems that others are likely facing, or will be soon. As India's fastest growing city, it now boasts "skyscrapers, shopping malls, and gated residential developments, a corporate park called 'Cyber City' housing some of the world's leading IT and commercial companies." But, along with outward symbols of progress, it now suffers from very serious public health challenges: "chronic water shortages, a power supply so erratic that business and private residents are obliged to provide their own backup generators and a drainage system so inadequate that in monsoon time sewage bubbles up on the pavements." Set against "pockets of immense wealth," abject squalor and deprivation abound. More than 200,000 migrants a year make their way into the city and are forced to live "in slums and squatter camps." A government report predicts that by 2021, Gurgaon's population will more than double "generating 533 million litres of sewage a day," but with a capacity of treating only 255 million liters and with the prospect of becoming "literally, a city drowning in its excreta."

While this "dystopian urban vision" may be changed by strategic public health interventions, including improved planning, systems, accountability, and addressing "bureaucratic inertia" while stamping out corruption, an underlying population problem is emerging: "an absence of community." As Pramod Bhasin, the nonexecutive vice-chairman of Genpact, a worldwide financial analytics and research company,

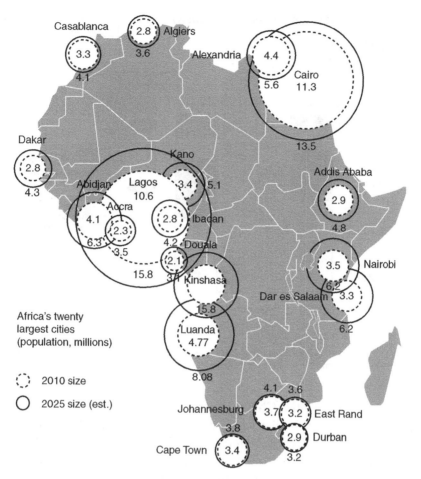

FIGURE 2.6 Growth of Africa's cities.

Source: Frontier Strategy Group, Capturing Africa's Transformative Urban Growth (2011; 27)

wisely infers, overcrowding coupled with lack of resources make "people selfish, concerned only for themselves . . . the breakdown of society," a problem "manufactured by society."

Similar issues are being faced in China, where by the end of 2012, the mainland had a total urban population of 712 million or 52.6% of the total population, rising from 26% in 1990, with a prediction that this will increase to nearly 70% by 2035 (31,32).

As shown in Figure 2.7, the McKinsey Global Institute projects that based "on current trends China's urban population will expand from 572 million in 2005 to 926 million in 2025," representing an increase of over 350 million Chinese city dwellers, which is "larger than the population of the United States today." And, "by 2030 China's population is on track to reach one billion" (33).

An example of moving millions from rural to urban areas in the southwest of China is the riverside city of Chongqing, selected in 2010 by Chinese leaders "in an attempt to find a low-carbon growth model that can be spread to the rest of the

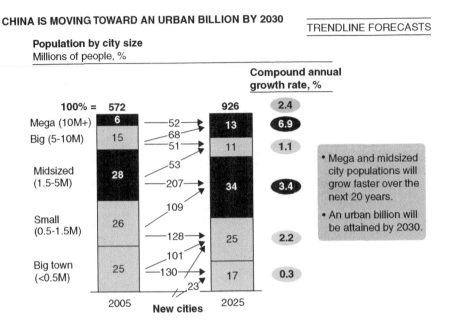

FIGURE 2.7 Number of cities in China.

Source: Exhibit from "Preparing for China's Urban Billion," February 2009, McKinsey Global Institute, www.mckinsey.com/mgi. Copyright © 2009 McKinsey & Company. All rights reserved. Reprinted by permission.

nation" (34). The city in central China (Figure 2.8) has a population of close to 33 million spread across a total of 36 districts and counties, straddling the Yangzi River, covering an area of 82,401 square kilometers, about the size of Scotland (35).

About 45% of Chongqing's people live in urban areas, but Chongqing's leaders are "determined to make their vast municipality an oasis of modernity in China's backward west." Their megacity dream is "that by 2020 the municipality must be 70% 'urbanised'" (36). However, like Gurgaon in India, Chongqing is struggling as "its socioeconomic development is characterized by fragmented growth, huge disparities between the rural and urban areas, enormous challenges in terms of energy, environmental protection, infrastructure and land-use as well as corruption and opacity problems" (37). In terms of cleaner air, commendably, "Chongqing first changed the fuel of its taxis, replacing their gasoline tanks with natural gas. Meanwhile, light rail was set to run up and down its hilly streets, luring private car drivers into mass transit. Heavy industries—all of them major polluters—were ordered to relocate to the outskirts in industrial parks with tighter environmental controls" (37).

Based on the goals of the 12th 5-year plan, there appear to be two priority areas: "becoming more service oriented"—"while letting the market play an increasingly larger role," thereby growing "a large private sector," shown to be possible in the south of China, "where an entrepreneurial spirit has played an important role through the last two decades." The other priority is "reducing the differences between the rural and urban population." Important measures to be undertaken may involve a better legal system and transparency, access to finance, and a better education system (37). Comparisons have been made with Chicago, "a gateway to vast and largely undeveloped lands to its west, a hub where the traffic of roads, rail lines and waterways

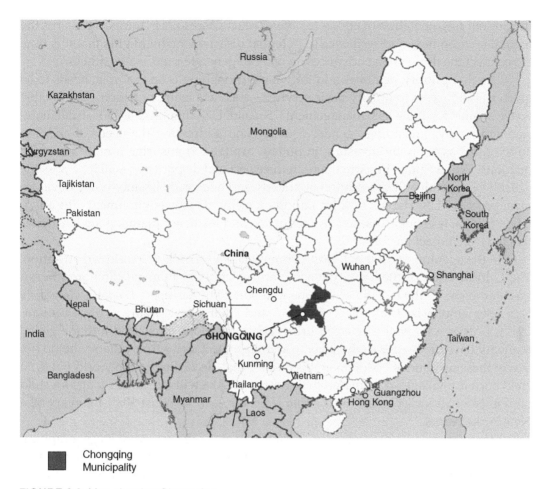

Chongqing
Municipality

FIGURE 2.8 Map showing Chongqing.

Source: Adapted from *Wikipedia*—Location map: China, Chongqing (Creative Commons Attribution-ShareAlike License).

converged, and a centre for business where ambition eviscerated risk." They have also been made with Detroit, as Chongqing is "China's third- or fourth-biggest car manufacturing centre" (36).

While these aspirations are laudable, lessons may be learned from other cities that have or are experiencing a "boom and bust cycle" that may become more commonplace as we continue into this century. As one example, in the United States, the world's wealthiest nation, Detroit, "the engine-room of the nation's 20th century economic boom," in the 20th century experienced "a rude awakening from the American dream," filing for bankruptcy in July 2013 owing US$20 billion to 100,000 creditors, caused largely by "abandonment, racial tensions and financial missteps" (38).

As executive director of the United Nations Human Settlements Programme (UN-Habitat), the UN agency for human settlements and sustainable urban development, Dr. Joan Clos stresses that "it is in cities around the world that the pressures of globalization, migration, social inequality, environmental pollution and climate change and youth unemployment are most directly felt" (39). He further asserts that "good urban development is key to achieving global sustainable development." Recognizing the present fragmentation of efforts to deliver practical results in terms of poverty, the natural environment and resilience to potential disasters, he highlights that it is time "to connect the dots, so that advances on one can generate progress on others."

The first priority, he notes, and for which Chongqing is an example, needs to be given to the "access to quality basic services—such as health, nutrition, safe potable water, sanitation, and waste management." Second, UN-Habitat calls "for social inclusion and equity," including "gender equality, and addressing the needs of children and youth," as "only by investing in human capital and ensuring a more equitable distribution of wealth—in particular to reduce national disparities—will it be possible to achieve a sustainable eradication of poverty and a territory balance of the development process." UN-Habitat's "third important element is the environment. The adaptation to climate change, disaster risk reduction and resilience planning are key issues that have an impact on cities."

In the opening chapter of *Global Urbanization*, (40) entitled "World Urbanization: The Critical Issue of the Twenty-First Century," authors Eugenie Birch and Susan Wachter reference the World Development Report 2009: *Reshaping Economic Geography* (41). They emphasize that "place matters," and "that people living in highly urbanized countries with well-connected urban agglomerations integrated into the global economy have higher per capita income and life expectancies than others who do not live in these conditions." Moreover, they assert that, according to the World Bank, "a child born in a village far from Zambia's capital Lusaka will live half as long as a child born in New York City—and during that short life, will earn just $0.01 for every $2 a New Yorker earns."

The ultimate goal, they observe, is that "any city—regardless of its geographical location—would be proud to achieve. . . . an inclusive, vibrant economy; environmentally responsible development; and an infrastructure resilient in the face of continued population growth and natural disaster." Moreover, they highlight that "responding to this growth and its environmental and societal challenges requires better governance and economic solutions as well as an enhanced capacity to plan at all levels of government."

Joan Clos identifies a number of planning measures that Gurgaon planners could consider (39). These include adopting a green economy, building effective partnerships, encouraging citizen participation, and the development of global urban roadmaps and national urban strategies in general. These might be appropriate not only for cities like Gurgaon but also for economically emerging or poorer countries. Indeed, they might also be instrumental in averting future disasters in the richer nations as is the case with Detroit (38).

2.4 OUR FRAGILE ECOSYSTEMS: ENSURING PLANETARY HEALTH AND WELL-BEING

The planet's ecosystems are highly vulnerable, and with increases in greenhouse gas emissions, there are good reasons for concern. As an example, carbon dioxide (CO_2) levels in the atmosphere, which remain in the atmosphere for about 100 years, reached a significant milestone this year as the amount of CO_2 in the atmosphere was at the

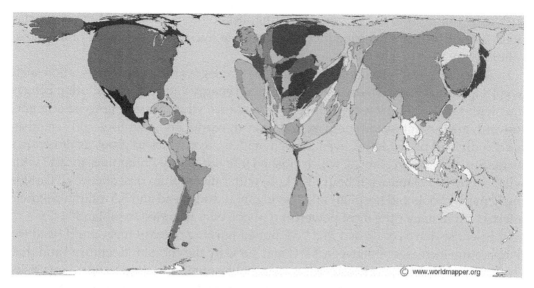

FIGURE 2.9 Release of sulfur dioxide (territory size shows the proportion of all sulfur dioxide emitted from the burning of coal, lignite, and petroleum products there).

Source: Worldmapper.org. Map 301, Sulfur Dioxide. © Copyright SASI Group (University of Sheffield) and Mark Newman (University of Michigan). Reproduced under Creative Commons license https://creativecommons.org/licenses/by-nc-nd/3.0.

highest levels in 5 million years at 400 parts per million, compared to about 300 parts in 1958 and an increase of about 40% since the Industrial Revolution. As shown in Figure 2.9, the result of human activity, for example, burning fossil fuels—petrol, diesel, and kerosene to heat homes, businesses, and power factories—releases CO_2 stored millions of years ago and erodes the plant gas exchange (respiration and decay), which "is almost perfectly balanced" (42).

Climate researchers predict that climate change may have "unequal impacts globally," and potential health threats experienced by many could include inter alia, increases in skin cancers, cardiorespiratory disease, flooding, droughts, storms, and damage to food and water supplies and health. Those living in poor and developing countries may be "less able to adapt to the changes" (31).

A recent report by the WHO International Agency for Research on Cancer (43,44) should help raise awareness and accelerate global government action. In their report, the research agency classified "air pollution by exhaust fumes and industrial waste as carcinogens to humans," responsible in 2010 "for the deaths of 223,000 lung cancer patients around the world" and possibly "an increased risk of bladder cancer."

A notable concern, according to Dr. Markus Reichstein, from the Max Planck Institute in Germany, is that "as extreme climate events reduce the amount of carbon that the terrestrial ecosystems absorb, and the carbon dioxide in the atmosphere therefore continues to increase, more extreme weather could result" (45). Moreover, researchers from the Potsdam Institute found that "3 sigma events—heatwaves that should occur in a particular region less than once a century—would double in frequency by 2020 and quadruple by 2040." Given "that everything we do in the modern world increases the burden of carbon dioxide in the atmosphere—burning fossil fuels, such as petrol in cars, gas in central heating, heating boilers and coal in power stations" as well as manufacturing processes and that livestock are a source of methane, solutions are hard to implement.

The public health solution is of course to "urge governments to take action such as cutting carbon emissions by using more green energy and curbing polluting behaviour with taxes" (46). However, these interventions, while appearing to be straightforward, are not in today's complex and uneven world, and countries and scientists remain divided on the issue, even though evidence continues to grow, as illustrated by the Super Typhoon Haiyan, which crashed into the central Philippines in 2013 with winds of up to 195 miles per hour (300 kph) with catastrophic consequences, "flattening homes, schools and hospitals and leaving thousands dead and 5.5 million children affected." It remains "the most powerful typhoon ever recorded to hit land" (47).

Scientists have concluded that "continued burning of fossil fuels could [lead to] temperature increases of between 3.7°C and 4.8°C by the end of the century" and that "warming beyond 4°C would likely result in 'substantial species extinction, large risks to global and regional food security, impacts on normal human activities'" (48).

As a welcome sign that climate change is being taken seriously, almost 200 governments "have agreed to try to limit global warming to below 3.6°F (2°C) above pre-industrial times, which is seen as a threshold for dangerous changes including more droughts, extinctions, floods and rising sea that could swamp coastal regions and island nations" (49).

According to scientists, it would take about 5,000 years for all the ice—most of which is concentrated in the East Antarctic ice sheet on earth—to melt as it did during the Eocene Epoch (Figure 2.10)—a period of increased temperatures 34 million years ago. Sea levels could rise by 216 feet, "changing shorelines and engulfing entire cities worldwide" (50). As examples, The Netherlands, Denmark, and large parts of eastern England and London would disappear. "The entire Atlantic seaboard would vanish along with Florida and the Gulf coast. In Asia, land now inhabited by 600 million Chinese people would flood, as would all of Bangladesh and much of coastal India" (51).

Dr. Ted Nield, a geologist and editor of *Geoscientist*, affirms that according to sediment cores taken from the Atlantic, what is happening now—"a greenhouse world," injecting carbon into the atmosphere "at about the same rate as today"—has happened before, "55 million years ago" (52). "And the results then weren't pretty. . . . global temperatures shot up. Water close to the ocean floor rose from (an already very high) 11°C (this was already a 'greenhouse' world) to 15°C" and "in a direct mirror of modern times, sea levels rose to a degree that would displace 90 per cent of the present world's population."

Dr. Nield's response to the way forward is to accept that if "we are responsible for global warming, then we are able to do something about it." Alternatively, he concludes that "if it's all down to changes in the Sun, or in the Earth's orbit, or any of the other things that climate-change deniers assert, then we are in serious trouble."

Evidence for this assertion abounds, with California experiencing the worst drought (a "megadrought") in 500 years, leading "to fierce wildfires, water shortages and restrictions, and potentially staggering agricultural losses," impacting on loss

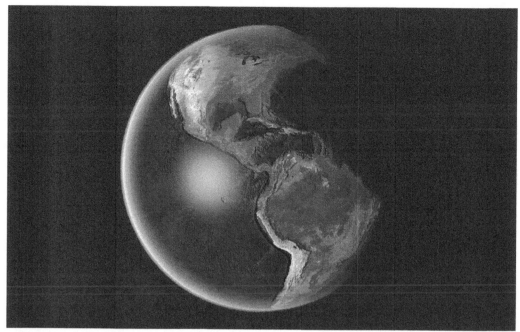

Western

Near Eastern

FIGURE 2.10 An earth without ice: potential flooding of coastlines. (*continued*)

Far Eastern

FIGURE 2.10 (*continued*) An earth without ice: potential flooding of coastlines.

of jobs and economic activity (53); and Delhi, India, now exceeding Beijing's pollution levels (Figure 2.11; 54). These are extremely dangerous as they consist of sulfate, nitrates, ammonia, and carbon particles under 2.5 microns in diameter that are small enough to pass into the bloodstream and cause premature deaths from diseases such as lung cancer and emphysema.

A former Chinese health minister, Chen Zhu, now president of the China Medical Association, reported that "air pollution in China is killing as many as half a million people each year" (55) and that China continues to "confront the same trade-off as its

FIGURE 2.11 Beijing: View of skyline after rain and on a sunny day.

Source: Bobak Ha'Eri, https://commons.wikimedia.org/wiki/File:Beijing_smog_comparison_August_2005.png.

predecessors between soaring economic growth and the nation's health." He further observed that China spewed out more of the main pollutants than any other country, but that "prevention and control of environmental pollution in China is difficult because there are multiple pollution sources and pollutants across cities and regions." Beijing has committed US$277.5 billion over 5 years to preventing and controlling air pollution, and if targets are met, 200,000 fewer people would die prematurely each year, according to *The Lancet* article. It said the main polluters in the country were industry, coal, and vehicles.

There can be little doubt that most pollution stems from uncontrolled technology. While some may be reluctant to connect atmospheric changes with extreme weather patterns, our planet's ecology seems increasingly to be under threat. Ignoring this truth is definitely not an option, despite some in "big business" wanting us to think otherwise.

Referenced previously, the most recent UN Intergovernmental Panel on Climate Change (IPCC) report, released in November 2014 in Copenhagen, Denmark, warns that the world can expect "'severe and perverse' negative impacts from climate change unless rapid action is taken to cut greenhouse gas emissions" (48), including "flooding, dangerous heatwaves, ill health and violent conflicts."

In May 2014, the U.S. Global Change Research Program released its third National Climate Assessment report (56), which, after extensive research involving over 300 scientists, corroborates the IPCC findings, making it very clear that while climate change is being caused by natural influences, the greatest contributors are of human origin (Figure 2.12), based on "multiple lines of independent evidence . . . of the past 50 years."

Since the stakes for the planet are high, it seems crucial that the two governments—the United States and China—"have agreed to cooperate, and the US is

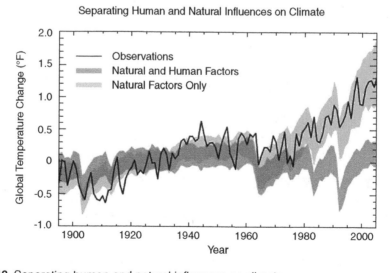

FIGURE 2.12 Separating human and natural influences on climate.

Source: Adapted from M. Huber and R. Knutti, "Anthropogenic and Natural Warming Inferred From Changes in Earth's Energy Balance," *Nature Geoscience* (2011). U.S. Global Change Research Program, 2014 (56). http://www.globalchange.gov/browse/multimedia/%EF%BF%BCseparating-human-and-natural-influences-climate

prioritizing an international agreement in Paris." In addition, "61 of the 66 countries responsible for 88 per cent of the world's emissions have passed legislation to control them: in all, nearly 500 laws have been adopted worldwide" (57).

There appears to be considerable urgency in matching evidence to action, as shown in Figure 2.13. According to data released by the National Oceanic and Atmospheric Administration in their report, *The Earth Just Had Its Warmest "Year" on Record*,

> The past 12 months—October 2013–September 2014—was the warmest 12-month period among all months since records began in 1880, at 0.69°C (1.24°F) above the 20th century average. This breaks the previous record of +0.68°C (+1.22°F) set for the periods September 1998–August 1998, August 2009–July 2010; and September 2013–August 2014. (58)

And while activists and skeptics remain unconvinced about the effects of climate change, they might take a moment to browse through the latest edition of the World Wildlife Fund (WWF) *Living Planet Report* (59) discussed further in Section 7.3.

Marco Lambertini, Director General of WWF International, highlights that "in less than two human generations, population sizes of vertebrate species have dropped by half. These are the living forms that constitute the fabric of the ecosystems which sustain life on Earth–and the barometer of what we are doing to our own planet, our only home. We ignore their decline at our peril."

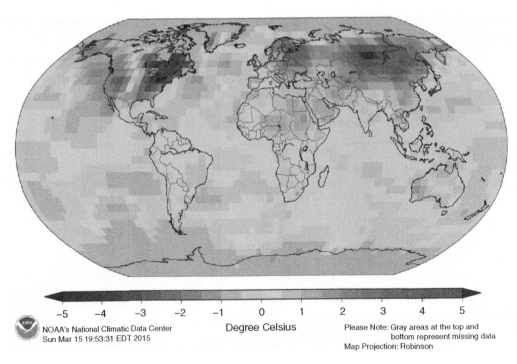

NOAA's National Climatic Data Center
Sun Mar 15 19:53:31 EDT 2015

Degree Celsius

Please Note: Gray areas at the top and bottom represent missing data
Map Projection: Robinson

FIGURE 2.13 Land and ocean temperature departure from average, January through February 2015 (with respect to a 1981–2010 base period).

Source: National Oceanic and Atmospheric Administration's National Climatic Data Center, 2015.

2.5 PROBLEMS OF MODERNITY: GENETIC INCONGRUENCE?

Societal Evolution

Beginning with the 17th century Age of Enlightenment, which radically transformed primary and secondary European social institutions, modernity is generally associated with industrialization and capitalism from the 18th to the 21st centuries, "culminating in the current, post-modern state of globalisation which shapes contemporary society" (60). Sociologist Keeley Knowles has traced the four main phases of societal evolution from about 12,000 BCE to today's information age in Box 2.3.

Progress toward modernity, including "the realisation of democracy," has come at a steep price. While these human costs are still taking their toll today in Europe, Africa, the Middle East, and other parts of the world, modernity is also exacting another cost—highlighted in Box 2.3—undermining the health and well-being of both rich and increasingly poor countries through economism, materialism, and individualism (61).

In keeping with Keeley Knowles's overview, Ulrich Beck, author of *Risk Society: Towards a New Modernity* (61), posits that toward the later years of the 20th century,

BOX 2.3

Evolutionary Stages of Society

Until about 12,000 BCE
Families lived as hunter-gatherers—"kinship based with the family traditionally taking responsibility for gathering and distributing food, educating, and bestowing essential survival skills on their children."

Around 5,000 years ago in the Middle East
Hunter-gatherer societies transformed into an agrarian society, characterised by large-scale farming "and additional scientific advances, for example the use of the wheel, and irrigation, thereby transforming 'all areas of social life'."

Mid 18th century
The beginning of the industrial era "saw an unparalleled shift in familial life, leading to a loss of traditional values, changes in working patterns and the kinds of work available, and urbanisation—overall, a more impersonal, individualistic way of life."

Today
Our "post-industrial, information-based society" is "dominated by computer-linked technology: an age of globalisation," and "the interconnectedness of the world" best understood perhaps "through the imagery of global multicultural companies such as McDonald's," whereby "the process by which the principles of the fast-food restaurant are coming to dominate more and more sectors of American society as well as the rest of the world."

mainly in Europe and North America, "the overall frameworks and assumptions of early modernity were questioned and radically changed. Individualism deepened its hold on the western imagination" along with "the emergence of a highly educated *information* society which displaced the older manual worker society of the previous period."

The most significant shift, he alleges, was the decrease in "long term loyalty to the corporate institutions and structures of the 20th century" as "these new classes of people in the information society *reflected* (hence reflexive modernity) back on their relationships with these *institutions* concluding that they no longer needed to make them primary in order to maximize their own individual self development and biographies." To some extent, it may be argued that this transformation is continuing to shape nations in the Middle East and Eastern Europe, to mention several regions.

While physical suffering continues unabated in many global regions, we are increasingly having to adapt to the complexities and pressures of modern life, but without the evolutionary capacity or makeup to do so. The consequences can be damaging to the human mind and body spirit, exacerbated by, what seems for some, an often uncaring, competitive society, where materialism outweighs compassion and, as Keeley Knowles observed, "a loss of traditional values," beginning in the industrial era (60).

Fundamentally, it may be argued that in all global societies and economies, health and well-being—or the "'well-ness' of the persons' being" (62) are at risk and demand radically different solutions than we are used to providing, but these were more prominent in traditional societies that "shaped people's lives" and "gave them the symbols that provided meaning, place and purpose in society" along with "institutions that gave order to people's lives and [formed] tight social communities" (63).

Retaining Our Humanity

The current global situation, where personal "meaning and identity are grounded in *the self as the primary agent* of meaning" has become so tenuous that some writers are calling for "a new image of what it is to be human to begin to address the challenges of promoting well-being." Along similar lines, others encourage us to view ourselves "as human beings within a 'caring' context" (63) and within an integrated society.

The vital importance of retaining our humanity was exemplified by Edmund Husserl (1859–1938), a mathematician, founder of the 20th century philosophical school of phenomenology, and one of the most influential philosophers of the 20th century. Disenchanted with the importance given to quantitative measures at the expense of "the qualities of the human experience" (63), he asserted that "any human view of the world without subjectivity has excluded its basic foundation from the beginning."

Long-term solutions to the profound health and well-being challenges facing society globally have yet to be uncovered but belong squarely in the realms of improved collaboration, open and transparent governance, and more innovative and outcomes-based enabling action through public and population health. What is clear and discussed further in this book, however, is that "'experts' giving advice to those who need 'fixing'" does not solve population-based problems that are beyond civil engineering, scientism, restructuring or "risk" theory (63).

As we peer into this century, what seems paramount, according to Dr. Ann Hemingway from the Centre for Well-being and Public Health at Bournemouth University in England, is learning "from and with others to find a vision for the future" and focusing "on the way in which we as human beings experience our world." Further, she explains

> If we persist in viewing public health interventions as independent of their contexts where the prescribed elements of the program are more important than local human experiences and beliefs, we are at risk of ignoring the human assets when arguably these are the very strengths upon which a solution needs to build. How can we promote well-being freedoms within and across communities without knowing what it is like in human terms to live there? (62)

It appears that what the developed and developing worlds have in common at the beginning decades of the 21st century is an urgent need to find answers to a set of very different circumstances. Both could benefit substantially, however, from accelerating and strengthening change through public health organizations by increasingly sharing expertise along with environmental and epidemiological R&D and lessons learned in the 20th century about improving conditions for planet and population health and well-being.

Some of the priorities, as discussed later in this section, are those that are becoming more prevalent at the population level, such as mental health and addictive behaviors, and those that challenge the expertise of most professionals. These deep-seated problems—referenced earlier—may be indicative of a genetic and environmental dissonance or incongruence (64). In other words, the argument put forward is that, going back to Knowles's hunter and gatherer society (60), which stretched over millions of years, "we are biologically and psychologically 'hard–wired' in a way that does not suit the modern world" (64), and conventional wisdom or application of the standard public health intervention strategy—"understand, predict, control, provide," generally patterned after a reductionist view of reality, could have limited success (64). The global obesity epidemic may be a prime example of a mismatch between our evolutionary makeup and the lifestyle—food, activity, and values—that now confronts our species.

The Obesity Epidemic

While acknowledging the "good news that Canadians are living longer than ever before," a letter by the president of the Ontario Medical Association (OMA) to the editor of the Canadian *Maclean's Magazine* also provides some "concerning news"—more than half of the Canadians "are now overweight or obese" (65). The findings from the Canadian study could be a "wake-up call" for many nations.

According to the U.S. Centers for Disease Control and Prevention, a person's body mass index (BMI) is "calculated as weight in kilograms divided by height in meters squared, rounded to one decimal place. Obesity in adults is defined as BMI greater than or equal to 30" (66). Examples of adult obesity cut points at specific heights are shown in Table 2.1.

TABLE 2.1 Obesity Cut Points for Adults 5′4″ and 5′9″

HEIGHT	OBESITY WEIGHT RANGE
5 feet 4 inches or 1.63 meters	174 pounds or more, or 79 kilograms or more
5 feet 9 inches or 1.75 meters	203 pounds or more, or 92 kilograms or more

Table 2.2 shows recent combined data of the Organisation for Economic Co-operation and Development (OECD) of adults who are overweight and obese across 40 nations (67). Of these, nine are in the 60%+ range with Mexico an the U.S. heading the list at 69.5% and 69.2%, respectively.; 12 in the 50%+ range; and 13 in the 40%+ range with most edging toward 50%. Only six nations are in the 30% range, with

TABLE 2.2 OECD Data of Adults Who Are Either Overweight or Obese

		TOTAL OVERWEIGHT AND OBESE			TOTAL OVERWEIGHT AND OBESE
1.	Australia	61.2	22.	Japan	25.3
2.	Austria	47.7	23.	Korea	30.2
3	Belgium	46.9	24.	Luxembourg	59.1
4.	Brazil	48.1	25.	Mexico	**69.5**
5.	Canada	60.0	26.	Netherlands	48.2
6.	Chile	64.5	27.	New Zealand	64.7
7.	China	18.9	28.	Norway	46.0
8.	Czech Republic	55.0	29.	Poland	52.2
9.	Denmark	46.7	30.	Portugal	51.6
10.	Estonia	48.6	31.	Russian Federation	44.0
11.	Finland	59.2	32.	Slovak Republic	51.5
12.	France	42.9	33.	Slovenia	55.1
13.	Germany	51.4	34.	South Africa	42.4
14.	Greece	55.7	35.	Spain	53.6
15.	Hungary	61.6	36.	Sweden	46.9
16.	Iceland	58.5	37.	Switzerland	37.3
17.	India	10.9	38.	Turkey	49.9
18.	Indonesia	13.4	39.	United Kingdom	62.8
19.	Ireland	61.0	40.	United States	**69.2**
20.	Israel	50.1		EU Average	52.7
21.	Italy	46.0		OECD Average	52.7

Source: OECD, Factbook 2013: Economic, Environmental and Social Statistics. http://www.oecd-ilibrary.org/sites/factbook-2013-en/12/02/03/index.html?itemId=/content/chapter/factbook-2013-100-en.

the lowest being Japan at 25.3%. Japan and Korea have the lowest overweight and obesity rates. Japan also has the highest life expectancy. If trends continue, then it is conceivable that many other nations will soon see rates increasing to 70% and beyond.

A recent analysis by the Overseas Development Institute (ODI; 68) corroborates the findings from Table 2.2 (67). As shown in Figure 2.14, using data from Stevens et al. (69) and as reported by ODI (68), "globally, the percentage of adults who were overweight or obese"—classed, and mentioned previously—having a body mass index greater than 25, "grew from 23% to 34% between 1980 and 2008" (68).

Moreover, the report concludes (68):

- The number of overweight and obese adults in the developing world has almost quadrupled to around 1 billion since 1980.
- One in three people worldwide are now overweight. The majority of this increase is seen in the developing world, particularly in countries where incomes are rising, such as Egypt and Mexico.
- A total of 904 million people in developing countries are now classed as overweight or above, with a BMI of more than 25, up from 250 million in 1980. This compares to 557 million in high-income countries. Over the same period, the global population nearly doubled.
- Regionally, the greatest increases have been in North America, with the highest percentage of overweight adults at approximately 70% and regions such as Australasia and southern Latin America, which are now not far behind at 63%. Latin America, North Africa, and the Middle East are now on a par with Europe at around 58%.

While "under-nourishment is still recognised to be a problem for hundreds of millions of people in the developing world, particularly children," the greatest growth in overweight people occurred in southeast Asia, where the percentage tripled from a lower starting point of 7% to 22%. Further, "among individual countries, the report found that

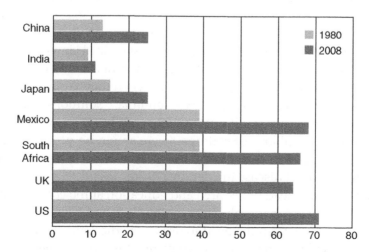

FIGURE 2.14 Percentage of overweight and obese adults with BMI greater than 25, by country.
Sources: Overseas Development Institute (ODI; 68); Stevens et al (69).

overweight and obesity rates had almost doubled in China and Mexico, and risen by a third in South Africa since 1980" along with many countries in the Middle East (68).

The causes of obesity are complex and diverse. As one example, Kate Smith, a research economist at the Institute for Fiscal Studies (IFS) and a contributing author of the report *Food Expenditure and Nutritional Quality Over the Great Recession* (70), notes that because of rising grocery bills and stagnant incomes, "households bought fewer calories and have switched to cheaper calories. This has coincided with a switch towards more calorie-dense types of food and substitution to more calorific food products within food types." Moreover, the report contends that "pensioners, households with young children and single-parent households experienced a larger decline in the nutritional quality of the foods they purchased."

Another trigger may be stressful lifestyles, often compounded by feelings of unhappiness and depression; as a consequence, these may lead to the temptation to overindulge. Professor Buckroyd notes that "a number of studies have highlighted the fact that obesity and overeating are attempts to 'control an overwhelming internal anxiety state'" and that these people believe they are trying to make themselves feel better, even if, of course, they are not doing this in reality (71). Social distress caused by rising youth unemployment in European countries undergoing severe austerity measures is also a major cause for concern and may have health implications (72).

For some, "a treat can repeatedly turn into a full-blown food binge," thereby putting themselves at other "serious health risks associated with obesity, including type 2 diabetes, high cholesterol, heart and gallbladder disease" (73). In type 2 diabetes, "the hormone insulin can't properly transport glucose from the bloodstream to muscles and cells . . . worsened by carrying extra weight, being inactive and eating lots of saturated fat." A key problem relates to "the damage to blood vessels that occurs when blood glucose levels remain high for long periods of time," leading to "heart disease, kidney disease, eye damage and circulation problems" (73).

The food-bingeing behavior, which may be "a genetically-determined problem," or, according to some experts, may be "more the product of our food-rich environment" (71), or perhaps both, has become so prevalent that the diagnosis of "'binge eating disorder' has now been added to the U.S. *Diagnostic and Statistical Manual of Mental Disorders* [Fifth Edition]" (74), alongside anorexia and bulimia.

Christopher Fairburn, professor of psychiatry at Oxford University and an expert in binge eating, advises that "people suffering from binge eating disorder tend to be overweight and, in addition to this, have phases when they regularly binge eat—but without the purging behavior associated with bulimia." Solutions, according to campaigners, demand "a return to traditional outdoor childhoods" as well as better eating, as evidence shows that millions of children "were shunning vegetables and exercise in favour of fizzy drinks in front of the television," thereby increasing their chances of developing coronary heart disease in later life (75,76).

Dr. Adam al-Kashi, head of research and education at the charity BackCare, cautions that while "there are many pluses to modern life and technology. . . the darker side is how it divorces us from the need to use our bodies and exert ourselves physically. . . . we are now living dangerously convenient lifestyles where you don't even have to move to exist" (77). The key lesson for us, he comments, is "that too much of something is bad. Most of today's advances only require us to exert comparatively minimal effort to get things done, depriving our bodies of the need for adequate movement to remain healthy."

Providing a rather frank and introspective perception of familial eating habits, columnist Dominic Lawson, in his article "Fat Is a Self-Control Issue—Take It From Supersize Me" (78), references his paternal great-grandfather, who died "because he was too corpulent for the surgeons of the day to operate on successfully." His main thesis is that "the greatest prejudice against the morbidly obese [is] that this condition is the outcome of a dreadful absence of self-control," suggesting further "that binge-eating, like alcoholism, is generally caused by deep unhappiness of some sort." The problem, he argues further, "is one of delayed gratification. Or, more precisely, those of us who overeat are revealing a rather childish inability to defer pleasure," a trait "that was demonstrated by the hugely influential Stanford marshmallow experiment "of the 1970s, that children who were able to defer eating marshmallows demonstrated "higher academic performance and lower levels of uncontrolled *aggression and impulsiveness*." Given the evidence base for overeating, health care provider support for obesity is astonishing or bewildering. As one example, in all of Derbyshire, a county in England, ambulances "are to be equipped to carry patients weighing up to 50 stone" (700 pounds) by 2016 at a cost of approximately £100,000 per ambulance and a total cost of approximately £27 million. Additional costs will also need to be borne by hospitals where "necessary equipment, from trolleys to beds to operating tables, will also need adapting" (79).

Journalist India Knight may be speaking for many when she posits that "Weight is an indicator of social class, and what an ugly, messed-up portrait it paints" (80). Obese children tend to come from poorer families, who eat a diet of cheap filling rubbish that makes them fat and ill. The classic profile of an eating disordered child is one who is from a "high achieving and middle-class family, although there is overlap in both directions." She also emphasizes that "healthy eating habits start in babyhood and that there is not much to be gained by pandering to a fussy eater. And, while eating 'more veg' and running 'around more' are fine . . . 'none of it is going to amount to much if we don't also address the question of unhappiness that surrounds the issue."

Approaches to addressing obesity seem to have limited success as recent data indicate. Mexico has now surpassed the United States, and an astounding number of boys and girls—82%—are now overweight or obese in Greece (Table 2.3).

The Sugar Epidemic

To tackle the growing crisis, the Mexico Congress "has imposed a hefty tax on sugary drinks and junk food in an effort to trim the nation's bulging waistline, drawing the attention of public health experts worldwide": 1 peso-per-liter tax on soft drinks and an 8% levy on fatty foods (81). Moreover, "according to a report by news service Reuters, Mexicans are the world's greatest soft drink consumers, guzzling on average 7,070.24 litre servings per person each year, compared with an average 701 servings in the United States. The move makes Mexico the first of the world's large soft drink markets to impose such a tax, which has been proposed in several countries grappling with the health effects of high calorie diets."

TABLE 2.3 Overweight and Obesity Rates in Children

COUNTRY	YEAR	AGE (YEARS)	OVERWEIGHT (INCLUDING OBESE)	
			BOYS	GIRLS
Australia	2007	2–16	22.0	24.0
Belgium	2010	10–12	16.9	13.5
Canada	2004	6–17	28.9	26.1
Czech Republic	2005	6–17	24.6	16.8
Denmark	1996/1997	5–16	14.1	15.3
England	2009	5–17	21.8	26.1
France	2006–2007	3–17	13.1	14.9
Germany	2008	4–16	22.6	17.7
Greece	2010	10–12	44.4	37.7
Hungary	2010	10–12	27.7	22.6
Iceland	1998	9	22.0	25.5
India	2007–2008	2–17	20.6	18.3
Ireland (Republic)	2003–2004	5–12	19.4	28.9
Italy	2008	7	37.2	34.7
Japan	1996–2000	6–14	16.2	14.3
Mexico	2006	6–17	28.1	29.0
Netherlands	2010	10–12	16.8	15.4
New Zealand	2007	5–14	28.2	28.8
Norway	2010	10-12	15.1	13.8
Poland	2000	7–17	16.3	12.4
Portugal	2008	6–8	30.0	26.1
Slovakia	2001	7–17	17.5	16.2
Slovenia	2010	10–12	31.7	22.5
Spain	2012	8–17	32.3	29.5
Sweden	2000	10	17.0	19.5
Switzerland	2007	6–13	16.7	13.1
Turkey	2001	12–17	11.3	10.3
United States (1)	2003–2004	6–17	35.0	35.9

Note: All rates use International Obesity Taskforce (IOTF) reference to overweight and obese.

Source: M. Shields, M. S. Tremblay, "Canadian Childhood Obesity Estimates Based on WHO, IOTF and CDC Cut-Points," *International Journal of Pediatric Obesity.* 2010;5(3):265–273 (65).

There is overwhelming evidence that "fat and sugar—[which] trigger the release of endorphins and dopamines—the body's feel-good chemicals, inducing a natural high" (71)—contribute to obesity, diabetes, cardiovascular disease, and tooth decay. In fact, the *New York Times* reports that tooth decay in kids as young as 2 years is becoming more and more common (82). According to the *Times*, severe tooth decay in young kids can be caused by "endless snacking and juice or other sweet drinks at bedtime, parents who choose bottled water rather than fluoridated tap water for their children, and a lack of awareness that infants should, according to pediatric experts, visit a dentist by age 1 to be assessed for future cavity risk, even though they may have only a few teeth."

The harm done by sugar is corroborated by the American Dental Association, which cautions that "each and every time bacteria come in contact with sugar or starch in the mouth, acid is produced, which attacks the teeth for 20 minutes or more. This eventually can result in tooth decay." Published studies show that "tooth decay is the most common chronic disease on the planet, affecting five billion people, or nearly 80 percent of the world's population" (83).

In 2010, the global Alliance for a Cavity-Free Future that promotes an integrated clinical and public health effort was formed, with a global declaration signed by members of the World Health Organization, Pan American Health Organization, FDI World Dental Federation, and the International Association of Dental Research (IADR; 83).

Recognizing that most people do not do enough to prevent caries, the Alliance "calls for joint action to challenge leaders and stakeholders in the community to learn the importance of caries as a disease continuum by recognising that cavities are preventable and that in the early stages caries is reversible, and to develop comprehensive programs for the prevention and management of dental caries appropriate for individual regions" (83). Their ultimate aim is that "every child born from 2026 should stay cavity free during his or her lifetime." As noted in Box 2.4, their strategy builds incrementally with targets set for 2015, 2020, and 2026 and is based on five key interventions.

Governing their global approach, which may resonate with other public health issues and health/social care systems, discussed further in Chapter 8.0, is the importance of educating "dental professionals and the public on the importance of preventative measures designed to stop caries before they ever develop, or at the very least identify and fight them at their early stages" (Box 2.5; 83).

BOX 2.4

Global Alliance for a Cavity-Free Future: Long-Term Goals

- By 2015, 90% of dental schools and dental associations should have embraced and promoted the "new" approach of "caries as a continuum" to improve dental caries prevention and management.
- By 2020, regional members of the *Alliance for a Cavity-Free Future* should have integrated, locally appropriate, comprehensive caries prevention ad management systems and monitoring developed and in place.
- Every child born in 2026 should stay cavity-free during his or her lifetime.

BOX 2.5

Global Alliance for a Cavity-Free Future: Prevention Strategy

- Launching four local chapters in Latin America and an upcoming launch of a chapter in China
- Launching in-local-language Web-based content for professionals and families
- Partnering with local Ministries of Health and other local stakeholders
- Working to standardize the caries curriculum at key academic institutions
- Developing intervention models that can be used to address oral health in early childhood (83)

The WHO is advocating reducing the worldwide recommended level of free sugars (all sugars—"added to foods by the manufacturer, cook, or consumer, plus sugars naturally present in honey, syrups and fruit juices") from 10% to 5% (about five teaspoons per day) of total energy intake (84).

Disturbingly, and raising concerns about corporate social responsibility, in Mexico, "Coke Fesma told the market it would pass the tax onto consumers by increasing the cost of its products by between 12 and 15%" (85). There are also fears now that "imposing a tax on sugar in drinks could push manufacturers into looking at alternatives, or encourage consumers to spend more on soft drinks and less on other items, including possibly more healthy food." In the United States, the sugar industry "threatened to lobby for America to cut £260 m of funding to WHO when its experts recommended cutting sugar consumption to 10% in 2003."

Speaking at a conference in June 2013, WHO Director-General Margaret Chan stressed that "it is not just 'Big Tobacco' any more" but that "public health must also contend with Big Food, Big Soda, and Big Alcohol. All of these industries fear regulation and protect themselves by using the same tactics," which, like the tobacco industry, "tried to suppress scientific evidence that smoking was bad for people's health" (86).

Rob Moodie, professor of public health at the University of Melbourne, in his paper, "Unhealthy Big Business Spreading Great Harm," observes that "tobacco, alcohol, and diabetes related to overweight and obesity all have one feature in common. They are each largely driven and, in the case of tobacco, completely caused by powerful commercial interests in the form of transnational corporations. It has been said that China's booming economy has brought with it a medical problem that could bankrupt the health system" (87).

Further, he concludes (highlighted further in Chapter 7.0) "we now face a major dilemma: unrestrained commercial development is pitted against the health and well-being of populations. This dilemma is not new—opponents of the abolition of slavery complained it would ruin the economy—but it is manifesting in more obvious ways in the 21st century." However, what makes the battle even harder is that "the major tobacco, food, and alcohol companies have assets that are greater than many countries and can wield this power in parliament, law courts and the media, against the interests of the public's health."

Current Global Versus Paleolithic Diet

While the world has progressed on many fronts, our sedentary and food-rich lifestyle may become our downfall when we compare ourselves to hunter-gatherer societies, from which we inherited our congenital traits. Their food intake consisted of about 35% plant and 65% animal foods compared, for example, to the current African diet, which is based on cereals (46%), roots and tubers (20%), and very few animal products (7%; 88).

As shown in Figure 2.15a (88), today's average global diet consists largely of cereals (51%), oils, fats, and sugars (19.5%), and milk, fish, and eggs (13.5%), with 8.2% fruits, vegetables, pulses, and nuts, and only 5.3% roots and tubers—quite different from the Paleolithic (Old Stone Age) diet that may be more in harmony with our genetic makeup (Figure 2.15b; 89).

Loren Cordain, professor and researcher in the Health and Exercise Science Department at Colorado State University, argues that "when cereal grain calories reach 50% or more of the daily caloric intake, humans suffer severe health consequences. . . . such as the severe pellagra epidemics of the late 19th century in America and the beri-beri scourges of southeast Asia" (90).

It is significant that globally at least 20% of our present diets consist of processed "oils, fats, and sugars," which research has linked to the rapid rise of NCDs. According to the ODI (91), the world's top sugar consumers include the United States, Belgium, The Netherlands, New Zealand, Costa Rica, and Mexico. For many doctors and academics, sugar has become the new tobacco "now pressed on unsuspecting parents and children by a cynical industry focused on profit not health" (92).

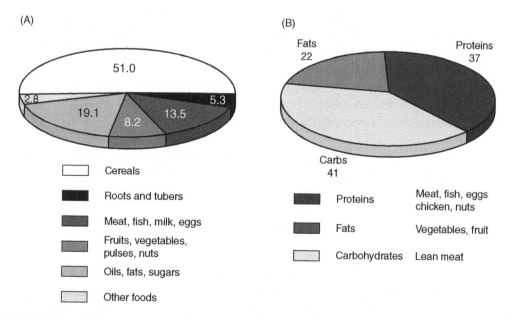

FIGURE 2.15 (A) World average diet versus (B) Paleolithic diet. Numbers represent percentages.

Source: (A) Food and Agricultural Organization (88), (B) Adapted from Eaton SB et al, "Paleolithic Nutrition Revisited: A Twelve-Year Retrospective on Its Nature and Implications." *Eu J Clin Nutr.* 1997 (89).

TABLE 2.4 Classification of adult underweight, overweight and obesity according to BMI and risk of obesity-related comorbidities

CLASSES	BMI (KG/M2)	RISK OF COMORBIDITIES
Underweight	<18.5	Low (but risk of other clinical problems increased e.g., anorexia nervosa)
Normal	18.5–24.9	Normal
Overweight	25.0–29.9	Increased
Obese	≥30.0	
Class I	30.0–34.9	Moderate
Class II	35.0–39.9	Severe
Class III	≥40.0	Very Severe

Source: Adapted from World Health Organization, *Obesity: Preventing and Managing the Global Epidemic. Report of a WHO Consultation* (94).

Sugar manufacturers reject claims by health experts and—similar to ongoing battles with the tobacco industry—assert that the scientific evidence does not support the correlation between foods and disease. Their arguments are in sharp contrast to those of people engaged in research and treatment (93), including Professor Shrinath Reddy, president, Public Health Foundation of India (PHFI), formerly head of the Department of Cardiology at the All India Institute of Medical Sciences (AIIMS) and a prominent cardiologist at the Harvard School of Public Health, who concluded that there was "overwhelming evidence coming out about sugar-sweetened beverages and other sugar consumption links to obesity, diabetes and even cardiovascular disease" (92). As illustrated in Table 2.4, the consequences of continued escalation of obesity and other conditions could be disastrous.

Steve Wiggins, one of the authors of the ODI report (68) previously cited, concludes that while a few countries are managing to curtail rises in obesity, most have not been successful in stemming the worldwide trend:

> Governments have focused on public awareness campaigns, but evidence shows this is not enough. The lack of action stands in stark contrast to the concerted public actions taken to limit smoking in developed countries. Politicians need to be less shy about trying to influence what food ends up on our plates. The challenge is to make healthy diets viable whilst reducing the appeal of foods which carry a less certain nutritional value.

Simon Gillespie of the British Heart Foundation, which conducted a study with the University of Oxford, concurs that the present "situation" is unsustainable and emphasizes early interventions; to start with, "our expectations of what childhood is have to change . . . it's not a question of turning back the clock, it's a question of regaining that balance," including promoting a more active lifestyle (75).

In the same article, Professor John Ashton, president of the UK Faculty of Public Health, also made a strong economic argument that may resonate with other nations, emphasizing that as a country we "need to compete with China and India," and that means "we need fit, healthy adults," not "obese and de-energised people," who are "likely to be less productive over their lives" (75).

Similar productivity concerns have been voiced in the United States, where a study on absenteeism; the economic impact of obesity, including such factors as presenteeism (less productive in the workplace); and premature mortality concluded that the total annual economic costs is in excess of $215 billion (95). In Europe, the European Agency for Safety and Health at Work (EU-OSHA) highlighted that "studies from Europe and beyond provide evidence that the financial burden on societies and organisations related to stress and psychosocial risks at work is considerable. Moreover, there is evidence suggesting that appropriately planned and implemented workplace interventions focusing on preventing stress, improving psychosocial work environment and promoting mental health are cost-effective" (96).

For UK physician Dr. Max Pemberton, obesity is "not a disease, it's a mindset—and that means it can be changed" (97), thereby averting, as journalist Janice Turner asserts, "breeding the next generation of sugar junkies and contributing to the devastation of our collective health" (98). As the president of the Ontario Medical Association affirmed, although "medical advances are allowing . . . patients to live longer than ever before," we need to be mindful that "a long life isn't always a good life when you are seriously impacted by a debilitating disease," and prevention is always the best option (65).

These conclusions were also reached at the inaugural World Innovation Summit for Health (WISH) in Qatar, December 10–11, 2013 (99), where Professor Shiriki Kumanyika of the International Obesity Task Force, University of Pennsylvania, and Obesity Forum Chair, firmly declared

> Public recognition of obesity as an important and non-communicable health crisis is not a debatable issue anymore. One of the main recommendations is for nations to find innovative and economically viable ways to address obesity, promote forces in the food environment and learn from successes in similar countries.

In the words of Dr. Margaret Chan, Director-General of WHO, NCDs are "the diseases that tax health systems to the breaking point. These are the diseases that break the bank" (100). In light of growing global concerns, the WHO has developed a global action plan for Member States "for the prevention and control of NCDs (including heart disease, stroke, diabetes, cancer and chronic lung diseases)" (101), with a view to setting the world on a new course to achieve nine globally agreed targets for NCDs, including a reduction in premature mortality from NCDs by 25% in 2025.

Supporting these enabling actions, there is also "a monitoring framework, including 25 indicators to track mortality and morbidity; assess progress in addressing risk factors, and evaluate the implementation of national strategies and plans" (101). Progress reports on the implementation of the action plan are due in 2016, 2018, and 2021.

Global, regional, and national initiatives to tackle increasing levels of obesity are timely, crucial, and commendable. However, alongside raising awareness, new policies, and guidelines, there may be a number of lines of inquiry that could benefit from further research in uncovering the underlying or deep-seated causes of obesity, including finding out the following:

- Whether there is a link or relation between "an overwhelming internal anxiety state" (78), "a rather childish inability to defer pleasure" (78), and "the question of unhappiness that surrounds the issue" (80)
- Whether these are by-products of our genetic ancestry or are environmentally determined or both
- Whether we might be able to evolve collaborative population-based interventions, guided by fundamental life-sustaining principles and actions, broached to some extent in Chapter 7.0, that could potentially make a profound difference to the health and well-being of society in the long run

There is little time to waste as we are reaching the tipping point. Making the case for fundamental change in our lifestyle, Dr. Robert Lustig, author of *Fat Chance*, says: "In 2011, there were 366m diabetics in the world—more than double the number in 1980" (102).

Furthermore, he asserts, "the food industry has contaminated the food supply with added sugar to sell more products and increase profits. Of the 600,000 food items in American grocery stores, 80% have been spiked with added sugar; and the industry uses 56 other names for sugar on the labels. They know when they add sugar, you buy more. And because you do not know you're buying it, you buy even more."

It is shocking to discover that by the age of 15, 21st century British boys typically have a 40 kg-a-year sugar habit, the equivalent of 1,000 cans of cola or 11,800 sugar cubes (103).

Mental Health and Substance Abuse

In a crisp piece, "The Stress of Modern Life Makes People Sick With Worry," David Reid (104) emphasizes that "anxiety and stress are at the root of all kinds of other problems, including insomnia, agoraphobia, road rage, panic attacks, OCD and many more." He attributes the main causes to modern life, which "places great expectations on us . . . to be good-looking, successful, ambitious and clever . . . popular, appreciated, slim, and looked up to or envied by our peers." Of course, he says, most of us are not "super-beings," and trying to be so results in anxiety and stress. While he uses "hypnotherapy as a stress busting guide" and is able to "help many sufferers," modern society, as we have seen in the previous section, has made available numerous other ways of coping, some positive, for example, exercise, meditation, and psychotherapy; but also many negative, involving potentially destructive behaviors.

His observations are corroborated by Professor Colin Espie at Oxford's Nuffield Department of Clinical Neuroscience (105) who reflects that "most people have an easier life than they would have 100 years ago. Then, the pressures were very real. Child mortality was high, there were fewer treatments for illnesses, greater poverty."

Moreover, he affirms one of the key themes in this book: "The problems we have now are more self-inflicted. We put ourselves under a huge amount of pressure and fail to take full advantage of having more free time to live a full and healthy life. We are victims of failed expectations and disappointments, and we end up with a lot of essentially psychological problems."

Substance abuse compromises individual good health and draws heavily on health and social care services, thereby impoverishing state coffers. For John Seffrin, chief executive of the American Cancer Society, smoking—which the WHO refuses to discuss—remains "the biggest public health disaster in the history of the world," killing "more than half of all smokers" (106). The habit (addiction?) is on the rise with more than 30 million new smokers each year, "killing some 1.7 million people, with almost a million dying from lung cancer." Attendees at a recent high-level forum of the world's 100 leading cancer experts affirmed that—unless strong measures are taken worldwide—about 1 billion people will die from smoking in this century, the cause of about a quarter of all cancer deaths.

One of the most distressing findings is that a lot more young people are starting to smoke each year than are quitting. Dan Siegel, professor of psychiatry at the University of California, codirector of the UCLA Mindful Awareness Research Center, and executive director of the Mindsight Institute, in *Brainstorm: The Power and Purpose of the Teenage Brain* (107), provides a physiological explanation for adolescent risk-seeking behavior. His research traces behavioral changes to structural changes in the brain—rather than the conventional hormone attribution. These changes occur mostly in the frontal lobe, the "control center" that regulates reasoning, starting at about age 11 for girls and age 12 for boys, and lasting, surprisingly, to about age 24, with the time from childhood to adulthood taking much longer than 100 years or so ago. The adolescent years, often characterized by a time of recklessness and impulsivity, are actually essential in the "testing of boundaries, the passion to explore what is unknown and exciting" and "can lay the stage for the development of core character traits that will enable adolescents to go on to lead great lives of adventure and purpose." It is also a time when reward and risk-taking may be compromised, making adolescents potentially more disposed to addictive behavior.

There are a number of key messages in this work for parents or guardians: One of these is to try to see the world from the perspective of the son or daughter, building a "collaborative interdependent relationship" and trying to better understand how their emotions and reasoning are developing. Another important "take-away" message is Professor Siegel's suggestions for the need to balance simple daily activities to ensure optimum personal health and brain development—"healthy mind platter," he calls the concept, that is, emphasizing the importance each day of getting the right "mix" of quality "sleep time, physical time, focus time, connecting time, playtime, down-time and time-in" (inner reflection). Adults guiding adolescents through these transition years, Professor Siegal says, will have greater influence aiming for something rather than imposing inhibitions. As one example, he references a teen antismoking campaign, which became successful only after it switched its focus from saying "no" to smoking to a positive value and raising awareness about advertising campaigns whose main goal (largely through manipulation) was to entice smokers.

In their paper, "The Rise of the Knowledge Organization," Alex and David Bennet—experts in knowledge management and organizational development—identify key factors that characterize modern life and may make Professor Siegel's crucial "healthy mind platter" more difficult to attain, especially in a world where "Time accelerates. Distance shrinks. Networks explode. Information overwhelms. Interdependencies grow geometrically. Uncertainty dominates. Complexity boggles the mind" (108).

It is difficult to say whether these global trends are the root cause of unhealthy coping behaviors, such as smoking, but certainly they cannot be ruled out as contributors. Professor Rob Moodie observes that "two-thirds of Indonesian men smoke and more than half of Chinese men smoke. Even more disturbing is that 40 per cent of 13–15-year-old Indonesian boys smoke." He further poses an important question, "How have these levels been reached while the world has known for more than 50 years that tobacco is such a deadly habit?" (87).

It is noteworthy that in the United States, life expectancy for poor White Americans has decreased by about 5 years since 1990. Possible reasons for this reduction "include a spike in prescription drug overdoses among young white women, rising obesity, and a steady increase in the number of the least educated Americans who lack health insurance" (109). Overall, researchers conclude that "in 2008 US adult men and women with less than twelve years of education had life expectancies not much better than those of all US adults in the 1950s and 1960s." According to the researchers, "the message for policy makers is clear: implement educational enhancements at young, middle, and older ages for people of all races, to reduce the large gap in health and longevity that persists today" (110).

Emotional and mental health needs are also on the rise. In *When the Money Runs Out: End of Western Affluence* (111), Stephen King, chief economist at HSBC, predicts that in the West, "weak growth will mean less prosperity to go round. People will be stripped of their 'entitlements' . . . resulting in greater pressure for equality" and possibly, a return to "protectionism," thus undermining "globalisation."

There is no doubt that socioeconomic factors—unemployment and poverty, along with an aging population—all play their part, leading to increases in such conditions as dementia/Alzheimer's disease and depression. Depression is a "significant contributor to the global burden of disease," "estimated to affect 350 million people worldwide," with depressive disorders often starting at a young age and posing "a substantial public health challenge, both at the social and economic levels as well as the clinical level" (112).

Dr. Beverley Barnett, Pan American Health Organization (PAHO)/WHO Guyana Country Office Representative (113), confirms that preventive programmes are best implemented at community levels by "strengthening of protective factors, including school-based programmes targeting children and adolescents, as well as exercise programmes for the elderly," along with reducing risk by "identifying children with behavioural problems" and provision of "information and training in behavioural child-rearing strategies, which may reduce parental depressive symptoms and improve outcomes in the children, regarding their cognitive, problem-solving and social skills." The causes of rising depressive disorders are complex, but experts suggest that "modern childhoods had become increasingly stressful with pressures from social media and cyber-bullying, school testing and rising family breakdowns among factors behind mental health problems."

Applying psychosocial interventions (e.g., cognitive behavioral therapy and family-based approaches)—often used alongside psychopharmacological interventions (e.g., antidepressants)—for mental illnesses "assume that there is a complex interplay between biological, environmental and sociological factors and that ambient stress together with certain life events may trigger an onset or relapse of mental health problems in some people" (114). Taken together, these interventions may lead to a healthier lifestyle and well-being. One study concluded that family doctors "are 46 times more likely to prescribe medication of depression and other mental illnesses instead of suggesting exercise, which has been shown to be no less effective in some cases" (115).

A previous study concluded that "schizophrenics in poor countries were doing a lot better than those in rich countries" (116). According to the research, the difference may be attributed to how, in the Western world, mental illness has been turned into a "system" and that patient care might be "better provided by former patients and . . . peers than by doctors and nurses" along with "giving mental health patients a sense of control."

Dr. Tanya Byron, a leading child psychologist in the United Kingdom, observes that "mental health problems are 'escalating' with a growing number of children arriving at her clinic with a range of disturbing symptoms, including pulling out their hair and eyelashes, tics, fasting and extreme anxiety disorders" (117). Further, she is concerned that "illnesses usually associated with teenagers are now affecting children as young as seven or eight." Substance misuse in boys and anorexia in girls tend to be on the increase. She also makes the point that "adults are transferring their own anxieties to their children," caused by living in a "risk-aversive" society where children "have no freedom" and are heavily monitored by their parents, thereby not learning to manage risk and learning how to become more resilient (118).

Referencing the controversial *Doctoring the Mind: Is Our Current Treatment of Mental Illness Really Any Good* (119), the present approach, according to Dr. Bentall, professor of Clinical Psychology at the University of Liverpool in the United Kingdom, places "people into diagnostic groups according to the symptoms and then say that they are cured only when they disappear. If we define recovery as the capacity to live a meaningful life even as the symptoms persist (which is what, in effect, happens in countries with less expensive services) people tend to get better."

Further, he argues that "studies on the connection between mental illness, brain chemistry and heritability remain inconclusive" and that "the connection between serotonin deficiency and depression, a connection presumed by drugs like Prozac, has never been proven" (120). And perhaps significantly in terms of "tackling the wicked problems" of the present book, while there appears to be "a weak genetic component in severe mental illness," there may be "a much stronger correlation with environmental stress." As one example, Dr. Bentall observes that "the rate of psychosis in adults who were sexually abused as children was 15 times the national average," and that "a Finnish study of 11,000 children born in 1966 and followed up 28 years later found that the risk of developing psychosis increased fourfold among those adults whose mothers hadn't wanted them."

He also laments the fact that while "mental illness is more common and more costly than cancer," the illness "attracts a fraction of the research, money or sympathy." Further, he observes "there is not a single physical condition in which recovery in the developed world trails the developing world, but it does in mental illness. It's an astonishing and shaming fact." A study investigating "the success rate of drug-based psychiatry in treating serious psychoses . . . found it was not much better than the old astrologers and apothecaries." From the research, it is clear that there are severe limitations to the pill culture that has been entrenched worldwide, where "the annual global market for antipsychotic drugs reached approximately \$US15 billion" in 2008 (120).

It is telling that more than 4 billion prescriptions, "not counting over-the-counter drugs or vaccine shots," for medications were written in the United States in 2011 for about 314,000 people (121); these "taken as directed" kill about "100,000 Americans a year" "from known side effects" (122). "That's one person every five minutes" (121) or about "13 prescriptions for each man, woman, and child" (122).

Melody Petersen, author of *Our Daily Meds* (123), notes that from 1980 to 2003, Americans "increased their spending on prescription drugs by 17 times," twice "what they spent on cars." She is particularly concerned about the older generation who "move through time, often from physician to physician . . . they are at increasing risk of accumulating layer upon layer of drug therapy, as a reef accumulates layer upon layer of coral."

Similarly, in the United Kingdom, the number of prescription drugs increased from 927 million in 2010 to 961 million in 2011, costing taxpayers £8.8 billion—a nearly 70% rise over a decade! In 2012, there were 50 million prescriptions for antidepressants alone compared to 20 million in 1999 (123). Repeat prescriptions for young patients with attention deficit hyperactivity disorder (ADHD)—to counter "hyperactivity, a short attention span and restlessness"—are also on the rise, but, according to Dr. Martin Scurr, a well-known UK general practitioner (GP), the condition is often "misdiagnosed, wrongly labelled," and children "are given tablets linked to insomnia, irritability, abnormal heart rhythms, and other undesirable side-effects" (124). The statistics are alarming, and there is now plenty of evidence that we—families, doctors, and pharmaceuticals—may all be complicit in "medicalizing" society. The costs in terms of health and well-being and financials are extraordinary and may backfire in human terms.

A major concern for all of us, according to Professor Dame Sally Davies, chief medical officer in the United Kingdom, is that "the power of these drugs may be coming to an end" as "we have taken antibacterial and antimicrobial drugs for granted for too long. We have misused them through overuse and false prescription, and as a result, the bugs are growing in resistance and fighting back" (125). In addition, she reminds us that "if we allow resistance to increase, in a few decades we may start dying from the most commonplace of ailments that can today be treated easily." For Professor Davies, this "global threat" is "as important and deadly as climate change and international terrorism."

The first WHO *Antimicrobial Resistance: Global Report on Surveillance 2014* (126), involving 114 countries and demanding an international effort modeled on the fight against AIDS, substantiates Professor Davies's fears.

According to Dr. Keiji Fukuda, WHO's Assistant Director-General for Health Security,

> without urgent, coordinated action by many stakeholders, the world is headed for a post-antibiotic era, in which common infections and minor injuries which have been treatable for decades can once again kill.
>
> Effective antibiotics have been one of the pillars allowing us to live longer, live healthier, and benefit from modern medicine. Unless we take significant actions to improve efforts to prevent infections and also change how we produce, prescribe and use antibiotics, the world will lose more and more of these global public health goods and the implications will be devastating. (127)

Among findings, the report highlights that "resistance to the treatment of last resort for life-threatening infections caused by a common intestinal bacteria, *Klebsiella pneumoniae*–carbapenem antibiotics–has spread to all regions of the world. *K. pneumoniae* is a major cause of hospital-acquired infections such as pneumonia, bloodstream infections, infections in newborns and intensive-care unit patients."

For Professor Tim Walsh, a microbiologist at Cardiff University in Wales, "We're up against a foe and it is a scenario combined with antibiotic industries around the world pumping out drugs and polluting environments, as well as overuse in our communities. . . . It's almost like a perfect storm" (128).

Impact of the Internet and Social Media on Health and Well-Being

Unquestionably, the Internet has had an enormous impact on our daily lives. At its most fundamental, and as shown in Figures 2.17 and 2.18 (129), it has changed and continues to transform the way at least 3 billion people (out of over 7.3 billion) think, communicate, study, work, and play. It differs from the television revolution in the

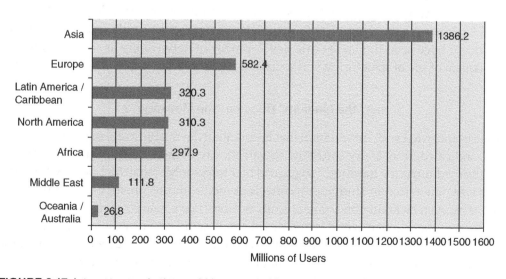

FIGURE 2.17 Internet users in the world by geographic regions—2014, Q2.

Note: 3,035,749,340 Internet users estimated for June 30, 2014.

Source: Internet World Stats (www.internetworldstats.com/stats.htm). Copyright © 2014, Miniwatts Marketing Group.

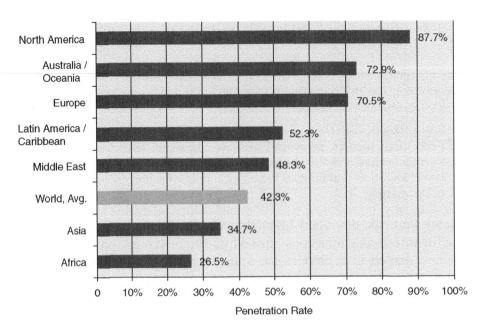

FIGURE 2.18 World Internet penetration rates—2014, Q2.

Note: Penetration rates are based on a world population of 7,182,406,565 and 3,035,749,340 estimated Internet users on June 30, 2014.
Source: Internet World Stats (www.internetworldstats.com/stats.htm). Copyright © 2014, Miniwatts Marketing Group.

1950s, not only in terms of global reach but also driven by technological advances with regard to the immediacy of information and services—instant access to people worldwide, banking, shopping, and education, to name but a few areas. We also have front-row seats to sports and entertainment—sitting just a click away from world poverty and the continuing cruelty and inanity of wars and conflicts. For Manuel Castells, who is the Wallis Annenberg Chair Professor of Communication Technology and Society at the University of Southern California, "what is clear is that without the Internet we would not have seen the large-scale development of networking as the fundamental mechanism of social structuring and social change in every domain of social life" (130).

Has "the Medium" Become "the Message"?

We are bombarded with information that is potentially available to all, regardless of race, color, and creed, from every sphere of human endeavor. Indeed, the controversial mantra, "the medium is the message," suggested by Professor Marshall McLuhan, who in the 1960s was "interested in studying the effects of media and technology on humankind" (131), may even be taking on a ring of truth. Seeing "Poe's maelstrom as a metaphor for the chaos of the modern world; a whirlpool swallowing and destroying everything of value," his "survival strategy" for dealing with this "chaos" may be a timely spark for contemplation or discussion: "It's inevitable that the whirl-pool of electronic information movement will toss us all about like corks on a stormy sea, but if we keep our cool during the descent into the maelstrom, studying the process as it happens . . . we can get through." While his optimism is shared today (130), research also suggests a darker side.

Internet Engagement and Well-Being

As one example, journalist Judith Woods notes the extent to which the Internet has infiltrated our moods, stating that it "makes us feel so fabulously omnipotent most of the time that when it doesn't work, the feelings of outraged impotence are overwhelming." Moreover, she references "new research from Public Health England," which has found "a clear relationship between the amount of time spent on social media sites" and "lower levels of well-being" (132).

Moreover, evidence is mounting that violent video games played over many hours may indeed be "re-wiring the human brain" and, arguably, translating into anti-social behavior and possibly insensitivity to the needs of others (133). A case example involved a model student aged 15 who robbed a bank as if he were in a video game. According to a judge, the boy was "motivated by greed and immaturity" (134). It is a sign of the times that, while in the United States Internet addiction is not officially recognized for insurance purposes, for the first time, and while only mentioned in the Appendix, requiring further "scientific evidence," the condition (Internet Gaming Disorder) is mentioned in the revised *Diagnostic and Statistical Manual of Mental Disorders* (5th ed.). According to the well-known American psychiatrist, Dr. Keith Ablow, Internet addiction, which another psychiatrist labeled "electronic cocaine," "will lead to the greatest psychiatric epidemic of all time," causing a "loss of reality and sense of self" (135). Another distressing development that counters many of the advantages gained by social media engagements is the growth of cyberbullying. The term refers to "the act of abusing another person through the use of web-related avenues of communication" (136) and is becoming another epidemic across the globe and is certainly one of the "wicked" problems of our times.

In a study by Ipsos (137) involving 18,687 people around the world, as shown in Figure 2.19, 1 in 10 parents (12%) say their child has experienced cyberbullying and "24% say they know of a child who has experienced the same in their community."

Moreover, "three quarters (77%) of world citizens say cyberbullying needs special attention and cannot be addressed through existing anti-bullying measures," as confirmed by 91% of the respondents in Japan; 89% in Indonesia, as well as a strong majority in Spain (84%), Argentina (83%), France (83%), and Italy (83%). Children in India have the highest number of children experiencing cyberbullying and also the highest number of parents who are aware of this national problem.

The Ipsos MORI study also revealed that social networking sites, like Facebook, play a major part in the increase of cyberbullying. As examples, "in South Africa (63%), Russia (59%), South Korea (48%) and Japan (47%) parents report the primary way kids are being cyberbullied is through their cellular or mobile devices while in China the top media is online chat rooms (83%) and in India it is evenly split between social networking sites (55%) and online chat rooms (54%)."

Cyberbullying can take many forms (136), including, inter alia:

- Sending mean messages or threats to a person's e-mail account or cell phone
- Spreading rumors online or through text
- Posting hurtful or threatening messages on social networking sites or web pages

Has a child in your household ever experienced cyberbullying?

	Yes, on a regular basis	Yes, sometimes	Yes, once or twice	NET (Yes)	No/Never/DK
Total	3% 3% 6%	12%			88%
India	13% 6% 13%	32%			68%
Brazil	10% 2% 7%	20%			80%
Saudi Arabia	4% 6% 9%	18%			82%
Canada	7% 11%	18%			82%
United States	5% 4% 6%	15%			85%
Indonesia	2% 4% 7%	13%			87%
Australia	4% 9%	13%			87%
Sweden	1% 12%	13%			87%
Poland	4% 8%	12%			88%
China	3% 4% 4%	11%			89%
Belgium	1% 9%	11%			89%
South Africa	2% 2% 6%	10%			90%
Great Britain	2% 1% 7%	10%			90%
Argentina	5% 2% 2%	9%			91%
Mexico	1% 2% 5%	8%			92%
Japan	1% 6%	8%			92%
South Korea	1% 7%	8%			92%
Germany	1% 2% 4%	7%			93%
Hungary	6%	7%			93%
Spain	3% 5%	5%			95%
Turkey	3% 5%	5%			95%
France	1% 4% 5%				86%
Russia	1% 4% 5%				95%
Italy	2%				95%

DN4_1. To the best of your knowledge, has a child in your household ever experienced cyberbullying? What about another child in your community? - My child

Base: Parent or guardian of any child(ren) under the age of 18 (unwtd) n=6502

A Global @dvisory – December 2011 – G@27

CYBERBULLYING

FIGURE 2.19 Cyberbullying—a global phenomenon.

Source: Ipsos. One in Ten (12%) Parents Online, Around the World Say Their Child Has Been Cyberbullied, 26% Say They Know of a Child Who Has Experienced Same in Their Community; 2013 (137).

For clinical social worker Victor Sims in New Orleans (138), "bullying is a power issue common among adolescents ages 13 to 18, causes low self-esteem and happens for any reason that makes a child different. He said bullies bully other children for things like wearing glasses, being shorter than they are, for not being athletic or for earning higher grades . . . technology now makes it easier to bully." Victims are "being told that they're not worthy, or that they're nothing. They don't even need to come to school anymore and some as far as the cyber bullying is concerned, some have even gotten messages like, 'Why don't you just take yourself out?' "

Indeed, according to the U.S. Centers for Disease Control, "bullying victims are 2 to 9 times more likely to commit suicide or attempt it than those who do not experience bullying" (136). Dr. Hinduja and Dr. Justin Patchin of the Cyberbullying Research Center have no doubt that "the nature of adolescent peer aggression has evolved due to the pro-liferation of information and communications technology (139). There have been several high-profile cases involving teenagers taking their own lives in part because of being harassed and mistreated over the Internet, a phenomenon we have termed *cyberbul-licide*—suicide indirectly or directly influenced by experiences with online aggression."

This may have been the case for a 14-year-old, a gifted pupil with ambitions to go to Oxford University, whose heartbreaking suicide poem (Box 2.6) moved Britain (140).

Experts advise there are a few things parents and teens can do that may "help reduce the cyber bullying statistics." Among these, there is an urgent need for schools, parents, and health professionals to talk about "cyber bullying, explaining that it is wrong and

BOX 2.6

"I Give Up"

I GIVE UP
By Izzy Dix

I arrive,
Happy and fresh,
Ready and excited
To celebrate the goodness.
I am eager and keen to have a good time.
As I smile from the bubbles of anticipation whizzing around my stomach,
I begin to see the crowd...
I see more people,
Many are happy and joyful.
They're there like me,
To celebrate...
I smile at them and say hello to the many faces I see,
They look shocked and surprised to see me...
I question their judgemental glares as I wonder,

'What have I done wrong?'
I see their drinks swilling in their fingers as their backs begin to face me.
I try to edge my way back into the circle of giggles and talking,
They push me away.
I stand still,
My eyes glazed and absent.
Suddenly they call me over,
I think, 'yes! They've noticed me!'
But then it begins,
They start to ask questions,
As to why I am there.
They begin to tell me that nobody wants me there,
They tell me to leave and that I am not wanted,
Not there, not anywhere...
My heart,
My head,
My body,
Numb...

I feel pricks of stinging begin to pinch my eyes as cheeks begin to burn.
'Don't let them see you,
Don't show them that you're weakened,
Weakened by their remarks'.
'Stay strong' I think...
But it's too late,
My palms, clammy,
My cheeks, streaming,
My neck, sweating.
I walk quickly away from the chanting and laughing,
My vision, spinning,
My heart, beginning to break.
I look down and walk,
My eyes drowning in a sea of emotion.
Another piece of me chiselled away by their cruel remarks and perceptions...
I give up.

Source: Daily Mail, Mail OnLine, 2013 (140).

can have serious consequences" (136). Prevention through policies, consequences, and family education can have positive outcomes, but perhaps, most important, according to a high school principal in Iowa City, is "to establish a learning environment and school climate where students treat each other with respect and kindness" (141).

At the global level, the WHO has recognized that much more attention needs to be given to mental health and well-being and has developed a comprehensive mental health resolution and action plan for 2013 to 2020 with four major objectives (142):

- Strengthen effective leadership and governance for mental health
- Provide comprehensive, integrated, and responsive mental health and social care services in community-based settings
- Implement strategies for promotion and prevention in mental health
- Strengthen information systems, evidence, and research for mental health

Adopting this plan, which also proposes indicators and targets to gauge its implementation, is significant on at least two counts: First, it provides "a central role for provision of community-based care and a greater emphasis on human rights." And, second, it emphasizes "the empowerment of people with mental disabilities and the need to develop strong civil society and health promotion and prevention activities."

Australia's final report, *A Healthier Future for All Australians* (2009; 143) recognizes the importance of "encouraging good mental health in young people" and posits that "most new cases of what become chronic mental illnesses—including psychotic disorders such as schizophrenia—emerge in late adolescence and the early adult years." One of their key recommendations, therefore, calls for "national implementation of youth-friendly, community-based services providing information and screening for mental disorders and sexual health, and specialist clinical services for prevention of, and intervention for, early psychosis" (143).

Influenced by the media, including social, that all-too-often promote a cult of "perfectionism" or "a cult of personality," rather than emphasizing the valuing and building of character and resilience, the younger generation continues to be at risk, confirmed, as one example, by a survey conducted by Public Health England (PHE; 144). A key finding was that each hour spent online "puts children at greater risk," increasing the possibility of "mental illnesses and social problems, such as loneliness, depression, anxiety, low self-esteem and heightened aggression" with "750,000 teenagers" believing "things are so bad that they 'have nothing to live for'."

It is unlikely that the British findings are unique across the globe; those who have influence and power—political, social, and economic—must urgently make the health and well-being of the current and future generations their top priority, especially stressing the importance of family well-being and finding ways of reducing the "anxiety and stress" that comes from modern life, including "heavy web use," that may result "in online bullying, suicidal thoughts and self-harm."

Jenni Russell, a journalist, may have said it best in her article on the profound importance of children's self-worth set against "efficiency":

> We need a revolution in official thinking—one that understands that people are much more like hedgerow plants than chess pieces. Rip us out of the ground and we do not only lose leaves, roots and branches, but damage all those with whom we are intertwined. It's

not enough for politicians to play at being "master strategists." We desperately need them to start acknowledging that individuals and communities are organic and delicate and that they need careful nurturing too. (145)

2.6   SOCIAL INTOLERANCES AND CHALLENGING SOCIAL NORMS

Violence against women both violates and impairs or nullifies the enjoyment by women of their human rights and fundamental freedoms. . . . In all societies, to a greater or lesser degree, women and girls are subjected to physical, sexual and psychological abuse that cuts across lines of income, class and culture.

Beijing Declaration and Platform for Action, paragraph 112 (146)

As the cases in Box 2.7 illustrate, the types of abuse inflicted on innocent victims are shocking and a chilling reminder why "real change" needs to happen around the globe to eradicate gender-based violence (GBV) and outlaw social intolerances.

While armed conflicts represent the extremes of "social intolerances" affecting all genders and age groups, as illustrated in Box 2.8, violence against women, identified

BOX 2.7

Cases of Abuse

A 15-year-old girl was locked up in the basement of her in-laws' house, starved, and had her nails pulled out. The girl was married off to a 30-year-old man last year. Authorities said the girl reportedly was tortured after she refused to submit to prostitution (147).

A young woman was sentenced to 12 years in prison after she reported that her cousin's husband had raped her. Her plight attracted international attention when it came out that she had agreed to marry her attacker to gain her freedom and legitimize a daughter conceived in the attack (148).

BOX 2.8

Violence Against Women

Childhood: Female infanticide, emotional and physical abuse, differential access to food and medical care

Adolescence: Dating and courtship violence, economically coerced sex, sexual abuse in the workplace, rape, sexual harassment, forced prostitution

Reproductive: Abuse of women by intimate partners, marital rape, dowry abuse and murders, partner homicide, psychological abuse, sexual abuse in the workplace, sexual harassment, rape, abuse of women with disabilities, abuse in the workplace, forced prostitution

Old Age: Abuse of widows, elder abuse (which affects mostly women)

Source: United Nations Economic Commission for Europe (149).

as "the most pervasive yet least recognized *human rights* abuse in the world," cuts across "all socio-economic groups." Its dimensions include "physical, sexual and psychological/emotional violence in the family and community, as well as such violence perpetrated or condoned by the State" (149). Like wars, abusive acts of violence impact all ages.

The United Nations Population Fund

The United Nations Population Fund (UNFPA) estimated that globally "as many as one in every three women has been beaten, coerced into sex, or abused in some other way—most often by someone she knows, including by her husband or another male family member; one woman in four has been abused during pregnancy." Violence evidenced in percentage terms globally in Figure 2.20, varies "within and between communities, countries and regions with highest occurrence in the WHO Southeast Asian Region, followed closely by the African and the Eastern Mediterranean Regions."

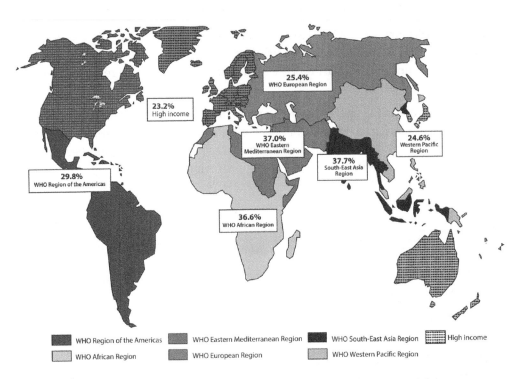

FIGURE 2.20 Global map showing regional prevalence rates of intimate partner violence by WHO region.

Source: World Health Organization, *Global and Regional Estimates of Violence Against Women: Prevalence and Health Effects of Intimate Partner Violence and Non-Partner Sexual Violence* (2013). http://www.who.int/reproductivehealth/publications/violence/9789241564625/en

Causal Factors Behind Gender-Based Violence

The main reason behind gender-based violence, the UNFPA concludes, is that gender-based violence "serves—by intention or effect—to perpetuate male power and control." At its most fundamental, the main causal factor relates to "the way men view themselves as men, and the way they view women"; both determine "whether they use violence or coercion against women." Finding solutions to ending this form of violence "will mean changing cultural concepts about masculinity, and that process must actively engage men, whether they be policy makers, parents, spouses or young boys" (149).

Report on Global and Regional Estimates of Violence Against Women

Corroborating the UNFPA findings, a recent report by the WHO, the London School of Hygiene & Tropical Medicine, and the South African Medical Research Council (150) focuses on the prevalence of two forms of global violence against women—intimate partner violence and nonpartner sexual violence (Figure 2.20). The study, summarized in Box 2.9, "presents the first global systematic review and synthesis of the body of scientific data on the prevalence of two forms of violence against women—violence by an intimate partner (intimate partner violence) and sexual violence by someone other than a partner (non-partner sexual violence)."

The authors of the report also posit that the "evidence highlights the need to address the economic and sociocultural factors that foster a culture of violence against women." Key recommendations include the importance of "challenging social norms that support male authority and control over women and sanction or condone violence against women; reducing levels of childhood exposures to violence; reforming discriminatory family law; strengthening women's economic and legal rights; and eliminating gender inequalities in access to formal wage employment and secondary education"

In addition, "services also need to be provided for those who have experienced violence" and there is an "urgent need to integrate issues related to violence into clinical training."

BOX 2.9

Summary: Intimate Partner Violence and Non-Partner Sexual Violence

- Overall, 35% of women worldwide have experienced either physical and/or sexual intimate partner violence or non-partner sexual violence. Most of this violence is intimate partner violence.
- Globally, as many as 38% of all murders of women are committed by intimate partners.
- Women who have been physically or sexually abused by their partners report higher rates of a number of important health problems.
- Globally, 7% of women have been sexually assaulted by someone other than a partner (150).

UN Security Council: GBV—A Crime Against Humanity

Most recently, the UN Security Council reaffirmed its commitment to end sexual violence, but remained deeply concerned "over the slow implementation of important aspects of resolution 1960 (2010) to prevent sexual violence in armed conflict and post-conflict situations and noting as documented in the Secretary-General's report that sexual violence occurs in such situations throughout the world," and, inter alia, "that sexual violence can constitute a crime against humanity or a constitutive act with respect to genocide" (151).

Resolution 2106 (2013) also highlights that "women who have been forcefully abducted into armed groups and armed forces, as well as children, are especially vulnerable to sexual violence in armed conflict and post-conflict situations and as such *demands* that parties to armed conflict immediately identify and release such persons from their ranks." The Council also underlined "the important roles that civil society organizations, including women's organizations, and networks can play in enhancing community-level protection against sexual violence in armed conflict and post-conflict situations and supporting survivors in accessing justice and reparations."

Declaration of Commitment to End Sexual Violence in Conflict

Another important step was taken in 2013 when 113 members of the United Nations, a clear majority, endorsed a historic new "Declaration of Commitment to End Sexual Violence in Conflict," sponsored by the UK Foreign & Commonwealth Office with the support of the Department for International Development (152).

The declaration (Box 2.10) is intended to send "an important message to the victims of these crimes that the international community has not forgotten them, and to the perpetrators of rape that they will be held to account."

Moreover, the declaration "contains a set of practical and political commitments to end the use of rape and sexual violence as a weapon of war, which terrorises and destroys communities during conflict."

BOX 2.10

Declaration of Commitment to End Sexual Violence in Conflict

- Ensure that sexual violence prevention and response efforts are prioritized and adequately funded from the first phase and throughout all responses to conflict and humanitarian emergencies.
- Provide better, more timely and comprehensive assistance and care, including health and psychosocial care that addresses the long-term consequences of sexual violence in conflict, to female, male and child victims and their families, including children born as the result of sexual violence.
- Ensure that all peace, security and conflict mediation processes explicitly recognize the need to prevent, respond to and reduce crimes of sexual violence in conflict and stress the need to exclude such crimes from amnesty provisions.

- Promote women's full participation in all political, governance, and security structures, as well as all decision-making processes, including peace negotiations, peace-building, prevention and accountability efforts, recognizing the important contribution that National Action Plans on UN Security Council Resolution 1325 can play in this regard, and ensure that such processes also take into full consideration the needs and rights of women and children.
- Strengthen UN efforts to address sexual violence in conflict and provide further support to the Special Representative of the Secretary-General on Sexual Violence in Conflict as chair of UN Action gainst Sexual Violence in Conflict.
- Strengthen and support the efforts of regional organizations to prevent and respond to sexual violence in conflict in their peacemaking, peacekeeping and peace-building initiatives.
- Support conflict-affected states in strengthening their capacity to prevent and respond to sexual violence in conflict and to develop and implement national security sector and justice reform programmes that take into full consideration the needs and rights of women and children.
- Support the deployment of national and international expertise at the request of host governments, the UN and other international organisations to build national capacity to hold perpetrators to account and to improve the response and support to victims and their access to justice.
- Ensure our national military and police doctrine and training is in accordance with international law so as to enable a more effective prevention and response to sexual violence in conflict.
- Encourage and improve the safe and ethical collection of data and evidence relating to acts of sexual violence committed in conflict, to inform national and international responses.
- Encourage, support and protect the efforts of civil society organizations, including women's groups and human rights defenders, to improve the monitoring and documentation of cases of sexual violence in conflict without fear of reprisal and empower victims to access justice.
- Support and encourage the development of the International Protocol on the documentation and investigation of sexual violence in conflict at national, regional and international levels, with a view to its conclusion in 2014. (152)

Breaking the Silence on Violence Against Indigenous Girls, Adolescents, and Young Women

The UNICEF report, *Breaking the Silence on Violence Against Indigenous Girls, Adolescents and Young Women* (153) sought to generate a deeper understanding of the magnitude, nature, and context of violence experienced by indigenous girls, adolescents, and young women through illustrative examples from Africa, Asia Pacific, and Latin America.

It also identified a set of guiding principles and recommendations "to accelerate progress and action to protect and prevent violence against indigenous girls and women in all its forms, including accountability, equity and non-discrimination, gender equality, respecting the collective and individual rights of indigenous peoples, participation and empowerment, and the integration of inter-cultural perspectives." The recommendations are grouped into four broad areas of concern identified in the report:

- Research, monitoring, and reporting
- Prevention
- The provision of age, gender, and culturally appropriate comprehensive services
- Enhancing capacities, coordination, and cooperation

The authors conclude, "violence prevention requires the changing of attitudes, challenging stereotypes and building the capacities of communities to appreciate the adverse consequences of violence against women and girls. It also requires women and girls to be empowered socially, economically and politically to overcome their subordinate position in society."

UN Women

Taking on board the findings of previous studies and reports, global efforts toward eliminating gender-based violence are being spearheaded by UN Women, created in July 2010 by the United Nations General Assembly (154). UN Women is the United Nations' "Entity for Gender Equality and the Empowerment of Women." Bringing together four previously distinct parts of the UN system, including the UNFPA, the main roles of UN Women are:

- To support intergovernmental bodies, such as the Commission on the Status of Women, in their formulation of policies, global standards and norms.
- To help Member States to implement these standards, standing ready to provide suitable technical and financial support to those countries that request it, and to forge effective partnerships with civil society.
- To hold the UN system accountable for its own commitments on gender equality, including regular monitoring of system-wide progress.

UN Women, led since 2013 by Executive Director Phumzile Mlambo-Ngcuka, recognizes that "gender equality is not only a basic human right, but its achievement has enormous socio-economic ramifications," as "empowering women fuels thriving economies, spurring productivity and growth" (155). UN Women is also acutely aware that

> gender inequalities remain deeply entrenched in every society. Women lack access to decent work and face occupational segregation and gender wage gaps. They are too often denied access to basic education and health care. Women in all parts of the world suffer violence and discrimination. They are under-represented in political and economic decision-making processes.

Giving women "a powerful voice at the global, regional and local levels" and "grounded in the vision of equality enshrined in the UN Charter," UN Women, among other aims, works for the:

- Elimination of discrimination against women and girls
- Empowerment of women
- Achievement of equality between women and men as partners and beneficiaries of development, human rights, humanitarian action and peace and security

One of the main roles of UN Women has been monitoring progress toward eliminating gender-based violence. And, although the 2000 to 2015 Millennium Development Goals (MDGs) will be discussed later in Section 4.1, there is global evidence that progress toward meeting the MDGs for women and girls remains slow and "uneven" and "in many areas far from sufficient" (156). Three of the MDGs may be particularly germane to the present discussion, MDG 1, MDG 3, and MDG 5 (156,157).

MDG 1 focuses on the eradication of extreme poverty and hunger. "MDG 1 aims to halve world poverty by 2015." And, "while there has been progress on the target of reducing the proportion of people living on less than $1.25 per day, progress is uneven between and within countries. The largest declines in proportions of undernourished people occurred in Asia," while the "numbers of people in extreme poverty actually increased from 290 million in 1990 to 414 in 2010" (157).

MDG 3 is "the overarching gender equality goal, which encompasses parity in education, political participation, and economic empowerment." Its main targets are to "eliminate gender disparity in primary and secondary education, preferably by 2005, and in all levels of education no later than 2015" (155).

Indicators include "the share of women in wage employment in the non-agricultural sector and the proportion of seats held by women in national parliament." According to UN Women, while "gender parity in schooling worldwide is closest to being achieved at the primary level . . . only 2 out of 130 countries have achieved that target at all levels of education." Moreover, "globally, 40 out of 100 wage-earning jobs in the non-agricultural sector are held by women" and "women still enter the labour market on an unequal basis to men, even after accounting for educational background and skills."

The conclusions of a study "Challenges and Achievements in the Implementation of the Millennium Development Goals for Women and Girls" (158), providing background information for the delegation of the Committee on Women's Rights and Gender Equality of the European Parliament, noted that

> the existence of MDG 3 was important in raising political profile and funding for gender equality. Some progress has been made on gender equality, particularly in relation to education, but much more needs to be done with both a broadening and deepening of the issues. Gender was insufficiently mainstreamed across the MDGs. Substantial lessons can be learnt from the experience of the MDGs, particularly in relation to the need to address more issues, and to tackle the root causes of inequality.

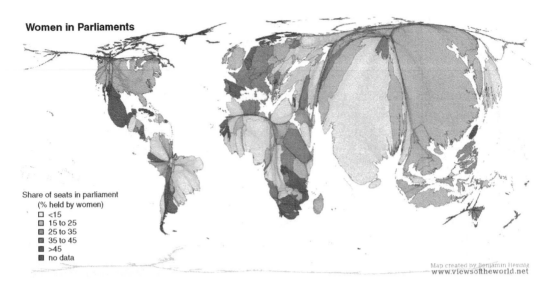

Women in Parliaments

Share of seats in parliament
(% held by women)
☐ <15
▨ 15 to 25
▨ 25 to 35
▨ 35 to 45
■ >45
■ no data

Map created by Benjamin Hennig
www.viewsoftheworld.net

FIGURE 2.21 Proportion of seats held by women in single or lower houses of national parliament, 2000 and 2014 (percentage).

Note: Basemap: Gridded population cartogram giving every person en equal amount in the map.

Source: Benjamin Hennig, viewsoftheworld.net, 2014. Data from United Nations Human Development Report 2014 (159).

As indicated in Figure 2.21 (159), slow progress is also being made with regard to the proportion of women in parliament from 2000 to 2013; as a result, women continue to be under-represented in decision-making and are "also absent from senior positions in judicial systems, executive branch of governments, and the civil service" (155). At the current rate, "it will take nearly 40 years to reach the parity zone in parliaments" (155).

According to a Gallup poll (Table 2.5; 160), "in every region of the world, men surpass women when it comes to having a 'good job'—that is, full-time work for an employer." Gallup's study applied "the Payroll to Population (P2P) employment rate. Worldwide, the P2P employment rate for men is 34%; it is 18% for women." It is noteworthy that "globally, full-time employment for an employer sits at 26%—but it is even lower for the world's women, who lag far behind the percentage of men who have a "good job." While "the gender gap in full-time employment for an employer (out of the entire population) is worst in South Asia and in non-EU European countries, with more than 20 percentage points separating men from women," we may well ask, how long will it take for the global workforce to also "reach the parity zone"?

The UN Women Policy Division (161) cites the European Parliament report (162) and highlights that "the narrow focus of Goal 3 fails to address such critical issues as violence against women, inequalities in the division of unpaid care work, women's limited access to assets, violations of women's and girls' sexual and reproductive health and rights, and their unequal participation in private and public decision-making beyond national parliaments."

MDG 5 focuses on improving maternal health. And, while globally there were about 287,000 maternal deaths, a decrease of 47%, the MDG target to reduce the maternal mortality ratio—stemming to a large extent from unsafe abortions, lack of

TABLE 2.5 Regional Payroll to Population Employment Rates (Good Jobs), by Gender

	MEN	WOMEN	WOMEN'S DEFICIT
GLOBAL	34	18	−16
South Asia	36	10	−26
Non-EU Europe	51	29	−22
Latin America and the Caribbean	41	21	−20
Northern America	52	33	−19
Middle East and North Africa	27	8	−19
European Union	41	26	−15
Southeast Asia	28	14	−14
East Asia	33	22	−11
Balkans	33	25	−8
Commonwealth of Independent States	42	34	−8
Sub-Saharan Africa	15	8	−7

Note: % Full-time employment for an employer, among the entire adult population, ranked by deficit.
Source: Gallup World Poll, 2012 (159).

contraception, and early marriage—by three quarters by 2015 will not be reached, although all regions have made progress.

It is because of the slow and uneven progress made across most of the MDG 2015 goals, including the "freedom from violence against women and girls," that UN Women is calling for a post-2015 "transformative stand-alone goal [Sustainable Development Goal (SDG)] on achieving gender equality, women's rights and women's empowerment" to address the structural causes of gender-based discrimination and to support "transformation in gender relations" (161).

A key lesson learned from the 2000–2015 MDG process is to "broaden and deepen indicators to measure progress," particularly in areas ensuring "quality" postprimary education; economic empowerment, especially "on women's control over, and access to, assets and decent work; and political participation," particularly measuring "women's effective participation and influence at international, national and community levels" (162).

The UN Women proposal urges "concrete actions to eliminate the debilitating fear and/or experience of violence," which "must be a centrepiece of any future framework." Two main priorities frame the UN Women SDG proposal (161):

- Gender equality in the distribution of capabilities—knowledge, good health, sexual and reproductive health, and reproductive rights of women and adolescent girls; and access to resources and opportunities, including land, decent work, and equal pay to build women's economic and social security.

- Gender equality in decision-making power in public and private institutions, in national parliaments and local councils, the media and civil society, in the management and governance of firms, and in families and communities.

From the numerous studies and reports in the past few decades and the ongoing UN Women as well as other global, regional, and national initiatives, it is becoming clear that freedom from gender-based violence is now being taken very seriously worldwide, heightened significantly recently by the abduction of more than 200 girls from a school in Northern Nigeria (163).

Two major challenges confront decision makers in making real progress with respect to the post-2015 SDG agenda. One is the need "to address the economic and sociocultural factors that foster a culture of violence against women" (149). The other demands recognition that violence prevention requires the changing of attitudes, challenging stereotypes, and building the capacities of communities (145).

Thoraya Ahmed Obaid, executive director of the UNFPA from 2000 to 2010, in the foreword to *Programming to Address Violence Against Women: 10 Case Studies* (164), several years ago highlighted the purpose of the text:

> It is intended primarily for development practitioners and others seeking to change attitudes and practices that have been passed on through generations. Breaking the cycle of violence is a necessary—and urgent—task, if the realization of women's human rights is to become a reality in this generation.

Then and as is the case now, violence against women remains "a multidimensional problem that requires a multidimensional response. Adding to the complexity is the fact that every culture has its own set of attitudes and reactions to it, which must be thoroughly understood by anyone attempting to tackle the problem in an effective and sustainable way" (164).

Resources, such as the excellent WHO and UNAIDS-sponsored *16 Ideas for Addressing Violence Against Women in the Context of the HIV Epidemic: A Programming Tool* (165), are available to provide support and—along with alliances or collaborative partnerships—need to be optimized by nation states in order to achieve the post-2015 SDG agenda.

In addition, there are policy levers that nations might put in place. As one example, Britain dispenses "about £11 billion of aid a year across the globe." A new Act of Parliament will ensure that Britain "becomes the first nation in the world to make respecting "the basic human rights of the female . . . a legal condition" (166) and "will end what the former U.S. President Jimmy Carter has described as "the worst and most pervasive and unaddressed human rights violation on Earth." (167).

Mariella Frostrup, a trustee of The Great Initiative, a UK-based gender equality charity, observes that "the impact of putting gender equality at the heart of development aid has a similar potential to influence global policy as William Wilbeforce's Slave Trade Act of 1807—a historic precedent of legislation that set a precedent for all other nations to follow" (168).

REFERENCES

1. Lusher A. Kids these days: A portrait of childhood around the world. *The Telegraph.* September 23, 2013. http://www.telegraph.co.uk/news/worldnews/10317562/Kids-these-days-A-portrait-of-childhood-around-the-world.html. Accessed September 30, 2014.

2. Phillips C. How many more? Syria conflict refugees top 2 million [Weblog]. http://blog.amnestyusa.org/middle-east/how-many-more-syria-conflict-refugees-top-2-million. Accessed September 5, 2013.

3. Dockery M. Sad, lonely, bewildered: The children of Syria who left me lost for words. *Daily Mail.* November 30, 2013. http://www.dailymail.co.uk/news/article-2516071/Sad-lonely-bewildered-The-children-Syria-left-lost-words-Michelle-Dockery.html. Accessed December 2, 2013.

4. Driscoll M. Pouring out the horror on paper. *The Sunday Times.* December 15, 2013. http://www.thesundaytimes.co.uk/sto/public/charity/article1352776.ece. Accessed December 20, 2013.

5. Shah A. Poverty facts and stats. *Global Issues.* March 28, 2010. http://www.globalissues.org/article/26/poverty-facts-and-stats. Accessed June 20, 2013.

6. World Health Organization (WHO). Closing the gap in a generation: Health equity through action on the social determinants of health; 2008. http://apps.who.int/iris/bitstream/10665/43943/1/9789241563703_eng.pdf. Accessed August 10, 2014.

7. Hall GH, Patrinos HA, eds. *Indigenous peoples, poverty, and development.* New York, NY: Cambridge University Press; 2012.

8. Fonn S, Ravindran TKS. The macroeconomic environment and sexual and reproductive health: A review of trends over the last 30 years. *Reprod Health Matters.* 2011;19(38):11–25.

9. Soros, G. The plight of the Roma. *Projectsyndicate;* 2010. http://www.project-syndicate.org/commentary/the-plight-of-the-roma. Accessed November 13, 2013.

10. Dahlgren G, Whitehead M. Tackling inequalities in health: An agenda for action. Working paper prepared for The King's Fund International Seminar on Tackling Inequalities in Health, September 1993, Ditchley Park, Oxfordshire. London: The King's Fund. In: Dahlgren G, Whitehead M, eds. *Levelling up (Part 2): European strategies for tackling social inequities in health.* Copenhagen, Denmark: WHO Regional office for Europe; 2007. http://www.who.int/social_determinants/resources/leveling_up_part2.pdf

11. Centers for Disease Control and Prevention. *Fact Sheet—CDC Health Disparities and Inequalities Report—U.S., 2011.* http://www.cdc.gov/minorityhealth/CHDIR/2011/FactSheet.pdf. Accessed November 13, 2013.

12. Oakesshott I, Grimston J. Social mobility in reverse for middle class. *The Sunday Times.* October 13, 2013. http://www.thesundaytimes.co.uk/sto/news/uk_news/Society/article1326894.ece. Accessed October 16, 2013.

13. Evans-Pritchard A. Eurozone cannot recover while cancer of unequal competition remains. *The Daily Telegraph.* September 5, 2013: B2.

14. Blakely, R. Soup kitchens across America are under siege. *The Times.* November 29, 2013. http://www.thetimes.co.uk/tto/news/world/americas/article3935010.ece. Accessed December 3, 2013.

15. Støre J. Address by Mr Jonas Gahr Støre, Foreign Minister of Norway at the 65th World Health Assembly. Geneva, Switzerland: World Health Organization; 2012. http://www.who.int/mediacentre/events/2012/wha65/jonas_gahr_store/en/. Accessed July 29, 2013.

16. Horton, R. Global Burden of Disease 2010: Understanding disease, injury, and risk. *The Lancet.* 2012;380(9859):2053–2054.

17. Worldmapper. The world as you've never seen it before. http://www.worldmapper.org/display.php?selected=219. Accessed November 20, 2013.

18. Worldmapper. The world as you've never seen it before. http://www.worldmapper.org/display.php?selected=216. Accessed November 20, 2013.

19. Bhaumik S. WHO: Global initiative for emergency and essential surgical care. *Your Health.* 2012;61(12):7–8.

20. Bloom DE, Bloom D, Cafiero E, et al. *The global economic burden of non-communicable diseases.* Geneva: World Economic Forum; 2013. http://www3.weforum.org/docs/WEF_Harvard_HE_GlobalEconomicBurdenNonCommunicableDiseases_2011.pdf. Accessed September 25, 2013.

21. Global burden of disease: The key data. http://www.theguardian.com/global-development/poverty-matters/2012/dec/13/global-burden-disease-data

22. Loney T, Aw T, Handysides DG, et al. An analysis of the health status of the United Arab Emirates: The 'Big 4' public health issues. *Global Health Action.* 2013: 6. http://www.global-healthaction.net/index.php/gha/article/view/20100. Accessed February 7, 2007.

23. Bliss, KE. *Health in Latin America and the Caribbean: Challenges and opportunities for U.S. engagement.* Washington, DC: Center for Strategic and International Studies; 2009. http://csis.org/files/media/csis/pubs/090422_bliss_healthlatinamer_web.pdf. Accessed March 12, 2014.

24. OECD. Diabetes prevalence and incidence. In: *Health at a glance 2013: OECD indicators.* Paris: OECD Publishing; 2013. http://www.oecd.org/els/health-systems/Health-at-a-Glance-2013.pdf. Accessed February 20, 2014.

25. Kemper, T. Monitoring urbanization in the 21st century. *Earthzine.org.* January 21, 2013. http://www.earthzine.org/2013/01/21/monitoring-urbanization-in-the-21st-century/. Accessed June 15, 2013.

26. United Nations Department of Economic and Social Affairs. World urbanization prospects, the 2011 revision. http://www.un.org/en/development/desa/publications/world-urbanization-prospects-the-2011-revision.html. Accessed June 25, 2013.

27. Frontier Strategy Group. Capturing Africa's transformative urban growth. http://blog.frontier-strategygroup.com/2011/08/capturing-africa%E2%80%99s-transformative-urban-growth/. Accessed June 25, 2014.

28. Traynor, I. Europe of the future: Germany shrinks, France grows, but UK population booms. *The Guardian.* August 27, 2008. http://www.theguardian.com/world/2008/aug/27/population.eu. Accessed November 20, 2013.

29. The World Bank. *What climate change means for Africa, Asia and the Coastal Poor.* http://www.worldbank.org/en/news/feature/2013/06/19/what-climate-change-means-africa-asia-coastal-poor. Accessed July 10, 2013.

30. Brown M. Growing pains. *The Telegraph.* May 25, 2013: 24–33.

31. Hillman B, Unger J. *The urbanisation of rural China.* https://crawford.anu.edu.au/files/uploads/crawford01_cap_anu_edu_au/2013-09/cp2013-3_special_feature.pdf. Accessed July 10, 2014.

32. UN Habitat. *The state of China's cities 2014/2015.* http://unhabitat.org/publications-listing/state-of-china-cities/. Accessed November 12, 2014.

33. McKinsey Global Institute. Preparing for China's Urban Billion. http://www.mckinsey.com/~/media/McKinsey/dotcom/Insights%20and%20pubs/MGI/Research/Urbanization/Preparing%20for%20Chinas%20urban%20billion/MGI_Preparing_for_Chinas_Urban_Billion_full_report.ashx. Accessed February 20, 2014.

34. Liu C. Built in a dirty boom, China's biggest city tries to go green. *E&E Publishing LLC.* September 26, 2011. http://www.eenews.net/stories/1059954131/print. Accessed October 20, 2013.

35. China Discovery. *Chongqing Maps 2014: Updated, detailed and downloadable.* http://www.china-discovery.com/chongqing-tours/maps.html. Accessed May 5, 2014.

36. The Economist. Urbanisation in China: China's Chicago. *The Economist.* July 26, 2007. http://www.economist.com/node/9557763. Accessed November 13, 2013.

37. Dobreva E. *Chongqing: Future challenges to sustainable growth.* Budapest: CEU Business School; 2011. Student research project No. 051. http://www.ceibs.edu/images/bmt/research/2012/02/08/0D3A51C6126E1A48FF9D6DA0F6AF25BC.pdf. Accessed July 13, 2014.

38. Kurth J, Wilkinson M, Aguilar L. Six decades in Detroit: How abandonment, racial tensions and financial missteps bankrupted the city. *The Detroit News.* October 4, 2013. http://www .detroitnews.com/article/20131004/METRO01/310040001#ixzz2sw3KuiCt. Accessed December 2, 2013.

39. Clos J. United Nations Non-Governmental Liaison Service (NGLS). *Interview with the executive director of UN-Habitat Joan Clos.* http://www.un-ngls.org/rioplus20/newsletter/issue5/article3 .html. Accessed November 4, 2013.

40. Birch EL, Wachter SM, eds. *Global urbanization.* Philadelphia, PA: University of Pennsylvania Press; 2011. https://cis.uchicago.edu/outreach/summerinstitute/2011/documents/sti2011 -clark-world_urbanization.pdf. Accessed August 18, 2013.

41. Global Taskforce of Local and Regional Governments for Post-2015: Development Agenda Towards Habitat III. *Our achievements.* http://www.gtf2016.org/#!about/csgz. Accessed November 16, 2014.

42. Oremus W. *Carbon dioxide in atmosphere hits 400 PPM for first time in human history* [Weblog]. http://www.slate.com/blogs/future_tense/2013/05/10/atmostpheric_carbon_dioxide_ hits_400_ppm_for_first_time_in_human_history.html. Accessed January 2, 2014.

43. Germanos A. Air pollution a leading cause of cancer: World Health Organization. *Common Dreams.* October 17, 2013. http://www.commondreams.org/news/2013/10/17/air-pollution-leading-cause-cancer-world-health-organization. Accessed October 18, 2013.

44. International Agency for Research on Cancer (WHO). *World Cancer Report.* http://www.iarc .fr/en/publications/books/wcr/. Accessed July 17, 2015.

45. Whipple T. Extreme weather may trigger more climate change. *The Times.* August 15, 2013. http://www.thetimes.co.uk/tto/environment/article3843213.ece. Accessed September 20, 2013.

46. Gray R. Why the UN's climate experts still believe the heat is on. *The Daily Telegraph.* September 28, 2013: 4.

47. Collins N. Global warming 'unequivocal,' say scientists. *The Daily Telegraph.* September 28, 2012: 4.

48. Gosden E. UN climate change report to warn of 'severe, pervasive' effects of global warming. *The Telegraph.* November 1, 2014. http://www.telegraph.co.uk/news/earth/environment/ climatechange/11202987/UN-climate-change-report-to-warn-of-severe-pervasive-effects-of -global-warming.html. Accessed November 2, 2014.

49. Allen N. Climate change: Forecast for 2100 is floods and heat…and it's man's fault. *The Telegraph.* August 16, 2013. http://www.telegraph.co.uk/earth/environment/climatechange/ 10248747/Climate-change-forecast-for-2100-is-floods-and-heat-…-and-its-mans-fault.html. Accessed September 20, 2013.

50. Woollaston V. Would YOUR house be underwater? Terrifying map reveals the devastation that would occur if ALL the world's ice melted. *Daily Mail.* November 6, 2013. http://www.dai-lymail.co.uk/sciencetech/article-2488452/Map-reveals-devastation-worlds-ice-melted.html. Accessed November 29, 2013.

51. Gill K. An earth without ice. http://blog.apoapsys.com/2013/08/19/an-earth-without-ice/. Accessed November 20, 2014.

52. Nield T. Rocks hold the truth about climate change. *The Telegraph.* November 18, 2013. http:// www.telegraph.co.uk/earth/environment/climatechange/10458235/Rocks-hold-the-truth-about-climate-change.html. Accessed January 10, 2014.

53. Rice D. California's 100-year drought. *USA Today.* September 3, 2014. http://www.usatoday .com/story/weather/2014/09/02/california-megadrought/14446195/. Accessed September 3, 2014.

54. Varandani S. Polluted cities, to experience worse air quality during diwali. *International Business Times.* October 22, 2014. http://www.ibtimes.com/new-delhi-one-worlds-most -polluted-cities-experience-worse-air-quality-during-diwali-1709641. Accessed October 22, 2014.

55. Chen Z, Wang JN, Ma GX, Zhang YS. China tackles the health effects of air pollution. *The Lancet.* 2013;382(9909):1959–1960.

56. U.S. Global Change Research Program. National Climate Assessment and Development Advisory Committee. http://www.globalchange.gov/ncadac. Accessed June 2, 2014.

57. Lean G. Global warming—there's hope amid the gloom. http://www.telegraph.co.uk/news/earth/environment/globalwarming/10730590/Global-warming-theres-hope-amid-the-gloom.html

58. Holthaus E. *The earth just had its warmest "year" on record* [Weblog]. October 20, 2014. http://www.slate.com/blogs/future_tense/2014/10/20/climate_change_records_the_earth_just_had_the_warmest_12_month_period_recorded.html?wpsrc=fol_tw. Accessed November 5, 2014.

59. World Wildlife Fund (WWF). *Living planet report 2014.* http://wwf.panda.org/about_our_earth/all_publications/living_planet_report/. Accessed October 23, 2014.

60. Knowles K. *What is 'modernity' and why have sociologists been so interested in it?* Colchester, UK: University of Essex. https://www.essex.ac.uk/sociology/documents/pdf/ug_journal/vol1/KeeleyKnowles_SC111_2008.pdf. Accessed May 20, 2014.

61. Beck U. *Risk society: Towards a new modernity.* London: Sage Publications Ltd; 1992.

62. Hemingway A. Lifeworld-led care. Is it relevant for well-being and the fifth wave of public health action? *International Journal of Qualitative Studies on Health and Well-Being.* 2011;6(4):10364. http://www.ncbi.nlm.nih.gov/pmc/articles/PMC3235359/. Accessed May 16, 2013.

63. Roxburgh A. *A summary of Ulrich Beck–risk society: Towards a new modernity.* http://www.nextreformation.com/wp-admin/resources/risk-society.pdf. Accessed October 30, 2012.

64. Hanlon P, Carlisle S, Hannah M, Lyon A. *The future public health.* Maidenhead: Open University Press; 2012.

65. Shields M, Tremblay MS. Canadian childhood obesity estimates based on WHO, IOTF and CDC cut-points. *International Journal of Pediatric Obesity.* 2010;5(3):265–273.

66. Ogden CL, Carroll MD, Kit BK, Flegal KM. Prevalence of obesity among adults: United States, 2011–2012. Centers for Disease Control and Prevention. NCHS Data Brief No. 131; October 2013. http://www.cdc.gov/nchs/data/databriefs/db131.pdf. Accessed October 16, 2014.

67. OECD. *OECD factbook 2013: Economic, environmental and social statistics.* http://www.oecd-ilibrary.org/sites/factbook-2013-en/12/02/03/index.html?itemId=/content/chapter/factbook-2013-100-en. Accessed September 20, 2014.

68. Keats S, Wiggins S. Future diets: Implications for agriculture and food prices. http://www.odi.org/sites/odi.org.uk/files/odi-assets/publications-opinion-files/8776.pdf. Accessed March 15, 2014.

69. Stevens GA, Singh GM, Lu Y, et al. National, regional and global trends in adult overweight and obesity prevalences. *Popul Health Metr.* 2012;10(1):22.

70. Griffith R, O'Connell M, Smith K. *Food expenditure and nutritional quality over the great recession.* London: Institute for Fiscal Studies; 2013. IFS Briefing Note BN143. http://www.ifs.org.uk/bns/bn143.pdf. Accessed November 20, 2014.

71. Keeling J. Comfort eating: The new mental illness. You eat a biscuit–then can't stop until you finish the packet. Don't assume it's lack of willpower. Doctors now say it's a psychiatric condition that needs treatment. *Daily Mail.* October 29, 2013. http://www.dailymail.co.uk/health/article-2478592/Comfort-eating-classified-doctors-psychiatric-condition-needs-treatment.html#ixzz2mPj7k78f. Accessed October 30, 2013.

72. King SD. *When the money runs out: The end of western affluence.* London: Yale University Press; 2013.

73. Kelly T. Diabetes: Separating fact from fiction. *Daily Express.* October 29, 2013. http://www.express.co.uk/life-style/health/439843/Diabetes-Separating-fact-from-fiction. Accessed October 30, 2013.

74. American Psychiatric Association. *Diagnostic and Statistical Manual of Mental Disorders* (5th ed.). http://www.terapiacognitiva.eu/dwl/dsm5/DSM-5.pdf. Accessed June 28, 2014.

75. Smyth C. Obesity will send today's children to early grave. *The Times*. August 12, 2013. http://www.thetimes.co.uk/tto/health/child-health/article3840186.ece. Accessed August 12, 2013.

76. Rudolf M. Tackling Obesity through the Healthy Child Programme: A Framework for Action. http://www.noo.org.uk/uploads/doc/vid_4865_rudolf_TacklingObesity1_210110.pdf. Accessed June 29, 2014.

77. Luck's Yard Clinic. *Back pain 'time bomb'.* http://www.lucksyardclinic.com/back-pain-time-bomb. Accessed May 20, 2014.

78. Lawson D. Fat is a self-control issue–take it from supersize me. *The Sunday Times*. January 5, 2014. http://www.thesundaytimes.co.uk/sto/comment/columns/dominiclawson/article1359025.ece. Accessed January 6, 2014.

79. Jones C. Ambulances to carry 50st patients as obesity soars. *Derby Telegraph*. October 1, 2013. http://www.derbytelegraph.co.uk/Ambulances-carry-50st-patients-obesity-soars/story-19868404-detail/story.html. Accessed October 14, 2014.

80. Knight I. The scoffing, starving kids are trying to tell us something. *The Sunday Times*. October 13, 2013. http://www.thesundaytimes.co.uk/sto/comment/columns/indiaknight/article1326475.ece. Accessed October 14, 2013.

81. Rollins A. *Mexico taxes soft drinks, junk food as obesity rates go loco.* https://ama.com.au/ausmed/mexico-taxes-soft-drinks-junk-food-obesity-rates-go-loco. Accessed November 19, 2013.

82. Saint Louis C. Preschoolers in surgery for a mouthful of cavities. *New York Times*. March 6, 2012. http://www.nytimes.com/2012/03/06/health/rise-in-preschool-cavities-prompts-anesthesia-use.html?pagewanted=all&_r=0. Accessed November 10, 2013.

83. Dental Products Report. *Alliance for Cavity-Free Future reports progress.* http://www.dental-productsreport.com/dental/article/alliance-cavity-free-future-reports-progress. Accessed November 10, 2013.

84. World Health Organization (WHO). *Nutrition.* http://www.who.int/nutrition/topics/5_population_nutrient/en/index1.html. Accessed August 15, 2014.

85. Guthrie A. Mexican Coke bottler warns about soda tax. *The Wall Street Journal*. October 24, 2013. http://www.wsj.com/news/articles/SB10001424052702304799404579155801193822712. Accessed October 28, 2013.

86. Chan M. *WHO Director-General addresses health promotion conference.* http://www.who.int/dg/speeches/2013/health_promotion_20130610/en/. Accessed June 25, 2013.

87. Moodie R. Unhealthy big business spreading great harm. *The Age*. January 6, 2014. http://www.theage.com.au/comment/unhealthy-big-business-spreading-great-harm-20140105-30bnk.html. Accessed January 10, 2014.

88. Food and Agriculture Organization of the United Nations. *Staple foods: What do people eat?* http://www.fao.org/docrep/u8480e/u8480e07.htm. Accessed May 5, 2009.

89. Eaton SB, Eaton SB III, Konner MJ. Paleolithic Nutrition Revisited: A Twelve-Year Retrospective on Its Nature and Implications. *Eu J Clin Nutr*. 1997;51(4):207–216.

90. Cordain L. The late role of grains and egumes in the human diet, and biochemical evidence of their evolutionary discordance. *World Review of Nutrition and Dietetics*. 1999;84:19-73. http://www.beyondveg.com/cordain-l/grains-leg/grains-legumes-1a.shtml. Accessed January 29, 2009.

91. Overseas Development Institute (ODI). *Overweight and obese adults reaching almost a billion in developing countries, as numbers continue to grow in richer nations.* http://www.odi.org/news/703-overweight-obese-adults-reaching-almost-billion-developing-countries-as-numbers-continue-grow-richer-nations. Accessed June 14, 2014.

92. Nestle M. *Action on sugar to the food industry: Reduce sugar now!* http://www.foodpolitics.com/2014/01/action-on-sugar-to-the-food-industry-reduce-sugar-now/. Accessed March 20, 2014.

93. Hughes M. *The World Health Organisation takes a tough stand on sugar. It's about time we listened.* http://blogs.crikey.com.au/croakey/2014/01/06/the-world-health-organisation-takes-a-tough-stand-on-sugar-it%E2%80%99s-about-time-we-listened/. Accessed March 20, 2014.

94. World Health Organization. *Obesity: Preventing and Managing the Global Epidemic. Report of a WHO Consultation. World Health Organ Tech Rep Ser*. 2000;894:1–253.

95. Hammond RA, Levine R. The economic impact of obesity in the United States. *Diabetes, Metabolic Syndrome and Obesity: Targets and Therapy*. 2010;3:285–295.

96. Hassard J, Teoh K, Cox T, et al. *Calculating the cost of work-related stress and psychosocial risks.* Luxembourg: Publications Office of the European Union; 2014. https://osha.europa.eu/en/tools-and-publications/publications/literature_reviews/calculating-the-cost-of-work-related-stress-and-psychosocial-risks. Accessed August 16, 2014.

97. Pemberton M. If doctors like me are nice to fatties, they'll just get FATTER: A provocative view by Dr Max Pemberton. *Planning for Care*. http://www.planningforcare.co.uk/BlogView.asp?id=9074. Accessed February 20, 2013.

98. Turner J. We are too sweet on sugar to give it up easily. *The Times*. January 11, 2014. http://www.thetimes.co.uk/tto/opinion/columnists/article3972227.ece. Accessed January 11, 2014.

99. World Innovation Summit for Health. *Obesity is a global public health pandemic.* http://wish.org.qa/media-center/news-details?item=34&backArt=71. Accessed January 17, 2014.

100. Chan M. *Best days for public health are ahead of us, says WHO Director-General.* http://www.who.int/dg/speeches/2012/wha_20120521/en/. Accessed June 10, 2012.

101. World Health Organization. Sixty-sixth World Health Assembly closes with concern over new global health threat. http://www.who.int/mediacentre/news/releases/2013/world_health_assembly_20130527/en/

102. Lustig RH. *Fat chance: Beating the odds against sugar, processed food, obesity and disease.* New York, NY: Penguin Group; 2013.

103. Public Health England, Food Standards Agency. *National Diet and Nutrition Survey: Results from years 1 to 4 (combined) of the rolling programme for 2008 and 2009 to 2011 and 2012.* https://www.gov.uk/government/statistics/national-diet-and-nutrition-survey-results-from-years-1-to-4-combined-of-the-rolling-programme-for-2008-and-2009-to-2011-and-2012. Accessed June 3, 2014.

104. Reid D. The stress of modern life makes people sick with worry. *Daily Mail*. May 15, 2014:61.

105. Betts H. Is there any way to cure insomnia? *The Telegraph*. September 14, 2013. http://www.telegraph.co.uk/health/wellbeing/10304984/Is-there-any-way-to-cure-insomnia.html. Accessed October 2, 2013.

106. Connor S. Smoking will 'kill up to a billion people worldwide this century.' *The Independent*. October 28, 2012. http://www.independent.co.uk/life-style/health-and-families/health-news/smoking-will-kill-up-to-a-billion-people-worldwide-this-century-8229907.html. Accessed November 20, 2012.

107. Siegel DJ. *Brainstorm: The power and purpose of the teenage brain.* New York, NY: Penguin Group; 2013.

108. Bennet D, Bennet A. The rise of the knowledge organization. *International Handbook on Information Systems*. 2004;1:5–20. http://link.springer.com/chapter/10.1007/978-3-540-24746-3_1#page-1. Accessed January 20, 2007.

109. Tavernise S. Life spans shrink for least-educated Whites in the U.S. *The New York Times*. September 20, 2012. http://www.nytimes.com/2012/09/21/us/life-expectancy-for-less-educated-whites-in-us-is-shrinking.html?pagewanted=all&_r=2&. Accessed February 10, 2013.

110. Olshansky SJ, Antonucci T, Berkman L, et al. Differences in life expectancy due to race and educational differences are widening, and many may not catch up. *Health Aff*. 2012;31(8): 1803–1813.

111. King SD. *When the money runs out: End of western affluence.* London: Yale University Press; 2013.

112. Marcus M, Yasamy MT, Ommeren M, Chisholm D, Saxena S. *Depression: A global public health concern.* Geneva: World Health Organization, Department of Mental Health and Substance Abuse, 2012. http://www.who.int/mental_health/management/depression/who_paper_depression_wfmh_2012.pdf. Accessed March 20, 2014.

113. World Health Organization. *Prevention of mental disorders: Effective interventions and policy options*. Geneva: World Health Organization; 2004. http://www.who.int/mental_health /evidence/en/prevention_of_mental_disorders_sr.pdf. Accessed January 18, 2014.

114. Gamble C, Hart C. The use of psychosocial interventions. *Nurs Times*. 2003;99(9):46–47.

115. Devlin H. GPs 'too quick' to prescribe pills for depression. *The Times*. October 14, 2013. http:// www.thetimes.co.uk/tto/news/uk/article3893944.ece. Accessed October 17, 2013.

116. Smith BL. Inappropriate prescribing. *American Psychological Association*. 2012;43(6):36–41.

117. Bennett R, Thompson A, Sylvester R. 'Nightmare situation' as mental illness in children escalates. *The Times*. March 1, 2014. http://www.thetimes.co.uk/tto/health/mental-health /article4019994.ece. Accessed March 2, 2014.

118. Sylvester R, Thomson A. More young children are getting extreme anxiety…their parents are terrified. *The Times*. March 1, 2014.

119. Bentall RP. *Doctoring the mind: Is our current treatment of mental illness really any good?* New York, NY: New York University Press; 2009.

120. Halliwell E. Psychiatric diagnoses are less reliable than star signs. http://edhalliwell.com/ richard-bentall-interview.html. Accessed May 7, 2010.

121. Rappoport J. Mind-boggling report: How many drug prescriptions written in the US every year? *Natural News*. http://www.naturalnews.com/037226_drug_prescriptions_medical_news_pills .html. Accessed November 10, 2013.

122. Perdomo D. 100,000 Americans die each year from prescription drugs, while pharma companies get rich. *Alternet*. http://www.alternet.org/story/147318/100,000_americans_die_each_year_ from_prescription_drugs,_while_pharma_companies_get_rich. Accessed February 28, 2014.

123. Petersen M. *Our daily meds: How the pharmaceutical companies transformed themselves into slick marketing machines and hooked the nation on prescription drugs*. New York, NY: Sarah Crichton Books; 2008.

124. Hope J. We're a nation of pill poppers: New figures reveal Britons are prescribed a record 1,900 tablets every MINUTE. *Daily Mail*. July 30, 2013. http://www.dailymail.co.uk/health /article-2381450/Were-nation-pill-poppers-New-figures-reveal-Britons-prescribed-record-1 -900-tablets-MINUTE.html. Accessed August 30, 2013.

125. Davies S. The drugs don't work. *The Sunday Times*. September 15, 2013. http://www.thesun-daytimes.co.uk/sto/newsreview/features/article1313446.ece. Accessed October 20, 2013.

126. World Health Organization. WHO's first global report on antibiotic resistance reveals serious, worldwide threat to public health. http://www.who.int/mediacentre/news/releases/2014/ amr-report/en/. Accessed May 10, 2014.

127. World Health Organization. *Antimicrobial resistance. Global report on surveillance*. http://apps .who.int/iris/bitstream/10665/112642/1/9789241564748_eng.pdf?ua=1. Accessed May 5, 2014.

128. Shute J. Antibiotic resistance: Death of a wonder drug. *The Telegraph*. http://s.telegraph.co.uk/ graphics/projects/antibiotic-resistance/. Accessed March 20, 2014.

129. Miniwatts Marketing Group. Internet users in the world and Internet penetration rates by geographic region – 2104 Q2. http://www.miniwatts.com/. Accessed July 30, 2014.

130. Castells M. The impact of the Internet on society: A global perspective. *MIT Technology Review*; 2014. https://www.bbvaopenmind.com/en/article/the-impact-of-the-internet-on-society-a -global-perspective/?fullscreen=true. Accessed October 28, 2014.

131. Munday R. Marshall McLuhan declared that "the medium is the message." What did he mean and does this notion have any value? http://www.aber.ac.uk/media/Students/ram0202.html. Accessed September 26, 2013.

132. Woods J. Impotent rage at the click of a button. *The Telegraph*. May 16, 2014. http://www .telegraph.co.uk/technology/internet/10836810/Impotent-rage-at-the-click-of-a-button.html. Accessed May 18, 2014.

133. Greenfield S. *You and me: The neuroscience of identity.* London: Notting Hill Editions; 2011.

134. Narain J. Model pupil 15, robbed bank as if he was in a video game – then mum shopped him. *Daily Mail.* September 25, 2013: 5.

135. Allen N. Help at last for the addicts enslaved by the Internet. *The Telegraph.* June 2, 2013. http://www.telegraph.co.uk/technology/10093011/Help-at-last-for-the-addicts-enslaved-by-the-internet.html. Accessed November 18, 2013.

136. Skye J. Cyber bullying statistics. http://safety.lovetoknow.com/Cyber_Bullying_Statistics. Accessed May 3, 2014.

137. Ipsos. One in Ten (12%) Parents Online, Around the World Say Their Child Has Been Cyberbullied, 26% Say They Know of a Child Who Has Experienced Same in Their Community; 2013. http://www.ipsos-na.com/news-polls/pressrelease.aspx?id=5462. Accessed September 9, 2013.

138. WDSU 6 News. *Experts: Bullying victims more prone to commit suicide.* http://www.wdsu.com/Experts-Bullying-Victims-More-Prone-To-Commit-Suicide/10974412#ixzz2mQYb9kn8. Accessed January 13, 2014.

139. Hinduja S, Patchin JW. Bullying, cyberbullying and suicide. *Arch Suic Res.* 2010;14(3):206–221. http://www.cyberbullying.us/cyberbullying_and_suicide_research_fact_sheet.pdf. Accessed March 26, 2014.

140. Salkeld H. Schoolgirl, 14, hanged herself after years of abuse that started when she was at primary school 'because she had a different accent.' http://www.dailymail.co.uk/news/article-2522712/Schoolgirl-Izzy-Dix-14-hanged-years-abuse.html. Accessed December 15, 2013.

141. Abromeit L. School officials discuss social media bullying. *The Daily Iowan.* November 4, 2013. http://www.dailyiowan.com/2013/11/04/Metro/35511.html. Accessed December 10, 2013.

142. World Health Organization. *Comprehensive mental health action plan 2013–2020.* http://www.who.int/mental_health/action_plan_2013/en/. Accessed December 3, 2013.

143. National Health and Hospitals Reform Commission. *A healthier future for all Australians—Final report June 2009.* http://www.health.gov.au/internet/nhhrc/publishing.nsf/Content/nhhrc-report. Accessed March 15, 2014.

144. Public Health England. How healthy behaviour supports children's wellbeing. https://www.gov.uk/government/publications/how-healthy-behaviour-supports-childrens-wellbeing. Accessed September, 2013.

145. Russell J. The care system neglects children's self-worth. *The Times.* May 15, 2014. http://www.thetimes.co.uk/tto/opinion/columnists/article4089965.ece. Accessed May 16, 2014.

146. PublicHealthWatch. Twenty five shocking facts about violence against women. June 18, 2014. https://publichealthwatch.wordpress.com/2014/06/18/twenty-five-shocking-facts-about-violence-against-women/. Accessed August 25, 2014.

147. CNN. Afghan police: Man kills wife for giving birth to daughter instead of son. http://news.blogs.cnn.com/2012/01/31/afghan-police-man-kills-wife-for-giving-birth-to-daughter-instead-of-son/. Accessed February 20, 2013.

148. One Free World International. *Religious freedom in Afghanistan and Pakistan.* http://www.onefreeworldinternational.org/wp-content/uploads/2012/06/2012-USC-print-dbl-sided.pdf. Accessed May 22, 2013.

149. United Nations Economic Commission for Europe (UNECE). About violence against women. http://www.unece.org/fileadmin/DAM/stats/gender/vaw/about.html. Accessed April 25, 2014.

150. World Health Organization. Global and regional estimates of violence against women: Prevalence and health effects of intimate partner violence and non-partner sexual violence. http://www.who.int/reproductivehealth/publications/violence/9789241564625/en/. Accessed September 20, 2014.

151. United Nations Security Council. Resolution 2106 (2013). http://peacemaker.un.org/sites/peacemaker.un.org/files/SC_ResolutionWomen_SRES2106%282013%29%28english%29.pdf. Accessed September 20, 2014

152. Gov.uk. 113 countries pledge action to end sexual violence in conflict #timetoact. https://www.gov.uk/government/news/113-countries-pledge-action-to-end-sexual-violence-in-conflict-timetoact. Accessed October 10, 2014.

153. United Nations Children's Fund (UNICEF). *Breaking the silence on violence against indigenous girls, adolescents and young women.* http://www.unfpa.org/sites/default/files/resource-pdf/VAIWG_FINAL.pdf. Accessed December 10, 2014.

154. UN Women. About us. http://www.unwomen.org/en/about-us. Accessed December 10, 2014.

155. UN Women. Progress towards meeting the MDGs for women and girls. http://www.unwomen.org/en/news/in-focus/mdg-momentum. Accessed December 10, 2014.

156. United Nations. The Millennium Development Goals Report 2013. http://www.un.org/millenniumgoals/pdf/report-2013/mdg-report-2013-english.pdf. Accessed November 17, 2013.

157. United Nations. *The Millennium Development Goals Report 2014.* http://www.un.org/millenniumgoals/2014%20MDG%20report/MDG%202014%20English%20web.pdf

158. UN Women. Challenges and achievements in the implementation of the Millennium Development Goals. http://www.unwomen.org/~/media/headquarters/attachments/sections/csw/58/csw58-stakeholdersforum-conceptnotediscussionguides-en%20pdf.ashx. Accessed April 10, 2014.

159. Hennig B. Women in Parliament (map). http://www.viewsoftheworld.net/?p=4406. Accessed November 20, 2014.

160. Marlar J, Mendes E. Globally, men twice as likely as women to have a good job—women's deficit in the "good jobs" market is biggest in South Asia. *Gallup.* 2013. http://www.gallup.com/poll/164666/globally-men-twice-likely-women-good-job.aspx. Accessed Septemeber 23, 2014.

161. UN Women Policy Division. A transformation stand-alone goal on achieving gender equality, women's rights and women's empowerment: Imperatives and key components. http://www.unwomen.org/en/digital-library/publications/2013/7/post-2015-long-paper. Accessed November 20, 2014.

162. European Parliament. Challenges and achievements in the implementation of the Millennium Development Goals for women and girls from a European Union perspective. http://www.europarl.europa.eu/RegData/etudes/etudes/join/2014/493049/IPOL-FEMM_ET%282014%29493049_EN.pdf. Accessed October 15, 2014.

163. Amnesty International. Nigeria: Find and protect abducted schoolgirls. http://www.amnesty.org.uk/groups/bloxham/nigeria-find-and-protect-abducted-schoolgirls. Accessed May 15, 2014.

164. United Nations Population Fund (UNFPA). *Programming to address violence against women: 10 case studies.* https://www.unfpa.org/publications/programming-address-violence-against-women. Accessed November 12, 2014.

165. World Health Organization. *16 Ideas for addressing violence against women in the context of the HIV epidemic: A programming tool.* http://apps.who.int/iris/bitstream/10665/95156/1/9789241506533_eng.pdf. Accessed November 10, 2014.

166. HM Government. A call to end violence against women and girls. https://www.gov.uk/government/uploads/system/uploads/attachment_data/file/287758/VAWG_Action_Plan.pdf. Accessed December 10, 2014.

167. Culp-Ressler T. Jimmy Carter: Violence against women is the most pervasive human rights violation in the world. *Thinkprogress.* http://thinkprogress.org/health/2014/03/24/3418277/jimmy-carter-gender-inequality/. Accessed March 30, 2014.

168. Frostrup M. Britain shows the world the way—again. *The Times.* March 8, 2014. http://www.thetimes.co.uk/tto/opinion/columnists/article4026828.ece. Accessed November 15, 2014.

3.0

Public Health:
The Impending Financial Crisis

3.1 AFFORDABILITY OF AN AGING POPULATION: SHOULD WE BE WORRIED?

"A Situation Without Precedent"

The authors of *Global Health and Aging* (1) observe that "the world is facing a situation without precedent: We soon will have more older people than children and more people at extreme old age than ever before" (Figure 3.1).

As shown in Table 3.1, Professor David Bloom and colleagues at Harvard's Department of Global Health and Population (2) observe that population aging is now a concern for every country in the world.

Three main factors appear to be at the root of an aging population in developed nations:

- Increased longevity: The average age increased from 48 years in the 1950s to 68 years in the first century of this decade to about 76 years in the present.
- Declining fertility: The average family consisted of 5 children per woman in 1950 to roughly 2.5 today with an estimate of about 2.2 by 2050.
- Aging of "baby boom" generations: Post-World War II saw the birth of large cohorts of children.

Globally, Professor Bloom et al. posit that "the number of those over age 60 is projected to increase from just under 800 million today (representing 11% of world population) to just over 2 billion in 2050 (representing 22% of world population)" (2). While the "world population is projected to increase 3.7 times from 1950 to 2050 . . . the number of those aged 60 and over will increase by a factor of nearly 10." However, "among the elderly, the 'oldest old'—that is, those aged 80 and over—is projected to increase by a factor of 26," along with the "compression of morbidity" due to antiaging technologies and healthier lifestyles.

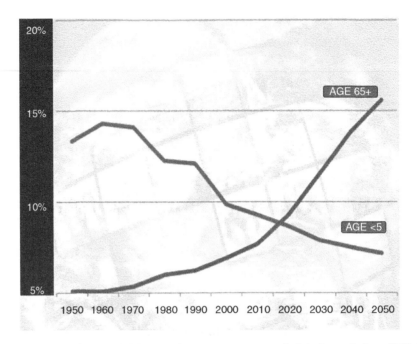

FIGURE 3.1 Young children and older people as a percentage of global population: 1950–2050.

Source: United Nations Department of Economic and Social Affairs, Population Division. *World Population Prospects: The 2004 Revision.* New York: United Nations, 2005 (2a).

Summarized in Table 3.1, "the 10 countries with the highest shares of 60+ population in 2011 are all in the developed world (or are countries in transition)" (2). By 2050, the United Nations (UN) predicts that "there will be 42 countries with higher shares of the 60-plus group than Japan has now." Figure 3.2 illustrates that the highest age range

TABLE 3.1 Countries With the Highest Shares of 60+ Population in 2011 and 2050 (percent; among countries with 2011 population of 1 million or more)

2011		2050	
Japan	31	Japan	42
Italy	27	Portugal	40
Germany	26	Bosnia and Herzegovina	40
Finland	25	Cuba	39
Sweden	25	Republic of Korea	39
Bulgaria	25	Italy	38
Greece	25	Spain	38
Portugal	24	Singapore	38
Belgium	24	Germany	38
Croatia	24	Switzerland	37

Source: United Nations, Department of Economic and Social Affairs, Population Division. *World Population Prospects: The 2010 Revision.* New York: United Nations, 2011 (3).

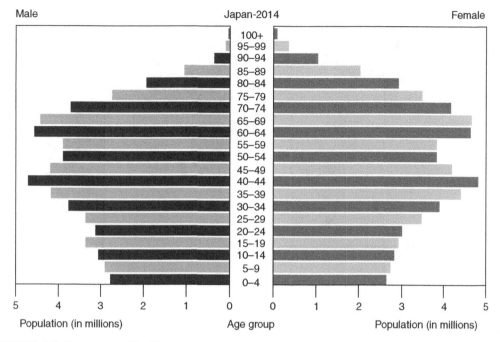

FIGURE 3.2 From tree to kite (Japanese population pyramid, millions).

Source: Central Intelligence Agency, *The World Factbook*, https://www.cia.gov/library/publications/the-world-factbook/index
.html (4).

for both males and females is now between ages 4 and 44, followed by those in the 60
to 64 and 65 to 69 ranges.

Although population growth is occurring mostly in developing nations, decline
in population is in the cards, perhaps increasingly, for many others—mainly Russia,
Japan, Ukraine, and South Africa, along with others. As austerity measures deepen
in Europe, more will seek employment opportunities abroad. Indeed, some "are witnessing an historically unprecedented demographic phenomenon: Simultaneous
population aging and population decline." As illustrated in Figure 3.3, "more than
20 countries are projected to experience population declines in the upcoming decades.
Russia's population, for example, is expected to shrink by 18 million between 2006 and
2030, a decrease of nearly 13 percent. Nine other countries are projected to experience
a decline of at least 1 million people during the same period" (5).

It is widely held that an aging population will severely impact the economic
health of a nation (6). The main reason put forward is that "the number of suscep-
tible individuals at older ages increases the overall incidence and prevalence of noncommunicable diseases" (1), which adds significantly to the cost of care. Another
argument is that fewer people working will reduce tax contributions and make affordability of health and social care more difficult as projected in the Dependency Ratio,
"calculated by dividing the number of people of working age by the number of people
of retirement age" (7).

Bloom, Canning, and Fink refute the argument that costs will become unsustainable, observing that "because of falling fertility rates" worldwide, "the labor force as
a share of total population has been increasing and is expected to continue increasing

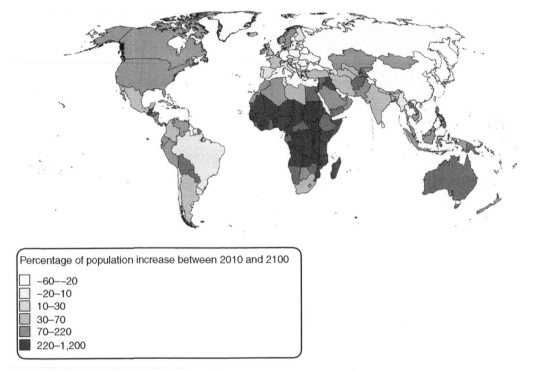

Percentage of population increase between 2010 and 2100

- ☐ −60−−20
- ☐ −20−10
- ☐ 10−30
- ☐ 30−70
- ☐ 70−220
- ☐ 220−1,200

FIGURE 3.3 Projected population growth, 2010 to 2100.

Note: The boundaries on this map do not imply official endorsement or acceptance by the United Nations.

Source: United Nations, Department of Economic and Social Affairs, Population Division, *World Population Prospects: The 2012 Revision.* New York: United Nations, 2013 (7a).

through 2050" (8). Further, they conclude that "one of the most widely cited fears about population aging—that there will be a crushing rise in elderly dependency unless the labor force participation of the elderly drastically increases—appears to be unfounded for the world as a whole—notwithstanding very steep increases in particular countries such as Italy and Japan," as illustrated in Figure 3.2. Part of the rebalancing may also eventually be attributable to "the reduction in mortality from infectious diseases and maternal and childhood conditions."

National policy responses to counter the effects of an aging population include raising the retirement age, removing incentives to retire early, encouraging immigration to aging societies and changing business practices, worker wellness programs, and increasingly valuing the role of the older worker (9,10).

In the United Kingdom, "recovery," according to Emma Duncan, deputy editor of *The Economist*, "is based on much the same froth as before the crisis—consumer credit and a housing boom" (11). Complicating matters is the aging population, which, she asserts, "is a drag on the economy," and while "pushing up the state pension age" is one way of dealing with the financial strains, "older people, even if they keep their noses to the grindstone, are not as productive as younger ones." And, while we may feel that we are in the midst of "astonishing technological change," the changes we are "seeing now are less fundamental, and less productive, than they have been in the past," when we consider "the spread of electricity, the car, the plane and modern medicine. At the end of the 20th century we saw computers revolutionizing offices. The big advance of the 21st century? Facebook and Twitter."

Gradually, it appears that more attention is being paid to "measures that reduce the risk of disease and promote the maintenance of function, confidence and engagement that can support healthy ageing and ease the pressure on healthcare systems. Most notable are health promotion and disease prevention programs that target the main causes of morbidity and premature mortality, in particular obesity and hypertension, as well as mental health" (12).

With regard to nations experiencing huge drops in the size of population in the next 40 or 50 years, Japan may be a case to watch and may hold serious lessons for the other countries listed in Table 3.1. A recent report spells out the risks involved. Japan has "one of the lowest fertility rates in the world, and at the same time, one of the highest longevity rates. As a result, the population is dropping rapidly, and becoming increasingly weighted toward older people." The country's population currently stands at 128 million, but that "has been falling—and is on a path to decline by about a million people a year. By 2060, the government estimates, there will be just 87 million people in Japan; nearly half of them will be over 65" (13). Its national debt is estimated at 196% of GDP in 2012 (940 trillion yen).

The long-range outlook, which may impact in the same measure on the other countries (Table 3.1), is that "without a dramatic change in either the birthrate or its restrictive immigration policies, Japan simply won't have enough workers to support its retirees, and will enter a demographic death spiral" (14). Its present strategy is to raise its sales tax from 5% to 10% (13).

While there is cause for concern for these demographic developments, a factor that may contribute to impoverished standards of living is "secular stagnation," a term "coined in the 1930s by Alvin Hansen, a disciple of Keynes." The theory holds that "as population growth and technological progress slowed, so would economic growth." This may be the case already on both sides of the Atlantic, as Larry Summers, the former U.S. Treasury secretary, observed "that although the financial had ebbed, there is really no evidence of growth that is restoring equilibrium" (15).

"Dementia: The Modern Plague"

Expectations of what health and social care systems should deliver are rising, while at the same time, the resources for treating patients and caring for the most vulnerable are becoming scarce (16). Of particular concern is the increase in dementia ("amyloid plaque—sticky damaged protein associated with dying neurons"), the "modern plague" (17), estimated globally at 44 million in 2013, an increase of 22% in only 3 years and rising to 135 million by 2050. Similar to other noncommunicable diseases (NCDs), dementia is "a mark of progress that in rich countries growing numbers of people are dying of the diseases of prosperity rather than those of poverty" and "the most frightening aspect is that nothing can be done to stop its onset."

Research has shown that "diet and regular exercise, eating fruit and vegetables, staying slim, light drinking and not smoking" instead of new drugs "will bring greatest progress in the fight against the condition" and that "middle-aged people must take responsibility for *preventing* the diseases rather than waiting for a cure" (18), discussed further in Chapter 6.0. Taking on these behaviors will also cut the number of people with diabetes, heart disease, and cancers.

David Smith, emeritus professor of pharmacology at Oxford University and founder of the research project OPTIMA (Oxford Project to Investigate Memory and Ageing) put it bluntly: "We've been waiting for a breakthrough drug treatment for Alzheimer's for decades. An astonishing £25 billion has been spent worldwide on trying to develop one, and yet we still don't have anything that can slow down, let alone stop, the disease. . . . What we should have spent some money on is research into prevention. If you can't reverse the damage, the obvious step is to stop it from happening at all." In the United Kingdom and likely in other developed countries, the story may be the same—out of the £140 million spent on studying Alzheimer's, "just 1p in every £1,000 went on prevention" (19).

Driven by the world's expanding middle class and the economic growth in developing nations, the Institute for Healthcare Informatics (IMS) estimates that global spending on prescription drugs will likely reach $1.2 trillion (£0.7 trillion; €0.9 trillion) by 2017, an increase of $205 billion to $235 billion from 2012 (20). How much of this would be better spent on prevention, we might ask.

And, as Philip Collins reminds us—discussed further in Section 3.2—"Across industrialized countries as a whole, only 3 per cent of the health budget is spent on prevention." Moreover, he argues that "health services need now to be reconfigured for an era in which people cope with a liveable disease for a large minority of their life span" (21).

A national study in the United States involving 17 counties (22) showed that efforts to reduce health risk factors had an empowering effect and clearly demonstrated that

- Communities and stakeholders were more willing and interested in participating in health promotion activities in a sustained manner.
- Alliances and collaborations were strengthened.
- Communication channels were opened.
- Municipalities were stimulated to review their planning and implementation processes in order to incorporate health promotion principles.

Similar findings underpinned the preparation for the G8 dementia summit, which took place in December 2013 in London. Signatories (Britain, France, the United States, Italy) called "for governments to invest more in teaching the public, including children, about the benefits of a healthy diet and lifestyle" (23).

Dr. Aseem Malhotra, a cardiology registrar at the British Croydon University Hospital, and one of the individuals who signed the letter, provided a compelling argument for depending less on pills and more on following a healthy diet, in particular the Mediterranean diet "in preventing all of the chronic diseases that are plaguing the Western world" (24). His main concerns are that "we are not going to overcome the increasing burden of chronic diseases by prescribing more pills. The medical profession has itself been guilty of placing too much emphasis on drugs, the benefits of which are often grossly exaggerated and fuelled by a powerful pharmaceutical industry, who naturally wish to expand the use of their drugs for financial gain" (23).

His comments resonate with those of Dr. David Zigmond (25), who cautions that dementia cannot be tackled head-on, as can HIV and some cancers, as "much dementia goes together naturally with advanced age and is not necessarily a pathological variation" and that "medical technology has little to offer directly to most cases. What helps is sensitive and imaginative guidance and containment" as "this is a matter of pastoral healthcare and welfare." What appears to be most important is not "a tranche of dementia clinics, consultants and brain scanners," but to find again social workers and other health professionals, who "can build personal relationships with patients, their families and communities—often over years."

These messages appear to have been taken on board by the G8 dementia summit decision makers—led by the United Kingdom, Japan, Canada, and France—whose international response to dementia (Declaration and Communiqué) rightly emphasized cross sector partnerships and innovation and included that in finding a cure by 2025 (26), priority be given to

- *Research* to elucidate the mechanisms underlying the initiation and progression of neurodegeneration as a basis for identifying new targets for therapeutic development
- *Prevention* of dementia
- Making timely *diagnosis and early intervention* feasible, affordable, and cost-effective
- Facilitating the *integration of care* and helping individuals and their carers access care and social services in their homes and communities
- Making care homes more *responsive to needs*

However, despite these good intentions, a fundamental issue that may challenge most countries throughout the 21st century remains: Given diminishing resources and, as projected in Table 3.1, will countries be able to support health and long-term care considering the growing number of dementia sufferers along with the increasing number of patients with diabetes, arthritis, and high blood pressure?

Less funding for health and social care at all levels triggers cost cutting, affecting populations and in particular the most vulnerable (27). The urgency of rebalancing global and national budgets in line with actual population health and social care needs could not be greater. In terms of public services, scaling up provider capacity—aligning population needs with sensible and sensitive community responses and interventions underpinned by rethinking of education and training approaches—must surely become a top priority for all planners and decision makers.

"Population Aging and Public Policy Options"

As previously cited, a few years ago, a WHO policy brief "Health Systems and Policy Analysis: How Can Health Systems Respond to Population Ageing?" (16) focused on health and long-term care services for the elderly population. Affordability—as was the case then and remains an exponentially growing concern now—depends on public policy options, which are increasingly constrained by competing national priorities and reduced funding. The main aims, while highly commendable, including ensuring that "elderly people will enjoy a better health status, have less need of health and long-term care services, and be supported by a balanced and integrated provision of care," are elusive for many nations caught in the midst of austerity measures.

The authors propose three ways of making efficiency savings:

First, given a growing number of chronic conditions and comorbidities, improving coordination among social and health care services is becoming crucial.

Second, the authors assert that it is essential to reduce "the inappropriate use of hospital services, including early transfer to people's own homes or to other appropriate types of accommodation (such as nursing homes or sheltered dwellings), demanding closer integration with the long-term care sector."

Third, emphasis should also be given to "interventions to tackle obesity and hypertension, immunizations, and fall prevention programmes" along with exercise to "reduce cognitive decline [and] vascular damage to the brain," thereby also bringing "wider economic benefits, as people who can expect to live a long and healthy life have a strong incentive to invest in developing their skills when younger and to extend their working lives."

As a whole, these policy priorities will have significant implications on how health and social care professionals are prepared. Discussed further in Chapter 8.0, there is an urgent need to enhance the skills and knowledge of health and social care professionals by improving student selection procedures and restructuring the curricula to meet the actual population needs of the 21st century (28). Continuing to educate and train health care students in silos is not only costly but also undermines the learning experience essential to supporting population health and well-being. Education providers need to play a more pivotal part not only in accelerating better understanding of disease prevention and in the main causes of morbidity and mortality but also to "minimize the cost pressures associated with ageing."

"The Bottom Line": Social Discrimination Versus Compassionate Care

Much has been written about the importance of greater compassion and understanding of the growing number of elderly patients as traditionally, health and social care have been about the young and those in the most productive years of their lives. Confirming the need for changes in the education of health professionals, Dr Iain Wilkinson, whose "interests concern social suffering, the politics of compassion, the sociology of health, the sociology of risk and social theory" (29), points out that "care is taken as read with healthcare professionals but I am not sure it should be—most junior doctors and nurses these days have had relatively little exposure to care. Medical students often spend less than a month on care of the elderly wards in their training. There seems to be little leading on care."

According to a study in Canada, ageism remains "the most widely tolerated form of social discrimination" (30). To combat this bias, the International Federation on Ageism (IFA) initiated the "Age Is More Film Project" to challenge "the negative attitudes, stereotypes and preconceptions that prevent older persons from living their lives to the fullest." The outcome was a series of 3-minute films, which saw "20 aspiring young documentarians [paired] with an older counterpart" living in retirement facilities and sharing glimpses of their lives.

Suggested Long-Term Outcome Measures
Underpinning Strategies for an Aging Population

As most countries are experiencing an aging of their population, the question of affordability is of paramount concern, especially at a time when poverty, austerity measures, unemployment, and increases in chronic illnesses and other NCDs are on the rise. While many will agree that a declining working-age population will lead to less income to pay for government services, the impact on health and social care still seems surprisingly less clear, despite the findings of the *World Alzheimer Report 2010: The Global Economic Impact of Dementia* (31). The report, issued several years ago, found that "Alzheimer's disease and other dementias are exacting a massive toll on the global economy, with the problem set to accelerate in coming years." The report also revealed that

- The worldwide costs of dementia will exceed 1% of global gross domestic product (GDP) in 2010, at US$604 billion. If dementia care were a country, it would be the world's 18th largest economy. If it were a company, it would be the world's largest by annual revenue, exceeding Walmart (US$414 billion) and Exxon Mobil (US$311 billion).
- The number of people with dementia will double by 2030 and more than triple by 2050.
- The costs of caring for people with dementia are likely to rise even faster than the prevalence, especially in the developing world, as more formal social care systems emerge and rising incomes lead to higher opportunity costs.
- Reports from individual countries such as the United Kingdom suggest that dementia is one of the costliest illnesses, and yet research and investment are at a far lower level than for other major illnesses.

For these reasons, the G8 dementia conference was held in London in late 2013, leading to the key recommendations. In monitoring progress, government and service consideration might especially be given to finding out whether the following outcomes are being achieved:

1. *The extent to which* governments and social care and health professionals have taken on board the importance of disease prevention and health promotion, targeting "the main causes of morbidity and premature mortality, in particular obesity and hypertension, as well as mental health"
2. *The extent to which* policies and plans for long-term care have been collaboratively drafted that "have an explicit focus on supporting family caregivers and ensuring social protection of vulnerable people with Alzheimer's disease and other dementias"

3. *The extent to which* systems of formal care are being developed and funded "in low and middle income countries which lack adequate systems of formal care"
4. *The extent to which* measures are being put in place to allow for most treatments out of hospital
5. *The extent to which* health and social care undergraduate and postgraduate education and training programs have been structured to optimize collaborative learning in elderly care
6. *The extent to which* measures have been implemented to reaffirm "a simple truth: every patient is a person. . . . A person with a name. A person with a family. Not just a body harbouring a pathology, not a diagnostic puzzle, not a four-hour target or an 18-week problem; not a cost pressure—and most certainly not a 'bed-blocker'" (32).

"An Old Lady's Poem"

"When an old lady died in the geriatric ward of a small hospital near Dundee, Scotland, it was felt that she had nothing left of any value. Later, when the nurses were going through her meager possessions, they found this poem. Its quality and content so impressed the staff that copies were made and distributed to every nurse in the hospital. One nurse took her copy to Ireland. The old lady's sole bequest to posterity has since appeared in the Christmas edition of the *News Magazine of the North Ireland Association for Mental Health*" (Figure 3.4; 33).

> And now this little old Scottish lady, with nothing left to give to the world, is now the author of this simple, yet eloquent, poem traveling the world by Internet. Goes to show that we all leave "SOME footprints in time."

3.2 FUNDING OF PUBLIC HEALTH: REBALANCING THE EQUATION?

Forces Shaping the 20th Century

Dr. Rolf Sattler, distinguished Canadian morphologist, biologist, philosopher, prolific author, and global educator, maintains that from a historic perspective "the 20th century was a most extraordinary century. It was also marked by horrible events: two world wars, the holocaust and other genocides and atrocities. Soviet communism with its regime of terror eventually collapsed, but capitalism became deeply entrenched and the poor remained poor or became even poorer" (34), an observation shared by President Barack Obama in his sixth State of the Union address (35).

> Average wages have barely budged. Inequality has deepened. Upward mobility has stalled. The cold hard fact is that even in the midst of recovery, too many Americans are working more than ever just to get by—let alone ahead. And too many aren't working at all.

The three main forces that, according to Dr. Sattler, shaped the 20th century—science/technology, capitalism, and the mass media (34)—continue to spread their influence in the early decades of the 21st century and are most likely central factors

An Old Lady's Poem

What do you see, nurses,
what do you see?
What are you thinking
when you're looking at me?

A crabby old woman,
not very wise,
uncertain of habit,
with faraway eyes?

Who dribbles her food
and makes no reply
When you say in a loud voice,
"I do wish you'd try!"

Who seems not to notice
the things that you do,
and forever is losing a
stocking or shoe.....

A woman of thirty,
my young now grown fast,
bound to each other
with ties that should last.

At forty, my young sons
have grown and are gone,
but my man's beside me
to see I don't mourn.

At fifty once more,
babies play round my knee,
again we know children,
my loved one and me.

Who, resisting or not,
lets you do as you will,
with bathing and feeding,
the long day to fill....

Is that what you're thinking?
Is that what you see?
Then open your eyes,
nurse;you're not looking at me.

I'll tell you who I am
as I sit here so still,
as I do at your bidding,
as I eat at your will.

I'm a small child of ten ....
with a father and mother,
brothers and sisters,
who love one another.

A young girl of sixteen,
with wings on her feet,
dreaming that soon now
a lover she'll meet.

A bride soon at twenty --
my heart gives a leap,
remembering the vows
that I promised to keep.

At twenty-five now,
I have young of my own,
who need me to guide
and a secure happy home.

Dark days are upon me,
my husband is dead;
I look at the future,
I shudder with dread.

For my young are all rearing
young of their own,
and I think of the years
and the love that I've known.

I'm now an old woman ....
and nature is cruel;
'Tis jest to make old age
look like a fool.

The body, it crumbles,
grace and vigor depart,
there is now a stone
where I once had a heart.

But inside this old carcass
a young girl still dwells,
and now and again,
my battered heart swells.

I remember the joys,
I remember the pain,
and I'm loving and living
life over again.

I think of the years ....
all too few, gone too fast,
and accept the stark fact
that nothing can last.

So open your eyes, people,
open and see,
not a crabby old woman;
look closer ..see ME!!

FIGURE 3.4 "An Old Lady's Poem, Anonymous".
Source: Care Pathways, http://www.carepathways.com/anoldladyspoem.cfm.

contributing to global and national socioeconomic inequities and imbalances in both poor and rich nations.

"A Report Card for Humanity: 1900–2050" (36)

Interestingly, while the short- and medium-term view of the planet's future looks unsettling, public health trends over the next 40 or so years become more positive—at least when viewed through the optimistic eyes of 21 economists who crunched "the numbers on 10 of the world's most bedeviling problems" for *A Report Card for Humanity: 1900–2050* (36), published by *The Atlantic*. Their main trigger research question was, "Will we be living better in 2050 than our predecessors did in 1900?" in terms of important problems—"including health, education, air pollution, and climate change—on a comparable scale," applying "classic economic valuations" to "everything from lost lives to bad health, considering factors including forfeited income from illiteracy and increased hurricane damage from global warming." In short, the economists identified the cost of each problem from 1900 to 2013 and then projected these costs to 2050, comparing the magnitude of each problem to "the total resources available to fix it" in GDP percentage terms. Overall, the method yields favorable results across the 10 indicators. However, additional input data might have changed the findings somewhat, taking "human health" as an example. The economists rightly acknowledge that "humans have made great strides in healthcare" since 1900 and posit that

> in economic terms, the cost of poor health at the outset of the 20th century was a staggering 32 percent of global GDP. Today, it is down to about 11 percent, and by 2050 it will be half that. One manifestation of this trend is that we are all living far longer. In 1900, the average person lived 32 years; today it's 69 years, and by 2050 it will be 76. Advances are so rapid that for every month you live, medical science adds a week to your life expectancy.

Longevity is a positive indicator of strengthened global health, but as we have seen in the previous section, it may also exact a price, such as increases in dementia and other comorbidities. In addition, emerging psychosocial conditions or illnesses, many of which may stem from the pressures of "modernity," are already adding considerably to health expenditures. The report card's future statistical projections may be overly optimistic and in many nations could once again be pushing beyond 32% of the GDP levels in 1900.

As one example, the U.S. expenditure on health care is now close to 18% of GDP (37); that is about 18 cents of every dollar earned or received in the form of pensions, for example. As shown in Figure 3.5, health care spending will likely rise by about 7%

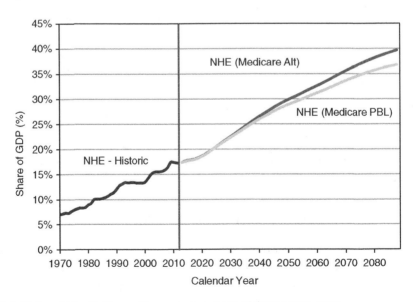

FIGURE 3.5 National Health Expenditures as a percent of GDP 1970–2088.

Note: Historical data is used before 2013 and projections from 2013 forward.

Source: Center for Medicare & Medicaid Services, Office of the Actuary, The Long-Term Projection Assumptions for Medicare and Aggregate National Health Expenditures. https://www.cms.gov/Research-Statistics-Data-and-Systems/Statistics-Trends-and-Reports/ReportsTrustFunds/Downloads/ProjectionMethodology2014.pdf

by 2030 and near 40% by 2080 or so on the CMS [Centers for Medicare & Medicaid Services] forecast. It is noteworthy that none of the forecasts predicts health spending below 35% of GDP; the Congressional Budget Office's (CBO's) assumption is close to 50% of GDP.

These increases in health will unquestionably have additional staggering consequences, requiring "funding equal to 36 percent of federal income taxes by 2030, based on the CMS [Centers for Medicare & Medicaid Services] forecast"; and "almost 70 percent of federal income taxes by midcentury, based on the CBO forecast"(37).

Along with other nations heading in these directions, there is no doubt that "tough choices will have to be made" and "framed in public policy."

Approaches for Reducing Future Health Costs: Addressing the Symptoms But Not the Disease?

McKinsey & Company, in partnership with the World Economic Forum, carried out a study of future public and private spending on health care across 21 developed nations (38,39). Highlighting the main drivers of change—rising patient expectations, a growing burden of disease, suboptimal allocation of resources, and rising unit costs of care—their analysis provides two main ways forward for dealing with increased spending on health care:

- Doing less: for example, by rationing access to care, imposing budgets, and allowing waiting times to rise; or shifting the financial burden to employers or households
- Doing more: by, for example, increasing financing for health through taxation or by boosting the budget by prioritizing health care over other public expenditure (40).

While these are logical scenarios, both lead to negative consequences, and neither appears to address the underlying problems that are causing the rapid rise in costs (human and financial) in health and social care. There are no "quick fixes," but it may be "time to think differently" and seriously reflect on the sustainability of global health and well-being.

"Health and Health Care for All the People"

In his paper, "Health and Healthcare for the 21st Century: For All the People" (41), the late Charles Everett Koop, a former vice admiral in the Public Health Service Commissioned Corps and a former surgeon general of the United States (1982–1989), reflected on his more than six decades of public health. And, while "awed at what has been achieved," he was equally "shocked at what has not." His main regret was that although "we can prevent and treat diseases formerly considered capricious death sentences. . . . Many proven strategies for preventing disease and disability sit on the shelves." His main longstanding concern was that "our capability to prevent and treat disease seems to exceed our willingness to apply our interventions."

The reasons why governments, health services, and many people are still drawn to curative interventions over preventive approaches to health care are complex but appear to "have a social basis" (42), influenced throughout the 20th century, as Dr. Sattler observes, by the expansion of science/technology, capitalism, and the media.

Certainly, "the power and status of the medical profession and the health industry in general" are key factors. Through scientific research, regulation, practice, and training, they define "the experience of being 'ill' and decide what treatment is required" (42). Spilling into the 21st century, the overall approach to health care is "the long-standing biomedical model of disease," most often also associated with the "latest technology or innovation in medical practice, [which] confers responsibility for good health on the system, not on the individual." Another explanation for the status quo in health care dependency is the mindset—originating in the late 19th century—that cure lies outside the body because of "ignorance of anatomy" (43). The stethoscope invented by Theophile Laennec (1781–1826) in 1816 could give access "to body noises—the sounds of breathing, the blood gurgling around the heart," as well as help diagnose bronchitis, pneumonia, and tuberculosis (phthisis or consumption), but was not able to provide effective and long-term solutions for treating sufferers. Today's parallel might be many of the chronic diseases and NCDs that are impacting society, such as dementia and anxiety disorders in their varied forms.

So it was over a hundred years ago, when in 1873 Sir John Erichson (1818–1896), surgeon to the University College Hospital, London, declared "the abdomen, the chest and the brain [will] be forever shut from the intrusion of the wise and human surgeon." Specializations also continued to struggle, as in 1900 when the *General Practitioner* said of specialists, "their minds are narrowed, judgment biased and unbalanced by disproportionate knowledge of one subject," and the patient would suffer because the specialist "knows nothing of the constitutional idiosyncrasies of the individual, which are essential to correct diagnosis and treatment" (43).

While medical practice was slow to change, scientific discoveries in the late 19th century, such as those of Rudolf Virchow (1821–1902), an eminent German "pathologist, anthropologist, and social thinker," widely regarded as one of the most influential physicians in history who made advances in cell theory and chemical pathology, profoundly altered the understanding of the human body and disease (44). These breakthroughs eventually translated into treatment and changed the role and public perception of doctors.

As examples, bacteriologist Paul Ehrlich in 1909 synthesized arsphenamine, a drug to destroy the syphilis-causing organism *Treponema pallidum*, and Gerhard Domagk, a German physician, developed the first useful sulfa drug or sulfonamide, "which was used to treat streptococcal disease," while in 1929, Alexander Fleming discovered penicillin to destroy various bacteria, "purified, manufactured on a large scale, and shown to be safe and effective in treating a host of diseases, including gonorrhea, syphilis, and meningitis" (46). In 1943, "the first antibiotic effective against tuberculosis" and against "a number of other bacteria not affected by penicillin" was discovered by the microbiologist Selman Waksman (46). These pioneers paved the way for the understanding and elimination of many diseases. Smallpox has now disappeared from the planet, and in the developed world "a number of childhood diseases such as poliomyelitis, rubeola (measles), rubella (German measles), diphtheria, and mumps now occur infrequently and sporadically."

However, given the time lapse between scientific discoveries and therapies to treat diseases in the 18th and 19th centuries, for the most part, credit must be given to public health measures for reducing the severity of epidemics and endemics, including the "*cordon sanitaire* along the Habsburg border with the Ottoman empire," that ran from the Danube to the Balkans, in the 18th century and the smallpox vaccinations from the early 19th. The well-known epidemiologist Thomas McKeown (1912–1988), reflecting on public health, concluded that "reductions in deaths associated with infectious diseases (air-, water-, and food-borne diseases) cannot have been brought about by medical advances, since such diseases were declining long before effective means were available to combat them." Moreover, he "concluded that resistance to infectious disease must have increased through improved nutrition" and "mapped out three phases: a rising standard of living from about 1770; sanitary measures from 1870; and better therapy during the twentieth century" (43).

Successes and Limitations of Modern Medicine

Continuing well into this century, medical research is pressing forward, trying, as one example, "to better understand the immune system which underpins many diseases such as AIDS, rheumatic fever, rheumatoid arthritis, and lupus erythematosus with a view to treating these 'through direct intervention, using the techniques of genetic engineering'" (42). Because of these and other life-saving discoveries, "several natural body chemicals have become available in quantity, including insulin, interferon, clot-dissolving enzymes, and human growth hormone" (46). The search for the fundamental—that is, "genetic—basis of human pathology is on whether the target is cancer, AIDS, or Alzheimer's disease" (42).

This scientific and technocratic world, dominated by resource-intensive, groundbreaking research, which makes few allowances for subjectivity is, according to Bilton et al. "about expertise, not tradition; about critical inspection, not folk beliefs; about control through scientific and technical regulation of the body, not customs and mistaken notions of healing" (42).

Roy Porter highlights that "modern medicine" has been successful on many fronts as "for almost all diseases something can be done; some can be prevented or fully cured" (43). Yet, despite a century of intense research and resources, many of the major killers in the developed and the developing worlds—cardiovascular diseases, cancer, HIV/AIDS, viral hepatitis, and chronic degenerative diseases—remain incurable and in some cases are on the increase. One reason why there has been "little success in eradicating them" may be "because the strategies which earlier worked so well for tackling acute infectious diseases have proved inappropriate for dealing with chronic and degenerative conditions," whose victims fill our hospitals, "and it has been hard to discard the successful 'microbe hunters' formula."

The problem, contends Sir David Weatherall, Regius Professor of Medicine at Oxford, is that "although we have learned more and more about the minutiae of how diseases make patients sick, we have made little headway in determining why they arise in the first place." "Cancer patients can, to some degree, be 'patched up'," . . . "but only at the price of 'the spiralling cost of health care, which threatens to cripple our economy'" (43).

Traditional curative medicine is going through a fundamental crisis brought on, especially in the West, by "the price of progress and its attendant inflated expectations." While its mission was clear in the last century—to care for the sick—its mandate has become "muddled," in the past few decades, particularly in the richer countries, and it is now difficult, agreeing with Roy Porter, to differentiate whether its prime function is "to keep people alive as long as possible, willy-nilly, whatever the circumstances," "to *make* people lead healthy lives," or "is it but a service industry, on tap to fulfil whatever fantasies its clients may frame for their bodies, be they cosmetic surgery and designer bodies or the longing of post-menopausal women to have babies?" The answer is likely a qualified "yes" to all three, depending on where we live and personal priorities. In addition, "Immense pressures are created—by the medical profession, by the media, by the high pressure advertising of pharmaceutical companies to expand the diagnosis of treatable illnesses."

In poor nations—those in conflict or responding to natural disasters, in fact, much of the world's population today!—just helping others to survive continues to be medicine's top priority. However, generally speaking, in both more developed and developing nations, demands for care far exceed the resources available, and many conventional clinical interventions are having limited success not only with "killer" diseases but also with many stubborn communicable diseases, such as HIV/AIDS, malaria, and tuberculosis (TB), that are still far from being resolved in many nations. These countries are also feeling the effects of modernity, where "patch'" or Band-aid solutions, often involving expensive changes in technology and infrastructure or pharmaceutical intervention, may not be addressing the real health care issues, which are not about "things," but about people, their relations with each other, community–state "power" balances, global/national social accountabilities, and leadership.

Three immediate enabling actions that global decision makers, in collaboration with local representatives, might consider are: first, to delve beyond the uncomfortable WHO health statistics shown in Table 3.2; second, to debate the impact these "hard" data are having on the lives of people living in these regions; and third, to identify practical and consequential ways forward to make a meaningful difference reflected in year-on-year improvements. Hopefully, the Sustainable Development Goals post 2015, discussed in Section 4.1, will be informed by these types of inquiries.

In the final analysis, it is all about the "faces" and "lives" behind the statistics and not simply the numbers that tend to attract most attention by economists and policy makers.

Global Imbalances in Health Care Spending

Across 194 nations, health expenditure costs vary enormously and disparities are striking, as shown in Table 3.2, with the highest annual spending per person on health in the United States, US$8,362, and the lowest in Burma-Myanmar, with a population of about 60 million, US$2.00 per year. In 2013, government spending on health care was 3.9% and

TABLE 3.2 Spending on Health: A Global Overview, April 2012

TOTAL GLOBAL EXPENDITURE FOR HEALTH	US$6.5 TRILLION
Total global expenditure for health per person per year	US$948
Country with highest total spending per person per year on health	United States (US$8,362)
Country with lowest total spending per person per year on health	Eritrea (US$12)
Country with highest government spending per person per year on health	Luxembourg (US$6,906)
Country with lowest government spending per person per year on health	Myanmar (US$2)
Country with highest annual out-of-pocket household spending on health	Switzerland (US$2,412)
Country with lowest annual out-of-pocket household spending on health	Kiribati (US$0.2)
Average amount spent per person per year on health in countries belonging to the Organisation for Economic Co-operation and Development (OECD)	US$4,380
Percentage of the world's population living in OECD countries	18%
Percentage of the world's total financial resources devoted to health currently spent in OECD countries	84%
WHO estimate of minimum spending per person per year needed to provide basic, life-saving services	US$44
Number of WHO Member States where health spending—including spending by government, households, and the private sector and funds provided by external donors—is lower than US$50 per person per year	34
Number of WHO Member States where health spending is lower than US$20 per person per year	7
Percentage of funds spent on health in WHO's Africa Region that has been provided by donors	11%

Source: World Health Organization, *Spending on Health: A Global Overview* (Fact sheet No. 319), April, 2012.

over 20% on the military in Burma-Myanmar. According to a *Lancet* article, "Life expectancy is 56 years, 40% of all children under the age of 5 are moderately stunted, and Burma has more than 50% of all malaria-related deaths in Southeast Asia. This is in part due to poor diagnosis and treatment, but also to the widespread prevalence of counterfeit anti-malarial medication" (47). Average per person spending across the OECD countries is roughly US$4,380, but globally it is only US$948. Developing countries account for 82% of the world population and 84% of the total disease burden *but only 16% of total global health spending.*

As Figure 3.6 indicates, there is a strong relationship between wealth and spending on health with the top nation, the United States, allocating the most.

As illustrated in Figure 3.7, most spending on health occurs in northern and western regions and least is spent in southern and eastern regions, especially in Africa and Southeast Asia.

These inequities are further reinforced in Figure 3.8 (48), which again shows that global spending is disproportionate to the size of populations and disease burden (49). With combined populations of over 2 billion people, the regional spending in Africa,

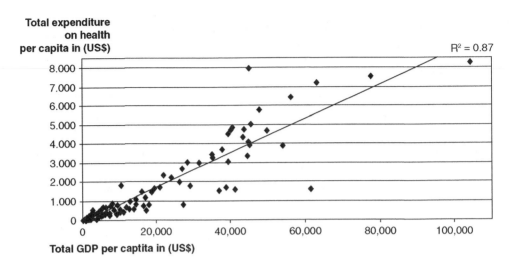

FIGURE 3.6 Wealth and health expenditure are correlated (2009).

Abbreviation: GDP, gross domestic product.

Source: World Health Organization, Spending on Health: A Global Overview (Fact sheet No. 319, Figure 1), April, 2012.

Southeast Asia, and the Eastern Mediterranean region falls far short of expenditures in Europe and the Americas, which also have the lowest disease burden.

Trend analyses of global expenditures by the World Bank over the past few years are indicative of challenges facing all economies (51):

> In rich and poor countries alike, health needs are changing in response to lower fertility rates, longer life expectancies, and the shifting burden of illness toward chronic diseases and injuries. These demographic and epidemiological transitions will pose health challenges for countries at every income level. In high-income countries, aging populations, rapidly increasing health costs, and shrinking numbers in the workforce will put increasing pressure on publicly

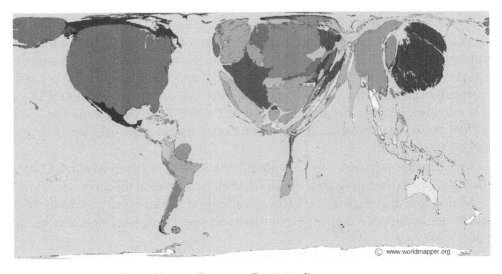

FIGURE 3.7 Global public health spending according to territory.

Source: Worldmapper.org (50). © Copyright SASI Group (University of Sheffield) and Mark Newman (University of Michigan). Reproduced under Creative Commons license https://creativecommons.org/licenses/by-nc-nd/3.0

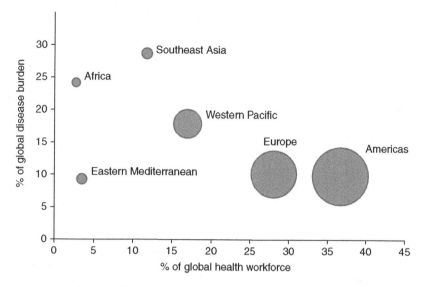

FIGURE 3.8 Distribution of health workers by level of health expenditure and burden of disease, by WHO region.

Source: World Health Organization, "Health Workers: A Global Profile," *World Health Report 2006.* Geneva, Switzerland (50). http://www.who.int/whr/2006/media_centre/06_chap1_fig06_en.pdf?ua=1. Accessed March 20, 2009.

financed healthcare systems. In some middle-income countries and in most low-income countries, which already are hard pressed to provide even the most basic health services, meeting projected health needs is likely to require additional funds from external financing sources.

Factors that contribute to high costs in the United States (Figure 3.9) are the costs of liability insurance as well as administration. In contrast, France spends only US$300 per person on the use of information and communication technology (52).

Moreover, the data records that the United States does more tests than other OECD countries and charges more for clinical procedures compared to other OECD nations (52).

It is difficult to trace or relate these data to causative factors and areas where disease prevention measures could have made a difference. Nevertheless, a correlation between rising levels of obesity in the United States (27.1% in 2013; 27.7% in 2014) and the demand for medical equipment, tests, and surgical procedures might be a possibility. Obesity can trigger diabetes and cardiac problems as well as the need for knee and hip replacements.

Tonsillectomies, the most common procedure requiring anesthesia for children, "spiked by 74 percent between 1996 and 2006" in the United States; they are also twice the OECD average (53). According to David Goodman, "It's a silent epidemic of unnecessary care. . . . In most instances, it's done for patients with much less recurrent symptoms than should be indicated. I think a lot of this is unbeknownst to providers."

Table 3.3 provides a summary of the annual U.S. health spending. In 2013, the total U.S. budget was $3.652 trillion. Sixty percent of the total budget was allocated to "necessary expenditures" and 40% to long-term care (54).

Most funding (in billions) was allocated to hospital care ($819), physician and clinical services ($516), supervisory care ($492 for family members and community

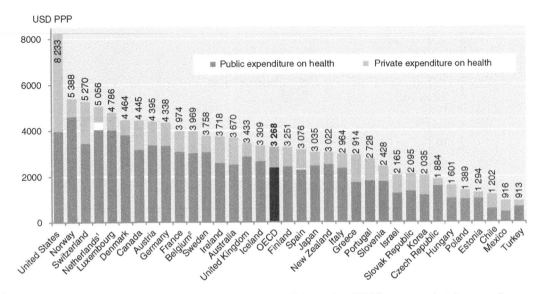

Total health expenditure per capita, public and private, 2010 (or nearest year)

FIGURE 3.9 The United States spends two-and-a-half times the OECD average (total per capita, public and private, 2010 [or nearest year]).

Note: 1. In the Netherlands, it is not possible to clearly distinguish the public and private share related to investments.
2. Total expenditure excluding investments.
Information on data for Israel: http://dx.doi.org/10.1787/888932315602

Abbreviation: OECD, Organisation for Economic Co-operation and Development; PPP, Purchasing Power Parity.

Source: Organisation for Economic Co-operation and Development (OECD), *Health at a Glance 2011: OECD Indicators,* OECD Publishing. http://www.oecd.org/els/health-systems/49105858.pdf

care services—three times the amount spent on nursing homes—a clear sign of a movement away from institutional care), prescription drugs ($259), nursing homes ($143), dental services ($105), and home health care ($70). (55)

TABLE 3.3 Annual U.S. Health Care Spending[a]

	2013	2014	2015
CMS-projected NHE	$2.915	$3.093	$3.273
Sustainable Growth Rate (SGR)	$0.116	$0.116	$0.116
Deloitte additional direct costs[b]	$0.129	$0.129	$0.129
Deloitte imputed indirect costs[b]	$0.492	$0.492	$0.492
	$3.652	$3.830	$4.010

[a]All numbers in trillions.
[b]2012 Deloitte Study: The Hidden Costs of U.S. Health Care.

Abbreviations: CMS, Centers for Medicare & Medicaid Services; NHE, National Health Expenditure.

Source: Adapted by Dan Munro (54) from Deloitte Study: "The Hidden Costs of U.S. Health Care: Impacts and Implications of Rising Out-of-Pocket Health Care Costs." http://www2.deloitte.com/content/dam/Deloitte/us/Documents/life-sciences-health-care/us-lchs-dig-deep-hidden-costs-112414.pdf. Accessed February 19, 2014.

Of the total U.S. health budget, ~$2 billion was spent on health reduction programs, ~$2 billion on health publications, and ~$2 billion on nutrition/supplements. Only about 3% of the total budget was allocated to public health or on disease prevention and health promotion. Recent data concerning the impact of programs on levels of obesity affecting all groups—all societal groups, that is, not only groups "identifiable by race, ethnicity, income, education or geography" (55)—confirms that much more quantitative, and certainly more qualitative, research is required to better understand the causes of and deep impact on society.

In light of emerging information on the state of population health in the United States, it is not surprising that health costs continue to rise and now stand at US~$3.8 trillion per year, combining the Sustainable Growth Rate deficit (SGR) (accrued over 10 years) with the U.S. National Health Expenditure in 2014. Spending growth at 3.7% is the "slowest growth rate on record," but a projection of ~$5 trillion by 2022 makes the U.S. "annual healthcare spending . . . an economic unit larger than the GDP of Germany (which is itself the 4th or 5th largest GDP on the planet)" (56).

Reducing Costs of Health Care

In terms of reducing costs, Mark Pearson, head of Division on Health Policy at OECD, cites policies in France and Japan and mentions several approaches being used elsewhere (52):

- A common fee schedule so that hospitals, doctors, and health services are paid similar rates for most of the patients they see.
- Flexibility in responding if they think certain costs are exceeding what they budgeted for.
- Unlike the United States, they depend less on private health insurers, which continually face a choice between asking health care providers to contain their costs and passing on higher costs to patients in higher premiums.
- Technology: In Sweden, all drug prescribing is done electronically—a message is sent directly from the doctor's office to the pharmacy.
- Strict price controls: In Switzerland, the national government provides a ranking of hospital services from most expensive to least expensive. Groups of insurers and hospitals across different regions then use the national government's ranking to negotiate the prices they ought to pay across the board.

While these systemic measures are constructive in curtailing spending, it is unlikely that they will go far enough in dealing with the severity of population health issues. Fundamentally, as argued in Chapter 6.0, their main drawback is that they are based on societal thinking that continues to espouse the biomedical or "sick" model of health care even though governments are unable to sustain health budgets for populations facing increasing morbidity and mortality. Our short-term thinking, as Prince Charles, heir to the British throne, controversially noted at an awards ceremony to a group of green entrepreneurs, is that "we spent the best part of the past century enthusiastically testing the world to utter destruction; not looking close enough at the long-term impact our actions will have" (57).

His comments certainly are in line with the perspectives of others on global health in the last century. Professor Ulrich Beck, professor of sociology at Munich University and visiting professor at the London School of Economics (LSE), points out that "the improved capacity to diagnose illnesses has not necessarily been accompanied by the presence or even the prospect of any effective measures to treat them" (58). Distinguishing between acute and chronic illnesses, he observes that at the beginning of the 20th century, 40 out of 100 patients died of acute illnesses, which in 1980 "constituted only 1% of the causes of mortality." On the other hand, he notes that "chronic illnesses" increased "from 46 to over 80%," making a "cure in the original sense of medicine . . . more and more the exception."

Improving Population Health and Patient Care by Strengthening the Education and Training of the Health Care Workforce

A critical area for ensuring improved health care delivery, discussed further in Chapter 8.0, lies with placing greater emphasis on how the health care workforce is prepared. In the preface to this book, Dr. George Thibault, president of the U.S. Josiah Macy Jr. Foundation, makes this clear when he says: "We will not have enduring health care delivery reform without changes in the preparation of health professionals" (59).

Areas that may need attention include workforce planning (60); identifying health concerns at the national level but also drawing on regional and global intelligence; and translating health and social/welfare trends and issues into viable program frameworks, aims, and learning outcomes that lead to engaging learning strategies (61–63), such as blended (face to face and Internet) inquiry-based learning and performance-based self- and peer assessment or evaluation.

Reforms to the "transformed" 21st century health care curricula—requiring a major boost in institutional faculty and educational development—will also need to place much more importance on interprofessional "team learning" applied to academic learning and, in practice, on disease avoidance and health promotion (64,65). This could have a major impact on enhancing population health and well-being and the quality of patient care, which increasingly necessitates multidisciplinary interventions, building collegial relations among team members, and reducing costs. Blurring of health care roles and primary care practitioners working alongside public health professionals will likely become the norm in community settings.

Collaborative learning activities might be extended to student-run clinics, team-based placements, joint assessments of patients with complex conditions, and interprofessional problem-based learning sessions (66). An obstacle that may impede progress in this direction relates to the traditional "rivalry between professional groups," which Audrey Leathhard (67) describes "as a form of social Darwinism of occupations"—in other words, a 20th century "dinosaur" that has no place in modern health practice!

Spending on Health Care Prevention Programs Across OECD Nations

Figure 3.10 shows the amount spent on preventive measures across OECD nations (68). Romania allocates the highest amount, 6.2%, while Croatia spends the least. The European average is 2.5%.

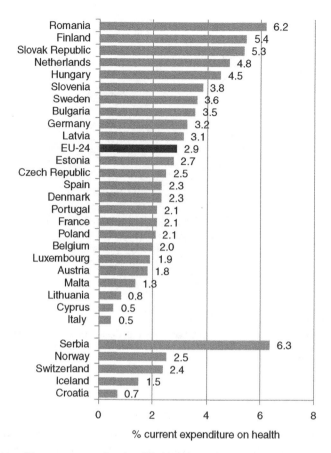

FIGURE 3.10 Expenditures on organized public health and prevention programs (2010 or nearest year).

Source: Organisation for Economic Co-operation and Development (OECD), *Health at a Glance: Europe 2012*, OECD Publishing. http://www.oecd-ilibrary.org/social-issues-migration-health/health-at-a-glance-europe-2012_9789264183896-en

Figure 3.11 makes it clear that most spending is on hospitals, ambulatory (out-patient) care, and drugs with *least* spending on public health, which, interestingly, in the United States is combined with administration—which arguably appears as an "add-on" rather than being considered as part of central health care delivery (52). It is noteworthy that Japan spends the least across all categories but has the longest life expectancies.

Governments' Reluctance to Prioritize Prevention Over Cure

Further to interviews with seven Harvard public health professors, in a thought-provoking article, "Public Health and the U.S. Economy" (69), Michael Blanding, then a freelance writer for the Harvard School of Public Health (HSPH), stresses that "more than 17 percent of the U.S. Gross Domestic Product is spent on health care—in many cases, for conditions that could be prevented or better managed with public health interventions. Yet only 3 percent of the government's health budget is spent on public health measures."

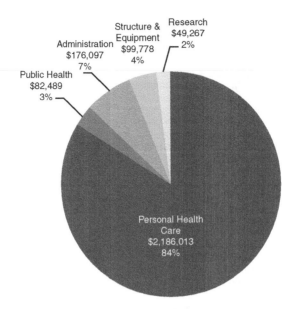

FIGURE 3.11 U.S. health care spending (2010).

Source: Analysis by The Knowledge Agency® of data published by the U.S. Centers for Medicare & Medicaid Services, the U.S. Bureau of Economic Analysis, and the International Monetary Fund. http://www.knowledgevaluechain.com/2012/03/05/health-care-spending-i-where-does-it-go

The author offers several reasons why these figures matter, noting, first, that "a healthier workforce is a more productive workforce," and that "according to an April 2012 report from the Institute of Medicine (IOM), the indirect costs associated with preventable chronic diseases—costs related to worker productivity as well as the resulting fiscal drag on the nation's economic output—may exceed $1 trillion per year."

He further argues that "the costs of health care are built into the price of every American-built product and service. And the per capita cost of health care in the U.S. is higher than in any nation in the world." And, "if the U.S. can reduce the costs of health care over the long term—by preventing diseases that require costly medical procedures to treat and by making our existing health systems more efficient—the costs of American products can become more competitive in a global marketplace."

Contributing to Michael Blanding's article, Professor Norman Daniels at Harvard's Department of Global Health suggests that governments are reluctant to admit that prevention is better than cure. One of the reasons is that, although "risk reduction . . . has the greatest impact on people's health," it does not necessarily provide a visible return on investment. There is therefore, he contends, "enormous pressure" on politicians "to heavily invest in medicine" rather than public health (69).

His argument is also substantiated by Dr. Sylvia Karpagam (70), a community health physician in India. In her blog, she observes that while India was a signatory at the First International Conference on Primary Health Care at Alma Ata, Kazakhstan, in 1978 (71), which called for an urgent and concerted effort by governments and the world community to protect and promote the health of all people, the recommendations of the Reorientation of Medical Education (ROME) in 1991 were not pursued as was the case with other nations who attended.

Furthermore, agreeing with Professor Daniels' argument, she comments that "although prevention is clearly the most effective and cheapest way of fighting ill health and reducing the high cost of secondary and tertiary care, it means that the medical profession would stand to lose financially if India's preventive services were extremely good. The highly lucrative, complex and expensive treatments offered at secondary and tertiary care become a good incentive for market forces to ignore the preventive and primary component of healthcare." As one example, she points out that "a patient educated about the ill-effects of smoking and supported to quit or reduce, is less lucrative to the health market than a terminally ill lung cancer patient requiring extensive lung resection surgeries and respiratory support."

Unfortunately, she concludes that "unscrupulous market agencies have converted health into a commodity that must exist for the market to survive. Ill-health therefore becomes an incentive for the private player; the more illness, the better, because the profits rise. Ill-health is therefore propagated and people become victims of the curative syndrome where they believe that they need to be cured to be healthy" (70).

Rebalancing Curative and Preventive Health Care Support

In terms of matching resources to actual population health needs, there can be little doubt that spending on curative approaches to health care and spending on disease prevention/health promotion are proportionately misaligned.

Twentieth-century assumptions about population health and well-being have been readily transported into this century at both education and service levels with potentially devastating consequences evidenced by current statistics. NCDs have overtaken communicable diseases worldwide as the main cause of mortality and morbidity, with projections estimating at least an additional $30 trillion to be spent in the next 20 years (72). Perhaps the "wake up" call for decision makers is that most of these conditions—type 2 diabetes, cancers, cardiovascular diseases, and HIV/AIDS as examples—are preventable, and proceeding along the current trajectory is financially unsustainable for most nations.

It is estimated that of the global health budget that stands at over US$7 trillion, a mere 3% is allocated to preventive measures and only about 2% to the training of the health workforce—mostly doctors and nurses in developed nations (62)—close to 12 million health workers in the United States alone (73), while the greatest burden of disease lies with the majority of people living in underdeveloped and developing countries. The remaining funding—around 95%—is geared toward infrastructure costs—buildings, equipment, medication, and salaries, again mainly in the West and North. Exacerbating the budget shortfalls is the fact that the majority of the health systems are funded on an activity, not on an outcome or evidential "improving the quality of life basis."

With a fast-aging population, comorbidities will accelerate and demand funding that far exceeds the state's capacity to deliver. It has increasingly been recognized that most conditions—especially those that arise from modernity and an aging population—are better treated in the community and that individuals need to take greater personal responsibility for their own health and well-being.

"Models of Public Health Education: Choices for the Future"

In *Models of Public Health Education: Choices for the Future?* (74), Professor Elizabeth Fee and Dr. Liping Bu trace the history of public health, beginning with the establishment of the Johns Hopkins School of Hygiene and Public Health in 1916, a time when the United States was "woefully lacking both in laboratories of hygiene and in opportunities for training in public health work."

What followed was extraordinary, as public health gathered momentum worldwide. With the support of the Rockefeller Foundation and guided by "two remarkable public health leaders, John B. Grant and Andrija Stampar," other schools were soon established in the 1920s and 1930s, including schools in the United States, Brazil, China, and in the former Yugoslavia. Dr. Grant believed firmly "that public health was an integral part of socioeconomic progress and that health care could be best achieved by combining preventive and curative medicine through a community 'health station' "—an idea he brought to fruition in 1925, creating "a health demonstration station . . . for training public health professionals and medical students of Peking Union Medical College," later extended to rural China and India (75).

Professor Fee and Dr. Bu suggest "that there are many possible models for public health education" and that "in the future, perhaps we will develop new and innovative models adapted to the needs of diverse societies," especially when "the flow of information and technology across national borders takes place at unprecedented speeds."

Similar to developments in the 1920s and 1930s, there is now pressing justification and growing momentum (75) for enlarging and strengthening the public health workforce worldwide, especially in tackling the spread of NCDs and addressing chronic illnesses. However, funding is tight and innovative approaches need to be explored, some of which could benefit from the far-sighted vision of previous pioneers. As one example, it might be instructive and timely to consider fundamentals that motivated John Grant's thinking with regard to establishing multidisciplinary and multipurpose—preventive and curative—community-based health centers, thereby not only improving access to more personalized health care but also reinforcing the view through localized initiatives that prevention is always a better option than cure.

As argued, provision of more realistic funding for training and service provision will need to be central in realizing population health and well-being in this and subsequent decades, regardless of future public health education models that are evolved or chosen. The bigger questions for health systems is not only how to find the funding to operate existing health care provision but also—and likely more significant in the long run—how to tackle the health and social care problems that are much more deeply rooted in contemporary society.

In conclusion, this chapter has highlighted the pressing need for the rebalancing of funding in health care, shifting the emphasis from secondary and tertiary care to primary care and public health. Doing so will require greater awareness and understanding by decision makers—who place the planet's future well-being above corporate wealth and self-interest—of the political, economic, and social forces shaping this century and a genuine commitment to sustaining the health and well-being of this and future generations. Continuing as they are can no longer be a long-term option for most nations.

In this regard, the WHO has shown considerable foresight in reprioritizing its global health funding commitments (76) and setting out strategies for tackling NCDs (77). Similar plans need to be put in place at all regional, national, and community levels. The challenge is of course to initiate these much sooner than later and to make them work in this decade and beyond.

Perhaps focusing on the early years of child development as a major pillar of health and well-being might help to "'kick-start" a global strategy toward the creation of a "social contract for health" with a view to ensuring "greater justice for all," underpinned by international human rights law. The proposition for a "global social contract" has been put forward in a working paper by Dr. Gorik Ooms et al. at the Belgium Department of Public Health, "Global Health: What It Has Been So Far, What It Should Be, and What It Could Become"(78).

Positioning child development at the center of a global UN/WHO social contract initiative might help to reinforce and reconcile the competing rights and interests— social, economic, and political—of health partnerships, strongly advocated, as one example, by Ban Ki-moon, secretary-general of the UN. Urgency for nations to raise the profile of children's well-being is made clear by the appalling life and living conditions affecting the millions of children caught in poverty and increasingly in war-torn nations.

At a national level, and thinking long term and about life satisfaction generally, the case for prioritizing the physical and emotional changes that occur in children from birth to adolescence has also been argued fervently by Dr. Deborah Allen, Director of Child, Adolescent and Family Health at the Boston Public Health Commission in the United States:

> Let's invest now for a benefit that may not emerge for many years. Let's create the conditions for healthy birth, healthy infancy, and healthy childhood. The payoff is extraordinary in terms of lifetime health status and averting the need for extraordinarily costly, often ineffective intervention at the later stages of life. It also creates a population that has a much higher quality of life (69).

REFERENCES

1. World Health Organization (WHO). Global health and aging. http://who.int/ageing/publications/global_health/en/index.html. Accessed March 15, 2014.
2. Bloom DE, Boersch-Supan A, McGee P, Seike A. *Population aging: Facts, challenges and response* (Program on the Global Demography of Aging, Working Paper No. 71). Cambridge, MA: Harvard University; 2011. http://www.aarp.org/content/dam/aarp/livable-communities/learn/demographics/population-aging-facts-challenges-and-responses-2011-aarp.pdf. Accessed March 16, 2015.
2a. United Nations Department of Economic and Social Affairs, Population Division. *World Population Prospects: The 2004 Revision*. New York: United Nations, 2005.
3. United Nations, Department of Economic and Social Affairs, Population Division. *World Population Prospects: The 2010 Revision*. New York: United Nations, 2011.

4. Central Intelligence Agency. *The World Factbook*. Washington DC: Author. https://www.cia.gov/library/publications/the-world-factbook/index.html. Accessed August 30, 2015.

5. National Institute on Aging, National Institutes of Health, U.S. Department of Health and Human Services, U.S. Department of State. *Why population aging matters: A global perspective*. Washington, DC: National Institute on Aging. https://www.nia.nih.gov/research/publication/why-population-aging-matters-global-perspective. Accessed March 15, 2014.

6. Magnus G. *The age of aging: How demographics are changing the global economy and our world*. Singapore: Wiley and Sons; 2008.

7. Charles J. *Key influences on future trends in healthcare*. Cardiff: National Public Health Service for Wales; 2008.

7a. United Nations, Department of Economic and Social Affairs, Population Division. *World Population Prospects: The 2012 Revision*. New York: United Nations, 2013.

8. Bloom DE, Canning D, Fink G. *Implications of population aging for economic growth* (NBER Working Paper No. 16705). Boston, MA: National Bureau of Ecomonic Reseach. http://www.nber.org/papers/w16705. Accessed January 20, 2013.

9. Report of the Premier's Council on Aging and Seniors' Issues. Aging well in British Columbia. http://www2.gov.bc.ca/gov/content/family-social-supports/seniors/about-seniorsbc/seniors-related-initiatives/premier-s-council-on-aging-and-seniors-issues/aging-well-in-british-columbia-report-summary-and-recommendations. Accessed May 24, 2014.

10. Trajanovska I. *Impacts of population ageing in the European Union: Responses of Germany and France* [master thesis]. Nice, France: Centre international de formation européenne. http://www.ieei.eu/Ressources/file/memoires/2013/TRAJANOVSKA_Thesis.pdf. Accessed June 15, 2015.

11. Duncan E. Osborne's festive bells simply don't ring true. *The Times*. December 9, 2013. http://www.thetimes.co.uk/tto/opinion/columnists/article3943346.ece. Accessed September 15, 2014.

12. Rechel B, Doyle Y, Grundy E, McKee M. *How can health systems respond to population ageing?* Copenhagen: World Health Organization. http://www.euro.who.int/en/health-topics/Life-stages/healthy-ageing/publications/2009/how-can-health-systems-respond-to-population-ageing. Accessed July 10, 2011.

13. Eberspacher S. Everything you need to know about Japan's population crisis. *The Week*. January 11, 2014. http://theweek.com/article/index/254923/everything-you-need-to-know-about-japans-population-crisis. Accessed June 20, 2014.

14. Brunner EJ. Japan's answer to the economic demands of an ageing population. *BMJ*. 2012;345:e6632. http://www.bmj.com/content/345/bmj.e6632. Accessed June 20, 2014.

15. Summers L. On secular stagnation. *Reuters*. November 16, 2014. http://blogs.reuters.com/lawrencesummers/2013/12/16/on-secular-stagnation/. Accessed September 15, 2014.

16. Rechel B, Doyle Y, Grundy E, McKee M. *How can health systems respond to population ageing?* (Health Systems and Policy Analysis Policy Brief 10). Copenhagen: World Health Organization. http://www.euro.who.int/__data/assets/pdf_file/0004/64966/E92560.pdf. Accessed April 5, 2009.

17. Smyth C. Crisis over '21st-century plague' of dementia. *The Times*. December 10, 2013. http://www.thetimes.co.uk/tto/health/news/article3944446.ece. Accessed December 14, 2013.

18. Brown L. Revealed: The five lifestyle rules that can beat dementia. *The Daily Mail*. December 10, 2013. http://www.dailymail.co.uk/health/article-2521125/Revealed-The-lifestyle-rules-beat-dementia.html. Accessed December 14, 2013.

19. Smith D. Stop trying to cure Alzheimer's—and prevent it instead: One of Britain's top dementia experts says we've wasted BILLIONS on useless drugs. *The Daily Mail*. December 10, 2013. http://www.dailymail.co.uk/health/article-2521024/Stop-trying-cure-Alzheimers-prevent-instead-says-dementia-expert.html. Accessed December 12, 2013.

20. IMS Institute. IMS Health Study Forecasts Global Spending on Medicines to Reach $1 Trillion Threshold in 2014, Driven by Greater Access. http://www.imshealth.com/portal/site/imshealth/menuitem.c76283e8bf81e98f53c753c71ad8c22a/? Accessed November 20, 2013.

21. Collins P. We can't wait for a miracle cure for old age. *The Times*. December 13, 2013. http://www.thetimes.co.uk/tto/opinion/columnists/article3947548.ece. Accessed December 15, 2013.

22. National Association of County Behavioral Health and Developmental Disability. *Directors. Issue brief: Harnessing community support for health and well-being*. Washington, DC: ACMHA Policy Forum. http://www.nacbhdd.org/portals/0/PDF/NACBHDD%20Newsletter_February%20 2013.pdf. Accessed December 28, 2013.

23. Collins N. Mediterranean diet key to dementia battle, PM told. *The Telegraph*. December 8, 2013. http://www.telegraph.co.uk/health/10504774/Mediterranean-diet-key-to-dementia-battle -PM-told.html. Accessed December 10, 2013.

24. Collins N. Dementia should be fought with diet, U.K.'s top doctors urge: 'We are not going to overcome chronic diseases by prescribing pills'. *The Telegraph*. December 8, 2013. http://news .nationalpost.com/2013/12/09/dementia-should-be-fought-with-diet-u-k-s-top-doctors-urge- we-are-not-going-to-overcome-chronic-diseases-by-prescribing-pills/. Accessed December 10, 2013.

25. Zigmond D. Those caring for people with dementia do not know where to turn. *The Telegraph*. December 14, 2013. http://www.telegraph.co.uk/comment/letters/10516647/Those-caring- for-people-with-dementia-do-not-know-where-to-turn.html. Accessed December 16, 2013.

26. Department of Health. Policy paper: G8 dementia summit communiqué. https://www.gov.uk/ government/publications/g8-dementia-summit-agreements/g8-dementia-summit-communi- que. Accessed December 12, 2013.

27. Coates S, Smyth C. Doctors fear cash crisis if funds are used for socialcare. *The Times*. May 20, 2014: 23.

28. Lueddeke G. *Transforming medical education for the 21st century: Megatrends, priorities and change*. London: Radcliffe Publishing; 2012.

29. Wilkinson I. The politics of compassion. http://www.youtube.com/watch?v=nMya-A0CMD8

30. International Federation on Ageing (IFA). Age is more film project. http://www.ifa-fiv.org/age- is-more-film-project-a-partnership-between-revera-inc-reel-youth/. Accessed April 20, 2014.

31. Alzheimer's Disease International. *World Alzheimer report 2010: The global economic impact of dementia*. http://www.alz.co.uk/research/world-report-2010. Accessed June 25, 2011.

32. Shipman T. NHS must treat its patients 'as people and not body parts. *The Daily Mail*. January 23, 2014. http://www.dailymail.co.uk/news/article-2544279/NHS-treat-patients-people-not -body-parts-Hunt-calls-end-ping-pong-referrals-speaks-plans-single. Accessed January 28, 2014.

33. Care Pathways. An Old Lady's Poem, Anonymous. http://www.carepathways.com/anoldlady- spoem.cfm. Accessed February 14, 2014.

34. Sattler R. Materialism, Holism, and Mysticism—A Mandala. http://www.beyondwilber.ca/ bookpre/mandala/mandala_of_life_and_living.html. Accessed November 6, 2013.

35. Montgomerie T. Forget the family, forget about social mobility. *The Times*. January 30, 2014. http://www.thetimes.co.uk/tto/opinion/columnists/article3989777.ece. Accessed February 10, 2014.

36. Lomborg B. A report card for humanity: 1900–2050: Economists crunch the numbers on 10 of the world's most bedeviling problems. *The Atlantic*. January 8, 2014. http://www.theatlantic.com/ international/archive/2014/01/a-report-card-for-humanity-1900-2050/282928/. Accessed January 10, 2014.

37. Centers for Medicare and Medicaid Services, Office of the Actuary. National Health Expenditures as a Percent of GDP1970–2088.

38. Kibasi T, Teitelbaum J, Henke N. (2012). *The financial sustainability of health systems: A case for change*. Geneva: World Economic Forum and McKinsey & Company.

39. Appleby J. *Spending on health and socialcare over the next 50 years. Why think long term?* London: The King's Fund; 2013. http://www.kingsfund.org.uk/sites/files/kf/field/field_publication_file/ Spending%20on%20health%20...%2050%20years%20low%20res%20for%20web.pdf. Accessed January 10, 2014.

40. The King's Fund. The financial sustainability of health systems. http://www.kingsfund.org.uk/time-to-think-differently/publications/spending-health-and-social-care-over-next-50-years/financial-sustainability-health-systems. Accessed January 10, 2014.

41. Koop CE. Health and healthcare for the 21st century: For all the people. *Am J Public Health.* 2006;96(12):2090–2092.

42. Clarke J. *Health, illness, and medicine in Canada.* 5th ed. Toronto: Oxford University Press; 2012.

43. Porter R. *The greatest benefit to mankind: A medical history of humanity from antiquity to the present.* 2nd ed. London: Fontana Press; 1997.

44. Weisenberg E. Rudolf Virchow, pathologist, anthropologist, and social thinker. *Hektoen International Journal.* http://www.hektoeninternational.org/Journal_Rudolf_Virchow.html. Accessed May 6, 2009.

45. Vasudevan S, Skreekumari S, Vaidyanathan K. *Textbook of biochemistry for medical students.* New Delhi: Jaypee Brothers Medical Publishers. http://www.shvoong.com/medicine-and-health/comparative-medicine/191779-medicine-20th-century. Accessed Januray 26, 2014.

46. Freedman AD. History of medicine. http://go.grolier.com/print?id=0189112-0&type=0ta&product_id=gme&authcode=gme. Accessed March 29, 2014.

47. Karen News. Facts on Burma. http://karennews.org/facts-on-burma/. Accessed May 27, 2014.

48. World Health Organization. *Spending on health: A global overview.* Geneva: World Health Organization. http://www.who.int/mediacentre/factsheets/fs319/en/. Accessed May 12, 2012.

49. World Health Organization. *World Health Report 2006–working together for health.* Geneva: World Health Organization. http://www.who.int/whr/2006/en/. Accessed February 25, 2007.

50. Worldmapper. The world as you've never seen it before. http://www.worldmapper.org/display.php?selected=213. Accessed November 20, 2013.

51. World Bank. *Health transitions, disease burdens, and health expenditure patterns.* Washington, DC: World Bank. http://siteresources.worldbank.org/INTHSD/Resources/topics/Health-Financing/HFRChap1.pdf. Accessed October 20, 2013.

52. Kane J. Health costs: How the U.S. compares with other countries. *PBS.* October 22, 2012. http://www.pbs.org/newshour/rundown/health-costs-how-the-us-compares-with-other-countries/. Accessed November 24, 2012.

53. Kliff S. What tonsillectomies tell us about the future of health care. *The Washington Post.* April 25, 2012. http://www.washingtonpost.com/blogs/wonkblog/post/what-tonsillectomies-tell-us-about-the-future-of-health-care/2012/04/25/gIQAt2pHhT_blog.htm. Accessed May 23, 2012.

54. Munro D. Annual U.S. healthcare spending hits $3.8 trillion. *Forbes.* February 2, 2014. http://www.forbes.com/sites/danmunro/2014/02/02/annual-u-s-healthcare-spending-hits-3-8-trillion/. Accessed March 2, 2014.

55. Deloitte Center for Health Solutions. The hidden costs of U.S. health care: Consumer discretionary healthcare spending. http://www.deloitte.com/assets/Dcom-UnitedStates/Local%20Assets/Documents/us_dchs_2012_hidden_costs112712.pdf. Accessed January 20, 2012.

56. Healio. Causes of rising obesity in U.S. often incorrect. http://www.healio.com/orthotics-prosthetics/health-care-updates/news/online/%7B1173f69a-aba4-40ee-b46f-24d30f3a021d%7D/causes-of-rising-obesity-in-us-often-incorrect. Accessed June 3, 2014.

57. Revell T. Prince Charles attacks 'headless chicken' climate change deniers. *Blue & Green Tomorrow.* February 2, 2014. http://blueandgreentomorrow.com/2014/02/02/prince-charles-attacks-headless-chicken-climate-change-deniers/. Accessed February 3, 2014.

58. Beck U. *Risk society: Towards a new modernity.* London: Sage Publications Ltd; 2005. http://www.nextreformation.com/wp-admin/resources/risk-society.pdf. Accessed February 7, 2014.

59. Thibault GE. Innovations in medical education: Aligning education with the needs of the public. Presented at: the American Medical Association 'Accelerating Change in Medical Education' Conference; October 3–5, 2013; Chicago, IL. http://www.ama-assn.org/sub/accelerating-change/pdf/thibault.pdf. Accessed November 19, 2013.

60. Centre for Workforce Intelligence (CFWI). What's new in horizon scanning? http://www.cfwi
    .org.uk/publications/horizon-scanning-a-strategic-review-of-the-future-healthcare-workforce
    -informing-the-nursing-workforce. Accessed June 20, 2013.
61. Lueddeke G. *Transforming medical education for the 21 century: Megatrends, priorities and change.*
    London: Radcliffe Publishing; 2012.
62. Frenk J, Chen L, Bhutta ZA, et al. Health professions for a new century: Transforming education
    to strengthen health systems in an interdependent world. *Lancet.* 2010;376(9756):1923–1958.
63. Czabanowska K, Rethmeier KA, Lueddeke G, et al. Public health in the 21st century: Working
    differently means leading and learning differently. *Eur J Public Health.* 2014;24(2):1–6. http://
    eurpub.oxfordjournals.org/content/early/2014/04/07/eurpub.cku043.abstract. Accessed April
    7, 2014.
64. Institute of Medicine (IOM). Global Forum on Innovation in Health Professional Education.
    http://www.iom.edu/Activities/Global/InnovationHealthProfEducation.aspx. Accessed
    January 10, 2014.
65. The Josiah Macy Foundation. Interprofessional care coordination: Looking to the future. http://
    macyfoundation.org/publications/publication/interprofessional-care-coordination-looking-to-
    the-future. Accessed January 10, 2014.
66. Bainbridge L. Interprofessional education for interprofessional practice: Will future health
    care providers embrace collaboration as one answer to improved quality of care? *UBCMJ.*
    2010;2(1):9–10.
67. Leathard A. *Interprofessional collaboration: From policy to practice in health and socialcare.* Sussex, UK:
    Psychology Press; 2003.
68. OECD. Health at a glance. http://www.oecd.org/health/health-systems/health-at-a-glance.
    htm. Accessed February 14, 2013.
69. Blanding M. Public health and the U.S. economy. *Harvard Public Health Magazine.* 2012. http://
    www.hsph.harvard.edu/news/magazine/public-health-economy-election/. Accessed May 16,
    2013.
70. Karpagam S. Medical education in India and its discontents. http://drsylviakarpagam.wordpress
    .com/2014/07/02/medical-education-in-india-and-its-discontents-book-chapter-higher-stud-
    ies-in-india/. Accessed November 2, 2014.
71. WHO. Declaration of Alma Ata. http://www.euro.who.int/__data/assets/pdf_file/0009/
    113877/E93944.pdf?ua=1. Accessed May 25, 2014.
72. Institute for Health Metrics and Evaluation (IHME). Global burden of disease study. http://
    www.healthdata.org/gbd. Accessed September 17, 2011.
73. The Henry J. Kaiser Foundation. Total healthcare employment. http://kff.org/other/state-indi
    cator/total-health-care-employment/. Accessed July 14, 2014.
74. Fee E, Bu L. Models of public health education: Choices for the future? *Bull World Health Organ.*
    2007;85(12):977–979. http://www.who.int/bulletin/volumes/85/12/07-044883.pdf. Accessed
    May 24, 2014.
75. Bjegovic-Mikanovic V, Vukovic D, Otok R, et al. Education and training of public health profes-
    sionals in the European Region: Variation and convergence. *Int J Public Health.* 2013;58(6):801–
    810. http://www.ncbi.nlm.nih.gov/pubmed/23132128. Accessed January 16, 2013.
76. WHO. Proposed WHO programme budget 2014–2015. *Inis Communication.* http://www.inis-
    communication.com/inis-news-and-comment/307-who-budget-2014-2015.html. Accessed June
    20, 2014.
77. WHO. *Global action plan for the prevention and control of NCDs 2013–2020.* Geneva: WHO. http://
    www.who.int/nmh/en/. Accessed June 20, 2014.
78. Ooms, G, Hammonds R, Decoster K, Damne WV. *Global health: What it has been so far, what it
    should be, and what it could become.* Belgium: Department of Public Health, Institute of Tropical
    Medicine; 2011. www.itg.be/WPshop. Accessed June 20, 2014.

4.0

World Health Reforms (UN, WHO, and The World Bank) in the Early Years of the 21st Century

4.1 PROGRESS ON THE UN MILLENNIUM DEVELOPMENT GOALS AND POST-2015 SUSTAINABLE DEVELOPMENT GOALS: "BACK TO THE FUTURE?"

The adoption of the Millennium Declaration in 2000 by all United Nations Member States marked an historic moment, as world leaders committed to tackle extreme poverty in its many dimensions and create a better life for everyone. (1)

The eight Millennium Development Goals (MDGs) and indicators (2) "arguably, the most politically important pact ever made for international development" (3), were adopted on a voluntary basis by 189 nations to "free a major portion of humanity from the shackles of extreme poverty, hunger, illiteracy and disease" (4), recognizing several fundamental human rights, such as health and education, to be achieved by 2015.

In the Foreword to the *Millennium Development Goals Report 2015* (5), Ban Ki-Moon, Secretary-General of the United Nations (UN), asserts that "the Millennium Development Goals (MDGs) have been the most successful global anti-poverty push in history." He further adds: "there have been visible improvements in all health areas as well as primary education."

Progress on the Millennium Development Goals

According to the World Health Organization (WHO) Director-General, Dr. Margaret Chan, while "all eight of the MDGs have consequences for health," "three put health at front and centre—they concern child health (MDG 4), maternal health (MDG 5), and the control of HIV/AIDS, malaria, tuberculosis and other major communicable diseases (MDG 6)" (6).

MDG 1, "eradicating extreme poverty and hunger," is on course to being achieved and has fallen to 14% in 2015 from 47% in 1990 (5), but remains a very serious problem in Oceanian nations, according to World Bank estimates. Aside from "North Korea and Somalia," where "the poor are getting poorer," Matt Ridley, in his article, "Start

Spreading the Good News on Inequality," observes that global income inequality is "plunging downwards" (7).

From an MDG perspective, Professors Ulrich Laaser and Helmut Brand point out these advances cannot be attributed to MDG commitments per se (8). Their analysis shows that "the goal of 21% living below the poverty line defined as 1.25 USD/day was within reach in 2005. However, this was calculated from a baseline set at 1990, that is, a decade before the MDGs were declared. If one compares the progress between 1990 and 1999 of 11 percentage points to the progress between 1999 and 2005 of 6 percentage points, then it becomes apparent that the pace of development has been quite similar before and after the MDG commitment in the year 2000" (8). In addition, the authors highlight "the largest chunk of progress is due to the over-achievement of China, not only halving but quartering its poorest population." The same argument can be made for malnutrition, according to the authors, standing at "19.8% in the developing countries in 1990 coming down to 16.8 in 1995 and remaining stagnant at 15.5% in 2006. However, the sheer numbers of malnourished remain stable at 848 million in 1990 vs. 850 in 2008. In sub-Saharan Africa the numbers even increased in the last period (2003–2008) from 211 to 231 million" (9).

Reducing by half the proportion of people without sustainable "access to drinking water has been achieved" (5), although the number of people without a "safe drinking water source" is still steadily increasing; by mid-2014 there were close to 800,000 deaths from water-related diseases (10), with more than 10% occurring among those who did not have access to safe water.

In terms of **MDG 2**, "significant steps towards achieving universal primary education have also been made with 'more than 9 million children . . . enrolled in primary education and more than 720, 000 primary school teachers have received training (2004–2009)'" (11). Progress has been slowest in the sub-Saharan Africa as well as the Middle East and North Africa regions. However, according to the European Union Gender Equality report, "the heavy focus on enrollment rates has come at the cost of educational quality and retention disproportionately affecting girls" (11).

Furthermore, the report underlines that "secondary school completion is particularly important for gender equality and should command increasing attention."

The aim of **MDG 3** is "to promote gender equality and empower women." And, while the targets and indicators within MDG 3 are important they were, according to the European Union study (11), "narrowly defined." Along with most other MDGs, "progress has been uneven both between and within countries, and indicators were inadequate to capture the lagging behind of the most marginalised groups and those facing multiple discrimination."

All sub-Saharan African countries are lagging behind the MDGs, especially with regard to **MDG 4** "to reduce child mortality" and **MDG 5** on maternal mortality, which calls for "a reduction in the number of child deaths from 12 million in 1990 to fewer than 4 million by 2015" (11), although the decline falls short by about 2 million (i.e., 6 million projected) in 2015 globally (5). And, although "all regions have made progress, with the highest reductions in Eastern Asia (69%), Northern Africa (66%) and Southern Asia (64%)" (11) since the turn of the millennium, progress toward MDG 5 is "well below the target to reduce the maternal mortality ratio by three-quarters by 2015" and "on current trends, this is one of the targets least likely to be met by 2015" (11).

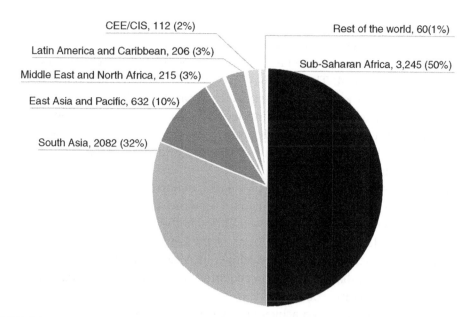

FIGURE 4.1 Number in thousands and percentage (of global total) of under-five deaths by region (2012).

Source: UNICEF, *A Promise Renewed: A Global Movement to End Preventable Child Deaths*, 2013. http://www.unicef.org/lac/Committing_to_Child_Survival_APR_9_Sept_2013.pdf

As shown in Figure 4.1, "significant disparities in infant mortality persist across regions. In sub-Saharan Africa, one in every 10 children born still dies before their fifth birthday, nearly 16 times the average rate in high-income countries" (12), although "71 per cent of births were assisted by skilled health personnel globally in 2014, an increase from 59 per cent in 1990" (5). Faster progress in other regions has seen the burden of global under-five deaths shift increasingly to sub-Saharan Africa, although it must be said that "the annual rate of reduction of under-five mortality was over five times faster during 2005–2013 than it was during 1990–1995" (5).

The approach taken by the Partnership for Maternal, Newborn and Child Health (PMNCH) may hold important lessons for other MDGs (13). The PMNCH's main aim is to enable "partners to share strategies, align objectives and resources, and agree on interventions to achieve more together than they would be able to achieve individually." Partners have joined from various organizations, including those from "the reproductive, maternal, newborn and child health (RMNCH) communities" to form "an alliance of more than 500 members, across seven constituencies: academic, research and teaching institutions; donors and foundations; health-care professionals; multilateral agencies; non-governmental organizations; partner countries; and the private sector."

Their evidence-based approach made clear the urgency of their work as studies revealed inter alia that "nearly nine million children under the age of five die every year," with "around 70% of these early child deaths . . . due to conditions that could be prevented or treated with access to simple, affordable interventions." Alarmingly, "over one third of all child deaths are linked to malnutrition" and "children in developing countries are ten times more likely to die before the age of five than children in developed countries."

Developed within the framework for the "Every Woman, Every Child initiative" (14), their concerted action has been successful and led to the "Every Newborn Action Plan," which was endorsed by the 194 member states at the 67th World Health Assembly (WHA) in 2014. The plan now paves "the way for national implementation and monitoring of key strategic actions to improve the health and well-being of newborns and their mothers around the world" (15). Translating vision into reality includes establishing "effective quality improvement systems," "competency-based curricula," "regulatory frameworks for midwifery and other healthcare personnel" and "multidisciplinary teams" (15).

MDG 6 focuses on combatting "HIV/AIDS, malaria and other diseases." Michel Sidibé, UNAIDS Executive Director, in his Foreword to the *UNAIDS Report on the Global AIDS Epidemic 2013* (16), reflects that "over the years, the gloom and disappointments chronicled in the early editions of the UNAIDS have given way to more promising tidings, including historic declines in AIDS-related deaths and new HIV infections and the mobilisation of unprecedented financing for HIV-related activities in low- and middle-income countries."

In his view, much has been achieved since "the dawn of this century" when there was "a lack of critical HIV treatment and prevention tools," which "often hindered efforts to respond effectively to the epidemic." Today, he posits "we have the tools we need to lay the groundwork to end the AIDS epidemic." Achievements such as "the sharp reductions in the number of children newly infected with HIV" and "life-saving antiretroviral therapy" can be traced to the synergistic efforts of diverse "stakeholders—the leadership and commitment of national governments, the solidarity of the international community, innovation by programme implementers, the historic advances achieved by the scientific research community and the passionate engagement of civil society, most notably people living with HIV themselves." As with the PMNCH initiative (13), an important element for advancing the MDGs/Sustainable Development Goals (SDGs) lies with forming committed and workable alliances, which have a common cause.

While acknowledging the significant progress that has been made toward reducing new HIV infections; zero discrimination; and zero AIDS-related deaths, he is concerned that "in several countries that have experienced significant declines in new HIV infections, disturbing signs have emerged of increases in sexual risk behaviours among people."

This ongoing uneasiness was highlighted at the Prince Mahidol Award Conference in 2014 in Thailand with the overall theme, Transformative Learning for Health Equity (17). At this event Dr. Anthony Fauci, director of the U.S. Institute of Allergy and Infectious Diseases, outlined the challenges remaining in ending the HIV/AIDS pandemic, citing that in 2012 there were over "70 million total HIV infections; 36 million total AIDS deaths; 35.5 million people living with AIDS" killing 1.6 million in 2012 alone; and 2.3 million new HIV infections.

The intervention model adopted by the institute places reliance on treatment and prevention with basic and clinical research given the highest priority, especially regarding antiretroviral drugs, with 12.7 million people receiving these in 2012 compared to about 200,000 in 2002. Furthermore, as mentioned, while treatment is providing good results in some areas, preventive measures are faring less well as fewer "than

10 percent of people in the world who are at risk of HIV infection are reached with prevention services." This low number is disappointing, especially after "the global approach to HIV prevention" in the past three decades "has moved from a fragmented one, initiated by different communities affected by HIV, to a unified approach led by international and national organisations and governments" (18).

Two conclusions that may be drawn from these cautiously optimistic statistics are, first, that "expansion of the combination prevention approach is essential to avoid future HIV infections and for the health and well-being of people living with HIV." Second, As is the case for malaria and tuberculosis, both showing significant decreased mortality rates (5), prevention needs to be given much more priority, especially in terms of resources for educational measures with a view to "empowering communities who are affected by HIV to deliver the prevention techniques that work for them."

Progress with **MDG 7**, which seeks "to ensure environmental sustainability," is however, "sluggish" in sub-Saharan Africa, southern and western Asia, and Oceanian countries. As one example, "the proportion of people with sustainable access to safe drinking water increased from 76% to 89% between 1990 and 2011" [currently 91% (5)] but "accounts for just 63% in sub-Saharan Africa" (11). In addition, "while access to sanitation improved from 49% to over 60%, it remains well below the target of 75%," although "Globally, 147 countries have met the drinking water target, 95 countries have met the sanitation target and 77 countries have met both" (5).

The number of people living in slums in developing nations "fell from approximately 39.4 per cent in 2000 to 29.7 per cent in 2014." (5). High rates of deforestation hamper progress with regard to MDG 7. By mid-2014, losses in forest over a 6-month period were 2,187,086 hectares and land lost to soil erosion was 2,944,409 hectares (10).

MDG 8 "relates to the need to develop a global partnership for Development" but "is conspicuous by the absence of any indicators to monitor progress" (11). However, the MDG 2015 report highlights that "official development assistance from developed countries increased by 66 per cent in real terms between 2000 and 2014, reaching $135.2 billion." Moreover, the report stresses that "in 2014, 79 per cent of imports from developing to developed countries were admitted duty free, up from 65 per cent in 2000" (5).

A Millennium Development Goal "Report Card"

Table 4.1 shows average ratings of progress toward each of the eight MDG-2015 goals based on an informal survey involving 24 members of a Universitas 21 Health Sciences MDG workshop group meeting in Dublin, Ireland (19). The main focus of the United Nations Millennium Development Goals (UNMDG) initiative, which comprises a network of 27 global research-intensive universities, is to facilitate incorporation of the UNMDGs (future SDGs) into health care curricula through the use of interprofessional case-study pedagogy. To this end, in the past few years the UNMDG team, drawn from members across the world, has conducted workshops in Dublin, Hong Kong, Nottingham, Melbourne, and Lund, to name several locations. In addition, members have contributed to global MDG projects focusing on raising awareness about the UNMDGs and networking with similar groups. MDGs 3, 6, and 8 received the highest scores but are still well below acceptable levels. MDGs 1, 3, and 4 seem to fare slightly better than MDGs 5 and 7.

TABLE 4.1 Universitas 21 Health Sciences MDG Report Card

MDG	CURRENT	REPORTED AS OUTSTANDING	SCORE-CARD 1(BEST) – 5 (WORST)
(1) Eradicate Poverty and Hunger	1990–2004: poverty fell from almost a third to less than a fifth.	Africa poverty rise; 36 countries (90% of world's undernourished children); 1 out of 8 people remain hungry; 2.5 billion lack improved sanitation facilities—1 billion practice open defecation, a major health/environmental hazard.	3.1
(2) Achieve Universal Primary Education	Children in school in developing countries increased from 80% in 1991 to 88% in 2005.	Approximately 72 million children of primary school age (57% girls) not being educated as of 2005.	3.1
(3) Promote Gender Equality	Tide turning slowly for women in the labor market.	Far more women than men—worldwide more than 60%—are contributing as unpaid family workers (World Bank Group Gender Action Plan).	2.8
(4) Reduce Child Mortality	Some improvement in survival rates globally. Deaths of children less than 5 years of age fell from 12 million in 1991 to 6.9 million in 2005.	Accelerated improvements needed urgently in South Asia and sub-Saharan Africa; approximately 10 million children <5 years old died in 2005; most deaths were from preventable causes (2014: 3.1 million).	3.1
(5) Improve Maternal Health	Most of about 500,000 women who die during pregnancy or childbirth every year live in South Asia and sub-Saharan Africa.	Probably one of the least likely MDGs to be met. Numerous causes of maternal deaths require a variety of health care interventions to be made widely accessible. Fewer than 50% of births attended in the African WHO Region.	3.4
(6) Combat HIV/AIDS, Malaria, and Other Diseases	2012: over 70 million total HIV infections; 36 million total AIDS deaths; 35.5 million living with AIDS and killing 1.6 million; and 2.3 million new HIV infections.	AIDS is the leading cause of death in sub-Saharan Africa (1.6 million in 2007), 36 million cases of HIV/AIDS. 300–500 million cases of malaria each year leading to more than 1 million deaths. Treatment meets only 30% of need.	2.9
(7) Ensure Environmental Sustainability	Continuing losses of forests, species, and fish stocks across the globe.	World is already experiencing the effects of climate change.	3.4
(8) Increase Global Partnership for Development	Donors have to fulfill their pledges to match the current rate of health care program development.	Emphasis on partnerships, e.g., The Global Partnership for Education and the World Bank.	2.9

Source: Notes (facilitator/GR Lueddeke) from Universitas 21 Health Sciences MDG workshop, Dublin, Ireland, 2013.

Lessons Learned From the MDG Initiative

A key question the WHO Director-General raises in her introduction to the *World Health Report 2013, Research for Universal Health Coverage* (6), is how lessons learned in other nations can help to reduce deaths everywhere. One answer appears to be making better use of community-based interventions, which according to "randomized controlled trials provide the most persuasive evidence for action in public health."

By 2010, findings from "18 such trials in Africa, Asia and Europe had shown that the participation of outreach workers, lay health workers, community midwives, community and village health workers, and trained birth attendants collectively reduced neonatal deaths by an average of 24%, stillbirths by 16% and perinatal mortality by 20%. Maternal illness was also reduced by a quarter." These trials clearly do not give all the answers—for instance, the benefits of these interventions in reducing maternal mortality, as distinct from morbidity, are still unclear—but they are a powerful argument for involving community health workers in the care of mothers and newborn.

Contributors to a study conducted by the University of London International Development Centre (LIDC) and published with *The Lancet*, "The Millennium Development Goals: A Cross-Sectoral Analysis and Principles for Goal Setting After 2015" (3), identify difficulties with the MDGs in four areas: "conceptualisation, execution, ownership, and equity." In their view, the goals were "too narrow and fragmented, leaving gaps in which other important development objectives are missing." Rather than focussing on the wider vision of the Millennium Declaration, the MDGs concern only "development and poverty eradication," not "peace, security and disarmament, and human rights." Moreover, investments have focussed on vertical versus horizontal components (e.g., communicable diseases) with "variable effect on improving national health systems." Education targeted mostly primary education and MDG 2 "underdevelops secondary and tertiary education, for which opportunities to create substantial improvements in incomes and health are greatest," including the development of skilled workers. Fragmentation between such areas as "education, poverty reduction, health and gender" at national and local levels with "responsibilities of different line ministries nationally, subnationally, and locally" [means] "that the potential for simultaneous actions in the same location, working with the same communities and households, is unlikely." The same separation holds true for environmental sustainability "with potentials for synergies across sectors."

Ownership has also been problematic as input from developing countries to the MDG framework "was small . . . mixed and often weak," along with "territorial issues with leadership," with examples from communicable diseases (HIV/AIDS, tuberculosis [TB], malaria), professional groups, the maternal and child health communities, and the pharmaceutical industry.

Another central issue for the MDGs is equity, mainly because in their initial formulation the MDGs targeted poverty reduction and development goals aimed at poor countries rather than "global goals for all countries," usually associated with economic aspects (e.g., income, education) and also distribution.

The main shortcoming of the current MDG framework is that it is concerned "with just adequate provision for some, ignoring the needs of those who are too hard to reach and not addressing the difficulties of inequality in societies that have deleterious consequences for everyone, not only the poorest people."

It is clear that the MDGs have had considerable impact by "focusing resources and efforts on important development goals," and more generally "in raising public and political interest in the development agenda, engaging for the first time a wide range of sectors and disciplines in a concerted effort."

However, in the light of difficulties with "conceptualisation, execution, ownership, and equity," there appears to be a need for new MDG directions post-2015. The contributors to the LIDC MDG report concluded that "future development goals should be framed by a vision of global justice at the present moment, when there are no appropriate institutions to deliver this vision." An important feature of their thinking is that "it is important to focus on the choices that are actually on offer in a globally-inter-related world," including plurality of principles and procedures and "permissibility of partial resolutions (i.e., that making some things a bit better is better than waiting for the best solutions)."

The core of their thinking lies in the definition of "development," which they define "as a dynamic process involving sustainable and equitable access to improving wellbeing." Drawing on Amartya Sen's work, *The Idea of Justice* (20), in which he views wellbeing as a combination of the aspiration that "human lives can go much better," they agree that "improvement can be brought about through a strengthening of human agency, a person's capability (vs capability deprivation) to pursue and realise things that he or she values and has reason to value," thereby linking "wellbeing with the capability to make choices and act effectively with respect to, for example, health, education, nutrition, employment, security, participation, voice, consumption, and the claiming of rights."

Finally, the authors suggest that future developments of millennium goals should follow—and ideally be measured through a lens consisting of five guiding principles:

- Holism—avoiding "gaps in a development agenda and realising synergies between components," acknowledging that "people's wellbeing and capabilities depend on human development, social development and environmental development."
- Equity—achieving "the development of a more equitable world, built on more equitable societies in which there are adequate flows of information, understanding, resources, training, and respect to enable diverse individuals to attain a decent quality of life."
- Sustainability—delivering "an outcome such as wellbeing, in terms of its capacity to persist, and to resist or recover from shocks that affect[s] its productivity" [and] is "both viable in social and economic terms."
- Ownership—beginning "from a comprehensive conceptualisation of development and the core development principles proposed to govern both the specifications of development goals and the processes by which they are specified."
- Global obligation—arguing "for the importance of a position on global obligation that values human rights with respect to human, social, and environmental development," ensuring that "concerns with wellbeing are not just limited to the obligations we have to citizens of our own country, but to individuals anywhere."

To a large extent, the LIDC report findings are echoed by Dr. Tewabech Bishaw, managing director of the Alliance for Brain-Gain & Innovative Development and secretary general of the African Federation of Public Health Associations (AFPH) in Ethiopia.

In her keynote address at the seventh Public Health Association of South Africa (PHASA) conference (2011), titled "What Public Health Actions Are Needed in African Countries to Confront Health Inequalities?"(21), she discusses the gaps that need to be addressed and shares her thoughts on public health actions "that could contribute to redressing existing gaps and inequalities."

With dismay she observes that by 2011 "out of the twelve MDG targets many of the countries in Africa have scored positively on only two—children completing a full course in primary school and achieving gender equality in primary school." Calling for urgent action, she also notes that "Many of the health problems that developing countries in Africa are faced with are preventable. Emerging new communicable diseases and expansion of the old due to climate change has doubled the challenge. In addition, the increasing burden of non-communicable diseases alongside the communicable diseases is further burdening the health system making the situation more challenging. Many of the unnecessary and unjustified deaths especially death of newborns, children and mothers could be averted. Many young talents are wasted due to poverty, environmental degradation, ill health, under nutrition, lack of access to health services, clean water, hygienic living conditions, education and other essential services. Unemployment continues to weaken productive human resources with disabilities worsening the vicious circle of unproductively leading to perpetual poverty."

Her recommendations reflect many of the guiding principles of the LIDC MDG report for redressing inequalities and other challenges, highlighting especially the importance of health being fundamentally "a human rights issue." In addition, she advocates the need for prioritizing policy, strategy, and action based on accurate analysis of reliable health information and epidemiological data; engaging in collaborative partnerships and networks; promoting good governance and accountability; using national think-tank groups; scaling up and sustaining critical intervention for sustainable health development; promoting and supporting problem-solving research; and developing and using participatory monitoring and evaluation systems.

A theme that weaves through her keynote address is the need to listen to and learn from many voices in trying to address the deep-seated and pressing issues facing Africa. Her determination is in keeping with Professor David Griggs, director of the Monash Sustainability Institute (MSI) in Australia (22). He cites Albert Einstein, who reportedly "once said that if he had just one hour to find a solution on which his life depended, he would spend the first 55 minutes defining the problem," and "once he knew the right question to ask, he could solve the problem in less than five minutes." Professor Griggs emphasizes that "today, humanity faces such a life-threatening problem: How are we to provide adequate nutrition and a decent quality of life to a global population that is set to surpass nine billion by 2050, without irreparably damaging our planetary life-support system?" It seems highly unlikely that even Einstein's huge thinking capacity could easily resolve issues facing the planet and its people today.

This question is, of course, one of many that confront the post-2015 SDG deliberations. In retrospect, while there is wide variability among global regions with regard to meeting the MDGs, according to some, by and large, they "did a good job in increasing aid spending and led to improved development policies, but left many of the bigger issues unresolved" (23).

The main critique of the cross-sectoral analysis is that the MDG goals were "too narrow and fragmented," and that they concern only "development and poverty eradication not peace, security and human rights." Other weaknesses are that investments focused on vertical versus horizontal components (e.g., communicable diseases) and that education targeted primary education and not secondary and tertiary education.

The United Nations Conference on Sustainable Development

The United Nations Conference on Sustainable Development (UNCSD)—also known as Rio 2012 and Rio-20, from 13 to 22 June 2012, with 192 attending nations and about 45,000 participants—made a commitment to the promotion of a sustainable future through SDGs (24).

Redefining the SDGs as "development that meets the needs of the present while safeguarding Earth's life-support system, on which the welfare of current and future generations depends" (25), a group of international scientists go further than focusing just on improving people's lives. They posit that "countries must now link poverty eradication to protection of the atmosphere, oceans and land" and propose six SDGs, as indicated in Box 4.1.

Taking into consideration the latter and other contributions, the mechanism to evolve new SDG goals has been through a two-phase process by the UN General Assembly (UNGA) Open Working Group (OWG), co-chaired by Csaba Kőrösi, Hungary ambassador to the UN, and Macharia Kamau, Kenya ambassador to the UN: The first phase focused on "stocktaking" from March 2013 to February 2014, followed by phase two from February to September 2014, which concentrated on the development of the report for the 68th meeting of the UNGA in September 2014 (26).

While the deliberations are ongoing, the MDG interim report in June 2013 concluded that "wide support" exists for a "single post-2015 UN development framework containing a single set of goals," which are universally applicable but adaptable to

BOX 4.1

Proposed Post-2015 Sustainable Development Goals
Goal 1: Thriving lives and livelihoods
Goal 2: Sustainable food security
Goal 3: Sustainable water security
Goal 4: Universal clean energy
Goal 5: Healthy and productive ecosystems
Goal 6: Governance for sustainable societies

national priorities (27). In addition, the report proposes "the need for a narrative that frames and motivates the SDGs, in particular to focus on poverty eradication as the overarching objective and central proposal of the Goals." However, while this focus remains crucial, it is vital to emphasize that sustainable global poverty reduction can only be accomplished in a world that makes "peace, security and human rights" its core aspiration, as advocated by the contributors of the LIDC MDG cross-sectoral analysis (3).

These global ideals, so claim Lant Pritchett and Charles Kenny, both senior fellows at Harvard's Center for Global Development, also recalling *The Lancet* report, could "put into measurable form the high aspirations countries have for the well-being of their citizens" (28), thereby offering "a rationale for upper middle-income engagement with the post-2015 development agenda," and providing "the rationale for a far broader engagement with development on the behalf of rich countries than attempting to kink progress through aid transfers."

"The World We Want"

However, their proposal may need to remain a future possibility as the UN's top priorities through "The World We Want" (29) and "Beyond 2015" (30) lie with supporting 88 of the poorer countries "to convene national consultations on the post 2015 development agenda." Stakeholder inputs are requested "on current and emerging challenges in respect to eleven defined substantive issues":

- Inequalities
- Health
- Population Dynamics
- Education
- Energy
- Water
- Environmental Sustainability
- Food Security and Nutrition
- Conflict and Fragility
- Growth and Employment
- Governance

The overall aim is to build "a global, multi-stakeholder civil society movement for a legitimate post-2015 framework" (30,31). The national consultations—essentially a "global conversation"—are "organized by UN Country Teams, under the leadership of the UN Resident Coordinator," which "are working with a wide range of stakeholders including governments, civil society, the private sector, media, universities and think tanks." To date, over 2 million have contributed to the exercise, including considerable input through the MyWorld Survey (32). It is pleasing to note the interest taken by the younger generation as 50% of the voters to date have been between 16 and 30 years of age. Their top priority is Education (254,505), followed by Health Care (210,550), Job Opportunities (195,117), Honest and Responsive Government (189,311), Protection Against Crime and Violence (156,687), and Clean Water and Sanitation (152,434).

Conciliation Resources, a peace-building nongovernmental organization (NGO), reminds us that "War shatters lives. It creates poverty and wastes billions every year. The people living in the midst of the violence often have the greatest insight into its causes. Yet they are often excluded from efforts to find a resolution" (33). In relation to the MDGs, Dr. Teresa Dumasy, working on policy change and learning in the field of peace building at Conciliation Resources, draws attention to the 2011 *World Development Report* (34), which highlighted that "no conflict-affected or fragile state has achieved a single MDG, nor are they expected to do so by 2015. Of the 42 countries at the bottom of UNDP's Human Development Index, 29 are fragile states. Countries where people are feeling the socially debilitating effects of fragility and conflict have simply been left behind."

She further notes that "experience shows that the targets set within the current MDGs have not proved sufficiently relevant to those countries grappling with the peace building and state building issues so central to their recovery." Moreover, she posits that the MDGs "speak to the symptoms, rather than the drivers of conflict" (33).

Referencing a statement by civil society organizations, "Bringing Peace Into the Post-2015 Development Framework: A Joint Statement by Civil Society Organisations" (35), she mentions key elements "that address the fundamental notion of 'fairness,' the absence of which can drive conflict and that should be included in any successor framework." These elements can be found in the goals set out in the New Deal for International Engagement in Fragile States, supported by more than 40 government and multinational organizations" (34).

- Legitimate politics—foster inclusive political settlements and conflict resolution
- Security—establish and strengthen people's security
- Justice—address injustices and increase people's access to justice
- Economic foundations—generate employment and improve livelihoods
- Revenues and services—manage revenue and build capacity for accountable and fair service delivery

Conciliation Resources contend that "the post-2015 targets must be much more broadly owned and also relevant to countries affected by fragility and conflict, as they persevere in their efforts to attain lasting peace and a significant reduction in poverty levels." The importance that Conciliation Resources places on the causes and consequences of conflicts is echoed by War Child International (36), a specialist agency working in countries devastated by armed conflict such as Iraq, Afghanistan, Democratic Republic of Congo, Uganda, Central African Republic, and Syria.

According to War Child International, and as mentioned earlier, without focusing on the plight of children in conflict areas, there is no hope of achieving the MDGs, nor the SDGs, one may add. However, if we are to optimize the success of the post-2015-SDGs, we may need to learn to work differently. This message is conveyed by Dr. Samantha Nutt, a founder of the international agency War Child, who, after close to 20 years visiting conflict zones, reflects on shortcomings of international aid, concluding that: "We're not spending enough time, effort and resources on the preventive aspects of it: programs that focus on education, people's employment and income opportunities for women and young people. . . . Something happens in the news and we throw money at it and a year later we expect it to be better. Until you start investing in the local community organizations and addressing these structural deficits, you'll always be chasing your tail" (37).

Her concern with "scaling up" community support and development is in keeping with WHO Director-General Dr. Chan's reflections on how MDG/SDG interventions can be improved (5), and will assuredly contribute to "the process of setting the SDG agenda," discussed at the 67th WHA in Geneva (38). At the latter WHA, member states also agreed that health needs to be "at the core of the post-2015 development agenda" including "the unfinished work of the health Millennium Development Goals, newborn health, as well as an increased focus on non-communicable diseases, mental health and neglected tropical diseases along with the importance of universal health coverage and the need to strengthen health systems."

Completing the outstanding MDG work is of course of vital importance to ensuring global population health and well-being. However, taking into account lessons learned from the MDGs 2000 to 2015, achieving the "health" goals will depend largely on significant and expeditious progress being made alongside the other 10 thematic indicators underpinned by "The World We Want" initiative.

Dr. Tewabech's keynote at the PHASA conference is a case in point (21). Little progress has been made since 2011, and some areas have actually worsened despite timely and realistic strategic plans for improving health care. The gap between good intentions, meaningful application, and outcomes remains vast, and, as argued compellingly by the LIDC (3), Conciliation Resources (33), and War Child International (36), the SDGs-2015 need to be conceptualized and enacted through a wider lens that subsumes, expands, and interrelates the MDGs in a framework with a view to realizing "fairness" and "Global Social Justice—underpinned by Peace, Security and Basic Human Rights."

As one example, MDG 1 on poverty and MDG 3 on gender equality could become part of the Inequalities indicator. It is of course too late from a planning perspective, but recognizing the threats imposed by "modernity," discussed in Chapter 2.0, an additional thematic indicator could have drawn attention to "Modern Lifestyle and Well-Being," the probable cause in the rise of noncommunicable diseases (NCDs) or conditions.

To this end, and as an illustrative example, Figure 4.2 juxtaposes goal guiding principles from *The Lancet* report (3) and 11 indicators that underpin "The World We Want" (29). Emerging indicators, such as Population Dynamics and Growth and Employment, would require considerable global analyses of scope, priorities, and enabling actions based to a large extent on the MDG experience.

Above all, the framework is intended to highlight that the overarching global goal toward which national governments and bodies, such as the UN, need to strive is "global social justice," underpinned by peace, security, and respect for basic human rights. Many of the global disparities or inequities, whereby only ~1.5 billion people of ~7.3 billion reap the benefits of a modern world, are outlined in Chapter 2.0.

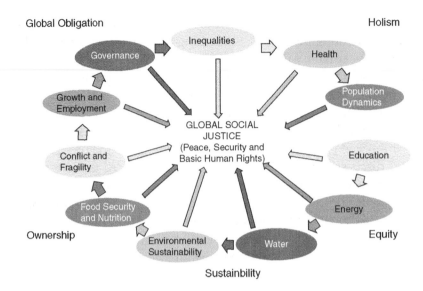

FIGURE 4.2 Toward an integrated sustainable development goals framework.

Source: G. Lueddeke (S. Carr, illustration), 10th Public Health Association of South Africa (PHASA) Conference, 2014. http://www.phasa.org.za/global-health-issues-responses-paradigm-shifts-needed

A working hypothesis for realizing a much-needed rebalancing of the global population, burden of disease, and health workforce is based on the robust worldwide implementation of strategic, multi-faceted, and interdependent holistic approaches to improve the quality of life at all levels, starting particularly at local levels and moving outward to regional and national levels. These initiatives, which should underpin the post-2015 Sustainable Development Goals (SDGs), must prioritize ensuring the essentials of daily life for everyone on the planet, especially recognizing the imperatives of personal security, well-being, as well as future life satisfaction, nourished above all by improved food security, health care, education, and employment opportunities.

Fundamentally, it may be argued that it is only through these means that the world can overcome the threats from terrorism and extremism (violent and non-violent) facing us today. Encouraging youth to reflect on these means and providing alternative life-enhancing or peaceful paths to personal well-being, rather than death and destruction, along with respecting the basic human rights of others, including actively supporting the sustainability of our planet for which we share a common destiny, appears to be our most important challenge in this decade and beyond.

The African "Health for All People" Campaign

Universal health coverage (UHC), discussed further in the next section, is about achieving health equity worldwide; it is also, to a large extent, an essential ingredient or "stepping stone" of a longer term global aim for global justice "peace, security, and basic human rights."

Jonathan Jay, coordinator of the Health for All Post-2015 campaign (39) launched in March 2014, commends policy makers for the progress achieved by the MDGs in areas such as "AIDS, childhood immunization, access to family planning and reproductive healthcare," along with helping to usher in a "Golden Age." However, he also points out that "the rapid scale-up was leaving people behind," and that "health inequalities continued to grow, both within and across countries," (and) "advances in child survival and maternal care left a concentration of deaths in the poorest regions, with persistent gaps in access."

Furthermore, while acknowledging considerable progress with regard to preventing and controlling AIDS/HIVs, "hot spots of increased risk among groups that are marginalized and vulnerable" remain. These health concerns are now also being exacerbated by the increase in "non-communicable diseases," which he labels a "growing hidden iceberg" in developing countries—so daunting a global health challenge that many key players have been virtually paralyzed. The global civil society campaign, Health for All Post-2015, that is now under way in Ethiopia, Nigeria, and Kenya calls "for an approach that would correct inequities and bring everyone along—ushering not just the next era, but truly a new era in global health."

Achieving "A New Era in Global Health"

Echoing the goals of international scientists (25), according to a global alliance of research institutes, the Independent Research Forum (IRF), "sustainable development can only be achieved if four foundations exist" (40), as shown in Box 4.2.

Achieving the SDGs that are more inclusive and integrated in terms of "planet and population" sustainability, as indicated in Box 4.1, according to the IRF, will be optimized if eight major shifts take place, as summarized in Box 4.3.

Bringing "Fairness" and "Civil Society Goals" Into the Development Framework

Unquestionably, in order to meet UN and other SDG challenges "much depends on the fulfilment of MDG-8—the global partnership for development" (5), rightly recognized as a key factor by UN Secretary-General Ban Ki-Moon in 2012. These "global partnerships," he asserts, should stretch beyond volunteerism—and could be greatly enhanced if "fairness" and the civil society goals, mentioned previously (35), were simultaneously advanced by global advocates (41–44)—especially by those who value the importance of working toward "global social justice—peace, security and basic human rights."

BOX 4.2

Four Foundations of Sustainable Development

- Economic progress
- Equitable prosperity and opportunity
- Healthy and productive ecosystems
- Stakeholder engagement and collaboration

BOX 4.3

Main Shifts Required to Meet Post-2015 Sustainable Development Goals (SDGs)

- From donor/beneficiary country relationships to meaningful international partnerships
- From top-down decision making to processes that involve everyone
- From economic models that do little to reduce inequalities to those that do
- From business models based on enriching shareholders to models that also benefit society and the environment
- From meeting relatively easy development targets—such as improving access to financial services—to actually reducing poverty
- From conducting emergency response in the aftermath of crises to making countries and people resilient before crises occur
- From conducting pilot programs to scaling up the programs that work
- From a single-sectoral approach, such as tackling water shortage through the water ministry, to involving various sectors, like the agriculture and energy sectors, which also depend on water

With proposed "global social justice" at its SDG core, supported by a set of 11 thematic indicators to ensure "sustainable development," depicted in Figure 4.2, the MDG refrain "progress has been uneven both between and within countries" should no longer be an acceptable option or convenient "escape route." The global challenge is huge, but the rewards for this and future generations are much greater.

4.2 UNIVERSAL HEALTH COVERAGE (UHC): "MYTH OR REALITY?"

I felt like I had traded my mother's health for my children's schooling.
It was a tough choice, and I cried every day. (45)

This heartfelt comment was made by a Kenyan mother who "had been forced to choose between paying for her children's education or her mother's urgently needed medical treatment. She could not afford both." Having to make this type of agonizing decision clearly demonstrates the global urgency behind UHC.

Universal Health Coverage and Public Health

Speaking at the 65th WHA in May 2012, it is, therefore, not surprising that WHO Secretary-General Dr. Margaret Chan declared that "Universal health coverage is the single most powerful concept that public health has to offer" (46). Because her view is shared by many nations "from every corner of the globe," including the United States, the United Kingdom, South Africa, and Thailand, in 2012 the UNGA adopted a resolution on affordable universal health care. The resolution urges "member states to develop health systems that avoid significant direct payments at the point of delivery and to have a mechanism for pooling risks to avoid catastrophic healthcare spending and impoverishment" (47). At present, "more than 3 billion people have to pay for healthcare themselves, forcing (as the introductory example illustrates) many—particularly women and children—to choose between healthcare and education . . . widely acknowledged as the most regressive form of health financing" (48).

As mentioned in the previous section, considerable progress has been made on several MDGs and targets, such as an increased number—10 million—on AIDS treatment since 2003, and deaths from measles dropping by more than 70% (48). However, there are still far too many who do not have access to any kind of health service or have very poor quality of health care despite additional funds that have been poured into health coffers worldwide "rising threefold during the first decade of the twenty-first century" (49).

Global Health System Imbalances and Progressing UHC

Although funding has increased, there are many areas—Myanmar, sub-Saharan Africa, and the Philippines, for instance—where there has been negligible or no impact on improving population health. In sub-Saharan Africa, the ratio of inhabitants to doctors remains as high as 50,000:1 (e.g., Malawi, Tanzania) with many at 33,500:1 (e.g., Burundi, Ethiopia, Liberia, Mozambique) and many in the 20,000:1 range, compared to around 300:1 in most developed nations (50). As illustrated in Table 4.2, an outstanding global issue is that many of the poorest nations are sending health workers to some of the richest (51).

The urgency of putting into place UHC is highlighted by MDG 3 and 4, as discussed in the previous section. Most deaths of children under 5 years of age are preventable, including maternal deaths, as shown in Figure 4.3, caused in the main by hemorrhaging. Although "between 1990 and 2013, maternal mortality worldwide dropped by almost 50%" (52), the present situation is still unacceptable when we consider that "99% of all maternal deaths occur in developing countries" and that in sub-Saharan Africa, as in one example, births "attended by skilled health workers increased from 44% to only 45% between 2000 and 2010 in sub-Saharan Africa" (48).

It is estimated that implementing strategies to advance UHC would prevent the deaths of at least 1.8 million children and 100,000 mothers annually (47). Moreover, each year over 150 million people face financial crises and 100 million are pushed into poverty due to high out-of-pocket spending on health care, which is widely acknowledged as the most regressive form of health financing (48).

Although there has been "considerable progress since 2005 when WHO members made the commitment to universal health coverage, the coverage of health services and financial risk protection currently fall far short of universal coverage" (47). As one example shows, "nearly half of all HIV-infected people eligible for antiretroviral therapy were still not receiving it in 2011!"

TABLE 4.2 Mobility of Health Professionals

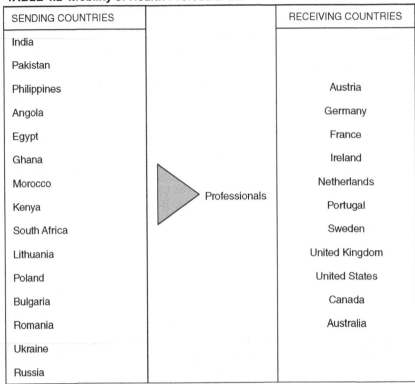

SENDING COUNTRIES		RECEIVING COUNTRIES
India		
Pakistan		
Philippines		Austria
Angola		Germany
Egypt		France
Ghana		Ireland
Morocco	Professionals	Netherlands
Kenya		Portugal
South Africa		Sweden
Lithuania		United Kingdom
Poland		United States
Bulgaria		Canada
Romania		Australia
Ukraine		
Russia		

Concerns over the years have also been voiced that there has been too much emphasis in health systems on disease management or, as one medical historian put it, "paying the wages of disease"(43) rather than prevention and dealing with underlying structural conditions. However, things may be changing. As one example, the report

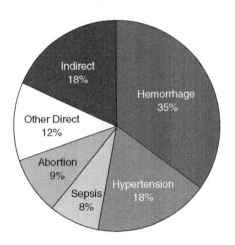

FIGURE 4.3 Global estimates of the causes of maternal deaths, 1997–2007.

Source: World Health Organization, *Countdown to 2015 Decade Report (2000–2010)*, (2010; 52).

by the Council of Foreign Relations, *The New Global Health Agenda—Universal Health Coverage* (53), acknowledges "in the last few decades we are also witnessing a shift in focus from disease-driven initiatives to projects aimed at increasing the sustainability and strengthening of health systems" and "a crucial component to this is universal health coverage (UHC)."

UHC and Historical Contexts

Many proponents of UHC argue that wider implementation of UHC is long overdue given the concept's appearance in Germany in the form of social or national insurance on the world stage more than a hundred years ago in keeping with social reforms in Europe at that time (54).

About 50 years later, Germany's lead was followed by such countries as the Soviet Union (1937 and 1969), the United Kingdom (1948), Nordic countries (1955–1964), Japan (1961), Canada (1968–1972), Southern European countries (1978–1986), Australia (1974, 1984), and Asian countries, such as Taiwan (1995) (54,55). In most countries, UHC has been achieved by a mixed model of funding, including private (e.g., compulsory insurance as in Switzerland and the United States) and public contributions (general taxation). In the United Kingdom, there is a single-payer health care system whereby the government (vs. insurers) pays for all health care costs (56).

Today's view of UHC, therefore, builds on the early attempts at "income stabilization and protection against the wage loss of sickness" (54), and sees health as a basic human right consisting of "two interrelated components: coverage with needed health services (prevention, promotion, treatment, rehabilitation and palliative care) and coverage with financial risk protection, for everyone" (57).

Health funding is the prerogative of each state and, of course, the poorer the country, the more the need for health care, but also the less probability of implementing UHC, particularly where health services are virtually nonexistent or where conflicts have impeded any support of its citizens, as in Syria.

Furthermore, as mentioned previously, the report, "Financing Global Health 2012" estimates that while "DAH (development assistance for health) reached a historic high of $28.2 billion in 2010," it "fell in 2011 for the first time since DAH could be tracked" and "projections for further cutbacks in development assistance do not augur well for a return to the rapid growth that punctuated the 2001 to 2010 era" (49).

Advancing UHC: Services, Costs, and Population

Given today's realities, it becomes clear that UHC is not about 'a one size fits all' approach to health care or "achieving a fixed minimum package," but rather requires

a process that needs to progress on several fronts: the range of services that are available to people (consisting of the medicines, medical products, health workers, infrastructure and information required to ensure good quality); the proportion of the costs of those services that are covered; and the proportion of the population that is covered. (57)

One of the greatest challenges facing UHC—especially for the most vulnerable countries—is that "these gains need to be protected during financial or economic downturns" (58,59).

Furthermore, although progress is being made as countries "as diverse as Brazil, China, Ecuador, Ghana, Indonesia, Morocco, Rwanda, Sierra Leone, Thailand and Turkey are among those [that] have taken steps to modify their health systems in order to move closer to universal coverage" (57), now also including the United States, much work remains to be done if the movement is indeed to emerge as a "reality" rather than an unattainable goal or indeed a "myth" for many in this decade and beyond. Regions that are of particular concern include Africa, Middle and Far East as illustrated in Figure 4.4, which differentiates between nations that have achieved UHC and those that are in the process of doing so.

By 2010 "of 192 nations studied, 75 had legislation mandating universal access to healthcare services independent of income. Of these, 58 met the criteria based on available measures of coverage (including >90% of the population having access to skilled birth attendance and insurance coverage) which serve as broader proxies for access to care" (60).

From 2010 to 2012, some types of UHC became particularly evident in Brazil, as well as Saudi Arabia, and there was progress toward a decrease in out-of-pocket expenditures on health (61), as shown in Figure 4.5.

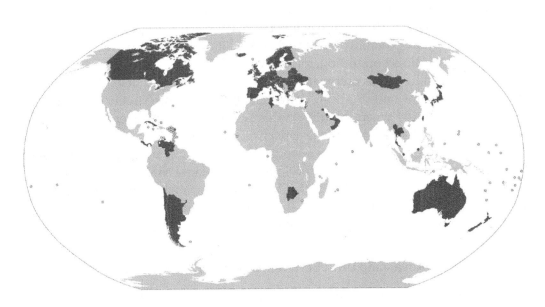

■ 58 countries with legislation mandating UHC, and
>90% health insurance coverage, and
>90% skilled birth attendance.

FIGURE 4.4 Global Prevalence of Universal Health Care in 2009.

Source: D. Stuckler, et al., *The Political Economy of Universal Health Coverage*. Background paper for the First Global Symposium on Health Systems Research. http://www.pacifichealthsummit.org/downloads/UHC/the%20political%20 economy%20of%20uhc.PDF

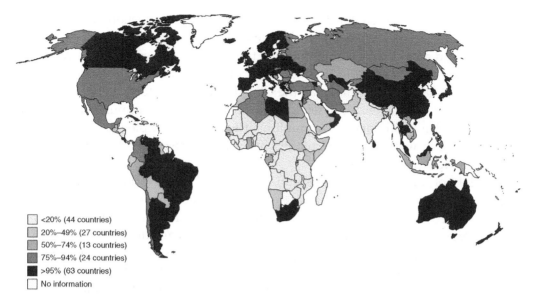

FIGURE 4.5 World: Out-of-pocket expenditure on health as a percentage of private expenditure on health (%), 2013.

Source: World Health Organization, Global Health Observatory. http://gamapserver.who.int/mapLibrary/Files/Maps/ OutPocketPercentagePrivate_2013.png

Achieving substantial reductions in health expenditures (e.g., India) will depend, as Dr. Laurie Garrett, senior fellow at the Council on Foreign Relations, argues in the Preface to *The New Global Health Agenda* (53), on "three bottom-line needs."

- Health financing schemes that cover the costs of care without putting health consumers, governments, or providers at risk of bankruptcy or severe economic hardship
- Systems of health care delivery that can absorb the many now-fragmented services and provide accessible treatment and prevention universally to those in need
- A health care workforce worldwide that should be at a minimum 5 million persons larger than it is currently, that displays a deeper range of skills, and that features greater attention to health management and community-based caregivers

UHC and Workforce Development

Dr. Garrett's third point strongly underscores the need to develop a competent workforce through appropriate education and training (42,43), a key factor to achieving UHC.

In her analysis, she reflects on a typical scenario in sub-Saharan Africa where "health-care facilities are in place and coverage is provided through a variety of financing schemes, but clinics are staffed by grossly undertrained personnel and lack even rudimentary medical supplies. In this scenario, the mother and baby may die, despite having affordable access to care, because the health providers were incompetent or inadequately supplied" (53).

A major concern, then, for those contemplating the introduction of UHC relates to the critical shortages of health workers, especially finding it hard to retain them in underserved areas (62). An ambitious yet timely and vital response to strengthening workforce capability, a fundamental tenet of the proposed 2015 MDG "capability approach," has been articulated in the Global Health Workforce Alliance (GHWA) Strategic Plan (63), which broadly sets out the main directions to be pursued from 2013 to 2016. The plan highlights the "commitment to train and deploy 2.6 to 3.5 million additional health workers," underpinned by evidence-based HRH plans in at least 75% of the HRH priority countries.

In light of the criticality of this initiative, in 2012 "the World Health Assembly adopted a resolution on the importance of educating health workers as part of universal health coverage" (64). Moreover, in the resolution member states "emphasized that universal health coverage is not just about health financing but requires strong health systems to provide a range of quality, affordable services at all levels of care." Recognizing the importance of achieving UHC for all member states, delegates also "expressed strong support for WHO's action plan and reiterated their call for a monitoring framework to help them to track progress towards universal health coverage." In addition, delegates expressed support that "universal health coverage should feature in the post-2015 development agenda."

The four global contributors to the report, *Universal Health Coverage: A Commitment to Close the Gap (48)*, reached a number of conclusions, including the need for the health sector to pool resources across the population "to allow the redistribution of resources and cross-subsidisation by the healthy and wealthy to cover the costs of care for the poor and sick."

They are also concerned with quality of service delivery "to secure progressive pathways towards UHC."

To this end, the *WHO Initiative on Transformative Scale-up of Health Professional Education* through provision of evidence-based education guidelines (65)—discussed further in Section 8.10—should make "a significant contribution to the challenging task of reshaping the health workforce of countries for the benefit and well-being of their citizens."

Other lessons that the authors of *Universal Health Coverage: A Commitment to Close the Gap* (48) emphasize concern ensuring that "poor and vulnerable benefit first," and progressively increasing "funding for the health sector . . . at least for vulnerable populations and priority services."

Gaining Broader Support for UHC

In an informative blog, Jonathan Jay observes that as part of the evolving SDGs framework "the global UHC movement can gain broader support by refining its messages to connect with the core values of civil society and provide reassurance that UHC is feasible for low-income countries" (66).

He also cites American economist Professor Jeffrey Sachs, who is director of the Earth Institute at Columbia University and special adviser to the UN Secretary-General on the MDGs. While speaking at "A Healthy Future for All: Making UHC a

Post-2015 Priority" event, Professor Sachs "framed the potential of UHC for uniting global health advocates" and envisioned the movement toward UHC as "bringing everyone together under one big tent," advocating six dimensions of "universal":

- People everywhere, but especially those in poor countries
- All people, regardless of class, race, ethnicity, gender, and geography
- All ages, from prenatal and newborn conditions to diseases of older adults
- All diseases
- All stages of health: promotive, preventive, curative, rehabilitative, and palliative
- All sectors, recognizing the health impact associated with environmental pollutants, climate change, the food industry, and others

These dimensions emphasize global inclusivity and are extremely crucial to achieving UHC. However, as argued in the previous section, much more emphasis in the post-2015 SDGs must be placed on health inequities, human rights, international cooperation, and systemic dysfunctions of global governments. Inspired by a vision for global justice—peace, security, and basic human rights, discussed in Section 4.1—the SDGs should ideally become catalysts or seed carriers for constructive social change and social stability.

The main obstacle to adopting UHC originates—according to the *Lancet–*University of Oslo Commission on Global Governance for Health report *The Political Origins of Health Inequity: Prospects for Change* (67)—from "conflict with powerful global actors in pursuit of other interests such as protection of national security, safeguarding of sovereignty, or economic goals." It is telling that some of these impediments were already identified almost a decade ago by the lead authors of *Who's Got the Power? Transforming Health Systems for Women and Children* (68). Then, as is the case now, to achieve the post-2015 SDG agenda, to make UHC truly universal, enabling actions need to go beyond a simplistic "both the SDGs and UHC" and focus on finding ways of overcoming, above all, the disconnect or delinking of "mainstream development practice . . . from the broader economic and political forces."

Examples of Emerging UHC

It appears that Nigeria after "ten years in the making" might see "an end in sight" (69). After many failed attempts since 2004, essentially, "the bill is set to provide a platform for efficient coordination of the Health System and the delivery of a Minimum Package of Essential Health Services. It also makes provision for social inclusion, addresses the issue of equity in Health and seeks to protect families from catastrophic health expenditure and impoverishment due to high cost of healthcare, accelerating Nigeria's progress towards Universal Health Care."

According to Felix Abrahams Obi, a physiotherapist and member of the Research Policy Group in Nigeria, "Some health economics experts project that implementation of the provisions of the bill can help save 3,131,510 lives of mothers, newborns and under 5s by 2022; thus helping to reverse the poor health indices in Nigeria as well as providing a better legal basis to address conflicts among health professionals in Nigeria." Furthermore, he reflects that

> as we look back from 2014 to the beginnings in 2004, we are confronted by the political realities that make Nigeria unique, and are appalled at how much resources and opportunities have been wasted to reform and strengthen our health system and improve the really poor health outcomes for which Nigeria has been known globally. We hope the Bill will indeed be signed into law this time and more importantly, help change the way healthcare is provided and managed in Nigeria! One day we will count how many lives could have been saved in those years. We hope the Bill will indeed be signed into law this time and more importantly, help change the way healthcare is provided and managed in Nigeria!

> One day we will count how many lives could have been saved in those 10 years.

Given the length of time it has taken Nigeria to implement a package of essential health services, it may be important to recall that adoption of UHC is not an issue restricted only to poor nations. The main obstacle in the United States, as one example shows, may be traced to ideological differences held by different parties in the government. Two central questions surrounding the issue are whether UHC is a basic human right and whether it is affordable.

After several failed attempts, most notably spearheaded by President Franklin D. Roosevelt in 1944 and First Lady Hillary Clinton in 1993 with the proposed Health Security Act—opposed by both conservatives and libertarians, as well as the health insurance industry—President Obama was finally able to sign the Affordable Care Act into law in 2010 (70). The outcomes to date are generally positive as "ten million Americans who had no insurance do so now" and "the rate of the uninsured has fallen from 20 per cent to 15 per cent along with the creation of nine million jobs." A major challenge remains in reducing the uninsured even further.

Progress with UHC is also being made in other regions of the Americas. In a *Lancet* article, Professor Julio Frenk, dean of Harvard's School of Public Health, draws together the findings of a series of *Lancet* articles on UHC and focuses "on actions that could help reach the goal of universal health coverage in Latin America" (71). As was the case in the United States, he stresses that "traditional health insurance is leaving the poor and those without salaries behind" and maintains that countries proceeding through the democratization process need "to build their universal health care efforts on value platforms that assume health care as a social right." Moreover, he underscores that "intersectorial cooperation alongside transparency, accountability and social participation are required to advance effective and equitable extension of coverage in the region" and in particular to "address health risks and social determinants of health." One way forward, Professor Frenk concludes, is to build health systems that incorporate three essential functions—stewardship (ministry of health), financing (public funds), and delivery (public and private providers, "supervised by a regulatory body")—and apply them to the whole population. For Professor Frenk "universal health coverage" is not only a "right" but also a "reality" or decidedly "a reachable objective," subject to 10 specific actions, as shown in Box 4.4, which may also hold valuable lessons for other nations.

BOX 4.4

Actions to Achieve Universal Health Care

1. Avoid the establishment of separate coverage schemes for different population groups and, if they already exist, design initiatives to reduce segmentation.
2. Continue to implement social protection schemes that reduce the burden of out-of-pocket payments.
3. Increase financing for health and, over time, increase the proportion of universal health coverage financing from general government revenues.
4. Design upstream interventions to address the determinants of health and downstream initiatives to deal with both the unfinished agenda and the emerging challenges related to noncommunicable diseases, injuries, and mental diseases.
5. Establish effective mechanisms to monitor and ensure quality of care, both in its technical and its interpersonal dimensions.
6. Improve the training, availability, and distribution of human resources for health.
7. Strengthen the key health system functions (stewardship, financing, and delivery) to expand choice, increase effectiveness and efficiency, promote equity, and improve accountability for results.
8. Design policies to strengthen the role of the state as the key steward of the national health system.
9. Invest in information systems, health systems research, and rigorous assessment.
10. Promote the introduction of transparency and accountability procedures, and stimulate the participation of civil society organizations in the design, implementation, and monitoring of universal health coverage initiatives.

Source: J. Frenk, "Leading the Way Towards Universal Health Coverage: A Call to Action," *The Lancet* (72).

Power and Transformative Change

For both the SDGs and the UHC initiatives, a fundamental question, raised by the authors of *Who's Got the Power* (68), still stands, and that is to what extent will

> the global community, particularly those who hold power in countries both rich and poor, have the courage to make the decisions, to challenge the status quo, to guide the transformative change necessary to advance the vision. Will those whose lives and health depend on these actions have the space, the leverage, and the will to demand and ensure that they do?

In Project Syndicate, a World Opinion blog, Professor Jeffrey Sachs cites John F. Kennedy, who observed that "man holds in his mortal hands the power to abolish all forms of human poverty and all forms of human life" (72).

He adds that "those words speak to us today with special urgency" as we have now entered 'The Age of Sustainable Development' in terms of "a way of understanding the world and a way to help save it." Moreover, he predicts that "sustainable development will become the organizing principle for our politics, economics, and even ethics in the years ahead," and that "all of us will have to become leaders in sustainable development in our homes, communities, and countries."

To this end, Professor Sachs contends solving problems "of climate change, water, energy, transportation, and education" necessitates engaging with "all stakeholders—government, communities, experts, business, and non-governmental organization." It also requires a better understanding of the world and SDGs, which could be greatly facilitated through "open on-line education" reaching thousands of cities and close to 200 nations.

Moving toward the SDGs and UHC is vital for both the planet and its people, including the "powerful global actors in pursuit of other interests" (71).

For all of us there really is no other choice—in the long run.

4.3 THE GLOBAL STRATEGY AND PLAN OF ACTION ON PUBLIC HEALTH, INNOVATION, AND INTELLECTUAL PROPERTY (GSPA-PHI): "GRAPPLING" WITH PRINCIPLES AND PRACTICE

Rationales for a Global Strategy

Access to high quality and affordable medicines, restricted to a large extent by "limited generic availability and limited price reductions" (72), remains a critical issue. The problems are exacerbated, particularly in developing nations where more than a billion people "don't have access to healthy water . . . 2.6 billion lack basic sanitation." It is estimated that "2.2 million children die each year because they are not immunized" (73).

The WHO's formal attempts to increase the availability of affordable, safe, and effective medicines globally go back to an information document on intellectual property, innovation, and public health. The paper was prepared by the WHO Secretariat for the 56th WHA in 2003 and established the Commission on Intellectual Property Rights, Innovation and Public Health (CIPIH) in early 2004. The CIPIH reported in 2006 on this issue and made "some 60 detailed recommendations." Its central recommendation, however, was that "WHO should develop a Global Plan of action to secure enhanced and sustainable funding for developing and making accessible products to address diseases that disproportionately affect developing countries" (74).

On May 27, 2006, the WHA adopted a resolution setting up an Intergovernmental Working Group on Public Health, Innovation and Intellectual Property (IGWG-PI). The remit of the IGWG was to "draw up a global strategy and plan of action in order to provide a medium-term framework." More specifically, the main aims of the strategy were to "promote new thinking on innovation and access to medicines," and provide "a medium-term framework (2008–2015) for securing an enhanced and sustainable basis for needs driven essential health R&D relevant to diseases which disproportionately affect developing countries, proposing clear objectives and priorities for R&D, and estimating needs in this area" (75).

In setting out its rationale for a global strategy, the WHO reminded member states that:

Today, 4.8 billion people live in developing countries and 2.7 billion of them (43%) live on less than US$ 2 a day. Communicable diseases account for half of the diseases in these countries. Recognizing that poverty, among other issues, affects access to health products and that new products to fight diseases affecting developing countries are needed; governments, the pharmaceutical industry, foundations, NGOs and others have undertaken initiatives in recent years to address these challenges. But more needs to be done. (76)

Further to the discussion in Chapter 2.0, Africa is a case in point as it is "home to 11% of the world's population" but "consumes less than 1% of global health expenditure. Yet, it carries 25% of the world's burden of disease." As identified in the final report, *Strengthening Pharmaceutical Innovation in Africa: Designing Strategies for National Pharmaceutical Innovation: Choices for Decision Makers and Countries"* (77), major contributors to this disease burden include:

- Diseases of poverty, such as malnutrition
- Infectious diseases, such as HIV/AIDS, malaria, diarrheal diseases, pneumonia
- Neglected tropical diseases (NTDs)
- Diseases predominantly affecting African populations, such as sickle cell disease
- NCDs, which are on the rise

Moreover, the authors observe "these problems are further compounded by limited access to safe, effective, quality and affordable medicines, vaccines and diagnostic tools. Africa's disease burden raises concern on many fronts. Unmet health needs result in high morbidity and mortality, creating a vicious cycle of poverty, disease, disability and death."

Adoption of the strategy and implementation plan after lengthy and intense negotiations was considered a landmark agreement, especially with its focus on "improving availability, affordability, access and acceptability of existing products."

At its most fundamental, it was widely agreed that "the inaccessibility of medicines for poor people directly impedes the realization of human rights including the right to health and development, and enjoyment of the benefits of scientific progress. It poses an insurmountable obstacle to meeting the health-related Millennium Development Goals at a time when the scope of health challenges for low and middle income countries is even growing wider." In essence, the strategy is in response to a global "lack of innovation and access to existing health products, including diagnostics, vaccines and Medicines" (78).

Reviewing the IGWG-PI report from a right-to-development perspective (79), Lisa Forman, then a Canadian Institutes of Health Research postdoctoral fellow, concluded that medicines are "by far the most significant tool that society possesses to prevent, alleviate and cure disease." She further noted that "access to medicines bears particularly upon individual abilities to alleviate poverty, since pharmaceuticals can consume fifty to ninety percent of out of pocket expenditures for the poor in developing countries." It is for these reasons that the strategy and action plan represents "a critical milestone in global policy on medicines in developing countries" because it aims to "meaningfully reform the failure of global R&D to produce medicines for diseases of the developing world, and to ensure more public health consistent applications of intellectual property rights protected under international and bilateral trade agreements."

Problem Focus

The crux of the problem that the global strategy seeks to address relates to the pricing of pharmaceuticals "determined by patents, which are protected internationally under the World Trade Organization's (WTO) Agreement on Trade-Related Aspects of Intellectual Property Rights (TRIPS)." And, while "the TRIPS agreement requires WTO members to provide twenty-year exclusive patent protection to pharmaceuticals preventing non-consensual use," TRIPS also provides "flexibilities," which permit "limits to exclusive patent protection to enable governments to meet public-health needs" (80).

Along with international treaties with public health implications, the discussion also "includes various regional and bilateral trade arrangements with IP provisions impacting public health, technology transfer efforts to resource-poor countries, data-exclusivity provisions and patent linkage requirements in drug registration systems, and new and innovative forms of IP management (such as the Medicines Patent Pool)" (80). Ms 't Hoen cites the international president of Médecins sans Frontières (Doctors Without Borders), who in her view "hit the nail on the head":

> At the moment medical innovation is financed through high drug prices backed up by patent monopolies, at the expense of patients and governments in developing countries who cannot afford those prices. Instead of seeking to abuse the patent system by bending the rules and claiming ever longer patent protection on older medicines, the pharmaceutical industry should focus on real innovation, and governments should develop a framework that allows for medicines to be developed in a way that also allows for affordable access. (81)

It is precisely because of these dynamics and complexities that "the appropriate role of innovation and intellectual property (IP) in global public health is a controversial issue. Discussion is one-sided, with potential benefits advocated by industry in stark contrast to condemnation by certain civil society players" (80).

Plan of Action

Responsibility for implementation of the Global Strategy and Plan of Action on Public Health, Innovation and Intellectual Property (GSPOA) strategy was "scattered among a large number of diverse stakeholders, including governments, academia, civil society organizations, international intergovernmental organizations and the private sector" (82). The strategy's principal objectives and priorities include

> setting the R&D needs-based agenda, for promoting innovation and associated skills in countries, for sharing existing knowledge through technology transfer initiatives and the management and application of intellectual property rights according to pro-public health criteria, to improve access to medicines as well as to mobilize resources. (82)

More specifically, the strategy document sets out eight elements that will be implemented to ensure "access and innovation for needed health products and medical devices," with particular emphasis on the needs of developing countries.

Adopting both a short-term and a long-term approach, including a "3D" innovation cycle or process (Figure 4.6)—discovery, development, and delivery—key elements of the global strategy and plan of action encompass:

Element 1—Prioritizing Research and Development Needs
Element 2—Promoting Research and Development
Element 3— Building and Improving Innovative Capacity
Element 4—Transfer of Technology
Element 5—Application and Management of Intellectual Property Rights
Element 6—Improving Delivery and Access
Element 7—Promoting Sustainable Financing Mechanisms
Element 8—Establishing Monitoring and Reporting Systems

Implementation of the global strategy began in November 2008 when the WHO established an Expert Working Group (EWG) on R&D Financing, consisting of 24 experts and policy makers. The remit was to examine "current financing and coordination of research and development, as well as proposals for new and innovative sources of funding to stimulate research and development related to Type II and Type III diseases and the specific R&D needs of developing countries in relation to Type I diseases" (83).

The EWG submitted its report in 2010, concluding that "there is no global coordination of research and development for major diseases," and that "the global health research and innovation system" is "highly fragmented" (84).

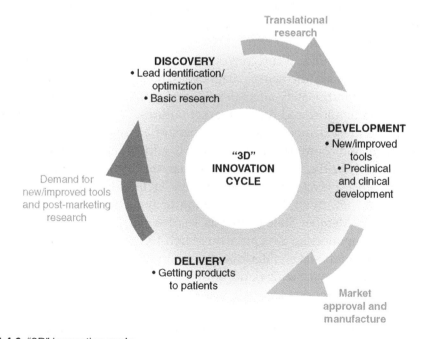

FIGURE 4.6 "3D" innovation cycle.

Source: World Health Organization. *Report of the Commission on Intellectual Property Rights, Innovation and Public Health* (74). http://www.who.int/intellectualproperty/documents/thereport/ENPublicHealthReport.pdf

Furthermore, members highlighted that

the system has four kinds of failure that lead to lack of effective treatment for health problems and the persistence of health disparities within and between populations: failures in science, in the market, in public health and in collecting, consolidating, interpreting and disseminating information.

To address these failures, the EWG proposed "a globally coordinated approach to research and development." Pursuant to their report, a Consultative Expert Working Group (CEWG) on Research and Development: Financing and Coordination was established by the WHO in 2010. Its principal task was to deepen "the analysis and work done by the previous Expert Working Group on Research and Development: Coordination and Financing (EWG)." The CEWG reported in April 2012 that the time had "come for Member States to begin a process leading to the negotiation of a binding agreement on R&D relevant to the health needs of developing countries" (85).

In addition, the CEWG recommended that countries should consider specific spending targets, a global health observatory, and invest in capacity building and technology transfer to developing countries as well as development of human resources and expertise, institutional and infrastructure development, and sustainable medium–long-term collaborations.

In March 2013, the WHO Director-General issued a follow-up to the CEWG report in preparation for the 66th WHO. The request from the Executive Board was for the Director-General to facilitate through regional consultations and broad engagement of relevant stakeholders the implementation of a few health research and development demonstration projects to address identified gaps that disproportionately affect developing countries, particularly the poor, and for which immediate action can be taken (86).

Moreover, the Executive Board conveyed that "these projects should aim at developing health technologies (medicines, diagnostics, medical devices, vaccines, etc.) for diseases that disproportionately affect developing countries and for which identified R&D gaps remain unaddressed due to market failures." The board also emphasized that "the projects must demonstrate effectiveness of alternative, innovative and sustainable financing and coordination approaches to address identified R&D gaps."

On January 24, 2014, the board "requested the Director-General to consider *the 7+1 demonstration projects in the order identified by the Global Technical Consultative Meeting of Experts*" (87) with "the participation of the Chair and Vice-Chair of the CEWG as well as 1 Member State (acting as an observer) from each of the six WHO regions." A follow-up meeting took place on March 10, 2014, which approved four out of eight proposals, with stakeholder discussions in early May. The 67th WHO held May 18–24, 2014 in Geneva, Switzerland, adopted "more than 20 resolutions on public health issues of global importance" (88), including:

- Giving "a firm go-ahead on the implementation of innovative health R&D demonstration projects" by establishing "a pooled fund for voluntary contributions towards R&D for diseases of the poor"

- Approving "WHO's strategy to help countries improve access to essential medicines"
- Continuing "to ensure the quality, safety and efficacy of selected priority essential medicines, diagnostics and vaccines and future progressive transition of prequalification to networks of strengthened regulatory authorities"
- Supporting "capacity-building for health technology assessment in countries"

An official WHO NGO side session, hosted by The Council on Health Research for Development (COHRED), along with the Global Health Council (GHC), the Drugs for Neglected Diseases *initiative* (DND*i*), the International AIDS Vaccine Initiative (IAVI), and the Global Health Technologies Coalition (GHTC), explored "the role of R&D in the post-2015 development agenda." More specifically, the NGO "focused on the critical role of global health research, development and innovation (R,D&I) in accelerating and sustaining progress in global health within the post-2015 development framework." Panelists included representatives from "high-, low-, and middle-income country stakeholders from both public and private sectors" (89). In their "Statement on the Role of Research and Innovation to Achieve Health for All and Sustainable Development," they assert that

> Achieving equitable and sustainable Health for all requires continued support for Research and Development for new or improved medicines, vaccines, diagnostics, devices and other health tools that work for and are accessible to those most in need. Continuous investment of human and financial resources in science, technology and innovation to improve health *and equity is essential to achieve economic and social development.*

Along with additional funding, the panelists also call for "a commitment to the development and implementation of policies that facilitate capacity building, collaboration and knowledge and technology sharing." Considered collectively, the panelists argue for "strong political leadership, as well as international and multi-sectoral collaboration" in order to achieve "innovations in healthcare and delivery."

In conclusion, it is reassuring that after more than a decade of deliberations, some progress on a global scale is finally being made in terms of priority science-based demonstration projects, although developments are still at Element 1 stage of the eight-phase "3D" innovation cycle, depicted in Figure 4.6.

However, the fundamental purpose of a global strategy and plan of action identified in 2003 for WHO to "develop a Global Plan of action to secure enhanced and sustainable funding for developing and making accessible products to address diseases that disproportionately affect developing countries" (74) seems to have been largely set aside. Moreover, the R&D aspirations of COHRED and others, mentioned earlier, reflect similar observations made by the IGWG-PI in 2006.

On the other hand, establishing a pooled fund at the Special Programme for Research and Training in Tropical Diseases (TDR) is a step in the right direction, especially if the fund is informed by the WHO Call for Proposals that highlights the need for projects that (a) "address identified R&D gaps that disproportionally affect developing countries, particularly the poor, and for which immediate action can be taken";

(b) use "collaborative approaches"; (c) "promote the de-linkage of the cost of R&D from product price"; and (d) are able to secure "innovative and sustainable financing mechanisms" (86).

However, the time—over 10 years—that this "chain of decision-making" has taken is a cause for concern at least on three fronts: Taking pediatric HIV/AIDS, as one example, in sub-Saharan Africa, health workers see "1,200 new paediatric infections every day" and "over 85% of infected children are not treated" (72). Dengue vaccine development is rightfully given priority in the list of demonstration projects, but what about long-standing "diseases of poverty," such as malnutrition, and other infectious diseases, referenced earlier?

Second, there is no mention of R&D projects in relation to NCDs, discussed extensively in Chapter 2.0. The latter were identified as representing high risk as long ago as 2002 when the then Director-General Dr. Gro Brundtland observed that "risks more commonly associated with wealthy nations . . . are becoming more prevalent in the developing world where they create a double burden on top of the infectious diseases that still afflict poorer countries" (90).

Although, as mentioned in Sections 4.1 and 4.2 of this chapter, there are examples that the world is moving forward on a number of important fronts, difficult challenges with NCDs, malnutrition, unemployment, and poverty remain in developing nations and are increasing in developed countries as austerity takes hold and uncertain economies flounder.

Third, the demonstration projects, while appropriately identifying treatments for diseases that are rampant in poorer nations, do not, as advocated by the CEWG, include projects that would help poorer countries "build and improve innovative capacity," in particular to "meet research and development needs for health products" and support "investment by developing countries in human resources and knowledge bases, especially in education and training including in public health."

It appears that in some quarters global agreements count for little. As one example, "in June 2013, member states of the World Trade Organisation (WTO) agreed to extend the transition period for adherence to the Agreement on Trade-Related Aspects of Intellectual Property Rights (TRIPS) among least-developed countries (LDCs)" (91).

Yet, this welcome agreement—though arguably 2021 is too short a time scale—was challenged recently in South Africa where the Director-General, joined by many other nations—"Namibia, Brazil, Cuba, India, Argentina, Nigeria, Bolivia, and Zimbabwe"—condemned "a global pharmaceutical campaign aimed at derailing efforts by the South African government to revise its intellectual property policy" (92). According to one African nation, this situation was "an unfortunate attack on a sovereign state and an attack on the right to life in the interest of profit."

WHO Director-General Margaret Chan, in her support of the South African position "while developed countries remained silent on the subject," was adamant, noting that "I have been following the event in South Africa and I was very struck by what is happening and I have said so in other contexts and I will repeat again: no government should be intimidated by interested parties for doing the right thing in public health." And, thanking "governments for their solidarity with South Africa," she stated that "nobody should be denied access to life-saving intervention or medical products."

In conclusion, four direction-setting questions might benefit from further discussion or debate:

1. When will the global strategy and plan of action (GSPOA) actually begin to make a difference to the lives of people who urgently need "access to essential, high-quality, effective and affordable medical products?"
2. To what extent are the pharmaceutical companies collaborating with each other to hasten the supply of generic drugs to benefit those in greatest need and investing ever-increasing profits in R&D?
3. Since NCDs and conditions are now the main cause of mortality and morbidity in both the developed and developing worlds, what preventive measures are being advocated at global, regional, and national levels?
4. How could WHO decision-making be expedited given life-enhancing population needs and delays (for example, the costly, >US$100 million, GSPOA reviews agreed for 2015–2018; 93,94)?

Dr. Gro Brundtland, former Norway prime minister and WHO Director-General, reminded us several years ago that "in our interconnected and interdependent world, bacteria and viruses travel almost as fast as e-mail messages and money flows" (90). Furthermore, although we can respond effectively and efficiently to viral epidemics when our own lives are threatened, as the severe acute respiratory syndrome (SARS) outbreak demonstrated in 2002 and the Ebola virus in West Africa more recently, our responses to severe "human" crises—conflicts, poverty, sanitation, including access to appropriate medicine—are much too slow. We have the data, knowledge, technology, products, and dedicated professionals, but, more often than not, we are reluctant to assert our collective political will—despite many decision makers personally acknowledging that basic human rights and lives are at stake.

However, in terms of access to medication, a turning point may be in sight as demonstrated "by the landmark decision of the Indian Supreme Court in Delhi to uphold India's Patents Act in the face of a seven-year challenge by Swiss pharmaceutical company Novartis" (91). The ruling "is a major victory for patients' access to affordable medicines in developing countries, according to Médecins Sans Frontières (MSF)" and "marks the first time that a decision by a judicial authority from a developing country in the area of intellectual property has been so closely scrutinised and so extensively commented upon internationally" (95).

In "Not Just a Tragedy: Access to Medications as a Right under International Law" (96), Alicia Yamin, a lecturer at Harvard's Department of Global Health and Population, and director, Program on the Health Rights of Women and Children, reminds us that access to medications is not just "a matter of fundamental human rights." But, that it

> forces us to face the momentous suffering and loss of life that is occurring in developing countries due to HIV/AIDS, tuberculosis, malaria, and other diseases as not just a tragedy; it forces us to recognize it as a horrific injustice.

4.4 THE WORLD BANK: HISTORICAL PERSPECTIVES AND REVITALIZING FOR THE 21ST CENTURY

Created in 1944, the World Bank Group and the International Monetary Fund (IMF), which focuses on surveillance, technical assistance, and lending programs, are both headquartered in Washington DC, United States. Founded at the United Nations Monetary Conference in Bretton Woods, New Hampshire, United States, their main mission was to promote reconstruction and economic recovery after World War II. The mandates of these institutions (known as the "Bretton Woods Institutions") have now "evolved to focus on promoting global economic stability and poverty reduction" (96).

The World Bank Group (WBG), owned member companies, now comprises "five complementary but distinct entities" (97): the World Bank, consisting of two development institutions—the International Bank for Reconstruction and Development (IBRD) and the International Development Association (IDA). In addition, the bank is closely affiliated with three other organizations—the International Finance Corporation (IFC); the Multilateral Investment Guarantee Agency (MIGA); and the International Centre for Settlement of Investment Disputes (ICSID), all of whom support reducing global poverty, guided by the achievements and targets of the present MDGs and future SDGs.

A common aim that weaves through these corporate entities is "fostering a climate conducive to investment, job creation and sustainable growth" (see Table 4.3). Moreover, the WBG "seeks to empower the less fortunate, through the provision of health services, education and other social services, to enable them to participate in development" (97).

In its early years, other than its first loan to France in 1945, the World Bank's main loan recipients were non-European nations as Europe received aid from the post-WW2 Marshall Plan, which came into effect in 1947. Priority loans were then allocated "for the construction of income-producing infrastructure, such as seaports, highway systems, and power plants, that would generate enough income to enable a borrower country to repay the loan" (97).

Further, in the 1950s, many developing countries could not afford (and still are unable to—as shown in Figure 4.7) the high interest rates provided by the IBRD and established the IDA to alleviate poverty "by providing interest-free credits and grants," offering "25- and 40-year interest-free loans" and focusing "on countries with annual per capita income of less than US$1,195. . . . eighty-two countries are currently eligible to receive IDA resources" (98).

Figure 4.8 clearly illustrates the extent to which sub-Saharan African countries are taking advantage of IDA loans, with sub-Saharan Africa receiving "the largest share of IDA resources in 2013—US$8.2 billion, or 50.3 per cent of total commitments," whereas "South Asia received 25.1 per cent of new commitments, totalling US$4.1 billion."

Emphasis in the 1980s was on "lending to service Third-World debt, and structural," investing "in education, health, and infrastructure. The loans can also be used to modernize a country's financial sector, agriculture, and natural resources management as the bank's goal is to "bridge the economic divide between poor and rich countries, to turn rich country resources into poor country growth and to achieve sustainable poverty reduction" (99).

TABLE 4.3 Background Information and a Glimpse of World Bank Operations (2013)

	WORLD BANK				
	1. INTERNATIONAL BANK FOR RECONSTRUCTION AND DEVELOPMENT (IBRD)	2. INTERNATIONAL DEVELOPMENT ASSOCIATION (IDA)	3. INTERNATIONAL FINANCE CORPORATION (IFC)	4. MULTILATERAL INVESTMENT GUARANTEE AGENCY (MIGA)	5. INTERNATIONAL CENTER FOR SETTLEMENTS OF INVESTMENT DISPUTES (ICSID)
Established	1944	1960	1956	1988	1966
Members	188	172	184	179	149 full members; 157 signatories
Mission	Broad poverty reduction	Broad poverty reduction	Promote sustainable private sector investment to help support economic growth, reduce poverty, and improve people's lives	Promote foreign direct investment in developing countries to help support economic growth, reduce poverty, and improve people's lives	Facility to resolve international investment disputes

Source: Department of Finance Canada, *Canada at the IMF and World Bank Group 2012-2013* (Part 2 of 3; 98). http://www.fin.gc.ca/bretwood/bretwd12-02-eng.asp

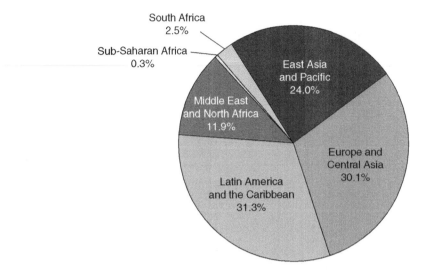

FIGURE 4.7 The International Bank for Reconstruction and Development (IBRD) lending (2013, by region).

Source: Department of Finance, *Canada at the IMF and World Bank Group 2012–2013: Part 2 of 3* (98). www.fi n.gc.ca/bretwood/bretwd12-02-eng.asp

To achieve this goal, as summarized in Box 4.5, the bank focuses on six strategic priorities (100):

As indicated, a key mechanism in meeting these goals has historically been through the provision of loans and grants, which have been gradually decreasing after reaching their peak in 2010 at US$58.01, dropping to US$43.01 in 2011, US$35.34 in 2012, US$31.55 in 2013, and US$19.09 in 2014 (Table 4.4).

Considering its own accounts, while other operations increased slightly from 2012 and 2013, the IBRD lending decreased by approximately US$5 billion.

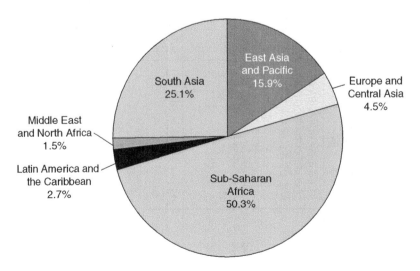

FIGURE 4.8 The International Development Association (IDA) lending (2013, by region).

Source: Department of Finance, *Canada at the IMF and World Bank Group 2012–2013: Part 2 of 3* (98). www.fi n.gc.ca/bretwood/bretwd12-02-eng.asp

BOX 4.5

World Bank Strategic Priorities

1. Overcome poverty by **spurring growth** in the poorest countries, focusing on **Africa.**
2. Offer **reconstruction** to poor countries emerging from war, a major contributing factor to extreme poverty.
3. Provide a **customized development** solution to help middle-income countries overcome problems that could throw them back into poverty.
4. Spur governments to act on preventing **climate change**, controlling **communicable diseases** (especially HIV/AIDS and malaria), managing **international financial crises**, and promoting **free trade.**
5. Work with the League of Arab States to improve **education,** build **infrastructure**, and provide **microloans** to small businesses in the Arab world.
6. **Share** its **expertise** with developing countries, and its knowledge with anyone via reports and its interactive online database.

As shown in Figure 4.9, China's investments in Africa have been growing as it seeks "to secure access to the continent's raw materials and new markets for its manufactured goods" (102). According to Fitch Ratings, State-owned "Export-Import Bank of China (EXIM) extended $12.5 billion more in loans to sub-Saharan Africa in the past decade than the World Bank, and lent about $67.2 billion to the world's poorest region between 2001 and 2010 (mostly for infrastructure projects) compared with the World Bank's $54.7 billion" (102). Regular recipients of these loans since 1994 have included Angola, Ethiopia, Nigeria, and Sudan with a more even distribution across other African countries currently. China's loans are also popular because of "absence of political strings, competitive interest rates and flexible repayment schedules" (102).

TABLE 4.4 Lending Commitments by Year

WORLD BANK GROUP COMMITMENTS FISCAL YEARS 2013 AND 2012 (IN US$ BILLIONS)		
WORLD BANK GROUP	FY 13*	FY 12*
IBRD	15.2	20.6
IDA	16.3	14.7
IFC+	18.3	15.4
MIGA	2.8	2.7
TOTAL	52.6	53.4

*Preliminary and unaudited numbers.
+Own account only. Excludes nearly $6.5 billion in FY13 and nearly $5 billion in FY12 in funds mobilized from other investors.
Source: The World Bank, "In Fight to Improve Lives of the World's Poor, World Bank Group Delivers Nearly $53 Billion in Support to Developing Countries in FY13 (2013; 101).

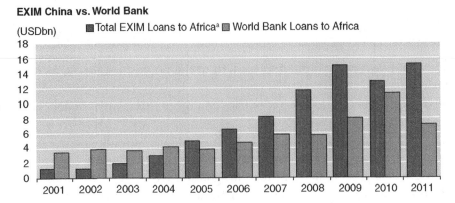

^a Fitch estimates derived from sources stated

FIGURE 4.9 Export-Import Bank of China (EXIM) investment versus World Bank.
Source: Fitch Ratings, 2015. https://www.google.co.uk/search?q=Fitch+%2B+EXIM+China+vs.+World+Bank&espv=2&biw=8
19&bih=542&source=lnms&tbm=isch&sa=X&ved=0CAcQ_AUoAmoVChMlho2Q7KDTxwlV6hTbCh0G6w0g&dpr=1.25#imgrc=f
KmMGd7vpvGJrM%3A

Global Projects

Along with a sizeable loan program, the World Bank is widely involved in global projects with a view to poverty reduction and economic development. From 1947 onwards there have been 11,874 projects in 172 countries (103). Three in particular may demonstrate the reach and impact of the types of projects in which the bank engages:

- Global burden of disease (GBD) studies
- Governance and anticorruption strategies
- The World Bank Institute (WBI) and the Global Development Learning Network (GDLN)

Global Burden of Disease (GBD) Studies

The original GBD study (1993), funded by the World Bank, in collaboration with the Institute for Health Metrics and Evaluation (IHME) (104), culminated in a landmark report, "World Development Report 1993: Investing in Health" (105). The study, which "had a profound impact on health policy and agenda setting," globally "served as the most comprehensive effort up to that point to systematically measure the world's health problems, generating estimates for 107 diseases and 483 sequelae (non-fatal health consequences related to a given disease) in eight regions and five age groups" (105).

Building on the 1993 study, GBD 2010, funded by the Bill & Melinda Gates Foundation, "provided estimates for 291 diseases and injuries, 1,160 sequelae, and 67 risk factors for 20 age groups and both sexes for 1990, 2005, and 2010, across 187 countries and 21 regions" (106). Recognizing the need for monitoring trends and continuously updating data, on September 4, 2013, the World Bank and IHME—led by Dr. Chris Murray, IHME Director, and Dr. Timothy Evans, Director of Health, Nutrition, and Population at the World Bank—"launched a series of six regional reports based on the findings from the latest Global Burden of Disease (GBD 2010) study" (106).

The reports, one for each World Bank region—the Middle East and North Africa, Latin America and Caribbean, East Asia and Pacific, sub-Saharan Africa, South Asia, and Europe and Central Asia—incorporate "cutting-edge measurement science; and benefitted from input from nearly 500 co-authors worldwide as well as philosophers, ethicists, and economists." As with GBD 1993, the GBD 2010 and subsequent reports will without a doubt have an equally "profound impact on health policy and agenda setting" worldwide in the next few years.

Improving Governance and Controlling Corruption

A significant project initiated in 2007 relates to the World Bank's adoption of the "Strengthening World Bank Group Engagement on Governance and Anticorruption (GAC)" strategy (107). The project's main aim is "to help develop capable and accountable states and institutions that can devise and implement sound policies, provide public services, set the rules governing markets, and combat corruption, thereby helping to reduce poverty."

The need for the project is premised on several factors: One is that the "quality of governance and development outcomes" are largely determined by "the behaviour of the state and other stakeholders such as private and financial institutions." The World Bank's experience in influencing governance and corruption has been "mixed," and generally ad hoc rather than applying a systematic and consistent approach across all nations. A priority is to expand private sector engagement and engaging more "systematically with a broad range of stakeholders at project and global levels" (108).

The strategy is also groundbreaking in the way the bank "does business"— "providing incentives to managers and staff, addressing staffing, skills and resource needs, strengthening country monitoring and evaluation systems, partnerships with institutions such as universities, civil society groups and businesses, in particular to support research on causes and effects of governance and corruption and their links to growth and developments" (108,109).

In 2012 the bank updated the strategy further to feedback from countries and online consultations, culminating in the report, "Strengthening Governance, Tackling Corruption: The World Bank's Updated Strategy and Implementation Plan" (110). The report recognizes the "changing global landscape" since adopting the original strategy in 2007, emphasizing the "fundamental changes [that] have swept the world." In particular, the report highlights "the implications of the 2008 financial crisis . . . continuing uncertainties in the Euro-zone, nervousness in the financial markets, and fragile growth in most of the developed world."

In terms of ways forward, the bank will continue to focus its attention on systematically mainstreaming "governance and anticorruption elements," especially "systems and processes within countries" which "are the key; drivers of development," underpinned by "transparency and openness." Among other priorities, the 2012 strategy underscores the need for "a more rigorous framework to measure results" and "for the private and financial sector to identify a practical set of indicators to measure institutional quality."

Locations of currently debarred firms

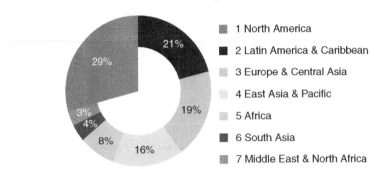

- 1 North America
- 2 Latin America & Caribbean
- 3 Europe & Central Asia
- 4 East Asia & Pacific
- 5 Africa
- 6 South Asia
- 7 Middle East & North Africa

FIGURE 4.10 Locations of currently debarred firms.

Source: Freshfields Bruckhaus Deringer, 2015 (111). http://www.freshfields.com/uploadedFiles/SiteWide/Knowledge/ World%20Bank%20sanctions%20-%20blacklist%20revisted.pdf

Two fundamental precepts that guide the strategy emphasize, first, "the Bank's policy of zero tolerance, wherever instances of fraud and corruption are discovered [and taking] decisive measures . . . to address these," as demonstrated by the number of debarments in Figure 4.10; and second, the World Bank's insistence to remain "absolutely committed to the highest fiduciary standards in all its work."

Given the data (Figure 4.10) provided by the international law firm Freshfields Bruckhaus Deringer (112), the 2007 strategy with further robust tightening in 2013 is making a difference. It is noteworthy that "as much as $40bn worth of aid is estimated to have been stolen from some of the poorest nations in the world over the last seven years." Sectors involved, in descending order of the World Bank's investigations for debarment, include "health care, water, energy, transport and agriculture," which "make up 2/3" of the total (111). Most debarred firms are now in North America, Latin America, and the Caribbean, followed by the East Asia and Pacific regions. Africa, South Asia, and the Middle East account for only 8%, 4%, and 3% of debarred firms, respectively.

More specifically, according to *The Economist* (112), by September 2013, "the international lending organization debarred over 250 individuals and companies from participating in projects that it finances—as many as over the previous seven years combined." It is salient that "the bank invested around $200 billion in poor countries in the past five years, and conducted over 600 investigations of misconduct."

Significant progress is being made not only on the loan front but also in terms of improving global governance. Tactics that are being rolled out include embedding "governance dimensions into global programs," strengthening "training programs of staff," establishing "clear accountabilities that align resources with priorities," and integrating "monitoring and reporting into regular management systems" (110).

The World Bank Institute (WBI) and Global Development Learning Network (GDLN)

Established on March 11, 1955, with the support of the Rockefeller and Ford Foundations, the WBI, formerly known as Economic Development Institute (EDI), "creates learning opportunities for countries, World Bank staff and clients, and people committed to poverty reduction and sustainable development" (113). With an overarching role as a "global connector of knowledge, learning and innovation for poverty reduction," its work program includes training, policy consultations, and the creation and support of knowledge networks related to international economic and social development. Four major strategies underpin its approaches to development problems: innovation for development, knowledge exchange, leadership and coalition building, and structured learning.

Complementing the work of the WBI and initiated in June 2000, a third major undertaking is the GDLN, which is "a global partnership of over 120 learning centers (GDLN Affiliates) that offer the use of advanced information and communication technologies to people working in development around the world" (114). The services of the GDLN, which collaborates with universities, think tanks, governmental organizations, and others, range from "the design of learning events, the management and coordination of learning events, the development of learning and support materials, and event promotion and marketing services."

Priorities of the GDLN include health, poverty reduction, private sector development, urban development, economics, social development, education, entrepreneurship, environment, technology, population, development finance, and governance.

Recognized in 80 nations as "a channel for development learning and knowledge exchange," what seems to make the GDLN unique is its global capacity to promote learning and change and "its innovative way of doing development cooperation," creating "opportunities to connect with and engage in joint development learning and knowledge exchange activities." Another strength is offering "its members an attractive platform to work with like-minded development learning organizations around the world" (114). At the regional level, the network is governed by its Regional Associations, while the GDLN Board is responsible on the global level. The GDLN also offers "direct access to local, regional and international development experts, provide tailored learning programs, knowledge or technical assistance programs, and state of the art facilities for multi-point videoconferencing and internet-based learning."

There are now more than 500 access points around the world, including affiliates "as diverse as the Korean Development Institute, the Kenya School of Government—eLearning and Development Institute, the Energy and Resource Institute in India or the Instituto Tecnológico de Monterrey in Mexico." Remarkably, these affiliates "put on 1000+ learning multi-country dialogues and virtual conferences." Key topics of universal concern have focused on issues such as the food crisis, climate change, water, HIV/AIDS, the China–Africa partnership, and women's dialogue (114).

Corporate Scorecard

"Designed to provide a snapshot of the Bank's overall performance, including its business modernization, in the context of development results," the Corporate Scorecard initiated a print version in 2011 and an electronic version for user access in 2012 (115). The scorecard "monitors performance, including its business modernization, in the context of development results" (116).

Summary of the Corporate Scorecard

FIGURE 4.11 The World Bank Corporate Scorecard (2013).

Source: World Bank Corporate Scorecard, September, 2013. (116). https://openknowledge.worldbank.org/bitstream/handle/10986/15780/WBCorporateScorecard_Sept13.pdf?sequence=1

Extending this approach to all operations (Figure 4.11), the scorecard "presents a high-level view" and "monitors, at an aggregate level, whether the Bank is functioning efficiently and adapting itself successfully (Tier IV), and whether it is managing its operations and services effectively (Tier III) to support countries in achieving results (Tier II) in the context of global development progress and priorities (Tier I)." One of its strengths is that "it facilitates strategic dialogue between Management and the Board on progress made and areas that need attention."

The summary (Figure 4.11) shows that scores for Tier III, Development Outcomes and Operational Effectiveness, show improvement or are on track for Knowledge Activities and Use of Country Systems but indicates that further improvement in areas related to Development Outcomes Rating and Lending Operations is required. Similarly, the scores for Tier IV show improvement for Resources and Alignment and Sector Actions Related to Post-Crisis Directions, but there do not yet appear to be clear trends with regard to Capacity and Skills and Business Modernization.

Future Considerations From National Members

Canada's Minister of Finance, the Honorable James M. Flaherty, observes that "Achieving the World Bank Group's goals by 2030 will not be an easy task. In his view, the World Bank will need to ensure that every dollar contributed through replenishments and trust funds is linked to demonstrable results within an environment of continuous learning and improvement," in particular strengthening "results-based management frameworks, both at the corporate and project level" (97).

Former Colombian finance minister Professor José Antonio Ocampo, one of the three contenders for heading the World Bank, in a recent analysis of World Bank operations argues that "a basic lesson the bank needs to re-learn is never to impose any particular development model," especially in the light "of the changes now taking place in the world economy," calling for "adapting the World Bank to the changing needs of the international community," and "in some cases, taking the institution back to its roots" (117). While progress has been made across all nations, he reminds us "over two billion people still live in poverty," and "countries have made very uneven economic and social progress, and the development gap between rich and poor countries remains unacceptably wide." For Professor Ocampo "this means that the World Bank's core mandate must remain that of reducing poverty," focusing "not only on the poorest countries . . . but also to middle-income countries, where most of the world's poor are in fact to be found." A priority is to "design mechanisms that mainstream equity objectives into economic policy-making . . . by putting the creation of quality jobs at the centre of the development agenda, favouring small producers, developing universal education, health and social protection systems and eradicating gender inequalities."

Furthermore, in his analysis, he advocates inter alia "changes in its lending practices," and "a fresh focus on industrialisation and technological upgrading." Echoing some of the rationales for refocussing the purpose of the post-2015 SDGs discussed in Section 4.1, he stresses the need to "address the enormous long-term global challenges of our time," including "the food and financial crises" and "the visible effects of climate change."

Revitalizing the World Bank

After becoming the 12th president of the World Bank Group on July 12, 2012, but the first "elected" president, one of Dr. Jim Yong Kim's chief aims "has been the development of a 'Common Vision' to bring efficiency and focus to the operations of the World Bank Group." To this end, "In Spring 2013, the Development Committee of the Boards of Governors of the World Bank Group and the International Monetary Fund (IMF) endorsed two overarching goals to guide the direction of the World Bank Group through the next phase of the global economic recovery and beyond" (118).

- Eradicating extreme poverty within a generation, by reducing the percentage of people living with less than US$1.25 a day to no more than 3% by 2030; and
- Promoting shared prosperity, by ensuring that economic growth and job creation are experienced by those in the bottom 40% of the population in every country.

These aims, replacing "a complex 'matrix' structure with a system of expertise-based 'global practices' " (119), which were also likely informed by the 2013 World Bank Corporate Scorecard, triggered the bank's first restructuring in nearly two decades. The essence of the plan, according to Annie Lowrey, a reporter in the Washington bureau of *The New York Times*, is "to keep it relevant at a time when even the poorest countries can easily tap the global capital markets" (120).

The reporter cites an interview with Dr. Kim where he defended his strategy, indicating that the "overarching goal is to break down the bank's regional 'silos' " . . . thereby discouraging, "for instance, experts who are working on mobile banking in sub-Saharan Africa from sharing best practices with experts handling the same issue in Central America." In response, and in an effort to strengthen "moving knowledge throughout the world," he "has created more than a dozen new global practices (121)—on subjects like trade, health and infrastructure" impacting 15,000 bank employees effective from July 1, 2014. In addition, "to squeeze out inefficiencies" $400 million have been cut from the bank's operating budget. These changes have caused considerable turmoil among employees, although many agreed that there was little choice as the "bank is losing its relevance in middle-income countries . . . India, China and Brazil," where there are now a "lot of indigenous capacity to analyze and make technical decisions."

Beginning July 1, 2014, the overarching goal, in line with the bank's website, "is to build on the current country-driven model, but to strengthen this with a more systematic, evidence-based and selective approach to goal setting and prioritization" (122). The bank's technical staff will report to the new global practices, each headed by global practice senior directors. In addition, the bank's new "Standardized Operational Risk-Rating Tool" will be implemented "to help the World Bank consistently assess and monitor risks across all operational instruments and country programs." Simplifying bureaucratic procedures and practices is also in the cards (119).

Achieving the bank's goals in the next 15 years may depend on at least four key factors:

- Building on strengths (Knowledge Activities, Country Systems, Resources and Alignment, Post-Crisis Directions [114]) and projects that are making a difference (e.g., GBD studies, governance and anticorruption strategies, the WBI, and the GDLN).

- Ensuring, as Professor José Antonio Ocampo contends, that "the creation of quality jobs" is placed "at the centre of the development agenda, favouring small producers, developing universal education, health and social protection systems and eradicating gender inequalities" (117). As discussed in Section 4.1, these goals, targets, and indicators could be optimized if the bank's overarching mission focused on supporting "Global Social Justice," underpinned by peace, security, and human rights. This broader remit would make its continuing contribution unique among emerging global financial infrastructures (e.g., Brazil, Russia, India, China, and South Africa [BRICS] and the China-led Asian Infrastructure Investment Bank).

- Making certain, as Canada's Minister of Finance, the Honorable James M. Flaherty, purports, "that every dollar contributed through replenishments and trust funds is linked to demonstrable results within an environment of continuous learning and improvement" (116). This challenge may be tested with the recent announcement that the bank has "committed a record-breaking $15.3 billion to sub-Saharan Africa's development in fiscal year 2014 (July 2013 to June 2014) supporting shared prosperity in the Region and focusing on increased efforts to reduce poverty." According to Makhtar Diop, World Bank Vice President for the Africa Region, the bank is "stepping up the momentum to innovate and think big in order to help our clients achieve their development goals" (123).

- Implementing managerial practices that foster people-centered decision making or engagement at all levels, thereby facilitating communication, teamwork, trust, and help collectively to fulfill the bank's central mission: to save and improve the lives of billions of people by strengthening the effectiveness of its operations.

Thinking Globally but Acting Locally

The Ebola crisis may have demonstrated the ongoing contribution to global health and well-being that the World Bank is capable of making. With reduced trade and travel, estimates of negative financial impact stand at $32.6 billion "for the immediate affected area alone that assumes containment by the end of the year," and much worse to come if the disease spreads more widely. The rationale for overseas aid is made clear as "relatively small amounts of investment in African healthcare and infrastructure could save the West incalculable costs further down the line" (124).

Perhaps the focus of World Bank projects in the immediate future should not just lie with "thinking big," especially in the light of urbanization, food security, and climate change, but also making sure that population health and well-being, especially involving poor communities, remains the top priority. Containing problems like Ebola and, most importantly, preventing or at least reducing the severity of pandemics from occurring and spreading in the first place should be the first order of business for the World Bank.

In collaboration with national and local stakeholders, the establishment of community health or "wellness" center networks, staffed by trained community health workers with appropriate medical support across sub-Saharan African and South-East Asian nations, as examples, might be a good start.

The centers might be patterned after existing models whose missions generally focus on "health promotion, harm reduction, education, community development, and advocacy, and through the provision of medical, nursing, dental and counseling services" (125).

Objectives for such a network might include the capacity to "offer services and programs necessary to improve the quality of life; help secure a wider primary health care system that provides services and programs that are accessible, meet the changing health needs of communities and people"; and "respect, honour and integrate traditional and alternative approaches to health care." While the two main World Bank aims—"eradicating extreme poverty" and "promoting shared prosperity" by 2030— are commendable, some may agree that unless concrete measures are taken to reduce or prevent diseases—mostly in poor but also in middle- and high-income nations— that can threaten the lives of people globally, neither of these two well-intentioned goals will be achievable.

Following a meeting in 2013 of the World Bank's 188 member countries in Washington DC (126), Dr. Kim reiterated his resolve to address his current priorities: "ending extreme poverty by 2030, boosting shared prosperity for the bottom 40% of the population in developing countries and implementing a set of sweeping internal reforms that aim to make the organization more efficient and better able to achieve its ambitious goals."

Reinforcing Professor José Ocampo's earlier assertion (117), Dr. Kim's mantra "no one size fits all—every country is different" might just pave the way for the World Bank Group to adopt much-needed, unique approaches to address poverty and prosperity globally, thereby also strengthening "cross-fertilization of knowledge between the regions" (125,126,127).

4.5 TOWARD A REVITALIZED WORLD ORDER: "THE END OF AN ERA BUT A SALUTARY WAKE UP CALL"? (126)

Two potentially global "game-changing" developments appear to be in line with this thinking, both of which are welcomed with "open arms" by Dr. Kim as president of the World Bank, as they could impact significantly on making a real difference in fighting global poverty, which, the World Bank estimates, presently requires around US$1.5 trillion in infrastructure (128). One of these is the establishment of an Asian Infrastructure and Investment Bank (AIIB), led by China, "with more than 50 countries and regions signing on as members" from "New Zealand to Denmark" (128), including, among others, the UK, France, Israel, Germany, and Italy (129); the other is the creation of the New Development Bank (NDB), established by the BRIC nations (Brazil, Russia, India, and China; 130).

Larry Summers, a former U.S. Treasury secretary and one of the most influential American economists, contends that March 2015 "may be remembered as the moment the United States lost its role as the underwriter of the global economic system" (130). Underscoring that "the global economic architecture needs substantial adjustment" and advocating "a comprehensive review of the US approach to global economics," his leadership precepts include the establishment in the United States of "a bipartisan foundation at home" that is "free from gross hypocrisy" and is "restrained in the pursuit of self-interest" (130). His global priorities call for approaches that serve "the working class in industrialized nations (and rising urban populations in developing ones)" as well as "the promotion of investment rather than austerity." His rationale is that "we may be headed into a world where capital is abundant and deflationary pressures are substantial" and that it may be time to shift from "the present system" that "places the onus of adjustment on 'borrowing' countries" to "a symmetric system, with pressure also placed on 'surplus' countries." In Professor Summer's view, given the magnitude of the financial issues facing the world, there can be little doubt that the new financial structures—AIIB and the NDB—are "probably the most obvious sign yet that the global financial system is in for a giant reset" (130).

While these readjustments may prove difficult for the West, they are unavoidable in a world that is in need of rebalancing given population densities and inequities in terms of safety and security, health and education, employment opportunities, labor market shortages, and rising consumer demands. Ideally, these financial reorientations will enable closer collaboration between regional and national economic as well as political forces, informed, above all, by genuine societal needs rather than government, corporate, or individual self-interests or externally driven hegemonic interventions.

To this end, the top priority, as advocated by the World Bank, for all stakeholders—including the new banks—should surely be on "ending extreme poverty" for close to 1 billion people and boosting "shared prosperity for the bottom 40% of the population in developing countries" (126), underpinned by internal reforms. Dr. Kim affirms that meeting these targets by 2030, which complement the UN's post-2015 SDGs, may become "humankind's most significant and memorable achievement" (129). Indeed, for many they represent a vital step toward global social justice, peace, and ensuring basic human rights for all that has eluded previous attempts, including the 192 nations' MDGs initiative.

However, realizing these ambitions in the next 15 years or so will necessitate what seems to be the view of a growing number of pundits, overcoming "transnational paralysis." For many it is time to hold those who for their own gains "behave with savage abuse of power towards their fellow citizens" (131), rather than the good of the country or the world, to account.

Marcus Tannenberg, project coordinator at The Quality of Government Institute at the University of Gothenburg, Sweden, argues that, alongside business, government, and civil society, universities have a central role to play in this regard (132). That is, "instead of continuing with an educational system that produces individuals geared towards narrow self-interests, higher education should adopt a more holistic approach, with an emphasis on ethics and anti-corruption in an attempt to promote social capital and subsequently health and development." A beginning step "encapsulated in the Poznan Declaration" (133), endorsed by the 68 member universities of the Compostela Group of Universities, the World University Consortium, the World Academy of Art and Science, and Transparency International, is the development

"more ethically aware and critically thinking graduates," who would be in a better position to confront corrupt and "morally reprehensible behaviour" that undermines global population health and well-being.

How the new world economic order and the roles played by the World Bank, the AIIB, and the NDB evolve will emerge only over time.

In light of China's growing "feverishly speculative market," the fear that "the markets will become a lot more volatile, and a lot more politically directed" (134) appears to be well founded. One consequence may be that it will take more years than anticipated before the Shanghai Index will be replacing the Dow "as the key driver of global sentiment" and before the Shanghai Composite "will be where the biggest companies are traded" (135).

Finally, in their briefing paper on implementing "AAAA (Addis Ababa Action Agenda) and the Sustainable Development Goals (SDG) Vision and Words with Action" (137), Lanre Rotimi, director, and Peter Orawgu of the International Society for Poverty Elimination/Economic Alliance Group, highlight the findings of the International Development Cooperation Scorecard (1960–2009). Over the past 6 years, they observe that lessons relating to global Development Cooperation appear to have not been learned, and that the grades given for Policy, Program, and Project evaluation and implementation were rated "flawed" or "failed" by a majority of the respondents— that is, by most of the 193 UN Member States.

Unless "village to global stakeholders jointly agree to face new directions and adopt new priorities," by "addressing all fundamental issues," the authors of the briefing contend, the same scores may be repeated in 2030 and 2059. For them, the key lies in "transformative change" at local, national, regional, and global levels, guided by the UN SDGs, indicators, and corresponding criteria (2016–2030).

In 2015, the stage has been set for global initiatives to promote "integrated approaches to the interconnected economic, social and environmental challenges confronting the world" (136) and now really is the time to turn "vision and words into action," thereby sustaining the planet and its people for future generations.

REFERENCES

1. Zagaya. United Nation's Millennium Development Goals. http://www.zagaya.org/news-and-events/united-nations-millenium-development-goals/. Accessed April 10, 2014.
2. United Nations. *We can end poverty: Millennium Development Goals and beyond 2015.* New York: United Nations; 2013. http://www.un.org/millenniumgoals/. Accessed January 20, 2014.
3. Waage J, Banerji R, Campbell O, et al. The Millennium Development Goals: A cross-sectoral analysis and principles for goal setting after 2015. *Lancet.* 2010;376:991–1023.
4. United Nations. *The Millennium Development Goals report 2009.* http://www.un.org/millenniumgoals/pdf/MDG_Report_2009_ENG.pdf. Accessed February 12, 2014.
5. United Nations. *The Millennium Development Goals report 2015.* http://www.un.org/millenniumgoals/2015_MDG_Report/pdf/MDG%202015%20rev%20(July%201).pdf. Accessed July 27, 2015.
6. World Health Organization. *The World Health report 2013: Research for universal health coverage.* Geneva: World Health Organization. http://apps.who.int/iris/bitstream/10665/85761/2/9789240690837_eng.pdf. Accessed March 6, 2014.
7. Ridley M. Start spreading the good news on inequality. *The Times.* June 2, 2014. http://www.thetimes.co.uk/tto/opinion/article4106191.ece. Accessed June 3, 2014.

8. Laaser U, Brand H. Global health in the 21st century. *Glob Health Action*. 2014;7:23694. http://www.globalhealthaction.net/index.php/gha/article/view/23694/html. Accessed May 12, 2014.

9. Laaser U, Epstein L. Threats to global health and opportunities for change: A new global health. *Public Health Reviews*. 2010;32:54–89.

10. *Worldometers. Real time world statistics*. http://www.worldometers.info/. Accessed June 1, 2014.

11. Kabeer N, Woodroffe J. *Challenges and achievements in the implementation of the Millennium Development Goals for women and girls from a European Union perspective*. Brussels: European Parliament; 2014. http://www.europarl.europa.eu/RegData/etudes/etudes/join/2014/493049/IPOL-FEMM_ET%282014%29493049_EN.pdf. Accessed May 29, 2014.

12. UNICEF. *A Promise Renewed: A Global Movement to End Preventable Child Deaths*. New York, NY: UNICEF; 2013. http://www.unicef.org/lac/Committing_to_Child_Survival_APR_9_Sept_2013.pdf. Accessed February 20, 2014.

13. World Health Organization. *Every newborn endorsed by World Health Assembly*. Geneva: World Health Organization; 2014. http://www.who.int/pmnch/media/events/2014/wha/en/index4.html. Accessed May 26, 2014.

14. United Nations Foundation. Every woman every child. http://www.unfoundation.org/what-we-do/campaigns-and-initiatives/every-woman-every-child/. Accessed May 12, 2014.

15. World Health Organization. Draft action plan. Every newborn: An action plan to end preventable deaths. http://www.who.int/maternal_child_adolescent/topics/newborn/enap_consultation/en/. Accessed May 5, 2014.

16. UNAIDS. *Global report-UNAIDS report on the global AIDS epidemic 2013*. http://www.unaids.org/sites/default/files/en/media/unaids/contentassets/documents/epidemiology/2013/gr2013/UNAIDS_Global_Report_2013_en.pdf. Accessed October 15, 2013.

17. Prince Mahidol Award Conference. *Report on the 2014 Conference on Transformative Learning for Health Equity*. http://www.healthprofessionals21.org/images/PMAC2014_Report.pdf. Accessed May 26, 2014.

18. Avert. HIV prevention strategies. http://www.avert.org/abc-hiv-prevention.htm. Accessed April 25, 2014.

19. Universitas 21. Fourth U21 European UNMDG Workshop, June 13–14, 2014, University College Dublin, Dublin, Ireland. http://www.u21mdg4health.org/others/?page=news_and_announcements&id=15. Accessed June 10, 2014.

20. Sen A. *The idea of justice*. Cambridge, MA: Harvard University Press; 2009.

21. Bishaw T. What public health actions are needed in African countries to confront health inequalities? Paper presented at: 7th Public Health Association of South Africa conference; 2011. http://www.phasa.org.za/what-public-health-actions-are-needed-in-african-countries-to-confront-health-inequalities/. Accessed February 14, 2014.

22. Griggs D. Redefining sustainable development. http://www.project-syndicate.org/commentary/redefining-sustainable-development-by-david-griggs. Accessed November 13, 2013.

23. Murphy T. Did the Millennium Development Goals make things better? http://www.humanosphere.org/basics/2013/08/did-the-millennium-development-goals-make-things-better/. Accessed March 12, 2014.

24. UN News Centre. At UN-backed conference, African countries adopt sustainable development measures. http://www.un.org/apps/news/story.asp?NewsID=42897&Cr=sustainable+development&Cr1=#.U6A6TyhRLSh. Accessed September 14, 2012.

25. Griggs D, Stafford-Smith M, Gaffney O, et al. Sustainable Development Goals for people and planet. *Nature*. 2013;495:305–307. http://sustainabledevelopment.un.org/content/documents/844naturesjournal.pdf. Accessed April 20, 2013.

26. National Resources Defense Council (NRDC). Sustainable Development Goals: "Focus areas" require commitments for a new global partnership. http://www.simplesteps.org/es/aggregator/sources/1. Accessed February 28, 2014.

27. International Institute for Sustainable Development (IISD). OWG issues interim progress report. http://post2015.iisd.org/news/owg-issues-interim-progress-report. Accessed September 16, 2013.

28. Kenny C, Pritchett L. Promoting Millennium Development ideals: The risks of defining development down. Washington, DC: Center for Global Development. http://www.cgdev.org/sites/default/files/Pritchett_Kenny_md-ideals_wcvr.pdf. Working Paper 338. Accessed May 20, 2014.

29. The World We Want. Dialogues on implementation of the post-2015 development agenda. http://www.beyond2015.org/who-we-are. Accessed June 5, 2014.

30. Beyond 2015. Who we are. http://www.beyond2015.org/who-we-are. Accessed June 5, 2014.

31. Beyond 2015. Values and targets. http://www.beyond2015.org/document/beyond-2015-values-and-targets. Accessed June 5, 2014.

32. United Nations. Have your say. The United Nations wants to know what matters most to you. http://vote.myworld2015.org/. Accessed April 15, 2014.

33. Conciliation Resources. Development, peace and security: The post-2015 framework. http://www.c-r.org/comment/development-peace-and-security-post-2015-framework-teresa-dumasy. Accessed February 13, 2014.

34. The World Bank. *World development report 2011: Conflict, security, and development.* Washington, DC: The World Bank; 2011. https://openknowledge.worldbank.org/handle/10986/4389. Accessed November 2, 2013.

35. Saferworld. Bringing peace into the post-2015 development framework: A joint statement by civil society organisations. http://www.saferworld.org.uk/resources/view-resource/692-bringing-peace-into-the-post-2015-development-framework. Accessed October 20, 2012.

36. War Child International. About us. http://www.warchild.org.uk/. Accessed November 20, 2013.

37. Turnbull B. Why emergency help is never enough in war-torn countries. *Toronto Star.* December 6, 2011. http://www.thestar.com/life/2011/12/06/why_emergency_help_is_never_enough_in_wartorn_countries.html. Accessed April 24, 2014.

38. Lueddeke G. Towards an integrative post-2015 sustainable development goal framework: Focusing on global justice–peace, security and basic human rights. *South East European Journal of Public Health 2014;* doi: 10.12908/SEEJPH-2014-26. http://www.seejph.com/wp-content/uploads/2014/06/2014-06-25-George-Lueddeke.pdf. Accessed November 20, 2014.

39. Jay J. A global UHC campaign launches: Health for all post-2015. http://healthforallcampaign.org/2014/03/04/a-global-uhc-campaign-launches-health-for-all-post-2015/. Accessed June 15, 2014.

40. Independent Research Forum (IRF) 2015. *Post2015: Framing a new approach to sustainable development.* http://sustainabledevelopment.un.org/content/documents/1690IRF%20Framework%20Paper.pdf. Accessed June 2, 2014.

41. Frenk J, Chen L, Bhutta ZA, et al. Health professionals for a new century: Transforming education to strengthen health systems in an interdependent world. *Lancet.* 2010;375:1137–1138.

42. Ottersen OP, Dasgupta J, Blouin C, et al. *The political origins of health inequity: Prospects for change.* Oslo, Norway: The Lancet-University of Oslo Commission on Global Governance for Health; 2014.

43. Lueddeke GR. *Transforming medical education for the 21st century: Megatrends, priorities and change.* London, United Kingdom: Radcliffe Publishing; 2012.

44. World Health Organization. *Health workforce governance and leadership capacity in the African region: Review of human resources for health units in the ministries of health.* Geneva, Switzerland: WHO Document Production Services; 2012.

45. Chelsey Canavan C, Lemma A. Waking up to universal health coverage in Kenya. https://www.msh.org/blog/2014/05/05/waking-up-to-universal-health-coverage-in-kenya. Accessed June 10, 2014.

46. Chan M. Best days for public health are ahead of us, says WHO Director-General. Paper presented at: World Health Assembly, Geneva. http://www.who.int/dg/speeches/2012/wha_20120521/en/

47. WHO. *World Health report 2013: Research for universal health coverage.* Geneva: WHO. http://www.who.int/whr/2013/report/en/. Accessed September 20, 2013.

48. Rockefeller Foundation, Save the Children, the United Nations Children's Fund (UNICEF) and the World Health Organization (WHO). *Universal health coverage: A commitment to close the gap.* https://everyone.savethechildren.net/sites/everyone.savethechildren.net/files/library/Universal_health_coverage.pdf. Accessed June 15, 2013.

49. Institute of Health Metrics and Evaluation. *Financing global health 2012: The end of the golden age?* http://www.healthdata.org/policy-report/financing-global-health-2012-end-golden-age. Accessed February 20, 2013.

50. Jacobs F. The patients per doctor map of the world. *Big Think.* http://bigthink.com/strange-maps/185-the-patients-per-doctor-map-of-the-world. Accessed March 15, 2008.

51. Tjadens F, Weilandt C, Eckert, J. *Mobility of health professionals.* Berlin Heidelberg: Springer-Verlag; 2013. http://www.springer.com/medicine/book/978-3-642-34052-9. Accessed November 17, 2013.

52. WHO. *Countdown to 2015 Decade report (2000–2010): Taking stock of maternal, newborn and child survival.* http://www.countdown2015mnch.org/documents/2010Report/2010_Report_nopro-files.pdf. Accessed February 28, 2014.

53. Ahoobim O, Altman D, Garrett L, Hausman V, Huang Y. *The new global health agenda: Universal health coverage.* New York, NY: Council on Foreign Relations. http://www.cfr.org/health-policy-and-initiatives/new-global-health-agenda/p27998. Accessed May 15, 2012.

54. Palmer K. *A brief history: Universal health care efforts in the US.* http://www.pnhp.org/facts/a-brief-history-universal-health-care-efforts-in-the-us. Accessed December 19, 2012.

55. Abel-Smith, B. Social welfare; Social Security; benefits in kind; national health schemes. In: *The new Encyclopaedia Britannica.* 15th ed. Chicago, IL: Encyclopaedia Britannica; 1987.

56. World Health Organization. *The world health report: Health systems financing: The path to universal coverage: World health report 2010.* Geneva: WHO. http://www.who.int/whr/2010/en/. Accessed January 19, 2013.

57. WHO. Universal health coverage: Report by the Secretariat. http://apps.who.int/gb/ebwha/pdf_files/WHA66/A66_24-en.pdf. Accessed April 15, 2013.

58. WHO. WHO/World Bank ministerial-level meeting on universal health coverage. http://www.who.int/mediacentre/events/meetings/2013/uhc_who_worldbank_feb2013_background_document.pdf. Accessed April 14, 2014.

59. WHO. Health financing for universal coverage. http://www.who.int/health_financing/en. Accessed June 20, 2014.

60. Stuckler D, Feigl AB, Basu S, McKee M. *The Political Economy of Universal Health Coverage.* Background paper for the First Global Symposium on Health Systems Research, 16–19 November 2010, Montreaux, Switzerland. http://www.pacifichealthsummit.org/downloads/UHC/the%20political%20economy%20of%20uhc.PDF

61. WHO. Global Health Observatory (GHO) data. http://www.who.int/gho/health_financing/out_pocket_expenditure/en/. Accessed September 6, 2015.

62. Dayrit MM, Braichet J-M. *Increasing access to health workers in remote and rural communities through improved retention: Global recommendations.* Geneva: WHO; 2010.

63. Global Health Workforce Alliance. *The Global Health Workforce Alliance strategy 2013–2016. Advancing the health workforce agenda within universal health coverage.* Geneva: WHO; 2012. http://www.who.int/workforcealliance/knowledge/resources/ghwastrat20132016/en/index.html. Accessed December 10, 2012.

64. WHO. Sixty-Sixth World Health Assembly closes with concern over new global health threat. http://www.who.int/mediacentre/news/releases/2013/world_health_assembly_20130527/en/. Accessed June 19, 2012.

65. WHO. WHO Initiative on transformative scale-up of health professional education. http://www.who.int/hrh/education/planning/en/. Accessed December 5, 2012.

66. Jay J. Rallying for UHC (IV): Aligning UHC with civil society priorities. http://www.msh.org/blog/2013/10/02/rallying-for-uhc-iv-aligning-uhc-with-civil-society-priorities. Accessed April 15, 2014.

67. Governance Lancet/Oslo Commission: The political origins of health inequity. http://pnhp.org/blog/2014/02/11/lancetoslo-commission-the-political-origins-of-health-inequity/. Accessed February 28, 2014.

68. United Nations. *Who's got the power? Transforming health systems for women and children.* London: Earthscan; 2005. http://www.unmillenniumproject.org/reports/tf_health.htm. Accessed July 25, 2006.

69. Obi FA. The national health bill: After ten years in the making is an end in sight? *Nigeria Health Watch.* http://nigeriahealthwatch.com/the-national-health-bill-after-ten-years-in-the-making-is-an-end-in-sight. Accessed November 5, 2014.

70. Collins P. Yes he could. Obama is a truly great president. *The Times.* November 7, 2014; p. 27 (Opinion).

71. Sachs JD. The age of sustainable development. http://www.project-syndicate.org/commentary/jeffrey-d--sachs-proposes-a-new-curriculum-for-a-new-era. Accessed July 2, 2014.

72. Frenk J. Leading the way towards universal health coverage: A call to action. *Lancet.* 2014. S0140-6736(14)61467-7. http://www.thelancet.com/journals/lancet/article/PIIS0140-6736(14)61467-7/fulltext. Accessed October 10, 2014.

73. 't Hoen E. The medicines patent pool increasing access, stimulating innovation consultative expert group on R&D financing and coordination; April 5–7, 2011. WHO, Geneva. http://www.google.co.uk/webhp?nord=1#nord=1&q=ellen+t+hoen+medicines+patent+pool%2Bpower+point. Accessed March 27, 2012.

74. WHO. Public health innovation and intellectual property rights: *Report of the Commission on Intellectual Property Rights, Innovation and Public Health.* http://www.who.int/intellectualproperty/documents/thereport/ENPublicHealthReport.pdf. Accessed April 3, 2014.

75. WHO. Intergovernmental Working Group on Public Health, Innovation and Intellectual Property (IGWG). http://www.who.int/phi/igwg/en/. Accessed April 3, 2014.

76. WHO. The global strategy and plan of action on public health, innovation and intellectual Property. http://www.who.int/phi/implementation/phi_globstat_action/en/. Accessed April 3, 2014.

77. African Union, Council on Health Research for Development, and NEPAD Agency of the African Union, with contributions from the George Institute for International Health. *Strengthening Pharmaceutical Innovation in Africa. Designing strategies for national pharmaceutical innovation: Choices for decision makers and countries.* Final study report: Revised after review by the Extended Technical Committee on the Pharmaceutical Manufacturing Plan for Africa, 2010. http://www.nepad.org/system/files/str.pdf. Accessed April 4, 2014.

78. WHO. The global strategy and plan of action on public health, innovation and intellectual property: A new roadmap to reconcile needs-driven health innovation and access to essential medicines innovation and access to essential medicines http://apps.who.int/medicinedocs/documents/s18255en/s18255en.pdf. Accessed April 5, 2014.

79. Forman L. *Desk review of the intergovernmental working group on public health, innovation and intellectual property from a right to development perspective.* Geneva: WHO; 2009. http://www2.ohchr.org/english/issues/development/right/docs/A-HRC-12-WG2-TF-CRP5-Rev1.pdf. Accessed April 6, 2014.

80. Mackey TK, Liang BA. Promoting global health: Utilizing WHO to integrate public health, innovation and intellectual property. *Drug Discov Today.* 2012;17(23–24):1254–1257. http://www.ghd-net.org/sites/default/files/Promoting%20global%20health.pdf. Accessed April 6, 2014.

81. 't Hoen E. A victory for global public health in the Indian Supreme Court. *J Public Health Policy.* 2013;34(3):370–374. http://www.ipwatch.org/weblog/wpcontent/uploads/2013/05/NovartisCase_IndianSupremeCourt_tHOEN.pdf. Accessed April 10, 2014.

82. Nannei C. Monitoring and evaluation framework for the global strategy and plan of action on public health, innovation and intellectual property. http://www.who.int/phi/implementation/ME_framework_and_implementation_final.pdf. Accessed April 5, 2014.

83. WHO. *Research and development to meet health needs in developing countries: Strengthening global financing, and coordination.* Executive summary: Report of the Consultative Expert Working Group on Research and Development: Financing and Coordination. http://apps.who.int/gb/ebwha/pdf_files/WHA66/A66_23-en.pdf; http://www.who.int/phi/CEWG_Report_Exec_Summary.pdf. Accessed April 4, 2014.

84. WHO. The Expert Working Group on Research and Development Financing. *Research and development: coordination and financing: report of the expert working group.* http://www.who.int/phi/documents/RDFinancingwithISBN.pdf. Accessed April 4, 2014.

85. WHO. World Health Organization's consultative expert working group on R&D financing releases its report. http://www.keionline.org/node/1398. Accessed April 4, 2014.

86. WHO. Call for proposals for R&D demonstration projects. http://www.wpro.who.int/health_research/call_proposal_2013/en/. Accessed February 6, 2014.

87. WHO. CEWG demonstration projects: Background and process. http://www.who.int/phi/implementation/cewg_background_process/en/. Accessed June 10, 2014.

88. WHO. World Health Assembly closes. http://www.who.int/mediacentre/news/releases/2014/WHA-20140524/en/. Accessed May 28, 2014.

89. Council on Health Research for Development (COHRED). Health research for all: The role of innovation in global health in the post-2015 development framework. http://blog.cohred.org/95/health-research-for-all-the-role-of-innovation-in-global-health-in-the-post-2015-development-framework. Accessed June 2, 2014.

90. Brundtland GH. Public health challenges in a globalizing world. *Eur J Public Health.* 2005;15(1):3–5. doi: 10.1093/eurpub/cki134. Accessed May 9, 2014.

91. Make medicines while the sun shines. http://www.thehindu.com/todays-paper/tp-opinion/make-medicines-while-the-sun-shines/article5066286.ece. Accessed April 5, 2014.

92. Saez C. WHO chief: No government should be intimidated for doing "right thing" in public health. http://www.ip-watch.org/2014/01/24/who-director-general-no-government-should-be-intimidated-by-interested-parties. Accessed February 2, 2014.

93. TWN Info Service on Intellectual Property Issues. WHO public health, innovation and IP programme to be reviewed. http://www.twn.my/title2/intellectual_property/info.service/2015/ip150507.htm. Accessed June 24, 2015.

94. Hutchinson E, Benson Droti, Gibb D, et al. *Translating evidence into policy in low-income countries: lessons from co-trimoxazole preventive therapy.* http://www.who.int/bulletin/volumes/89/4/10-077743/en/. Accessed March 25, 2011.

95. Menghaney L. Court decision on Novartis case: A victory for access to medicines in developing countries. *Mededcins Sans Frontieres.* April 1, 2013. http://www.equinetafrica.org/newsletter/index.php?srch=medicines&page=54. Accessed July 4, 2014.

96. Yamin AE. Not just a tragedy: Access to medications as a right under international law. *Boston Univ Int Law J.* 2003;21(2):325–372.

97. The World Bank. World Bank history. http://go.worldbank.org/2GIYUD9KB0. Accessed February 20, 2014.

98. Department of Finance Canada. *Canada at the IMF and World Bank Group 2012-2013: Part 2 of 3.* http://www.fin.gc.ca/bretwood/bretwd12-02-eng.asp

99. The World Bank. About us. http://go.worldbank.org/M1UXTKWPI0. Accessed May 20, 2014.

100. The World Bank. Supporting the World Bank Group's strategic directions. http://siteresources.worldbank.org/WBI/Resources/WBIAR08StrategicDirections.pdf

101. The World Bank. In fight to improve lives of the world's poor, World Bank Group delivers nearly $53 billion in support to developing countries in FY13. http://www.worldbank.org/en/news/press-release/2013/07/23/improve-lives-world-poor-world-bank-group-delivers-nearly-53-billion-support-developing-countries-fy13

102. Cohen M. China's EXIM lend more to sub-Sahara Africa than World Bank, Fitch says. *Bloomberg*. December 28, 2011. http://www.bloomberg.com/news/articles/2011-12-28/china-exim-loans-to-sub-sahara-africa-exceed-world-bank-funds-fitch-says

103. The World bank. Projects and operations. http://www.worldbank.org/projects?lang=es

104. WHO. National burden of disease studies. http://www.who.int/healthinfo/nationalburde-nofdiseasemanual.pdf

105. The World Bank (Open Knowledge Repository [OKR]). *World development report 1993: Investing in health*. https://openknowledge.worldbank.org/handle/10986/5976

106. Institute for Health Metrics and Evaluation (IHME). GBD history. http://www.healthdata.org/gbd/about/history

107. The World Bank. Implementation plan for strengthening World Bank Group engagement on governance and anticorruption. http://web.worldbank.org/WBSITE/EXTERNAL/TOPICS/EXTGOVANTICORR/0,,contentMDK:21447906~pagePK:210058~piPK:210062~theSitePK:3035864,00.html

108. The World Bank. Governance and anti-corruption—FM sector approach. http://web.world-bank.org/WBSITE/EXTERNAL/PROJECTS/EXTFINANCIALMGMT/0,,contentMDK:21387886~menuPK:4438069~pagePK:210058~piPK:210062~theSitePK:313218,00.html

109. The World Bank Group. Strengthening World Bank Group engagement on governance and anticorruption http://siteresources.worldbank.org/PUBLICSECTORANDGOVERNANCE/Resources/GACStrategyPaper.pdf

110. The World Bank. *Strengthening governance, tackling corruption: World Bank updated strategy and implementation plan*. http://web.worldbank.org/WBSITE/EXTERNAL/TOPICS/EXTPUBLICSECTORANDGOVERNANCE/0,,contentMDK:23086675~pagePK:210058~piPK:210062~theSitePK:286305,00.html

111. Freshfields Bruckhaus Deringer. *Location of currently debarred firms*. http://www.freshfields.com/en/insights/The_War_On_Corruption_%E2%80%93_World_Bank_Fights_Back/. Accessed February 20, 2015.

112. The Economist. World Bank robbers. http://www.economist.com/blogs/graphicdetail/2013/09/daily-chart-12. Accessed January 20, 2014.

113. The World Bank. *Corporate responsibility*. http://crinfo.worldbank.org/wbcrinfo2012/node/19

114. Global Learning Development Network. About GDLN. http://gdln.org/files/GDLN_Backgrounder-may2011.pdf

115. Global Learning Development Network. Connecting the world through learning. http://gdln.org/engage-gdln

116. The World Bank. Corporate scorecard 2013 indicators. http://data.worldbank.org/data-catalog/corporate-scorecard-2013-indicators

117. Ocampo JA. My blueprint for streamlining the World Bank. *Europe's World*. http://europes-world.org/2012/10/01/my-blueprint-for-streamlining-the-world-bank/#.U8PvOZRdVf8. Accessed June 14, 2014.

118. The World Bank. The World Bank Group goals end extreme poverty and promote shared prosperity. http://www.worldbank.org/content/dam/Worldbank/document/WB-goals2013.pdf

119. Igoe M. Jim Kim's moment of truth. *Devex*. July 1, 2014. https://www.devex.com/news/jim-kim-s-moment-of-truth-83759

120. Lowrey A. World Bank revamping is rattling employees. *The New York Times*. http://www.nytimes.com/2014/05/28/business/international/world-bank-revamping-is-rattling-employees.html?_r=0

121. World Bank appoints leaders of global practices, CAO. *The Bretton Wood Projects.* http://www.brettonwoodsproject.org/2014/05/world-bank-appoints-senior-leadership-global-practices-cao

122. The World Bank. Interim guidelines for systematic country diagnostic (SCD). http://www-wds.worldbank.org/external/default/WDSContentServer/WDSP/IB/2014/03/11/000333037_2014031116. Accessed March 11, 2014.

123. The World Bank. Africa: World Bank Group sets historic new development financing record for region. http://www.worldbank.org/en/news/press-release/2014/07/07/africa-world-bank-group-sets-historic-new-development-financing-record-for-region

124. Warner J. Ebola is a global economic crisis and requires a global response. *The Telegraph.* http://www.telegraph.co.uk/finance/comment/jeremy-warner/11154697/Ebola-is-a-global-economic-crisis-and-requires-a-global-response.html. Accessed October 12, 2014.

125. Queen West Community Health Centre. Central Toronto Community Center. http://www.ctchc.com/. Accessed October 15, 2014.

126. EY Dynamics. *The man with the plan.* http://www.ey.com/Publication/vwLUAssets/Dynamics_collaborating_for_growth/$FILE/EY-Dynamics%20African%20dawn.pdf. Accessed Janury 20, 2014.

127. The World Bank. *Indicators.* http://data.worldbank.org/indicator#topic-11. Accessed March 15, 2015.

128. The World Bank. *Speech by World Bank Group President Jim Yong Kim: Ending extreme poverty by 2030: The final push.* http://www.worldbank.org/en/news/speech/2015/04/07/speech-by-world-bank-group-president-jim-yong-kim-ending-extreme-poverty-final-push. Accessed April 10, 2015.

129. Black S. It just happened: "The moment the United States lost its role...". http://www.sovereignman.com/trends/it-just-happened-the-moment-the-united-states-lost-its-role-16693/. Accessed April 10, 2015.

130. Summers L. *Time US leadership woke up to new economic era.* http://www.ft.com/cms/s/2/a0a01306-d887-11e4-ba53-00144feab7de.html#axzz3WvES2WnK. Accessed April 6, 2015.

131. Phillips M. *Putin has us dancing like a puppet on a string.* http://www.thetimes.co.uk/tto/opinion/columnists/article4409128.ece. Accessed April 13, 2015.

132. Tannenberg M. *Role of universities in the fight against corruption.* http://www.universityworldnews.com/article.php?story=20141113110707222. Accessed November 20, 2014.

133. Compostela Group. *The Poznan Declaration.* http://revistas.usc.es/gcompostela/en/activities/PoznanDeclaration.html. Accessed April 14, 2015.

134. The Telegraph. Three ways the rise of China's stock market will change the world. http://www.telegraph.co.uk/finance/china-business/11533317/Three-ways-the-rise-of-Chinas-stock-market-will-change-the-world.html. Accessed April 15, 2015.

135. Lynn M. Get ready for Shanghai to become the world driver. *The Daily Telegraph.* Tuesday 14 April 2015: B2.

136. Rotimi L and Orawgu P. Briefing #6: How to Implement AAAA and SDG Vision and Words with Action? Akure, Nigeria: International Society for Poverty Elimination and the Economic Alliance Group, 2015. http://developmentchangechampions.blogspot.co.uk/2015_08_30_archive.html. Accessed September 5, 2015.

5.0

Contemporary Approaches
to Public Health Issues

5.1 FROM HORIZONTAL POLICIES TO SHARED SOCIETAL GOALS

The importance of intersectoral collaboration in addressing health and well-being concerns through policy and health services delivery was rooted historically in such reports as the Canadian Lalonde report in 1974 (1), with the acknowledgement that determinants of health existed outside of the health care systems, and the Declaration of Alma-Ata (1978) (2), discussed in Chapter 2.0. This was also reinforced at other World Health Organization (WHO)-sponsored global conferences in the past few decades. These include the First International Conference on Health Promotion (2) held in Ottawa, Canada, resulting in the proclamation of the Ottawa Charter for Health Promotion (1986), which "stated unequivocally that health is created in the context of everyday life where people live, love, work and play." The Ottawa Charter also called for five key action areas for health promotion; it is summarized in Box 5.1.

The charter made an additional fundamental contribution by expanding "the concept of health determinants to include environmental challenges and people's empowerment." Other international conferences (2) have followed, and it is noteworthy that, viewed as a whole, identical themes have been emerging pre- and post-2000—at conferences in Mexico (2000), Bangkok (2005), and Nairobi, Kenya (2009—first in Africa!) with emphasis on social responsibility and accountability, community action, and collaboration, along with "horizontal policy-making and implementation."

Considered collectively, these and other conference reports, previously mentioned, including an analysis "Crossing Sectors" (3) by the Public Health Agency of Canada, further underscored that over the past decades the balance appears to be shifting from "intersectoral action for health" and moving toward "intersectoral action for shared societal goals."

BOX 5.1

Ottawa Charter Enabling Actions

- Building healthy public policy
- Creating supportive environments
- Strengthening community action
- Developing personal skills
- Reorienting health services

5.2 PERVASIVE INFLUENCE OF HEALTH IN ALL POLICIES (HiAP)

These developments clearly informed the organizers of the Health in All Policies International Meeting, held in Adelaide, Australia (April 15–19, 2010) (4). The WHO meeting, attended by "100 senior experts from a wide range of sectors and countries," and co-hosted by the Government of South Australia, culminated with the Adelaide Statement or Declaration on "Health in All Policies" (HiAP) based on policies and services "developed and tested in a number of countries," emphasizing the "interface between health, well-being and economic development" along with the need for "joined-up government." From precursor national projects (5) and as mirrored in the declaration, it appears that the HiAP approach is optimized in contexts listed in Box 5.2.

Following closely on the heels of the Adelaide deliberations came the report *Implementing Health in All Policies: Adelaide 2010* (6), led by Professor Ilona Kickbusch, director, Global Health Program, Graduate Institute of International and Development Studies, Geneva, and Dr. Kevin Buckett, director, Public Health, Department of Health, South Australia.

Dr. Timothy Grant Evans, then Assistant Director-General (Information, Evidence and Research) of WHO, introduced the report (6), and in his opening remarks referenced the seminal report, "Closing the Gap in a Generation: Health Equity Through Action on the Social Determinants of Health" (7), issued 2 years earlier. One of the main conclusions reached by Sir Michael Marmott and other commissioners, according to Dr. Evans, was that "the true upstream drivers of health inequities reside in social,

BOX 5.2

Optimizing the "Health in All Policies" (HiAP) Approach

- A clear mandate makes joined-up government an imperative.
- Systematic processes take account of interactions across sectors.
- Mediation occurs across interests.
- Accountability, transparency, and participatory processes are present.
- Engagement occurs with stakeholders outside of government.
- Practical cross-sector initiatives build partnerships and trust.

economic and political environments" and that "these environments are shaped by policies, which make them amenable to change." In addition, echoing the 2008 "World Health Report on Primary Care," he further stressed that progress on population health and well-being depended to a large extent on understanding the frameworks within which multisectoral groups operate, in particular in terms of "using their language, based on their desired outcomes (8)."

The transition from a concern strictly with health improvement and health care systems to the broader community is most recently echoed in the book *Health in All Policies (HiAP): Seizing Opportunities, Implementing Policies* (9), published by the Ministry of Social Affairs and Health of Finland, under the auspices of the European Observatory on Health Systems and Policies. In terms of HiAP, the central message of the book for policy makers appears to be "the need to be prepared and quick to seize windows of opportunity arising from the convergence of problems, policies and politics." Moreover, the authors contend that the HiAP approach is strengthened significantly when health systems and decision makers accept that "health"

- Is largely created by factors outside health care services
- Builds on a strong foundation of human rights and social justice
- Is a focus for policy making with a view to enhancing health and other important societal goals; and seeks to avoid harmful impacts on health

Taking these principles on board, Finland's Prime Minister, Jyrki Katainen, in the Foreword is clear about his government's priorities: "a reduction of poverty, inequality and social exclusion; the consolidation of public finances; and enhancement of sustainable economic growth."

In the past few years, the HiAP concept and approach have had a pervasive influence across nations. As one example, all European Union (EU) "policies are now required by the EU treaty to follow the *'Health in all Policies'* (HIAP) approach and involve all relevant policy areas, **in** particular social and regional policy, taxation, environment, education, and research (10)." However, "to be fully effective," the European Commission insists "this approach needs to be extended to national, regional and local policies." HiAP also underpins *Europe 2020*, the EU's 10-year economic-growth strategy (11), mirrored by member states, which "has set five ambitious objectives— on employment, innovation, education, social inclusion and climate/energy—to be reached by 2020." Similarly, the American Public Health Association (APHA) has adopted *Health in All Policies: A Guide for State and Local Governments*, written by the public health facilitators of the California Health in All Policies Task Force (12). The comprehensive guide "is geared toward state and local government leaders who want to use intersectoral collaboration to promote healthy environments" and focuses largely on promoting equity, "a key strategy for addressing major population health issues rooted in socioeconomic inequalities facing the United States."

Stressing that "equity and sustainability are core components of a healthy community," the authors of the guide highlight that health inequities "are a result of systemic, avoidable and unjust social and economic policies and practices that create barriers to opportunity." They further clarify that "*sustainability* refers to the need of society to create and maintain conditions so that humans can fulfill social, economic, and other requirements of the present without compromising the ability of future generations to meet their own needs."

Globally, the overarching HiAP approach is supported extensively by increasing attention on the social determinants of health (SDH), discussed in Chapter 2.0. As one example, the WHO Rio de Janeiro (2011) conference (2) focused on the worldwide issues relating to SDH, and the five action areas identified in the Rio Political Declaration, also referenced in the Epilogue. In May 2013, the 66th World Health Assembly of the WHO approved the report on the progress of action on SDH, and through the Secretariat Report (13) highlighted major global developments that have taken place since the world conference in 2011. Examples demonstrate commitment to addressing SDH primarily through need assessments and planning frameworks. However, for most nations, enabling actions are yet to be evolved and need to be guided by Dr. Chan's astute caveats mentioned earlier, and particularly informed by *Health in All Policies (HiAP): Seizing Opportunities, Implementing Policies* (9), mentioned previously.

Snapshots of regional progress with regard to addressing SDH are provided in the Secretariat's report (13):

> The Regional Office for Europe: "commissioned a review of the social determinants of health in order to measure and explore the causes of the health divide among and within its 53 Member States. Using the conceptual framework created by the Commission on Social Determinants of Health, the review identified new evidence and recommended actions that were incorporated into Health 2020, the new European policy framework for health and well-being which was adopted by the Regional Committee for Europe in September 2012 addressing the social determinants of health by 'whole-of-government' and 'whole-of-society' approaches and improved governance for health."
>
> WHO's Country Office in India: "has begun work on a study of barriers to access to health services for selected chronic diseases' services in order to analyse the wider social determinants of health influencing access to health care. This study is built on one of the themes of Rio Political Declaration 'further reorient health sector towards reducing health inequities' and aims to prepare the way towards universal health coverage, with a focus on noncommunicable diseases."
>
> The Regional Office of Africa: "has established a program on determinants and risk factors in order to accelerate the response to the main determinants associated with priority public health conditions. Four countries in the African Region, namely Botswana, Kenya, Uganda and Zambia, organized multistakeholder meetings with representatives of the public and private sectors, bodies in the United Nations system, academia and civil society to examine how they could work on the social and economic determinants of health in order to improve health and well-being of populations."
>
> The Pan American Health Organization (PAHO): "has created a Cross-Organizational Team on the Determinants of Health and Risks, which promotes interprogrammatic and intersectoral work inter alia on the concept of health in all policies."

Recognizing the importance of sharing research, issues, and case studies, the WHO Secretariat is also working toward facilitating an informal global network for capacity building on the SDH. Initially, this network will include leading capacity-building institutions, primarily, schools of public health and civil society organizations (professional as well as grassroots bodies) that have the interest, capabilities, resources and close linkages to public policy on the SDH in different regions (13). It is significant that tackling SDH has been identified as being "a fundamental approach to the work of WHO and a priority area in the draft 12th WHO general programme of work 2014–2019." In order to raise the profile of HiAP, a global web-based consultation, initiated by the Health Promotion and Social Determinants of Health Units of WHO in 2012, resulted in a new definition of HiAP (14), emphasizing the importance of creating "shared" policies that focus on "population health and health equity."

HiAP is an approach to public policies across sectors that systematically takes into account the health implications of decisions, seeks synergies, and avoids harmful health impacts, in order to improve population health and health equity.

The preceding examples illustrate that HiAP has become a global imperative. The case studies in *Health in All Policies (HiAP): Seizing Opportunities, Implementing Policies* (9), which built on the WHO booklet "Intersectoral Action on Health: A Path for Policy-Makers to Implement Effective and Sustainable Action on Health" (15), *a few years earlier,* attest the value ascribed to the approach.

However, as evidenced in Chapter 4.0, making concrete headway globally continues to be a struggle. In developing nations, poor sanitation, communicable diseases, conflicts, ideational differences, and lack of educational opportunity continue to be endemic. Many developed and economically emerging nations are also experiencing the consequences of financial austerity, rapid growth of an aging population, and increases in noncommunicable diseases, many caused by the lack of availability and high cost of good nutritious foods and sedentary lifestyles. WHO Secretary-General Dr. Margaret Chan makes the challenges facing us clear in her opening remarks to the Adelaide 2010 report (4):

> Growing evidence shows that economic growth in an interconnected world creates an entry-point for the rise of diseases such as heart disease, stroke, diabetes and cancers (especially cancers linked to tobacco use and obesity) and that these are the diseases that break the bank. In some countries, care for diabetes alone consumes as much as 15% of the national health-care budget.

These expanding health issues are, in Dr. Chan's view, "largely beyond the power of ministries of health," and while "health and medical professions can plead for lifestyle changes and tough tobacco legislation," she asserts it is not possible to "re-engineer social environments in ways that encourage healthy behaviours" or "open opportunities for people to work (or educate) their way out of poverty."

Dr. Chan probably has identified one of the main hurdles to overcome: that is, while rational well-crafted policies, developed by "relevant actors" across key societal sectors, provide direction based on health systems data "on harmful health impact" they may not be able to address "the underlying causes of poor health——physical, social or emotional."

In short, conventional approaches to ensuring population health and well-being may have limited success with many emerging population-related health and well-being issues—obesity, depression, pollution, corruption, conflicts, to name several—despite "managerial capacities, legal backing; and monitoring and evaluation." The following case examples may help to illustrate why some public health projects have succeeded, while others have not.

5.3 CASE EXAMPLES OF PREVENTIVE STRATEGIES

The North Karelia Project

A disease prevention and health promotion project that achieved considerable success close to 40 years ago—in many ways a "classic" forerunner of the HiAP approach—was *The North Karelia Project*. The project, documented in *The North Karelia Project: From North Karelia to National Action* (16), ran from 1972 to 1977, and "is widely seen as a model for successful population-based prevention of cardiovascular and other non-communicable diseases" (17).

Led by Professor Pekka Puska, as director and principal investigator of the project, the Finnish experts were concerned with improving eating habits "in a region covered by snow half of the year and with limited productive capabilities." Strategies included "a broad communication campaign, focusing on community organizations and the training of peer-to-peer leaders." Furthermore, the experts were able to convince local producers "to reduce the fat content of local milk and sausages and to decrease the salt content in bread and pastries, and encouraging local producers to reduce reliance on 'the dairy and meat industry' and concentrate more on the production of rape seed oil and berries" along with "introducing healthier school food and changing workplace menus." Finally, "a third element of the approach was the implementation of a national legal framework"—emphasizing "health promotion and tightening tobacco legislation."

The results confirmed that "the intervention was a success: cardiovascular mortality decreased by 82%, a consequence of marked reductions in cholesterol levels, smoking prevalence and blood pressure. The project was later expanded to the whole country, which has experienced similar achievements." "The biggest innovation," in Professor Puska's opinion,

> was massive community-based intervention. We tried to change entire communities. Instead of a mass campaign telling people what not to do, we blitzed the population with positive incentives. Villages held "quit and win" competitions for smokers, where those who quit for a month won prizes. Entire towns were set against each other in cholesterol-cutting contests. We would go in, measure everyone's cholesterol, then return two months later. The towns that cut cholesterol the most would win a collective prize. We didn't tell people how to cut cholesterol, they knew how to do that. It wasn't education they needed, it was motivation. (17)

Several recommendations and conclusions were made with regard to "a successful community intervention programme," summarized in Box 5.3.

Moreover, overall project findings demonstrated that

- "a comprehensive, determined and theory-based community program can have a substantially positive effect on risk factors and lifestyles";
- "such developments are associated with correspondingly favourable changes in chronic disease rates and population health";
- a major national demonstration program can be a powerful tool for generating favorable nationwide developments in chronic disease prevention and health promotion.

BOX 5.3

North Karelia Project Recommendations and Conclusions

- A sound and comprehensive understanding of the community ("community diagnosis"), close collaboration with various community organizations, and full participation by the local people themselves
- Utilizing the appropriate medical/epidemiological frameworks in selecting the intermediate objectives, and the relevant behavioral/social theories for designing the actual intervention program
- A need to combine well-planned media and other messages with broad-ranging community activities involving sectors such as primary health care, voluntary organizations, food manufacturers and supermarkets, worksites and schools, the local media, etc., and
- A system of reliable and first-rate monitoring and evaluation, both for continuous follow-up of the change process and for more comprehensive summative evaluations.

There are many reasons why the North Karelia Project merits ongoing attention, particularly at a time when the rise of noncommunicable diseases appears to be unstoppable in most nations that have adopted the Western lifestyle.

A crucial aspect of its overall success as a public health intervention is that the project was "initiated following a petition from local people requesting government action to reduce high rates of cardiovascular disease in the area" (18). This concern for maintaining good health and well-being appears to be lacking across the globe, exacerbated by the fact that differences "in socioeconomic status correspond with differences in health status." Moreover, it may be important to mention that many public health projects do not succeed because "they fail to engage communities in such a way that will change the social norms, attitudes and patterns of behaviour that reinforce unhealthy lifestyles."

It is also noteworthy, and as discussed further in Box 5.3 that

> the intervention began with the premise that behaviour cannot simply be changed by providing information. Rather people need to be persuaded to act in new ways and that these new ways are socially acceptable—for example, that the food is as good and activities as enjoyable. Central to achieving this was the involvement of opinion leaders from formal and informal groups to increase the credibility of the messages. (18)

Cross-Cultural Interventions: A Global Online-Based Education Project for Caregivers of Children Who Lost Parents

Another project that adheres to the current WHO spirit and definition of the HiAP approach, and from which lessons about public health interventions might be drawn, focuses on "designing and testing a non-profit education curriculum for orphanage and foster family staff and leaders in quality care" (19). Three online-based training programs have been developed so far: *www.train.fairstartedu.us*, aimed at training groups in care for infants and toddlers; *www.fairstart-train4care.com*, training care for children aged 0 to 17 years, in versions for both institutions and foster care; *www.fairstartglobal.com*, aimed at spreading the programs in the local languages of all developing countries. All programs are open source, in local user language versions, and only require the Internet, a projector, and a short period of training. The purpose of the programs is to set global, research-based standards for professional care of children without parental care, and initiate the growth of local care system competences.

Guided by principles and practices in the book *Severe Attachment Disorder in Childhood* (20), the first Fair Start program was developed during 2008/2010 with the cooperation of governments and associations in five EU partner countries globally. The dialogues in the researcher's network later inspired a special issue of *Infant Mental Health Journal*, co-edited by Niels Peter Rygaard, Christina Groark, and Robert McCall.

In the paper "Global Research, Practice, and Policy Issues in the Care of Infants and Young Children at Risk" (21), the authors highlight some of the main causes that are putting children's lives at risk along with consequences, noting that

> across the world, urbanization, migration, armed conflict, epidemics, and famine disrupt families. Add poverty, abuse, neglect, and parental incapacity due to substance abuse and mental health problems, and the result is millions of children without parental care who come under governmental responsibility, often to be reared in institutions, and at risk for long-term developmental deficiencies and problems.

Recent statistics, as shown in Box 5.4, corroborate the magnitude of this global tragedy, summarized by SOS Children's Villages (20,22), and confirm the growing urgency for intervention.

There is considerable evidence that children at "high risk of deprivation" experience developmental delays in terms of "physical, personality and social development" and that "the single most important factor in child development is social and emotional long term relations with caregivers." Unquestionably, the role of "professional caregiver"—with particular emphasis "on the dimensions of secure attachment caregiver behavior in relations"—is crucial in supporting children who lost parental care (23).

Unfortunately, according to Niels Rygaard, given the low socioeconomic status of the caregiver role, formal education of these professionals has not been allocated a high priority by most governments, thereby raising the risk of institutions and poorly managed foster care still practicing from "outdated care concepts" and "organisational principles harmful to the child" (19).

The overall aim of the project was to "provide a free on-line orphan care education globally available to local care givers, their supervisors and foster care families." With emphasis on competences relating to caregiver attachment behavior, physical stimulation, and social relations training, the pilot program engaged leader and staff in 15 "short workplace learning sessions, combined with practice and leadership development and video production of new local practices" (19).

BOX 5.4

The Plight of Children Worldwide

Africa:
- In sub-Saharan Africa 1 out of 9 children dies before the age of 5 (UNICEF).
- sub-Saharan Africa has the highest risk of first-day-death for infants, and is the region showing the least progress towards ending infant mortality (UNICEF).
- Malaria is a leading killer of children under 5 in Africa, leading to over 600,000 deaths in 2010 (UNICEF).
- In Egypt, 9 out of 10 children at our SOS Villages were born out of wedlock and abandoned (SOS).
- In Zimbabwe, 66% of children in SOS Families have lost both parents (SOS).
- The highest youth unemployment rates are in the Middle East and Africa, where 1 in 4 young people cannot find work (ILO).

Asia:
- Asia is home to the largest number of orphaned children in the world; 60 million, at last count (UNICEF).
- 30 million children in East Asia suffer from at least one severe deprivation (UNICEF).
- In the Russian Federation alone, 140,000 children with disabilities live in institutional care (UNICEF).
- Under-5 deaths are increasingly concentrated in Southern Asia—India and China are two of the countries with the highest rates of early childhood mortality (UNICEF).
- Almost 30% of neonatal deaths occur in India (UNICEF).

Latin America:
- 7.5 million girls are married before age 18 in Latin America and the Caribbean (UNICEF).
- There are 10.2 million orphaned children in Latin America, 5% of all children in the region (UNICEF).
- Women and children are especially vulnerable in Latin America; underage minors represent 50% of people living in extreme poverty (World Bank).

United States:
- There are over 120,000 orphans in America, while another 400,000 children live without permanent families (HHS; AFCARS).
- It is common for children in foster care to age out, leaving them with little financial or emotional support. 27,000 children age out of the system every year (AFCARS).
- Almost 25% of youth aging out did not have a high school diploma or GED (University of Chicago).

Note: The term "orphan" is common, but covers a range of causes for placement in an orphanage or foster care. In developing countries, many parents give their children to orphanages, hoping that this will give them better education. In fact, some 90% of these children are estimated to have parents alive. For this reason, orphan children' has been replaced by the terms "children without parental care" and "children in residential/foster care." (Personal communication from Niels Rygaard, [July 28, 2014])

Underpinned by several organizational and management models (23), the initial project—developed in cooperation with the School for Social and Health education in Aarhus (Denmark)—involved eight countries from 2008 to 2010, with five testing an Internet version in eight languages, and has proven to be very successful; results indicate "high motivation from users" and the need to develop a global program version aimed at developing world child care professionals and foster families (24). The second Fair Start program was started in another EU project, TRANSFAIR 2012–2014, where the aim was to extend the use of the program further in Europe and develop two versions: one for institutions, and another for foster families (24).

Most recently, the nongovernmental organization (NGO) FairstartGlobal was established in 2012; its main "purpose is to create and develop a global forum where researchers, decision-makers and caregivers can find free resources, share experiences and can be inspired to develop local care environments in the developing world to the work with children without parents and to create local multidisciplinary focus groups so that they get the necessary care during childhood."

The programs are now used in 12 EU countries globally by the SOS Children's Villages, Adoption Center Denmark, and local aid and professional organizations. As one example of its reach and success, in Indonesia a local language version is now the government standard for all staff members in the 8,000 Indonesian orphanages.

Medicaid Childhood Obesity Prevention Pilot

The complexities of dealing with lifestyle changes—and that appear to confirm Dr. Chan's apprehension about our present capacity to address "underlying causes of poor health—physical, social or emotional"—involved the Medicaid Childhood Obesity Prevention Pilot (25), funded by the Texas Health and Human Services Commission.

According to the commission's final report, "20.4 percent of Texas children aged 10 to 17 are obese; since 1980, the rate of obesity among U.S. children and adolescents tripled; obese children have an 80 percent chance of staying obese their entire lives." In addition, across the United States "average healthcare spending for obese individuals was $1,429 or 41.5 percent higher than that of non-obese persons in 2006" and "could cost Texas businesses $32.5 billion annually by 2030, if current trends in obesity and healthcare costs continue."

The report also makes it clear that "causes of overweight/obesity are multifaceted," and that "children today, generally, are thought to eat too much high-calorie fast food, exercise too little, and spend too much of their time in sedentary activities."

Given these concerns—now shared by most other developed and increasingly developing nations—the aims of the project were threefold: "decrease the obesity rate of children in the Children's Health Insurance Program (CHIP) and the Medicaid program; improve nutritional choices and increase physical activity levels; and achieve long-term reductions in CHIP and Medicaid program costs incurred by the state as a result of obesity." The program model included "visits with a primary care provider; assessments; care coordination; and a menu of enhanced community services." The contract, signed in August 2010, proposed "a pilot group of 350–400 participants (ages 6–11) completing 6 months in the program and a minimum of 300 participants completing 12 months of the program." The pilot ran from November 1, 2010, and concluded on October 31, 2012.

Regrettably, although supported by a multidisciplinary team of professionals, the pilot study experienced a major problem right from the start "enrolling clients into and retaining them." Only 124 children completed the 12-month program, making "data interpretation unreliable."

There appear to be two major factors for the pilot's failure: "lack of interest among parents and children" and "lack of interest among physicians in participating in the pilot," as "there was no incentive provided to physicians . . . *other than an educational opportunity.*" It may also be of particular concern that "parents did not believe that their children in the 'overweight' or 'at-risk' categories needed the program."

A more comprehensive and systematic approach to tackling obesity in Texas is suggested by the authors of "Combating Childhood Obesity With a Multiprong Attack" (26). Focusing on a Central Texas Mind, Exercise, Nutrition, Do It! (MEND) Partnership, they acknowledge that "childhood obesity is caused by a complex combination of nutritional, health, educational, economic, cultural, and social factors" and that "no single approach can serve as a 'magic bullet' cure."

Their findings point toward the development of multidimensional strategies that incorporate progressive screening by health professionals, "health plans" that "focus on creating opportunities and incentives for families to initiate healthier lifestyles." Moreover, they affirm that community-based organizations "are in the best position to advise on what social and cultural factors should be addressed in an obesity program," and, perhaps most importantly, they can facilitate connecting "with hard-to-reach populations."

5.4 REFLECTIONS ON CURRENT INTERVENTIONS

As the interventions (national, international, and local) demonstrate, tackling the difficult or "wicked" health and well-being problems of our age is proving difficult and is determined largely by the wider context—political, economic, and cultural—in which a particular measure takes place. Fundamentally, what distinguishes the North Karelia project from the *Medicaid Childhood Obesity Prevention Pilot* is that the former depended on implementing an intersectoral "shared policy" while the latter, although supported by government action, not by a "shared policy," driven, for example, by the school leaders, parent groups, and health care profession, was much more narrowly focused. Perhaps, most important, the Texas project illustrated the gap between political will and valuing good health at the local level.

Michael Blomfield and Harry Cayton, in their "Community Engagement Report for the Health Foundation," observe that "there are strong correlations between self-reported health status and social class, and between social class and self-perceived control over health." Further, they note that "there might also be a link between self-perceived health status and self-perceived control over health." Based on these premises, the argument for "engaging people in their health, to increase their self-perceived control over it, could have the effect of improving their perceptions of their health and, among those with long-term conditions, lower its negative impact on their daily lives." Perhaps the Texas project could have been strengthened considerably had there been a concerted community effort on raising awareness about the causes and impact of poor health on the lives and well-being of the children before starting the project. This phase would be in keeping with the views espoused in *Health in All Policies (HiAP): Seizing Opportunities, Implementing Policies* (9), recognizing the importance of "early involvement of relevant actors; a high level of political and public support; technical, administrative and managerial capacities across government sectors; complementary interventions; legal backing; and monitoring and evaluation." While the North Karelia project integrated these features, the Medicaid project did not. As a result, it was unable to achieve its commendable aims lacking most of these elements, including the necessary background research exemplified by the cross-cultural orphanage initiative.

Both the North Karelia and "children without parental care/children in residential/foster care projects" made community and multisectoral engagement a top priority, evidently "learning many of the key lessons from integrated community-led approaches" (18). Moreover, education played a significant part in achieving their overall aims. The North Karelia project relied on psychological models and included "four steps of training to smooth the transitions in behaviour" (18):

1. Demonstration of the new patterns of actions and responses.
2. Guided and progressively more independent practicing of these new behaviors.
3. Feedback on the appropriateness of responses.
4. Reinforcement through support and encouragement that is withdrawn as the new behavior becomes habitual.

Similarly, the Danish Fair Start pilot program engaged staff in "short workplace learning sessions, combined with practice and leadership development and video production of new local practices."

It is telling that while the intended participants in the American obesity study have many life choices, those who are without parental care have very few, if any. The lack of interest among parents and physicians in the Medicaid project is especially disappointing as the need for adults and health professionals to act as family and community role models sends a powerful message to children that their health and quality of life can be compromised by eating the wrong foods and engaging in too many sedentary activities. These deep-seated attitudes may send warning signals to the organizers of the U.S. *Healthy People 2020* project (27).

The importance of "focusing on the social context in which individual action occurs and is maintained, rather than on increasing the knowledge of individuals" (28) is also central to the North Karelia, the Fair Start, and MEND interventions. According to the authors of "Community-Based Noncommunicable Disease Interventions: Lessons From Developed Countries for Developing Ones" (29), key elements for successful community interventions include "a good understanding of the community (community diagnosis)" and "close collaboration with various community organisations, and full participation of the people themselves."

In conclusion, from the literature, it is clear that "fundamentally, behaviour change programmes targeted at individuals do not alter the social and environmental conditions that promote and maintain the behavioural risks that are the focus of intervention" (28). However, it is less apparent how we might go about tackling the difficult health and well-being issues that confront us, especially in light of the forces that want to retain the status quo and that place profits over people's well-being.

As noted in the Texas MEND project, a key aspect for achieving positive health outcomes is to find ways of engaging "communities in such a way that will change the social norms, attitudes and patterns of behaviour that reinforce unhealthy lifestyles" (18).

5.5   BRIDGING THE "INGENUITY GAP"

Chapter 2.0 identified areas that are proving difficult to address, given today's prevention approaches or tools. A case in point relates to the U.S. National Prevention Strategy (30) that was agreed upon in 2011 and is supported by the National Prevention, Health Promotion, and Public Health Council, established by the Affordable Care Act. The Council includes 20 heads of federal agencies. Although an earlier study concluded that obesity rates among young Americans had fallen, a subsequent study published in the medical journal *JAMA Pediatrics* reversed this finding. The new study "found increases in obesity for children age 2 to 19, and a marked rise in the percentage who were severely obese," particularly "among black boys, Hispanic girls and white girls" (31). Overall the authors conclude:

> Nationally representative data do not show any significant changes in obesity prevalence in the most recently available years, although the prevalence of obesity may be stabilizing. Continuing research is needed to determine which, if any, public health interventions can be credited with this stability. Unfortunately, there is an upward trend of more severe forms of obesity and further investigations into the causes of and solutions to this problem are needed.

Along with other nations, now also including many in the developing world, the United States appears to be facing an "ingenuity gap" when it comes to dealing with rising levels of people who are overweight or obese and affected by many other chronic conditions.

According to Professor Thomas Homer-Dixon, Centre for International Governance Innovation Chair of Global Systems at the Balsillie School of International Affairs in Waterloo, Ontario, Canada, the phrase "ingenuity gap" denotes the space between a challenge and a solution (32). His argument is that as the complexity of the world increases, our ability to solve the problems we face is becoming critical and that our "challenges require more than improvements arising from physics, chemistry and biology, as one will need to consider the highly complex interactions of individuals, institutions, cultures, and networks involving all of the human family around the globe."

On deeper reflection, most population- and planet-centered issues now seem to fall into this category as many public health professionals and other cross-sectoral practitioners appear stymied when faced with complex people problems that are multifaceted, interdependent, and potentially life-threatening, such as malnutrition, obesity, urbanization, pollution, political conflicts, and pandemics, to name but a few.

Professor Kickbusch and Dr. Buckett (6) pinpoint some of the reasons why translating policy relating to socioeconomic determinants of health into enabling action on the ground is difficult.

> Issues such as income, employment, education and environment are complex and multifactorial. The time between cause and effect is generally long (especially compared to the political cycle), evidence is often incomplete or weak, and associations are often difficult to explain. Working across government sectors is also difficult—'ownership', funding, reporting arrangements, departmental or agency culture, and language all present challenges for joined-up government. Government departments are often said to operate as 'silos', which need to be bridged to achieve joined-up government. In reality, government departments often work more like castles and keeps than silos, being actively defended to resist distraction from 'core business' and sectoral interests.

REFERENCES

1. Lalonde MA. *New perspective on the health of Canadians.* Ottawa: Minister of Supply and Services; 1974. http://www.phac-aspc.gc.ca/ph-sp/pdf/perspect-eng.pdf. Accessed June 6, 2014.
2. WHO. Global conferences on health promotion. http://www.who.int/healthpromotion/conferences/en/. Accessed June 6, 2014.
3. Public Health Agency of Canada. Crossing sectors: Experiences in intersectoral action, public policy and health. http://www.unnaturalcauses.org/assets/uploads/file/Canada-Crossing%20 Sectors.pdf. Accessed June 6, 2014.
4. WHO. Adelaide statement on health in all policies moving towards a shared governance for health and well-being. http://www.who.int/social_determinants/hiap_statement_who_sa_final.pdf. Accessed June 6, 2014.
5. WHO. Intersectoral action on health: A path for policy-makers to implement effective and sustainable action on health. http://www.who.int/kobe_centre/publications/intersectoral_action_health2011/en/. Accessed June 6, 2014.
6. WHO and the Government of South Australia. *Implementing health in all policies: Adelaide 2010.* http://www.who.int/sdhconference/resources/implementinghiapadel-sahealth-100622.pdf. Accessed June 15, 2014.
7. WHO. Closing the gap in a generation: Health equity through action on the social determinants of health. http://www.who.int/social_determinants/thecommission/finalreport/en. Accessed June 15, 2014.
8. WHO. Primary healthcare now more than ever. http://www.who.int/whr/2008/whr08_en.pdf. Accessed June 15, 2014.
9. Leppo K, Ollila E, n Pe¯na S, Wismar M, Cook S. *Health in all policies (HiAP): Seizing opportunities, implementing policies.* Finland: Ministry of Social Affairs and Health; 2013. http://www.euro.who.int/en/about-us/partners/observatory/studies/health-in-all-policies-seizing-opportunities,-implementing-policies. Accessed May 10, 2014.
10. European Commission. Public health: Health in all policies. http://ec.europa.eu/health/health_policies/policy/index_en.htm. Accessed June 28, 2014.
11. European Commission. *Health 2020.* http://ec.europa.eu/europe2020/index_en.htm. Accessed June 28, 2014.

12. Rudolph L, Caplan J, Ben-Moshe K, Dillon L. *Health in all policies: A guide for state and local governments.* Washington, DC: American Public Health Association and Public Health Institute; 2013. http://www.phi.org/uploads/application/files/udt4vq0y712qpb1o4p62dexjlgxlnog-pq15gr8pti3y7ckzysi.pdf. Accessed June 28, 2014.

13. WHO. Social determinants of health. Report by the Secretariat. http://www.who.int/social_determinants/B_132_14-en.pdf?ua=1. Accessed June 3, 2014.

14. Baltic Region Healthy Cities Association. Health in all policies approach reinforced during the Global WHO Conference in Helsinki; June 10–14, 2013; Helsinki. http://www.marebalticum.org/brehca/index.php?option=com_content&view=article&id=318:health-in-all-policies-approach-reinforced-during-the-global-who-conference-in-helsinki&catid=1&Itemid=100050. Accessed June 28, 2014.

15. WHO. Intersectoral action on health: A path for policy-makers to implement effective and sustainable action on health. http://www.actionsdh.org/Contents/Action/Governance/Building_governance/Health_in_All_Policies_approach3.aspx. Accessed June 28, 2014.

16. National Institute for Health and Welfare. http://www.thl.fi/en_US/web/en/whatsnew/events/ncdseminar/nkproject. Accessed June 5, 2014.

17. McAlister A, Puska P, Salonen JT, Tuomilehto J, Koskela K. Theory and action for health promotion illustrations from the North Karelia Project. *Am J Public Health.* 1982 January;72(1):43–50.

18. Blomfield M, Cayton C. *Community engagement report for the Health Foundation.* London: The Health Foundation; 2009. http://www.health.org.uk/public/cms/75/76/313/576/Community_engagement.pdf?realName=KGmZpr.pdf. Accessed June 28, 2014.

19. Rygaard NP. Designing the Fair Start project: A free E-learning and organizational development program for orphanages and foster families in quality care giving. *Child Youth Care Practice,* 2011;24(3). http://aieji.net/wp-content/uploads/2012/02/Fair-Start.pdf. Accessed April 17, 2014.

20. Rygaard NP. *Severe attachment disorder in childhood.* New York, NY: Springer Verlag; 2006. http:www.attachment-disorder.net/. Accessed April 17, 2014.

21. McCall RB, Groak CJ, Rygaard NP. Research, practice, and policy issues in the care of infants and young children at risk. *Infant Ment Health J.* 2014;35(2):87–93. http://onlinelibrary.wiley.com/doi/10.1002/imhj.21441/full. Accessed April 17, 2014.

22. SOS Children's Villages. Children's statistics. www.sos-usa.org/our-impact/childrens-statistics. Accessed April 14, 2014.

23. Rygaard NP. Emergent dynamics of cross-cultural interventions (unpublished). Accessed April 17, 2014.

24. Fairstart Global. http://www.fairstartglobal.com/. Accessed April 18, 2014.

25. Health and Human Services. *Commission. Medicaid Child Obesity Prevention Pilot report to the Texas legislature.* Austin, TX: Health and Human Services Commission. http://www.hhsc.state.tx.us/reports/2012/Medicaid-Child-Obesity-Prevention.pdf. Accessed May 26, 2014.

26. Reddy S, Finley M, Alloju S, Rohack J., MD. Combating childhood obesity with a multiprong attack. *Ted Med.* 2012;108(6):e1–e8. http://www.texmed.org/June12Journal/. Accesed May 25, 2013.

27. U.S. Department of Health and Human Services. *Healthy People 2020.* http://www.healthypeople.gov/2020/. Accessed May 26, 2014.

28. Swerissen H, Crisp BR. The sustainability of health promotion interventions for different levels of social organization. *Health Promot Int.* 2004;19:123–130. http://heapro.oxfordjournals.org/content/19/1/123.full. Accessed October 28, 2009.

29. Nissinen A, Berrios X, Puska P. Community-based noncommunicable disease interventions: Lessons from developed countries for developing ones. *Bull World Health Organ.* 2001;79:963–970. Accessed May 26, 2014.

30. National Prevention Council. National prevention strategy. http://www.surgeongeneral.gov/initiatives/prevention/index.html. Accessed May 26, 2014.

31. Skinner AC, Skelton JA. Prevalence and trends in obesity and severe obesity among children in the United States, 1999–2012. *JAMA Pediatr*. 2014;168(6):561–566. http://archpedi.jamanetwork.com/article.aspx?articleid=1856480&resultClick=. Accessed July 10, 2014.
32. Homer-Dixon T. *The ingenuity gap*. New York, NY: Vintage Books; 2002.

6.0

Community-Centered Care and Evolving "Fifth" Wave Interventions in Public Health

6.1 PROFESSOR CARL E. TAYLOR: PIONEER IN GLOBAL HEALTH

Few people may be described as unique but the late Professor Carl E. Taylor (1916–2010) certainly can be. Born in India, the son of medical missionaries for the Reformed Presbyterian mission in the Himalayas, he graduated from Harvard's medical school in 1941, then earned a master's degree in public health (Master of Public Health [MPH]) in 1951 and a doctorate (Doctor of Public Health [DPH]) in 1953 (1).

Dedicating "his life to improving the healthcare of people throughout the world," his philosophical and practical leanings were built "on the principle of equity." His concept of health equity underscored the criticality of providing "health benefits according to measurable need rather than on the basis of political or economic status . . . concentrating on those with the greatest problems" (1). His clear vision enabled him "to find new ways of helping developing countries improve the health of their citizens."

Among his many achievements was his contribution to the field of international health, becoming the first director of the Department of International Health (DIH) at Johns Hopkins School of Hygiene and Public Health (now the Johns Hopkins Bloomberg School of Public Health) in 1961. DIH was "the first department of its kind at any school of public health," helping to "establish international health as a distinct academic field in the United States" (1).

Over the next 40 years, "his pioneering research and service work in more than 70 countries brought lifesaving medical care to marginalized populations across the globe and inspired generations of students" (2). On his return to India, as head of a preventive social medicine department, he demonstrated "the value of recruiting and training villagers to deliver basic healthcare in poor communities." It is noteworthy that "children who received preventive care in his study (1960–1975) had increased height and weight and reduced mortality compared with those in a control group."

In the late 1970s he was the primary World Health Organization (WHO) consultant and one of the architects for the Alma-Ata World Health Conference in 1978 on

Primary Health Care (PHC), attended by representatives from 134 nations, discussed earlier in Chapter 1.0 (Section 1.2). The Declaration's "advocacy of community participation in health care," influenced considerably by his research, "remains a guiding tenet of public health" (3). Subsequently, he served as United Nations Children's Fund (UNICEF) Director for China in the 1980s.

"A man of spiritual conviction" (4), central to his beliefs were the importance of "exploring innovative and sustainable solutions," "building partnerships," and adapting solutions "to the local situation and owned by the local community" (1). In a 2005 interview he wisely remarked "what makes a difference in improving health is not so much what physicians do, but what communities do."

6.2 ORIGINS OF COMMUNITY-BASED PRIMARY CARE AND PUBLIC HEALTH

Over 2,500 years separated Professor Taylor and Hippocrates (460–377 BCE). However, Hippocrates, frequently called the "father of medicine" was well ahead of his time in the practice of "community-based primary health care." Indeed, Marketa Houskova, a master's student at Johns Hopkins, in a blog discussed a videotaped lecture by Dr. Taylor on "Health For All" (HFA) and came to the conclusion that Hippocrates was essentially the founder of community-based PHC (5). As one example, she cites his approach to health care, which included treating "sick people in the open as in village squares where every person from the village could come and offer advice on treatment and getting better!"

Moreover, she noted that "by not isolating the sick"—germ theory was unknown, of course—Hippocrates demonstrated "his initial foresight of holistic/community approach to healing and showed his outlook to the future foundation for community-based primary health care." Interestingly, in her blog she queried whether he was also "the original public health care worker" as "he started to recognize that different geographical areas meant different patterns of diseases—a major fork in the road for healthcare where medicine has clearly different goals and different strategies from community-based primary health care" (5).

Although the separation of primary, preventive, and basic curative practice continues to be the norm across the world, there are contemporary models for improving integration leading to positive health outcomes. As one example, the Cuban health system with its emphasis on polyclinics and the Doctor Family program has consistently been "endorsed by the World Bank and held up as an example for Latin American countries" (6). Although centuries apart, both Hippocrates and Professor Taylor would likely have endorsed the "outreach" Cuban model as they well understood "the core idea that community is at the center of 'health and well-being' of an individual (and) thus of the collective 'health' of the whole community" (5).

An early forerunner of this concept was the "Community Oriented Primary Care" (COPC) approach, originating in South Africa, which embraced all aspects of health—"based upon principles derived from epidemiology, primary care, preventive medicine, and health promotion" (7).

Here the work of Dr. Sydney Kark in the 1940s/50s, which "showed dramatic positive changes in the health status of the population of Pholela, South Africa" (7) applying COPC, is particularly significant. Sydney Kark's and others' contributions to health care arose from the "farseeing recommendation in 1945 of a nationwide network of community health centres (8,9), the establishment in 1946 of the Institute for Family and Community Medicine (IFCH) in Durban (headed by Sidney Kark) to train doctors, nurses, community health educators, and other personnel to work in these centres." Their efforts culminated in "the development of more than 40 centres (of the over 200 planned) . . . and the establishment in 1954 of the Department of Social, Preventive and Family Medicine chaired by Sidney Kark at the Natal University Medical School in Durban."

Figure 6.1 illustrates how male worker migration to urban communities in the 1940s impacted on rural communities or villages, leading to serious consequences in terms of increases in mental health conditions, infectious diseases, poverty, and malnutrition. It is especially notable that Sydney Kark's "broad view of the social, cultural, economic, and political determinants of health" in the South African context, "with its inequalities, cultural differences, and striking differences in health patterns," seems as relevant today globally as it was in the mid-20th century.

Dr. Kark's vision of epidemiology and community-oriented health care may help to inform necessary transformations in public health practice and education, in particular in terms of ensuring that the post-2015 Sustainable Development Goals (SDGs) and targets are conceptualized and enacted holistically as discussed in Section 4.1.

It is noteworthy that similar positive outcomes in using the COPC model were achieved in the United States with regard to "the health status of poor and underserved populations. . . ." Indeed, according to the Institute of Medicine (IOM), "the results were so impressive," that the organization "recommended widespread application of COPC in the United States" (7). The expansion of COPC was not realized,

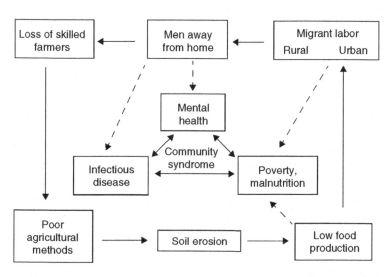

FIGURE 6.1 The determinants of a community syndrome of malnutrition, communicable diseases, and mental ill-health in a rural area in South Africa (approximately 1940). The collapse of successful farming.

Source: Adapted from S. L. Karl, *Epidemiology and Community Medicine.* New York: Appleton-Century-Crofts 1974, p. 272.

however, perhaps partly because it required "considerable external funding from private and government sources" and caused controversy about its "feasibility of implementation in mainstream primary care practices" (7). In addition, it was difficult to develop "COPC in schools of medicine and the discipline of family medicine within traditional medical school and residency structures" (7).

More than likely, lack of political and professional will to change a hospital-based system of care to community-driven models continues to be a key factor in not "achieving widespread application of COPC," despite, arguably, the unjustifiability and unaffordability of maintaining the status quo.

While the latter remains the case, the need for improving the "recognition of and intervention in community health problems" and much better "coordination of community health resources" (7) persists as the top priority for most nations, and, as John Whalley, professor of International Public Health at Leeds University and former chair of the Lancet Alma-Ata Working Group, affirms: "The emphasis must shift from single intervention to creating integrated, long-term sustainable and ethical health systems" (10).

6.3 THE ALMA-ATA DECLARATION

An attempt to reconcile this divide was the Alma-Ata Conference in 1978, to which Professor Taylor made a major contribution, and which resulted in the Alma-Ata Declaration (11,12). According to Professor Marcus Cueto, well known for his pioneering contributions in the field of history of medicine and public health in Peru, three major ideas arose at this "watershed" conference (13):

1. The need to shift from "disease technology" to "appropriate technology" that is scientifically sound and culturally acceptable.
2. The need to eradicate elitism and medical overspecialization, including top-down health campaigns and shift to community participation and work with traditional medicine.
3. The need for development of a public health center concept, a new center of the public health system, characterized by an intersectoral approach to health and that is part of a social and political movement for development.

Regrettably, "shortly after its appearance the primary health care (PHC) concept was criticized for being too broad, idealist and having an unrealistic timetable" (13). As a result, the declaration was unsuccessful in terms of implementing the key principles and targets relating to Disease Prevention and Health Promotion, Equity, Appropriate Technology, Community Participation, Intersectoral Coordination, and Decentralization (13). Key elements of the PHC strategy called for embracing total health and covering all elements of public health care, involving the community, ensuring equitable distribution of resources, facilitating effective referral systems, and making PHC the main priority.

A number of obstacles countered the implementation of the PHC strategy, including misinterpretation of the PHC concept, misconception that PHC is second rate health care for the poor, resistance to change, and lack of political will (13).

In its place the concept of "Selective PHC Strategies," "a package of low cost interventions" (13) was adopted, offering treatment and preventive strategies in areas that were "cost-effective and practical . . . easy to monitor and evaluate" (13): "growth monitoring—identifying at an early stage children who were not growing as they should, because of poor nutrition; oral rehydration to control diarrheal diseases with ORS, a mixture of water, salt and sugar that could be prepared by mothers; breast feeding of infants as a means to prevent diseases; immunization—vaccines, especially against diseases of childhood (measles, diphtheria, tetanus, polio, tuberculosis and whooping cough) along with Food supplementation, Female literacy and Family planning" (13).

Weaknesses of the "Health For All" (HFA) approach, which also impacted on the 2000–2015 Millennium Development Goals (MDGs), included inter alia continuance of the disease versus preventive model of health care and growing inequities, donor priority versus community involvement, and top-down decision making (13).

Because of the lack of progress on many fronts, discussed in Chapter 4.0, the ideas behind the Alma-Ata Declaration appear to be "going through a re-birth of sorts as more and more studies show that Dr. Taylor's SEED-SCALE approach (directing community change through existing human energy and resourcefulness), which clearly encompasses the South African COPC model, is an approach that takes all other, not only health and disease, but also other social determinants of health in account when dealing with 'health'" (5).

Indeed, the authors of "Primary Health Care: Making Alma-Ata a Reality" (10) argue that "primary healthcare is an approach to achieve both the MDGs and the wider goal of universal access to health through acceptable, accessible, appropriate, and affordable health care." Writing in 2008, in their view the MDGs for 2015 would "not be met in most low-income countries without substantial acceleration of primary health care." Reasons are numerous and include "insufficient political prioritisation of health . . . poor governance . . . population growth . . . inadequate health systems and scarce research and assessment on primary health care."

Their proposal for revitalizing PHC highlighted the need for improved infrastructure, intersectoral action, and greater community participation, particularly "linking health and development, . . . better water" along with "sanitation, nutrition, food security, and HIV control . . . chronic diseases, mental health, and child development" with "progress . . . measured and accountability assured."

6.4 "RESTORING HEALTH TO HEALTH REFORM"

These findings are supported in the paper "Restoring Health to Health Reform: Integrating Medicine and Public Health to Advance the Population's Wellbeing" (14), drafted by Lawrence Gostin, Georgetown University Law Center (GLC), Peter Jacobson, University of Michigan School of Public Health, Katherine Record (GLC), and Lorian Hardcastle (GLC). In their well-argued article, the authors contend that "by focusing nearly exclusively on health care, policy makers have chronically starved public health of adequate and stable funding and political support."

Furthermore, they posit that "the lack of support for public health is exacerbated by the fact that health care and public health are generally conceptualized, organized, and funded as two separate systems, and "in order to maximize gains in health status and to spend scarce health resources most effectively, healthcare and public health should be treated as two interactive parts of a single, unified health system."

A central point they make is that "at their broadest level, public health and healthcare confront the same challenge—injury and disease—and act in furtherance of the same overarching goal—improving health." And, while both have different ways of achieving this goal, "these disciplines share more similarities than differences." A provocative challenge they pose is to "think about starting a health system from scratch. Would policymakers opt for two separate systems or one that integrates population and individual health? We argue that an integrated health system would bring benefits to patients and populations and reduce overall cost."

They offer three major policy reforms, which they assert "would facilitate integration and dramatically improve the population's health, particularly when compared to the health gains likely to be realized from a continued focus on access to healthcare services":

- Changing the environment to incentivize healthy behavioral choices
- Strengthening the public health infrastructure at the state and local levels
- Developing a health-in-all policies strategy that would engage multiple agencies in improving health incomes

Implementing these and possibly other reforms will not be easy, as in the 20th century most nations separated curative from preventive approaches. In the United States and across the globe, the main catalyst was the 1915 Welch–Rose Report (15; discussed in Section 1.4), which clearly has had major implications in the way health systems and education programs are organized and delivered, with most funding allocated to hospital infrastructure and treatment (estimated at about 97% of health budgets) and the "silo" preparation of practitioners. Both aspects are based on 20th century assumptions— many scientifically-driven—about the best way to respond to individual patient and population health requirements.

To this day Johns Hopkins—along with most other schools of public health—distinguishes between the role of the medical field and public health, stating that "in the medical field, clinicians treat diseases and injuries one patient at a time. But in public health, we prevent disease and injury. Public health researchers, practitioners and educators work with communities and populations. We identify the causes of disease and disability, and we implement large scale solutions (16)."

6.5 INTEGRATED SERVICE DELIVERY: THE "MISSING LINK?"

Authors of a WHO technical brief, "Integrated Health Services—What and Why?" (17) define the term "Integrated Service Delivery" (ISD) as "the management and delivery of health services so that clients receive a continuum of preventive and curative services, according to their needs over time and across different levels of the health system." Their reasons reveal a concern over the need to better balance "single-disease or population-group-specific programs" (e.g., HIV/AIDS, malaria) and "less well-funded health priorities." In addition, say the authors, "more attention has to be paid to low income countries." And, third, the MDG process has identified factors that are common across several technical programs, such as "well-functioning workforce of nurses and an efficient pharmaceutical distribution system," indicating a need for interventions that cut across several program or projects.

While these rationales are justifiable, throughout the WHO brief it seems that not enough importance is ascribed to the impact that ISD could actually have on population health and well-being if fundamental rethinking of tackling health issues occurred. The idea of seeing ISD on a continuum of preventive and curative services rather than as an integrated/nonintegrated concept is useful, but at the moment ISD is almost totally geared toward the cure end of the continuum and not on prevention, based on research funding, the types of health care interventions, and national financial allocations, discussed in Chapter 3.0.

The authors are also right that "not everything has to be integrated into one package" and that "integration isn't a cure for inadequate resources." However, regardless of the varied components of each package and resource constraints, rebalancing is required to ensure that preventive measures play a much higher part than cure than they do now in both developing and developed nations.

The observation that there are "more examples of policies in favour of integrated services than examples of actual implementation" demonstrates the difficulty of translating rhetoric into meaningful enabling action in support of population and individual health and well-being.

Finally, key actions in the wider application of ISD that governments could take may be twofold: first, increase understanding of the ISD concept and its relationship to people's health, especially the vital role that disease prevention and health promotion can play; and, second, develop approaches that are effective and efficient with regard to policy, implementation, and evaluation.

6.6 CASE EXAMPLES OF SHIFTING TOWARD "PREVENTION OVER CURE" IN DEVELOPING AND DEVELOPED NATIONS

The Nicaraguan Health System

The need for reorientation of priorities is made clear in Dr. Leonel Arguello's paper, "The Health System Nicaragua Needs Is Preventive Not Curative" (18). Dr. Arguello is a general practitioner specializing in epidemiology; he has worked for the health ministry (Ministerio de Salud; MINSA), as well as served as a director of a national and international nongovernmental organization (NGO) for 19 years. He is currently president of the Nicaraguan General Medicine Society.

Dr. Arguello reflects that "health systems implement models that combine preventive and curative care in different proportions." This proportionality "depends on political, economic, social and cultural factors." Furthermore, he emphasizes that the term "prevention" has a different meaning in developing countries compared to the developed. As an example, he observes that when sewage systems were installed in Europe many illnesses were prevented, such as poliomyelitis, "without the need for a single vaccine." However, "in Nicaragua, 64% of the population—as is the situation in many other countries—still isn't hooked up to a sewage system" and "more energetic preventive actions" need to be taken, including "vaccinating against polio and many other illnesses."

Recalling the 1980s and the war when much progress was made on the health front in Nicaragua, he stresses that major changes came about because of three main factors: prevention, mass health education, and popular participation. As a result, "doing those things drastically reduced infant mortality; controlled practically all immuno-preventable illnesses such as polio, diphtheria, whooping cough and measles; lowered diarrhea-related mortality; did education on preventive health; and established an internationally recognized primary healthcare model." Of note are his observations that "illnesses don't have political preferences and exclusion is a deadly poison in the area of health," and that "health is everyone's problem and you can only move forward with broad participation, because everything is interrelated."

Sharing timely information with doctors and health workers while simultaneously alerting the population early enough "about what might happen" is crucial in terms of preparatory steps. "In public health," he stresses, "you have to act based on information, not go around looking for guilty parties or blaming one government or another. We have to work for the people and if we're clear about that basic principle then we already have a common starting point, which we have to strengthen and exploit."

In addition, he maintains "in public health you also have to take into account our lackadaisical, shrug-off-the-consequences culture, according to which people wait for the nurse to come to their home to vaccinate their children rather than taking them to the health center." For Dr. Arguello, it is a matter of taking personal responsibility and eliminating "that kind of dependence" and placing responsibility on "fathers and mothers to fulfill our obligation to care for our own and our children's health."

Noting consequences of the war in the 1980s—amputations of legs and feet from landmines and, after the war, now diabetes, he reflects on the high costs of supporting a patient with a diabetic foot. He points out that it would be much less "costly to conduct information campaigns to ensure that diabetics manage their eating habits and medications better" and that we "need information to put prevention into practice." A major outstanding problem is that universal access to health care with reduced funding is proving difficult where most of the budget is allocated "for operating costs—salaries, fuel, stationery—rather than increasing the medications, promoting their rational use or including other culturally-acceptable complementary therapies."

Broadening the Concept of Public Health in England and the United States

In developed nations, there is now considerable evidence that new ways of thinking and acting are emerging. In England, for instance, commenting on the sociohistorical changes impacting on public health, Dr. Sally Davies, chief medical officer, highlights that "most of the factors that shape public health can't be altered by central government actions" (19). The concept of "public health" is now also more encompassing as "these days, public health is about how we live our lives—and that takes in urban planning, our interactions with each other; loneliness; well-being." "What's required," she says, is a "much more holistic approach"—and that means passing the lead role to those best placed to occupy it, including linking health and education as "they're inextricably linked."

Without question her observations make it clear that public health—which has traditionally focused mostly on population health—must now also embrace "individually oriented health work" as "part of the public health toolbox" (19) and assume much greater visibility and responsibility among the nations and communities it serves while adopting new models of delivering health care, as shown in Figure 6.2 (20).

Anita Charlesworth, then chief economist of the UK National Health Service (NHS), in a blog titled "The Lost Decade," recalling the nation's budget difficulties since 2008, and thinking about the future, counsels that "the challenge is not to get through four or five difficult years and then everything returns to normal but rather to try to deliver a step change in the productivity of health services. So beyond the current pay policy we need a productivity plan . . . if we are to deliver a step change in the productivity of the NHS we need to look at primary care's role as the front-line provider of health care" (21).

She further opines that "without an effective primary care service with the capacity and skills to support patients with chronic health conditions and the frail elderly more effectively, it's difficult to see how the NHS can manage with such a long period of constrained funding."

These directions are also gaining momentum in the United States where the Institute of Medicine's report, *Primary Care and Public Health: Exploring Integration to Improve Population Health*, (22) argues for the closer assimilation of these functions. Justification for this shift appears to be based on "the likely market dynamics of U.S. healthcare reform and the productive intersection of the principles of healthcare management and public health," along with "greater value for the healthcare dollar" (22).

The longer term view—The Triple Aim—of the health care and public health integration is that this merger would improve population health, care for individuals (better access and quality) as well as cost reduction as the United States now has the highest cost for health care globally, while achieving poorer results on a number of indicators, including life expectancy.

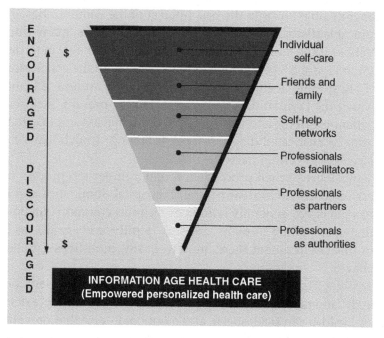

FIGURE 6.2 Industrial age medical model versus information age health/social care model.
Adapted from T. Ferguson, Consumer Health Informatics. *Healthcare Forum J*. 1995;Jan-Feb:28–33.) (20).

The timing for these reorientations also seems to be propitious. According to Dr. Donna Petersen, who is dean of the College of Public Health at the University of South Florida (USF) as well as the senior associate vice president of USF Health and chairs the *Framing the Future Task Force*, launched by the Association of Schools of Public Health (23):

- Both health and nonhealth professions are seeking to integrate more public health content in their academic programs.
- The academy continues to honor its historic commitment to the traditional public health workforce.
- Other sectors, including the community at large, are increasingly calling for public health guidance in, and more familiarity with, whole person, prevention-oriented, and population health concepts.
- Fellow health professions desire more team-based, interprofessional collaboration with public health.
- Global health is becoming more prominent as is the globalization of public health education and practice.
- The structure of education and its delivery and access points are undergoing rapid transformation.

6.7 TRANSITIONING FROM A "SICK" CARE TO A "WELL-BEING" CULTURE

Elaborating on and underpinning Dr. Petersen's last point, a fundamental aspect of embracing the interdependency between population and individual health is recognition that the 20th century or "industrial" model of health care that places responsibility for "patient" care on the health care provider—primary, secondary, and tertiary care—is no longer viable for or in the best interest of the communities, given the rise in noncommunicable diseases (NCDs) and chronic conditions, many due to an aging population. Neither is the biomedical model of health sustainable in terms of funding.

As shown in Figure 6.3 (24), which may resonate with the conclusions drawn by the authors of "Restoring Health to Health Reform: Integrating Medicine and Public Health to Advance the Population's Wellbeing" (14), the present "sick" care system is essentially "patient-centred," and involves a fundamental assumption that a person is unwell and, after sophisticated diagnoses, needs "fixing" (much like a car that needs repair or replacement of certain parts).

The patient's journey then proceeds through a three-step process from diagnosis of an illness or condition to treatment with hospital dominance and follow-up, if necessary, which, in effect, generally reinforces the most common outcome of patient–doctor consultations, leading in many cases to "a pill for every ill," as discussed in Section 2.5. In this environment there are few, if any, incentives for changing one's lifestyle or behavior.

Alternatively, a 21st century health biopsychosocial (25) reorientation would be "people-centred," and take at its starting point that there are multiple determinants of good and poor health—physical, social, and emotional—and that prevention is much more powerful than cure. As Marketa Houskova points out:

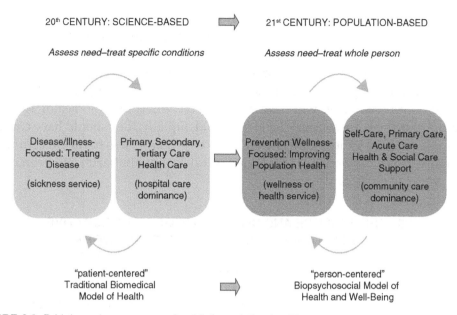

FIGURE 6.3 Bridging primary care and public/population health.

Source: Adapted from G. Lueddeke keynote presentation, "Perspectives on Current and Future Issues facing Medical and Health Professions' Education in the Developed and Developing Worlds," Accelerating Change in Medical Education (ACE). American Medical Association (AMA); 2013 (24). Lueddeke (2014).

Health does not happen in a vacuum! Very rarely do people get sick out of nowhere. . . . 'Health' happens as a result of . . . or a consequence to . . . certain political actions or social events. The primary public healthcare problem . . . is a problem originating in poverty, lack of potable water, lack of safe environment, lack of developed infrastructure, lack of knowledge and awareness, and lastly, as a lack of political will. (26)

The underlying premise behind a more holistic and person-centered biopsychosocial approach to health care is that it recognizes the multifaceted physical and social factors—that is, the effects of harmful physical and social environments—that determine individual and, by extension, community health and well-being. Fundamentally, the model resonates with the sentiments proposed by Professor Julio Frenk, former dean of the Harvard T.H. Chan School of Public Health and now president of the University of Miami. In essence, he envisions public health as "a crossroads where multiple dimensions intersect: biology and society, individual and population, evidence and ethics, analysis and action" (27).

In Canada, aspects of these transformative philosophical foundations are being translated into coordinated interventions. As one example, the Association of Health Centres (AOHC) in Ontario advocates "health promotion and illness prevention through a strong focus on the determinants of health" (28). The AOHC rightly assumes that good health and personal well-being depend on much more than visits to a local clinic and diagnostic physical examination and, as shown in Figure 6.2, "begin in our homes, our schools, in our workplace and in the communities where we live." The organization, therefore, advances public policy for "integrated, caring, and compassionate

Health and social care support . . . through the provision of medical, nursing, dental and counseling services." These focus largely on "health promotion, harm reduction, education, community development, and advocacy" and are provided through community health centers. Unquestionably, changing public expectations of health services and encouraging members of the public to take greater responsibility for their own health and well-being will have a "knock-on" effect on how health and social service professionals are socialized and educated. Equally, they should have considerable impact on how society addresses the need for doing "less harm" in community and family life, and, in particular, how the functions of public health and primary care can be productively optimized.

6.8 THE ESSENCE AND DIMENSIONS OF AN INTEGRATIVE AND ECOLOGICAL PUBLIC HEALTH FRAMEWORK

This latter aspiration is also implicit in *The Future Public Health* (29), based on a 6-year project, funded by the Scottish government, whose main argument is that change is needed to "move us beyond the technical and reductionist mindsets that have characterised modernity and produced our current ingenuity gap." Introduced in Chapter 1.0 and illustrated in Figure 6.4 (24), in developed nations public health has moved through four main stages or metaphorical "waves" since the Industrial Revolution that began in the late 18th century—the First Wave (c. 1800–1890), noted for Great Public Works, water/sanitation, germ theory; the Second Wave (c. 1890–c. 1950), typified by "medicine as science" and scientific breakthroughs; the Third Wave (c. 1940–c. 1960), which saw the birth of the welfare state and social security; and the Fourth Wave, with its focus on systems thinking, risk factors, and lifestyle.

And, while most interventions in the first three "waves" followed the traditional public health approach—Understand, Predict, Control, Provide—during the fourth "wave," it became apparent that managing the complexities of many illnesses and conditions—"obesity, depression, addiction, loss of wellbeing"—"which sap the

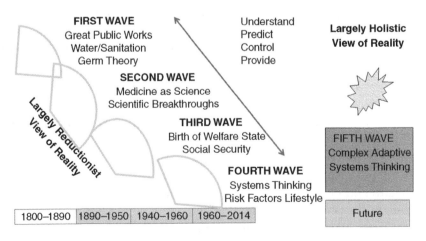

FIGURE 6.4 Waves of public health improvement (1800–2015+).

Source: Adapted from P. Hanlon et al., Making the Case for a "Fifth" Wave in Public Health, 2011 (30).

resources and spirit of modern practitioners" (29), was becoming increasingly difficult. Assumptions that governed decision making throughout the 20th century, premised largely on reductionist views of reality, could no longer be assumed as correct or appropriate, and a more holistic view of public health issues and interventions was required, rooted in more complex adaptive thinking. In the authors' view, "healthy, equitable and sustainable ways of living should be an individual and communal goal."

To this end, Professor Phil Hanlon and colleagues evolved an integrative and ecological framework based on the three fundamental Platonic principles—The "True" (Science), The "Good" (Moral), and Aesthetics (Beauty, Art). These principles were likely selected by Professor Hanlon and colleagues from Plato's lifelong search for an answer to the question: "What is the nature of norms and values for the constitution of human society and culture?" (31) The fundamental principles, according to T. K. Seung, a Korean American philosopher and author of *Plato Rediscovered: Human Value and Social Order*, reign "over the entire domain of human knowledge, practical as well as theoretical," reflecting the "ultimate themes that run through all his (Plato's) dialogues" (31).

As shown in Figure 6.5, the authors propose an integrated and ecological framework that essentially views public health interventions through a lens that is informed by current and emerging science, current and emerging ethics, and current and emerging aesthetics. The framework is intended to move us from our present, often reductionistic, thinking about how we conceptualize, organize, and implement public health measures to an emerging, holistic thought process applying "a much wider range of paradigms, methods and mindsets." The overarching aim is to build a future that is characterized by "better health equity and sustainability" and that "raises our spirits" as well as "fires our imagination."

Echoing the need for a more integrated United Nations Sustainable Development Goal framework, as proposed in Section 4.1, the authors emphasize the integrative aspect of their approach to public health, as they "perceive separation and fragmentation to be fundamental to the mindset that has created our most challenging problems." Their integrative framework is essentially "a summary of activities that will

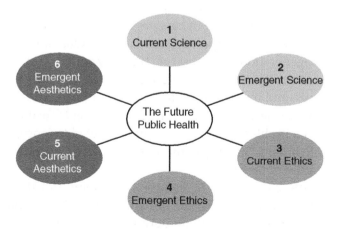

FIGURE 6.5 Integrative and ecological public health framework.

Source: Adapted from P. Hanlon et. al., *The Future Public Health*, 2012 (29).

BOX 6.1

Features of an Integrative and Ecological Public Health Framework

- **Integrative**—science, ethics, and aesthetics
- **Ecological**—recognizing "limits to growth and engaging with other complex adaptive systems that influence human health"
- **Ethical**—"respecting individual human rights and raising human consciousness that is global"
- **Creative**—"envisioning a better future and unblocking the forces that impede creativity"
- **Aesthetic**—"of a possible future that has greater health, equity and sustainability—'raises our spirits,' 'fires our imagination'"

need to come together to create the concept of health and well-being required for the successful navigation of a change of age."

The authors further suggest that interventions need to be guided by five fundamental features or dimensions, as shown in Box 6.1.

In addition, public health practitioners and others engaged in public health are encouraged to model or "embody" the change "they want to see in the world," to become more reflexive and "more self-aware of their own mindset." Moreover, the researchers advocate, they need to pay more attention to understanding others' perspectives on change.

6.9 APPLYING "FIFTH" WAVE THINKING TO COMPLEX PUBLIC HEALTH PROBLEMS OR ISSUES

Similar to addressing global governance issues (29,32,33), applying the integrative framework to particular societal problems, many of which are global in character, demands a high level of understanding of "historical, cultural and psychological factors" that inform today's complex problems.

The *Future Public Health* (29) researchers provide several insightful examples with regard to the limitations of contemporary interventions. One of these relates to inner city regeneration. Regeneration, they observe, typically suffers "from high unemployment, low levels of amenities or services, high levels of crime, low levels of trust, poor educational outcomes, and much else, including poorer health outcomes." The problem with present approaches, they argue, is that governments treat regeneration "as if it were only a material problem" rather than a multifaceted (science, moral, aesthetic) public health problem, and "for regeneration to be effective, these dimensions also have to be considered, but rarely are."

Another example considers "the complex aetiology and drivers of obesity," whose likely origin lies with "the fast changing human socio-economic and cultural systems, as conditions associated with modernity (improved technology, consumerism, economism, individualism and breakdown of social capital) appear to be the drivers." Although the epidemic is complex, widespread and costly, the authors conclude that "public health policies and programmes are riddled with loopholes and seem uncoordinated" applying control strategies that are "inconsistent and not holistic."

The integrative framework appears to be a useful guide to examine current issues relating, as one example, to rising levels of obesity and identifying ways forward in moving toward more positive future scenarios, that is, through horizontal and vertical policies and enabling actions. In terms of the former, WHO has identified sugar as a key culprit in causing obesity, dental problems for young children, and other illnesses. And, while the science has clearly confirmed causation, there has been very little discussion on the ethics of governments and manufacturers in continuing to promote high sugar content in their products alongside other issues relating to fat, salt, and nutrition generally.

6.10 ADVANCING SOCIAL ACCOUNTABILITY AND HUMAN RIGHTS AT NATIONAL AND COMMUNITY LEVELS— DR. GERALD PACCIONE: PHYSICIAN "EXTRAORDINAIRE"

The voices for social accountability or, broadly defined, "the obligation of power-holders to take responsibility for their actions" (34) must become much louder than at present. To strengthen these voices and social accountability interventions, which basically are rooted in ethics and morality, according to a recent report by the United Nations Development Program (UNDP), we require "capacity development, not just for communities and individuals engaged in monitoring but also with subnational officials who must be willing and incentivized to create space for enhanced participation by the community." More specifically, UNDP highlights

> it is important to analyse the incentives that local officials may have for accountability and to understand the lines of accountability that may run upward to central government and also outward to communities. Local officials must have the financial and human resources and capacities to respond to community demands if they are to be held accountable for delivery. An important lesson is to be aware that new mechanisms of social accountability may threaten existing structures of power and thus place government bureaucrats under pressure not to comply with public demands. These pressures must be understood in a programme's design.

Moreover, UNDP stresses that "a rights-based approach to social accountability is highly important" in further enhancing "social accountability initiatives," particularly as "the concept of accountability is at the core of both democratic, rights-based governance and equitable human development." Human rights are fundamental to "the way people perceive themselves and are perceived by government or donors. Instead of talking about 'beneficiaries with needs' or 'consumers with choice', the rights-based approach speaks of 'citizens with rights'. With this perspective, people are seen as active subjects in the political sphere and not objects of pity, charity or the benevolent intervention of government programmes or passive choosers in the marketplace" (34).

A crucial component in facing contemporary global public health issues, as Dr. Gunhild Stordalen and colleagues with regard to climate change point out—a recurring theme throughout this book—is the fundamental importance of inter-sectoral or integrated approaches—across "academia, enterprise, governments, and global agencies" (35). An inherent demand for social accountability must be built into all these collaborations and partnerships at all levels in order to ensure transparency, equity, and fairness for those who are the beneficiaries of collective interventions.

Along with the need for information and engaging with governments, an essential element of a social accountability initiative "includes raising the awareness of citizens, building confidence and capacity for engagement, building networks and coalitions" (34). In terms of recognizing the interdependency between personal and population health and well-being, few seem to have been as successful in demonstrating this abil-ity as Dr. Jerry Paccione, an internist and professor of clinical medicine at the Einstein Medical Faculty in New York, who recently received the Honorary Alumnus Award at the university's 2014 commencement ceremony (36).

Graduating from Harvard Medical School in 1975, his contributions over 40 years have been many—from volunteering "to provide primary care and help organize a nutrition program in a remote region of Guatemala" to creating "student and resident training opportunities abroad, initially in South America and eventually around the world." In addition, Dr. Paccione "founded the primary care residency program, later directing the merged program of primary care/social internal medi-cine" for Einstein. The launch of "special clinics for immigrants" and "for victims of international human rights abuse" has also been commendable. Moreover, for the past 15 years, he has led a collaborative group, including the "international advocacy group Doctors for Global Health to help staff a public hospital in the impoverished, rural Ugandan district of Kisoro," only one of two hospitals "serving a population of 270,000" with only two physicians and "nursing staffing levels at 60% of capacity." His fellowship program "brings faculty members, students and residents to work on the hospital wards and to team with village health workers on public health projects in dozens of surrounding communities" and over the past eight years "has served tens of thousands of patients, while providing real-world training for more than 200 students and residents."

For Dr. Paccione the program seems to reflect the growing interest and changes in global health. "No longer just looking at tropical diseases like malaria," they are "also looking at disparities in health that are due to abject poverty—HIV, TB, malnutrition."

"Health," he insists, "is not just about medicine; it's primarily about social issues." Moreover, "technological advances and other changes have 'shrunk' the world, increasing awareness of global health problems and making it easier for scien-tists and clinicians to combat them. . . . Now going off to work in global health doesn't have to be like going into exile. It can be like taking the subway."

> It's a joy to practice medicine with your hands and with your eyes, . . . You learn the importance of the physical exam, of relying on your own judgment. You're really practic-ing medicine on the frontier, and this gives you a different perspective on diseases.

Finally, this chapter has explored a number of themes that underpin the future of public health. In particular, it has reviewed the links between community-based primary care and its relationship to public health as well as the potential of using "fifth" wave thinking in addressing health and well-being issues and social accountability obligations. It has also profiled two global leaders in public health, both of whom exemplify virtuous, visionary, courageous, altruistic, and collaborative leadership qualities, and who are rightly recognized for their service to humanity and helping to ensure a more equitable and sustainable future for all.

REFERENCES

1. Center for Global Health Faculty. Carl Taylor. http://www.jhsph.edu/news/stories/2010/carl-taylor.html. Accessed May 14, 2012.

2. Johns Hopkins Bloomberg School of Public Health. A tribute to Carl Taylor 1916–2010. http://www.jhsph.edu/news/stories/2010/carl-taylor-tribute.html. Accessed July 20, 2014.

3. Gellene D. Carl E. Taylor, leader in global health care, is dead at 93. *The New York Times*. March 12, 2010. http://www.nytimes.com/2010/03/13/world/13taylor.html?_r=1&. Accessed May 14, 2012.

4. American Public Health Association. Dr Carl Taylor obituary. http://www.future.org/news/20110111/american-public-health-association-commemorates-carl-e-taylor-annual-meeting. Accessed October 20, 2013.

5. Houskova M. Hippocrates, the original public health care worker? http://marketahouskova.com/2014/02/23/hippocrates-the-original-public-health-care-worker/. Accessed March 15, 2014.

6. Bose S, Chan C, Crass D, et al. Analysis of health system in Cuba. http://www.slideshare.net/dcrassa/PresentationHealth-System-in-Cuba-VERSION-32811?related=1. Accessed May 19, 2014.

7. Longlett SK, Kruse JE, Wesley RM. Community-oriented primary care: Historical perspective. *J Am Board Fam Pract*. 2001;14;54–63. http://www.jabfm.org/content/14/1/54.full.pdf+html.

8. Kark JD, Abramson S. Sidney Kark's contributions to epidemiology and community medicine. *Int J Epidemiol*. 2003;32(5):882–884. http://ije.oxfordjournals.org/content/32/5/882.full. Accessed May 14, 2014.

9. Gluckman H. *The provision of an organized national health service for all sections of the people of the Union of South Africa, 1942–1944. Report of the National Health Services Commission*. Pretoria, South Africa: Government Printer; 1944.

10. Walley J, Lawn JE,, Anne Tinker A, et al. Primary health care: Making Alma-Ata a reality. *Lancet*. 2008;372(9642):1001–1007. http://www.ncbi.nlm.nih.gov/pubmed/18790322. Accessed November 20, 2009.

11. WHO. WHO called to return to the Declaration of Alma-Ata. http://www.who.int/social_determinants/tools/multimedia/alma_ata/en/. Accessed April 20, 2014.

12. Arshad U. Primary health care. http://www.powershow.com/view1/26a3e7-ZDc1Z/ALMA_ATA_DECLARATION_powerpoint_ppt_presentation. Accessed April 20, 2014.

13. Cueto M. *The origins of primary health care and selective primary health care*. AM J Public Health. 2004;94(11):1864–1874. http://www.who.int/kms/initiatives/ghhcueto.pdf. Accessed June 20, 2013.

14. Gostin L, Jacobson P, Record K, Hardcastle L. Restoring health to health reform: Integrating medicine and public health to advance the population's wellbeing. *Univ PA Law Rev*. 2011;159(6):101–147. http://papers.ssrn.com/sol3/papers.cfm?abstract_id=1780267. Accessed April 22, 2014.

15. Sommer A, Fee E. The Welch-Rose report: A public health classic. http://www.deltaomega.org/documents/WelchRose.pdf. Accessed May 10, 2011.

16. Johns Hopkins Bloomberg School of Public Health. What is public health? http://www.jhsph.edu/about/what-is-public-health/. Accessed April 20, 2013.

17. WHO. Integrated health service–what and why? http://www.who.int/healthsystems/service_delivery_techbrief1.pdf. Accessed January 19, 2014.
18. Arguello L. The health system Nicaragua needs is preventive not curative. http://www.envio.org.ni/articulo/4113. Accessed February 17, 2013.
19. Matt Ross. Interview: Sally Davies. http://www.civilserviceworld.com/interview-sally-davies. Accessed February 20, 2014.
20. Greenhalgh T, Hinder S, Stramer K, et al. Adoption, non-adoption, and abandonment of a personal electronic health record: Case study of HealthSpace. *BMJ*. 2010; 341:c5814. (Figure adapted from Ferguson T. Consumer health informatics. *Healthcare Forum J*. 1995;Jan-Feb:28–33.)
21. Charlesworth A. The lost decade. *Nuffieldtrust*. http://www.nuffieldtrust.org.uk/blog/lost-decade. Accessed April 12, 2013.
22. Institute of Medicine. *Primary care and public health: Exploring integration to improve population health*. Washington, DC: The National Academies Press; 2012.
23. Petersen D. Framing the future: The second hundred years of education for public health. www.scctv.net/league-dl/ppt/INV2012/625.pptx. Accessed February 20, 2013.
24. Lueddeke GR. 'Perspectives on Current and Future Issues facing Medical and Health Professions' Education in the Developed and Developing Worlds,' Accelerating Change in Medical Education (ACE) Conference. American Medical Association (AMA); 4 October, 2013.
25. Engel G. The clinical application of the biopsychosocial model. *Am J Psychiatry*. 1980;137(5):535–544.
26. Houskova M. Educate/influence make a difference. http://marketahouskova.com/tag/primary-health-care/. Accessed June 20, 2014.
27. Frenk, J. A Message from the Dean Julio Frenk. http://archive-edu.com/page/5063374/2014-12-08/; http://www.hsph.harvard.edu/deans-office/. Accessed October 20, 2014.
28. Association of Ontario Health Centres (AOHC). Leading Transformative Change. Strategic Plan 2012–2015. http://issuu.com/aohc_acso/docs/aohc_2012-2015_report_-_english_-_f. Accessed July 23, 2015.
29. Hanlon P, Carlisle S, Hannah M, Lyon A. *The future public health*. London: Open University Press; 2012.
30. Hanlon P, Carlisle S, Hannah M, Reilly D, Lyon A. Making the case for a 'fifth wave' in public health. *Public Health*. 2011;125(1):30–36. http://www.ncbi.nlm.nih.gov/pubmed/21256366. Accessed March 12, 2011.
31. Seung TK. *Plato rediscovered: Human value and social order*. Lanham, MD: Rowman & Littlefield; 1996.
32. Ottersen OP. Rector of the University of Oslo. Personal communication. April 4, 2014.
33. Ottersen P, Frenk J, Horton R, et al. The Lancet-University of Oslo Commission on Global Governance for Health, in collaboration with the Harvard Global Health Institute. *The Lancet*. 2011;378(9803):1612–1613.
34. United Nations Development Program (UNDP). Reflections on social accountability: Catalyzing democratic governance to accelerate progress towards the Millennium Development Goals. http://www.undp.org/content/dam/undp/documents/partners/civil_society/publications/2013_UNDP_Reflections-on-Social-Accountability_EN.pdf. Accessed August 20, 2013.
35. Stordalen GA, Rocklöv J, Nilsson M, Peter Byass P. Only an integrated approach across academia, enterprise, governments, and global agencies can tackle the public health impact of climate change. *Global Health Action*. 2013. http://www.globalhealthaction.net/index.php/gha/article/view/20513/html. Accessed March 22, 2015.
36. Paccione J. Reflections of a leader in global health. http://blogs.einstein.yu.edu/reflections-of-a-global-health-leader. Accessed June 20, 2014.

7.0

Toward a New Worldview

7.1 RATIONALES FOR FUNDAMENTAL PARADIGM SHIFTS

Planet and Population Health
and Well-Being: A Statistical Snapshot

It feels puzzling and disheartening that year on year real-time Worldometers statistics (1) that cover a range of indicators—economics, environment, food, and health, to name several—in the main do not show any downward trend. Indeed, across the globe there appears to be very little change or mostly increases in such crucial areas as the number of people undernourished and overweight, forest loss, toxic chemicals in the atmosphere, deaths from noncommunicable diseases, and world spending on illegal drugs despite rhetoric and expensive measures to counter growing health concerns. It is estimated that "in 2011, the world spent a total of US$6.9 trillion on health at exchange rates of I$ 7.2 trillion (International dollars taking into account the purchasing power of different national currencies)" (2). Today's estimate is over US$7.5 trillion.

On December 31, 2014, Worldometers provided the information summarized in Box 7.1. These figures remain largely unchanged year on year despite considerable expenditures in public health care, at about US$4.1 billion daily, and public education, at about US$3.6 billion daily. These are dwarfed, however, by world spending on illegal drugs, at close to US$400 billion in 2014, or over US$1 billion each day.

Leadership and "Seeking a Higher Purpose"

For some, such as Professor Jeffrey Sachs, economist and director of The Earth Institute at Columbia University, in his book *To Move the World: JFK's Quest for Peace* (3), a fundamental weakness in the United States has been leadership. He alludes to previous presidents in the United States in the 1980s and 1990s, who either undermined the public sector purpose or took a centrist approach that underscored the mantra "that

BOX 7.1

Worldometer Statistics *(December 31, 2014)*

World Population

7,284,811,575	Current world population
138,792,933	Births this year
147,371	Births today
57,267,629	Deaths this year
60,807	Deaths today
81,525,303	Net population growth this year
86,564 Net	Population growth today

Government and Economics

US$4,132,673,369	Public health care expenditure today
US$3,650,734,020	Public education expenditure today
US$1,860,191,286	Public military expenditure today

Health
Health statistics prove equally unsettling. Almost all deaths are preventable!

12,958,304	Communicable disease deaths this year
7,587,345	Deaths of children under 5 years this year
41,935,035	Abortions this year
343,162	Deaths of mothers during birth this year
36,840,493	HIV/AIDS infected people
1,678,031	Deaths caused by HIV/AIDS this year
8,198,110	Deaths caused by cancer this year
979,114	Deaths caused by malaria this year
5,819,880,836	Cigarettes smoked today
4,990,017	Deaths caused by smoking this year
2,496,583	Deaths caused by alcohol this year
1,070,414	Suicides this year
US$399,327,316,031	World spending on illegal drugs this year
1,347,462	Road traffic accident fatalities this year

greed was in, and that government's role was to get out of the way of Wall Street and the new economy."

His admiration for President John F. Kennedy (JFK) is unquestionable. The late president, he contends, "helped us to see how to live, both as individuals seeking a larger purpose, and as a society." Professor Sachs notes that only a few presidents (Lincoln, Teddy Roosevelt, and Franklin Delano Roosevelt [FDR]) could match "that measure of encompassing purpose—not only to have a vision, but to convince others to see it and embrace it."

In attempting "to move the world to a just and lasting peace," one of the president's most important contributions, asserts Professor Sachs, was that he "told us about our common purpose, always emphasizing that what unites us is vastly deeper than what divides us." His Peace Speech "on our common humanity" remains "of enduring importance."

> So let us not be blind to our differences, but let us also direct attention to our common interests and the means by which those differences can be resolved. And if we cannot end now our differences, at least we can help to make the world safe for diversity. For in the final analysis, our most common link is that we all inhabit this small planet. We all breathe the same air. We all cherish our children's future. And we are all mortal.

Modern Day Paradoxes

In Chapter 3.0, Dr. Rolf Sattler identified the three main forces that in his view shaped the 20th century—science/technology, capitalism, and the mass media (4). And, while these continue to exert their influence in this century, we appear to be at a "pivotal point in history." In terms of modernity, what we are witnessing is a double-edged phenomenon: while science and technology have made and are continuing to make huge strides, as discussed earlier, they may not be the panacea for what really ails the world at the moment as many of today's scientific innovations may be used for global good or global harm. As one example, many environmental threats are directly related to the industrialization of society, and many health and well-being concerns arise from the modern lives we lead. Mass and social media have given us the means to access information and people instantly but not necessarily the knowledge to use these wisely and for the benefit of society.

Capitalism and wealth creation are essential for addressing poverty and "access to education, health, water, sanitation and food security." As the chairman of the Ugandan National Planning Authority, Dr. Wilberforce Kisamba Yoweri underscores: "The focus on poverty eradication won't succeed until we blend it with wealth creation . . . the focus of the 2040 plan" (5).

However, while return on investments seems reasonable and may enable social improvement, there is a darker side to extreme capitalism, and there may be considerable justification, as Prince Charles, Britain's future king, urges, "for an end to capitalism as we know it to save the planet from global warming by protecting the environment, improving employment practices and helping the vulnerable" (6). Otherwise, he opines in his speech to business leaders "dangerously accelerating climate change" would "bring us to our own destruction."

For Dr. Ben Selwyn, a researcher at Sussex University in the United Kingdom, "The central paradox of the contemporary world is the simultaneous presence of wealth on an unprecedented scale, and mass poverty" (7). Further, he maintains that while "Capitalism's dynamism, evidenced by its ability to propagate rapid economic growth, technical change and wealth generation is pursued and achieved in the interests of capital firms and states," it is "not in the interests of the majority of the world's population." His conclusion is supported in Thomas Piketty's book, *Capital in the Twenty-First*

Century (8), which argues that "inequality was the great injustice of modern politics," "the gap between the rich and the poor is rising again," and that the "return on capital (property, share dividends, land and so on) is higher than the growth rate." Indeed, in Europe "the wealthiest 10 per cent take about 35 per cent of the income but 70 per cent of the wealth," while in the United States "Between 1977 and 2007 the richest 1 per cent . . . took an astonishing 60 per cent of the growth in national income."

In fact, statistics reveal that "The wealth of the richest 85 people in the world is greater than that of the 3.5 billion people who make up the bottom half of the world's population," which stands close to 7.4 billion. What is happening now is that capitalism has a tendency "to consume its own moral basis," possibly exemplified in a scene in the movie *The Wolf of Wall Street*: "We don't build anything, we don't create anything—purring" between "sips of martinis and snorts of cocaine. . . . You move the money from your clients' pockets into your pocket" (9). A similar narcissistic culture is also detected in the comments of a billionaire in London, "the most international, monied city the world has ever known": "We live in a capitalist world. It's every man, every country, every city for himself. We need to attract the wealthiest people. There's no point in screwing them for tax. They'll just go elsewhere" (10).

An alternate approach to the conventional form of capitalism, "humanistic capitalism," was proposed eloquently by Professor Willis Harman (1918–1997) several decades ago in his seminal paper "Humanistic Capitalism: Another Alternative" (11):

> Corporations [must] assume an active responsibility for creating a healthy society and a habitable planet—not as a gesture to improve corporate image or as a moralistically undertaken responsibility, but because it is the only reasonable long-run interpretation of "good business." In the end, good business policy must become one with good social policy.

In the intervening years, Professor Harman's clarion call seems to have evolved into a philosophy known as "conscious capitalism" (CC; 12). While there are similarities with the concept of corporate social responsibility (CSR) and "inclusive capitalism," which focuses on equality of outcomes, a concept Mark Carney, the governor of the Bank of England, seems to favor, CC differs sharply for "whom the programs are meant to benefit. CSR programs seek to benefit shareholders, while CC seeks to benefit 'all' stakeholders." CC therefore "is associated with self-awareness, personal development, the greater good, and a worldview that eschews competition, hierarchy, and materialism." In the introduction to their book, *Conscious Capitalism: Liberating the Heroic Spirit of Business*, John Mackey (co-founder of Whole Foods Market in 1978) and Raj Sisodia (professor of global business and Whole Foods Market research at Babson College) highlight the global benefits of CC made by Bill George, the former chief executive officer (CEO) of Medtronics: "Well run, values-centered businesses can contribute to humankind in more tangible ways than any other organization in society" (13).

Its key tenets include:

1. Operating with a higher purpose
2. Taking a total stakeholder orientation
3. Conscious leadership
4. Establishing a values-driven culture (14)

The philosophical underpinnings of CC may remind us of Professor Sachs's comments about JFK, whose leadership was able "to join practical politics with our highest ethical calling." Similarly, paralleling the practical and the ethical, CC is "not about being virtuous or doing well by doing good. It is a way of thinking about business that is more conscious of its higher purpose, its impact on the world, and the relationships it has with its various constituencies and stakeholders. It reflects a deeper consciousness about *why* businesses exist and how they can create more value."

> Our dream for the Conscious Capitalism movement is simple: *one day, virtually every business will operate with a sense of higher purpose, integrate the interests of all stakeholders, elevate conscious leaders, and build a culture of trust, accountability and caring.* (14)

Interestingly, there may be another reason why CC should be preferable over conventional capitalism. A study by Professor Raj Sisodia concluded that those companies ("firms of endearment") that practice CC ("stated purpose, generosity of compensation, quality of customer service, investment in their communities, and impact on the environment") performed 10 times better over a 15-year period (13).

It is along CC lines that the founder of the Chinese telecoms equipment giant Huawei, Ren Zhengfei "has rejected the possibility of a stock market flotation to build trust in the company," fearing that "Huawei's long term growth strategy could be damaged by 'greedy' Western style market capitalism" (15). The perception that "shareholders possess this long-term view, they do not seek short-term benefits," and "make very reasonable and justified investments in the future," written in traditional textbooks, is not based on fact. "In reality," he says, shareholders "want to squeeze every bit out of a company as soon as possible." His argument certainly holds true for "the heart of the Western World's economic funk," according to Jeremy Warner, a leading British financial, business, and economics commentator, and assistant editor at *The Daily Telegraph* (16). More than 6 years since the financial crisis, the journalist laments the refusal of the private sector to "fund new investment, job creation and further innovation" and government's incapacity to look "beyond the next election."

Huawei "last year reported 8.5 percent revenue growth to £22.6 billion." Its "unusual structure, whereby he retains only a 1.4 per cent stake and the rest of the equity is distributed among Chinese employees, was vital to its success," perhaps a valuable lesson for many companies engaged in "corporate cash hoarding" and "risk aversion."

Huawei's altruistic values are also evident in Germany's *Mittlestand* firms—"the term commonly used to denote small and midsize family-owned export companies." These "churn out top-notch auto components, lasers, high-tech machinery and healthcare equipment." Employing "60% of the nation's workers" and contributing "more than half of Germany's economic output," the firms also "embody certain social and moral values, like thrift, conservatism, family orientation and long-term thinking," especially thinking about "the next generation" (17).

Finding an alternate approach to the present free market capitalist culture might also have well-being or psychological advantages, according to economists at Warwick University, United Kingdom. Their research clearly demonstrates that "life satisfaction appears to dip beyond a certain level of wealth." In other words, "the richer we get, the poorer our spirits" (18).

> *Ever more people today have the means to live, but no meaning to live for.*
> —Viktor E. Frankl, *Man's Search for Meaning*

Transforming Mindsets

The authors of *The Future Public Health* (19) posit that building an enduring future necessitates a new worldview, which is "compatible not only with our needs as human beings" but also "an outer world that is compatible with the needs of our ecosystem." The urgency of having to make major paradigm shifts—not just "doing things better" but also "doing better things" in all walks of life across the globe—may not seem as far-fetched as it may have been 10 or 20 years ago. This observation is made all the more poignant by Professor Kickbusch's exhortation:

> What we have yet to fully understand is how our way of life and use of energy in the 21st century is counterproductive to our health and wellbeing in a very direct way. We are at a turning point in health policy. It has become increasingly clear that changes in the existing healthcare system will not be sufficient to maintain and improve our health. Both our extensive knowledge about what creates health, as well as the exponentially rising rates of chronic disease, obesity and mental health problems, indicate that we need to shift course and apply a radically new mindset to health. (20)

Her concern for the potentially reduced life expectancy of the present generation of children, compared to that of their parents, which she says would be—"a phenomenal failure"—should also resonate strongly with community leaders and public health professionals (19). Indeed, as "exponential growth is unsustainable on a finite planet" (17), transforming how we see the planet and ourselves—characterized in the developed world largely by consumerism, materialism and individualism (21)—must become a top priority for this generation and the next.

According to Richard Eckersley, an Australian researcher on progress and well-being, promoting "images and ideals of 'the good life' that serve the economy but do not meet psychological needs or reflect social realities" is a form of "cultural fraud" (20). In his view, the "Task we face goes far beyond the adjustment of policy levers by government; it demands an open and spirited debate about how we are to live and what matters in our lives"(22).

7.2 THE "ONE HEALTH" MOVEMENT

Historical Perspectives

Professor David Waltner-Toews, an epidemiologist/veterinarian in the Department of Population Medicine at the University of Guelph, Ontario, Canada, highlights that there is now universal "recognition that the health of people, other animals and the ecosystems of which we are a part are inextricably woven together" (23). Moreover, he reminds us that this insight is not new and "is as old as culture." As examples, he takes us back more than 2,500 years to Hippocrates who "urged physicians to consider where their patients lived, the foods they ate and waters they drank, their lifestyles, and the seasons of the year." Another major proponent in the 19th century was Rudolf Virchow, a physician, who argued that "there should be no dividing line between human and animal medicine, and that the causes of human disease were social and political."

Regrettably, however, Professor Waltner-Toews notes

> Much of this integrative thinking was pushed into the background in the mid-twentieth century as many leaders and scholars were lured by the vision that infectious disease had been conquered, and that through basic scientific understanding, advanced technology and unlimited electrical power, humanity had somehow been freed from the bonds of nature. In the late 20th century, this vision was clearly demonstrated to be an illusion.

The global wake-up call came in 1999 with the West Nile virus outbreak in New York City, which prompted the establishment of the National Center for Zoonotic (spread from animals to humans) Vector-Borne, and Enteric Diseases, now the National Center for Emerging and Zoonotic Infectious Diseases, by the Centers of Disease Control and Prevention (CDC) (23,24). As shown in Figure 7.1, it is estimated that about 70% of global infections are zoonotic (of animal origin) (24).

The global One Health Initiative recognizes that "human health (including mental health via the human–animal bond phenomenon), animal health, and ecosystem health are inextricably linked" (25). Moreover, "One Health," a term coined by the late veterinary epidemiologist and parasitologist Dr. Calvin Schwabe at the University of California in the 1960s (25), seeks to "promote, improve, and defend the health and

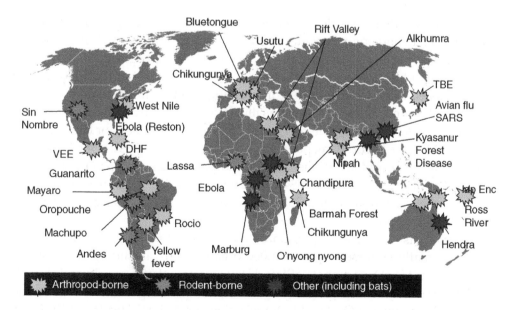

FIGURE 7.1 Emerging and reemerging infections—70% vector-borne or zoonotic.
Created by Thomas P. Monath, MD, for the One Health Initiative website.

well-being of all species by enhancing cooperation and collaboration between physicians, veterinarians, other scientific health and environmental professionals and by promoting strengths in leadership and management to achieve these goals" (25).

Formal Agreement to Connect Animal and Human Medical Communities

A significant breakthrough in bringing "the animal and human medical communities together" occurred in 2007 when Dr. Roger Mahr, president of the American Veterinary Medical Association (AVMA), met with the late Dr. Ronald Davis, president of the American Medical Association (AMA).

The discussion led to an agreement "that the best way for the AMA to get involved in such an endeavor would be to pass a formal landmark 'One Health' resolution" adopted in June 2007 (26,27), drafted by physician Dr. Laura Kahn and veterinarian Dr. Bruce Kaplan, co-founders of the One Health Initiative (26), with assistance from physician Dr. Tom Monath, an adjunct professor at the Harvard School of Public Health (26). The AVMA then "established a One Health Initiative Task Force and passed a One Health resolution analogous to the AMA's resolution in July 2008 (28). The task force became a One Health Commission (OHC), headed by Dr. Roger Mahr, headquartered at Iowa State University, and the first International One Health Conference took place in Melbourne, Australia (February 14–16, 2011; www.onehealthglobal.net/?p=475).

One Health approaches have found their way into health policies "that improve public health by incorporating human medicine, veterinary medicine, public health and environmental information," thereby allowing "practitioners to achieve optimal health for people, domestic animals, wildlife, and the environment, concurrently, over multiple scales" (29).

With One Health there is also increasing awareness that strategies need to involve not only the health and environmental science sides but also require "the cooperation of experts from numerous disciplines (e.g., social sciences, engineering, economics, education, and public policy, among others)" (29). The public health community will increasingly need to play a pivotal role in bringing together the human, animal, and environmental communities of practice, as illustrated in Figure 7.2 (30), with a view to focusing on human, animal, plant, and environmental health issues or concerns.

In June 2012, the World Bank published the economic benefits of One Health (31), concluding, as one example, "if one-half of mild pandemics are prevented, then the global net benefit is a substantial US$4.1 billion per year (i.e., 0.5 multiplied by 15, or US$3.4 billion). Prevention of all mild pandemics would yield a net global benefit of US$11.6 billion annually."

Reflecting its universal significance, the holistic One Health approach has now been formally endorsed by over 1,000 organizations, including the European Commission, the U.S. Department of State, U.S. Department of Agriculture, U.S. CDC, World Bank, World Health Organization (WHO), Food and Agriculture Organization of the United Nations (FAO), World Organisation for Animal Health (OIE), United Nations System Influenza Coordination (UNSIC), various universities, nongovernmental organizations (NGOs), and many others (30).

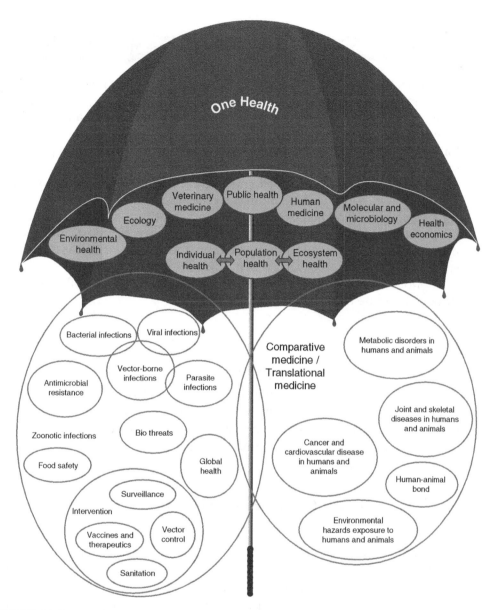

FIGURE 7.2 Scope of "One Health" according to the One Health Initiative.
Source: One Health Sweden.

Interrelationship Between Zoonotic Infections and Medicine

Today it is estimated that of the 1,415 microbes that are known to infect humans, more than 70% come from animals (25). Figure 7.2 illustrates the interrelationships between zoonotic infections and comparative medicine/translational medicine that go beyond "a relatively simple animal–human dyad," and consider "the roots of human well-being (and ill health) in the dynamics of complex ecological systems" (23).

BOX 7.2

One Health Initiative Global Strategies

1. Joint educational efforts among human medical, veterinary medical schools, and schools of public health and the environment;
2. Joint communication efforts in journals, at conferences, and via allied health networks;
3. Joint efforts in clinical care through the assessment, treatment, and prevention of cross-species disease transmission;
4. Joint cross-species disease surveillance and control efforts in public health;
5. Joint efforts in better understanding of cross-species disease transmission through comparative medicine and environmental research;
6. Joint efforts in the development and evaluation of new diagnostic methods, medicines, and vaccines for the prevention and control of diseases across species;
7. Joint efforts to inform and educate political leaders and the public sector through accurate media publications. (30)

The figure also highlights "that the health of people, wild and domestic animals, and ecosystems share a common fate," which is intensified by a new paradigm created by "a new global health environment," which challenges us "to again learn to live with an 'infectious uncertainty' and the potential worldwide impact of local crises." One Health Initiative global strategies are summarized in Box 7.2.

The U.S. One Health Commission (OHC)

Chartered in Washington, DC, on June 29, 2009, the OHC is "dedicated to promoting improved health of people, domestic animals, wildlife, plants and the environment" (32). Its board of directors is currently chaired by Dr. Joann Lindenmayer, and is supported by Dr. Cheryl Stroud, executive director, and Deeanna Burleson, associate executive director. The Commission is headquartered in the United States in North Carolina's Research Triangle Park region, Raleigh/Durham/Chapel Hill.

The mission/charter of the OHC is to "educate" and "create" networks to improve health outcomes and well-being of humans, animals, and plants and to promote environmental resilience through a collaborative, global One Health approach.

The commission will achieve its mission/charter with the following goals:

- *Connecting* One Health stakeholders
- *Creating* strategic networks/partnerships
- *Educating* about One Health issues to support a paradigm shift in information sharing, active health interventions, collaborations, and demonstration projects

More information is provided in Appendix A, "Profiles of Leading Health Organizations and Schools/Institutes of Public Health," and can be found at the OHC website (www.onehealthcommission.org).

Tackling the Fundamental Causes of
Global Health and Environmental Threats

In conclusion, contributing to *Jekel's Epidemiology, Biostatistics, Preventive Medicine, and Public Health* (32), Dr. Meredith Barrett and Dr. Steven Osofsky compellingly affirm that "Issues of global environmental change, global health, emerging disease, and sustainability present some of the most complex and far-reaching challenges of the 21st century." Furthermore, given the enormity of the universal transformation required in the decades ahead, they stress that "individual disciplines cannot address these issues in isolation" (32).

In addition, they contend that by tackling the fundamental causes of global health and environmental threats, "One Health offers a logical path forward by recognizing the interconnected nature of human, animal, and ecosystem health in an attempt to inform health and environmental policy, expand scientific knowledge, improve healthcare training and delivery, improve conservation outcomes, identify *Upstream* solutions, and address sustainability challenges" (32).

The key lies in prevention which could "not only reduce the response time to infectious disease outbreaks, but also predict and ideally prevent such disease emergence from occurring" in the first place, a lesson that we might take away from the Ebola crisis in West Africa and potential infections in the future.

7.3 TIMESCALING EVOLUTION AND RETHINKING
PUBLIC HEALTH INTERVENTIONS

Greenpeace International provides a timeline perspective on the planet's past and probable future—unless we change tack—reminding us that

> The earth is 4.6 billion years old. Scaling to 46 years humans have been here 4 hours, the Industrial Revolution began 1 minute ago, and in that time we have destroyed more than half the world's forests. (33)

This timescaling may prompt several basic questions: What happens in the next "15 to 30 seconds," and is there still time to turn things around globally? Against this time perspective, what also seems remarkable in the general scheme of things is the short time *Homo sapiens* have been around. As mentioned in the Preface, while modern humans evolved about 90 to 110 thousand years ago, they were anatomically and behaviorally more like us only around 50,000 years in Australia and perhaps 40,000 years in Europe. Most of the innovations and new technologies came about in the last nanoseconds or a few hundred years or so—especially in the last 50—and, ironically, while benefiting the developed world immensely, they have also simultaneously caused extensive damage to the planet in very little time.

Clearly, the current world ecological stressors, as illustrated in Figure 7.3 (34), are unsustainable and place a lot of responsibility and accountability (pressure) on global

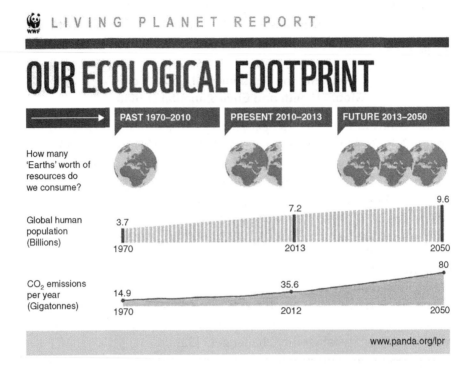

FIGURE 7.3 Our ecological footprint.

Source: World Wildlife Fund, *Living Planet Report 2014: Species and Spaces, People and Places* (34).

and national leadership to rise above partisan politics and profit margins and on the future of the planet and life as we know it.

The "bottom line" is that, if the globe and the people are already at risk from a 'sick' planet, then all the machinations; stocks and selling/purchasing powers; and self-interests will be in vain as future generations may not be around to appreciate or enjoy what the world has to offer—and then everyone loses.

"Thinking in Time"

Solutions are very much a case of "thinking in time" rather than "out of time," as Lee Smolin, an American theoretical physicist, in *Time Reborn: From the Crisis in Physics to the Future of the Universe* (35) suggests. In essence, the author argues that we must embrace the nature of time in a new way. In his view, we think outside of time when, "Faced with a technological or a social problem, we assume that the possible approaches are already determined as a set of absolute pre-existing categories." On the other hand, "thinking in time"—"a prototype for Darwinian evolutionary biology"—encourages us "to see everything that exists in nature, including ourselves and our technologies, as time-bound and part of a larger ever-evolving system" (35).

The continuing intentional separation of the "natural and the artificial" may have implications for public health interventions, discussed earlier, when considering an integrated and ecological public health framework. As one example, Professor Smolin cites climate change where we see "ourselves apart from nature and technologies as imposition on the natural world" rather than "muddying the distinction between the artificial and the natural," and thereby surmounting "the unprecedented problems raised by climate change," and likely most other complex and unpredictable social and political problems. He further affirms that "By assuming that nature and technology are mutually exclusive, both environmentalists who believe nature is paramount and those who see the world in purely economic terms miss the point."

Perhaps, above all, in the globe's next few "seconds," applying the 46-year timescaling model, our top priority needs to be, as emphasized earlier in this chapter, to turn around the present stance that "exploiting" the earth is an acceptable social norm to one that places the highest value on sustaining future generations and the planet (18).

The Folly of a "Limitless World"

It is noteworthy that as long ago as "1980 the WWF (established in 1961) World Conservation Strategy warned that humanity had no future unless nature and the world's natural resources were conserved" (36). It also introduced the concept of sustainable development—"living within the limits of the natural environment without compromising the needs of future generations—which has been central to WWF's thinking ever since." The WWF's "ultimate goal has always been 'people living in harmony with nature'—so we're about respecting and valuing the natural world and finding ways to share the Earth's resources fairly."

Unfortunately, in the past 30 years that has not been the case. "One key point that jumps out is that the Living Planet Index (LPI), which measures more than 10,000 representative populations of mammals, birds, reptiles, amphibians and fish, has declined by 52 percent since 1970" (34).

Marco Lambertini, director general of WWF International, highlights that "in less than two human generations, population sizes of vertebrate species have dropped by half. These are the living forms that constitute the fabric of the ecosystems which sustain life on Earth—and the barometer of what we are doing to our own planet, our only home. We ignore their decline at our peril" (37).

He further rightly asserts that "This has to make us stop and think" and queries, "What kind of future are we heading toward? And what kind of future do we want? Can we justify eroding our natural capital and allocating nature's resources so inequitably?"

His challenge for all of us is blunt, serious, and compelling:

We need a few things to change. First, we need unity around a common cause. Public, private and civil society sectors need to pull together in a bold and coordinated effort. Second, we need leadership for change. Sitting on the bench waiting for someone else to make the first move doesn't work. Heads of state need to start thinking globally; businesses and consumers need to stop behaving as if we live in a limitless world. (34)

7.4 PUBLIC HEALTH: A FORCE FOR SOCIAL CHANGE

In a paper identifying "the failings of past educational programs to address social and economic determinants of health" (37) Professor Donald Nutbeam, then at the Department of Public Health and Community Medicine at the University of Sydney in Australia, concluded that "Disappointingly, the potential of education as a tool for social change, and for political action has been somewhat lost in contemporary health promotion."

One of the reasons he gave for this lack of impact was that the provision of "supportive environments for health may have had the unintended consequence of leading to structural interventions 'on behalf' of people—health promotion which is done 'on' or 'to' people, rather than 'by' or 'with' people." In his article, he also called for the "rediscovery of the importance of health education . . . together with a significant widening of the content and methods used," a subject addressed in Chapter 8.0.

Reflecting on the present day, much of what Dr. Nutbeam, current vice-chancellor of the University of Southampton in the UK, observed in 2006 appears to still stand today and may very well be a major systemic failure in current public health interventions if we think for a moment about the global HIV/AIDS or the obesity epidemics. Rather than promoting prevention that is beyond public campaigns and focus on the person, we fund treatments in the form of medication or in the latter case even surgery (e.g., gastric bands).

However, case studies are emerging that are showing a much better understanding of the need to work closely with and through people if the goals of improving health and well-being are to be achieved.

In this section, case studies of initiatives in public health—with references or acknowledgments cited at the end of each scenario—have been provided by the Region of the Americas, India, and South Africa, respectively.

Region of the Americas: Pan American Health Organization (PAHO)

Case Study 1: *Using Health in All Policies as a Driver for Social Change*

By: Dr. Francisco Becerra-Posada (Assistant Director, PAHO, Washington, DC), Dr. Luiz Galvão (Chief, Sustainable Development and Environmental Health, Washington, DC), and Dr. Kira Fortune (Advisor, Determinants of Health, Washington, DC)

India: Public Health Foundation of India (PHFI)

Case Studies 2 and 3: *Indian Experiences With Action on the Social Determinants of Health: Risk-Factor-Based, Village-Level Decision Making, and Design of Urban Policy Making*

By: Dr. Devaki Nambiar (Research Scientist, PHFI, Delhi, India)

South Africa: Public Health Association of South Africa (PHASA)

Case Study 4: *Ideal Clinic Concept in South Africa*

By: Professor Stephen J. H. Hendricks (Public Health Management Policy Specialist, University of Pretoria, South Africa)

CASE STUDY 1

Using Health in All Policies as a Driver for Social Change

Francisco Becerra-Posada, Luiz Augusto Galvão, and Kira Fortune,
Pan American Health Organization (PAHO)

The world has progressed and changed substantially in recent decades. How to guarantee a world that is socially, economically, and environmentally sustainable is a question that governments, specialists, academics, businesses, and citizens around the world are trying to answer. As part of this debate, the United Nations (UN) has defined a package of Sustainable Development Goals (SDGs) to be adopted. In the deliberations leading up to the SDGs it was well recognized that the post-2015 agenda needed a rigorous framework that clearly articulated both how sustainable development differs from and is preferable to existing development models and how health and development are inextricably linked (1). Greater synergies between health and other sectors could be achieved by framing the goals in such a way that their attainment requires policy coherence and shared solutions across multiple sectors; that is, a Health in All Policies approach. Thus, as preparations for the post-2015 process continued to gain momentum, the public health community had an opportunity to secure a broader development framework that put equity at its very center, using multisectoral mechanisms such as the Health in All Policies (HiAP) Approach.

In 2013, countries agreed to the Helsinki Statement on HiAP, stating that "Health in All Policies is an approach to public policies across sectors that systematically takes into account the health implications of decisions, seeks synergies and avoids harmful health impacts in order to improve population health and health equity" (2). HiAP draws from national and international development in the area of health policy and comprehensive health care. This includes the Alma-Ata Declaration (3), the Ottawa Charter (4), and the Rio Political Declaration on Social Determinants of Health (5). The latter was adopted on October 21, 2011, during the World Conference on the Social Determinants of Health and expresses worldwide political commitment to implement an approach geared toward the social determinants of health, which are often better addressed through policies, interventions, and actions outside the health sector. To implement an HiAP approach it is paramount to identify common ground between the health sector and other sectors and build shared agendas and strong partnerships that promote policies aiming at improving the health and well-being of populations.

The Region of the Americas has played a key role in shaping the global discourse on HiAP. In February 2013, 30 PAHO/WHO countries met in Brazil for a regional consultation on HiAP. The consultation served to introduce the HiAP Conceptual Framework to key stakeholders in preparation for the 8th Global Conference on Health Promotion held in Helsinki in June 2013. The goal of the regional consultation was to discuss the conceptual framework with stakeholders

(continued)

CASE STUDY 1 (*continued*)

from the Americas and to formulate a regional position on HiAP. The outcomes of the consultation were later incorporated into the WHO HiAP Framework for Country Action (6) as well as into the final Conference Statement on HiAP (2). During the regional consultation, countries similarly recommended the need for a Regional HiAP Action Plan to ensure that this approach is applied in a consistent manner across the region.

Following up on these particular recommendations, the PAHO has, in close consultations with countries, partners, and stakeholders, developed a Regional Plan of Action on HiAP, which was adopted by PAHO's Directing Council in September 2014. The plan is informed by the WHO HiAP Framework for Country Action as well as evidence from the region itself. It contains region-specific recommendations for how to implement HiAP by setting specific goals and targets for a period of 5 years. This will not only further strengthen the HiAP agenda and the application of this approach in the region but also provide important insights so as to move the HiAP forward in a practical manner.

Most recently, countries in the region have gathered data and showcased regional evidence, providing concrete examples as to how countries have implemented the HiAP approach. Success stories such as Ecuador's National Plan for Good Living and Mexico's efforts to tackle obesity through an HiAP approach are just some examples of the rich evidence that exists within the Region of the Americas (see Box). A number of countries showcasing their evidence reported that successfully tackling health equity requires not only the acknowledgment that health is determined by factors that lie outside the health sector, but also the commitment of resources from government, private sector, academia, and civil society. Similarly, it was noted that recognition of the interdependence of all sectors in a community, region, and country is necessary to improve health, along with acknowledgment that a participatory approach including those communities that are most marginalized is needed to be successful in reducing health inequities. Thus, policy coordination is necessary to address the various social determinants of health and through integration of HiAP whether it be education, environment, employment, or transportation-focused. Within any proposed health governance structure, partnerships that include "unusual" or "unlikely" partners are essential for conducting a comprehensive approach to achieve health equity. This entails including representatives from other sectors as equal partners in the decision-making processes.

In shaping the post-2015 goals, the public health community now has had a unique opportunity to use a HiAP approach in informing policies and practices that recognize the importance of building partnerships and developing networks with and within different sectors of the society, with the ultimate goal of supporting health equity and promoting social change. The strength of the Region of the Americas is indeed its ability to build partnerships and develop networks

(*continued*)

CASE STUDY 1 (*continued*)

with different sectors of society to address the stark health inequities seen in the region through innovative, sustainable, and consensus-based public policies aimed at attaining the highest possible level of health for all. There is strength in unity, and with sufficient collaboration and multisectoral alliances, the Region of the Americas will continue to make great strides in promoting social change.

BOX

Integrated Policies and Social Action for Sustainable Development in Ecuador: The Case of the National Plan for "Good Living": As part of the reform, Ecuador's new constitution called for the democratization of right to water, land, credit, technologies, knowledge and information, and diversity. The *National Plan of Good Living* gives life to a new vision of the role of government in social policy and management. It calls for inclusive, multicultural, and sustainable development, presenting a new way for understanding growth, participation, and the distribution of its benefits. Development is defined in a broad manner, beyond the quantitative margins of the economic lens, moving toward an inclusive, sustainable, democratic, and economic strategy. By seeking to coordinate action among different sectors and levels of government, the *National Plan of Good Living* creates economies of scale and supports the efficient allocation of resources as well as multisectoral collaboration. It also entails a participatory methodology in the development of plans at national and local levels.

The National Agreement for Healthy Food: Strategies to Combat Obesity in Mexico: Mexico has one of the highest rates of overweight and obesity in the world. Since 1980, obesity and overweight prevalence have tripled in Mexico, especially among the adult population, with 70% of the population having a body mass index greater than the healthy range. This epidemic results in high costs for the health system, affects the sustainability of the social security system, and threatens the economic and social stability of the population. In 2010, the Mexican Government launched the National Agreement for Healthy Food, Physical Activity and Health for the Prevention for Chronic Diseases. The agreement, led by the Secretariat of Health, mobilized 15 heads of governmental agencies and received the support of the president at the time. This was the first time in Mexico that a healthy public policy was proposed to address the challenges of obesity through a multisectoral approach as well as by adopting mechanisms and actions that go beyond the scope of the health sector. As a result, there has been a reduction of salt, trans fat, sugar, and caloric sweeteners in processed food products as well as an increase in physical activity in schools and workplaces. The sustainability of the initiative is a result of the development of actions not only at the federal level, but also at state and local levels, and by establishing key norms and regulations that apply to a variety of sectors.

Source: Summary of Experiences from the Americas, 2013 (7).

(continued)

CASE STUDY 1 *(continued)*

References

1. The World We Want. *Health in the post-2015 agenda.* Report of the Global Thematic Consultation on Health; April 2013 [cited 2014 Nov 15]. Accessed from http://www.post2015hlp.org /wp-content/uploads/2013/04/health-in-the-post-2015-agenda_LR.pdf
2. World Health Organization. *The Helsinki statement on Health in All Policies.* The 8th Global Conference on Health Promotion, June 10–14, 2013, Helsinki, Finland. Geneva: WHO; 2013 [cited 2014 Aug 13]. Accessed from http://www.healthpromotion2013.org /images/8GCHP_Helsinki_Statement.pdf
3. World Health Organization. *Declaration of Alma-Ata.* International Conference on Primary Health Care, June 6–12, 1978, Alma-Ata, USSR. Geneva: WHO; 1978 [cited 2014 Aug 13]. Accessed from http://www.who.int/publications/almaata_declaration_en.pdf
4. World Health Organization. *The Ottawa charter for health promotion.* First International Conference on Health Promotion, November 21, 1986, Ottawa, Canada. Geneva: WHO; 1986 [cited 2014 Aug 13]. Accessed from http://www.paho.org/hiap/images/stories /PDFs/1986-OttawaCharterEN2.pdf
5. World Health Organization. *Rio political declaration on social determinants of health.* World Conference on Social Determinants of Health, October 19–21, 2011, Rio de Janeiro, Brazil. Geneva: WHO; 2011 [cited 2014 Mar 13]. Accessed from http://www.who.int/ sdhconference/declaration/Rio_political_declaration.pdf
6. World Health Organization. *Health in All Policies (HiAP) framework for country action.* Geneva: WHO; 2014 [cited 2014 Mar 13]. Accessed from http://www.who.int /cardiovascular_diseases/140120HPRHiAPFramework.pdf?ua=1
7. Pan American Health Organization. *Summary of experiences from the Americas.* The 8th Global Conference on Health Promotion, June 10–14, 2013, Helsinki, Finland. Washington, DC: PAHO; 2013 [cited 2014 Aug 13]. Accessed from http://www.paho.org/hq/index. php?option=com_docman&task=doc_download&gid=24430&Itemid=270&lang=en

CASE STUDIES 2 AND 3

Indian Experiences With Action on the Social Determinants of Health: Risk-Factor-Based, Village-Level Decision Making, and Design of Urban Policy Making

Dr. Devaki Nambiar, Public Health Foundation of India (PHFI)

1. Risk-Factor-Based: The Case of National Tobacco Control

Some lessons may be offered by India's approach to tobacco control efforts (1), which in fact predate India's allegiance to the WHO Framework Convention on Tobacco Control (FCTC). The precedent was initially set through Supreme and High Court mandated bans on smoking in public places, offices, restaurants, bars, and open streets. Following this, over the past decade, various ministries have developed policies. The Ministry of Railways has banned the sale of tobacco products on platforms and trains, the Ministry of Road Transport has designated

(continued)

public transport as smoke-free, and the Ministry of Home Affairs has done the same for prisons. Most central government offices as well as the army and navy headquarters require public servants to submit an undertaking that they do not use tobacco in smoke or smokeless forms. These efforts are buttressed by the mobilization and advocacy of civil society organizations. Food safety regulations have been used to prohibit the production, sale, and storage of smokeless tobacco products. These policy approaches are seen to be a model for multisectoral coordination for noncommunicable diseases (NCD) control in the country (1). Moreover, advancing tobacco control arguments, experts note that tobacco control has implications for addressing food insecurity, reducing poverty, and improving employment (in less mechanized industries) (2). The challenges of implementation certainly remain, but the policy precedent for multisectoral action has been set through these efforts.

2. Village-Level Action-Based: The Case of the State of Chhattisgarh
At subnational scales, there are critical experiences to draw from as well. In the central Indian state of Chhattisgarh, from 2006 onwards the State Health Resource Centre has steered the creation of a 26-indicator Village Level Health and Human Development Index (3). It was felt that a participatory platform was needed for accessible (i.e., not overly technical) information around key health issues and determinants. This scheme continues to run, and is facilitated by state cadres of some 67,000 community health workers who had a longer precedent of working closely with communities. In 2008, India's National Rural Health Mission began convening Village Health Sanitation and Nutrition Committees, and these formations were connected to Village Health Monitoring Registers. These registers monitored health status (such as cause-specific mortality), service access (immunization, drugs, and referral transport), and determinants (functionality of hand pumps, girls' school attendance, and rural employment) using basic counts in the previous month. The use of health equity data in this process is immediate; registers are used during committee meetings to create Village Health Action plans in a stepwise process of identifying a gap, its cause, a response, responsibilities of different stakeholders, and a timeline for joint action. Moreover, this is in keeping with India's 73rd constitutional amendment for decentralization of decision making at, as it were, the most local administrative unit, where health and its social determinants are in effect experienced in a conjoined fashion and where action can have the most immediate effect.

3. Urban Policy Planning: The Case of the National Urban Health Mission
In May 2013, India's National Urban Health Mission (NUHM) came into effect, placing emphasis on improving urban health infrastructure, health service

(continued)

provisioning, and financing, with a focus on the poor. Acknowledging both the diversity and complexity of urban poverty across Indian cities, a Technical Resource Group (TRG) was convened by the Ministry of Health and Family Welfare to support the process (4). Apart from typical policy recommendation exercises, detailed situational analyses of 30 Indian cities were carried out, comprising interviews and discussions with officials of local body and state departments, as well as vulnerable communities across residential/habitational, occupational, and social categories. This policy process thus sought to qualitatively understand the diversity and complexity of India's urban health scenario based on understanding the conditions and aspirations of highly vulnerable groups, as well as the challenges and demands of policy implementers. Limitations notwithstanding, this process resulted in nuanced, pragmatic, and locally customizable recommendations for NUHM. These include the procedure of mapping of vulnerable groups to siting, construction, timing, and staffing of urban health posts, from good practices in convergence for urban health to the identification of priority areas for policy making and governance reform. There are at least two key lessons from this exercise. First, at the outset, the intersectionality of the vulnerability of the urban poor was recognized as traversing habitational, occupational, and social domains, requiring attention across the housing, transport, nutrition, water, and sanitation sectors, as well as departments concerned with social justice and empowerment. Second, the processes of policy making can themselves be opportunity structures for expanding participation and stakeholdership. The Technical Resource Group of the NUHM, for instance, comprised not just state department officials, but also municipal corporation officials, technical experts, and civil society advocates; it also conducted direct interactions with citizens and beneficiaries of services. Efforts are now under way to ensure that both the letter and the spirit of these recommendations may be feasibly operationalized and customized based on the specific context of individual Indian cities.

References

1. Arora M, Chauhan K, John S, Mukhopadhyay A. Multi-sectoral action for addressing social determinants of noncommunicable diseases and mainstreaming health promotion in national health programmes in India. *Indian J Community Med.* 2011;36,Suppl S1:43–49.

2. Reddy KS, Yadav A, Arora M, Nazar GP. The future of tobacco control: Integrating tobacco control into health and development agendas. *Tob Control.* 2012;21:281–286. doi:10.1136/tobaccocontrol-2011-050419

3. Public Health Foundation of India/World Health Organisation Country Office. *PHFI/WHO consultative workshop on an Indian "health equity watch:" A report of proceedings.* New Delhi: PHFI; 2013.

4. National Urban Health Mission Technical Resource Group. *Making the system work for the urban poor: Recommendations of the National Urban Health Mission Technical Resource Group.* New Delhi: National Health Systems Resource Centre; 2014.

CASE STUDY 4

Ideal Clinic Concept in South Africa

Stephen J. H. Hendricks, Public Health Association of South Africa (PHASA)

These are extracts pieced together from the National Department of Health (NDOH) documents on the development and functioning of the proposed Ideal Clinic (IC) for South Africa.

Introduction

Since 1994, the new democratic government of South Africa has introduced various measures in primary health care (PHC) for facilitating access to service delivery with particular focus on the vulnerable including women and children. In particular, a policy was introduced, which provided for free health services for children under 6 years and for nursing mothers. While this policy was implemented, there was ongoing research and development on how the PHC system can be improved. A new development has been the IC.

The IC initiative was started in July 2013 by the NDOH1 as a way of systematically improving the deficiencies in PHC clinics in the public sector. The goal is high-quality PHC services universally available as in a "social franchise." Deficiencies in quality were picked up by the NDOH baseline audit in 2011–12 and the more recent inspections of the Office of Health Standards Compliance (OHSC). Over a period of 8 months, 196 elements (now), categorized into 10 components and 26 subcomponents were identified that needed to be fully functional if the clinic was to be "ideal." Behind each element was a set of questions (or criteria) that had been developed by teams of nurses and doctors who visited 10 study clinics on a regular basis over an 8-month study phase. Each element is scored as red (not present/not functional), amber (in process of being fixed), or green (present and functional). Process flows have been developed to clarify what is required for full achievement.

It is envisaged that the implementation of the IC concept will help to fix the system from the facility, district, and provincial levels and will also point to what needs to be corrected at the national level to fix the system. The concept will also help to understand and address the bottlenecks at all these levels that persistently hamper PHC facilities from providing quality services to the community they serve. The NDOH is striving through the IC process to provide an optimally functioning PHC service platform that will support health program managers to improve the health status of the population.

Description of an Ideal Clinic

An IC is a clinic where all the elements under the subcomponents under the 10 components in the following list are fully functional. Such a clinic is client-centered, works with the community it serves, applies all the relevant resources

(continued)

CASE STUDY 4 (*continued*)

at its disposal to provide a quality PHC service and optimally uses its referral network for the benefit of its clients. A clinic will be classified to have reached Ideal Clinic status when it scores 80% and higher in an OHSC inspection. Clinics and other PHC facilities will only be able to reach Ideal Clinic status if they are well supported by optimally functioning district health management, provincial health departments, and the national health department.

The IC components are:

i. Administration
ii. Clinical guidelines and integrated chronic disease management to arrive at integrated clinical service management
iii. The availability of a doctor
iv. Medicines, supplies, and laboratory support
v. Staffing and professional standards
vi. Infrastructure and support services
vii. Health information management
viii. Communication
ix. District health system
x. Partners and stakeholders

The IC components are aligned with the OHSC domains. It is not duplication, but it is not and cannot be the same process. The OHSC processes are about doing assessments (this includes self-assessments done by health facilities), while the IC processes are about correcting weaknesses. Addressing weaknesses is visualized to be a proactive process, which should not wait for negative findings by the OHSC before they are addressed. The IC process will also assist districts and their facilities to secure the required resources needed to address weaknesses.

Conclusion

The IC program is work in progress toward the realization of equitable access to quality health care that is affordable for the total population of South Africa.

Acknowledgment

The National Department of Health of South Africa is acknowledged for the information in the documentation obtained.

7.5 LEADING CHANGE IN A NEW ERA: TRANSFORMING MINDSETS AND "BUILDING THE NEW" THROUGH ONE HEALTH RESEARCH, EDUCATION, POLICY, AND PRACTICE

Education: The Key to Social Progress

Close to 20 years ago, United Nations Educational, Scientific and Cultural Organization (UNESCO) provided what some may regard as a definitive statement of placing education at the center for the advancement of social progress and the development of new forms of living together:

> Education is the most effective means that society possesses for confronting the challenges of the future. Indeed, education will shape the world of tomorrow. Progress increasingly depends upon the products of educated minds: upon research, invention, innovation and adaptation. Of course, educated minds and instincts are needed not only in laboratories and research institutes, but in every walk of life. Indeed, access to education is the sine qua non for effective participation in the life of the modern world at all levels. Education, to be certain, is not the whole answer to every problem. But education, in its broadest sense, must be a vital part of all efforts to imagine and create new relations among people and to foster greater respect for the needs of the environment. (38)

A few years later this resolve was also captured in the UN's Earth Charter, which in Principle 9 emphasized the importance of "integrating into . . . education and life-long learning the knowledge, values, and skills needed for a sustainable way of life" (39). More recently, the 2000–2015 Millennium Development Goals (MDGs; 40) emphasized the need to expand primary education while the post-2015 SDGs (41) have gone further reinforcing that by 2030

> all learners acquire knowledge and skills needed to promote sustainable development, including among others through education for sustainable development and sustainable lifestyles, human rights, gender equality, promotion of a culture of peace and non-violence, global citizenship, and appreciation of cultural diversity and of culture's contribution to sustainable development. (SDG 4)

The urgency of building on the considerable success of the MDG targets aimed at primary education (90% of children now enrolled in developing nations) and the unmet vocational needs of both younger and older generations cannot be overstated. In her closing remarks at the UN Economic and Social Council (ECOSOC) Youth Forum, Helen Clark, administrator of the UN Development Programme (UNDP), observed that "Today's generation of youth is the largest the world has ever known" (42) with most of the 75 million youth unemployed and living in developing countries affected by war and conflict, suffering from "widespread lack of access to education and other services."

The desperation felt by an estimated 50 million migrants of all ages attempting to relocate from south to north—"fleeing wars and repression in Syria, Eritrea, Libya and Iraq"—the largest number since the Second World War according to the International Organization for Migration (43), and Europe's reluctance to accept them may be a sign of a much larger issue undermining universal human rights. Columnist of the Year Caitlin Moran, who sees migration in a wider historical context, where "movement" has always been part of humanity's social "murmurations," concludes that "The boats will not stop coming, because there is nowhere else for these people, with their children to go." Coupled with "predictions about climate change," it is highly likely, the writer maintains, that "they will be joined, within a generation, by millions more fleeing drought, flood, or countries that have been inundated by the sea." Factors, such as oppression, poverty, malnutrition, and hopelessness, that are driving hundreds of thousands to seek a better life (or maintaining life itself!) must be seen in their entirety, not as singular, haphazard events. If so, it may be argued that present-day global responses to migration and other serious societal issues, many discussed in Chapter 2.0, require much better coordinated and compassionate public health and practical geopolitical interventions than are presently at hand in both the more developed and emerging nations, when the former are often the source of destabilization of the latter, and where surely a "barbed-wired Europe" cannot be the answer (44).

Gaining a much better understanding of the principles and approaches associated with "One World, One Health" through education from early childhood to postgraduate and nonformal lifelong learning could be a logical starting point for improving how we see the world and its future sustainability.

Translating "One Health" Possibilities Into Reality

In this regard, students from diverse disciplines might take the lead, collaborating closely on projects or studies with experts from the health, medical, and biological sciences, environmental and social sciences, engineering, economics, and education, among others, developing new lines and forms of inquiry, thereby also raising awareness about One Health possibilities in research, education, and practice arenas.

As one example, adopting a "bottom-up" change model approach, postgraduate students from Duke University, Oxford University, UNC Gillings School of Public Health, and North Carolina State University in a concept paper argued that "The collaborative groundwork for One Health could be developed through existing national and international resources" and incorporated into standard curricula (45). Their research revealed that currently "less than 3% of the total veterinary curriculum in the US is devoted to public health issues, resulting in fewer than 2% of current veterinarians working in public health." Perhaps unsurprisingly, the authors observe, given the "anthropocentrism" of traditional medical curricula and medical education, "medical training maintains a strict focus on human health." What may be equally disturbing in the light of the pressing "new challenges to human, animal and ecosystem health" is that "neither discipline receives training in basic environmental science, despite its proven relevance to each field and to global health." In addition, they report that with "limited time, disciplinary inertia, and lack of funding," "traditional Western medical education focuses solely on the human system, with a reactive rather than preventive approach." Furthermore, the students suggest curriculum delivery alternatives, including multidisciplinary common coursework, supplemental courses through distance learning, and summer electives.

Moreover, the student researchers propose that One Health could benefit significantly through the creation of national centers of excellence (centers of One Health excellence [COHE]), as shown in Figure 7.4, possibly with "seed" funding provided by a number of organizations (e.g., WHO, CDC, United States Agency for International Development [USAID], the UN's environmental program, foundations). These could collaborate with national, regional, and global and educational institutions, government agencies, and public–private partnerships to develop blended curricula, advance multidisciplinary research, and inform "plans that acknowledge the balance of the environment and health in achieving sustainable development."

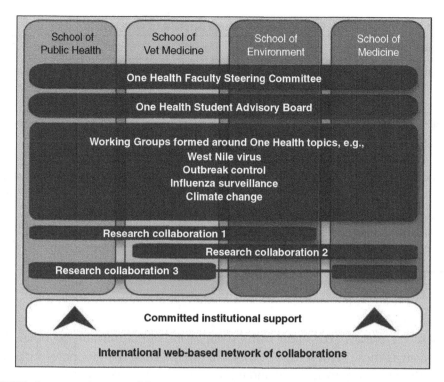

FIGURE 7.4 A proposed center of One Health excellence (COHE) collaborative structure designed to involve multiple disciplines around specific research collaborations.

Source: Adapted from M.E. Barrett et al., "Integrating a One Health Approach in Education to Address Global Health and Sustainability Challenges," *Frontiers in Ecology and the Environment*. 2010;9(4):239–245 (45).

The benefits of greater student engagement in One Health, which is closely associated with Conservation Medicine, EcoHealth, and Global Health, are many (46). For one thing, increasing involvement could enable them to assume the role of change agents and "become more effective health and environmental professionals." In addition, by working collaboratively "on real-life examples," students would be able to build on "a framework for problem-solving that they can bring into their professional or graduate training."

Bridging Reformed Corporate Values and One Health Aspirations

In advancing the goals of One Health, we might take a leaf from John Mackey and Professor Raj Sisodia's alternative to free enterprise capitalism, cited earlier (12). Their view is that while capitalism "has been the most powerful creative system of social cooperation and human progress ever conceived its perception and its role in society have been distorted," hence the need for more responsible or conscientious capitalism. They challenge business leaders "to rethink why their organizations exist, and to acknowledge their roles in the interdependent global marketplace." Their movement, as readers will recall, is based on four interconnected and mutually reinforcing core principles (12); see Table 7.1.

TABLE 7.1 Core Conscious Capitalism Principles Applied to One Health

CONSCIOUS CAPITALISM		ONE HEALTH (ILLUSTRATIVE EXAMPLES)
Higher purpose	→	Prioritizing interdependency of human/animal/plant needs and environmental requirements over political/personal gain
Stakeholder integration	→	Multidisciplinary involvement at all levels, resolving problems and sharing information, opportunities, political influence, and power
Conscious leadership	→	Inclusive/participatory visions and decision-making, and collaborative solutions with a view to creating a sustainable future
Conscious culture/management	→	Global ethical values rooted in interdependencies and the sanctity of life, translated into day-to-day thinking and actions

These "reformed" corporate values might also be applicable to other "public goods," such as those represented by One Health, guiding the rationales for adopting One Health in both organizational and educational circles, particularly with a view to "transforming mindsets and building the new."

Professor Waltner-Toews's critique of science and technology may strengthen the case. His main point is that today's health systems have also become "distorted" as too much faith in the 20th century, and to this day, has been placed in science/technological interventions alongside profit margins over altruistic humanitarian efforts (23). The Mackey and Sisodia core principles may be a way of transcending the narrow focus of health, as applied only to humans, by promoting broader perspectives that take public health in general and One Health approaches in particular to a more encompassing or holistic level of reality or engagement:

Preparatory Steps Toward "One World, One Health" Education

Developing the building blocks for incorporating One Health themes in early childhood and higher education is essential, calling for collective action by legislators, other public and private education providers as well as public health associations to develop progressive and comprehensive One Health learning opportunities beginning in preschool and continuing thematically to postgraduate education levels. The timing for considering these ideas may be especially propitious in the United States, where President Obama's recent proclamation on prevention over cure and making the United States the healthiest nation on Earth by 2030 is highly ambitious but commendable (47).

In terms of learning in the early years, students could benefit from discussing, as examples, the uniqueness of the planet, the importance and connection of all living things—learning about other cultures, animals, and plants alongside or contextualized within reading, language, and mathematical skills.

In later years, students could build on their broad foundation of One Health and continue to explore, ideally through active, collaborative, and interdisciplinary learning, topics that mirror, as one example, the proposed main themes of the SDG framework, that is, structuring curricula around the natural environment (e.g., climate change and impact on the world's ecosystem); global infrastructure (e.g., energy, economic growth, water, and sanitation), and well-being (e.g., poverty, equitable education, and peaceful, inclusive societies) (48). Rather than giving the students a fragmented view of reality where, as Peter Senge at Massachusetts Institute of Technology (MIT) observed, technical rationality remains "the prevailing epistemology, disconnecting theory from practice and sending young people into the world with heads full of ideas and 'answers' but little experience in producing more effective action" (49), One Health could act as a unifying concept and prompt the creation of novel collaborative experiential learning experiences.

There is no doubt that the paradigm shift to One Health will impact fundamentally on governance, policy, and practice, potentially extending the mission of the recognized "Health in All Policies (HiAP)" approach to inspiring a new global "One Health in All Policies (OHiAP)" framework.

Rebalancing Mindsets

Moving in these directions will be facilitated, so reason the authors of *The Future Public Health* (19), if we recognize that we "are not dealing with simple systems that can be predicted and controlled but complex adaptive systems with multiple points of equilibrium that are unpredictably sensitive to small changes within the system."

To a considerable extent, practicing public health and embedding One Health in this decade and beyond will also demand a new vision and rebalancing of our mindset: reorienting our thinking from a strictly disease-driven approach to health (human, animal) and the environment to taking a much more positive (pro vs. anti) stance that embraces prevention along with "well-being, balance, and integration." The 20th century focus on individualism and a "mechanistic understanding of the world and ourselves" would need to shift to prioritizing "the capacity to learn from and with others" and developing a more fluid or organic approach to decision making, drawing increasingly on "a future consciousness to inform the present." Implications for how we may live, learn, and work, discussed further in Chapter 8.0, are considerable.

Optimizing the Health and Well-Being of the Earth Community

At a global level, finding imaginative and alternative ways of tackling intractable issues or problems seems more crucial than ever before and may benefit from evolving "thinking" and "doing" patterns just discussed. Enacting positive transformative change—not only doing things better but doing better things—is no longer just wishful thinking but strikes at the heart of humanity's survival in this and future centuries.

To illustrate, although fewer people are in poverty since 1990 (down 50%) and there is progress with regard to polio (80% of the world is now polio-free) and HIV infections (38% decline), a Council of Councils report card (an initiative of the Council on Foreign Relations)—to which 26 major policy institutes contributed—concluded "that multilateral action on most of the critical transnational threats is sorely lacking" (50).

Although one bright spot is the curtailment of global nuclear proliferation with a grade of B−, survey report card respondents gave 8 of the 10 issues, including global economic systems, climate change, development, and global trade, only mediocre C+ grades, while cyber governance, transnational terrorism, and violent conflict among states were rated C−, and internal violent conflict received the lowest score, a D. Defusion of "the risk of great power conflict" was ascribed the highest priority in 2014.

Projected losses from noncommunicable diseases are estimated to be US$47 trillion by 2030 or 70% of lost output, with most costs due to a rise in mental ill-health and cardiovascular diseases. It is estimated that at least 40% of the costs—notwithstanding lives!—impact on "non-health-related areas of society, equal contributions from government, the private sector and civil society."

It may be noteworthy to mention how quickly world priorities change. In 2011, Dr. Ian Johnson, a British economist, then Secretary General of the Club of Rome and a former vice president of the World Bank, concluded that "The largest challenge we face will be to create the opportunities for meaningful employment across the globe for the maximum people." Fast forwarding to 2015, defusion of "the risk of great power conflict" is ascribed the highest priority by the Council of Councils. The affairs of the world pale in comparison when set against its potential destruction.

According to Professor Alexander Likhotal, president and CEO of Green Cross International (a "Red Cross for the environment") and former adviser to Mikhail Gorbachev, the first president of the Soviet Union, "The problem is not about the world; it is about us, it is about our inability to change our eternal belief that we will always be able to shape the world according to our needs" (51). He references the World Bank, which predicts that by 2050 "the GDP of the world will reach 200 trillion a year," meaning that "three worlds sitting on the resources we have today" (52). His main concern is that the costs far outweigh human capacity to respond to population needs "unless we change the way we deal with resources and energy."

Moreover, cautioning that "the world is headed into a perfect storm of an interconnected economic, ecological and social crisis," Professor Likhotal maintains that it has also become "clear that growth is unsustainable and de-growth is unstable" (53). Coping with these challenges, he says, "will depend on a different way of thinking about the economy and our ability to use the changes at hand for transformative change of the modern economic model—a renewables-based system, which enhances access, health and security, creates jobs and safeguards the environment." Above all, he concedes that achieving these ends requires building "human relationship with nature" (which) "crosses all boundaries and transcends all ideas of class" and necessitates "a solution that goes beyond good governance and good policy, and hinges on the shared responsibility for a sustainable and just future for all."

Along similar lines, authors Professor Julio Frenk, Dr. Octavio Gómez-Dantés, and Dr. Suerie Moon, of the article "From Sovereignty to Solidarity: A Renewed Concept of Global Health for an Era of Complex Interdependence" (54), provide a glimpse of how Professor Likhotal's "ends" might ideally be enacted in a world where issues "extend beyond the capacity of any one country." The authors' narrative transcends national goals and argues for a "unifying force to build a global society," not through "traditional framings of global transfers for health, development aid, and international cooperation," but by "building global solidarity," offering "a more symmetrical expression of mutual respect between members of a society," and addressing "the underlying conditions of interdependence in an unequal world." Underpinning the authors' focus on global health is the "realization of health as a human right based on a recognition of our common humanity." This fundamental valuing and acceptance by global leadership could easily be applied to other "key systemic barriers to sustainable development priorities" that lie before us: "inequality, unsustainable consumption patterns, weak institutional capacity, and environmental degradation that the MDGs neglected" (51).

Research findings are clear: "social, economic, political and educational inequalities within and between countries" are the root causes of most societal ills, undermining, as examples, social cohesion, poverty reduction, economic growth, and democracy (55). There are no easy answers to tackling these universal issues but "reinforcing the integration of culturally relevant education for sustainable development," discussed earlier in this chapter, must surely play a pivotal role. Given other potentially viable options, few may disagree that education remains the most compelling "vehicle or instrument for change" as well as the most vital "means of assuring a more sustainable future" (55).

To make a substantive difference, however, education in the 21st century, while meeting primary care and vocational needs, must be painted with a different, some say social constructivist, brush—one that honors multiple traditions and crossing of cultures, values different ways of looking at things, and encourages the trading of personal "stories" to create not only new forms of living together and organizations of the future but also new possibilities to sustain life (56).

REFERENCES

1. Worldometers. http://www.worldometers.info/. Accessed December 31, 2014.
2. World Health Organization. WHO global health expenditure atlas: September 2014. http://www.who.int/health-accounts/atlas2014.pdf. Accessed January 20, 2014.
3. Sachs J. *To move the world: JFK's quest for peace.* London: The Bodley Head; 2014.
4. Sattler R. Materialism, holism, and mysticism—A mandala. http://www.beyondwilber.ca/bookpre/mandala/mandala_of_life_and_living.html. Accessed November 6, 2013.
5. PMC Communication Ltd. Uganda—Vision 2040 builds on advantages. *The Daily Telegraph.* October 21, 2014.
6. Gosden E. Capitalism must change to save the planet, says Prince. *The Daily Telegraph.* May 28, 2014.
7. Selwyn B. *The global development crisis.* Oxford: Wiley; 2014.
8. Piketty T. *Capital in the twenty-first century.* Goldhammer A, trans. London, England: The Belknap Press of Harvard University Press; 2014.
9. Bond M. Film of the week: *The Wolf of Wall Street. The Mail on Sunday.* January 19, 2014:25.
10. Arlidge J. Dawn of a gilded age. *The Sunday Times Magazine.* May 11, 2014:17.
11. Harman W. Humanistic capitalism: Another alternative. *J Humanistic Psychol.* 1974;14:5–32. http://jhp.sagepub.com/content/14/1/5.full.pdf. Accessed August 20, 2014.
12. Mackey J, Sisodia R. *Conscious capitalism: Liberating the heroic spirit of business.* Boston, MA: Harvard Business School Publishing; 2013.
13. Schwartz T. Companies that practice "conscious capitalism" perform 10x better. http://blogs.hbr.org/2013/04/companies-that-practice-conscious-capitalism-perform/. Accessed August 20, 2014.

14. Simpson S, Fischer BD, Rohde M. The conscious capitalism philosophy pay off: A qualitative and financial analysis of conscious capitalism corporations. *J Leadersh Account Ethics.* 2013;10(4): 19–29. http://www.na-businesspress.com/jlae/simpsons_web10_4_.pdf. Accessed August 21, 2014.

15. Williams C. Huawei founder Ren Zhengfei rejects 'greedy' public markets. *The Telegraph.* http://www.telegraph.co.uk/finance/newsbysector/mediatechnologyandtelecoms/tele-coms/10804835/Huawei-founder-Ren-Zhengfei-rejects-greedy-public-markets.html. Accessed May 10, 2014.

16. Warner J. Obama's cash grab signals a wider assault on capital. *The Telegraph.* February 4, 2015:B2.

17. Foroohar R. Why Germany must save the euro. *Time.* August 12, 2013:26.

18. Centre for Competitive Advantage in the Global Economy. Economic development can only buy happiness up to a 'sweet spot' of $36,000 GDP per person. http://www2.warwick.ac.uk/fac/soc/economics/research/centres/cage/news/07-07-14-economic_development_can_only_buy_happiness_up_to_a_sweet_spot_of_36000_gdp_per_person/#sthash.EaF97Cdu.dpbs. Accessed August 20, 2014.

19. Hanlon P, Carlisle S, Hannah M, Lyon A. *The future public health.* Maidenhead, Berkshire, England: Open University Press McGraw-Hill Education; 2012.

20. Kickbusch I. *Healthy societies: Addressing 21st century health challenges.* http://apo.org.au/node/962. Accessed January 29, 2012.

21. Eckersley R. Is modern Western culture a health hazard? *Int J Epidemiol.* 2006;35(2):252–258. http://ije.oxfordjournals.org/content/35/2/252.full. Accessed June 20, 2014.

22. Eckersley R. About me. http://www.richardeckersley.com.au/main/page_about_me.html. Accessed June 20, 2014.

23. Waltner-Toews D. One Health for one world: A compendium of case studies. http://www.onehealthinitiative.com/publications/OHOW_Compendium_Case_Studies.pdf. Accessed June 22, 2014.

24. National Center for Emerging and Zoonotic Infectious Diseases. Our work, our stories 2011–2012. http://www.cdc.gov/ncezid/pdf/annual-report.pdf. Accessed August 20, 2014.

25. The American Veterinary Medical Association. One Health: A new professional imperative. One Health Initiative task force: Final report. July 15, 2008. https://www.avma.org/KB/Resources/Reports/Documents/onehealth_final.pdf. Accessed September 1, 2011.

26. One Health Initiative. One Health Initiative will unite human and veterinary medicine. http://www.onehealthinitiative.com/mission.php. Accessed July 25, 2014.

27. Kahn LH, Kaplan B, Monath TP, Steele JH. Teaching "one medicine, one health." *AM J Med.* 2008;121(3):169–170. http://www.amjmed.com/article/S0002-9343%2807%2901082-0/abstract. Accessed November 22, 2014.

28. JAVMA News. AMA adopts one-health policy—Physicians' association supports ties with AVMA. *J Am Vet Med Assoc (JAVMA).* 2007. https://www.avma.org/News/JAVMANews/Pages/070801b.aspx. Accessed August 25, 2014.

29. Barrett MA, Osofsky SA. One Health: Interdependence of people, other species, and the planet. In: Katz DL, et al., eds. *Jekel's epidemiology, biostatistics, preventive medicine, and public health.* 4th ed. Philadelphia, PA: Elsevier/Saunders; 2013. http://hss.ucsf.edu/PDF/article-OneHealthChapter_JekelEpi&PublicHealth_Barrett&Osofsky.pdf. Accessed August 19, 2014.

30. World Bank Group. *People, pathogens and our planet* (volume 2): *The economics of one health.* https://openknowledge.worldbank.org/bitstream/handle/10986/11892/691450ESW0whit0D0ESW120PPPvol120web.pdf?sequence=1. Accessed August 20, 2014.

31. The One Health Commission. Home Page. http://www.onehealthcommission.org/. Accessed August 25, 2014.

32. Wild D, Elmore J, Lucan S. *Jekel's epidemiology, biostatistics, preventive medicine, and public health.* Philadelphia PA: Elsevier Saunders; 2014:33.

33. Greenpeace Africa. Poster for Congo rainforest.

34. World Wildlife Fund (WWF). *Living planet report 2014: Species and spaces, people and places.* wwf.panda.org/about_our_earth/all_publications/living_planet_report. Accessed October 23, 2014.

35. Smolin L. *Time reborn: From the crisis in physics to the future of the universe.* London, Ontario, CA: Penguin Random House Canada; 2013.

36. World Wildlife Fund (WWF). A brief history of WWF. http://www.wwf.org.uk/about_wwf/history/. Accessed November 29, 2014.

37. Nutbeam D. Health literacy as a public health goal: A challenge for contemporary health education and communication strategies into the 21st century. *Health Promot Int.* 2015;15(3):259–267.

38. United Nations Educational, Scientific and Cultural Organization (UNESCO). *Educating for a sustainable future: A transdisciplinary vision for concerted action.* International Conference Thessaloniki, Greece; 1997. Accessed February 17, 2013.

39. Earth Charter Initiative. What is the Earth charter? http://www.earthcharterinaction.org/content/pages/What-is-the-Earth-Charter%3F.html. Accessed August 28, 2013.

40. United Nations. *The Millennium Development Goals report 2015.* http://www.un.org/millenniumgoals/2015_MDG_Report/pdf/MDG%202015%20rev%20(July%201).pdf. Accessed July 27, 2015.

41. United Nations. *Transforming our world: the 2030 Agenda for Sustainable Development.* http://www.un.org/ga/search/view_doc.asp?symbol=A/69/L.85&Lang=E. Accessed September 2, 2015.

42. Clark H. 'Youth lens' brings development challenges into sharper focus at UN forum. http://www.un.org/apps/news/story.asp?NewsID=49985#.VVZP3rlViko. Accessed February 28, 2015.

43. Moran C. 'Do not underestimate our anxiety-I am worried about our mental health.' *The Times Magazine.* May 9, 2015.

44. Purves L. I can't be proud of a barbed-wired Europe. *The Times.* August 31, 2015:25.

45. Barrett MA, Bouley TA, Stoertz AH, Stoertz RW. Integrating a One Health Approach in Education to Address Global Health and Sustainability Challenges. *Frontiers in Ecology and the Environment.* 2010;9(4):239–245.

46. Kaufman GE. Designing graduate training programs in conservation medicine-producing the right professionals with the right tools. *Ecohealth.* 2008;5(4):519–527. http://www.ncbi.nlm.nih.gov/pubmed/19212790. Accessed March 15, 2013.

47. The White House. Presidential proclamation—National public health week, 2015. https://www.whitehouse.gov/the-press-office/2015/04/06/presidential-proclamation-national-public-health-week-2015. Accessed April 7, 2015.

48. London International Development Centre (LIDC). Governing the UN Sustainable Development Goals: Interactions, infrastructures, and institutions. http://www.lidc.org.uk/news/governing-un-sustainable-development-goals-interactions-infrastructures-and-institutions. Accessed March 28, 2015.

49. Senge P. The academy as a learning community. In: Lucas AF, ed. *Leading academic change: Essential roles for department chairs.* San Francisco, CA: Jossey-Bass; 2000.

50. Council of Councils (An Initiative of the Council on Foreign Relations). Report card on national cooperation. http://www.cfr.org/councilofcouncils/reportcard/#!/. Accessed April 20, 2015.

51. Likhotal A. Environmental acceptability as the driver of new civilization. *CADMUS.* 2014;2(2):24–34. http://www.cadmusjournal.org/node/389. Accessed April 30, 2014.

52. Wang J. How much longer can the world support our way of life? http://www.scmp.com/comment/blogs/article/1302556/how-much-longer-can-world-support-our-way-life?page=all. Accessed October 20, 2013.

53. Likhotal A. New paradigm quest. *CADMUS.* 2015;2(4):43–47. http://cadmusjournal.org/node/458. Accessed April 29, 2015.

54. Frenk J, Gómez-Dantés O, Moon S. From sovereignty to solidarity: A renewed concept of global health for an era of complex interdependence. *Lancet*. 2014;383(9911):94–97. http://www.thelancet.com/journals/lancet/article/PIIS0140-6736%2813%2962561-1/abstract. Accessed January 20, 2014.

55. International Council for Science (ICSU). Review of targets for the Sustainable Development Goals: The science perspective. http://www.icsu.org/publications/reports-and-reviews/review-of-targets-for-the-sustainable-development-goals-the-science-perspective-2015/SDG-Report.pdf. Accessed May 20, 2014.

56. Gergen KJ. *Relational being: Beyond self and community*. New York, NY: Oxford University Press; 2009.

8.0

Building Public Health Capacity: "Working Differently Means Learning Differently"

8.1 DISEASE PREVENTION AND HEALTH PROMOTION: "A CONTINUING CRISIS OF LEGITIMACY?"

What Is New About the New Public Health?

Public health measures to prevent disease have been undertaken since antiquity, or as the authors of *Public Health in the Arab World* cite, "modern public health has old historical seeds" (1). Several years ago, Dr. Awofeso, in his paper, "What's New About the 'New Public Health'?" (2) traced the history of public health "from a time when public health was integral to societies' social structures, through the sanitary movement and contagion eras, when it evolved as a separate discipline, to the 'new public health' era, when health promotion projects like Healthy Cities appear to be steering the discipline back to society's social structure."

In his view, "public health seems to have come full circle" and prompted him to ask from an early 21st century perspective: "What's new about the 'new public health'?" And, while attempts through such initiatives as the 1978 Alma-Ata Declaration and the 1986 Ottawa Charter, which were instrumental in characterizing the "new public health" (both of which inter alia recognized the need for "involvement of all sectors in the promotion of health"), have raised the profile of health promotion, they have generally not succeeded on several fronts, including ensuring, arguably, the importance of "primary healthcare as the backbone of a nation's health strategy." His consternation may resonate with many who believe that much more priority needs to be given to community-based health care, with much greater emphasis placed on prevention rather than treatment.

However, making this shift is made more difficult because, according to Dr. Awofeso, contemporary health promotion suffers from a "crisis of legitimacy . . . providing a functionalist framework that detracts from the need for longer-term social, economic, and political change, as succinctly advocated by the Alma-Ata Declaration." Furthermore, he noted that "countries currently operate parallel systems of public health and health promotion, when unlike previous eras, the dominant paradigm and public health were generally coterminous."

Moreover, he argued that "public health theorists and commentators appeared to be losing confidence in the capacity of the health promotion paradigm to effectively address major contemporary public health threats, such as health inequalities and terrorism." Strengthening the health promotion movement would necessitate taking into account several perspectives, including:

- A need to define the philosophical basis of contemporary public health, thereby facilitating more effective monitoring of public health functions and a more secure basis for advocacy of public health funding
- A need to determine who exactly is a public health worker or specialist
- A need to acknowledge public health workers and activists who "lead from the front," rather than overrelying on the hierarchical structures of previous eras

Finally, he maintained that advancing "specific public health paradigms" could only be achieved by "addressing the structures of power and socioeconomic development within the history of national and regional cultures."

8.2 TOWARD A COMPREHENSIVE PUBLIC HEALTH APPROACH

Traditionally, public health has been defined along the lines of "the science and art which focuses on population health; human systems and interventions made to improve health, and interaction between these two systems" (3). The scope of this definition applies to all levels of population health at global, national, or local levels.

A Holistic Versus a Fragmented Approach to Public Health

As England's chief medical officer, Dr. Sally Davies, pointed out in an interview, "most of the factors that shape public health can't be altered by central government actions" (4). The concept of "public health" is now also more encompassing because "these days, public health is about how we live our lives—and that takes in urban planning, our interactions with each other; loneliness; well-being." "What's required," she says, "is a 'much more holistic approach'—and that means passing the lead role to those best placed to occupy it," including linking health and education as "they're inextricably linked."

Discussed previously, the Welch–Rose Report (1915) in effect separated "medicine's laboratory investigation of the mechanisms of disease and public health's nonclinical concern with environmental and social influences on health and wellness" (5). While this schism has endured for close to a century, its continuance is now questionable, and there is considerable justification—moral and financial—in realigning public and individual health care.

Professor Ulrich Laaser's tributes to Dr. Salomon Neumann (1819–1908) and Sir Geoffrey Rose (1926–1993) may help to strengthen the argument (6). Dr. Neumann devoted most of his life (Vienna, Paris, Berlin) to ensuring that "the state should ensure the basic human right to live a healthy life." One of his key contributions was "his understanding of 'medicine as a social science' which produces health, prevents disease and heals illness." It is noteworthy that his visionary ideas predate by well over a hundred years many of the conclusions reached by 134 nations at the Alma-Ata conference on primary care in 1978.

Sir Geoffrey Rose was an exceptional British epidemiologist who lectured at the London School of Hygiene and Tropical Medicine as well as at the Johns Hopkins School of Hygiene and Public Health. In his paper, "Relative Merits of Intervening on Whole Populations Versus High-Risk Individuals Only," he concluded that "most of these deaths (eg, cardiovascular) do not arise in the 'clinical' part of the range, where risks are high but numbers are few; most arise at lower levels, where the risk to an individual is small but the numbers are large," a formula which became known as the "preventive paradoxon."

Furthermore, Professor Laaser cites Sir Rose's views on the traditional preventive strategy, which "is concerned with identifying and helping minorities with special problems, by treating the risk factors or seeking changes in behaviour. The underlying aim is to truncate the risk distribution, eliminating the tail but not interfering with the rest of the population." However, as their findings showed, "the close link between mean and prevalence implies, that to help the minority the 'normal' majority must change. . . . The health of society is integral."

This retrospective tribute analysis gave Professor Laaser time to reflect on the future, where he asserted "what is a must for the next century is a new balance and linkage between individual medical care and Public Health, based on ethical norms which include efficiency in the sense that limited resources must not be reduced."

Regrettably, however, from the time Professor Laaser gave his tribute on behalf of the German Society for Social Medicine and Prevention in the early 1990s, except in a few successful models, discussed later in this chapter, it seems little has changed in cohering public and individual health care at institutional/academic or population service levels. The current relationships remain relatively unchanged with schools of medicine still following, by and large, a biomedical model of health care at a time when most illnesses or conditions do not have biomedical origins (the "preventive para-doxon" noted earlier). Unquestionably, the need for a more comprehensive preventive population health approach that joins "cross-disciplinary perspectives and action" to achieve the goal of "health for all," encapsulated in the World Health Organization (WHO) universal health care movement, remains a vital outstanding global issue, which will not go away in this century.

Adding to the momentum for broadening the scope of public health is the One Health movement which, as discussed in Chapter 7.0, "recognizes the interconnected nature of human, animal and environmental health in an attempt to inform health policy, expand scientific knowledge, improve healthcare training and delivery and address sustainability challenges" (7).

Characteristics of the New Public Health

Origins of the New Public Health Revisited

As mentioned in Chapter 1.0, Harvard's dean of the School of Public Health, Professor Julio Frenk, observed that globalization was the main factor in bringing about a renaissance of public health as the "new public health" (NPH) (8). More specifically, according to Drs. Theodore Tulchinsky and Elena Varavikova, NPH "links the classic public health issues of environmental sanitation, hygiene, epidemiology to the newer issues of universal health care, economics and management of health systems in a 21st century approach" (9).

Writing in *Public Health Reviews* (10), the authors highlight that NPH is "concerned with finding a blueprint to address many of the burning issues of our time, but also with identifying implementable strategies in the endeavor to solve these problems." It is new in the sense that it "links health promotion with healthcare access; it is an integration of transdisciplinary and multi-organizational work."

Public Health and Primary Care

These directions are also gaining momentum in the United States where the Institute of Medicine's report, "Primary Care and Public Health: Exploring Integration to Improve Population Health" (11), argues for the closer assimilation of these functions. Justification for this shift appears to be based on "the likely market dynamics of U.S. healthcare reform, the productive intersection of the principles of healthcare management and public health," along with "greater value for the healthcare dollar" (12).

Largely because of these reasons, the U.S. Centers for Disease Control and Prevention (CDC) and the Health Resources and Services Administration (HRSA) took public health a step further in asking the Institute of Medicine to investigate how the two national agencies "could work collectively to improve health through the integration of primary care and public health." Although there had been previous attempts at national levels, few had come to fruition beyond focusing on collaborative arrangements that went beyond specific health issues, in particular "chronic disease, prevention and health promotion, or the health of specific populations" (9).

While there are challenges to strengthening integration, such as existing fragmentation within public health and primary care and a lack of financial investment in both, "the central argument for greater integration" is that "each has knowledge, resources, and skills that can be used to assist the other in carrying out its roles." Further, as discussed in Chapter 2.0, given the rise of noncommunicable diseases and chronic illnesses, the biomedical model of health care that conceives disease "as something separate from social causes" is showing serious shortcomings in improving population health and reducing costs in this century.

In the United States, the longer term view—The Triple Aim—of health care and public health integration is that this merger would improve population health care for individuals (better access and quality) as well as provide cost reduction, because the United States now has the highest cost for health care globally, while achieving poorer results on a number of indicators, including life expectancy (12).

Professors Huda Zurayk, Rita Giacaman, and Ahmed Mandil, authors of "Graduate Education in Public Health: Toward a Multidisciplinary Model" (13), capture the essence of a more comprehensive and integrated approach to health through five key facets:

1. *The ecological model* (discussed in Section 6.8) with emphasis on "health determinants at various levels, including individual biological and behavioural factors, social and family factors, living and working conditions, as well as other broader societal factors influencing health" such as structural forces, especially "power."
2. *Multisectoral health practice,* involving public health professionals working alongside "a plurality of agents and stakeholders . . . across multiple sectors," requiring "graduate public health programs to produce a different kind of graduate," one grounded in the realities of public health practice linking "what they know" with what "they are able to do."
3. *People and communities at the center,* bringing the "public" back into public health by "situating populations in their community context," thereby ensuring that "individuals and communities become active participants in the public health system, not passive recipients of services."
4. *Different ways of knowing,* drawing on a "range of methods and approaches from disciplines as diverse as sociology, psychology, anthropology, economics, and political science," including recognizing the importance of localized approaches, people's lived experience, and community-based participatory research.
5. *Values,* ensuring that "the values of social justice and ethics are at the foundation of the approach" with "its central goal of addressing inequities in health," necessitating the "frank engagement with the politics of public health."

Public Health: "Critical Interface Arenas"

Several years ago, Professor Ilona Kickbusch, director of the Geneva-based Global Health Program at the Graduate Institute of International and Development Studies, identified three seminal "overlapping and mutually reinforcing" trends, which underpin the role of public health—globalization, consumerism, and inequalities (14). In her paper, she also highlighted that public health has "again prominently entered the political domain," involving discussions "beyond technical and medical journals" but which are "part of the debates of government leaders, private entrepreneurs, military strategists, social innovators, trade negotiators and development advocates."

However, while these are positive directions, she cautioned that there was not only a "crisis in global health governance" but also, as Dr. Awofeso affirmed, a "crisis in competency" in public health. This crisis, Professor Kickbusch observes, is due partly "because of the natural time lag between the real world and educational institutions," and partly it is "due to the lack of priority given to the political dimension of public health," demonstrated clearly in Section 3.2 with regard to global health funding priorities.

In her paper, she pointed out that "new types of public health pioneers and organizations have emerged in the last two decades" along with "three critical interface arenas for innovation in public health":

1. *The interface global–local*: requiring "a complementary approach of strong national and global institutions, mechanisms, instruments and funding, as well as commitments to both development and to global public goods";
2. *The interface public health and other sectors and actors*: requiring "a 'Health in All Policies' (HiAP) approach, network governance and broad public and private partnerships and accountabilities at all levels of governance";
3. *The interface technical excellence and political commitments*: with a view to "establishing its renewed ethical base . . . a political process that needs the strong voice and the support of civil society and of political and other leaders to address the equity, exclusion and human rights issues at stake."

Adopting the interface arena framework may be helpful in several ways as the arenas recognize: the dynamic interplay between local issues and global developments; the need for implementing HiAP universally through networking, partnerships, and governance, along with a strong ethical base in building of civil society and addressing fundamental human rights issues. Collectively, the interface arenas may precipitate new routes through intractable global health and well-being terrains. As one example, Professor Kickbusch focused on the need "of about one billion people . . . that are falling behind and sometimes falling apart in 50 different countries." An alternative strategy might be to use "a new approach that does not consider them country by country but as a joint global commitment to health as a global public good." Further, she draws on the work of the anthropologist Arjun Appadurai "to describe the major flows in the fluid and global world in which we live," defining "a variety of global 'scapes,' . . . an amalgam of *'healthscapes'* or as *'networks . . .'* which are more or less borderless and constantly in motion."

The adoption of a more comprehensive and integrated public health approach and emergence of the arenas in which the public must operate will no doubt have a profound effect on how the public health profession is conceptualized, how professionals function for optimal outcomes, and how professional roles are described, understood, enacted, and evaluated.

8.3 PUBLIC HEALTH PRACTITIONERS AND CONTEMPORARY PUBLIC HEALTH COMPETENCY

Core Public Health Functions

According to the U.S. Environmental Public Health Leadership Institute (EPHLI), the preparation of public health practitioners depends on three core public health functions—assessment, policy development, and assurance—illustrated in Figure 8.1, collectively underpinned by research (15).

Core Public Health Competencies: Global Comparisons

These three core functions provide the base for core public health competencies. Globally, Vesna Bjegovic-Mikanovic, president of the Association of Schools of Public Health in the European Region (ASPHER), analyzed documentation from four global providers

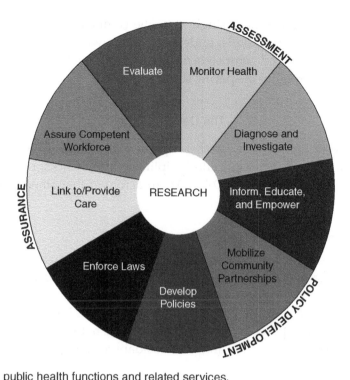

FIGURE 8.1 Core public health functions and related services.
Source: Centers for Disease Control and Prevention (15).

(16): WHO regional essential public health operations (EPHO), the Western Pacific essential public health functions (EPHF), the U.S. CDC essential public health services (EPHS), and the Pan American Health Organization EPHF. Perhaps unsurprisingly, the findings identified nine areas of overlap across all regions and only one area where only two regions identified "preparedness and planning for public health emergencies" as a priority. Functions of general agreement include *public health surveillance; health protection and health promotion; human resource development; core governance, financing, and quality assurance; social participation in health*; and the need for *health-related research*.

Frequently sponsored by national organizations, in the past few decades there has been a proliferation of competency frameworks that extend core competences in both medical and public health education. The main intent behind the competency movement is to ensure that the competencies will serve "as benchmarks" and would help to "standardize the criteria for change in education of public health professionals" as "there is a need for a rapid reform of the educational system as a result of economic and political changes or previous failure to meet employment market needs" (15). The frameworks also serve as a "roadmap" for the development of education and training programs, courses, or modules.

Approaches to Competency Framework Developments

Generally speaking, the resulting frameworks have been based on deliberations of curriculum committees or surveys of public health professionals and public health employers. These groups increasingly describe competencies in terms of "a holistic performance incorporating skills, underpinning knowledge and an integrated set of attitudes and values," and competence "as complex structuring of attributes needed for intelligent performance in specific situations" (17).

The Dacum Process

An innovative technique that has been proven to effectively and efficiently identify competencies and develop multidisciplinary frameworks, pioneered in Canada and the United States, is called *DACUM*, an acronym that stands for "Designing A CurriculUM" (18).

Key Assumptions Underpinning the Process

- Experts can define and describe their roles more accurately than anyone else.
- Any profession or occupation can be effectively described in terms of the competencies that successful professionals perform.
- All professions and occupations demand certain knowledge, skills, and attitudes from employees—and one that may be helpful to add.
- Roles develop over time and need to adapt to changing environments.

The Method

Curriculum mapping or functional analysis is simply a process that ensures that students, trainees, and supervisors know "where they are going, why they are going there, and what is required of them to get there." DACUM is primarily concerned with the first two questions and is a facilitated curriculum mapping or storyboarding process (Figure 8.2)—which normally takes 2 to 3 days to complete and can involve approximately 15 to 20 expert practitioners—early, mid, late career—drawn carefully from a cross-section of professional fields. With regard to potential public health analyses using DACUM, contributors would likely include public health practitioners, primary care doctors, nurses, psychologists, educators, midwives, pharmacists, radiologists, social workers, and lay representatives, to name several professions.

As shown in Figure 8.2, the main reason for coming together is to discuss, debate, define, and agree on core and interdependent competencies that are necessary, as an example, in public health. The resultant documentation or "blueprint"—normally a chart or profile providing a summary of major areas and intermediate areas of competencies—can then be validated or triangulated through additional survey research involving other practitioners, nationally or globally.

Benefits of Applying DACUM in Planning Public Health Curricula

The DACUM process is one of the few methods that engages stakeholders—local, national, and international—directly, builds understanding and commitment in relationships, helps to raise awareness of key issues, and begins the journey for further planning and decision making. Whereas surveys and interviews can take months to gather the data, and relying on texts that were published several years ago could be risky, the DACUM process takes only a few days to identify key competencies

FIGURE 8.2 Mapping competencies using the *DACUM* process.

Source: G. Lueddeke, *Transforming Medical Education for the 21st Century: Megatrends, Priorities and Change*. Radcliffe Publishing, 2012 (18).

and compile highly relevant and timely information to guide further instructional development.

Another strength of the approach is that it can promote discussion of transdisciplinary public health needs, where competencies are centered around issues, problems, needs, or themes. These then form the basis of the learning outcomes applied to a particular program. Moreover, participants who are involved in the process become—in a sense—leaders or "seed carriers" or catalysts for change. Their background and experience would also enable them to further advance the curriculum design or redesign. Assessments that are geared to the actual work environment are another key feature.

Who Are the Public Health Practitioners?

A crucial element in developing valid and reliable competency frameworks, such as the DACUM profiles, is ensuring that those participating in the analysis sessions are representative of all key stakeholders. The premise is simply this: given the "number of profound and dynamic challenges related to its goals to increase healthy life years and reduce health inequalities," only a participatory approach will work in order to address "multiple causes at socio-economic, environmental, and individual levels" (19).

Membership of multidisciplinary teams could involve "researchers, institutional decision-makers, professionals, representatives of civil society and the private sector."

In terms of public health interventions, these teams will be tasked with adopting new ways of thinking and working, moving away from 20th century fragmented reductionist approaches to 21st century "fifth" wave holistic, ecological, and systems orientations, as discussed in Chapter 6.0. This shift is fundamental as "empirical evidence suggests that major improvement of health does not come from new medical findings or cures, but from the broad development and application of population-based preventive programs" (20).

The argument for greater cohesion between curative and preventive measures, including organizational, is based on the generally acceptable findings that "health is determined not only by individual behavioral factors but also by population related social, economic, political, cultural, and environmental factors" (21).

It is for these reasons that "increasingly, public health includes," as shown in Table 8.1, "the role of the 'wider' workforce": people who can be grouped into three divisions: (a) "public health specialists"; (b) "people indirectly involved in public health activities through their work"; and (c) "people who should be aware of public health implications in their professional life" (16).

In terms of estimating national workforce requirements, a 2008 study in the United States may be helpful (16). The study estimated that "for a population of projected 325 million in 2010, a total of 715,000" public health practitioners would be required, "corresponding to 220/100,00 population." Compared to the population of the 27 European Union (EU) members states of 501 million (January 2011), this results in a "workforce of 1.1 million public health workers using the same ration." And, allowing for "an average attrition rate around 2% per year, up to 22,000 professionals would have to finish some education in public health each year to fulfill these needs." However, the average number of graduates per year across the EU is 43, and there are only 86 schools or departments of public health out of a total 467 schools or departments of public health worldwide. When we consider other highly populated nations or regions, for example, India or Southeast Asia, as outlined later in this chapter, it is clear that the imbalance between treatment and prevention is unsustainable.

TABLE 8.1 Possible Division of Public Health Professions

1) PH Specialists	2) Partial PH Role	3) Awareness of PH Issues
• Health professionals with specialization in public health • Health policy makers • Epidemiologists • Environmental health experts • Health economist • Health promotion specialists • Employees at local health agencies • (. . .)	• Physicians • Nurses • Dentists • Pharmacists • Midwives • Food inspectors • Nutritionists • Fitness instructors • Psychologists • (. . .)	• Police • Architects • Urban planners • Teachers • Welfare workers • (. . .)

Source: Adapted from M. Whitfield, "Public Health Job Market," in *Employment in Public Heath in Europe*. Jagiellonian University Press, 2004 (22).

8.4 COMPETENCY ANALYSIS EXEMPLARS: COMPARISONS ACROSS SEVEN NATIONS/REGIONS

Australia

Developed by 21 members of the Australian Network of Public Health Institutions (ANAPHI), the Competencies for Master of Public Health (MPH) Graduates, the emergent competencies were organized under the five core public health functions as defined by the former National Public Health Partnership (23) along with two generic competencies, summarized in Box 8.1.

Canada

Developed in consultation with more than 3,000 practitioners across the country, the *Core Competencies for Public Health in Canada* (Release 1.0 [2007], listed in Box 8.2) organizes 36 competency statements into seven categories (24).

BOX 8.1

Core Public Health Functions (Australia)

1. Health monitoring and surveillance
2. Disease prevention and control
3. Health promotion
4. Health protection
5. Health policy, planning and evaluation
   Two added key functions*:
6. Research methods
7. Professional public health practice

*Each of these functions was defined within the competency framework as an "area of practice" with a defined "practice goal" to be met by achieving the related "unit(s) of competency." Each "unit of competency" incorporates various "elements of competence."

BOX 8.2

Core Competencies for Public Health (Canada)

1. Public health sciences
2. Assessment and analysis
3. Policy and program planning, implementation, and evaluation
4. Partnerships, collaboration, advocacy
5. Diversity
6. Communication
7. Leadership

Public Health Canada highlights that "these core competencies, with their companion glossary, transcend the boundaries of specific disciplines and provide a baseline for all public health professionals."

Europe

In Europe, there has also been growing interest in moving away from "a traditional public health worker, a specialist physician, to a more generic worker, who will be expected to work across organizational boundaries with a vast array of professionals to promote the public health agenda" (25). The overall developments are informed by the Bologna Process, which "aims to create a European Higher Education Area based on international cooperation and academic exchange that is attractive to European students and staff, as well as to students and staff from other parts of the world." In addition, the developments are supported by the WHO Regional Office for Europe's New European policy for health—Health 2020—which is also being enhanced by further development of the "public health systems, capacities and functions and promoting public health as a key function in society" (16).

Started in 2006, the "process involved more than a hundred European public health teachers, scientists and practitioners," the leading competency framework is the *European Core Competencies for Public Health Professionals* (ECCPHP)—developed by ASPHER (25). The document provides a set of MPH program accreditation standards and procedures administered by the European Agency for Accreditation in Public Health.

Summarized in Box 8.3, there are six main domains, each supported by intellectual and practical competencies.

BOX 8.3

Core Competencies for Public Health Professionals (Europe)

1. Methods in public health—qualitative and quanititative
2. Population health and its social and economic determinants
3. Population health and its material-physical, radiological, chemical, and biological-environmental determinants
4. Health policy; economics; organizational theory and management
5. Health promotion: health education, health protection, and disease prevention
6. Ethics

In addition, additional mapping of public health education has shown the emergence of new trends and the need to strengthen capacities in areas such as:

- Informatics
- Genomics
- Communication
- Cultural competence
- Community-based participatory research
- Policy and law
- Global health and
- Ethics

India

In India, there is no institutionally agreed upon set of skills that a graduate must demonstrate to earn an MPH degree (26). Public Health Foundation of India (PHFI) was established to build Indian Institutes of Public Health (IIPHs) across the country. In an effort to develop a framework of competency for MPH programs, the IIPH followed a four-step approach: situation assessment of MPH programs in India; survey of public health care professionals; national consultation; and developing a framework.

In the first step of this process, 10 core public health areas of practice and functions were identified, as shown in Box 8.4.

Southeast Asia

In his direction-setting article, "Public Health Education in South Asia: A Basis for Structuring a Master Degree Course," Rajendra Karkee, then at the Koirala Institute of Health Sciences, Dharan, Nepal, highlights that "South Asian countries under the South Asian Association for Regional Cooperation (SAARC)" include "Afghanistan, Bangladesh, Bhutan, India, Maldives, Nepal, Pakistan, and Sri Lanka." He further observed that "excluding Maldives and Sri Lanka, the remaining six countries have nearly one-fifth of the world's population with about 27% of global disease burden (680,859 thousands disability-adjusted life years lost in 2010)" (27).

Similar to other developing nations, notably sub-Saharan Africa, "these countries are undergoing an epidemiological transition with a double burden of diseases, unfinished agenda of infectious diseases, nutritional deficiencies, and unsafe pregnancies, as well as the challenge of escalating epidemics of non-communicable diseases." Again, echoing health inequities and imbalances across the globe, developments and

BOX 8.4

Core Public Health Areas of Practice and Functions (India)

1. Monitoring of health status and identifying and prioritizing health problems in the community;
2. Investigating and diagnosing public health problems;
3. Communicating health problems to people and empowering the community;
4. Engaging the community to identify and solve public health problems;
5. Developing policies related to public health and ensuring the safety of people by implementing public health laws and regulations;
6. Applying a critical thinking and systems approach to the analysis of environmental and occupational determinants of disease and injury and suggesting suitable corrective measures;
7. Developing a competent and efficient public health workforce;
8. Evaluating public health programs, services, and policies;
9. Developing innovative and cost-effective locally relevant solutions;
10. Undertaking action research to guide public health policies and programs.

"despite this situation, public health education in these countries has largely been neglected compared with medical education until recently, resulting in inadequate public health schools and workforce."

In keeping with one of the main themes of this book, it is laudable that the "WHO Regional Office for South-East Asia has called for a paradigm shift in approach to public health by focusing on a preventive and promotive health system that can actively change conditions that make people sick and by producing a public health workforce through public health institutes and schools."

Figure 8.3 identifies the three domains of public health "to manage the wide nature of public health and to clarify its boundaries in terms of public health practice and public health education." The three domains "are inter-related with a common core, which includes research methods (epidemiology and biostatistics), ethics, and use of information." The health improvement domain "includes socio-economic influences and health promotion, tackling the underlying determinants of health," whereas the "health protection domain includes infectious diseases control, disaster prevention, environmental health regulation, and occupational health." The "health services domain includes healthcare system and policy, service quality, healthcare management, evidence-based practice, and health economics."

United Kingdom

In the United Kingdom, the Faculty of Public Health (FPH) of the Royal College of Physicians "oversees the quality of training and professional development of public health consultants," and "maintains the professional standards in the discipline. . . . Its overall approach is multi-disciplinary and applications are welcomed from both doctors

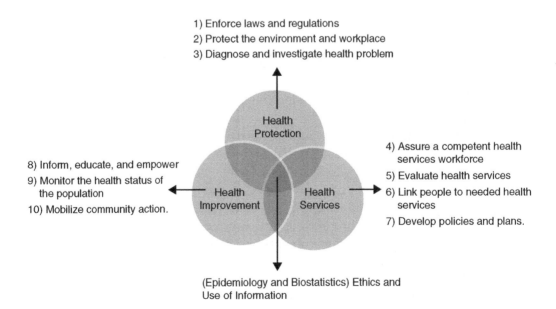

FIGURE 8.3 The 3 domains and 10 activities of public health practice (Southeast Asia).

Source: Adapted from R. Karkee, "Public Health Education in South Asia: A Basis for Structuring a Master Degree Course," *Frontiers in Public Health.* 2014;2:88 (27).

BOX 8.5

Public Health Academic Curriculum Areas (United Kingdom)

- Knowledge requirements to underpin specialist public health practice.
- Principles of ethical and professional practice through *Good Public Health Practice*.
- Curriculum core requirements described in nine key areas of public health practice.
  - Surveillance and assessment of the population's health and well-being.
  - Assessing the evidence of effectiveness of health and healthcare interventions, programmes, and services.
  - Policy and strategy development and implementation.
  - Strategic leadership and collaborative working for health.
  - Health improvement.
  - Health protection.
  - Health and social service quality.
  - Public health intelligence.
  - Academic public health.

and graduates from other backgrounds" (28). The highly detailed academic curriculum that leads to a certificate of completion of training (CCT) in public health covers broad competency areas, summarized in Box 8.5.

Learning outcomes—185 (18 ethical management of self; 121 core; 46 trainees selected) are divided into core (those which every trainee must have to gain a CCT) and trainee selected (these areas of optional special interest are available in addition to the core and allow development of special interest either in a particular area of public health practice or in a particular setting).

United States

Medicine

U.S. Learning Outcomes Model: Undergraduate

Inspired by the "Institute of Medicine's recommendation for an educated citizenry," in the United States, the Association of Schools of Public Health (ASPH) in collaboration with the Association of American Colleges and Universities, Association for Prevention Teaching and Research, and CDC, developed a learning outcomes model "designed to facilitate the introduction of public health for undergraduate students in two- and four-year colleges and universities" (29). The model (Box 8.6) "represents public health knowledge, concepts and skills that can be integrated into curricular and co-curricular undergraduate educational opportunities to enable students to become more active participants in their own and their community's health."

BOX 8.6

Undergraduate Public Health Domains (United States)

- Domain 1: knowledge of human cultures and the physical and natural world as it relates to individual and population health
- Domain 2: intellectual and practical skills
- Domain 3: personal and social responsibility
- Domain 4: integrative and applied learning

Core Competencies for Public Health Professionals

Established in 1992 and staffed by the Public Health Foundation (30), the Council on Linkages Between Academia and Public Health Practice (Council on Linkages) (31) is a "collaborative of 20 national public health organizations with a focus on improving public health education and training, practice and research." The Council on Linkages developed the Core Competencies for Public Health Professionals (Core Competencies), which are foundational and are intended "for the broad practice of public health in *any* setting to strengthen public health workforce development" (32).

The Core Competencies, which are informative in terms of planning public health programs and projects, along with drafting job descriptions (33), are organized into eight domains (Box 8.7) reflecting skill areas within public health, and three tiers, representing career stages for public health professionals. An example of the competencies, "Leadership and Systems Thinking Skills," is provided in Table 8.2 along with the description of tier responsibilities.

Commentary

Public health is at different stages of development across the globe. However, a fundamental correlation is easily made: the more populated and poorer the nation or region, the greater the challenge and the more urgent the need for public health interventions.

As summarized in Table 8.3, the language used to describe competencies across seven nations varies.

BOX 8.7

Core Competencies Domains

1. Analytical/assessment skills
2. Policy development/program planning skills
3. Communication skills
4. Cultural competency skills
5. Community dimensions of practice skills
6. Public health sciences skills
7. Financial planning and management skills
8. Leadership and systems thinking skills

TABLE 8.2 Example Competencies From Council on Linkages Core Competencies

LEADERSHIP AND SYSTEMS THINKING SKILLS		
TIER 1	TIER 2	TIER 3
8A1 Incorporates ethical standards of practice (e.g., Public Health Code of Ethics) into all interactions with individuals, organizations, and communities	8B1 Incorporates ethical standards of practice (e.g., Public Health Code of Ethics) into all interactions with individuals, organizations, and communities	8C1 Incorporates ethical standards of practice (e.g., Public Health Code of Ethics) into all interactions with individuals, organizations, and communities
8A2 Describes public health as part of a larger inter-related system of organizations that influence the health of populations at local, national, and global levels	8B2 Describes public health as part of a larger inter-related system of organizations that influence the health of populations at local, national, and global levels	8C2 Interacts with the larger inter-related system of organizations that influence the health of populations at local, national, and global levels
8A3 Describes the ways public health, health care, and other organizations can work together or individually to impact the health of a community	8B3 Explains the ways public health, health care, and other organizations can work together or individually to impact the health of a community	8C3 Creates opportunities for organizations to work together or individually to improve the health of a community
8A4 Contributes to development of a vision for a healthy community (e.g., emphasis on prevention, health equity for all, excellence, and innovation)	8B4 Collaborates with individuals and organizations in developing a vision for a healthy community (e.g., emphasis on prevention, health equity for all, excellence, and innovation)	8C4 Collaborates with individuals and organizations in developing a vision for a healthy community (e.g., emphasis on prevention, health equity for all, excellence, and innovation)
8A5 Identifies internal and external facilitators and barriers that may affect the delivery of the 10 Essential Public Health Services (e.g., using root cause analysis and other quality improvement methods and tools, problem solving)	8B5 Analyzes internal and external facilitators and barriers that may affect the delivery of the 10 Essential Public Health Services (e.g., using root cause analysis and other quality improvement methods and tools, problem solving)	8C5 Takes measures to minimize internal and external barriers that may affect the delivery of the 10 Essential Public Health Services (e.g., using root cause analysis and other quality improvement methods and tools, problem solving)

Note:

Tier 1: Front Line Staff/Entry Level. Responsibilities of these professionals may include data collection and analysis, fieldwork, program planning, outreach, communications, customer service, and program support.

Tier 2: Program Management/Supervisory Level. Responsibilities of these professionals may "include developing, implementing, and evaluating programs; supervising staff; establishing and maintaining community partnerships; managing timelines and work plans; making policy recommendations; and providing technical expertise.

Tier 3: Senior Management/Executive Level. Responsibilities of these professionals may include "overseeing major programs or operations of the organization, setting a strategy and vision for the organization, creating a culture of quality within the organization, and working with the community to improve health.

Source: Adapted from Public Health Foundation (PHF). *Core Competencies for Public Health Professionals.*
http://www.phf.org/resourcestools/pages/core_public_health_competencies.aspx

TABLE 8.3 Summary of Seven Health Competency Frameworks, Areas of Study or Domains

(A) AUSTRALIA	(B) CANADA	(C) EUROPE	(D) INDIA	(E) SOUTH EAST ASIA	(F) UNITED KINGDOM	(G) UNITED STATES
1. Health monitoring and surveillance 2. Disease prevention and control 3. Health promotion 4. Health protection 5. Health policy, planning, and evaluation 6. Research methods 7. Professional public health practice	1. Public health sciences 2. Assessment and analysis 3. Policy and program planning, implementation, and evaluation 4. Partnerships, collaboration, advocacy 5. Diversity 6. Communication 7. Leadership	1. Methods in public health, qualitative and quantitative 2. Population health and its social and economic determinants 3. Population health and its material-physical, radiological, chemical, and biological-environmental determinants 4. Health policy, economics, organizational theory, and management 5. Health promotion: health education, health protection, and disease prevention Ethics 6. Emergence of new trends: informatics, genomics, communication, cultural competence, community-based participatory research policy and law, global health and ethics	1. Monitoring of health status and identifying and prioritizing health problems in community 2. Investigating and diagnosing public health problems 3. Communicating health problem to people and empowering community 4. Engaging community to identify and solve public health problems 5. Developing policies related to public health and ensuring safety of people by implementing public health laws and regulations 6. Applying a critical thinking and systems approach to the analysis of environmental and occupational determinants of disease and injury and suggesting suitable corrective measures 7. Developing competent and efficient public health workforce 8. Evaluating public health programs, services, and policies 9. Developing innovative and cost effective locally relevant solutions 10. Undertaking action research to guide public health policies and program	Health protection 1. Enforce laws and regulations 2. Protect environment and workspace 3. Diagnose and investigate health problems Health Services 4. Assure a complete health service workforce 5. Evaluate health services 6. Link people to needed health services Health Improvement 7. Develop policies and plans Health Improvement 8. Inform, educate, and empower 9. Monitor health status of the population 10. Mobilize community	1. Surveillance and assessment of the population's health and well-being 2. Assessing the evidence of effectiveness of health and health care interventions 3. Policy and strategy development and implementation 4. Strategic leadership and collaborative working for health 5. Health improvement 6. Health protection 7. Health and social service quality 8. Public health intelligence 9. Academic public health	1. Analytical/assessment skills 2. Policy development/program planning skills 3. Communication skills 4. Cultural competency skills 5. Community dimensions of practice skills 6. Public health sciences skills 7. Financial planning and management skills 8. Leadership and systems thinking skills

Coding the competencies, using the constant comparative method (34), identified 10 areas, summarized in Box 8.8, where there is considerable consensus across the competency frameworks.

Public health sciences are mentioned in four frameworks, while "population health and its social and economic determinants are identified in only two (C and E)," arguably one of the most important priorities given the rise of noncommunicable diseases.

Collaboration (or word equivalents) is mentioned in only three frameworks, although this capacity is emerging as one of the most critical in the United States (35), where an expert panel, representing six national associations (Nursing, Osteopathic Medicine, Pharmacy, Dentistry, Medical Colleges, Public Health) have identified four Core Competencies, as summarized in Box 8.9, at general and specific levels for interprofessional collaborative practice.

A major milestone in accelerating interprofessional education (IPE), supported strongly by the Josiah Macy Jr. Foundation (36), was the creation of the U.S. National Center for Interprofessional Practice at the University of Minnesota. The center's main charge is to help "dismantle the silo approach to health professions education that has been our tradition and to promote culture and pedagogy that are more team-based to prepare professionals for collaborative practice." In terms of enacting improvements in the health system, Macy is encouraging the strategic step connecting education reformers with health system and health practice reformers so that they can

BOX 8.8

Competency Consensus Across Seven Nations

- Health monitoring or surveillance
- Health promotion
- Disease prevention
- Workforce development
- Public health sciences
- Policy development (including laws and regulations)
- Program planning
- Engaging the local community
- Communication
- Strategic leadership

BOX 8.9

Interprofessional Competency Domains (United States)

Competency Domain 1: Values/Ethics for Interprofessional Practice
Competency Domain 2: Roles/Responsibilities
Competency Domain 3: Interprofessional Communication
Competency Domain 4: Teams and Teamwork

"inform and influence each other to develop and strengthen IPE efforts with the goal of improving patient care."

Potential alliances of public health and primary care—both at the forefront in community care—are also not indicated. It is of course possible that these or similar phrases are found deeper in existing documents, but since they may become major future interventions then perhaps they should be profiled more in the frameworks, especially since these will underpin further curriculum planning and developments.

Workforce development is listed explicitly by three areas (C, D, E); research is identified by all; and communications by three (B, D, F). Only Europe identified other emerging areas, such as informatics, genomics, and ethics, and only the United States highlighted the need for "systems thinking skills."

Considered collectively, both India and Southeast Asia's competency frameworks appear particularly refreshing and echo many of the Alma-Ata values as well as strategies pioneered by Carl Taylor in India and Sydney Krak in sub-Saharan Africa, discussed earlier.

Building on the discussions in Chapters 5.0 and 6.0, in revising national frameworks authors might also give due regard to placing more emphasis on the development of integrative and ecological health models, such as those espoused through One Health. Pursuing this line of thinking appears crucial in addressing the "ingenuity gap" in relation to the complex issues facing us, along with advancing social accountability and human rights at all levels—local, national, regional, and global.

As illustrated in Table 8.3, the 10 common competencies in Box 8.8 are also generally corroborated in a study involving five participating institutions offering MPH programs (The Netherlands, South Africa, Vietnam, China, Sudan) (37). Drawing on the set of competencies of the Council on Linkages Between Academia and Public Health Practice as a reference, the researchers used a modified Delphi method to which public health experts and alumni contributed. Along with agreeing on the competencies, they also developed impact variables in terms of "impact on the workplace, such as developing improved working procedures within a work unit, and impact on the sector or society, such as improved quality of care for patients." It is noteworthy that "public health science skills" and "context sensitive competencies received the highest ratings from both experts and alumni."

To date, none of the competency frameworks, including the Core MPH competency synthesis based on a study involving the five nations, shown in Figure 8.4, allude to the One Health approach that "calls for a paradigm shift in developing, implementing, and sustaining health policies that improve public health by incorporating human medicine, veterinary medicine, public health and environmental information," although many organizations are aligned with it, including the WHO, American Veterinary Association, the World Bank, the American Medical Association, and Bill & Melinda Gates Foundation, to name several organizations.

Developing a Global Framework for Public Health (GFPH) Services and Functions

Rationales

According to Dr. Joanna Nurse—the author of a paper written on behalf of a task force for a Global Framework for Public Health that included Professor Ulrich Laaser and

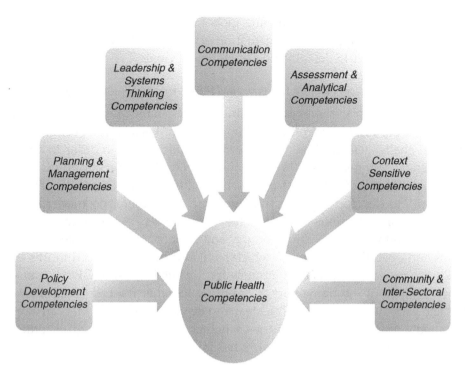

FIGURE 8.4 Core MPH competencies across five nations.

Source: P.A.C. Zwanikken, et al., "Validation of Public Health Competencies and Impact Variables for Low- and Middle-Income Countries," *BMC Public Health*. 2014;14:55 (37).

Dr. Ehud Miron of the World Federation of Public Health Associations (WFPHA)—there are a number of fundamental rationales for having "robust public health systems in place globally and within each country" (38).

This initiative is part of the policy education and training group's work on modernizing public health to address the challenges of the 21st century, and the task force for the global framework includes members from across the world.

The main arguments in the paper were confirmed most recently by the Ebola outbreak in East Africa, which, unquestionably, added to "old and new threats to global health security, and wider public health challenges, including inequalities and a demographic and disease shift towards non-communicable diseases." In addition, the author raises awareness of "the current reality," which "consists of fragmented, variable and incomplete public health services and functions, with little common understanding of what a good public health service looks like." Exacerbating the status quo, she points out that "Currently, there is no global agreement on what public health functions or services consist of, and the lack of a common vocabulary in public health adversely affects the efforts of public health systems, including security and workforce development and quality standards across the world."

In her view "*A Framework for Global Public Health Functions and Services (GPHFS) has the potential of becoming an established, widely accepted vocabulary that would allow public health systems to communicate globally, compare capacity and improve performance through systematic action.*" Taken as a whole, the author contends that "Adoption of a GFPH can contribute to strengthening global health security, the sustainability of health systems, including the implementation of Universal Health Coverage and contribute to wider post-2015 Sustainable Development Goals."

World Health Organization (WHO): Modernizing Public Health for Global Action

Given "the increasing complexity of public health challenges, the WHO Director General asked the World Federation of Public Health Associations (WFPHA) to consider global challenges and how to modernize public health in order to respond to these challenges." In response, "in 2013 the WFPHA's Working Group on Education and Training (WG-PET) launched the Global Public Health Framework Taskforce" with a remit "to develop a global framework to strengthen and modernize public health services and functions to address these challenges." After examining "current models" and building on "existing country and regional level essential public health functions and operations," many of which have also been referenced in this chapter, the task force produced the Global Framework for Public Health (GFPH) framework. The overall intent of the framework is "to bring together the best of all the existing models and provide a comprehensive, clear and flexible framework that can be applied globally and within individual countries, whether low, middle or high-income."

Strengthening the GFPH framework has involved

> a range of partners, so far including: the WHO (HQ Health Systems cluster), the International Association of Public Health Institutes, CDC, the World Bank, UNICEF, DFID, the Faculty of Public Health—UK, Public Health England, the Department of Health (UK), the Australian and the American Associations of Public Health and the European Association of Public Health Associations.

A Proposed Definition of "Public Health"

According to an agreed definition by the WFPHA, developed to reflect the framework:

> Public Health is the art and science of organizing collective efforts to promote well-being, protect health and prevent disease. These efforts should be based upon robust information and enabled by good governance, advocacy and the capacity to ensure fair, secure and sustainable health and well-being for all.

> (WFPHA Taskforce for a Global Public Health Framework, 2014)

The Global Framework for Public Health Policy (GFPH)

To advance further development of the framework and help inform policy deliberations, task force members have provided additional information on framework objectives, services/functions, GFPH headings, enabling action plans, and the establishment of a leadership forum.

Objectives of the Framework

1. To advance adoption of a globally recognized set of public health functions and definitions

2. To develop a flexible framework and tools that can be applied to different countries and settings to strengthen public health services and functions, including for assessment, planning, training, evaluation, and accreditation
3. To strengthen public health systems to improve global health security and to achieve sustainable and fair health outcomes, including the implementation of universal health coverage
4. To support wider economic growth and the post-2015 Sustainable Development Goals
5. To strengthen leadership and governance, "scale up" public health capacity building, standardize assessment, and improve quality of public health services

Proposed Functions/Services

- **Services**: A group of core services—intelligence, protection, prevention, and promotion
- **Functions**: A group of enabler functions—governance, advocacy, and capacity

Suggested Headings for the GFPH

There is overlap among all these services and functions, especially among health promotion, primary prevention, and environmental health, which benefit from a cross-sector approach (Figure 8.5). Specific public health topics require components drawn from across the range of services and functions.

1. **Governance**: public health legislation; health and cross-sector policy; strategy; financing; organization; quality assurance: transparency, accountability, and audit

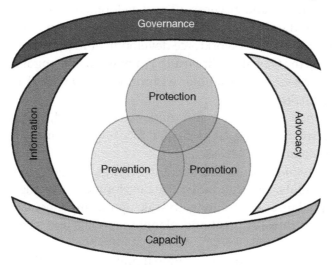

FIGURE 8.5 A global framework for public health services and functions.

Source: J. Nurse, "Developing a Global Framework for Public Health Services and Functions (GFPH)." *Personal communication* (May 28, 2015).

2. **Information**: surveillance, monitoring, and evaluation; research and evidence; risk and innovation; dissemination and uptake
3. **Protection**: international health regulation and coordination; communicable disease control; emergency preparedness; environmental health; climate change and sustainability
4. **Prevention**: primary prevention: vaccination; secondary prevention: screening; tertiary prevention: evidence-based, integrated, person-centered quality health care and rehabilitation; health care management and planning
5. **Promotion**: inequalities; environmental determinants; social and economic determinants; resilience; behavior and health literacy; life course; healthy settings
6. **Advocacy**: leadership and ethics; social mobilization and solidarity—people-centered approach and voluntary community sector engagement; communications; sustainable development
7. **Capacity**: workforce development for public health, health workers, and wider workforce; workforce planning: numbers, resources, and infrastructure; standards, curriculum, and accreditation; capabilities, teaching, and training

Actions to Advance the GFPH

1. **Sustainable, secure health systems:** To incorporate the GFPH and the relevant public health services and functions within the health systems strengthening approach, in order to support global health security and the sustainability of universal health coverage
2. **Building consensus:** To assist in developing a consensus on public health definitions, services, and functions and facilitate the promotion of a World Health Assembly resolution and action plan for a GFPH, to gain international consensus
3. **Communications and advocacy:** The development of communications materials for the GFPH, to raise awareness and scale up action
4. **Workforce:** To scale up workforce development in public health:
   - To embed the Global Public Health Framework into ongoing workforce planning processes—for example, within the WHO Global Human Resources for Health Strategy
   - Based upon pilots, tools, and guidance developed, scale up public health system strengthening, in particular, focusing assistance for low and middle income countries (LMICs)
   - Capability of the workforce to address surge and emergency challenges
5. **Guidance, tools, and standards:** The development, piloting, and publication of tools, guidance, and training, to scale up the implementation of the GFPH:
   - Public health assessment and planning toolkits and application for health impact assessments
   - Guidance for strengthening national public health policy and services
   - Capacity building at country level, twinning, and multicountry initiatives
   - Standards for accreditation and quality improvement

6. **Investment in public health:** To develop, pilot, and advance the case for investment in prevention and public health policy, to create investment models for modernizing and strengthening public health services for a range of settings

Development of a Leadership Forum

The first global public health leadership forum was established at the 14th WFPHA Congress in India (February 2015). The aim of the leadership forum was to provide leadership and strategic direction, and facilitate resource mobilization for the advancement of the proposed actions to take forward the GFPH services and functions, in collaboration with partners.

Feedback

Organizations, countries, or individuals interested in advancing the GFPH are asked to contact Dr. Joanna Nurse (j.nurse@commonwealth.int).

8.5 PUBLIC HEALTH: AN EXPERT OCCUPATION, A PROFESSION, OR BOTH?

An underlying assumption of the GFPH is the determination to strengthen public health as a "profession" in its own right. Indeed, judging by the growing government and other agency interests in planet and population health, epitomized by the WFPHA and the One Health movement, the proliferation of job descriptions that internalize many of the key competencies, and the expansion of public health education at bachelor, master, and doctoral levels, the field is quickly gaining recognition as a "profession" comprising "expert occupations," founded on "social justice and fairness for all." According to Richard Horton et al., the main focus of public health is on the collective actions of interdependent and empowered peoples and their communities. Its objectives are to "protect and promote health and well-being, to prevent disease and disability, to eliminate conditions that harm health and well-being, and to foster resilience and adaptation" (39).

Elton Freidson (40) observed that an occupation becomes a "profession" when it evolves "a set of values, behaviors, and relationships that underpin the trust of the public, " demonstrated to a large extent in Box 8.8 as well as Figures 8.4 and 8.5.

Ralph Rowbottom and David Billis in *Organisational Design: The Work-Levels Approach* (41) highlight that the role of a professional "is complex; the practitioner has to respond to novel situations which he must analyze and categorize; work with incomplete or inchoate information," requiring "judgement," calling upon a body of theoretical knowledge to inform such judgments (that is, they are not based only on personal experience) and is "guided in his/her judgement by a set of ethics."

Moreover, "the connection between the response which the practitioner makes and the effect of that response is not absolute; that is, the effect of action taken or treatment offered is not predictable except in probabilistic terms." In addition, professionals are "committed to a calling . . . where self interest must take second place" (41).

While public health draws on "experts" from a range of professions—indeed, it is this element that makes public health unique—it is their collective "professional" approach to complex societal problems that raises the public health profile from that of an "occupation," concerned largely with reductive tasks per se, to a "profession," potentially with the capacity to apply a wide range of holistic competencies, underpinned by a consensual understanding of and commitment to values that focus on health equity.

8.6 *THE LANCET* COMMISSION FINDINGS: SYSTEMIC FAILURES IN GLOBAL HEALTH EDUCATION, REFORMS, AND ENABLING ACTIONS

Systemic Failures in Health Care and Need for a Broad Reform Movement

Echoing findings from the WHO 2008 *World Health Report* (42), the 20 professional and academic leaders of *The Lancet*-commissioned report, "Health Professionals for a New Century: Transforming Education to Strengthen Health Systems in an Interdependent World" (43), concluded that the problems with 21st century health care education stem mostly from systemic failings, as shown in Box 8.10.

According to the report, changes are needed in medical education "to overcome dysfunctional and inequitable health systems because of curricular rigidities, professional silos, static pedagogy, insufficient adaptation to local contexts, and commercialism in the professions. Breakdown is especially noteworthy within primary care, in both poor and rich countries."

To address these issues (Figure 8.6), the commission calls for a broad reform movement, encompassing instructional design (what we teach and how) and institutional design (schools or universities that should carry out instructions). In terms of instructional design, the approach should be competency-based and interprofessional, bringing together health professionals to work as a cohesive team. It should use information technology (IT) to empower health professionals during training and in the field (43).

Implications for Public Health Instructional and Institutional Reforms

To achieve the overarching goal "transformative and interdependent professional education for equity in health," the commission set out reforms and enabling actions with

BOX 8.10

Systemic Failures in Health Professionals' Education and Training

Mismatch of competencies to needs
Weak teamwork
Gender stratification
Hospital dominance over primary care
Labour market imbalances
Weak leadership for health system performance

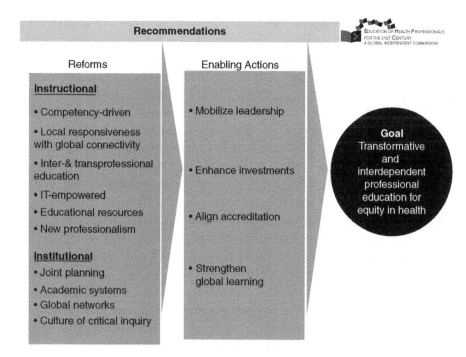

FIGURE 8.6 *The Lancet* report—instructional and institutional reforms and enabling actions.

Source: Adapted from J. Frenk J, L. Chen, Z.A. Bhutta, et al., "Health Professionals for a New Century: Transforming Education to Strengthen Health Systems in an Interdependent World," *The Lancet*. 376(9756):1923–1958. doi:10.1016/S0140-6736(10)61854-5 (43).

regard to instructional reform and institutional reform, as shown in Figure 8.6. The commission uses a wide lens in seeking instructional reform, which needs to consider "the entire range from admission to graduation, to generate a diverse student body with a competency-based curriculum that, through the creative use of information technology (IT), prepares students for the realities of teamwork, to develop flexible career paths that are based on the spirit and duty of a new professionalism."

Moreover, the commissioners emphasize that in order to improve health care education through "institutional design" much tighter coordination is needed between education and the health sector to ensure that the type of health professionals trained matches the health needs in every country. In addition, global coalitions, associations, and networks are needed to better leverage educational resources from around the world. With the aim of developing transformative and interdependent professional education, as shown in Figure 8.6, the authors have also identified four key enabling actions or strategies: the need to mobilize leadership, enhance investments, align accreditation, and strengthen global learning.

The commission reforms raise a number of questions with regard to present-day public health curricula that program planners may wish to consider in reviewing their programs at undergraduate and postgraduate levels. More specifically, discussions might revolve around themes relating to the following:

- *Competency-based curricula*: To what extent are existing courses "responsive to rapidly changing needs rather than dominated by static coursework?"

- *Interprofessional and transprofessional education*: To what extent do the program and its courses break down "professional silos while enhancing collaborative and non-hierarchical relationships in effective teams?"
- *Exploitation of the power of IT*: To what extent is IT used "for learning through development of evidence, capacity for data collection and analysis, simulation and testing, distance learning, collaborative connectivity, and management of the increase in knowledge . . . teaching students how to think creatively to master large flows of information in the search for solutions?"
- *Adaptation locally but harnessing resources globally*: To what extent does the program confer the "capacity to flexibly address local challenges while using global knowledge, experience, and shared resources, including faculty, curriculum, didactic materials and students linked internationally through exchange programs?"
- *Promoting a new professionalism*: To what extent are competencies used as "the objective criterion for the classification of health professionals, transforming present conventional silos" with a view to developing "a common set of attitudes, values, and behaviors . . . as the foundation for preparation of a new generation of professionals to complement their learning of specialities with their roles as accountable change agents, competent managers of resources, and promoters of evidence-based policies?"

Institutional Reforms

These reforms call for aligning "national efforts through joint planning especially in the education and health sectors, engage all stakeholders in the reform process, extend academic learning sites into the communities, develop global collaborative networks for mutual strengthening and lead in promotion of the culture of critical inquiry and public." Again, institutional decision makers might find the following *Lancet* queries helpful in evaluating the status quo:

- *Establishment of joint planning mechanisms*: To what extent does the country "engage key stakeholders, especially ministries of education and health, professional associations, and the academic community, to overcome fragmentation by assessment of national conditions, setting priorities, shaping policies, tracking change, and harmonizing the supply of and demand for health professionals to meet the health needs of the population?"
- *Expansion from academic centers to academic systems*: To what extent is "the traditional discovery-care-education continuum in schools and hospitals" being extended "into primary care settings and communities, strengthened through external collaboration as part of more responsive and dynamic professional education systems?"
- *Alliances and consortia*: To what extent are educational institutions worldwide linked "across to allied actors, governments, civil society, organizations, business and media," particularly "in view of faculty shortages and other resource constraints" making it unlikely for every country "to train on its own the full complement of health professionals that is required?"
- *Nurturing of a culture of critical inquiry*: To what extent is this culture "a central function of universities and other institutions of higher learning, which

is crucial to mobilize scientific knowledged social, ethical deliberation, and public reasoning and debate to generate enlightened social transformation?"

As decision making and funding will increasingly move from central budgets toward local communities, public health professionals will need to play a central role, becoming more knowledgeable about resource planning, working with structures and organizations that support localized population health and social care. Educational research to evaluate progress and identify potential solutions should become a "built-in" requirement of all initiatives, according to *The Lancet* commissioners (43).

The Lancet Commission Vision for all Health Professionals and Curriculum Reform

The Lancet report commissioners also put forward their own vision for "all health professionals in all countries" in the early decades of this century. In their view, and consistent with leadership capacity required to lead change in a new era, transform mindsets, and "build the new," emphasized in Section 7.4, graduates should be

> Educated to mobilize knowledge and to engage in critical reasoning and ethical conduct so that they are competent to participate in patient and population-centred health systems as members of locally responsive and globally connected teams.

> The ultimate purpose is to ensure universal coverage of the high-quality comprehensive services that are essential to advance opportunity for health equity within and between countries.

Realizing this vision would be optimized if program developers adopted a systems and competency-based approach in designing curricula, as shown in Figure 8.7, and by strengthening local–global links.

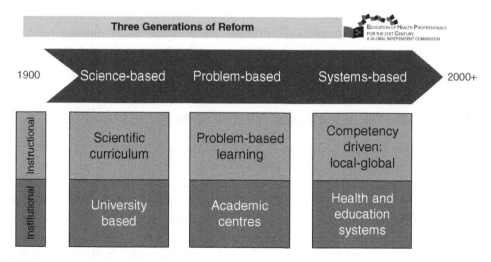

FIGURE 8.7 Three generations of reforms.

Source: Adapted from J. Frenk J, L. Chen, Z.A. Bhutta, et al., "Health Professionals for a New Century: Transforming Education to Strengthen Health Systems in an Interdependent World," *The Lancet*. 376(9756):1923–1958. doi:10.1016/S0140-6736(10)61854-5 (43).

8.7 APPLYING *THE LANCET* COMMISSION VISION OF "HEALTH PROFESSIONALS FOR A NEW CENTURY" TO THE TRADITIONAL "MASTER OF PUBLIC HEALTH" (MPH) DEGREE

The Lancet vision and reforms may be especially applicable to informing traditional MPH program development, paying particular regard to potentially strengthening capacities involving knowledge dissemination, critical reasoning, ethical conduct, health system involvement, interconnecting locally and globally, and advancing health equity globally.

From the evidence gathered by the commission, it appears that many health programs fall short in meeting these criteria, also affirmed by conclusions reached in the report, "Policy Summary: Addressing Needs in the Public Health Workforce in Europe" (16). In terms of public health, across the European Union there are "large gaps . . . in both numbers and professionals trained and the kind of training that exists" with "education . . . still largely characterized by a traditional and limited public focus" (16).

The gaps tend to be much wider, of course, in India, China, and sub-Saharan Africa. In 2010, *The Lancet* Commission reported that "worldwide" there were "2420 medical schools, 467 schools or departments of public health, and an indeterminate number of postsecondary nursing educational institutions" (43). These "train about 1 million new doctors, nurses, midwives, and public health professionals every year" (43).

Further, the commissioners emphasized that "severe institutional shortages are exacerbated by maldistribution, both between and within countries." Four countries (China, India, Brazil, and the United States) each have more than 150 medical schools, whereas 36 countries have no medical schools at all. Twenty-six countries in sub-Saharan Africa have "one or no medical schools." Unsurprisingly, "in view of these imbalances medical school numbers do not align well with either country population size or national burden of disease." Needless to say, the number of schools of public health—most in the West—across regions of about 6 billion people falls far short of what is required and adds to the difficulties associated with meeting the post-2015 Sustainable Development Goals (SDGs). Certainly, a major aim in the coming decade is to fund schools of public health across all nations in the developing world and closely associate these with expanding primary care facilities.

The Traditional Master of Public Health (MPH) Degree

The MPH is considered to be the most widely recognized professional credential for leadership in public health. In the main, MPH and other public health programs are offered through schools of public health whose main remits include "training for research and services, monitoring population health community oriented interventions, liaising with public health associations, and consulting with decision makers" (16).

In most nations, MPH degrees are structured around core requirements, following standards set by accreditation bodies. For example, in the United States students may gain an MPH degree in biostatistics, epidemiology, environmental health sciences, health services and administration, and social and behavioral sciences, along with practice and culminating experience components. Core courses to complete the typical program generally include an Introduction to Health Policy and Management, Determinants of Health, Introduction to Environmental Health, Statistical Methods in Health Research, Fundamentals of Epidemiology for Public Health, a Field Practicum, and a Capping Project. Accreditation for the MPH is through the U.S. Council on Education for Public Health (CEPH), sponsored by the American Public Health Association and the Association of Schools and Programs of Public Health (ASPPH; 44). The MPH generally carries 42 credits, although some schools (e.g., Johns Hopkins) demand as many as 80. In Canada, credits average around 45.

In Europe, the master's level is accredited by the Agency for Public Health Education Accreditation (APHEA) (45), an initiative undertaken by the Association of Schools of Public Health in the European Region (ASPHER), together with partners the European Public Health Association (EUPHA), the European Public Health Alliance (EPHA), the European Health Management Association (EHMA), and EuroHealthNet—and in consultation with WHO Europe and the EU Commission. The curriculum required by APHEA is "based on the core subject domains from the list developed in the European Public Health Core Competences Programme, although slightly regrouped." Core subject areas include Introduction to Public Health, Methods in Public Health, Population Health and Its Determinants, Health Policy, Economics and Management, Health Education and Promotion, Cross-Disciplinary Themes (mandatory or elective courses), and internship/final project resulting in thesis/dissertation/memoire attracting 90 to 120 European Credit Transfer System (ECTS) credits, with a minimum of 60 credits earned between 1 and 3 years (compared to the bachelor level; 180–240 ECTS credits, usually awarded in 2–3 years).

Limitations of the Traditional MPH Degree

While nations are increasingly adopting the MPH, many countries and regions, including Canada, Germany, Singapore, and France, have only come on board in the first decade of this century (46). In the Arab region, as in other nations, public health is still mostly taught in medical schools. In fact, throughout the entire Arab region, there is "only one independent graduate public health program at the University of Alexandria" which also "offers the only doctoral program in public health outside medical schools in the Arab world" (1).

Reasons for the delay in progressing more quickly with the expansion of the MPH degree may be both politically and professionally motivated.

Many European nations favored a more centralized and practical approach to public health training through the establishment of a national system with central national schools acting as the focus for a network of state schools. Some were also not prepared to separate medicine from public health practice, possibly believing that there was no need to change as public health was already being taught in academic programs within other university departments such as medicine, social work, and kinesiology (46). And, although public health played an important role in the 20th century, particularly with the development of toxoids and the capability inducing "immunity to a disease," in the early decades of the 20th century it gradually moved "into a background role" as "the growing effectiveness and technological sophistication of clinical medicine captured the public imagination" (24).

After insulin came sulfa drugs and penicillin, and then a massive armamentarium of antibiotics, including treatments for tuberculosis. Surgical and related techniques blossomed. Open heart surgery, dialysis, joint replacement, pacemakers, kidney transplantation—these and other innovations featured prominently in the mass media of the 1950s and 1960s.

In the decades leading to the millennium and beyond, the emphasis on the scientific basis of medicine and health care has continued while relations between practitioner and patient widened, caused in large measure by the predominance of the hospital system, specialization, medicalization, and technology. At the same time it became widely recognized that the causes of many illnesses or conditions were associated with social determinants of health, discussed in Chapter 2.0, and that in many cases—cancer, cardiovascular disease, and type 2 diabetes—prevention was more effective than trying to find a cure, calling for a different approach in the education and training of health professionals, including much more emphasis on population health and well-being.

The crux of the current problem for many nations, discussed in Chapter 3.0, is that most government and private funding (approximately 95%) flows to conventional health infrastructure, systems, and treatment services along with health education providers at a time when new population health needs have changed. While communicable diseases remain a serious issue in poor nations, these have been compounded by the steep rise in noncommunicable diseases and global health generally, the cause of most global mortalities and morbidities, that are much more in the realm of public or population health and where real differences (e.g., obesity, depression) could be made, especially if public health and primary care were twinned more closely, and if funding followed population health needs and not provider priorities, which are seldom the same. As one example, most primary care budgets have been cut (in the United Kingdom, the budget is only about 8% of the total health budget—reduced from around 11%) at a time when their services are in greatest demand.

Although the number of MPH degrees and courses offered are on the rise, few schools have moved toward providing "a comprehensive, multidisciplinary education beyond the focused biomedical framework and to teach the notion of health as produced in, and determined by, society"(1). The biomedical model, as reflected in Chapter 6.0, which takes a "disease-specific perspective" "represents only one approach to health and health improvement and is not sufficient for addressing population health as we understand it today."

As the authors of *Public Health in the Arab World* (1) maintain, the paradigm's main "concern is with disease risk factors and emphasizing medical, environmental, and individual behavioral lifestyle factors," thereby delivering "a narrowly defined set of health services as the main intervention."

Another major limitation of the biomedical model is that it sees the social determinants of health through "the lens of biomedicine" rather than the fact that "key determinants of individual and population health lie in the circumstances in which people live, and those circumstances are affected by the social and economic environment, causing premature disease and suffering" (1).

While some MPH programs are showing more integrated course delivery, especially ones that offer online blended learning degrees, according to Professor Bjegovic-Mikanovic, president of ASPHER, "most" are still "driven by the strengths and capacities of the teachers and staff instead of actual need. Old epidemiological models prevail together with traditional administrative and management approaches to health care. Little focus is paid to needs analysis with respect to required competences and skills, especially at the level of continuous professional education" (16). No programs appear to have adopted principles and practices associated with One Health.

Remarkably, the university as a social institution has remained "by and large stable in its forms, structures and governance. In the Western world perhaps only the military and the papacy have enjoyed such longevity" (47). Most master's programs still follow the standard university calendar consisting of 2 years, 4 semesters, each with discrete courses, rooted historically, according to some, in medieval times. James Duderstadt, former president of the University of Michigan, observed that "in a very real sense, the industrial age bypassed the university (and we) continue to favor programs and practices based more on past traditions than upon contemporary needs" (48).

Another main concern with this four- or five-century-old course format is that students acquire knowledge in one course but seldom are able to synthesize or transfer what they are learning to other course content or, aside from capstone projects in public health, to the program as a whole. That is, for many students in health professions, learning and assessment often appear fragmented rather than the pursuit of interdependent or interconnected themes. A further limitation is that discipline-specific cohorts seldom tend to have the opportunity to mix with other disciplines or to gain multidisciplinary perspectives on issues that are crucial in resolving so many problems in an interdependent global world (49).

8.8 EMERGING INNOVATIVE HEALTH PROGRAM MODELS

The Latin American School of Medicine (ELAM) Program (CUBA)

The medical school founded in 1999 has graduated more than 12,000 doctors from 64 countries and "is the world's largest and most diverse medical school" (50). Its medical school program is 6 years long and focusses on "fostering equity and improving individual and population health outcomes." Distinctive features are summarized in Box 8.11 that could help to inform health educators in both developing and developed nations (51,52).

ELAM is part of a socially accountable medical school consortium, Training for Health Equity Network (THEnet—see Appendix C, "Global Partnerships for Transformative Education Initiatives"), with schools in Australia, Africa, Asia, Europe,

BOX 8.11

Distinctive Features of the Latin American School of Medicine (ELAM) Program

- Recruiting students from rural, remote, and other disadvantaged communities with the greatest need
- Providing full 6-year scholarships to all students
- Encouraging students to commit to practice as primary care physicians in underserved areas upon graduation
- Integrating concepts of prevention, social determinants of health, and active community partnering into curriculum design
- Using a community based, service-led learning methodology, preparing student to resolve local health problems
- Providing post-graduate clinical, research and continuing education opportunities

and the Americas "to promote the innovations needed to confront the global crisis in health resources for health."

Gillings School of Public Health (United States)

The Gillings School of Public Health at the University of North Carolina offers three MPH concentration areas—Leadership (which includes focus areas in Field Epidemiology, Global Public Health, Public Health Nursing, and Public Health Practice); Health Care and Prevention; and Occupational Health Nursing. The MPH is available in both distance and residential formats, with the exception of the Health Care and Prevention Concentration, which is offered only on campus (53).

The school also offers an integrated Executive MPH program, which focuses on improving decision making and leadership skills. Key features include:

- Applied leadership integrative simulations held at the end of each term to test concepts learned
- Classes held online in real time with faculty and students
- Immediate application of new skills and knowledge to the work environment

Moreover, students are taught by a world-class faculty who use a variety of learning approaches.

University of Heidelberg Institute of Public Health (Germany)

The Institute of Public Health (IPH) is part of the medical school/medical faculty (54). Its mission "is to contribute to the improvement of health through research, teaching and direct services (patient care, consulting) in developing countries and at home." The

IPH also seeks "to look at health and health systems from an international perspective, linking experience in the north and south." Another important dimension at the institute "is the linkage between different disciplines. Health economists, epidemiologists, anthropologists, political scientists, sociologists, mathematicians, geographers, management specialists and biologists work closely together with public health and clinical physicians." Staff work within six thematic units: Epidemiology and Biostatistics, Health Systems Research, Global Health Policies and Systems, Disease Control, Global Environmental Change and Human Health, and Junior Group of Health Economics and Health Financing.

James P. Grant School of Public Health (Bangladesh)

Combining classroom and field-based learning, the James P. Grant School of Public Health in Bangladesh uses "innovative pedagogic methods—through problem-solving, case-study and community-based experiential learning, BRAC Institute of Global Health (the world's largest NGO), government and other NGO sites (74 global and local partnerships)" (55). Its orientation is "a global classroom targeting students from the Americas, Asia, Africa and Europe." Faculty members are drawn from Berlin, Heidelberg, Harvard, Johns Hopkins, Stanford University, London School of Hygiene and Tropical Medicine, Public Health Foundation of India, and the World Bank. To date, over 300 students from 24 countries have graduated.

Maastricht University CAPHRI School of Public Health and Primary Care (The Netherlands)

Seated within Maastricht University's CAPHRI School for Public Health and Primary Care, the Health Education and Promotion program highlights that "A gram of prevention is worth a kilo of cure" (56). Furthermore, in their description, the promoters acknowledge that "helping people to live a healthier lifestyle is not an easy task," especially since health promotion, according to the WHO definition, involves "the process of enabling people to increase control over, and to improve, their health." "Combining elements of psychology, communications, epidemiology, biomedicine, sociology, political science," their interdisciplinary Master of Health Education and Promotion focuses on "health interventions at both the behavioural and environmental levels."

Similarly, their master's program in European Public Health offers "an integrated curriculum which is based on a combination of different educational methodologies, specifically Active and Self-Directed Learning (ASDL), Problem-Based Learning, tutorials and lectures, while also offering the opportunity to pursue research under the supervision of experts" (57). Commendable is the emphasis on students taking "an active role in the learning process, and to join forces to approach a particular problem—analysing it from the widest possible range of perspectives, using many sources of information, and together devising potential solutions."

University of New Mexico Medical School (United States)

Another innovative approach for combining traditional medical education and public health has taken place at the University of New Mexico Medical School, where the 2020 vision of Physicians and Public Health comprises not only clinical expertise but also the integration of a public health focus into all years of the medical school curriculum (58) with regard to the following:

- Disease prevention
- Health promotion and protection
- Health policy development/advocacy
- Awareness of behavioral, environmental, and other social determinants on health and disease
- Population focus to augment the effectiveness of individual practice
- Community participation
- Social responsibility
- Emergency preparedness
- Interprofessional development

University of Wisconsin School of Medicine and Public Health (UWSMPH, United States)

Another educational innovation that is proving to be transformative in bridging medicine and public health is the use of Public Health Integrative Cases (59) at UWSMPH "in which first- and second-year medical students examine an issue or case from many perspectives, including basic science, clinical, public health, social/ethical issues and healthcare systems." An important feature of the case-based program is that "the cases bring students together with community public health practitioners as well as clinicians and scientists across the campus." Cases are faculty-led in small discussion groups over a 2-day period where "students discover many factors influencing health and wellbeing, the interconnections between those factors, and important roles for physicians in promoting health and wellbeing for both individuals and populations that extend beyond traditional ideas of clinical medical care."

Topics have included:

- Determinants of health
- Healthy birth outcomes
- Drunk driving—impact and prevention
- Poverty and health
- Tuberculosis—social, ethical, legal, and global issues
- Cost of care
- Health policy advocacy

Master of Public Health (Southeast Asia)

Building on the three domains Health Improvement, Health Protection, and Health Services (Figure 8.8), the MPH consists of three parts: core course, electives, and thesis

HEALTH IMPROVEMENT	HEALTH PROTECTION	HEALTH SERVICES
Primary health care Public health nutrition • Maternal and child nutrition • Nutrition policy and programming • Nutrition assessment and malnutrition Medical sociology and anthropology Health promotion Health education and behavior change	Advanced epidemiology and biostatistics • Design and analysis of epidemiological studies • Statistical methods in epidemiology • Designing disease control programs • Infectious diseases epidemiology • Non-communicable diseases epidemiology AIDS Disaster and post-disaster management Environmental health • Medical entomology • Hygiene, water, and sanitation interventions Occupational health Globalization and health	Health care policy and management • Health leadership and management • District health management • Health systems design and management • Health system research Maternal and child health • Integrated management of childhood illness • Safe motherhood and prenatal health Reproductive/sexual health • Family planning programs Health economics • Health care financing • Health sector reform and financing • Health care evaluation Hospital administration

FIGURE 8.8 Categorizing services within health improvement, health protection, and health services (Southeast Asia).

(27). The core course focuses on "basic knowledge and skills needed to perform all public health services in all the three domains" and includes "basic knowledge in epidemiology; biostatistics; health policy, management, and economics (health services administration); social and behavioral sciences (medical sociology, health education, health promotion, behavior change); and environmental health."

Summit on Innovations in Graduate Public Health Education (United States)

As discussed, public health schools are now seriously challenged "with how to innovate to best meet the health needs of the 21st century." This concern was the key theme of a national conference in 2012, titled "Innovations in Public Health Education," sponsored by the University of Columbia Mailman School of Public Health (60). Attended by deans and associate deans from 47 of the 50 member schools of the ASPPH (see Appendix A2), the one-day summit focused "on innovations in graduate public health education" and the themes of "leadership and meeting future needs." Challenges that Dean Linda Fried highlighted in her opening remarks included "the health effects of globalization; urbanization; aging and migration; chronic disease and obesity; climate and other environmental changes; as well as pre-existing health needs." Moreover, she said "graduates must acquire new technical skills" and "must be adept with cutting-edge scientific methods, including a life-course approach to prevention and systems science, and leadership education."

She also observed "that redesigned graduate public health education would provide an incentive for the federal government to meet *The Lancet* Commission's call for highly scaled-up investment in training a workforce that is ready to serve in more effective health systems." In his keynote address, Dr. Howard Koh, assistant secretary of health in the U.S. Department of Health and Human Services, emphasized that leadership was key in public health but that "in several important ways . . . public health schools haven't given students the skills to navigate the reality of public health work."

And, while the summit identified innovations across many areas (e.g., "leadership education at the University of California Berkeley School of Public Health, systems science at the University of Pittsburgh, and teaching innovative thinking at the University of Texas"), perhaps the most radical was the restructuring of the MPH at the Mailman School of Public Health, representing "a breakthrough MPH curriculum that sets a new standard for public health education."

The innovative structure of the 2-year MPH program integrates six components, so that learning in one part of the program informs activities and assignments in another. The core curriculum, taken by all incoming students in their first semester, consists of six broad areas of study, known as "studios," each associated with a number of independent modules: Foundations of Public Health; Quantitative Foundations, Evidence, and Policy; Biological & Environmental Determinants of Health; Social, Behavioral, & Structural Determinants of Health; Health Systems; and Systems and Methods for Public Health Planning. Subsequent semesters focus on the integration of science and practice (case studies), leadership (leading teams in a variety of settings, working effectively as a team member, and implementing fresh, innovative ideas within an organization or larger community), and the discipline that students choose as the focus of their studies (academic hub), and the practicum—essentially an internship in the field, a required component of an MPH degree. Year 2 includes a certificate program that provides training in a second, more focussed area of expertise, leading to a Columbia University approved credential, and continuation of the discipline focus as well as preparation for the capstone project or thesis.

Framing the Future for Public Health (United States)

In 2011, the ASPPH established an interprofessional task force on framing the future for education in public health (61). The task force was formed in recognition of the "rapidly changing environment for education in public health" and the fact that "a consequence of the unprecedented upheavals both in healthcare and in higher education." required a different approach. Members were drawn "from major public health organizations, private sector foundations, sister health professions organizations, undergraduate programs, the Association of American Colleges and Universities, the League for Innovation in the Community College, and the Council on Education for Public Health (CEPH)."

The task force conducted its work through a series of expert panels, one of which was devoted to the MPH degree. Recommendations in this report, as indicated in Box 8.12, include reorientation from the five traditional core public health disciplines to a focus on institutional strengths and actual community needs.

BOX 8.12

Framing the Future Task Force Recommendations on the MPH Degree

- A set of core professional skills, attitudes, and values in addition to a shared foundational knowledge base;
- An integrated common core rooted in professional practice (and not in the traditional five core disciplines); a clear emphasis on preparing professionals with a definitive area of expertise beyond the core;
- Practice-based field and culminating experience requirements linked directly to the area of specialization;
- The liberation of graduate programs from the requirement that they offer the MPH degree in the five core disciplines toward encouraging the creation of concentrations more reflective of the strengths of the institutions and the needs of the communities each serves.

There is much to commend within the task force report, in particular, encouraging MPH programs to deviate from the traditional core disciplines, and introducing common core "rooted in professional practice and emphasis on field experience."

In addition to the expert panel reports on various aspects of education in public health, the complete report of the "Framing the Future" task force addresses emerging educational technologies, new pedagogical techniques, and the rapidly changing community of learners, many of whom prefer distance-based education or are demanding credit for previously acquired experience and knowledge.

Concluding Comments on Building Program Curriculum Capacity

Across many health and social care program providers, there is now increasing awareness that the quality (effectiveness and efficiency) of health and social care provision depends to a large degree on the capacity—knowledge, skills, and attitudes—of health and social care professionals. Their effectiveness is based on the quality of their preparation in becoming a health/social care practitioner, including access to timely and high-quality continuing professional development (CPD) activities.

Two fundamental aspects should govern the education and training of health/social care professionals to ensure that learning is "fit for purpose": First, there needs to be much greater emphasis on the socioeconomic and sociopolitical determinants of health and well-being (in particular the One Health concept and practice) in structuring the curriculum. The greatest burdens of disease are in the poorest countries as has once again been clearly demonstrated with the Ebola outbreaks in Western Africa. And, second, prevention through health improvement, health protection, and health services must assume a much greater priority in academic learning and practice. Knowledge in these areas is seldom assessed and hence found to be of little importance by the students.

More specifically, fundamental curriculum dimensions should ensure:

- Placing people and communities at the center (social accountability)
- Ensuring competencies are based on actual population needs (bridging primary care and population health)
- Optimizing collaborative interprofessional, interdisciplinary, global, and digital learning
- Recognizing different ways of knowing, drawing on a range of methods and approaches from disciplines (e.g., sociology, psychology, medicine, nursing, anthropology, economics, and political science)
- Prioritizing a strong emphasis on value formation—competence, compassion, respect, dignity, and recognizing that the values of social justice and ethics are the central goal of addressing inequities in health
- Emphasizing blended, active, and deep learning (vs. surface): face to face, small group, online, community engagement, metacognition, and reflective practice
- Placing an emphasis on problem-based learning (PBL) through realistic scenarios or cases
- Integrating the development of generic or cross-cutting skills (e.g., communication, negotiating skills, ethics)

8.9 INTEGRATING LEARNING, RESEARCH, AND PRACTICE

Informative, Formative, and Transformative Learning

Dr. Eliudi Eliakimu at the Tanzania Ministry of Health and Social Welfare and a global think-tank contributor for this book's Epilogue on "Global Health, Governance, and Education" observes that in low- and middle-income countries there are "manifest limitations to public health training" (62). As one example, there is an urgent need "to reconnect public health education and research with public health practice." His conclusion may be equally valid or appropriate for high-income nations.

A key obstacle, as discussed earlier, relates to how curricula in higher education are conceptualized, structured, and delivered. Faculty members generally divide programs into discrete blocks and themes, and identify courses (subthemes) that logically relate to the main themes. Each course has its own learning outcomes, not necessarily work-related competencies, teaching activities, resources, and assessments, and is given a credit weighting depending on total course hours or relative importance. Many courses also expect students to complete research-based assignments. Other than the capstone component in the final year, application of the competencies acquired throughout a course is seldom practiced immediately or, if they are, there may not be a direct correlation between what has been learned in lectures or class and the practical experience. The latter observation may apply to many health and other disciplines and is counter to one of the key principles of learning*: the importance of frequent

---

*Others are: Active Involvement, Patterns and Connections, Informal Learning, Direct Experience, Reflection, Compelling Situation, and Enjoyable Setting

feedback on what students need to retain, including "explicit cues about how to do better, such as that provided deliberately (or unconsciously) by a teacher or peer" (63).

From Passive "Surface" to Active "Deep" Learning

The Lancet Commission differentiated between informative learning, formative learning, and transformative learning, noting (43) that:

- Informative learning is about acquiring knowledge and skills; its purpose is to produce experts.
- Formative learning is about socializing students around values; its purpose is to produce professionals.
- Transformative learning is about developing leadership attributes; its purpose is to produce enlightened change agents.

Building each level on the previous one, achieving transformative learning requires, say the commissioners, three basic shifts:

- From fact memorization to searching, analysis, and synthesis of information for decision making
- From seeking professional credentials to achieving core competencies for effective teamwork in health systems
- From noncritical adoption of educational models to creative adaption of global resources to address local priorities

Because of the limitations of the traditional teaching model, over the past four decades many universities moved toward PBL, especially in medical schools. According to researchers, the main difference between inquiry-based learning (IBL) and problem-based learning (PBL) is that IBL is "driven on raising (deductive) questions based on real observations," whereas PBL focusses on "the solution of ill-structured problems" (64).

The approaches share many similarities—both have been informed by the work of the American pragmatic philosopher John Dewey in the 20th century; both rely on minimally direct instruction, and both see the teacher's main role as a facilitator or coach rather than as a disseminator of information. So, while IBL is considered the "best learning approach for human nature," PBL may provide "the best outcomes and learning for problem solution."

Problem-Based Learning Versus Didactic Teaching

A central assumption underlying student-centered PBL is that "learning is an active, integrated, and constructive process influenced by social and contextual factors" (65). Open-ended problems serve as the initial stimulus. In PBL, these are called "ill-structured" in the sense that they may "have multiple solutions and require students," working in small groups, "to look at many methods before deciding on a particular solution."

Finding solutions may require research, possibly in small teams (e.g., online, expert interviews, community contact), following several lines of inquiry outside the discipline. Groups reconvene, discuss their findings, and may be asked to draft a research report, which may then be presented to the whole group.

According to Dr. Michael Copland, then a faculty member in the School of Education at Stanford, "creating ill-structured problems takes time and creativity but can be extremely rewarding when students achieve their learning goals" (65,66).

> The key thing in making [PBL] successful is the amount of time and energy that goes into the creation of the project. Finding a problem that really means something to the participants is absolutely critical. Once you find a very salient problem, then structure the learning objectives around that problem and find resources that inform students' thinking about the problem . . . chances are it's going to have some success.

Assessment mirrors the "PBL philosophy of active learning rather than passive reproductive learning" and entails assessing both content and process objectives, which focus on the "kinds of problems embraced by specific disciplines and professions, and the means by which practitioners go about solving them." A strength of PBL is that many cross-cutting skills could be integrated into the case studies and benefit from authentic assessments. That is, assessments, which could include peer feedback, "should be structured so that students can display their understanding of problems and their solutions in contextually-meaningful ways."

Research on Teaching and Learning

There is considerable consensus that PBL is one of the most effective ways of linking learning, research, and practice. Most research in the early decades of the 20th century focused on teaching or what the teacher did in the classroom or the transmission conception rather than on learning and what the student does (67). This reorientation is consistent with research in the neurosciences, which suggests that there is very little value "in giving students ready made meaning (*surface learning*) as this passive process seldom leads to deep learning" (68). In contrast, active learning triggers "a virtual explosion of neural activity, causing synapses to form, neurotransmitters to activate and blood flow to increase" (69). This engagement can be strengthened further through collaboration and team-based projects.

The shift to a learner-centered orientation can be analyzed from three main perspectives: research on cognition and learning, research on motivation and learning, and research on the social context of learning (67).

Although didactic teaching (or preaching?) is still widely practiced—"teaching is telling" in terms of cognition and learning, "research no longer supports a transmission model (memorization and reproduction)" (67). Findings have shown that learners "must learn by interacting with and transforming received information so as to own it and make it personally meaningful" (68) and to "help bridge the gap between the structures of the discipline and the structures in the students' minds" (70).

Motivation was generally viewed as a "trait inherent in students . . . or as determined by factors in the environment." However, similar to knowledge acquisition motivation is now considered "in a dynamic way based on a process of self-appraisal of situations" (71) or basically what the "students perceive as important—which is determined by personal *needs and values*."

The social context of learning has also been recognized as playing a key role in learning. The main finding is that "learning takes place essentially through interaction with others and with the wider social culture in departments and institutions." Rather than being a dispenser of information, the teacher's or lecturer's main role in PBL is as a facilitator of learning, encouraging "contacts between students and staff," developing "reciprocity and cooperation among students," communicating "high expectations," and respecting "diverse talents" (72).

In conclusion, it is argued that PBL could be an important step in enhancing informative and formative learning in public health. It could provide a strong foundation on which to build transformative learning, ensuring that today's public health students become the leaders and change agents of tomorrow.

David Perkins, professor at the Harvard Graduate School of Education, contends that this approach to learning is about "playing the whole game," or "learning by wholes," rather than learning disconnected and isolated knowledge or skills or discrete topics. The "bottom line" in his book, *Making Learning Whole: How Seven Principles of Teaching Can Transform Education* (73), is that "elements don't make much sense in the absence of the whole game" or understanding the wider context. This observation may be particularly true for public health education.

8.10 GLOBAL HEALTH WORKFORCE CRISIS AND WHO GUIDELINES FOR SCALING UP EDUCATION AND TRAINING FOR HEALTH WORKERS: INFORMING DIALOGUE AND ENABLING ACTION

Global Health Worker Crisis

Several years ago Dr. Michele Frank, a Cuban physician, and Gail Reed, both editors for the *MEDICC REVIEW* (*Health and Medical News of Cuba*), pinpointed "the core problems that keep us from achieving health for all" (74). "Front and centre," they asserted, "among them is that there are simply not enough health workers, not trained or distributed well enough, nor with sufficient equity, to staff the health systems of the world, particularly those of developing countries."

Exacerbating the situation, they observed "health systems are understaffed, poorly led and organized, and inequitable in providing services—incapable of cure, let alone prevention, and thoroughly unsustainable. These problems may be more acute and urgent in the Third World—especially where whole populations are being decimated by HIV-AIDS—but they exist within rich countries as well, in countries whose historical policies also bear responsibility for the global disaster."

With findings released at the Third Global Forum on Human Resources for Health (HRH; 75) "together with recommendations on actions to address workforce shortages in the era of universal health coverage," it is estimated that by 2035 the world will have a shortage of 12.9 million health care workers, with a current shortage of about 7.2 million worldwide.

The report, *A Universal Truth: No Health Without a Workforce* (76), identifies several main causes, including:

- An ageing health workforce with staff retiring or leaving for better paid jobs without being replaced

- Not enough young people are entering the profession or being adequately trained
- A growing world population with risks of noncommunicable diseases (e.g., cancer, heart disease, stroke, etc.)
- Internal and international migration of health workers

Two of the most crucial recommendations call for "Maximizing the role of mid-level and community health workers to make frontline health services more accessible and acceptable" and "Providing mechanisms for the voice, rights and responsibilities of health workers in the development and implementation of policies and strategies towards universal health coverage." As shown in Figure 8.9, the greatest health workforce shortage is in sub-Saharan Africa, India, and Southeast Asia.

According to Dr. Marie-Paule Kieny, WHO Assistant Director-General for Health Systems and Innovation, "the foundations for a strong and effective health workforce for the future are being corroded in front of our very eyes by failing to match today's supply of professionals with the demands of tomorrow's populations. . . . To prevent this happening, we must rethink and improve how we teach, train, deploy and pay health workers so that their impact can widen" (77). And, while "more countries have increased their health workforce, progressing towards the basic threshold of 23 skilled health professionals per 10 000 people, there are still 83 countries below this basic threshold."

Although "shortages in numerical terms are expected to be in parts of Asia," sub-Saharan Africa will be impacted the most. The report, *A Universal Truth: No Health Without a Workforce*, highlights that "in the 47 countries of sub-Saharan Africa, just 168 medical schools exist. Of those countries, 11 have no medical schools, and 24 countries have only one medical school."

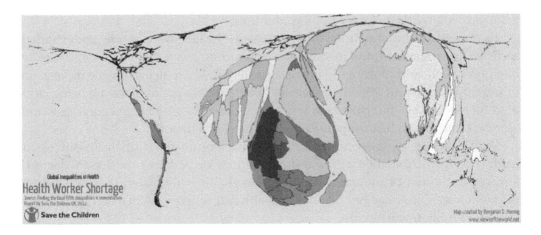

FIGURE 8.9 Health worker shortage, 2012.

Source: Map created by Benjamin D. Hennig (www.viewsoftheworld.net) for *Finding the Final Fifth: Inequalities in Immunisation*, published in May 2012 by Save the Children.

For Dr. Carissa Etienne, WHO Regional Director for the Americas, "one of the challenges for achieving universal health coverage is ensuring that everyone—especially people in vulnerable communities and remote areas—has access to well-trained, culturally-sensitive and competent health staff" and "the best strategy for achieving this is by strengthening multidisciplinary teams at the primary healthcare level." Making primary care the main catalyst for supporting population health and well-being is particularly crucial as "around 90% of all maternal deaths and 80% of all still births occur in 58 countries, largely because those countries lack trained midwives. Also, of the 6.6 million under-five-year olds who died in 2012, most deaths were from treatable and preventable diseases."

Global Health Workforce Alliance (GHWA): First Phase (2006–2011): "Scaling Up, Saving Lives"

Global recognition of the urgency behind workforce shortages and its impact on the lives of billions began in 2006 when WHO "alerted the world to a shortfall of 4.3 million trained health workers globally with the worst shortages in the poorest countries" (78). As a result, the Global Health Workforce Alliance (GHWA) was launched at the World Health Assembly in Geneva. The GHWA "set up task forces to address specific aspects of the problem such as health-worker education and training, migration and financing," thereby initiating the first phase (2006–2011) of the HRH movement (79).

In 2008, the Task Force for Scaling Up Education and Training for Health Workers, co-chaired by Lord Nigel Crisp, former National Health Service (NHS) chief executive, now a crossbench peer, and Bience Gawanas, a lawyer who formerly served as a member of the Namibian government and then as an African Union commissioner, presented their findings. Focusing on countries with the worst health workforce crisis—severe shortage of doctors, nurses, midwives, and other skilled health workers, particularly in Africa—the task force concluded that "policies and plans" were failing and that "the number of people being educated and trained" was "too small to make a difference." Moreover, they found that the problem was exacerbated due to a lack of "international coordination of effort and, all too often, differential salary scales between public sector, international and private organizations, which drive up costs and lead to movement from the public sector, poor working conditions, and significant international migration of workers."

GHWA Strategy for the Second Phase (2013–2016)

While there were a number of significant achievements during Phase 1 of the GHWA strategy (78), such as HRH mainstreaming "into the global health policy and development discourse," establishing "thematic task forces" that progressed "seminal work on health worker education," task shifting and the role of community health workers, and universal access to HIV prevention and treatment service, more work remains to be done, as summarized in Box 8.13.

BOX 8.13

A Vision for Success in 2016

In 2016, the alliance will collectively consider its mission accomplished if the following results are achieved:

- Commitments to train, deploy, and retain at least an additional 2.6 million health workers, in support of the United Nations Secretary-General's *Global Strategy for Women's and Children's Health* and universal health coverage, are delivered and being implemented;
- Evidence-based quality HRH plans, developed through inclusive mechanisms of coordination among HRH stakeholders, are integrated within national health strategies and implemented in at least 75% of the alliance's priority countries;
- A new, equitable, long-term vision for HRH, that seeks to eliminate avoidable morbidity and mortality and promote well-being, is firmly embedded in the post-2015 development agenda;
- Accountability for HRH results is ensured as an integral part of existing health governance and monitoring platforms;
- HRH stakeholders mobilized to take proactive roles in support of national HRH development priorities within a health system strengthening framework.

Source: WHO, Transformative Education for Health Professionals, (80).

The alliance intends to realize its vision "by providing an enabling environment to mobilize global, regional and national leadership to adopt and invest in the most appropriate and effective policy options for health workforce development, in collaboration with relevant domestic stakeholders and the international community, through three core objectives."

Transforming and Scaling Up Health Professionals' Education and Training

Responding to the severe global health workforce crisis and at the request of its member states and partners, WHO developed "policy guidelines to assist countries, development partners and other stakeholders in efforts to expand the health workforce and improve the alignment between the education of health workers and population health needs" (81). In the Foreword to "Transformative Education for Health Professionals," WHO Director-General Dr. Margaret Chan notes that "In virtually every country, shortages have been accompanied by an imbalance in skill mix of teams and uneven geographical distribution of health professionals, leaving millions without access to health services."

Further, she highlights: "More professional health workers are needed, but it has become clear that efforts to scale up health professionals' education must not only increase the quantity of health workers, but also address issues of quality and relevance in order to address population health needs." She underscores that educational institutions not only need to increase their capacity to teach in terms of infrastructure but also improve the competencies of existing staff and increase their numbers; reform admissions criteria; strengthen health professionals' competencies by revising and updating curricula on a regular basis; and link the disease burden to training needs.

Purpose of the Guidelines

Calling "for new approaches in health professional education, the guidelines focus on transforming systems and encourage the move away from the traditional focus on tertiary care hospitals to initiatives that foster community engagement."

More specifically, the purpose of the guidelines is to:

- Provide sound policy and technical guidance in the area of pre-service education, particularly to countries experiencing shortages of doctors, nurses, midwives, and other health professionals
- Guide countries on how to integrate (CPD) as part of medical, nursing, midwifery, and other health professional education scale-up

These aims are crucial "in order to ensure excellence of care, responsive health service delivery and sustainable health systems." To achieve these goals, "Country ownership in determining priorities and setting policy is required in each of the five identified guideline domains:

1. Education and training institutions
2. Accreditation, regulation
3. Financing and sustainability
4. Monitoring and evaluating
5. Governance and planning"

Achieving the broader vision for transformative education will necessitate a number of system-wide enabling actions, as shown in Box 8.14.

BOX 8.14

Enabling System-Wide Reforms to Achieve Transformative Education

- Greater alignment between educational institutions and the systems that are responsible for health service delivery.
- Country ownership of priorities and programming related to the education of health professionals with political commitment and partnerships to facilitate reform at national, regional, and local levels.
- Promotion of social accountability in professional education and of close collaboration with communities.
- Clinicians and public health workers who are competent and provide the highest quality of care for individuals and communities.
- Global excellence coupled with local relevance in research and education.
- Vibrant and sustainable education institutions with dynamic curricula and supportive learning environments, including good physical infrastructure, and
- Retaining faculty of outstanding quality who are motivated.

National Governance and Planning in Support of the Education Guidelines

Four good practice recommendations have been identified, including encouraging national political commitments, collaboration, and shared accountability among key ministries, national graduate planning, and strengthening national and subnational institutions "to support the implementation of the reform and scale-up plan (eg, legislation, policies, procedures)."

Meeting the Educational Challenges: India—A Case in Point

The WHO guidelines for scaling up the health care workforce become all the more crucial when set against the actual ambitions and realities facing many nations. India is a case in point. A few years ago, a United Kingdom–India Education and Research Initiative (UKIERI) submission for funding proposed "a high-impact skills development skills training programme across higher/further education and schools" (82). The aim was "to achieve a skilled workforce of 500 million by 2022. An interim target is for 70 million of new jobs to be created by 2012 in high growth industries such as automobiles, logistics, travel & tourism, media & entertainment and healthcare services. Five percent of these 70 million jobs would require a sector and skill specific trained workforce."

The gap between the government's ambition and reality on the ground is wide. As one example, "while 90 percent of the jobs in India are skill-based only 6 percent of the Indian workforce receives any form of vocational training." "The Government of India is looking to partner with the private sector to promote vocational skills by creating 1600 new Indian Technical Institutes."

Exacerbating the problem is that "Vocational education is also held as a low priority, lacking vertical mobility." India's plight is shared by all poor nations and makes sharing global success stories in scaling up and improving the global health workforce a matter of considerable urgency, especially if the GHWA 2016 vision is to be met. However, distinguishing India from many other nations in transition is that "more than half" of its "population of 1.2 billion is under the age of 25," along with "7.5 percent GDP growth," making it a prime target "for international investors." Focusing its strategic training priorities on the younger population and streamlining its "cumbersome bureaucracy" (83) could provide opportunities too important to waste.

8.11   MAKING A DIFFERENCE TO "LIFE AS IT IS LIVED"

Increasing and strengthening the health workforce globally remains a top priority not only because of the continuing struggle to combat communicable and rising noncommunicable diseases but also because billions of people are still deprived of even the most basic human needs—shelter, water, sanitation, food, safety.

In a LinkedIn discussion on nondisease public health priorities (84), Dr. Claudia Pagliari, a senior lecturer in primary care and program director of the MSc in Global eHealth at The University of Edinburgh, reminds us that providing essential life-sustaining and life-enhancing support is not necessarily a question of more funding for novel, often technologically driven and expensive, interventions but that true "innovation" will come from translating what we already know into practice in lower income countries, so as to address basic health needs and social equity. Digging wells, providing toilets, embedding condom use into cultural norms, and banning cigarette promotion are far more likely to impact public health than any amount of surgical tools or new drugs.

An editorial in *EcoHealth* (85) reinforces her argument. By and large, funding by the medical community in most developed countries over the past half century has been allocated to "emerging infectious diseases" (EIDs), as these originate "primarily in tropical regions where wildlife biodiversity and human population density are high." To combat EIDs among the world's poorest nations, the editors, Claire Standley and Tiffany Bogich at Princeton University, posit that health spending has been mostly on single diseases—"AIDS, malaria, TB and polio," a systemic weakness also identified in the 2000 to 2015 Millennium Development Goals (MDGs), discussed in Section 4.1— rather than on taking a more horizontal "integrated, ecohealth approach," that delves beyond superficial causes or symptoms—often deadly—and addresses actual deep-seated, multi-faceted causative structural factors, such as "destructive land-use change and biodiversity loss," identified by the editors. Further, they contend, as one signifi-cant change, that foreign aid should integrate "development objectives, particularly when they relate to human, animal, and wildlife health," by adopting "an ecohealth approach at an international development policy level," thereby "creating sustainable and integrated health systems" (85). With the latter in mind, in her LinkedIn comments, Dr. Pagliari emphasizes the importance of "encouraging coordinated health policies and integrated health systems underpinned by better information, knowledge and the principle of health as a fundamental human right" alongside "strengthening health system governance, including measures to counter corruption and fraud" (85).

For Dr. Pagliari, bolstering "health systems must surely start with strengthening the vision, knowledge, management and ethics of those at the top, whilst enabling coordinated and sustainable action requires overcoming siloed thinking and donor territoriality." Moreover, in line with the innovative approaches of global health pio-neers, such as Dr. Sydney Kark in South Africa in the 1940s/1950s, and Professor Carl Taylor in India several decades later (discussed in Chapter 6.0), and key conclu-sions reached more recently in *A Universal Truth: No Health Without a Workforce* (76), she points to the centrality of "empowering untrained community health workers to strengthen workforce capacity." There can be little doubt that this cohort will need to play a pivotal or leading role in the implementation of the WHO Education Guidelines and help to build curriculum "fit for purpose" to enable effective global health work-force developments and compassionate care.

And, while these transformations may be seen as belonging solely in the sphere of poor nations, they also hold valuable lessons for the more advanced economies, where poverty, social inequities, illnesses stemming from modernity, unrest, and fears of an uncertain future remain equally trenchant and unsettling.

REFERENCES

1. Jabbour S, Giacaman R, Khawaja M, Nuwayhid I, eds. Yamout R (associate editor). *Public health in the Arab world*. Cambridge: Cambridge University Press; 2012.
2. Awofeso N. What's new about the "New Public Health"? *Am J Public Health*. 2004;94(5):705–709. http://www.ncbi.nlm.nih.gov/pmc/articles/PMC1448321/. Accessed July 28, 2014.

3. Foldspang A, Otok R. ASPHER'S position paper concerning: The new European policy for health—Health 2020 (Draft 2) and the European action plan for strengthening public health capacities and services (17.02.2012). Brussels: ASPHER; 2012. http://www.aspher.org/foto/EB032014/ASPHER_Position_Paper_RE_Health2020.pdf. Accessed January 2, 2013.

4. Ross M. Interview: Sally Davies. http://www.civilserviceworld.com/interview-sally-davies. Accessed February 20, 2013.

5. Patel K, Rushefsky ME. *The politics of public health in the United States.* Armonk, NY: M.E. Sharpe; 2005.

6. Laaser, U. Appreciation Professor Geoffrey Arthur Rose CBE. http://www.researchgate.net/publication/21319321_Appreciation_Prof._Geoffrey_Arthur_Rose_CBE. Accessed May 30, 2014.

7. Barrett MA, Bouley TA, Stoertz HA, Stoertz WR. Integrating a One Health approach in education to address global health and sustainability challenges. *Front Ecol Environ.* 2011;9:239–245. doi: 10.1890/090159

8. Frenk J. The new public health. *Annu. Rev. Health.* 1993;14:469–490.

9. Tulchinsky TH, Varavikova EA. What is the "New Public Health"? *Public Health Reviews.* 2010;32:25–53.

10. Tulchinsky TH, Varavikova EA. *The new public health.* 3rd ed. San Diego, CA: Elevier, Academic Press; 2014.

11. Institute of Medicine. Primary care and public health: Exploring integration to improve population health. https://www.nap.edu/login.php?record_id=13381&page=http%3A%2F%2Fwww.nap.edu%2Fdownload.php%3Frecord_id%3D13381

12. Berwick DM, Nolan TW, Whittington J. The triple Aim: Care, health, and cost. http://content.healthaffairs.org/content/27/3/759.full. Accessed May 30, 2012.

13. Zurayk H, Giacaman R, Mandil A. Graduate education in public health: Toward a multidisciplinary model. In Jabbour S, Giacaman R, Khawaja M, Nuwayhid I, eds. Yamout R (associate editor). *Public health in the Arab world.* New York, NY: Cambridge University Press; 2012.

14. Kickbusch, I. In search of the public health paradigm for the 21st century: The political dimensions of public health. http://www.thinkers.sa.gov.au/lib/pdf/Kickbusch_Final_Report.pdf. Accessed July 25, 2014.

15. Centers for Disease Control and Prevention. Core functions of public health and how they relate to the 10 essential services. http://www.cdc.gov/nceh/ehs/ephli/core_ess.htm. Accessed July 30, 2014.

16. Bjegovic-Mikanovic V, Czabanowska K, Flahaut A, et al. *Addressing needs in the public health workforce in Europe* (Policy Summary 10). http://www.euro.who.int/__data/assets/pdf_file/0003/248304/Addressing-needs-in-the-public-health-workforce-in-Europe.pdf?ua=1. Accessed March 15, 2013.

17. Gonczi A. Competency based assessment in the professions in Australia. *Assessment in Education.* 1994;1(1):27–44.

18. Lueddeke G. *Transforming medical education for the 21st century: Megatrends, priorities and change.* Oxford, UK: Radcliffe Publishing; 2012.

19. Bjegovic-Mikanovic V, Vukovic D, Otok R, Czabanowska K, Laaser U. Education and training of public health professionals in the European region: Variation and convergence. *Int J Public Health.* 2013;58(6):801–810. http://www.ncbi.nlm.nih.gov/pubmed/23132128. Accessed January 16, 2013.

20. Institute of Medicine. *The future of the public's health in the 21st century.* Washington, DC: The National Academy Press; 2003.

21. World Health Organization. *Ottawa charter for health promotion.* Geneva, Switzerland: WHO; 1986.

22. Whitfield M. Public health job market. In Czabanowska K, Włodarczyk C, eds. *Employment in public heath in Europe* [Zatrudnienie w Zdrowiu Publicznym w Europie]. Kraków: Jagiellonian University Press; 2004:122–165.

23. Genat B, Robinson P, Parker E. *Foundation competencies for master of public health graduates in Australia.* Australian Network of Academic Public Health Institutions (ANAPHI). http://www.phaa.net.au/documents/ANAPHI_MPH%20competencies.pdf. Accessed January 20, 2010.

24. Public Health Agency of Canada. Core competencies for public health in Canada. http://www.phac-aspc.gc.ca/php-psp/ccph-cesp/about_cc-apropos_ce-eng.php. Accessed June 15, 2014.

25. Birt C, Foldspang A, European core competences for public health professionals (ECCPHP). *ASPHER's European public health core competences programme.* ASPHER Publication No. 5. Brussels: ASPHER; 2011.

26. Sharma K, Zodpey S, Gaidhane A, Syed ZQ, Kumar R, MD; Morgan A. Designing the framework for competency-based master of public health programs in India. *J Public Health Manag Pract.* 2013;19(1):30–39. https://www.academia.edu/2712006/Designing_the_Framework_for_Competency-Based_Master_of_Public_Health_Programs_in_India. Accessed June 20, 2014.

27. Karkee R. Public health education in South Asia: A basis for structuring a master degree course. *Front Public Health.* 2014;2:88. http://journal.frontiersin.org/Journal/10.3389/fpubh.2014.00088/full. Accessed July 15, 2014.

28. Faculty of Public Health of the Royal Colleges of Physician of the United Kingdom. Public health specialty training program 2010. http://www.fph.org.uk/uploads/2010MASTERPHCurriculum0610b.pdf

29. Association of Schools of Public Health. Undergraduate public health learning outcomes FINAL model version 1.0. http://www.phf.org/news/Documents/UGPHLearningOutcomes_ModelVersion1%200_FINAL.pdf. Accessed August 15, 2012.

30. Public Health Foundation (PHF). About PHF. http://www.phf.org/AboutUs/Pages/default.aspx. Accessed June 20, 2014.

31. Council on Linkages Between Academia and Public Health Practice. Overview. http://www.phf.org/programs/council/Pages/default.aspx. Accessed June 20, 2014.

32. Council on Linkages. About the core competencies for public health professionals. http://www.phf.org/programs/corecompetencies/Pages/About_the_Core_Competencies_for_Public_Health_Professionals.aspx. Accessed June 20, 2014.

33. Council on Linkages. Competency-based job descriptions. http://www.phf.org/resourcestools/pages/competency_based_job_descriptions.aspx. Accessed August 20, 2014.

34. Maykut P, Morehouse R. *Beginning qualitative research: A philosophic and practical guide,* London: The Falmer Press; 1994.

35. Josiah Macy Jr. Foundation. *Accelerating interprofessional education. 2012 annual report.* New York, NY: JMJF;2012.

36. Josiah Macy Jr. Foundation. *Accelerating interprofessional education.* 2012 Annual Report. http://www.macyfoundation.org/docs/annual_reports/macy_AnnualReport_2012.pdf. Accessed 27 February, 2013.

37. Zwanikken PAC, Alexander L, Huong NT, et al. Validation of Public Health Competencies and Impact Variables for Low- and Middle-Income Countries. *BMC Public Health.* 2014;14:55. http://www.ncbi.nlm.nih.gov/pmc/articles/PMC3899921/#!po=43.1818. Accessed February 25, 2014.

38. Nurse J. *Global public health: definitions and challenges.* Module N 1.2. http://www.seejph.com/wp-content/uploads/2015/02/N-1.2-Nurse-PH-Definitions-150207.pdf

39. Horton R, Beaglehole R, Bonita R, Raeburn J, McKee M, Wall S. From public to planetary health: A manifesto. *The Lancet.* 2014;383(9920):847. http://www.thelancet.com/journals/lancet/article/PIIS0140-6736(14)60409-8/fulltext. Accessed May 18, 2014.

40. Freidson E. The theory of professions: State of the art. In Dingwall R, Lewis P, eds. *The sociology of the professions.* London: Macmillan; 1993.

41. Rowbottom R, Billis D. *Organizational design: The work levels approach.* Aldershot, Hants: Gower; 1987.

42. WHO. *Now more than ever* (The world health report 2008: Primary health care). http://www.who.int/whr/2008/en/. Accessed October 4, 2009.

43. Frenk, J, Chen L, Bhutta ZA, et al. Health Professionals for a New Century: Transforming Education to Strengthen Health Systems in an Interdependent World. *The Lancet.* 2010;376(9756): 1923–1958.

44. Association of Schools and Programs of Public Health (ASPPH). http://www.aspph.org/. Accessed April 10, 2011.

45. The Agency for Public Health Education Accreditation (APHEA). About APHEA. http://www.aphea.net/index.php?id=3. Accessed June 20, 2013.

46. Global Knowledge Exchange Network. An overview of education and training requirements for global healthcare professionals. http://www.gken.org/Docs/Workforce/Public%20Health%20FINAL%20092709.pdf. Accessed April 25, 2014.

47. Lueddeke G. Applying a constructivist framework to strategic change and innovation in research-intensive universities. *Int J Knowledge, Culture Change Manag.* 2006;6(7):199–212.

48. Duderstadt J. *A university for the 21st century.* Ann Arbor, MI: The University of Michigan Press; 2000.

49. Gnagey LT. Projects selected, RFP announced. Multidisciplinary Learning and Team Teaching Initiative. http://www.ur.umich.edu/0607/Jan22_07/02.shtml. Accessed October 31, 2005.

50. Frank M, Reed GA. Doctors for the (developing) world. http://www.medicc.org/publications/medicc_review/0805/spotlight.html. Accessed May 18, 2014.

51. Gorry C. Cuba's Latin American medical school: Can socially-accountable medical education make a difference? *Medicc Review* 2012;14(3):5–11.

52. Huish R, Kirk JM. (2007). Cuban medical internationalism and the development of the Latin American school of medicine. *Latin American Perspectives.* 2007;34(6):77–92.

53. UNC Gillings School of Global Public Health. Degrees and certificates. http://sph.unc.edu/epid/epid-degrees-and-certificates. Accessed January 15, 2014.

54. University of Heidelberg Institute of Public Health. Institute of Public Health (IPH). http://www.klinikum.uni-heidelberg.de/Institute-of-Public-Health.5358.0.html. Accessed May 20, 2014.

55. James P. Grant School of Public Health. What's new? http://sph.bracu.ac.bd/. Accessed May 26, 2014.

56. Maastricht University Faculty of Health, Medicine and Life Sciences. Health education and promotion. http://www.maastrichtuniversity.nl/web/show/id=349069/langid=42. Accessed May 24, 2014.

57. Maastricht University Faculty of Health, Medicine and Life Sciences European Public Health. http://www.maastrichtuniversity.nl/web/show/id=927947/langid=42. Accessed May 24, 2014.

58. University of New Mexico School of Medicine. MD/MPH program. http://som.unm.edu/education/md-mph.html. Accessed May 15, 2014.

59. University of Wisconsin-Madison. Integrative cases exemplify school's transformation. http://www.med.wisc.edu/quarterly/integrative-cases-exemplify-schools-transformation/31469. Accessed May 27, 2014.

60. Columbia University Mailman School of Public Health. Summit on public health education sets course for change. http://www.mailman.columbia.edu/news/summit-public-health-education-sets-course-change. Accessed November 17, 2013.

61. Petersen DJ, Weist EM. Framing the future by mastering the new public health. *J Public Health Manag Pract.* 2014;20(4):371–374. http://www.ncbi.nlm.nih.gov/pmc/articles/PMC4032212/#!po=45.0000. Accessed July 24, 2014.

62. Eliakimu E. Principal medical officer, ministry of health & social welfare, Tanzania. Personal communication. April 4, 2014.

63. intime. Principles of learning. http://www.intime.uni.edu/model/learning/freq.html. Accessed August 20, 2014.

64. Oğuz-ünver A, Arabacioğlu S. Overviews on inquiry based and problem based learning methods. http://web.deu.edu.tr/baed/giris/baed/ozel_sayi/303-310.pdf. Accessed January 20, 2014.

65. Stanford University. Problem-based learning. https://www.arrs.org/uploadedFiles/ARRS/Life_Long_Learning_Center/Educators_ToolKit/STN_problem_based_learning.pdf. Accessed July 16, 2008.

66. Barrows HS. Problem-based learning in medicine and beyond: A brief overview. In Wilkerson L & Gijselaers WH, eds. *Bringing problem-based learning to higher education: Theory and practice.* San Francisco, CA: Jossey Bass; 1996: 3–12.

67. Nicol DJ. Research on learning and higher education teaching. UCoSDA Briefing Paper 45; April 1997.

68. Ramsden P. *Learning to teach in higher education.* London: Routledge; 1992.

69. Ginnis P. *The teacher's toolkit.* Bancyfelin, Carmarthen, Wales: Crown House Publishing Ltd; 2002.

70. McKeachie WJ. Recent research on university teaching and learning: Implications for practice and future research. *Academic Medicine.* 1992;67(10):584–587.

71. Paris SG, Turner JC. Situated motivation. In Pintrich PR, Brown anf DR, Weinstein CE, eds. *Student motivation, cognition and learning.* Hillsdale, NJ: Erlbaum; 1994: 213–237.

72. Chickering AW, Gamson ZF. *Seven principles for good practice in undergraduate education.* Racine, WI: Johnson Foundation.

73. Perkins D. *Making learning whole: How seven principles of teaching can transform education.* San Francisco, CA: Jossey-Bass; 2009.

74. Frank M, Reed GA. Doctors for the (developing) world. http://www.medicc.org/publications/medicc_review/0305/pages/spotlight.html. Accessed June 15, 2014.

75. Global Health Workforce Alliance and WHO. Third global forum on human resources for health. http://www.who.int/workforcealliance/forum/2013/en/. Accessed January 10, 2014.

76. Global Health Workforce Alliance and WHO. *A universal truth: No health without a workforce* http://www.who.int/workforcealliance/knowledge/resources/hrhreport2013/en/. Accessed January 10, 2014.

77. WHO and Global Health Workforce Alliance. Scaling up, saving lives. Summary and recommendation. http://www.who.int/workforcealliance/knowledge/toolkit/42_2.pdf. Accessed September 5, 2008.

78. Global Health Workforce Alliance and WHO. *Strategy for the second phase 2013–2016: An illustration.* Geneva: WHO; 2011.

79. The Global Health Workforce Alliance Strategy 2013–2016. Advancing the health workforce agenda within universal health coverage. http://www.who.int/workforcealliance/knowledge/resources/ghwa_strategy_long_web.pdf.

80. WHO. Transformative education for health professionals. http://www.capacityplus.org/files/resources/who-recommendations-transforming-scaling-up-health-workforce-education.pdf. Accessed April 15, 2014.

81. Wheeler E. WHO recommendations for transforming and scaling up health workforce education, and for retaining health workers in rural and remote areas. http://www.capacityplus.org/files/resources/who-recommendations-transforming-scaling-up-health-workforce-education.pdf. Accessed April 18, 2014.

82. UK-India Education and Research Initiative (UKIERI). Skills development. http://www.ukieri.org/skills-development.html. Accessed December 20, 2011.

83. Pagnamenta R. Now is the right time for India to step out of its neighbour's shadow. *The Times.* August 31, 2015:39(Business).

84. Pagliari C. What are your top (not disease) public health challenges of the future? https://www.linkedin.com/groupItem?view=&gid=120372&type=member&item=5853221710899220480&commentID=-1&trk=groups_item_detail-b-jump_last#lastComment. Accessed August 21, 2014.

85. Standley CJ, Bogich TL. International development, emerging diseases, and ecohealth. *EcoHealth.* 2013;10:1-3. doi: 10.1007/s10393-013-0820-z. http://www.ecohealth.net/pdf/journal_pdf/Vol_10/10.1/ECH_10_1_Editorial.pdf. Accessed November 20, 2014.

9.0

Global Health Workforce Capacity and Transforming the Education of Health Professionals

9.1 "SCALING UP, SAVING LIVES" REVISITED

Cited in Chapter 8.0, a Global Health Workforce Alliance/World Health Organization (GHWA/WHO) report issued in 2008, "Scaling Up, Saving Lives" (1) addressed the critical shortage of health workers, stressing that in Ethiopia, for example, about 200 doctors are trained each year for a population of around 75 million while the United Kingdom trains more than 6,000 for about 60 million people. As a whole, according to a sub-Saharan African study of medical schools (2), in 2010 sub-Saharan Africa had 145,000 physicians to serve a population of 821 million. The physician-to-population ratio in sub-Saharan Africa is about "13/100,000, as compared to other countries, such as India (60/100,000), Brazil (192/100,000), and the United States (280/100,000)" with "Africa's poorest countries" facing "even greater physician workforce shortages." Exacerbating the situation is the fact that there are only "169 medical schools in the 48 countries" of sub-Saharan Africa, graduating about 10,000 physicians per year compared to India (381–49,000) and China (268–144,000) (3).

The "Scaling Up, Saving Lives" (1) findings indicated that from country cases, for example, the Brazil "Family Health Program" strategy in the 1980s, the Ethiopian "Health Extension Program" in 2003, and the Pakistan "Lady Health Worker" cadre in 1994, there are a number of crucial factors for the successful scale-up of the health workforce. According to the task force, critical factors underpinning successful scale-up include "sustained political commitment from the highest levels; rigorous workforce planning that ideally includes long-term 10 year plans of action; an enabling environment including sound management systems and a labour market with capacity to employ new workers."

Another WHO report, "Health Workforce Governance and Leadership Capacity in the African Region" (4), involving 26 of the 46 WHO member states, reiterated many of the findings of the 2008 "Scaling Up, Saving Lives" report. However, while "the capacity of Human Resources for Health (HRH) units is generally promising," the researchers concluded that "information regarding the overall status of HRH units has been generally lacking, especially in countries where the health workforce is in greatest need." Overall, they found that HRH functions reflected a "fragmented approach in managing the health workforce" and that "key functions such as monitoring and evaluation were virtually absent."

9.2 "A UNIVERSAL TRUTH: NO HEALTH WITHOUT A WORKFORCE"

The recent report *A Universal Truth: No Health Without a Workforce* (5), commissioned by the GHWA Secretariat and WHO "to inform the global community on how to attain, sustain and accelerate progress on universal health coverage," makes it clear that sub-Saharan Africa is far from being alone in terms of critical health workforce shortages.

The report was prepared "to inform proceedings at the Third Global Forum on Human Resources for Health," which took place in Recife, Brazil, from November 10 to 13, 2013. It was also meant "to inform a global audience and trigger momentum for action"; it suggests three guiding questions for decision makers.

1. What health workforce is required to ensure effective coverage of an agreed package of health care benefits?
2. What health workforce is required to progressively expand coverage over time?
3. How does a country produce, deploy, and sustain a health workforce that is both fit for purpose and fit to practice in support of universal health coverage?

To answer these questions, the researchers used "a conceptual framework that speaks to the key principles of both the right to health and minimum social protection floors: the availability (competencies and skill mix that correspond to the health needs of the population), accessibility (the equitable access to health workers), acceptability (dignity, trust, demand for services), and quality of health services (the competencies, skills, knowledge, and behavior of the health worker).

Confirming findings of the previously cited WHO workforce governance report, "few countries have a comprehensive and valid information base on available health workers." In order "to highlight the variation in health workforce availability," the authors of the report "created a global snapshot in comparison to three density thresholds of skilled health professionals (midwives, nurses and physicians) per 10,000 population . . . 22.8, 34.5 and 59.4 skilled health professionals per 10,000 population." Their analysis is shown in Box 9.1.

More specifically, the report concludes that

- Most (70%) of the countries with a density of skilled health professionals of less than 22.8 per 10,000 population and a coverage of births by skilled birth attendants below 80% are in Africa (31 countries, 57%) and in South East Asia (7 countries, 13%).

BOX 9.1

Variation in Workforce Availability

- 83 countries fall below the threshold of 22.8 skilled health professionals per 10,000 population.
- 100 countries fall below the threshold of 34.5 skilled health professionals per 10,000 population.
- 118 countries fall below the threshold of 59.4 skilled health professionals per 10,000 population.
- 68 countries are above the threshold of 59.4 skilled health professionals per 10,000 population.

- In South East Asia, the number of countries below 22.8 per 10,000 population and with a skilled birth attendant coverage below 80% is small, but they are some of the most populous (estimates for 2012): Myanmar (population 52.8 million), Bangladesh (154.7 million), Indonesia (246.9 million), and India (1,236.7 million).
- In contrast, 11 (48%) of the countries with a density below 22.8 per 10,000 but with a skilled birth attendant coverage exceeding 80% are in the Americas.
- Of the 68 countries that exceed the workforce-to-population ratio of 59.4 per 10,000 population, 36 are in the European region, and none in Africa, where only Algeria, Botswana, and Tunisia are above 22.8 per 10,000.

Overall, summary report findings common to most countries include:

- There are shortages of some categories of health workers, and more are forecast.
- Although skill-mix imbalances persist, advanced practitioners, midwives, nurses, and auxiliaries are still insufficiently used in many settings.
- Availability and accessibility continue to vary widely within countries because of difficulty in attracting and retaining workers.
- Adapting education strategies and the content of pre-service education is a major challenge.

The report provides "a 10-point agenda to strengthen human resources for health in the context of universal health coverage," highlighting above all "the centrality of the health workforce in translating the vision of universal health coverage into improved healthcare on the ground."

A beginning step is to identify "the gap between the need for a health workforce . . . and the population's demand for health services," followed by "human resources for health policy objectives that encapsulate the vision for the health system and services," monitoring "the policy objectives" and sustaining "effective management," along with the "technical capacity to design, advocate for and implement policies." Other enabling actions focus on gaining political support for universal health coverage, reforming governance, identifying costs, involving international partners in "building capacity for health systems," and "addressing transnational issues.

9.3 ADAPTING HEALTH EDUCATION AND TRAINING TO COMMUNITY NEEDS

Developed World

It is noteworthy that similar challenges that face developing nations in providing access to health care are also felt—on a much decreased population scale—in rural communities in the developed nations (6). A case in point is the vast region of Northern Ontario in Canada, where the Northern Ontario School of Medicine (NOSM) with a view to being responsive to people's needs has adopted a distributed model of community-engaged medical education and runs a range of educational programs spanning the undergraduate, postgraduate, and continuing professional phases of physician training (7).

The school was started in 2005 and it "became the first new medical school in Canada in over 30 years, and only the second new medical school in North America during a similar period. It is the first Canadian medical school hosted by two universities, over 1,000 kilometres apart. NOSM serves as the faculty of medicine for Lakehead University in Thunder Bay and Laurentian University in Sudbury." Because of the diverse population challenges, the NOSM curriculum, summarized in Box 9.2, had to be both innovative and worthy of Canada-wide accreditation.

The entire undergraduate medical curriculum is organized around five integrated themes. These are integrated into every module and clerkship of the MD program

BOX 9.2

Northern Ontario School of Medicine (NOSM) Curriculum

The 4-year MD curriculum is split into three phases: Phase 1 covers years 1 and 2 and involves a sequence of 11 modules with ongoing community integrated learning; Phase 2 involves learners undertaking an 8-month community-based longitudinal clerkship; Phase 3 consists of seven specialist clerkship rotations in larger hospital settings. The curriculum content is organized around five themes that link teaching, learning, and assessment into a single integrated curriculum.

Learners engage in a combination of small and large group teaching, practical and lab teaching, and a large quantity of community-based clinical experiences that combine clinical, medical, and human sciences into a powerful, innovative, and socially accountable program. At completion of the program, graduates will have earned an MD degree equivalent to all other Canadian medical schools and are ready and able to undertake postgraduate training anywhere in Canada, albeit with a special affinity for training and clinical practice in northern urban, rural, and remote communities.

for both teaching and assessment. The reinforcement of concepts across the themes ensures key learning outcomes are being achieved with an emphasis on medical and clinical topics.

Theme 1: Northern and rural health
Theme 2: Personal and professional aspects of medical practice
Theme 3: Social and population health
Theme 4: Foundations of medicine
Theme 5: Clinical and communication skills in health care

In terms of learning, Phase 1 employs four distinct types of learning opportunities at the medical school: large group sessions, small group facilitated sessions, structured clinical skills sessions, and community interprofessional learning sessions.

A key feature of the program, discussed in Chapter 8.0, is case-based learning (CBL) whereby each week students meet with a facilitator in groups of no more than eight for a 2-hour session. Through a model of guided discovery that is designed to support self-directed research, students consider a complex case, which directs the learning for the module.

Student practical experience is gained in a number of settings:

- Year 1: Aboriginal communities
- Year 2: Small rural/remote communities
- Year 3: Large rural and small urban communities
- Year 4: Urban communities

The school brings together over 90 community partners; over 1,300 clinical, human, and medical sciences stipendiary faculty; and more than 200 employees. Its "success is very much a result of many partnerships and collaborations with individuals, communities and organizations including Aboriginal and Francophone, hospitals and health services, physicians and other health professionals, universities and colleges, information communication technology organizations, and other medical schools."

According to the website, "NOSM is a made-in-the-North solution that is attracting attention from around the world for its innovative model of community-engaged medical education and research, while staying true to its social accountability mandate of contributing to improving the health of the people and communities of Northern Ontario."

There are many elements that make this program stand out:

- Focus on meeting health needs of people in large remote/rural communities
- Integrated curriculum—varied learning approaches—small and large groups
- Learning in context
- CBL
- Longitudinal learning
- Community-engaged clerkships
- Extensive community partners and faculty members

In many ways, the school's overall approach could be a blueprint for others to follow in both developed and developing nations.

9.4 APPROACHES TO THE EDUCATION AND TRAINING OF HEALTH PROFESSIONALS: CHINA, INDIA, AND SOUTH AFRICA

China: A Case Example

A 1998 reform initiated in China, highlighted in a paper published in *The Lancet*, "Transformation of the Education of Health Professionals in China: Progress and Challenges," called for "an increase in the quality of higher education . . . not only health professional education" by encouraging "all health professional schools . . . to be integrated with universities" (3). Both 3-year and 7- to 8-year medical programs operate in China where "curricular reform has been a slow and steady continuing process, not sudden or dramatic like the administrative reform." In terms of content, the overwhelming emphasis continues to be "on basic biomedicine, medical technology, and clinical medicine" with very little "student exposure to the humanities, social sciences, ethics, public health, psychology, communication skills and professionalism" and "very little time is given to social medicine." Given the huge class sizes, the main teaching approach "consists usually of didactic lectures requiring rote-memorization" with "limited faculty–student and student–student interactions for creativity and innovation," possibly underpinning "the emerging crisis of violence against medical workers" with "48% of hospitals" reporting "violent attacks against healthcare workers."

China has now set a national target of 300,000 general practitioners (GPs) by 2020. The aim is "to train GPs with 5 years of medical education and a bachelor's degree followed by 3 years of residency training."

It has also become apparent that other reforms are essential, focusing on public health and addressing population concerns relating to "non communicable diseases, geriatrics and ageing, and management of disabilities."

India: Need for a More Socially Accountable Medical Education Curricula

In her book, Dr. Sylvia Karpagam laments that colonial allopathic systems "wreaked havoc on traditional healing systems that have been in existence for centuries" (8). Her main concern is that health care has been monopolized by allopathic practitioners and that it is biased toward "elistist urban clients" alongside the caste system, thereby not serving most of the Indian population. In addition, "the westernized 5-year medical education programs," she stresses, do not include "ethics, primary health care or social determinants of health," graduating doctors who are mostly inexperienced, insensitive, and ignorant of many of the larger social and structural issues that are intrinsically linked to health in India, which "go largely unrecognized by medical councils and health departments," which "protect their own and the doctors' interests more than the rights of patients," she asserts.

The curriculum draws on British or American resources, which prepare graduates more for migration "to a developed country rather than practise in India." "Trained in tertiary hospitals on allopathic clinical care using expensive equipment to diagnose Western diseases," graduates lack the capacity to treat "diseases that cause death and disability in India." Moreover, India is "the biggest exporter of trained physicians among developed countries," accounting for "4.9% and 10.9% of American and British physicians respectively"; in addition, "almost 54% of AIIMS students who graduated during 1989 to 2000 now reside outside India." The Indian medical education system is "in stark contrast to Cuban medical internationalism which has provided almost 42,000 workers in international collaboration with 103 countries to provide substantial medical aid and relief to vulnerable communities and populations."

Discriminatory practices also appear to impact on "students from marginalized communities," including "inferior primary and secondary education, discrimination during the course period and segregation," including spilling over "into the recruitment of medical teachers as well."

Sub-Saharan Africa: Strengthening Collaboration, Advocacy, and Networking

In her paper, "Linking Public Health Training and Health Systems Development in Sub-Saharan Africa: Opportunities for Improvement and Collaboration" (9), Professor Sharon Fonn reminds us that many African countries are "not on track to achieve the Millennium Development Goals," and that reasons "relate fundamentally to poorly functioning health systems" and, consequently, despite investments "in TB, maternal health, reproductive health, childhood issues, and HIV-related services . . . health gains have been below expectations." One of the main flaws, she argues, lies with the "one-size-fits-all approach" and "the creation of vertical programs that duplicate and work around existing health systems," drawing health workers away "toward the better funded health interventions rather than building the overall health system serving the multiple health needs in a particular country."

In terms of public health training, she reinforces key themes of this book (Chapter 8.0) and those of *The Lancet* Commission report on the education of health professionals. Her four public health training priorities include the development of public health competencies and approaches that

1. create "the conditions in which people can achieve health";
2. focus "on the local disease burden" ensuring that "graduates have knowledge and skills appropriate to environments in which they will work";
3. train graduates to be "change agents" and "be equipped to think critically, make decisions, work as team members, and provide leadership"; and
4. "provide leadership in health and contribute to the local health system" by understanding "the social determinants of the disease burden to enable them to identify intersectoral partners to work with."

Realizing these goals will necessitate collaboration, advocacy, and networking across and beyond South Africa, involving, as examples, universities and health science faculties, national science and medical councils, ministries of education, health, and finance, as well as the African Union.

Another key area for strategic development relates to research "that is conceptualized, conducted, analysed and published by Africans" and training the next generation of researchers, which was strongly evidenced at the 10th anniversary Public Health Association of South Africa conference in Limpopo. Professor Fonn also calls for "a mechanism for individuals to move between academia, non-governmental organizations and government health services," patterned along similar lines as Oxford's St. Anthony's College Senior Associate Members Programme and The Woodrow Wilson International Center for Scholars in the United States. Shifting from "firefighting" to strategic and evidence-based rational decision making would help to strengthen "health service managers working in complex and under-functioning health systems," she posits.

9.5 PERSONAL REFLECTIONS ON FUTURE DIRECTIONS IN PROFESSIONAL HEALTH AND SOCIAL CARE EDUCATION AND TRAINING

Table 9.1 provides personal observations of education trends in terms of four categories: relationships; diseases and conditions; organizational aspects and education; training, research, and service (10).

Relationships

The health community is increasingly moving from centralized services and hierarchical decision making to devolved, person-centered care and social support based on principles and practices that value equality, mutual respect, and dignity. Top-down management and leadership is gradually being replaced by participatory planning at local levels and by self-care responsibilities. Other than specialized hospital care facilities, multipurpose hospitals will largely be replaced by community health or well-being centers.

Diseases and Conditions

While acute communicable diseases remain as serious problems in poorer nations, noncommunicable health concerns—obesity and type 2 diabetes, cancers, cardiovascular diseases, and chronic conditions, including mental health—have overtaken these across all nations and are the cause of most global mortalities and morbidities and are expected to rise significantly in this decade and next. As highlighted in Chapter 6.0, rather than treating specific symptoms or conditions, practitioners will be expected to view individuals holistically and respond to the health and well-being needs of the whole person. The One Health approach will increasingly recognize "the interconnected nature of human, animal, and environmental health in an attempt to inform health policy, expand scientific knowledge, improve healthcare training and delivery, and address sustainable challenges" (11).

Organizational

Health care and social care have been separated as distinct government entities in legislative and budgetary matters when they are in essence closely interconnected, and in

TABLE 9.1 Educational Trends in Health and Social Care (10)

FROM	TO
RELATIONSHIPS	
Hierarchial	Equality, respect and dignity-teamwork
Top-down management and leadership	Participatory management and leadership
DISEASES AND CONDITIONS	
Acute communicable infectious diseases	Noncommunicable diseases and chronic care
Treating specific health conditions or illness	Treating 'whole person' and supporting 'well-being'
ORGANIZATIONAL	
Health care	Health and social care
Hospital dominance	More community care and decision making
Secondary and tertiary clinical health care	More primary and public health and social care
Uni-disciplinary regulations and quality assurance	Multidisciplinary regulations and quality assurance
Funding based on activity	Funding based on outcomes
Closed systems	Open and transparent systems
EDUCATION/TRAINING/RESEARCH/SERVICE	
Teaching	Learning
Content-based	Competency-based
Specialism	More generalism
Training in silos	Interprofessional and multidisciplinary learning
Local and national networking and resources	Global networking, alliances, and resources
Quantitative research	More qualitative research
Hospital service	More local or community services

many nations it is time to merge the management of health and social care. The social determinants of health govern to a large extent the health and well-being of the population and impact directly on the services needed and provided. In the future, these two must be integrated, especially with an aging population that will rely increasingly on community and family involvement in individual care supported by primary care.

Most health and social care professions (medicine, nursing, social services) have their own regulatory frameworks that promote silo training and support. Moving toward holistic person care will mean integrating many of these functions to facilitate effective and efficient support with funding based on outcomes rather than activity. Government bodies in charge of discrete budgets will also need to be monitored and evaluated more closely and evidence transparency and accountability for policy decisions made and money spent.

Education and Training

The shift from didactic teaching to collaborative learning is beginning to accelerate as more education providers adopt models such as problem-based learning, increasingly embedded in blended learning environments (online and face to face). Learning will also be based increasingly on competencies that relate directly to population needs rather than being relegated to covering and memorizing content, much of which is not retained by students after a few days and therefore is not easily transferred to practice. With the rise of noncommunicable diseases, mental issues, and chronic illnesses—many of which can be attributed to modernity—the need for more generalism and interprofessional learning and working becomes clear in terms of structuring curricula and achieving cost savings by reducing unnecessary duplication, for example, separate anatomy classes for medical and nursing students. Developing multimediated resources can be very expensive, and in the future many more collaborative projects will be necessary, overcoming the "not invented here" syndrome.

The 20th century was indeed the science century, which understandably relied extensively on quantitative research. However, research in this century will need to investigate many problems that cannot be seen using the diagnostic tools or devices available as they may concern deeper social issues, including a growing crisis in the younger generation (e.g., eating disorders) and older population (e.g., dementia), and could benefit greatly from qualitative research—alongside quantitative, of course—that depends on personal stories or experience. Hospital hegemony will need to give way to community dominance where these stories can be heard firsthand and dealt with in a sensitive and multiprofessional capacity.

However, as highlighted in Chapter 7.0, the greatest challenge for public education may be moving away from a societal "sickness" culture or orientation to adopting personal values, attitudes, and behaviors that favor taking individual responsibility for one's health and well-being. Rather than thinking only in the "here and now," our survival as a species may also depend on developing "a future consciousness to inform the present, enabling innovation to feed the present" along with "rediscovering a reward system beyond the material."

9.6 CUBA'S HEALTH SYSTEM AND LATIN AMERICAN MEDICAL SCHOOL MODEL: DR. BREA BONDI-BOYD—AFFIRMING SOCIAL ACCOUNTABILITY IN HEALTH POLICY AND PRACTICE

Further to Section 8.8 and identification of innovative health education models, according to WHO, Cuba's health care system, despite limited resources and "more than 50 years of political enmity separating Cuba and the United States" (12), which are gradually becoming normalized, is an example for all countries of the world. Based on preventive medicine, its outcomes, such as an infant mortality rate of 4.2 per thousand births (13), are exemplary. WHO Director General Dr. Margaret Chan, who visited Cuba in July 2014, declared that the world should follow Cuba's model and replace the curative model, which is expensive and inefficient, with a prevention-based approach (13).

Underpinning Cuba's success in health care is a unique 6-year medical program in the Latin-American School of Medicine (ELAM) with "the central mandate of social accountability," recruiting "students from rural, remote, resource-scarce and other disadvantaged communities with the greatest health needs" (12,14). The curriculum design integrates "concepts of prevention, social determinants of health, and active community partnering" that optimizes "community-based, service-learning method-ology, preparing students to resolve local health problems."

Dr. Brea Bondi-Boyd, ELAM class of 2009, is one of these, and was "the first for-eign medical graduate (FMG) to have been accepted into California's Contra Costa County Family Medical Residency program in decades" (14). While well received, she found her "idealism, volunteerism and dedication to work with poor people," which she largely learned from her Cuban professors, was not generally the norm of U.S. applicants, going to the heart of "what distinguishes the training at a socially-account-able medical school from a traditional one," and the pivotal impact schools of medi-cine have on "the values, norms, behaviors, and worldviews held by key groups in the health system," influencing their graduates "with potentially wide-ranging effects throughout the health system."

It is noteworthy that in the United States the Contra Costa Family Practice Residency program in Martinez, California (15), where Dr. Bondi-Boyd completed her residence training, also makes "serving the underserved" their priority, and therefore her medical education well prepared her for the challenges. The ELAM curriculum "has both a classroom and practical component in different communities through-out Havana, and sets the stage for a community-based primary care orientation, the underpinning of the bio-psycho-social healthcare model." What makes the program unique is, according to Dr. Bondi-Boyd, "you're taught to look at patients in that same integrated way . . . not just what diseases they have, but how they function socially, in their homes, in their work environments, schools . . . and how as doctors, we can address all those things together" (15).

Chosen as a Youth Commissioner on the Lancet Commission on Health Professionals for a New Century (16), Dr. Bondi-Boyd contributed to shaping the com-mission's policy recommendations, in particular recognizing that "20th century edu-cational perspectives are unfit to tackle 21st century challenges" (14). Now practicing in primary care, she is convinced about "the possibilities of a universal health care system in low-resource settings."

Implementing universal health care worldwide, discussed in Section 4.2, may be facilitated through Cuba's outreach model, sending doctors and other health workers throughout the developing world to treat the poor. "Since its inception in 1998, ELAM has graduated more than 20,000 doctors from over 123 countries. Currently, 11,000 young people from over 120 nations follow a career in medicine at the Cuban institu-tion" (13). According to Ban Ki-moon, Secretary General of the United Nations, ELAM is "the world's most advanced medical school" (17).

REFERENCES

1. World Health Organization and Global Health Workforce Alliance. Scaling up, saving lives. http://www.who.int/workforcealliance/documents/Global_Health%20FINAL%20REPORT .pdf?ua=1. Accessed September 5, 2008.

2. SAMSS.org. The sub-Saharan African medical schools study. http://www.samss.org/. Accessed October 10, 2012.
3. Hou J, Michaud C, Li Z, et al. Transformation of the education of health professionals in China. Progress and challenges. *The Lancet.* 2014;384(9945);819–827.
4. World Health Organization. Health workforce governance and leadership capacity in the African Region. http://www.who.int/hrh/resources/Observer9_WEB.pdf. Accessed September 5, 2012.
5. World Health Organization and Global Health Workforce Alliance. *A universal truth: No health without a workforce.* http://www.who.int/workforcealliance/knowledge/resources/GHWA_AUniversalTruthReport.pdf. Accessed March 20, 2014.
6. Secretary of State for Health. *Government response to the House of Commons Health Select Committee first report of session 2012–13: Education, training and workforce planning.* London, UK: Controller of Her Majesty's Stationery Office, 2012. http://webarchive.nationalarchives.gov.uk/20140210084229/; http://www.official-documents.gov.uk/document/cm84/8435/8435.pdf Accessed July 29, 2012.
7. Northern Ontario School of Medicine. Innovative education and research for a healthier north. http://www.nosm.ca/about_us/default.aspx. Accessed September 18, 2014.
8. Karpagam S. Medical education in India and its discontents. In: Chacko J (ed.), *Higher studies in India.* 2014. https://www.academia.edu/8951568/Medical_education_in_India_and_its_discontents. Accessed November 15, 2014.
9. Fonn S. Linking public health training and health systems development in sub-Saharan Africa: Opportunities for improvement and collaboration. *J Public Health Policy.* 2011;32:S44–S51. doi:10.1057/jphp.2011.37
10. Lueddeke G. Perspectives on current and future issues facing medical and health professions' education in the developed and developing worlds. Paper presented at the American Medical Association, Accelerating Change in Medical Education conference; October 4, 2013; Chicago, IL.
11. Barrett MA, Bouley TA, Stoertz AH, Stoertz RW. Integrating a One Health approach in education to address global health and sustainability challenges. *Front Ecol Environ.* 2010;9:239–245. doi:10.1890/090159
12. Keck CW, Reed GA. The curious case of Cuba. *Am J Public Health.* 2012;102(8):e13–e22. http://www.ncbi.nlm.nih.gov/pmc/articles/PMC3464859/. Accessed October 20, 2014.
13. Lamrani S. Cuba's health care system: A model for the world. Oberg LR, translator. *The Huffington Post.* http://www.huffingtonpost.com/salim-lamrani/cubas-health-care-system-_b_5649968.html. Accessed October 5, 2014.
14. Gorry C. Cuba's Latin American medical school: Can socially-accountable medical education make a difference? *Medicc Review.* 2012;14(3):5–11. http://medicc.org/mediccreview/articles/mr_259.pdf. Accessed October 20, 2014.
15. Admin. From Cuba to Martinez. *The Martinez News-Gazette.* December 4, 2012. http://martinezgazette.com/archives/874. Accessed November 18, 2014.
16. Frenk J, Chen L, Bhutta ZA, et al. Health professions for a new century: Transforming education to strengthen health systems in an interdependent world. *The Lancet.* 2010;376(9756):1923–1958.
17. García NV. La escuela más avanzada del mundo. *Juventud Rebelde.* December 28, 2014. trans:operamundi. cuba: a model according to the World Health Organization. http://translate.google.co.uk/translate?hl=en&sl=pt&u=http://m.operamundi.uol.com.br/conteudo/opiniao/37220/cuba%2bum%2bmodelo%2bde%2bacordo%2bcom%2ba%2borganizacao%2bmundial%2bda%2bsaude.shtml&prev=search

10.0

Epilogue: Global Health, Governance, and Education

Ulrich Laaser, Vesna Bjekovic-Mikanovic, and George Lueddeke, with members* of the think-tank on Global Health, Governance and Education.

10.1 BACKGROUND INFORMATION AND ACKNOWLEDGMENTS

This Epilogue was prompted by a "core" paper drafted by Professor Ulrich Laaser and Professor Vesna Bjegovic-Mikanovic. To receive feedback on its contents, a think-tank, composed of 35 experts from 27 nations, representative of many fields involving global population health and well-being, was established (Appendix B, p. 453). Think-tank members as co-authors were then asked to participate in three Delphi rounds from October 2013 to April 2014, coordinated by the author.

The idea for an Epilogue arose at a later stage of the manuscript's progress. However, it was deemed essential that contributions from the world's key regions would help to confirm, critique, or advance some of the broader arguments rehearsed in the book, as seen through the unique lens of their own personal experience of public health systems and priorities for change and improvement.

A gratifying conclusion reached over the process is the high degree of shared consensus among think-tank participants with regard to "Global Health, Governance, and Education" issues and possible ways forward.

I extend my sincere gratitude to Professor Ulrich Laaser and Professor Vesna Bjegovic-Mikanovic, for their insights and for diligently and patiently taking on board the many, sometimes conflicting, comments that came their way, and allowing us to take part in this unique global "virtual" experience.

My warm appreciation also goes out to all of those listed in Appendix B (page 453) who took the time to read (and re-read!) the various versions of the Epilogue. Additionally, I thank Dr. Bernard Merkel, former Head of the Food Safety, Health and Consumer Affairs section of the delegation of the European Union to the United States, for reviewing and commenting on the draft Epilogue.

---

* See Appendix B, p. 453

As a result of these collective contributions, this final chapter has been deeply enriched and, it is hoped, will act as a catalyst for further debate and decision making that has at its main intent the improvement of worldwide population and planetary health and well-being.

George Lueddeke

10.2 INTRODUCTION

As demonstrated by the review of the Millennium Development Goals (MDGs) in Section 4.1, in terms of health, some progress has taken place across nations—especially with regard to child and also maternal health—but other goals remain elusive, such as those aspirations related to environmental sustainability and global partnerships for development.

It is regrettable that the world is still far removed from realizing William Nelson Joy's aspiration for a better world (1). Obstacles to a healthier and safer future for all appear to remain intransigent, caused no doubt in large measure by climate catastrophes, armed conflicts, and other public health emergencies; increasingly limited as well as inequitably distributed resources; and widespread corruption, inherent in both the developing and developed worlds.

Two themes that thread through several chapters in this book relate to broad limitations that constrain progress: first, in tackling many of the health problems caused by modernity and an aging society in many parts of the world; second, especially in poorer nations, closing the gap between the disconnect or delinking of "mainstream development practice . . . from the broader economic and political forces" (2).

In both rich and poor nations, the chasm between health and social policy aims and interventions leading to improved population health and wellness remains wider than ever, as affirmed by Dr. Margaret Chan, WHO Director-General, addressing the Sixty-Seventh World Health Assembly with the message: "Health has an obligatory place on any post-2015 development agenda" (3).

This Epilogue proceeds from a synthesis of the policy framework for global public health in Sections 10.3 to 10.5 to the discussion of key strategic areas for progress in Sections 10.6 to 10.8, and concludes with pragmatic recommendations in Section 10.9 that may help to inform and guide decision makers.

Regarding the terminology used, we consider that the health of the world's population depends on many determinants that include to some degree the provision of health care services, but even essential services are determined by the quality of governance, the availability of financial resources, the qualifying training of the staff, and so on. Therefore, components of the "new public health" (4) are important, including both the management (5) of health services and the setting of conditions that allow best for healthy living and improving the well-being of entire populations. Consequently, as the most comprehensive term, we use "global public health," which integrates the aim of an improved "global health" and the most important road toward it—setting up effective and efficient public health systems.

10.3   EPILOGUE RATIONALES AND AIMS

It is generally acknowledged that the key health problems of today transgress national borders, whether air and water pollution, climate change, demographic dynamics, infectious diseases, or financial crises that impact resources for health (6). Different health systems, behavioral cultures, resources, and governance may pose different challenges even between neighboring countries and within countries. The poor and other vulnerable groups, especially in the South East Asia Region and sub-Saharan Africa, are affected more than others. The people in these regions continue to have limited access to quality health care and public health services despite their recognized higher burden of morbidity and mortality. Many disparities exist in terms of health risks, health-seeking behavior, and access to services, responsiveness of the health system and health providers, and health outcomes. The barriers include multiple dimensions of social exclusion. Health disparities of various types appear to be widening rather than narrowing, suggesting that, as argued throughout this book, health and social systems are not addressing these problems effectively. Reversing health inequity and inequalities, whether among individuals or populations, require intersectoral action and larger and better-targeted investments in public health.

More specifically, the Epilogue explores such questions as:

- Who are the "real" global decision makers in terms of improving and sustaining population health and well-being?
- How can international aid become more responsible, equitable, and accountable in making a significant difference in people's lives?
- How can contributions of the civil society, in particular nongovernmental organizations (NGOs), be strengthened in terms of scope, impact, and integrity?
- Can best practices of regional cooperation show a way forward?
- To what extent can reconceptualizing of public health education and training help to transform and optimize public health performance in struggling communities?
- Which recommendations, agreed to in principle by think-tank members, could help to inform the thinking, acting, and debate of key decision makers at all global sociopolitical and socioeconomic levels?
- Why has the One Health approach become such an important global strategy adopted by health organizations and policy makers?

10.4   GLOBAL GOVERNANCE AND STRUCTURAL CHALLENGES

As outlined in Chapters 4.0 and 5.0, there have been many significant systemic public health interventions, including the primary health care (PHC) strategy inaugurated by the World Health Organization (WHO) in Alma-Ata 1978, the emergence of agencies such as the World Bank funding health sector development since the 1990s, and the MDGs agreed upon by the United Nations (UN) in 2000, as well as the recent attention to social determinants of health (Rio de Janeiro 2011) (7) and health in all policies (Helsinki 2013) (8). The Rio Declaration 2011 sets forth five action areas critical to addressing health inequalities: (a) to adopt better governance of health and development, (b) to promote participating in policy making and implementation, (c) to further reorient health sector toward reducing health inequalities, (d) to strengthen global governance and collaboration, and (e) to monitor progress and increase accountability. The participants of the Helsinki conference advocated along the same principles the urgent need to:

- "Commit to health and health equity as a political priority by adopting the principles of Health in All Policies and taking action on the social determinants of health.
- Ensure effective structures, processes, and resources that enable implementation of the Health in All Policies approach across governments at all levels and between governments.
- Strengthen the capacity of Ministries of Health to engage other sectors of government through leadership, partnership, advocacy and mediation to achieve improved health outcomes.
- Build institutional capacity and skills that enable the implementation of Health in All Policies and provide evidence on the determinants of health and inequity and on effective responses.
- Adopt transparent audit and accountability mechanisms for health and equity impacts that build trust across government and between governments and their people.
- Establish conflict of interest measures that include effective safeguards to protect policies from distortion by commercial and vested interests and influence.
- Include communities, social movements and civil society in the development, implementation and monitoring of Health in All Policies, building health literacy in the population."

In summary, the difficult challenges facing the global community appear to be threefold: (a) to identify and define precisely the threats that are undermining global population health and well-being along with opportunities; (b) to develop better global understanding and agreement about operational strategies; and (c) while achieving adequate funding is difficult enough, the real problem appears to be implementing effective and sustainable interventions that will make a significant difference to global population health and that recognize, as underscored in Chapter 6.0, that today's challenges cannot be solved with yesterday's solutions.

Unquestionably, achieving these ends is a long-term endeavor, a goal that we summarize under the term "good global governance (GGG)," therewith referring to effective governance structures at the global level. Therefore, a key condition for success is efficient and accountable governance over several years, if not decades, integrating the views of all stakeholders including civil society/NGOs.

10.5 DECISION MAKING IN GLOBAL PUBLIC HEALTH: COORDINATION AND IMPACT

The overarching question is: Who are the global decision makers guaranteeing stability over time in the early decades of the 21st century? (9) Are these the UN and their member governments, or more specifically in the field of health, the WHO and other

UN organizations, such as the United Nations Children's Fund (UNICEF), United Nations Population Fund (UNFPA), and Joint United Nations Programme on HIV/ AIDS (UNAIDS), to name several bodies? Are the "development banks" like the World Bank and the Asian and African Development Banks most influential, or the big philanthropic foundations and global NGOs like the Global Fund, Global Alliance for Vaccines and Immunisation (GAVI), the Ford Foundation or the Bill & Melinda Gates Foundation, or combined groups of partners such as the International Health Partnerships and related initiatives (IHP+) (10)? Or do the real powers reside with large corporations and the chase for profit margins?

Considered collectively from a perspective over the past few decades, it seems that global interventions succeeded only half-way, as Ban Ki-Moon, Secretary General, UN stated in 2012 (11):

> Projections indicate that in 2015 more than 600 million people worldwide will still be using unimproved water sources, almost one billion will be living on an income of less than $1.25 per day, mothers will continue to die needlessly in childbirth, and children will suffer and die from preventable diseases.

Further, he continued: "Achieving the MDGs by 2015 is challenging but possible. Much depends on the fulfilment of MDG 8—the global partnership for development." It seems that voluntary partnership is not enough vis-à-vis a reality which is characterized by "unevenness of progress within countries and regions, and the severe inequalities that exist among populations, especially between rural and urban areas."

If the health-related MDGs are achieved at the global level in 2015, which is doubtful, as discussed in Section 4.1, it will be due mainly to the overachievement of China (12). Especially MDG 5 on maternal mortality is lagging behind as larger investments are required to improve the clinical infrastructure (13). In order to accelerate progress, collaborative global decision making obviously is an essential requirement. However, whether the post-MDG agenda (14) will be based on firmer grounds of mutual responsibility remains an open question. Viewing it through today's lens, it is rather unlikely. What might be the principles of effective global decision making? In the regional context of the European Union (EU), two main expressions of mutual responsibility have been inbuilt to some degree: solidarity (15) and subsidiarity (16).

The broad concept of solidarity, which seems to be a more enlightened and less asymmetrical term than "aid," encompasses three major subfunctions: financing development, technical cooperation, and humanitarian assistance. In this last respect, human rights arguments dictate that the global community can become an agent for the dispossessed and act to protect certain populations in a variety of circumstances, as in the case of failed states that are chronically incapable of meeting the basic security needs of their own populations. A clear case for global solidarity occurs when public health preparedness in a country is insufficient or when it is overwhelmed by natural or human-made disasters, such as the armed conflicts in Iraq or earlier in Yugoslavia, which cost more lives than many of the unhealthy lifestyles.

Subsidiarity is an organizing principle of decentralization, stating that a matter ought to be handled by the smallest, lowest, or least centralized authority capable of addressing that matter effectively. The principle can be defined as the idea that a central authority should have a subsidiary function, performing only those tasks that cannot be performed effectively at a more immediate or local level. Subsidiarity is perhaps presently best known as a general principle of EU law. According to this principle, the EU may only act (e.g., initiate laws) where action of individual countries is insufficient. The principle was established in the 1992 Treaty of Maastricht (17).

Sovereignty is another important concept, debated especially regarding its impact on population health: Sovereignty is the right or capacity of countries to determine their own affairs. More specifically, it is the right of the supreme political authority—usually a government—to unqualified and unrivaled authority over its people and land. Sovereignty and the concept of the nation state are closely related. It is argued that globalization is eroding the world of sovereign states, and that many national decisions are now influenced by global forces (18) without democratic legitimization. As an example, a debate relates to whether World Trade Organization (WTO) trade agreements hurt or help WTO member states to exercise their health sovereignty (19). To fill in the widening sovereignty gap, global institutions increasingly exert stewardship. The fundament of a global society still has to be constructed, but certainly will be enhanced by growing social interaction at the global level. This links back to the principle of (global) solidarity as outlined above. Leadership and (health) diplomacy are keys to balance these three principles.

We also need a systematic strengthening of multilateralism in health as—for the World Bank—Prah-Ruger (20) has pointed out, arguing to focus on the following key areas of health policy: (a) helping countries to develop evidence-based analytical capacity, critical for health reform and policy implementation; (b) helping countries improve their budgetary planning and hence taking more responsibility in financing health care by increasing local funding per dollar from development partners; and (c) assisting countries to establish and strengthen good governance in health care. Gomez (21), on the other hand, has shed light on how we can better understand the stasis and change in international health agencies (IHAs). He has shown the potential of using the path dependency and institutional change theory in understanding IHAs, whereby the former provides historical perspectives on policy beliefs and decision making over time and the latter can better explain the complex internal and external sources on IHA and policy reform. The terminology of "smart sovereignty" is used to refer to the process of boldly reforming and strengthening global institutions in order to ensure that they can deal reliably—and with legitimacy—targeting globalization and global crises together, with the national governments.

In conclusion, an effective global framework for decision making in the way of GGG is not yet in sight, especially since the improvement of the population health does not depend primarily on the curative systems or on a national perspective, which is still occupying the minds of most decision makers. Are we capable of acting as a global community? Ilona Kickbusch identified the following mind changes required for this to occur (22), summarized as follows:

Politicians and electorates need to accept that in a global world we now have both national and global interests—and governments must be held accountable for both. There is a convergence of a set of key principles that form a global health ethics considering health as a human right, and framing the global equity gap in health as a major issue of social justice. We must have the courage to think beyond health and embrace a broad notion of sustainable development. Global health is dependent on a wide range of determinants and many other priority issues—for example, education, water, food, energy, and environment. Our debate must start, not end, with governance. No longer can we pretend that development is a purely technical and not a political process. The priority focus needs to be on the global public goods we all require in relation to health, climate, population, food, water, energy, conflict.

Ilona Kickbusch sees three new political spaces to take the global health agenda forward: the development paradigm of smart sovereignty, the post-2015 debates, and the increasing transborder challenges facing WHO (23). Finally we will require an agreement on how to jointly finance the global public goods we prioritize as a global community (24).

10.6   FUNDING OF GLOBAL PUBLIC HEALTH: THE INTERNATIONAL AID CONUNDRUM

Section 3.2 discussed the need, inter alia, to rebalance global and national health budgets—especially in the middle- and high-income nations—increasingly shifting funds from acute care to disease prevention and health promotion as most deaths are now attributable to noncommunicable diseases and chronic conditions. At a geopolitical level, another crucial area that urgently requires attention relates to the structures of international aid.

The temptation to accept international aid without conditions on the side of the beneficiary often disrupts national priorities, as is the case if money comes too easily. Loans, for example, of the World Bank—though at low interest rates—often put an underestimated burden on later years. Loans have two sides: Money is available now but has to be repaid later (especially if by others—taxpayers in the next generation). In addition, large portions of the money lent go via expert fees and purchase of equipment mainly back to the crediting countries. The resulting question is rarely asked: Is the long-term outcome worth the (national) investment? The answer depends also on the structural sustainability of projects, which in the majority of projects is impaired by the limited funding perspective of 2 or 3 years and disconnection of potential follow-up activity (25).

Conferences in Paris, 2005, and Accra, 2008 (26), and then in Busan at the end of 2011 (27), indicated some behavior change of donors and recipient countries as well along the so-called Paris indicators of Aid Effectiveness. The Paris Declaration on Aid Effectiveness was signed by more than 100 countries and international organizations and confirmed the five principles of ownership, alignment, harmonization, results, and mutual accountability. Indicators were set to monitor progress, which cater both to the needs of partner country and donors. From the side of partner countries, the indicators cover good national development strategies, reliable country systems for procurement and public financial management systems, development and use of result-based frameworks, and mutual assessment of progress. On the side of donors, the indicators cover the following issues: alignment with country priorities, joint analytic work, use of common arrangements and strengthened country systems, harmonized support for capacity building, and more predictable aid (28).

However, progress seems to be too small to reach the envisaged targets and may be fading, as concluded already in 2009 by Ravishankar et al. (29). Whereas there is some progress on operational development strategies (Indicator 1), the reliability of the public financial management systems in the recipient countries has improved only marginally (Aid Effectiveness Indicator 2a); also, "untying" aid has not improved (Indicator 8), although "earmarking" increasingly is seen as unethical (however, it is often indirectly done by expert-induced demand) (30). There are only marginal achievements with regard to the rest of the indicators, except Indicator 4 on coordinating technical assistance (where the target for some reason has been set to be equal to the baseline!). One of the key desiderata, coordination among donors and between government and donors, has made little to no progress as demonstrated by Indicators 3, 5a, 5b, and 9, whereas there is some progress for Indicator 6 although far from the target. Likewise, transaction costs for recipient countries by multiple missions (10a) and country studies (10b) are unchanged. However, tracking systems have to be improved to get an unbiased picture, as outlined by Vassall et al. (31).

Whereas in 2005, 32 countries participated in the OECD survey, 47 did so in 2007 and 76 in 2010. Some indicator values, as shown in Table 10.1, are based on lower participation.

In 2011, the co-chairs of the Busan conference summarized the achievements as follows (32): Progress has been made, but globally, donors and developing countries have fallen short of the goals that they set themselves for 2010. The findings from monitoring and evaluating the implementation of the Paris Declaration make for sober reading. Although the Accra Agenda for Action was adopted in 2008 to accelerate progress with a call for heightened focus on country ownership, more inclusive partnerships, and increased accountability for and transparency about development results, progress in 2010 was still lagging on the majority of the Paris Declaration commitments. Therefore, following commitments expressed at the Busan High Level Forum, the Global Partnership for Effective Development Co-operation has been mandated to support regular monitoring of progress in implementation (33). In 2014, before the first Global Partnership ministerial level meeting, its first report had been released (34). A set of 10 indicators partly based on those contained in the Paris Declaration on Aid Effectiveness are reported and grouped to reflect the ways forward in: (a) ownership and results of development cooperation, (b) inclusive development partnerships, (c) transparency and accountability for development results.

Country actions to implement the Busan commitments are seen in strengthening country-owned and country-led monitoring to support decision-making processes; improving country leadership to ensure the legitimacy of global monitoring efforts; and sharing of experiences and mutual learning among countries.

The foundations of the existing system of development assistance for health (DAH) and official development assistance (ODA) were built after the Second World

TABLE 10.1 Indicators for Monitoring the Paris Declaration

	INDICATORS 2005	PROGRESS			TARGET BY 2010	STATUS
		2007	2010			
1	Operational development strategies Percentage of countries having a national development strategy rated "A" or "B" on a five-point scale	19%	17%	37%	75%	Not met
2a	Reliable public financial management (PFM) system Percentage of countries moving up at least one measure on the PFM/Country Policy and Institutional Assessment (CPIA) scale since 2005	0%	–	38%	50%	Not met
2b	Reliable procurement systems Percentage of countries moving up at least one measure on the four-point scale since 2005	–	–	–	–	Too low sample of countries with data to allow for meaningful analysis
3	Aid flows are aligned on national priorities Percentage of aid for the government sector reported on the government's budget	44%	48%	41%	85%	Not met
4	Strengthen capacity by coordinated support Percentage of technical cooperation implemented through coordinated programs consistent with national development strategies	49%	60%	57%	50%	Met
5a	Use of country PFM systems Percentage of aid for the government sector using partner countries' PFM systems.	40%	–	48%	55%	Not met
5b	Use of country procurement systems Percentage of aid for the government sector using partner countries' procurement systems	40%	43%	44%	No target	–
6	Strengthen capacity by avoiding parallel project implementing units (PIUs) Total number of parallel PIUs	1,696	1,525	1,158	565	Not met
7	Aid is more predictable Percentage of aid for the government sector disbursed within the fiscal year for which it was scheduled and recorded in government accounting systems	42%	47%	43%	71%	Not met

(continued)

TABLE 10.1 Indicators for Monitoring the Paris Declaration (*continued*)

INDICATORS 2005		PROGRESS			TARGET BY 2010	STATUS
		2007	2010			
8	Aid is untied Percentage of aid that is fully untied	89%	85%	86%	>89%	Not met
9	Use of common arrangements or procedures Percentage of aid provided in the context of program-based approaches	43%	47%	45%	66%	Not met
10a	Joint missions Percentage of donor missions to the field undertaken jointly	20%	24%	19%	40%	Not met
10b	Joint country analytic work Percentage of country analytic work undertaken jointly	41%	44%	43%	66%	Not met
11	Result-oriented frameworks Percentage of countries with transparent and monitorable performance assessment frameworks	7%	–	20%	36%	Not met
12	Mutual accountability Percentage of countries with mutual assessment reviews in place	44%	–	38%	100%	Not met

Source: OECD, *Aid Effectiveness 2011: Progress in implementing the Paris Declaration*. Paris: OECD Publishing. 2012. http://dx.doi.org/10.1787/9789264125780-en (30).

War and decolonization, and initially framed as "foreign aid," with recipients in a hierarchical relationship of dependence on donors. Alternative framings have since emerged, including "cooperation," which implies a more equal relationship based on the principle of mutual benefit; "restitution," which emphasizes obligations to remedy past and/or ongoing wrongs; or "global solidarity," based on the notion of the emergence of a global society bound together by relationships of interdependence. Moon and Omole (35) summarized deficits in a most scholarly way:

- Existing financial resources dedicated to health fall short of needs.
- Aid disbursement is irregular and information on future financial flows is uncertain.
- External financing may displace rather than augment domestic financing for health.
- Donors continue to drive decision making at the cost of meeting recipients' greatest needs, which also undermines country ownership.
- Spending is not rationally allocated on the basis of objective indicators such as recipient income or disease burden.
- The proliferation of actors involved in DAH has exacerbated the problem of coordination among them, with the predictable consequences of system fragmentation, inefficiencies, confusion, gaps, and transaction costs.
- The existing DAH system has weak mechanisms of accountability.

It is clear that stewardship of the health system by governments should be promoted such that leadership, irrespective of whether the funding comes from the government or other sources, is evident in terms of vision, priorities, and regulatory climate, as well as transparent monitoring and evaluation (M&E). However, the top-down approach—strengthening governance (see Section 10.3/4) and regional cooperation (see Section 10.7)—has to be complemented by a bottom-up approach—strengthening civil society and particularly NGOs—in order to generate the necessary public pressure for change.

10.7 THE GROWING ROLE OF NONGOVERNMENTAL ORGANIZATIONS (NGOs)

A roadmap leading global health into the future will not become possible without a strong involvement of the civil society. The beginning of our century is connected to its rapidly growing role, especially in terms of private foundations and NGOs. This is obvious, referring to public–private partnerships between governmental institutions and organizations like the Bill & Melinda Gates Foundation, Greenpeace, or Medécins Sans Frontières (MSF) coping with emergency situations worldwide. In 1999, MSF received the Nobel Peace Prize for its work.

DAH has increased dramatically over the past two decades, almost doubling from US$5.7 billion in 1990 to US$10.8 billion in 2001, and nearly tripling to US$28.1 billion (2010 dollars) by 2011 (36). According to the recent reports, DAH slightly decreased in 2011 (37), and some global health activists expressed concern that the golden age of financing global health could come to its end. Whereas in 1990, NGOs and some smaller private foundations accounted for 11.2%, their share increased in 2000 to 19.8% and in 2011 to 30.6%, out of which NGOs accounted for almost one third, that is, 9.6%. In comparison, the entire UN organization contributed a share of 14.3%, the regional development banks 8.5%, and bilateral aid—including the EU—46.6% (38,39). An increasing amount of DAH is channeled outside governments (40).

Private foundations and NGOs shift the paradigm of global health aid away from governments or agencies and constitute as described a large piece of health assistance today. Accordingly there were also efforts to strengthen their role in the decision-making framework of WHO, proposing their participation as so-called "Table C" (41). However, the governmental constituency of WHO did not take this step forward. On the other hand, there are serious imbalances: DAH, over the past decade, obviously has been allocated not according to the highest disease burdens, which are found in South Asia and sub-Saharan Africa (42), but to other criteria, for example, political and economic interests (43). Analysis by IHME (25) in 2012 brought the conclusion that out of 20 countries with the highest all-cause disability adjusted life years (DALYs), only 12 are among the top 20 recipients of DAH.

NGOs and foundations are responsible to their constituencies but do not always feel such obligation toward their clientele and the general public. They usually act on their own and cooperate often on a case-by-case basis. This leads to extreme fragmentation and therefore ineffectiveness of international aid (44). Globally, 280 agencies, 242 multilateral funds, 24 development banks, 40 UN organizations, and thousands of NGOs can be identified. Thus, for example, in East Timor (approximately 1 million population) there are more than 1,200 donor-initiated studies, or one study on average for fewer than 1,000 inhabitants (45). That is a better coverage than the number of physicians in many rural regions in the world (in East Timor, one physician served a population of 10,000 in 2004) (46). In 2007, donors made more than 15,000 visits to 55 partner countries. Vietnam alone received 782 missions in 2007, more than two per working day. For under-resourced ministries in developing countries, these transaction costs can be unbearably high and reduce the value of the aid they receive to almost none. The sheer number of activities creates the need for greater harmonization between donors and alignment with partner country priorities (47). Especially in the indispensable state sector, knowledge and skills to secure coordination and collaboration in public health are limited, not only in transitional and developing societies. International and even more bilateral aid very often is disrupting coherent national development plans and priorities, especially in those countries that are highly dependent on aid (25,48), bringing in addition the burden of different reporting systems (49). Solutions are difficult but new initiatives focus increasingly on generating local production and income instead of perpetuating dependency on donors.

In this context, the role of a new generation of entrepreneurs to fill the gap between health decision makers and other stakeholders, including NGOs, can contribute to a solution. In fact, in developing countries (mainly in sub-Saharan Africa), where there is an evident lack of governance and accountability, strategic policies, and practices, the commitment of a new generation of entrepreneurs equipped with skills on governance, leadership, and management might be critical to move forward. This "independent" group of people with a mindset of engaged social entrepreneurship may drive and lead the implementation of good governance and accountability through good practices of business success! It should be investigated how a new emerging generation of entrepreneurs may serve and act as a relay or "transmission belt" between the government and civil society organizations. On the other hand, some may argue that this category would only be an additional intermediate and weigh down the mechanisms of functioning and communication. That might partially be true at first glance but considering the current dynamics, for example, in sub-Saharan Africa, where most countries have large numbers of young people, the potential of the emerging economy in the health market as well as entrepreneurship in these areas may be of benefit to all if they are more involved in health management. There is still an urgent need of partners in creating long-term solutions to public health problems. A new educated generation of entrepreneurs could be one among others.

In the 1990s, the limited capacity of many governments to coordinate among different governmental sectors as well as between ministries and the donor community became apparent. One of the most promising—however, rarely implemented—concepts to cope with these deficits has been the sector-wide approach (SWAp) (50,51). The SWAp can be described as an arrangement whereby donors work with the government to deliver a commonly agreed upon health policy and strategy, with the view to building ownership, enhancing aid effectiveness, and reducing transaction costs (52). All significant funding for the sector supports a single sector policy and expenditure program, under government leadership, adopting common approaches across the sector, and progressing toward government procedures to disburse and account for all funds. In exchange for giving up the right to choose projects according to their own priorities, donors gain a say in the development of national health policies and in decisions about how both external and domestic resources are allocated. However, the SWAp is not a blueprint but a programmatic focus on the intended policy, a direction of change rather than a specific program attainment.

One of the key principles and underlying mechanisms of a successful SWAp is a "three ones" approach, that is, one national strategy adopted, one national authority responsible, and one platform for M&E. Resources will be channeled increasingly through government systems (not parallel systems of donors)—for example, a strong project implementation unit—and consolidated joint accounts with a view toward overall budgetary support; in other words, an agreement on binding financial mechanisms. Common disbursement, accounting, reporting, auditing, and procurement systems are to be defined. Development budgets and recurrent budgets have to be separated. Those donors not participating in a basket approach (financial envelope for a common program agreed upon by multiple donors) should, not be excluded however, but rather integrated through a wider forum of interested parties (53). Improving government oversight, putting in place innovative institutional arrangements, and advocating for better discipline by donors toward more transparent negotiations in supporting the government constitute the nervous system for the future of SWAp (54). Following Rothman et al. (2011) even for fragile states, setting up a SWAp, can be a first step for regaining control (55).

Nevertheless, a sectoral program may not consider transversal interdependencies and the complexity of a social sector like health. Some recent impact evaluations point to weaknesses and strengths of SWAps (56,57), suggesting that—ideally—intersectoral coordination should be taken into account at a higher level according to the principle of health in all policies and of subsidiarity: If all activities are under one common sector-wide program, fully budgeted, and integrated into a Medium-Term Expenditure Framework (MTEF), the ministry of health becomes accountable to the population and not just to donors (25).

A code of conduct on cooperation with governments for national and international NGOs and a type of accreditation procedure at least at the national level are among the most urgent requirements for improving effective global governance. In strengthening the implementation of SWAp, some of the developing countries have produced a code of conduct between government ministries responsible for the health sector and development partners including NGOs. Tanzania is a good example for that. The code of conduct describes expectations and commitments on the sides of all parties. NGOs and foundations must be held accountable to the global public. Many countries have problems with NGOs, particularly when they compete for resources, appear not to respect national needs, fail to share information, and show lack of coordination. On the other hand, accredited NGOs very likely would get preferred access to funding and become trustworthy partners for their target groups, respective governments. Having laws governing operations of NGOs in a country is a cornerstone toward the accreditation procedure. To ensure better coordination, an umbrella body is an essential ingredient. In Tanzania for instance (58), NGOs are registered under the Non-Governmental Organisation Act, 2002. The Tanzania Association of NGOs (TANGO) is the umbrella body taking a leading role in organizing and coordinating participation locally and abroad. There is a global shift for more alignment between NGOs themselves. Bjegovic-Mikanovic et al. (2014) has assembled a list of global health networks including many NGOs (59).

10.8 ENHANCING REGIONAL COOPERATION

Two fundamental questions are important here. First, are the still relatively weak existing global structures able to direct implementation of policy and strategy? Second, are the smaller countries able to assemble the diversity of skills required? The conclusion could be that one should further strengthen regional collaboration not only on a fragile voluntary basis but organized also as long-term binding agreements.

The EU, with all its weaknesses, has, nevertheless, made progress despite considerable crises throughout the years. As examples, since the 1993 Treaty of Maastricht (in the Netherlands) (60), public health has been defined as a political mandate of the European Commission; and health issues are permanently on the table of the European Community. Along the same lines: when the Association of Southeast Asian Nations (ASEAN) was founded in 1967, there was a move to unify the region under the "ASEAN Way" (61), based on the ideals of noninterference, informality, minimal institutionalization, consultation and consensus, and nonuse of force and nonconfrontation. The principle of consultation and consensus brought about a considerable degree of harmonization among member states in the areas of economics, finances, and trade as well as in the area of education and human development, especially among universities. Perhaps, health practice will be determined as another key field requiring closer cooperation at regional levels, in particular addressing issues relating to improved integration of primary, secondary, and tertiary care, enhanced links between academia and public health, effective alliances for advocacy, and close cooperation with key health policy and decision makers.

For the nongovernmental sector, the World Federation of Public Health Associations (WFPHA) (62) may serve as an example. The WFPHA recently inaugurated a regionalization strategy for public health. The underlying concept behind the strategy is to initiate and support regional cooperation of countries with a related history and culture in order to identify common problems and solutions with a view to improving public health. The WFPHA was established in the same year (1967) as ASEAN.

The WFPHA is an international NGO composed of multidisciplinary national public health associations and is the only worldwide professional society representing and serving the broad field of public health, presently representing more than 80 national public health associations with more than a quarter million public health professionals. The federation is affiliated with WHO and holds consultation status with the UN Economic and Social Council (ECOSOC). Since the move of the main secretariat from Washington DC to Geneva in 2010, in addition to the pre-existing office of the European Public Health Association (EUPHA) (63) in Utrecht, The Netherlands, two regional secretariats have been opened: one in Beijing for the Asia-Pacific Region and the other in Addis Ababa for the African Region. The next step forward in regional cooperation was taken during the First Arab World Public Health Conference in Dubai early in April 2013, preparing the foundation of an Arab Public Health Federation. Similar developments are ongoing for the Pacific region and in Latin America.

When Ban Ki-Moon referred to the essential role of "global partnership" (64), he touched a key issue: with no doubt, regional cooperation is an essential intermediate step to enhance global partnership. Public health especially constitutes a neutral terrain and can open doors that otherwise would be kept closed.

Another excellent example is the institutional collaboration of postgraduate academic teaching for public health in the framework of the European Stability Pact for South Eastern Europe during the first decade of the 21st century (65), helping to reconnect the successor states of former Yugoslavia and their neighbors. Those involved will never forget when for the first time colleagues from Serbia attended a meeting in the Albanian capital of Tirana, and colleagues from there came to the Serbian Capital of Belgrade, followed by mutual first post-civil-war visits of public health professionals from all, now independent, countries of the region. All too often it is forgotten that, worldwide, armed conflicts have been responsible for more casualties than any single disease and for the huge waste of resources for armaments that could have been allocated to population health and well-being rather than death and destruction.

10.9 BUILDING CAPACITY FOR CHANGE: EDUCATION AND TRAINING

Affirmed in Chapter 8.0, to shape competent public health professionals (66) and other health and social care professionals, at least in the core subjects of health sciences (e.g., epidemiology, health promotion) education and training is the highest priority in order to transform the health systems and improve population health (67,68). One may add here the requirement of structured training opportunities for building leadership capacity (69), which can enables the transfer of concepts into reality. The central roles of education and capacity building for global public health are now recognized in most countries, along with worldwide efforts to reduce the burden of disease, strengthen health systems, and disseminate scientific innovation. Responding effectively and efficiently to these complex and comprehensive problems presents profound challenges for at least three reasons (70):

1. Multidisciplinary integration of primary care, social care, and public health and theory, practice, and research—stemming from mainly two contrasting philosophies: the medical and natural sciences (largely patient disease and cure-driven), on the one hand, and the social sciences (mainly "whole" person care, wellness and prevention-oriented), on the other. However, both focus on a common subject: the health and well-being of people.
2. The diversity of public health students and public health professionals—providing a very heterogeneous cohort—who must be able to handle population health problems as well as function within public health systems,

including clinical, and other human systems with health impact in a national and global context. Two of the key priorities in this decade and beyond are to help increase healthy life years and reduce health inequalities. To that end, they have to communicate with different actors and join multidisciplinary teams of researchers, institutional decision makers, and representatives of government, civil society, and the private sector.

3. Sustaining population health delivery systems when demand exceeds supply—providing innovative approaches in educating and training public and clinical health practitioners at a time when there are severe workforce shortages—both public and clinical in most non-European regions, and funding favors clinical support at a time when noncommunicable diseases and chronic care are the main health threats.

Especially from the perspective of low- and middle-income countries, the traditional approaches to public health training have manifest limitations. As mentioned previously, there is an urgent need to reconnect public health education and research with public health practice (71). As such, a combination of rigorous academic and supervised practical experience that orients individuals away from rote learning to becoming dynamic lifelong learners is needed, in other words, "focus on the capacity to pursue rather than memorize knowledge" (72). Some stark limitations relate to:

- The emphasis on epidemiology and biostatistics and the relative neglect of other public health sciences.
- The isolation from health ministries, other health providers, local communities, and other relevant disciplines that can impact on health.
- The emphasis on institution-based teaching and limited, if not complete lack of, direct field experience. Efforts such as the CDC Field Epidemiology and Laboratory Training program would be a redress to this.
- The scarcity (in some places, complete absence) of role models: public health practitioners in the field who can be looked upon as professional mentors.
- The consideration of public health as a medical specialty.
- The high cost of training programs.

Education and training of an adequate public health workforce, sufficient to operate globally, is, among others, the principal area of interest for the faculty of public health in the United Kingdom. Although in recent years there has been a massive worldwide expansion in the number of Master of Public Health programs, many of their graduates remain otherwise substantially untrained and unprepared for employment. In the United Kingdom, the faculty has developed an integrated multidisciplinary system of education and training that results in an output of public health professionals of high potential, who are much needed globally.

The ongoing debate on how to align different concepts in global health or, in other words, the complementarities in basic definitions of global health (73) is itself bringing together academic institutions all over the world and initiates a dialogue with the civil society, which becomes increasingly relevant for capacity building of public health professionals, and sharing good practice and lessons learned. Partnerships around education for public health will also stimulate the development of a code of ethics for population health (74) as different from biomedical ethics, essential for the self-understanding of the workforce engaged in global health.

The goals of public health training in the 21st century also seem highly applicable to global clinical training (75):

> to work collaboratively and with compassion, stimulate curiosity, to examine evidence and provide appropriate health interventions, to produce graduates who take initiative, accept risk and responsibility for failures, who are capable of making connections, understanding root causes of health and illness and able to refocus 'upstream and downstream' to ensure gains in population health, displaying self-confident behaviour when they advocate for health and human rights.

This debate relates also to the misunderstanding of primary health care (PHC) in the aftermath of Alma-Ata (1978) as health care exclusively at the primary level and separate from, if not in contradiction to, the public health services, discussed in some detail in Chapter 6.0. Unfortunately, PHC frequently is considered all that is needed for curative and preventive care, thereby minimizing the role of public health. This mainly affects allocation of budget in public health services that are not covered by PHC, for example, supporting lifestyle change. Today's thinking along a concept of universal health care requires strong cooperation between all levels of health care and health coverage, including health insurance systems. Transformative education for public health has to become universal itself in order to achieve a greater public health outcome, that of health for all.

Global cooperation as evidenced today has become possible only because of the wide availability of digital media since the 1990s. The new educational technologies allow for virtual universities/classrooms, guaranteeing equal opportunities and a much wider audience (76). In related terms, the relevance of a concept of lifelong learning has been recognized by all actors, particularly the EU. Supported by blended or hybrid learning and employing online technology, these developments will change the educational landscape for all professionals, their networks, and help make them more employable. However, the global community is still struggling to harmonize efforts, and is witnessing slow progress in reaching equal benefits for all countries from such partnerships.

A modernized teaching concept, based on core public health competencies as referred to in Chapter 8.0, also necessitates consensus between the most relevant international organizations and academia. Recently, also, and as illustrated in Chapter 8.0 using the Designing A CurriculUM (DACUM) process, future employers of public health professionals have been approached (77,78) to define their needs and expectations on public health performance in the field of public health and global health. In addition, the Bologna Declaration is setting a framework for Europe, signed by almost all states in the region. However, a globally harmonized public health terminology is still missing as is a global agreement on essential public health functions (EPHF) or on core competences for public health research and practice. Most relevant, the size and capacity of many schools of public health around the world are subcritical; the

European schools, for example, produce less than one third of the graduates required following U.S. estimates (79).

As public health opportunities and threats are increasingly global, schools of public health should look beyond the national boundaries and participate in global networks for education, research, and practice. This is underlined by the recent Charter of the Association of Schools of Public Health in the European Region (ASPHER) on the "The Global Dimension of Education and Training for Public Health in the 21st Century in Europe and in the World" (80).

It can be argued that current high visibility of many global health issues in today's headlines, whether related to avian flu, HIV/AIDS, Ebola, food contamination, the obesity epidemic, or air pollution in China, has created a critically important opportunity to use case studies to teach basic principles of public health to an audience much wider than those students destined for public health careers. Such awareness-raising efforts, whether they take the form of undergraduate courses, continuing education products, or online learning, will go a long way toward expanding public health "literacy" in pre-professionals in medicine, law, business, policy, engineering, and other sectors that will need to be partners in creating long-term solutions to public health problems. But they will also help to instill the basic notion that health is a prerequisite to—as opposed to a trickle-down result of—successful development in those who will be driving development efforts.

10.10 TOWARD A GLOBAL HEALTH ROAD MAP

The key to global health is improvement of population health in less developed and transition countries. However, as austerity bites hard, middle- and high-income nations are also feeling the brunt of the years of high spending and are a cause for health and social concern, especially among the unemployed younger generation and older adults, as evidenced in Chapter 2.0.

Many questions wait for an answer from the global community, especially on a more democratic, effective, and efficient global governance for health or in other words: What global, regional, national, and local structures, organizational principles, and mechanisms should ideally evolve in the early decades of this century to improve and sustain global health and well-being, including universal health coverage (UHC), and thereby inform policy makers?

With the latter query in mind, we offer 10 visionary recommendations for global decision makers at all levels, summarized in Box 10.1.

1. *Coordinate the creation of a collective public or population health and well-being vision underpinned by global social justice*, which is "fit for purpose" in rich, economically emerging and poor nations for the early decades of the 21st century with strong consideration, advocated in Chapter 6.0, for integrative, collaborative, ecological, and ethical dimensions that underpin global health development. Hopefully, the post-2015 debate could fulfill this expectation if it goes beyond the present status of the debate if it, for example, would include the issue of armed conflicts and consider the interrelatedness of the major global problems.

BOX 10.1

Ten Visionary Recommendations for Global Decision Makers

1. Coordinate the creation of a collective public or population health and well-being vision underpinned by global social justice
2. Inform the development of structures at the global level in terms of good global governance
3. Develop formalized structures of regional health cooperation
4. Accredit nongovernmental organizations
5. Harmonize global public health terminology
6. Register official development assistance (ODA) for health and development assistance for health (DAH) flows globally
7. Implement a Public Health Education European Review (PEER) "sur place" (country by country)
8. Correct the weaknesses of the DAH system
9. Transform traditional health and social care education and training programs through innovative practice, focusing on prevention and health promotion (versus cure), incorporating the One Health concept and approach
10. Implement fundamental change through collaborative and realistic scenario building and strategy setting: "thinking outside the mainstream" to help solve today's and tomorrow's public health challenges

2. *Inform the development of structures at the global level in terms of good global governance*, adding to the national context with a mandate to discuss any topic related to health and UHC, representing a broader membership than WHO including representatives of the civil society as full members, and going beyond WHO's strictly advisory mandate.
3. *Develop formalized structures of regional health cooperation* between countries as an intermediate step toward stronger global structures—public health as a neutral territory for piloting cooperation. This process may start with intensified networking, information sharing, and technology transfer across borders.
4. *Accredit NGOs* based on ethical criteria, especially with regard to administrative costs, brain drain of local staff, and participation in revitalized SWAps.
5. *Harmonize global public health terminology*, especially in terms of an agreement on a global framework for EPHF.
6. *Register ODA for health and DAH flows globally*, including a regular follow-up on the Monterrey and the Paris/Accra criteria, and zealous efforts to reach the Paris/Accra criteria and "making development cooperation more effective."
7. *Implement a Public Health Education European Review (PEER) "sur place" (country by country)* on invitation by professional teams, to advise on a set of pre-formulated issues in the health sector embracing the approach of UHC.

8. *Correct the weaknesses of the DAH system,* taking up proposals integrated by Moon and Omole 2013 (81), including considering proposals to improve national coordination by SWAps and, at the international level, recent initiatives such as the H8, an informal group of eight health-related organizations (82) formed in 2007 to improve coordination, especially on the health-related MDGs; and the H4+ for maternal and child health, created in 2010 (83) to coordinate support for countries with the highest infant and maternal mortality rates, as well as IPH+.

9. *Transform traditional health and social care education and training programs through innovative practice, focusing on prevention and health promotion (versus cure), incorporating the One Health concept and approach* by broadening opportunities for learning at all societal levels and across all nations. Chapters 3.0 to 9.0 dealt with a number of approaches for reforming health and social care curricula (84). These second-order changes (not only doing things better but also doing better things) are all the more pressing when we consider global imbalances, in particular recalling the discussions in Chapters 2.0 and 7.0.

   According to the recent WHO initiative *Transforming and Scaling Up Health Professionals' Education and Training: WHO Education Guidelines 2013* (85):

   > there are health workforce imbalances in terms of deficits, shortages or inequitable distribution of workers in all countries. Together with the imperative to deliver more and more effective health services, these imbalances create an urgent need to scale up the number of human resources for health, to adapt the education and training of health providers to the new epidemiological and demographic challenges, and ensure a proper skill mix, and to adopt measures and incentives to make the geographical and organizational distribution of health professionals more equitable. In many countries, this need has to be met in a context of difficult economic circumstances.

10. *Implement fundamental change through collaborative and realistic scenario building and strategy setting: "thinking outside the mainstream" to help solve today's and tomorrow's public health challenges.* Following the proposals in the foregoing chapters and the Epilogue, what has to be done to meet global public health issues is beginning to be recognized. However, what is the likelihood that recommendations will be implemented successfully and impact positively and ethically on people's lives? Progress has been slow, and agonizingly much too late in many instances, and calls for a new type of leadership that transcends self-interests, adopts planetary ecological perspectives, and strives "to make the quality of life and well-being of all people the top priority for public health" (9,86).

For each challenge we face—environmental threats; inequities and inequalities; population growth and aging; poverty; conflicts, bioterrorism, and human

TABLE 10.2 Elimination of Armed Conflicts and Their Death Toll

SCENARIO	STRATEGY
1. Armed conflicts between and within countries remain largely uncontrolled.	1. The present political and organizational arrangements are replaced by effective consensus building and reconciliation.
2. The use of military force becomes a sole prerogative of the United Nations (Security Council).	2. The military–industrial complex is dissolved.
3. Technological advance allows for use of force without taking lives.	3. The underlying reasons of armed conflict are removed (i.e., poverty, hunger, humiliation, lack of education).

security—one can imagine different scenarios for resolution, the probability of which generally depends on political will and strategies implemented.

As one example (Table 10.2), considering the challenge of "elimination of armed conflicts and their death toll" might lead us to imagine alternative scenarios and identify solutions.

Two more scenarios (Tables 10.3 and 10.4) should illustrate the issues at stake, one on health professional migration (from developing countries) and one on maternal mortality (in developing countries).

A central theme that emerges from reflections on these brief exemplars is that all three scenarios in global public health and possible solution strategies—and of course, there are so many more—require well-developed—*though nonexisting today*—global decision-making mechanisms that have enough leverage and expertise to carefully work through the delicate and complex decision-making processes needed to consider options or alternatives, inform planners and decision makers, and actually make a meaningful difference to the sustainability of life on this planet.

TABLE 10.3 Health Professional Migration (From Developing Countries)

SCENARIO	STRATEGY
1. Professional migration continues to deplete the sending countries which, therefore, lose their leadership and sink into civil war and poverty (leading to population moves).	1. The present political and organizational arrangements are replaced by effective consensus building and reconciliation.
2. The sending countries are fully compensated for their investments.	2. Health service industries move increasingly to countries with a cheaper workforce.
3. Professional migration is reducing because of a combination of economic growth in the sending countries and stricter rules in the receiving countries.	3. Professional migrants return to their home countries because of improved economic growth.

TABLE 10.4 Perspectives for Maternal Mortality Trends

SCENARIO	STRATEGY
1. Maternal mortality continues to decrease but at a higher rate than during the MDG period (up to 2015) because of highly improved gynecological services.	1. The present political and organizational arrangements are replaced by efective consensus building and reconciliation.
2. Unrest, social downgrading, and civil war in many countries destroy the clinical infrastructure and lead to a rise of maternal mortality in many countries.	2. The Medical–Industrial complex and its uncontrolled influence is contained.
3. Accepted technological advances in birth control and improvements in the education of potential parents eliminate the problem.	3. Economic improvements allow for more children born in safety.

10.11 ADDRESSING GLOBAL HEALTH CHALLENGES IN THE 21ST CENTURY THROUGH ONE HEALTH COLLABORATIVE NETWORKS

Perhaps, as highlighted in Sections 10.4 and 10.5 and recommendations 1 and 2 foregoing, emerging (that may be regional) public health structures along these lines—especially if they could network on an "issue-by-issue" basis—might be able to optimize in a realistic way their reach and impact by taking on the mantle of *apolitical* "learning organizations," as, for example, argued by *The Lancet*–University of the Oslo Commission on Global Governance for Health, which has made a compelling case for a global "Multi-Stakeholder Platform on Governance for Health" since its launch in February 2014 in Oslo (87). Following the One Health concept or approach, which advocates meeting "new challenges to human, animal and ecosystem health" through "novel solutions" (88), including improving interdisciplinary collaboration, these coordinating mechanisms—functioning possibly as "a collaborative education network"—could collectively support the training of a "new generation of One Health professionals" (89). In addition, they could liaise closely with other regional bodies and might also carry responsibilities for incentivizing schools of public health and associated organizations to identify, prioritize, and tackle the difficult public health issues of the day.

One of the more immediate priorities they might consider is to "unpack" (or simplify) the complexities of governance, including how it may be enabled to become more effective (doing the right things) and efficient (doing things right). This process might be maximized by collectively engaging in case-based scenarios, as advanced in Chapter 8.0, and by disseminating ideas through networked channels. Regional discussions on governance-related subjects might also be enlightened by the insights underpinning the recently announced WHO guidelines for transforming and scaling up health professionals' education and training (88), inspired to a large extent by *The Lancet* Commission report, "Health Professionals for a New Century" (90).

As Nyoni and Gedik observed on behalf of WHO in 2012 (91):

Good governance results from the combination of institutional and organizational mechanisms that support change, and the technical and political capacity and will to conduct change.

Knowing is not enough; we must apply.
Willing is not enough; we must do.
—Goethe

REFERENCES

1. Joy WN. Why the future doesn't need us. *Wired Magazine*; April 2000.
2. UN Millennium Project 2005. *Who's got the power? Transforming health systems for women and children. Task force on child health and maternal health.* Washington, DC: Communications Development Inc; 2005. http://www.unmillenniumproject.org/documents/maternalchild-frontmatter.pdf. Accessed June 15, 2014.
3. Chan M. Health has an obligatory place on any post-2015 agenda. http://www.who.int/dg/speeches/2014/wha-19052014/en/. Accessed June 15, 2014.
4. Frenk J. The new public health. *Annu Rev Public Health*. 1993;14:469–490.
5. Kerr C. Education for management in the new public health. *J Health Adm Educ*. 1991;9(2):147–161.
6. Horton R, Beaglehole R, Bonita R, et al. From public to planetary health: A manifesto. *Lancet*. 2014;383:847. doi:10.1016/S0140-6736(14)60409-8
7. WHO. World conference on social determinants for health: Rio political declaration on social determinants for health. www.who.int/sdhconference/declaration/en/. Accessed April 07, 2014.
8. WHO and Ministry of Social Affairs and Health, Finland. The Helsinki statement on health in all policies. Paper presented at: The 8th Global Conference on Health Promotion; June 10–14, 2013; Helsinki, Finland. www.who.int/healthpromotion/conferences/8gchp/8gchp_helsinki_statement.pdf. Accessed May 14, 2015.
9. Ottersen OP, Dasgupta J, Blouin C, et al. The political origins of health inequity: Prospects for change. *The Lancet*. 2014;383(9917):630–667. http://www.thelancet.com/pdfs/journals/lancet/PIIS0140-6736(13)62407-1.pdf. Accessed February 12, 2014.
10. IHP+Results. *Progress in the International Health Partnership & related initiatives (IHP+).* 2012 Annual performance report. http://www.internationalhealthpartnership.net/fileadmin/uploads/ihp/Documents/Results___Evidence/IHP__Results/IHP_Results_2012_Rpt.pdf. Accessed June 22, 2014.
11. United Nations. *The Millennium Development Goals report 2012.* New York, NY: United Nations; 2012. http://mdgs.un.org/unsd/mdg/Resources/Static/Products/Progress2012/English2012.pdf. Accessed February 10, 2013.
12. Bourguignon F, Bénassy-Quéré A, Dercon S, et al. *Millennium Development Goals at midpoint: Where do we stand and where do we need to go?* Brussels and Luxembourg: European Commission; 2008. https://ec.europa.eu/europeaid/sites/devco/files/study-millenium-development-goals-200810_en.pdf. Accessed January 11, 2014.
13. Trends in Maternal Mortality: 1990 to 2013. Estimates by WHO, UNICEF, UNFPA, World Bank, and the United Nations Population Division. Published May 2014; ISBN: 978 92 4 150722 6.
14. United Nations Economic and Social Council (ECOSOC). Millennium Development Goals and post-2015 development agenda. http://www.un.org/en/ecosoc/about/mdg.shtml. Accessed May 14, 2015.

15. Frenk J, Gomez-Dantes O, Chacon F. Global health in transition. http://inspvirtual.mx/espm30/docentes/formdocente/jd2011/pdf/ma1_2011_1.pdf. Accessed June 15, 2014.

16. Europa. Subsidiarity. http://europa.eu/legislation_summaries/glossary/subsidiarity_en.htm. Accessed June 15, 2014.

17. Europa. Treaty of Maastricht on European Union. http://europa.eu/legislation_summaries/institutional_affairs/treaties/treaties_maastricht_en.htm. Accessed January 14, 2014.

18. Frenk J, Gomez-Dantes O, Moon S. From sovereignty to solidarity: A renewed concept of global health for an era of complex interdependence. *Lancet*. 2014;383:94–97.

19. WHO. Sovereignty. http://www.who.int/trade/glossary/story082/en/. Accessed June 15, 2014.

20. Prah-Ruger J. The World Bank and global health: Time for a renewed focus on health policy. *J Epidemiol Community Health*. 2014;68(1):1–2. doi:10.1136/jech-2013-203266

21. Gomez EJ. Exploring the utility of institutional theory in analysing international health agency stasis and change. *Health Policy Plan*. 2013;28(7):769–777. doi:10.1093/heapol/czs117

22. Kickbusch I. A global system in the making—Six mind-changes. *Huffington Post*. May 13, 2013. http://www.huffingtonpost.com/dr-ilona-kickbusch/a-global-system-in-the-ma_b_3268370.html. Accessed June 22, 2014.

23. Kickbusch I. A game change in global health: The best is yet to come. *Public Health Reviews*. 2013; 35(1). http://www.publichealthreviews.eu/upload/pdf_files/13/00_Kickbusch.pdf. Accessed June 22, 2014.

24. Gostin LO, Ooms G, Heywood M, et al. *The joint action and learning initiative on national and global responsibilities for health. World Health Report 2010*. Background Paper 53. Geneva: WHO; 2010. http://www.who.int/healthsystems/topics/financing/healthreport/JALI_No53.pdf. Accessed June 22, 2014.

25. Laaser U, Epstein L. Threats to global health and opportunities for change: A new global health. *Public Health Reviews*. 2010;32(1):54–89. http://www.publichealthreviews.eu/show/f/32. Accessed June 22, 2014.

26. OECD. Aid effectiveness: A progress report on implementing the Paris Declaration. 3rd High Level Forum on Aid Effectiveness. September 2–4, 2008, Accra Ghana. www.worldbank.org/ACCRAEXT/Resources/Progress_Report-Full-EN.pdf. Accessed June 22, 2014.

27. OECD. (2011). 2011 Survey on monitoring the Paris Declaration. http://www.oecd.org/dac/effectiveness/2011surveyonmonitoringtheparisdeclaration.htm. Accessed June 22, 2014.

28. World Bank. *Paris Declaration at a glance*. Washington: World Bank; 2006. http://infoworldbank.org/etools/docs/library/238766/H&A%20Menu%20rev202%20English.pdf. Accessed June 22, 2014.

29. Ravishankar N, Gubbins P, Cooley RJ, et al. Financing of global health: Tracking development assistance for health from 1990 to 2007. *Lancet*. 2009;373:2113–2124.

30. OECD. *Aid Effectiveness 2011: Progress in implementing the Paris Declaration*. Paris: OECD Publishing. 2012. http://dx.doi.org/10.1787/9789264125780-en. Accessed June 22, 2014.

31. Vassall A, Shotton J, Klein-Reshetnyk O, et al. Tracking aid flows for development assistance for health. *Global Health Action*. 2014;7:23510. http://dx.doi.org/10.3402/gha.v7.23510

32. Progress towards more effective aid: What does the evidence show? Paper presented at: 4th High Level Forum on Aid Effectiveness. 29 Nov–1 Dec 2011; Bussan, Korea. http://www.oecd.org/dac/effectiveness/48966414.pdf. Accessed June 22, 2014.

33. OECD. Assessing progress towards effective AID. http://www.oecd.org/dac/effectiveness/assessingprogresstowardseffectiveaid.htm. Accessed June 22, 2014.

34. OECD/UNDP. *Making development co-operation more effective: 2014 Progress report*. Paris: OECD Publishing; 2014. http://dx.doi.org/10.1787/9789264209305-en. Accessed June 2014.

35. Moon S, Omole O. Centre on Global Health Security (The Royal Institute of International Affairs, Chatham House), Working Group on Financing, paper 1 (April 2013) Development assistance for health: Critiques and proposals for change. http://www.chathamhouse.org/sites/files/chathamhouse/public/Research/Global%20Health/0413_devtassistancehealth.pdf. Accessed June 22, 2014.

36. IHME DAH Database 2012. http://www.healthdata.org/sites/default/files/files/policy _report/2012/FGH/IHME_FGH2012_FullReport_HighResolution.pdf. Accessed June 22, 2014.

37. Institute for Health Metrics and Evaluation. *Financing global health 2012. The end of the golden age?* Seattle, WA: IHME (Institute for Health Metrics and Evaluation); 2012. http://www.health metricsandevaluation.org/publications/policy-report/financing-global-health-2012-end -golden-age. Accessed June 22, 2014.

38. Institute for Health Metrics and Evaluation. Financing global health. http://vizhub.healthdata .org/fgh/. Accessed May 14, 2015.

39. European Commission. EU aid explorer. https://euaidexplorer.jrc.ec.europa.eu/. Accessed June 16, 2014.

40. Jordan L, van Tuijl P, eds. *NGO accountability: Politics, principles & innovations.* Sterling, VA: Earthscan; 2006.

41. Silberschmidt G, Matheson D, Kickbusch I. Creating a committee C of the World Health Assembly. *Lancet.* 2008;371(9623):1483–1486.

42. Mathers CD, Lopez AD, Murray CJL. The burden of disease and mortality by condition: Data, methods, and results for 2001 (Figure 3.11). (Ch. 3 Relationship between health expectancies and health) In: Lopez AD, Mathers CD, Ezzati M, Jamison DT, eds. *Global burden of disease and risk factors.* Washington: IBRD; 2006. http://www.ncbi.nlm.nih.gov/books/NBK11808/#A323. Accessed June 22, 2014.

43. Ravishankar N, Gubbins P, Cooley RJ, et al. Financing of global health: Tracking development assistance for health from 1990 to 2007. *Lancet.* 2009;373:2113–2124.

44. Global Health Watch. Watching WHO. http://www.ghwatch.org/sites/www.ghwatch.org/ files/global%20health%20watch%203.pdf. Accessed June 22, 2014.

45. Bornhoft F, Knaup P. You are overtaxed [in German]. *Der Spiegel.* 2008;40:42–44. http://www .spiegel.de/spiegel/print/d-60666807.html. Accessed June 22, 2014.

46. UN Data. *Health workforce, infrastructure, essential medicines.* Physician density per 10,000 popula- tion, East Timor (p. 102). http://www.who.int/whosis/whostat/EN_WHS09_Table6.pdf?ua=1. Accessed June 22, 2014.

47. Laaser U, Brand H. Global health in the 21st century. *Glob Health Action.* 2014;7:23694. http:// dx.doi.org/10.3402/gha.v7.23694

48. Biehl J, Petryna A. *When people come first: Critical studies in global health.* Princeton, NJ: Princeton University Press; 2013. eBook | ISBN: 9781400846801

49. Horton R. Offline: The panjandrums of global health. *Lancet.* 2013;382(9887):112.

50. Council of Europe. Recommendation CM/Rec(2010)6 of the Committee of Ministers to member states on good governance in health systems (Adopted by the Committee of Ministers on 31 March 2010 at the 1081st meeting of the Ministers' Deputies): https://wcd.coe.int/ViewDoc. jsp?Ref=CM/Rec%282010%296&Language=lanEnglish&Site=COE&BackColorInternet=DBDC F2&BackColorIntranet=FDC864&BackColorLogged=FDC864. Accessed June 22, 2014.

51. Brown A, Foster M, Norton A, Naschold F. *The status of sector wide approaches.* London: Overseas Development Institute; 2001; Working Paper 142.

52. Hutton G, Tanner M. The sector-wide approach: A blessing for public health? *Bull World Health Organ.* 2004;82(12):893.

53. HLSP Institute. *Sector wide approaches: A resource document for UNFPA staff.* London: HSLP; 2005. http://www.unfpa.org/sites/default/files/pub-pdf/swap-unfpa2005eng.pdf. Accessed June 22, 2014.

54. Peters DH, Paina L, Schleimann F. Sector-wide approaches (SWAps) in health: What have we learned? *Health Policy and Planning.* 2013;28(8):884–890.

55. Rothman, I., Canavan, A., et al. (2011). *Moving towards a sector-wide approach (SWAp) for health in fragile states: Lessons learned on the state of readiness in Timor Leste, Sierra Leone and Democratic Republic of Congo.* KIT working Papers Series H5. Amsterdam, The Netherlands: KIT. http:// www.bibalex.org/Search4Dev/files/368176/206109.pdf. Accessed April 7, 2014.

56. Chansa C, Sundewall J, McIntyre D, Tomson G, Forsberg BC. Exploring SWAp's contribution to the efficient allocation and use of resources in the health sector in Zambia. *Health Policy and Planning*. 2008;23:244–251.

57. Pearson M. *Impact evaluation of the sector wide approach, Malawi*. London: DIFID and UKAID; 2010. http://41.87.6.35:8080/xmlui/bitstream/handle/123456789/903/Impact%20Evaluation%20of%20the%20Sector%20Wide%20Approach%20SWAP%20Malawi.pdf?sequence=1. Accessed June 22, 2014.

58. Nexus Commonwealth Network. Find civil society expertise in United Republic of Tanzania. www.commonwealthofnations.org/sectors-united_republic_of_tanzania/civil_societ. Accessed April 7, 2014.

59. Bjegovic-Mikanovic V, Jovic-Vranes A, Czabanowska K, Otok R. Education for public health in Europe and its global outreach. *Global Health Action*. 2014;7(special issue).

60. Summaries of EU Legislation. Treaty of Maastricht on European Union. http://europa.eu/legislation_summaries/institutional_affairs/treaties/treaties_maastricht_en.htm. Accessed June 22, 2014.

61. Goh G. The 'ASEAN way'. Non-intervention and ASEAN's role in conflict management. *Stanford Journal of East Asian Affairs*. 2003;3(1):113–118. http://web.stanford.edu/group/sjeaa/journal3/geasia1.pdf. Accessed June 22, 2014.

62. The World Federation of Public Health Associations. www.wfpha.org. Accessed June 22, 2014.

63. The European Public Health Association. www.eupha.org. Accessed June 22, 2014.

64. United Nations. *The Millennium Development Goals report 2012*. New York, NY: United Nations; 2012. http://mdgs.un.org/unsd/mdg/Resources/Static/Products/Progress2012/English2012.pdf. Accessed June 22, 2014.

65. Forum for Public Health in South Eastern Europe. Programmes for Training and Research in Public Health. http://www.snz.unizg.hr/ph-see/index.htm. Accessed June 22, 2014.

66. Czabanowska K, Laaser U, Stjernberg L. Shaping and authorizing a public health profession (Short report). *SEEJPH*. 2014. doi: 10.12908/SEEJPH-2014-23

67. Frenk J, Chen L, Bhutta ZA, et al. Health professionals for a new century: Transforming education to strengthen health systems in an interdependent world. *The Lancet*. 2010;376(9756):1923–1958.

68. Lueddeke G. *Transforming medical education for the 21st century: Megatrends, priorities and change*. London, England: Radcliffe Publishing Ltd.; 2012.

69. Czabanowska K, Rethmeier KA, Lueddeke G, et al. Public health in the 21st century: Working differently means leading and learning differently. *Eur J Public Health*. 2014;24(6):1047–1052. doi:10.1093/eurpub/cku043

70. Bjegovic-Mikanovic V, Jovic-Vranes A, Czabanowska K, Otok R. Education for public health in Europe and its global outreach. *Glob Health Action*. 2014;7:23570. http://dx.doi.org/10.3402/gha.v7.23570.

71. Bjegovic-Mikanovic V, Czabanowska K, Flahault A, et al. *Addressing needs in the public health workforce in Europe*. Copenhagen: WHO, ASPHER and the European Observatory on Health Systems and Policies, 2014. http://www.euro.who.int/en/about-us/partners/observatory/policy-briefs-and-summaries/addressing-needs-in-the-public-health-workforce-in-europe. Accessed June 22, 2014.

72. Beaglehole R, Bonita R. *Global public health: A new era*. 2nd ed. Oxford: Oxford University Press; 2009: 291.

73. Koplan JP, Bond TC, Merson MH, et al., for the Consortium of Universities for Global Health Executive Board. Towards a common definition of global health. *Lancet*. 2009;373:1993–1995.

74. Stapleton G, Schroeder-Baeck P, Laaser U, Meershoek A, Popa D. Global health ethics: An introduction to prominent theories and relevant topics. *Glob Health*. 2014;7:23569. doi: 10.3402/gha.v7.23569

75. McKee M. Seven goals for public health training in the 21st century. *Eur J Public Health*. 2013; 23(2):186–187.

76. Paucek C, Ferreira J, Johnson J, Yu C. Online education: From novelty to necessity. Chapter 8. In: *Education and skills 2.0: New targets and innovative approaches.* World Economic Forum; 2014. http://www.weforum.org/reports/education-and-skills-20-new-targets-and-innovative-approaches. Accessed June 22, 2014.

77. ASPPH. *Public health trends and redesigned education.* Blue Ribbon Public Health Employers' Advisory Board, summary of Interviews. http://www.aspph.org/educate/models/blue-ribbon-public-health-employers-advisory-board. Accessed January 14, 2014.

78. Vukovic D, Bjegovic-Mikanovic V, Otok R, et al. Which level of competence and performance is expected? A survey among European employers of public health professionals. *Int J Public Health.* 2013;59(1):15–30. doi: 10.1007/s00038-013-0514-x

79. Bjegovic-Mikanovic V, Vukovic D, Otok R, Czabanowska K, Laaser U. Education and training of public health professionals in the European region: Variation and convergence. *Int J Public Health.* 2013;58(6):801–810. doi: 10.1007/s00038-012-0425-2

80. Charter read at the occasion of the 6th European Public Health Conference; November 13–16, 2013; Brussels, Belgium. www.aspher.org. Accessed June 22, 2014.

81. Moon S, Omole O. Centre on Global Health Security (The Royal Institute of International Affairs, Chatham House), Working Group on Financing, paper 1 (April 2013). Development assistance for health: Critiques and proposals for change. http://www.chathamhouse.org/sites/files/chathamhouse/public/Research/Global%20Health/0413_devtassistancehealth.pdf. Accessed June 22, 2014.

82. WHO, UNICEF, UNFPA, UNAIDS, GFATM, GAVI, the Bill & Melinda Gates Foundation, and the World Bank.

83. WHO, UNFPA, UNICEF, UNAIDS, UN Women, and the World Bank.

84. Lueddeke G. Keynote address at the American Medical Association. Paper presented at: Accelerating Change in Medical Education (ACE) Conference; October 4, 2013; Chicago, IL. http://www.healthprofessionals21.org/index.php/news-views/commentaries-on-reform/356-healthcare-working-differently-in-21st-century-means-learning-differently. Accessed June 22, 2014.

85. World Health Organization: *Transforming and scaling up health professionals' education and training: WHO education guidelines 2013.* Geneva: WHO Publication Office; 2013. ISBN 978 92 4 150650 2.

86. Horton R, Beaglehole R, Bonita R, et al. From public to planetary health: A manifesto. *Lancet.* 2014;383:847. doi: 10.1016/S0140-6736(14)60409-8

87. *The Lancet.* UiO Commission on Global Governance for Health. www.med.uio.no/helsam/english/research/global-governance-health/about/. Accessed June 22, 2014.

88. Kaufman GE, Epstein JH, Paul-Murphy J, Modrall JD. Designing graduate training programs in conservation medicine–producing the right professionals with the right tools. *EcoHealth.* 2008;5(4):519–527. doi: 10.1007/s10393-008-0208-7

89. Barrett MA, Bouley TA, Stoertz AH, Stoertz RW. Integrating a One Health approach in education to address global health and sustainability challenges. *Front Ecol Environ* 2010;9(4):239–245. doi: 10.1890/090159

90. WHO. Transformative education for health professionals: Education guidelines. http://who-educationguidelines.org/. Accessed June 22, 2014.

91. Nyoni J, Gedik G. *Health workforce governance and leadership capacity in the African region. Review of human resources for health.* Geneva: WHO Publication Office; 2012.

THE PAST, THE PRESENT, AND THE FUTURE

SNIPPETS FROM THE PAST

Outlined in Section 1.3, public health has been a priority of ancient societies over the millennia (1). As one example, the early Romans recognized the importance of preventing disease and built aqueducts to transport water into the city, public latrines, bathhouses, and sewer systems. The need to curtail the spread of diseases was also understood during the various plague epidemics that ravaged Europe during the Middle Ages, as the dead were quickly buried and "doctors" wore birdlike masks to shield them from foul air, although the practices did little to control diseases and millions died, regardless.

The first modern public health intervention can arguably be traced to the English physician John Snow, recognized as one of the fathers of modern epidemiology. Through meticulous observation in 1854, he was able to trace a cholera outbreak in Soho, London, to a polluted public water pump. Removing the pump contained the cholera outbreak, thereby preventing many deaths. Scientific breakthroughs, such as the germ theory, provided a better understanding of the causes of disease and triggered the development of vaccines, as shown in Box A, throughout the last century, along with the increasing recognition of sanitation and the dangers of substance abuse (1).

Smallpox, which killed an estimated 300 million people in the 20th century, was globally eradicated in 1978. In addition, other conditions, such as polio and tuberculosis, became much less prevalent due to improved sanitation and breakthroughs in the development of vaccines and other forms of treatment, as shown in Box A.

Indeed, illustrated in Figure A, the 20th century saw the reduction of the top 10 causes of death in the United States, dropping from about 1,100/100,000 in 1900 to roughly 600/100,000 in 2010 (2).

BOX A

20th-Century Western Medicine Vaccines, Antibiotics, and the World's First Breakthroughs

- 1900—First human blood groups: O, A, and B (AB: 1902)
- 1903—First practical electrocardiogram (ECG)
- 1909—First antibiotic: salvarsan
- 1923—First vaccine: diphtheria
- 1927—First vaccine: tuberculosis
- 1928—Penicillin
- 1935—Prontosil: first of a class of antibiotic drugs known as sulfa drugs—beginning of modern medicine (antibacterial)
- 1948—Tetracycline: group of broad-spectrum antibiotics
- 1950—First kidney transplant (U.S.)
- 1952—First oral polio vaccine
- 1964—First vaccine: measles
- 1972—Computed tomography (CT)
- 1977—First magnetic resonance imaging (MRI)
- 1981—First vaccine: Hepatitis B
- 1982—HIV/AIDS (human immunodeficiency virus infection and acquired immune deficiency syndrome) are named and defined (U.S.)
- 1987—First heart, lung, and liver transplant (UK)
- 2007—Robotic treatments, gene therapy treatments; visual prosthesis (bionic eye)
- 2008—Laurent Lantieri performs the first full-face transplant
- 2013—First kidney grown in vitro in the United States; first human liver grown from stem cells in Japan
- 2015 and beyond—wearable technologies, remote patient monitoring, risk stratification, DNA vaccines . . .?

Source: G. Lueddeke, *Transforming Medical Education for The 21st Century: Megatrends, Priorities and Change,* 2012 (1).

SNAPSHOT OF THE PRESENT

Communicable diseases have largely been replaced by noncommunicable or lifestyle diseases, such as heart disease, cancers, diabetes, and mental illnesses. Chronic diseases, such as dementia, caused by an aging population are also on the rise. Moreover, globally, there are growing concerns with regard to the steep rise of diabetes mellitus type 2, HIV/AIDS, forms of the corona virus, and emerging diseases, such as the Ebola virus. Taken together, while we have generally been successful in treating many common 20th-century diseases or conditions, we have been less so, as the book argues, in tackling those associated with modern life despite (or because of?) our technologically advanced societies.

In an online survey, Professor Glenn Laverack at the University of Denmark posed the question "What are the top (not disease) public health challenges of the future?" (3). He received close to 500 responses from people living in many different countries

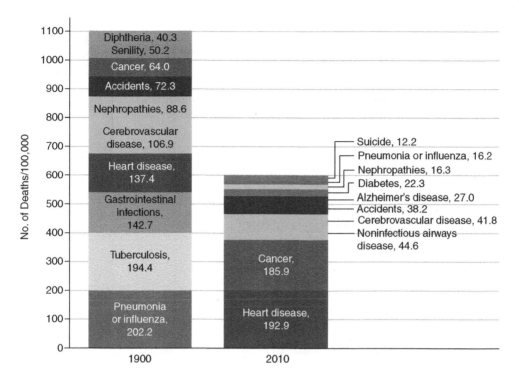

FIGURE A U.S. deaths per 100,000 people—1900 versus 2010.

Source: H. Blodget, What Kills Us: The Leading Causes of Death From 1900–2010 (2).

and at many different professional levels, with remarks of a very high standard and thought-provoking and evidence-based nature. He kindly prepared the summary that follows for this section of the book.

The key issues raised (not in order of importance) are shown in Box B:

BOX B

Key Global Issues Identified in LinkedIn Survey on Top Public Health (Nondisease) Challenges of the Future

- Health finance and insurance
- Inequalities
- Climate change
- Universal health coverage
- Health in all policies
- Workplace competencies
- Accountability and transparency
- Safe water supply, hygiene, waste disposal, and sanitation
- Food security
- Data analysis
- Human resources for health

(continued)

BOX B

Key Global Issues Identified in LinkedIn Survey on Top Public Health (Nondisease) Challenges of the Future (*continued*)

- The use of information and communication technologies
- Obesity
- Mental health
- Drowning
- Health education
- Applying an evidence-based approach
- Stigma, discrimination, and social isolation
- Risk communication and disaster slavery
- Tobacco control
- Management
- Corporate countertactics
- Resistance to antibiotics and insecticides
- Early years' intervention
- Social entrepreneurship
- Road traffic injuries
- Newborn health
- Gender violence including female genital cutting
- Implementing the International Health Regulations
- Volunteerism
- Patient empowerment
- Pollutants including protection against mercury compounds
- Access to essential medicines and strengthening of regulatory systems

Most responses could be differentiated between those having a direct practical solution such as improved drinking water supply and those requiring broader social and political action such as reducing poverty or inequality. Many issues were directly related to practice at a program level, including improved sanitation and hygiene. Other responses involved complex social processes such as gender violence and the stigmatization of people with infectious diseases.

There were local/national/international variations in the topics raised. In some countries, for example, the surge of obesity is a worrying development; in others, gender violence, sanitation, or poor access to health care is the primary concern.

A key challenge was seen as the commitment of governments to respond to, and have the financial capacity to, address local issues within a policy environment of often competing equal agendas. For example, how can public health issues such as violence against women and the resistance to antibiotics be prioritized as they are both equally important but resources are often limited?

A major theme was the need to help people at a local level to address their own health priorities versus broader issues at a population level. Some respondents were concerned that health systems do not allow both to occur at the same time. This is exacerbated by growing inequality and the poor intersectorial coordination between agencies and government departments. The implementation of a Health in All Policies approach was seen by some as a partial solution to these issues.

Some responses addressed innovative solutions to social problems by drawing upon appropriate thinking in all aspects of the business and nonprofit sectors including social entrepreneurship. *However, most survey participants did not see themselves as members of a civil society in which they could influence others, including those in government and a society in which corporate countertactics have a great deal of leverage in public health, for example, in tobacco control and fast-food manufacturing.*

Globalization, climate change, and inequalities were raised as the three largest future (nondisease based) challenges in public health. The discussants did identify that these challenges were dependent on political commitment and strong leadership, but saw them as issues beyond the control of most public health practitioners. It was, therefore, felt by most of the respondents that, at this point in time, public health practice did not have a direct role to play in addressing such broad issues as globalization, climate change, and inequalities.

> What was clear from the survey, according to Professor Laverack, is "that many discussants see public health as being political (vs. social, economic) in nature, and they were frustrated at the difficulty, in their everyday life and work, of making the changes necessary in, for example, policy and legislation to improve population health and well-being."

REFLECTIONS ON THE FUTURE OF POPULATION HEALTH AND WELL-BEING

The outcomes of Professor Laverack's survey reflect health inequities across the globe, distinguishing between issues that have "a direct practical solution" and those necessitating "broader social and political action." Figure B confirms these discrepancies, as the research findings correlate life expectancy with income per person with the highest attained in both areas in Japan, North America, Australia/New Zealand, and European countries and the lowest in Bangladesh, Pakistan, India, Indonesia, and sub-Saharan African nations (4). The findings indicate that the lower the income, the lower is the life expectation and the greater the need for immediate practical solutions. The Ebola outbreak in Western Africa is most pronounced in Sierra Leone and Guinea-Bissau, two of the poorest nations in the African continent.

Fundamental, broadly based social and political action also ranks high in terms of survey responses. Two key issues are that people are "not seeing themselves as members of a civil society," where those governing and corporate voices appear to have more influence than people being served as citizens or consumers. Second, this lack of societal connection has led to "frustration" felt in making changes in their daily lives, including the lack of public health influence in addressing "globalization, climate change and inequalities." This systemic dysfunction is also reflected in an article, "From Public to Planetary Health: A Manifesto," appearing in *The Lancet* (5). The authors observe that "we live in a world where the trust between us, our institutions, and our leaders, is falling to levels incompatible with peaceful and just societies, thus contributing to widespread disillusionment with democracy and the political process."

Life expectancy in years

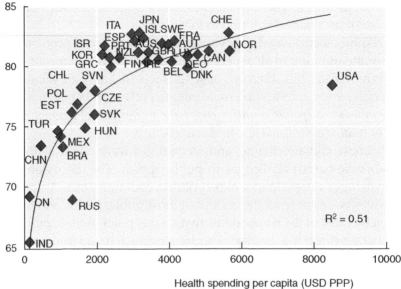

Health spending per capita (USD PPP)

FIGURE B Life expectancy at birth and health spending per capita, 2011 (or nearest year).
Source: OECD, Health at a Glance 2013: OECD Indicators (4).

Faced with growing public health issues, government challenges include the difficulty of responding to "competing equal agendas" at a time when resources are tight and finding a balance between meeting local and general population needs.

The UN post-2015 SDG deliberations confirmed that national priorities vary depending on social/economic/political circumstances (6). However, seven areas for fundamental global transformation in mindset or paradigms shifts (Box C) that cut across all 17 goals have been identified in this book and may be helpful guideposts for translating good intentions (SDGs, targets, indicators) into concrete and measurable enabling actions at global and national levels—moving from basic paradigms to implementation of policy and practice.

BOX C

Key Paradigm Shifts

- Recognizing global imbalances, in particular the reality that most people—about 5 billion out of c. 7.3 billion in 2015—live in developing and underdeveloped nations and that there is an *urgent* need for geopolitical momentum to end extreme poverty and strive toward *global economic and social justice,* within and across all nations, underpinned by the SDGs, targets, and indicators, perhaps following an incremental 5-year target and timescale to 2030.

(continued)

BOX C

- Placing much more emphasis on *humanitarian* agendas at the highest global decision-making levels and collectively adopting and implementing the principles and practices espoused in the UN Earth Charter and the SDGs: prioritizing ecological integrity, democracy, nonviolence, and peace (7).
- Turning from government and corporate demands for short-term gain, too often encompassing ruthless exploitation of resources (human and physical) in poor nations, to managing economic growth by adopting humane principles that underpin the UN Earth Charter and recognizing that government and corporate activity must operate for a *higher purpose* to sustain the planet and its species.
- Reorienting thinking from health as a strictly "human" concern to *One Health* that links *all living species*—human, animals (wildlife and domestic), plant, and the environment.
- Weaving the *One Health* concept throughout *early childhood, under-/postgraduate education, and lifelong learning,* including leadership development, fostering interdisciplinary collaborations and communications in all aspects and addressing many difficult problems facing the world.
- Shifting from a patient disease-driven (or "sickness") culture, dominated by costly centralized hospital care, to a *holistic "health and well-being" culture,* focusing on individual responsibility for health supported by families, communities, and information technology support that places a greater emphasis on *prevention* (physical, emotional) over curative measures, including global and national budgetary re-balancing.
- Replacing the unidimensional view of *public health,* based largely on 20th century assumptions and linear or reductionist practices, with a much more positive and *broader socioecological, multidimensional orientation* that has the potential of impacting significantly on social, economic, and political decision-making.

BUILDING A SOCIETY THAT IS TRULY "JUST AND CARING"

The World We Want as Seen Through the Eyes of Children

The post-2015 Sustainable Development Goals present a unique opportunity to make the world a better place, to create the "world we want" (8,9). This world is far different from the one we inhabit and that too many children experience today, highlighted in Section 2.1. The world envisaged by the current generation of children may have been best characterized in a recent survey involving 4,460 girls and boys, aged 8 to 18, summarized in Box D.

The concerns, passion, and commitment of the children's voices in delivering the post-2015 Development Agenda are real. It is for these reasons that global decision-makers must take their deeply felt "wants" or desires seriously and work toward these

BOX D

Summary of the World We Want 2015 e-Consultation With Children

- Love shared with family and friends
- Safety
- Healthy people and communities
- Play
- A clean environment
- Education
- Financial stability
- Equity and equality
- Good governments that respect children's rights
- To be listened to
- Better infrastructure

Source: United Nations, The World Children Want: Summary of e-Consultation With Children (8,9).

goals in the next 15 and more years—underpinned by initiatives that reclaim or restore basic human values—"the values of democracy, of the rule of law, of tolerance, of faiths, of equality of treatment" (10,11).

A Manifesto for Collective Public Health Action

The children's pleas are in harmony with the *Lancet* manifesto, which calls for a social movement to support collective public health action at all levels—"personal, community, national, regional, global and planetary" (15).

The manifesto spells out the disastrous consequences of not transforming our "attitude towards life" or "our values and our practices." We face two key threats: One is that "our patterns of overconsumption are unsustainable and will ultimately cause the collapse of our civilization," while the other relates to the creation of a "global economic system that favours a small, wealthy elite over the many who have so little."

And, while "the gains made in health and wellbeing over recent centuries . . . are not irreversible; they can easily be lost, a lesson we have failed to learn from previous civilisations" (5). The manifesto contributors posit that both public health and medicine, as "the independent conscience of planetary health," have a key role to play in realizing "a new vision of cooperative and democratic action at all levels of society. This vision embraces the a new principle of planetism and wellbeing for every person on this Earth—a principle that asserts that we must conserve, sustain, and make resilient the planetary and human systems on which health depends by giving priority to the wellbeing of all."

Finding a Better Way to Navigate the Complexities of Life

A reminder of a fundamental universal aspiration to build a just and caring society has been reinforced on numerous occasions by Pope Francis, the Argentinian pontiff.

As one example, in his New Year's greetings of peace on January 1, 2014, to the tens of thousands gathered in St. Peter's Square in Rome, he once again urged the world to listen to the "cry for peace" from those who are suffering and declared that "too many people are indifferent to wars, violence and injustice" (11).

Departing from his prepared text and calling for an end to violence, he agonized: *"What has happened in the hearts of man, in the heart of humanity? It's time to stop!!"* He emphasized that everyone must be committed to building a society that is "truly more just." After all, he avowed, "We belong to the same human family and we share a common destiny" (11). His exasperation with the state of things on Earth is clear, and many might agree that now is the time for the world to listen and "to turn the corner" before it really is too late.

According to acclaimed British writer, Rebecca Pearson, a promising approach to making the world a better place is through *mindfulness*—"realizing the importance of living wholeheartedly in the present" (12). The author contends that mindfulness could lead us to "a far more spiritually fulfilling way to navigate life, leading to a healthier, happier and more conscientious population." However, she emphasizes, making mindfulness "a vital component in our lives" requires us to accept that "it can't be bought or hurried; spirituality requires time and nurturing."

A consideration for those charged with developing primary school curricula is to introduce mindfulness—"being aware of what is happening as it is happening" (13,14) and focusing on "attention, balance and compassion" (13) in early childhood, ideally linking mindfulness to the unfolding of One World, Health values and dimensions. Developing children's "awareness of thoughts, emotions and worldview" appears to be a matter of considerable urgency not only for the younger generation but also for their parents, professionals, policy makers at all levels, and government leaders, some of whom may find "waking up from a life on automatic pilot" (15) personally liberating and gratifying.

In this regard, we might recall the words of the young Irish girl, who spoke from the heart at the 2013 G8 summit in Belfast, Ireland, before the keynote address by U. S. President Barack Obama. Her main hope was "to live in a society where we are safe and can be friends with everybody" (16). Her utopian world seems far-fetched when we consider today's realities and divisive factors. However, journalist Alice Thomson offers some optimism in this regard, saying that her children were "brought up in inner-city nurseries and schools, had multi-faith nativity plays. They pretended to be Hanukkah candles and the Hindu god Ganesh as well as angels and shepherds. They knew how to pronounce 'salwar kameez' before they could read the word 'Christmas' with the Oxford Reading Tree scheme" (17,18). In many ways they reflect much not only of the "world we want'" but also of the "world we need."

This aspiration could be more easily achieved, according to Professor Klaus Schwap, a German academic and founder in 1971 of the World Economic Forum (WEF), speaking at the opening of the 2015 forum, if we "recreate confidence in our future. Pessimism has become too much the *zeitgeist* of our time" (19). And here, U.S. President Barack Obama's incisive speech to the youth at the G8 Summit in Belfast, Ireland, on June 13, 2013, may provide a way forward for our increasingly divisive planet:

Ultimately, peace is just not about politics. It's about attitudes; about a sense of empathy; about breaking down the divisions that we create for ourselves in our own minds and our own hearts that don't exist in any objective reality, but that we carry with us generation after generation. (20)

A PIVOTAL MOMENT IN HUMAN HISTORY?

Finally, as the reports on the Millennium Development Goals and the post-2015 Sustainable Development Goals make clear, while progress in global health has been made, it has been uneven and fraught with many gaps; indeed, advances in strengthening population "well-being" have grown to be even more precarious than they were at the turn of the century. In the early decades of this millennium, the challenge that lies before us seems nothing less than ensuring the survival of our planet and all life upon it for this and future generations.

The megadrought now impacting on the United States and wreaking havoc on Brazil, along with a poverty-stricken Central America, are cause for alarm and should make us think about life and the way we are living it. According to environmentalists, the Brazil drought "has been caused by massive deforestation in the Amazon, where an area twice the size of Germany has been stripped of trees in the past 40 years," interrupting "a complex pattern of rainfall that once funnelled moisture from the Atlantic current through the rainforest and down to the farming regions" (21). Authorities warn that São Paulo, the largest city in the southern hemisphere, with more than 20 million inhabitants, "is sleepwalking into disaster" with potential rationing of water, turning "taps off for five days a week."

Perhaps we have now arrived at a pivotal moment—at a crossroads. More than ever before, the health and wellness of our planet lies in the hands of a few in positions of power and influence, some well-meaning and benign, but there are still far too many brutal dictatorships, corrupt oligarchies, and marauding or extremist factions responsible for human rights abuses and many guilty of war crimes against humanity.

As was the case last century in meeting global threats to freedom, and including current threats to European nations, the only tenable solution in this century once again is solidarity: that is, for freedom-loving nations to stand together as one, possibly spearheaded by a revitalized ("fit for purpose") and values-driven United Nations (UN) Security Council. The need for drastic re-thinking has been epitomized by the European migration tragedies and the "ravages of war" (22) that are keeping close to 14 million children in the Middle East—Syria, Iraq, Yemen, Libya, Sudan, and Lebanon—from school, thereby "crushing individual lives and futures" and "losing a generation of children" (23). Given global instabilities and the post-2015 SDGs, there is now considerable urgency by the UN General Assembly to review the composition of the permanent members of the UN Security Council (24), a post WW2 architecture, that does not include, for example, India with over 1.2 billion people, as well as the need to verify members' humanitarian commitment to peace and security (7).

Looking beyond 2015, Ban Ki-Moon, Secretary-General of the United Nations, provides a seminal definition of "sustainability" (25), highlighting principles of inviolability and challenging especially those responsible for continuing to allow "the women, men and children" to live "on a knife-edge of poverty, injustice and insecurity":

> At its essence, sustainability means ensuring prosperity and environmental protection without compromising the ability of future generations to meet their needs. A sustainable world is one where people can escape poverty and enjoy decent work without harming the earth's essential ecosystems and resources; where people can stay healthy and get the food and water they need; where everyone can access clean energy that doesn't contribute to climate change; where women and girls are afforded equal rights and equal opportunities.

This definition and its attributes are at the heart of the UN Sustainable Development Goals 2016–2030 framework, underpinned by the 5Ps: People, Planet, Peace, Prosperity, Partnership, as summarized in Box E.

BOX E

UN-Proposed Sustainable Development Goals	
Goal 1	End poverty in all its forms everywhere
Goal 2	End hunger, achieve food security and improved nutrition, and promote sustainable agriculture
Goal 3	Ensure healthy lives and promote well-being for all at all ages
Goal 4	Ensure inclusive and equitable quality education and promote lifelong learning opportunities for all
Goal 5	Achieve gender equality and empower all women and girls
Goal 6	Ensure availability and sustainable management of water and sanitation for all
Goal 7	Ensure access to affordable, reliable, sustainable and modern energy for all
Goal 8	Promote sustained, inclusive, and sustainable economic growth, full and productive employment, and decent work for all
Goal 9	Build resilient infrastructure, promote inclusive and sustainable industrialization, and foster innovation
Goal 10	Reduce inequality within and among countries
Goal 11	Make cities and human settlements inclusive, safe, resilient, and sustainable
Goal 12	Ensure sustainable consumption and production patterns
Goal 13	Take urgent action to combat climate change and its impacts
Goal 14	Conserve and sustainably use the oceans, seas, and marine resources for sustainable development
Goal 15	Protect, restore, and promote sustainable use of terrestrial ecosystems, sustainably manage forests, combat desertification, halt and reverse land degradation, and halt biodiversity loss

(continued)

UN-Proposed Sustainable Development Goals (*continued*)

Goal 16	Promote peaceful and inclusive societies for sustainable development, provide access to justice for all, and build effective, accountable, and inclusive institutions at all levels
Goal 17	Strengthen the means of implementation and revitalize the global partnership for sustainable development

Source: United Nations, *Transforming Our World: The 2030 Agenda for Sustainable Development*, https://sustainabledevelopment.un.org/post2015/transformingourworld.

However, translating these into reality across global communities requires addressing a fundamental issue, voiced recently, among many others, by the respondents to the LinkedIn survey on priority nondisease public health interventions (3), discussed earlier: rebuilding trust between all members of society and those that lead in social, political, and economic spheres. Far removed from bureaucratic "comfortable pews" or "win/lose power politics," there is a strong case to be made to reengage people directly and honestly to work with them closely through the tough daily problems they face.

There can be little doubt that given the economic crises in Europe and elsewhere, reestablishling—in many cases, establishing—trust between the increasingly urban poor and "politics as the agent of meaningful change," thereby bridging the divide between "politics and anti-politics" (26), remains one of the most crucial issues of our times.

According to Ms. Irina Bokova, UNESCO's first female director general, this fundamental reorientation calls for "a new humanism that reconciles the global and the local, and teaches us anew how to build the world" and that aspires "to peace, democracy, justice and human rights . . . tolerance, knowledge and cultural diversity . . . rooted in ethics and in social and economic responsibility." Further, she asserts the "new humanism" "comes into its own by extending assistance to the most vulnerable. It is at the heart of the commitment to struggle to face our greatest common challenges, particularly respect for the environment" (27).

This transformation worldwide continues to be difficult in light of financial and political turmoil, which have impacted deeply on society well-being. To make further progress in this decade and beyond, and as argued throughout this volume, global decision makers must pay much more attention to gaining deeper understanding of life in the modern age, where extreme austerity and poverty sit uncomfortably alongside unimaginable power and wealth.

What is perhaps most abhorrent and unacceptable is that an increasing number of the world's population are forced to survive in conflict zones and to raise families in intolerable—cramped and unsanitary—conditions, less tolerable for humans than those in the lives of the poorest in the 19th century! As one shocking example, the United Nations estimates that in Syria (28), out of about 23 million people, over 7.6 million are now internally displaced, an increase of more than 3 million in just a year, with many—over 3.8 million—escaping across the border, mostly to Jordan and Lebanon, many living in refugee camps without enough medical services and water, along with vanishing prospects for the future. Recalling "the worst exodus since the Rwandan genocide 20 years ago," there is no question that it is "the worst humanitarian disaster of our time," killing more than 220,000 to date. Unsurprisingly, "the youngest are confused and scared by their experiences, lacking the sense of safety and home they need. The older children are forced to grow up too fast, finding work and taking care of their family in desperate circumstances" (28).

And, while hard economic statistics matter with much new data confirming what we already suspect and statistical models doing very little in changing global track, it is perhaps by hearing "firsthand" the struggles of people—and raising world attention through real-life stories and anecdotes—that "head and heart" might best meet, connect with political leadership, curtail corruption and violence, hold individuals— "the good, the bad, and the ugly"—to public account, and find new ways of building new lives and battling hunger, disease, death, and fear. The impact of this approach was demonstrated recently at a closed meeting of the 15-member UN Security Council where a Syrian doctor "described desperate attempts to save dying children from chemical attacks"; all were affected by his briefing (29).

"THE RISE OF THE MACHINES" AND "STANDING UP" FOR HUMANITY

The need for reconnecting much more closely with communities—regaining public trust and developing an emotional connection—is made especially pressing when we consider the potential impact that technology and the rise of robots may have on our work and all societies, rich and poor, in this and coming decades. The new technology of the next quarter-century will present us, according to some, with the potential of creating a better world or, alternatively, humanity's greatest "existential threat" (30).

Economists Eric Brynjolfsson and Andrew McAfee have called our age "the second machine age" (31); the first being the Industrial Revolution. What distinguishes the latter from the former is that for the first time, it is "possible for humanity to create two of the most important one-time events in our history: the emergence of real, useful artificial intelligence (AI) and the connection of most of the people on the planet via common digital network."

Although the Internet has made important contributions in terms of e-mail and social networks, for columnist Matthew Lynn, its main added value has been in modifying "existing products rather than creating new ones" (32). "Robotics," he asserts, "is different," and as transformative as "the steam engine and electricity in the past." The field will create new products and new industries, increase productivity, and create "new industries of their own—driverless cars and robot childminders as well as robot manufacturers, many of which will likely emerge in the East."

And, while we could speculate that robotics may play a constructive role in helping to expedite infrastructure capacity in developing nations, as an example, the downside in both and developing nations may be the potential loss of skilled jobs and erosion of emotional well-being, as algorithms and cognitive systems replace human capital by "machine-centric capitalism," and further hasten inequality, as the world divides into those who are computer "savvy"—capable of exercising hegemony over global "tribal" communities—and those who are not, likely the vast majority (31).

The present directions prompt many questions: One is whether the rapid transition to the robotics age will exacerbate a 21st-century neo-Luddite societal response, that is, protests against labor-replacing machinery similar to the industrial backlash in the early 19th century, as technology turns from "disruptive innovation" to "devastating innovation" (33). If the possibility exists, how can repercussions be minimized?

Another relates to the impact that the proliferation of artificial intelligence (AI) may have on developing and underdeveloped nations,, most of which were only marginally affected by the Industrial Revolution, with many now connected virtually to today's (over 600 million mobile phone users in sub-Saharan Africa alone!) and tomorrow's world alongside heightened consumer expectations. These nations are already facing a triple burden: transitioning quickly but unevenly through "survival" public health phases or "waves" (e.g., tackling poor sanitation, health system, and workforce shortages), alongside an increasing use of communication and information technologies (C&IT), while simultaneously having to address both existing and emerging communicable and noncommunicale diseases. Based on past experience, solutions to these issues must include connecting political and developmental actors working collaboratively on strategies that take a horizontal versus vertical approach, focusing resources on building "healthy communities in healthy environments."

A third dimension is based on a working hypothesis that argues about the risks involved in adding the prospect of AI and robotics to the already precarious relationship between humans, animals, and the ecosystems (One Health). Devoid of any affective attributes—at least in the forseeable future—and recognizing the generating and degenerating (highlighted in Section 2.5) impact technology is already having through entertainment software and social media, we may ask to what extent AI has the potential of becoming, as Stephen Hawking has predicted, a more malevolent force rather than a benign public good. Indeed, he postulates that it has the capacity to wipe out the human race (34).

SUSTAINING HUMANITY IN A "SECOND MACHINE AGE"

The stakes for preserving humanity in the long run—possibly the most difficult "ingenuity gap" nations may need to confront later this century—are high. And, while progress in technology is inexorable, along with trying to implement and monitor the UN Sustainable Development Goals (Box E), world leadership may increasingly be tasked to proactively debate the consequences of uncontrolled technology, the ethics or morality of job losses (a Gallup estimate concluded that, worldwide, only 27% of men and fewer women currently work for one employer! [35]), and the impact on family health and well-being when algorithms supplant instinctive human empathy and care, potentially and ubiquitously destabilizing the human condition and spirit. The prospect of millions facing redundancies or "technological unemployment" is already being felt in large corporations, such as Amazon, Foxconn, and Bezos, and will likely impact on smaller service providers, for example, those employing security guards, fast-food cooks, and financial advisors (31).

Debates at national, regional, and global levels for finding more humanitarian or altruistic ways, such as conscious capitalism discussed earlier, to better manage the "emerging new robot economy" (31) may in due course need to take center stage along with a view and expectation to rebalance global inequities, especially in the light of shifting population densities, as shown in Figure C (36). While industry may want "a reliable, tireless workforce that doesn't require loo breaks, a canteen or a dormitory," according to experience to date, especially in China, the reality is that "robots must enter a factory slowly and in perfect harmony with the human beings" and that "for it to work best, the march of automation must be evolution, not a big bang" (37).

ADDRESSING INTERSECTING INEQUALITIES

John McDermott, a writer for the *Financial Times* and a former policy adviser in the U.K. government policy unit, in his article "Here Come the Robots" (38), notes that while some "techno-optimists" believe that "benefits of the machine age could be vast, bringing millions out of poverty across the world," others are more skeptical, believing it would lead to an "increase in inequalities of income, wealth and probably opportunity" and it is "not a world where everyone is going to feel comfortable"; it is one that "will look much more unfair and much less equal." One of the main reasons, as mentioned earlier, is that technology may lead to job losses and increasing poverty for the majority of people (38).

The situation may be further exacerbated as the world edges toward 9 to 10 billion people, primarily in developing nations such as sub-Saharan Africa and India, by 2050 (Figure C). Indeed, if current ratios of people living in developing and undeveloped nations are extrapolated, by 2050, more than 8.5 billion will be living in poor nations and about 4 billion in rich. The estimated cost of global health—currently around US$7.5 trillion annually—would also rise proportionately to an unsustainable US$13 trillion per year and likely much more unless steps are taken to address noncommunicable diseases and the costs of supporting an aging population.

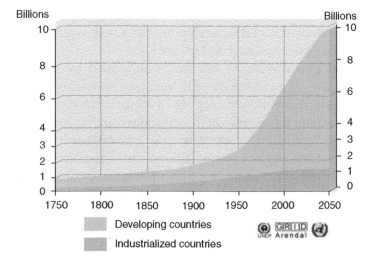

FIGURE C World population development, 1750–2050 (34).

Source: T. P. Soubbotina, K. A. Sheram, *Beyond Economic Growth: Meeting the Challenges of Global Development* (p. 16), The World Bank (36).

A recent report, *Strengthening Social Justice to Address Intersecting Inequalities*, sponsored by the Overseas Development Institute (ODI) and the Sustainable Development Goal Fund (SDGF), drew on the experience of seven nations (Brazil, Ecuador, Bolivia, India, Ethiopia, Pakistan, and Nepal); it identified key issues and suggested program interventions (39) to address inequalities. The writers' main concern was for those who are generally "most left behind by development" and who face "intersecting inequalities or economic deficits intersecting with discrimination and exclusion on the grounds of identity and locational disadvantage."

Their recommendations to tackle intersecting inequalities include

- Drawing on "social movements demanding changes in the 'rules of the game'"
- Advocating "political trajectories and processes of constitutional change that facilitate and actualize these changes" (e.g., social guarantees, opportunity enhancements, and developmental affirmative actions)
- Establishing "global norms which will support and encourage mobilisation to tackle intersecting inequalities, including a strong commitment to universal quality basic services, and the development of country-specific frameworks of targets and indicators monitoring intersecting inequalities"

TOWARD A WORLD WE NEED: GLOBAL SOCIOECONOMIC AND POLITICAL TRANSFORMATIONS IN THIS CENTURY

Global Projections

Contributors to the aforementioned inequality report may find that their recommendations take on considerable momentum as socioeconomic forces accelerate and impact on the lives of the world population. In this regard, given the speed of scientific and technological change in the past 20 years or so, the observations made by Professor Alexander Likhotal, president of Green Cross International, seem particularly timely (40). His overall view is that our world "will differ so much in 10 years that we will be surprised with our current concerns." Some of the global trends that we might expect, which essentially reflect the development of a new world economic, political, and social order, have been summarized in Box F.

An important global shift, he believes, exemplified by the U.S. One Health Commission and the global One Health Initiative, discussed in some detail in Chapter 7.0, relates to the world's managing "the imminent socio-economic transformations while respecting the realities of the natural world." In his view, the main lever will be through "reorienting and restructuring our economies on to a more reasonable, sustainable, balanced and inclusive path" through "the creation of a new developmental paradigm, which enhances access, health and security, creates jobs and safeguards the environment."

His analysis of sustainability proposes that the world's growing population demands at least two fundamental transformations: "to produce more in order to meet increasing demand while making less of an impact on resources (often referred to simply as 'decoupling')" and "to limit the increase in overall demand" requiring "nothing less than a revolution in the way we use natural resources." One of the strategic state roles might be to "create incentives for social and environmental transformation of

BOX F

Future Global Socioeconomic Transformations

- An integrated global economy functioning as a holistic entity will spur deep reframing of global governance;
- IT and communications revolution connecting billions of people to rapidly expanding volumes of data will evolve into a meta web that will change social standards and human behaviour patterns;
- A completely new balance of political, economic, and military power will shift "centres of gravity" from West to East, from North to South, and from nation-states to private actors;
- A radically new relationship between the aggregate powers of human civilization and the Earth's ecological systems on which humankind depends will force us to develop new patterns of production, trade, and consumer standards;
- A revolutionary new set of powerful biological, biochemical, genetic, and material science technologies, synthetic biology and human enhancement, will advance human capacities to—and possibly beyond—the limits of the traditional definitions of humanity.

Source: A. Likhotal, New Paradigm Quest. http://www.worldacademy.org/files/almaty_2014/New_Paradigm_Quest_A.Likhotal.pdf. 2015 (40).

business models adopting legal frameworks that make sustainability as strategic for business as customers and profits."

While the Sustainable Development Goals identify numerous goals and many more targets, Professor Likhotal places greatest priority on closing "the nexus between energy, health, food, education and water" by 2025. His arguments are rooted in two main assessments. One is that, according to the UN Food and Agriculture Organization, by 2025, it is estimated "1.8 billion people will be living in regions stricken with absolute water scarcity," and "two-thirds of the world population could be under stress conditions." In addition, the "United Nations Environment Programme (UNEP)" predicts that by then "water withdrawals will increase by 50 per cent in developing countries, and 18 per cent in developed countries."

World Issues and Transformational Change

It remains to be seen whether global responses to forces threatening the well-being of the planet and its population will be sufficient to avert global disasters. And, although many "good and workable ideas are already in the pipeline" (40), the signs are not as good as they might be. To illustrate, in an insightful article, James Rubin, assistant secretary of state for public affairs under President Bill Clinton, questions the lack of substance or resolve that came out of a recent G7 leaders' meeting in Bavaria, Germany (41). His main point is that despite "the explosion of instability and chaos" affecting major parts of the world, rather than "leadership to force debate and action," the outcome of the summit meeting was "just the opposite as self-satisfied governments touted the things they were already doing," and "no leader saw fit to push for any new steps." This lack of resolve led the author to question "whether the entire edifice of international security institutions, from the UN security council down, is overwhelmed" and "simply too weak." Trying to find a reason for their shortcomings, he opined that "they simply just don't have the capacity or the tools to deal with the multiple crises and the pervasive chaos and instability now plaguing so many parts of north Africa, eastern Europe, the Middle East and South Asia." Most fundamentally, he raised "the most cutting-edge question in international affairs these days," that is, "whether we face 'a crisis of international institutions.' " Alternatively, the G7 reticence may simply be that the "western publics want to stay out of long, messy international conflicts," and are therefore taking a "practical and cautious approach."

While his analysis is useful in presenting counter arguments behind the malaise of G7 decision making other than elections, he offers few alternatives for actually addressing the key issues facing the world. In fact, it is possible that the post-2015 Sustainable Development Goals will become "more and more side-lined by the multiplying economic, social and geopolitical problems" (40) including, most recently, the Council of Councils report card on international cooperation (42), referenced in Chapter 7, and the World Economic Forum *Global Risk 2015* report (43), with input from a panel of 900 worldwide business, governmental, and academic leaders. The latter report "for the first time listed interstate conflict in the top five list of risks in terms of likelihood . . . and put it at number one," followed by climate change, failure of national governance, state collapse or crisis, and high structural unemployment or underemployment.

Both reports demand urgent attention. Doing nothing or very little just to keep "the ship afloat," using a popular analogy, may not stop it from "taking on more water" and, unless more concerted and robust action is taken, may not keep it from sinking.

"THE CLOCK TICKS NOW AT JUST THREE MINUTES TO MIDNIGHT"

The authors of *The Bulletin of the Atomic Scientists* have reset the Doomsday Clock to 3 minutes to midnight as "unchecked climate change, global nuclear weapons modernizations, and outsized nuclear weapons arsenals pose extraordinary and undeniable threats to the continued existence of humanity, and world leaders have failed to act with the speed or on the scale required to protect citizens from potential catastrophe. These failures of political leadership endanger every person on Earth" (44). Since 1991, the clock has moved from "17 minutes to midnight" when the Cold War was officially over and when the United States and Russia began to make deep cuts to their nuclear arsenals to just a few minutes before catastrophe. The present environmental trends— rises in sea levels, atmospheric carbon dioxide, global temperature differences, and decreases in arctic sea level (44)—have added to the global conundrum.

For Professor Likhotal, there is only one choice: "between a perfect storm of progressively deepening set of crises or expanding perspectives of unprecedented opportunities" (45). The G7 meeting, along with UN vacillations on a number of high-profile issues (e.g., the Middle East, the Ukraine, migration), may contribute much more to the former than the latter, potentially leading to "a path to a systemic disaster of existential proportions." Transformational change that is beyond "rhetoric and political grandstanding" and "very powerful vested interests" is now a matter of considerable urgency.

To have any possibility of making a positive difference to the planet and its people, it now appears indisputable that world leaders need to be guided by two key priorities that drive all others: The first, as Dr. Likhotal emphasizes, calls for "adopting a truly holistic approach . . . linking areas previously considered unrelated such as energy and jobs, water and sanitation and healthcare, rural development and security, governance and development." Taking an integrated stance, he posits, "not only takes into account the interests of short-term growth, but provides the opportunity for sustainable and inclusive prosperity" (45). The second priority demands "a 'new humanism' . . . that reconciles the global and the local, and teaches us anew how to build the world" (27), reiterating UNESCO's Director General Irina Bokova's reflections on the world situation.

It is clear that the visions of these sage observers of the world we inhabit and attainment of a more desirable future are mutually inclusive. The past and present consistently demonstrate that economic prosperity for the few, which is not grounded in ethics and in social and economic responsibility, undermines "peace, democracy, justice and human rights" (27).

Time is not on our side, however, as the World Economic Forum *Global Risks 2015* report (43) concludes: "We're at the crossroads for humanity. It could be our best century but it could be our worst because our capabilities of spreading risk are greater than ever before." Scientists writing in the journal *Science Advances* (46) have warned that our planet "has entered its sixth 'mass extinction' phase with species—'essentially the walking dead'—disappearing up to about 100 times faster than the normal rate between mass extinctions." The main reason the scientists give is simple: "Humans have created a 'toxic mix' of habitat loss, pollution, and climate change."

Cornerstones for a better world must, therefore, reverse current trends and place the health and well-being of the planet and its people at the top of national and global socio-economic and geopolitical agendas. Echoing arguments rehearsed in Chapter 7.0, Dr. Likhotal asserts that "Actualizing the transformational change" will require "true political leadership, prophetic vision and courage, as well as a revitalized multilateral governance architecture adequate to meeting the interconnected challenges of the 21st century" (40). The changes that need to be made in the next few decades are profound, and perhaps the authors of a development report from India (47) say it best, affirming that there is a fundamental need to refashion our institutional systems and transform our current attitudes to virtually all aspects of society and the economy. This implies that the poorest and marginalized are put at the center of economic and social attention and the restoration and regeneration of natural systems become the boundary conditions that must not be transgressed, not just for future generations but also for those of today.

TRANSCENDING A "FUTURE BY INERTIA"

So, we may well ask "'what's holding us back, as a species" (22,48) from making these important global life-sustaining adjustments or decisions? In this regard, J. D. Moyer, music producer and writer, cofounder of Loöq Records in California, makes several insightful comments in his blogs that focus on "extended exploration of *how to live well*, both as individuals and collectively as a continually evolving species and systems for living well."

Being "cautiously optimistic about the future of humanity," he traces the main conflicts in making progress to two schools of thought: the Libertarian Space-Men versus the Gaia Collective (48). While the former are personified by such characteristics as "scientific research, technological innovation . . . economic expansion and growth," the latter adhere to principles related to economic justice, environmental sustainability, and an end to poverty, to name several goals. And, although the two have differing priorities, the author acknowledges that "both groups essentially have a 'realistic utopian perspective'" and "strive for a better future for humanity." His best-case future scenario for our species "includes strong influence from *both* groups."

The biggest problem, however, he sees, is that "most people, organizations, and institutions are a member of *neither* group, and don't care to think carefully and act intentionally in regards to the future of our species, planet, and global civilization" (48). As a result, he says, "we get future-by-inertia." And, rather than "an intentional future for our species and planetary civilization, we get a future that is a mash-up of special interest group squabbles, an extrapolation of existing trends, and rule by the lowest common denominator," which "might result in a 100 year dark age (or even worse, fascism, or global systemic collapse)."

What really scares him about a "future-by-inertia" is "a future created by powerful entities that don't think clearly about the global future *at all* (religious fundamentalists, profit-obsessed corporations, oligarchs, rabid nationalists, billionaire hedonists, etc.)." In his view, "putting us at risk for a great leap backwards" would be *"corporatism"*—"unchecked corporate power and amoral profiteering" (49,50).

These sentiments are reflected in Pope Francis's recent extraordinary encyclical on the environment (51). The pontiff does not mince his words: "The Earth, our home, is beginning to look more and more like an immense pile of filth. In many parts of the planet, the elderly lament that once beautiful landscapes are now covered with rubbish." For the Pope the "problems of environmental degradation and global poverty" are interrelated and reflect "a way of thinking that regards the world as a means, rather than an end." Clearly this thinking, or the "idea of infinite or unlimited growth, which proves so attractive to economists, financiers and experts in technology" cannot continue, as, according to the Pope, it is "based on the lie that there is an infinite supply of the earth's goods, and this leads to the planet being squeezed dry beyond every limit."

His incisive words bring to mind the last few lines of Percy Bysshe Shelley's 19th-century poem, *Ozymandius* (52), which may hold lessons for us all. The English poet reminds us that the "empires" we build are transient—they rise, peak, decline, and collapse. In the final analysis, ensuring "a future in which the children of the world of all colours, faith and races, can live together in grace and peace" (53) and where "we have a shared responsibility for others and the world" (51) are the only things that truly matter—reflections that global decision makers and world leaders might especially need to take to heart in this century.

> My name is Ozymandias, king of kings:
> Look on my works, ye Mighty, and despair!'
> Nothing beside remains. Round the decay
> Of that colossal wreck, boundless and bare
> The lone and level sands stretch far away."
>
> — Percy Bysshe Shelley, 1818

FIGURE D The pale blue dot.

A photograph of planet Earth taken on February 14, 1990, by the Voyager 1 space probe from a record distance of about 6 billion kilometers, as part of the NASA Family Portrait series of images of the solar system (54).

"Our planet is a lonely speck in the great enveloping cosmic dark. In our obscurity, in all this vastness, there is no hint that help will come from elsewhere to save us from ourselves."

—*Pale Blue Dot: A Vision of the Human Future in Space,* by Professor Carl Sagan (1934–1999)

REFERENCES

1. Lueddeke G. *Transforming medical education for the 21st century: Megatrends, priorities and change.* London: Radcliffe Publishing Ltd.; 2012.
2. Blodget H. What Kills us: The Leading Causes of Death From 1900–2010. Weblog. http://www.businessinsider.com/leading-causes-of-death-from-1900-2010-2012-6?op=1&IR=T. Accessed July 30, 2012.
3. Laverack G. *Survey on 'top (not disease) public health challenges of the future.'* Linked-In. https://www.linkedin.com/groups/What-are-your-top-not-120372.S.5853221710899220480?trk=groups_search_item_list-0-b-ttl
4. OECD. *Health at a glance 2013: OECD indicators.* Life expectancy at birth and health spending per capita, 2011 (or nearest year). http://www.oecd.org/els/health-systems/Health-at-a-Glance-2013-Chart-set.pdf. Accessed June 20, 2015.
5. Horton R, Beaglehole R, Bonita R, Raeburn J, McKee M, Wall S. From public to planetary health: A manifesto. *Lancet.* 2014;383(9920):847. http://www.thelancet.com/journals/lancet/article/PIIS0140-6736(14)60409-8/fulltext. Accessed May 18, 2014.
6. United Nations. *Transforming Our World: The 2030 Agenda for Sustainable Development.* https://sustainabledevelopment.un.org/post2015/transformingourworld. Accessed August 27, 2015.
7. Earth Charter International. *What is the Earth charter?* http://www.earthcharterinaction.org/content/pages/What-is-the-Earth-Charter%3F.html. Accessed June 20, 2014.

8. United Nations. The world we want 2015. http://www.worldwewant2015.org/. Accessed April 20, 2014.

9. United Nations. The World Children Want: Summary of e-Consultation With Children. http://www.worldwewant2015.org/node/464212. Accessed November 10, 2014.

10. Dominiczak P. Britain is facing the greatest terror threat of its history, warns the Home Secretary. *The Daily Telegraph.* p. 4. November 24, 2014. http://www.telegraph.co.uk/news/uknews/terrorism-in-the-uk/11249614/Theresa-May-Britain-is-facing-greatest-terror-threat-of-its-history.html. Accessed November 26, 2014.

11. Nicks D. Pope Francis: New year's message–"What is happening in the heart of humanity?" http://beforeitsnews.com/2012/2014/01/pope-francis-new-years-message-what-is-happening-in-the-heart-of-humanity-2448652.html. Accessed January 10, 2014.

12. Pearson R. A moment for meditation. *The Telegraph.* http://www.telegraph.co.uk/news/predictions/body-and-soul/11308040/healthy-mind-meditation.html. Accessed December 31, 2014.

13. Greenland S. The inner kids program. http://www.susankaisergreenland.com/inner-kids-program.html. Accessed October 15, 2014.

14. Mindfulness in Schools Project.Curricula. https://mindfulnessinschools.org/what-is-b/b-curriculum/. Accessed March 24, 2015.

15. Pearson R. The meaning of mindfulness. http://www.thebestbrainpossible.com/the-meaning-of-mindfulness-2/. Accessed September 20, 2014.

16. The Telegraph. Belfast schoolgirl Hannah Nelson upstages Barack Obama. http://www.telegraph.co.uk/news/worldnews/g8/10124626/Belfast-schoolgirl-Hannah-Nelson-upstages-Barack-Obama.html. Accessed June 20, 2013.

17. Thomson A. We may be Charlie but our children are not. *The Times.* January 14, 2015: 27.

18. Day I. Generation snapchat bins the American dream. *The Sunday Times.* January 25, 2015: 33.

19. Martin I. Does Davos ever make a difference? *The Daily Telegraph.* January 19, 2015:19.

20. The White House. Remarks by President Obama and Mrs. Obama in Town Hall with Youth of Northern Ireland. https://www.whitehouse.gov/the-press-office/2013/06/17/remarks-president-obama-and-mrs-obama-town-hall-youth-northern-ireland. Accessed June 23, 2013.

21. Hider J. Record drought seeps across the Americas. *The Times.* February 17, 2015: 35.

22. Unicef. *Education under fire: How conflict in the Middle East is depriving children of their schooling.* http://www.unicef.org/mena/Education-Under-Fire-English.pdf. Accessed September 5, 2015.

23. Aaronovitch D. We must rediscover the humanity of 1945. *The Times*, p. 25. September 3, 2015.

24. United Nations Security Council. The Security Council. http://www.un.org/en/sc/. Accessed 20 June, 2014.

25. Ki-Moon Ban. Big ideas 2015: Sustainability is common sense (blog). https://www.linkedin.com/pulse/big-idea-2015-sustainability-ban-ki-moon. Accessed January 15, 2014.

26. Clemente L. F. Party system stability in Latin America: A comparative study. https://books.google.co.uk/books?id=2y-GGOOC5jMC&printsec=frontcover#v=onepage&q&f=false. Accessed March 20, 2013.

27. UNESCO. UNESCO general conference: Irina Bokova sworn in as director-general. http://www.unesco.org/new/en/unesco/about-us/who-we-are/director-general/singleview-dg/news/unesco_general_conference_irina_bokova_sworn_in_as_director_general/#.VX8Rx_lViko. Accessed November 19, 2009.

28. MercyCorps. Quick facts: What you need to know about the Syria crisis. https://www.mercycorps.org.uk/articles/turkey-iraq-jordan-lebanon-syria/quick-facts-what-you-need-know-about-syria-crisis. Accessed May 25, 2015.

29. BBC News. Syria war: 'Chlorine' attack video moves UN to tears. http://www.bbc.co.uk/news/world-middle-east-32346790. Accessed April 17, 2015.

30. Keen A. The march of the robots. *The Sunday Times.* February 22, 2015: Section 4, p. 1.

31. Brynjolfsson E, McAfee A. *The second machine age: Work, progress, and prosperity in a time of brilliant technologies*. New York, NY: WW Norton & Company; 2014.

32. Lynn M. The Internet hasn't boosted productivity, but robots will. *The Daily Telegraph.* February 24, 2015: B1.

33. Appleyard, B. The new Luddites: Why former digital prophets are turning against tech. *The New Statesman.* September 20, 2014. http://www.newstatesman.com/sci-tech/2014/08/new-luddites-why-former-digital-prophets-are-turning-against-tech. Accessed September 28, 2014.

34. BBC News. Stephen Hawking warns artificial intelligence could end mankind. http://www.bbc.co.uk/news/technology-30290540. Accessed December 5, 2014.

35. Marlar J, Mendes E. Globally, men twice as likely as women to have a good job. http://www.gallup.com/poll/164666/globally-men-twice-likely-women-good-job.aspx. Accessed September 30, 2013.

36. Soubbotina TP, Sheram KA. *Beyond Economic Growth: Meeting the Challenges of Global Development* (p. 16). New York, NY: The World Bank, 2000. www.worldbank.org/depweb/beyond/beyond.htm. Accessed November 20, 2013.

37. Lewis L. Beware the rise of the robots or you'll rage against the machines. http://www.thetimes.co.uk/tto/business/columnists/leolewis/article4404421.ece. Accessed April 30, 2015.

38. McDermott J. Here come the robots. http://www.afr.com/technology/here-come-the-robots-20140501-iwug6. Accessed May 25, 2014.

39. Arauco VP, Gazdar H, Hevia-Pacheco P, et al. *Strengthening social justice to address intersecting inequalities.* http://www.odi.org/sites/odi.org.uk/files/odi-assets/publications-opinion-files/9213.pdf. Accessed October 15, 2014.

40. Likhotal A. New paradigm quest. http://cadmusjournal.org/node/458. Accessed June 4, 2015.

41. Rubin J. As the world goes up in smoke, G7 leaders swing into inaction. *The Sunday Times.* June 6, 2015, Comment p. 17.

42. Council of Councils. Council of Councils report card on international cooperation launch. http://www.cfr.org/councilofcouncils/videos/p36577. Accessed May 15, 2015.

43. World Economic Forum. *The Global Risks report 2015.* http://www.weforum.org/reports/global-risks-report-2015. Accessed May 20, 2015.

44. The Bulletin of the Atomic Scientists. *Timeline.* http://thebulletin.org/timeline. Accessed June 18, 2015.

45. The Climate Change Task Force. Alexander Likhotal. Intel. affairs expert "Address at the 15th Dehli Sustainable Development Summit–part 3." (February 15, 2015). http://www.climatechangetaskforce.org/blog/blog-view.php?Id=279. Accessed 20 February, 2015.

46. Ceballos G, Ehrlich PR, Barnosky, AD, et al. Accelerated modern human–induced species losses: Entering the sixth mass extinction. http://advances.sciencemag.org/content/1/5/e1400253. Accessed May 20, 2015.

47. Development Alternatives. To choose our future. https://www.dropbox.com/s/hf1mxsjacejn-brx/The%20DA%20Book.pdf?dl=0. Accessed May 28, 2015.

48. Moyer JD. What's holding us back, as a species? (Part I–Fight for the future). http://jdmoyer.com/2012/04/30/whats-holding-us-back-as-a-species-part-i-fight-for-thefuture. Accessed May 20, 2015.

49. Moyer JD. What's holding us back as a species? (Part II–Unpacking assumptions). http://jdmoyer.com/?s=What%E2%80%99s+Holding+Us+Back+as+a+Species%3F. Accessed June 4, 2015.

50. Moyer JD. 100-Year trends. http://jdmoyer.com/100-year-trends/. Accessed June 4, 2015.

51. The Vatican. Encyclical letter *Laudato Si'* of the Holy Father Francis on Care for our Common Home. http://w2.vatican.va/content/dam/francesco/pdf/encyclicals/documents/papa-francesco_20150524_enciclica-laudato-si_en.pdf. Accessed June 21, 2015.

52. The Literature Network. *Ozymandias.* http://www.online-literature.com/shelley_percy/672/. Accessed December 31, 2014.

53. Sachs J. Rabbi Lord Sacks: How to end the wars of hatred. http://www.telegraph.co.uk/news/religion/11665931/Rabbi-Lord-Sacks-How-to-end-the-wars-of-hatred.html. Accessed June 15, 2015.

54. NASA. Voyager celebrates 20-year-old valentine to solar system. http://www.jpl.nasa.gov/news/news.php?release=2010-048. Accessed March 15, 2010.

Appendix A

Profiles of Leading Health Organizations and Schools/Institutes of Public Health

INTRODUCTION

Worldwide, the number of health organizations are many and varied in terms of background, mission, values, aims, achievements, and strategic priorities. Most are located in developed nations. The main aim of these profiles is threefold: to raise awareness about their purpose and scope of activities, to identify common strategies, and to spot potential gaps in light of changing health/social care environments in developed and developing nations.

Appendix A1 provides brief profiles of 50 leading health organizations and associations that were selected based on two main criteria: (a) representative of global (n = 22[44%]); regional (n = 10[20%]); and national health organizations (n = 18[38%]); and (b) associations that differed in terms of principal remits: public health (n = 19[38%]); general health (human/animal) (n = 22[44%]); education/workforce development (n = 6[12%]); regulatory (n = 3[6%]). Given space constraints, aside from WHO no attempt was made to profile other multilateral and subsidiary agencies, bilateral agencies (e.g., United States Agency for International Development [USAID]), nongovernmental organizations (e.g., Project Hope, Oxfam), or additional donor organizations (e.g., Bill & Melinda Gates Foundation, International Medical Volunteers Association [www.imva.org/Pages/orgfrm.htm]).

The 15 schools and institutes of public health in Appendix A2 were selected mainly on the basis of recognized innovation in the field of public health.

There is no question that many other organizations could have been added to both profile listings but have been omitted owing to space constraints.

APPENDIX A1: PROFILES OF LEADING GLOBAL, REGIONAL, AND NATIONAL HEALTH ORGANIZATIONS

1. African Federation of Public Health Associations (AFPHA)
2. African Health Profession Regulatory Collaborative for Nurses and Midwives (ARC)
3. American College of Preventive Medicine (ACPM)
4. American Public Health Association (APHA)
5. American Veterinarian Medical Association (AVMA)
6. Asia Pacific Academic Consortium for Public Health (APACPH)
7. Association for the Study of Medical Education (ASME)
8. Association of Schools and Programs of Public Health (ASPPH)
9. Association of Schools of Public Health in the European Region (ASPHER)
10. Canadian Public Health Association (CPHA)
11. China Medical Board (CMB)
12. Chinese Preventive Medicine Association (CPMA)
13. Consortium of Universities for Global Health (CUGH)
14. Council on Linkages Between Academia and Public Health Practice (CLAPHP)
15. Euclid Consortium of Universities
16. European Association of Dental Public Health (EADPH)
17. European Public Health Alliance (EPHA)
18. European Public Health Association (EUPHA)
19. Faculty of Public Health (FPH[UK])
20. Foundation for Advancement of International Medical Education and Research (FAIMER®)
21. General Medical Council (GMC[UK])
22. Global Health Council (GHC)
23. Global Health Workforce Alliance (GHWA)
24. ICAP and the Nursing Educational Partnership Initiative (NEPI)
25. India Public Health Association (IPHA)
26. Institute of Medicine (IOM, U.S.)
27. International Association of National Public Health Institutes (IANPHI)
28. International Council of Nurses (ICN)
29. International Federation of Dental Educators and Associations (IFDEA)
30. International Union for Health Promotion and Education (IUHPE)
31. IntraHealth International (IHI)
32. Josiah Macy Jr. Foundation (JMJF)
33. One Health Commission (OHC)
34. One Health Initiative Movement (OHIM)
35. Open Society for Foundations (OSF)
36. Pan American Health Organization/WHO (PAHO/WHO)
37. People's Health Movement (PHM)
38. Public Health Association of Australia (PHAA)
39. Public Health Association of South Africa (PHASA)
40. Public Health England (PHE)
41. Public Health Foundation of India (PHFI)

42. Towards Unity for Health (TUFH)
43. United Nations Educational, Scientific and Cultural Organization (UNESCO)
44. World Bank (WB)
45. World Federation for Medical Education (WFME)
46. World Federation of Public Health Associations (WFPHA)
47. World Health Organization (WHO)
48. World Health Professions Alliance (WHPA)
49. World Health Summit (WHS)
50. World Organization of Family Doctors (WONCA)

1. African Federation of Public Health Associations (AFPHA)

Background

AFPHA is a nonprofit association composed of national associations of public health in Africa whose activities contribute to the strengthening of public health in the continent. Thirty-three years after the Alma-Ata Declaration of "Health for All" (HFA) by 2000, Africa and the world are still grappling with how to realize the primary health care (PHC) aspirations. Public health associations could be essential players to create the critical mass that would engage youth, women, leaders, administrators, policy makers, researchers, trainers, academicians, educators, practitioners, community members, and development partners, among others, to contribute to the realization of "Health for All"—Equity in Health.

Vision

The vision of the Federation is to work toward promoting public health policies, strategies, and practices in Africa and globally, through impacting on country action plans, and toward the attainment of the highest level of health for all African people.

Mission

The mission of the FPHA is to strive toward the improvement of the health of African populations. The Federation plans to help identify the best approaches to design better performing national health systems and to assist in their implementation.

To achieve these objectives FPHA will consider that:

- The equal access of all to health care is a requirement of social justice.
- Good governance and transparent accounts are a requirement.
- Confidence and community involvement constitute a necessity.
- Social and economic well-being is not possible without the involvement of the beneficiaries.

Values

Acknowledging that no social and economic welfare can be possible without responsible involvement of its vision, AFPHA's value is to create a stage where all African populations are healthy and productive and are found in optimal physical, mental, and intellectual conditions to actively participate in social and economic development, where each individual enjoys the opportunity to access quality services.

Achievements (in the Last 3 Years)

The accreditation of AFPHA by the Ethiopian Federal Ministry of Foreign Affairs is in its final phase. Minister of Foreign Affairs Dr. Tewodros Adhanom has approved the legal registration of the Federation in Addis Ababa, Ethiopia.

The Federation has established contacts with the WHO, the African Union, and other regional institutions.

Priorities

- Enhance the visibility and the credibility of the Federation
- Create the basis for the development and spread of the public health associations

Contact Information

President: Dr. Mathias Some (Burkina Faso)
Vice president: Dr. Flavia Senkubuge (South Africa)
Executive Director: Dr. Tewabech Bishaw (Ethiopia)

c/o Dr. Tewabech Bishaw, Secretary General, African Federation of Public Health Associations, Ethiopia
Ethiopian Public Health Association
Kirkos Sub City, P. O. Box: 7117, Ethiopia
Tel: +251-1- 416 60 83 / 41 / 88
Fax: +251-1- 416 60 86
E-mail: info@afphas.org
Permanent staff: bishawtewabech@yahoo.com

2. African Health Profession Regulatory Collaborative for Nurses and Midwives (ARC)

Strengthening Nursing and Midwifery Regulation and Standards Through South-to-South Collaboration

Background

To help achieve the vision of an AIDS-free generation, the U.S. President's Emergency Plan for AIDS Relief (PEPFAR) is working to strengthen the African health workforce—an essential element of expanding HIV care and treatment services. Accordingly, since 2011, PEPFAR and CDC have supported a regional health workforce initiative in sub-Saharan Africa entitled the African Health Profession Regulatory Collaborative for Nurses and Midwives or ARC. ARC is funded by CDC through PEPFAR, and is implemented in partnership with the Lillian Carter Center for Global Health & Social Responsibility at Emory University, the Commonwealth Nurses Federation, and the East, Central and Southern Africa Health Community—an intergovernmental regional coordinating body on health issues. ARC helps national nursing and midwifery leadership teams from

17 African countries identify and address regulatory bottlenecks to expanding and sustaining nurse and midwife-led models of HIV care and treatment services.

Vision/Mission/Values

ARC's vision is to strengthen national and regional nursing infrastructures by using a unique, collaborative approach that entails convening regional meetings or "Learning Sessions," providing targeted technical assistance, and awarding short-term grants that target identified professional challenges impeding PEPFAR's service delivery as well as nursing and midwifery professional development. Regional fora organized by ARC facilitate south-to-south sharing of best practices, thereby creating an environment that fosters African nursing leaders—a mission of the ARC initiative.

ARC core values include incorporating a Quality Assurance Approach, which is described below.

A Quality Assurance Approach

The ARC approach is adapted from the Institute for Healthcare Improvement (IHI) "Breakthrough Series" model for quality improvement collaboratives. (The Breakthrough Series: IHI's Collaborative Model for Achieving Breakthrough Improvement. Boston, MA: Institute for Healthcare Improvement; 2003.) The structure of IHI's quality improvement model is a series of alternating Learning Sessions and Action Periods. During the Learning Sessions, teams from participating organizations come together to learn about and discuss the chosen topic and plan changes to implement in their home institutions. During the Action Periods, the teams return to their home institutions and work together on the planned actions for change. At the conclusion of the collaborative cycle, participating organizations engage in a Summative Congress to share lessons learned and produce publications to disseminate their breakthrough improvements.

Achievements

Currently in its fourth year of activity, ARC has awarded over 35 short-term grants to nursing teams. Thus far, every country within the 17-country consortium has received a funded proposal, with several countries earning more than one award. In February 2015, the following countries were awarded Year 4 ARC grants to address the regulatory projects linked to improving prevention of mother-to-child transmission (PMTCT) and pediatric HIV care and treatment (specific focal area of the awarded activity is included within parentheses): Botswana (Scopes of Practice or SoP); Ethiopia (Continuing Professional Development or CPD); Kenya (CPD); Lesotho (HIV training); Mozambique (PMTCT Option B+); Rwanda (HIV training); Seychelles (CPD); South Africa (HIV/TB training); Tanzania (revising CPD program and national SoP); Zambia (CPD/SoP); Zimbabwe (HIV training).

Priorities for 2014–2015

The focus of this year's grant proposal is on:

- Building nursing and midwifery competency in implementing PEPFAR-supported programs, particularly those dedicated to preventing mother-to-child transmission of HIV (PMTCT B+) and improving pediatric HIV/AIDS programs

- Aligning professional pre-service and continuing education with current HIV and AIDS clinical content
- Facilitating the local regulatory environment with regard to ministry of health policies, professional licensure requirements, and nursing and midwifery scopes of practice

Other Information

The CPD Library is designed to serve as a "one stop shop" of peer-reviewed CPD offerings freely accessible to all nurses and midwives across the region. The CPD Library can be viewed at http://www.escacon.org.

Publications

A total of eight commentaries and research articles have been published since 2012, including a featured supplement of ARC accomplishments that appeared in the 2014 Spring issue of the *African Journal of Midwifery and Women's Health.*

Contact Information

Michelle Dynes, PhD, MPH, MSN, CNM
CDC/PEPFAR Technical Advisor for ARC
E-mail: mdynes@cdc.gov
and
Maureen Kelly, CNM
E-mail: makelle@emory.edu

3. American College of Preventive Medicine (ACPM)

Background

The ACPM is the national professional society for physicians committed to disease prevention and health promotion. ACPM was established in 1954. Its 2,500 members are engaged in preventive medicine practice, teaching, and research.

Mission

As the leader for the specialty of preventive medicine and physicians dedicated to prevention, the ACPM improves the health of individuals and populations through evidence-based health promotion, disease prevention, and systems-based approaches to improving health and health care.

Priorities

1. Promote the specialty of preventive medicine and preventive medicine physicians to assure an appropriate supply and demand of properly trained physicians to deliver effective and efficient health and health care.
2. Promote the advancement of scientific knowledge in preventive medicine and establish ACPM as the recognized leader for professional, multi-disciplinary, and public education, as well as collaboration and communication, in the areas of preventive medicine and public health.

3. Enhance member value by serving as the primary source for members to meet their professional needs, including but not limited to continuing medical education (CME), maintenance of certification (MOC), maintenance of licensure (MOL), career development, and practice tools.
4. Maintain and enhance the institutional stature and credibility of ACPM, professionally, financially, and politically, in order to maximally achieve its mission and goals.

Scope of Activities

ACPM plans and implements preventive medicine education programs on a wide range of topics, including ACPM's annual Preventive Medicine conference and Preventive Medicine Board Review Courses. Many more physicians access ACPM educational programs online via its e-portal education library, live and archived webinars, and web-hosted journal articles and practice tools. In addition, ACPM develops clinical and population-based practice guidelines consistent with the scientific principles of preventive medicine; carries out preventive medicine public policy activities such as analyzing and responding to regulations and legislation related to preventive medicine; educates public policy makers about preventive medicine and public health; facilitates the appointment of preventive medicine physicians to federal advisory committees, panels, and task forces; provides support and technical assistance to graduate medical education (GME) programs in preventive medicine; and co-sponsors the preeminent, peer-reviewed, scientific journal in preventive medicine, the *American Journal of Preventive Medicine*.

Preventive Medicine Annual Meeting

The Preventive Medicine annual meeting series is the preeminent conference for preventive medicine professionals. ACPM established the Preventive Medicine conference series to address the research, educational, and networking needs of those engaged in the practice of preventive medicine. Through the Preventive Medicine annual meeting series, ACPM provides a national conference that reaches more than 700 physicians and health professionals.

ACPM Newsletter

ACPM Headlines, the electronic newsletter for members of the ACPM, highlights recent happenings at the College, developments in preventive medicine, and ACPM member activities.

Contact Information

455 Massachusetts Avenue NW
Suite 200
Washington, DC 20001
Tel.: +1 202 466 2044
Fax: +1 202 466-2662
E-mail: info@acpm.org
Website: www.acpm.org

4. American Public Health Association (APHA)

Background

The APHA is a community of people and organizations interested in public health. Founded in 1872 by Dr. Stephen Smith, the Association champions the health of all people and all communities; strengthens the profession of public health; creates understanding, engagement, and support for key public health issues; and is the only organization that directly influences federal policy to improve public health. As the nation's leading public health organization, APHA is evidence based and speaks out for public health issues and policies backed by science. In addition to APHA's 25,000 individual members, the organization represents another 25,000 individuals and organizations who are members of affiliated state and regional public health associations.

- **Vision:** To create the healthiest nation in one generation
- **Mission:** To improve the health of the public and achieve equity in health status
- **Values:** Community, science and evidence-based decision making, health equity, prevention and wellness, and real progress in improving health

APHA publishes the field's most prestigious journal, the *American Journal of Public Health*, and the nation's most important public health newspaper, *The Nation's Health*. It also leads important national public awareness campaigns such as Get Ready, which encourages people to prepare for emergencies, and National Public Health Week, our nation's celebration of public health advances.

APHA is the largest national voice for public health advocacy. Its advocacy activities are guided by three overarching priority areas: building public health infrastructure and capacity, ensuring the right to health and health care, and creating health equity. Its 2014 legislative priorities include appropriations and funding for federal agencies that promote health, such as the U.S. Centers for Disease Control and Prevention, the Environmental Protection Agency, and the Health Resources and Services Administration; protecting the Affordable Care Act, particularly its Prevention and Public Health Fund; improving violence prevention; and promoting programs that address the social determinants of health.

APHA's Annual Meeting & Exposition serves as the home for public health professionals to convene, learn, network, and engage with peers. Each year, over 12,000 participants from across the United States and around the world convene to strengthen the profession of public health, share the latest research and information, promote best practices, and advocate for public health issues and policies grounded in research.

APHA publishes a monthly e-newsletter called *Inside Public Health* that communicates important activities and announcements to Association members. It also publishes *Public Health Newswire*, a leading source of news covering public health events, trends, and advocacy.

Contact Information

American Public Health Association
800 I St., NW
Washington, DC 20001
Tel.: +1 202 777 2742
E-mail: comments@apha.org
Website: www.apha.org

5. American Veterinarian Medical Association (AVMA)

Background

AVMA, founded in 1863, is one of the oldest and largest veterinary medical organizations in the world, with more than 85,000 member veterinarians worldwide engaged in a wide variety of professional activities and dedicated to the art and science of veterinary medicine.

Vision

AVMA's vision is to be the trusted leader protecting, promoting, and advancing a strong, unified veterinary profession that meets the needs of society.

Mission

AVMA's mission is to lead the profession by advocating for our members and advancing the science and practice of veterinary medicine to improve animal and human health.

Values

- Integrity: We act honestly and respectfully.
- Inclusiveness: We represent a diverse community of veterinarians with unique perspectives.
- Science based: We lead with science, providing trusted and evidence-based information.
- Animal focused: We support veterinarians in their stewardship of animal health and welfare and their role in promoting public health.
- Member focused: We seek input from and respond to the needs of our members.
- People: We invest in the development and support of our staff and volunteer leaders.
- Fiscal responsibility: We practice prudent financial decision making and accountability.
- Innovative culture: We advance through creativity and efficient processes to implement new ideas.

Achievements

- Successfully lobbied for the passage of the Veterinary Medicine Mobility Act, making it legal for veterinarians to provide complete medical care to their patients beyond their clinics and across state lines.
- Completed a workforce model and Economic Summit, providing an overview of the markets that affect veterinary medicine and educating the profession on factors that influence demand for their services, compensation, and employment rates.
- Launched award-winning Animal Welfare Hub that provides easy access to the AVMA's animal welfare policies, guidelines, literature reviews, and other trusted resources. It also includes a new discussion forum for AVMA and student AVMA members to exchange ideas on animal welfare-related issues.
- Launched Animal Connections: Our Journey Together, a traveling museum exhibit that emphasizes the rewarding connection between animals and humans and to promote the veterinary profession.
- AVMA has a leadership role in Partners for Healthy Pets, a collaboration of over 110 animal health organizations focused on promoting preventive care for dogs and cats. The mission is to ensure pets receive the preventive care they deserve through regular visits to a veterinarian.

Priorities 2015 and Beyond

- Advocacy efforts: Act on input from members to anticipate, identify, and address issues that could foster or inhibit their ability to provide crucial veterinary services in public, private, or corporate practice.
- Enhance the public image and reputation of veterinarians: Increase awareness of the important contributions veterinarians in all segments of the profession make to society.
- Provide valuable member products and services: Advance the knowledge and skills of veterinary professionals and improve the efficiency and effectiveness of member services.

Annual Conferences

- Annual AVMA Convention; July 10–14, 2015; Boston, MA

Newsletter/Key Publications

- *Journal of the American Veterinary Medical Association* (JAVMA)
- *American Journal of Veterinary Research* (AJVR)
- Monthly e-newsletter: *AVMA@Work*

Contact Information

Website: www.avma.org

6. Asia Pacific Academic Consortium for Public Health (APACPH)

Background

APACPH is an international nonprofit organization, comprising many of the largest and most influential schools of public health in the Asia Pacific region and dedicated to improving professional education for public health. It was launched in 1984 with just five members; APACPH now has over 81 member institutions in 23 countries throughout the Asia Pacific region, with regional offices in Bangkok, Beijing, Melbourne, California, Hawaii, Malaysia, and Tokyo. Through its activities, the members aim to tackle the unique public health challenges of the Asia Pacific region, for example, specific health issues of workers within the growing economies of the region.

Vision

To achieve the highest possible level of health of all the people of the nations of the Asia Pacific region.

Mission

To enhance regional capacity to improve the quality of life and to address major public health challenges through the delivery of education, research, and population health services by member institutions. APACPH has emphasized meeting the needs of health of disadvantaged people in the Asia Pacific region.

Objectives

APACPH encourages and supports the achievement of the following objectives through its member institutions:

1. To enhance the quality and relevance of educational and training programs in public health
2. To expand knowledge, improve skills, and demonstrate effective interventions
3. To raise awareness of current, emerging, and re-emerging public health issues and develop programs of action for their resolution
4. To enhance the capacity and sustainability of public health systems
5. To assist in policy and leadership development for health

Activities

- Holding an annual conference
- Publishing the *Asia Pacific Journal of Public Health*
- Running the International Cyber University for Health within APAPH and APACPH Young Carrier Network
- Cooperating with collaboration centers and hosting forums and workshops with member institutions

Contact Information

Website: www.apacph.org/wp

7. Association for the Study of Medical Education (ASME)

Background

ASME is unique in that it draws its members from all areas of medical education—undergraduate, postgraduate, and continuing—and from all specialties. It has a function as a forum for debate and exchange of information, and is building on its contacts in medicine and teaching in the UK, and among other networks, to promote knowledge and expertise in medical education.

Mission

To meet the needs of teachers, trainers, and learners in medical education by supporting research-informed best practice across the continuum of medical education.

Strategic Aim

To allow members to share and further best practice in medical education.

Values

- Education and learning are central to the delivery of high quality health care.
- Education must be an important component in the strategies of governmental and other health care organizations.
- Good health care educators are central in planning, delivering, and evaluating high quality health care.
- Individual members of ASME should be supported and developed.
- High quality research is necessary for the development of health care education.
- Vision, innovation, and leadership in health care education are to be fostered.

Goals

- Promote high quality research into medical education
- Provide opportunities for developing medical educators
- Disseminate good evidence-based educational practice
- Inform and advise governmental and other organizations on medical education matters
- Develop relationships with other organizations and groupings in health care education

What Does ASME Provide?

CPD, education and training, leadership development, research knowledge, skills and networks

Publications and Resources

ASME produces, in collaboration with Wiley, the journals *Medical Education* and *The Clinical Teacher*. We also offer a range of online resources to members.

Conferences

Annual scientific meeting/other

Contact Information

Nicky Pender, Chief Executive Officer
12 Queen Street
Edinburgh, EH2 1JE
Direct dial: +44 (0) 131 225 9133
E-mail: nicky@asme.org.uk
Website: www.asme.org.uk

8. Association of Schools and Programs of Public Health (ASPPH)

Background

ASPPH is the voice of Council on Education for Public Health (CEPH)-accredited public health education. ASPPH is committed to representing member schools and programs accredited by CEPH.

ASPPH strengthens public health schools and programs and improves global health by:

- Fostering quality education and practice-based training for the next generation of public health workers
- Promoting public health as a career option
- Monitoring trends relevant to public health education
- Facilitating collaborations across schools and programs
- Developing partnerships across the public, private, and nonprofit sectors

Advancing public health education that meets 21st-century demands is ASPPH's core mission. To ensure public health workers have the necessary knowledge, skills, and attitudes, ASPPH:

- Develops competencies and learning outcomes across the educational continuum
- Sponsors fellowships and internships that offer "real-world" practice experiences
- Promotes the Certified in Public Health (CPH) credential
- Leads *Framing the Future*, an interdisciplinary task force that is reconsidering public health education

As an advocate for the interests of academic public health, ASPPH:

- Safeguards and expands the US$1.5 billion-plus pool of federal grants and contracts to public health schools and programs for education, research, and practice
- Reviews existing and proposed federal laws and regulations and advances policy positions

Strategic partnerships power the ASPPH agenda, with collaborations across public health disciplines and the wider community of health professionals.

ASPPH is the successor to the Association of Schools of Public Health, established in 1953. In 2013, membership was expanded to include CEPH-accredited programs of public health.

Priorities

- Student recruitment
- Undergraduate CEPH-accredited public health education
- Data analysis and reports
- Digital resources
- Public health research
- Reframing public health education
- Global public health

Events

www.aspph.org/events

Contact Information

1900 M Street NW, Suite 710
Washington, DC 20036
Tel: (202) 296-1099
Fax: (202) 296-1252

9. Association of Schools of Public Health in the European Region (ASPHER)

Background

ASPHER is the key independent European organization dedicated to strengthening the role of public health by improving education and training of public health professionals for both practice and research. Founded in 1966, ASPHER has over 100 institutional members located throughout the European region of WHO. It is represented in 42 countries in Europe, with more than 5,000 academics employed in its member institutions.

Main Functions

The main functions of the Association are:

- To support the professionalization of the public health workforce in Europe, while respecting the diversity of national and regional contexts, in which each school of public health operates;
- To sustain capacity building in public health so that it balances with national and European population health challenges and threats, and is supported by best standards of public health education and training, scientific research, practice, and systems.

General Objectives

The general objectives of ASPHER are:

- To sustain, in theory and practice, member schools to achieve their missions of professional and graduate education, training, scientific research, and service
- To develop models for public health education and training at all professional and academic levels and the interaction of education and training with population health, health systems, and services
- To scrutinize and specify the competencies needed at all education and training levels and competencies necessary to carry out essential public health operations (EPHOs) corresponding to challenges in population health and in health systems
- To promote structured processes of sharing evidence-based public health models of innovation and good practice
- To build coalitions with other programs and public health organizations whose mission is to improve public health, specifically in an effort to put forth high standards and strengthen public health education and training, and to improve the quality of the public health workforce in Europe and its competitiveness globally

Participating in the Wider Public Health Movement

Though ASPHER's principal role includes the promotion of highest quality public health education/training and the highest standards of public health practice, it also assumes full participation in the wider public health movement, with direct concern for both quality of health and equity in health—in each country, across Europe, and globally—in order to achieve the goal of attaining a high level of health for all in Europe.

ASPHER is the founding member of the Agency for Public Health Education Accreditation (APHEA) consortium.

ASPHER currently also leads the work of WHO Europe in the area of EPHO 7 (workforce development) under the framework of the European Action Plan for Strengthening Public Health Services and Capacity.

The Association's two main yearly events, which provide a platform for meetings in which a greater part of its membership takes part, are: (a) the Deans' and Directors' Retreat (May); and (b) the Annual Forum at the European Public Health Conference (November).

ASPHER 2020 Strategic Objectives (Under Consultation)

1. Improving quality of academic programs and continuing professional development (CPD) for public health
2. Strengthening research capacity among members
3. Setting up a public health profession in Europe
4. Developing the global dimension of education and training for public health
5. Strengthening governance, management, and sustainable development of ASPHER

Contact Information

ASPHER Secretariat
UM Campus Brussels
10 Av de l'Armée
1040 Brussels, Belgium
Tel.: +32 2 735 0890
E-mail: office@aspher.org
President (2014–2015): Prof. Vesna Bjegovic-Mikanovic
Director: Robert Otok

10. Canadian Public Health Association (CPHA)

Founded in 1910, CPHA is the independent voice for public health in Canada with links to the international community. As the only Canadian nongovernmental organization (NGO) focused exclusively on public health, CPHA is uniquely positioned to advise decision makers about public health system reform and to guide initiatives to help safeguard the personal and community health of Canadians and people around the world. Our members represent more than 25 professions. CPHA is governed by a board of directors, which consists of the chair, chair elect, and six to eight directors (one of whom is a student member). The executive director is secretary to the board.

Vision

A healthy and just world.

Mission

CPHA's mission is to enhance the health of people in Canada and to contribute to a healthier and more equitable world.

Priorities

- Stakeholders across the continuum are mobilized in support of public health.
- Effective public health policy is being developed and implemented through an efficient public health structure at each level of government.
- The public health system is supported by sufficient, appropriately skilled public health practitioners.

Contact Information

Canadian Public Health Association
404-1525 Carling Ave
Ottawa ON
K1Z 8R9
Canada
Tel.: +1 613 725 3769
Fax: +1 613 725 9826
E-mail: info@cpha.ca

11. China Medical Board (CMB)

Background

The Rockefeller-endowed CMB is an independent American foundation with headquarters in Cambridge, Massachusetts, USA, and a new office in Beijing, China.

Vision

CMB aims to advance health in China and neighboring Asian countries through strengthening medical, nursing, and public health research and education. CMB is a highly focused foundation targeting its grant and support activities to carefully selected Asian grantees.

In 2008, CMB launched a fresh initiative to strengthen scientific excellence in "critical capacities" among Chinese and Asian institutions to address the premier health challenges of the 21st century—equitable access to primary and preventive health services in market-driven economies so that all can benefit from the advancement of knowledge. This work entails capacity strengthening in the fields of health policy and health systems and associated educational activities to advance health equity.

Achievements

In nearly a century of philanthropy, CMB has gifted hundreds of millions of dollars in grants and technical support to medical universities across the Far East and Southeast Asia. With an endowment of over $200 million, the CMB grants more than $10 million annually.

Priorities

CMB works in China and the five Mekong countries of Southeast Asia. In China, it prioritizes work in health policy and systems sciences (HPS) and health professional education (HPE).

- CMB's HPS program seeks to strengthen academic capacity to generate intelligence for guiding improved health policies and systems operations. The program supports two HPS centers and 8 to 10 collaborating programs to build institutional as well as individual capacities.
- In China, CMB also collaborates to pioneer reforms in HPE. The work entails promoting innovations in instructional and institutional design in public health, nursing, and medical education that prepares future health leaders.
- CMB's third program in Southeast Asia works to strengthen capacities in HPS and HPE in Myanmar, Laos, Thailand, Cambodia, and Vietnam. The Southeast Asia involvement focuses on these Mekong countries by building health policy capacity, reforming of health professional education, and strengthening of regional networks of collaboration.

Contact Information

Website: www.chinamedicalboard.org

12. Chinese Preventive Medicine Association (CPMA)

CPMA, established in 1987, is a nonprofit national academic institution comprised of voluntary scientific and technological workers in the fields of public health and preventive medicine. Under the direct administration of the Ministry of Health (MoH) and legally registered with the Ministry of Civil Affairs, CPMA is also a member of the China Association for Science and Technology (CAST). As such, it serves as an important social agent in promoting the development of public health and preventive medicine within China. Currently, all Chinese provinces, autonomous regions, and municipalities, as well as a large number of cities and counties throughout the country, have established preventive medicine associations. Consequently, China has been able to form a comprehensive network of preventive medicine across the nation. CPMA, which is headquartered in Beijing, has 1,486 organizational members and over 110,000 individual members at present, more than 10,000 of whom are well-known, preventive health professionals. With 47 professional branches, CPMA covers all disciplines in the field of preventive medicine and health care. It has also disseminated 70 publications, which includes 69 periodicals in specialized academic journals and one newspaper, *Healthcare Time*, in a popular science publication.

Vision

CPMA envisions uniting and organizing the vast number of scientific and technological workers in the fields of public health and preventive medicine; promoting and practicing medical ethics; advocating the development, popularization, and prosperity of public health and preventive medical science, according to national research priorities in science, technology, and health; improving the skills and capacity of scientific and technological personnel involved with preventive medical science; and improving the quality of health across all of China.

Mission

(a) Advocate scientific and technological advances in public health and preventive medicine; (b) promote the improvement and capacity of teams comprised of preventive medicine professionals; (c) carry out educational exchanges for members, as well as other scientific professionals working in preventive medicine; (d) serve as a link between the government and experts; (e) promote knowledge of, and technology in, preventive medicine to improve health services provided to persons of all nations; (f) apply preventive medicine science and technology to improve the production and development of China's economic services; (g) ensure the legal rights and interests of public health workers; and (h) promote international cooperation and exchanges.

Values

Prevention, healthy China

Achievements

1. Since 1996, CPMA has been a member of the World Federation of Public Health Associations (WFPHA), serving on the nomination committee and awards committee since 2006 and on the executive board from 2000. Since 2010, the WFPHA Asia-Pacific Regional Liaison Office (APRLO) has been operated. The secretariat was set up in CPMA. Dr. Cai Jiming, secretary general of CPMA, served as the director of APRLO.

2. The 4th CPMA Annual Conference was successfully held in 2013, and this event is now considered the most prominent conference in China for those working in the fields of public health and preventive medicine. This conference drew approximately 2,000 participants this time. In collaboration with other institutions, CPMA coordinates and carries out other interdepartmental and interdisciplinary conferences. Fifty-four winners were awarded in the Outstanding Contributions to the Development of Public Health and Preventive Medicine Award at the 4th annual conference in 2013.

3. CPMA holds 50 national-level projects and 100 association-level projects on continuing education each year.

4. CPMA has carried out more than 30 projects, in cooperation with the WHO, the United Nations Population Fund (UNFPA), the United Nations Children's Fund (UNICEF), the Joint United Nations Programme on HIV and AIDS (UNAIDS), the World Bank, the Asian Development Bank (ADB), the Capacity Building International, Germany (InWEnt), the Bill & Melinda Gates Foundation (B&MGF), and the China Medical Board (CMB), in the fields of disease prevention and control, health policy development, reproductive health, maternal and child health, environmental health, chronic disease prevention and control, public health education, AIDS prevention, and so on.

Priorities

(a) Academic activity; (b) international cooperation and exchange; (c) participating in the consultative activities of the United Nations; (d) journal publications and management; (e) capacity building; (f) IEC on preventive medicine science.

Contact Information

Yi Heya, Officer of International Cooperation Department
Tel.: +86 10 84037439
E-mail: shiwukeya@163.com
Website: www.cpma.org

13. Consortium of Universities for Global Health (CUGH)

CUGH began in 2008 as leaders from 24 academic institutions convened to create a leading global health organization that would work across disciplines to address global health challenges and reduce health inequities. It was based at the University of California San Francisco (UCSF) and was supported by grants from the Bill & Melinda Gates Foundation and the Rockefeller Foundation. In 2012, CUGH merged with the Global Health Education Consortium (GHEC) and kept the name CUGH. In September 2012, CUGH opened a permanent secretariat in Washington, DC, and hired its first executive director, Keith Martin, MD.

CUGH is a rapidly growing Washington, DC, nonprofit organization with a membership of over 100 academic institutions and other organizations from around the world, as well as an extensive international network of over 9,000 global health practitioners. CUGH works across disciplines in education, research, and service to address global health challenges internationally.

CUGH promotes mutually beneficial partnerships between universities and other sectors in high-, middle-, and low-income countries to strengthen human capital and institutional capabilities. As a source of training expertise across many fields, CUGH helps build capacity in resource-poor regions. CUGH has a knowledge hub of best practices and educational material and is committed to knowledge translation. We are dedicated to strengthening academic global health programs.

Vision

Making the university a transforming force in global health.

Mission

CUGH bridges the knowledge-needs gap by increasing access to innovations that address global health challenges; fostering the dissemination and implementation of evidence-based high impact interventions; and facilitating effective partnerships between institutions in high-, middle-, and low-income countries and between them and governments, foundations, NGOs, and the private sector to achieve these goals.

Achievements

- Convenes one of the leading global health conferences in the world: Montréal, Canada, in 2011; Washington, DC, in 2012 and 2013. The seventh annual conference will be held in San Francisco, April 8 to 11, 2016, and the eighth annual conference will be in Washington, DC, April 6 to 9, 2017
- Built collaborations with other consortia including the Canadian Consortia for Global Health Research, as well as Latin American consortia, ALASAG; it is a founding member of the World Federation for Academic Institutions for Global Health
- Doubled membership in the last year, with increasing membership from academic institutions overseas including those from low-income countries
- Organized special sessions and workshops on global cancer with the National Institutes of Health's National Cancer Institute, building a better global health professional with the Public Health Institution: Enabling Systems, and more.
- Created a mentorship program for global programs
- Sends out a bimonthly global health bulletin that is circulated worldwide

- Created a knowledge hub on its website www.CUGH.org, including an array of new training modules that are open source
- Developed and strengthened CUGH's committees in research, education, advocacy, and communications
- Advocated for funding for health research
- Worked with NGOs and governments to identify personnel who could volunteer for the response to the Ebola outbreak in West Africa

Priorities for the Next Year

- Completing a survey of global health programs in the United States.
- Engaging minority serving institutions to help strengthen their global health activities
- Expanding our engagement with institutions in low- and middle-income countries. Developing partnerships with institutions in these countries with a specific emphasis on building capacity across disciplines
- Setting up a webinar series and workshops
- Holding successful conferences in 2015 and beyond
- Expanding the knowledge hub including aggregating good/best practices across disciplines
- Expanding advocacy and communication efforts in global health using social networking tools and traditional media
- Strengthening our mentorship program

Contact Information

Executive Director: Keith Martin, MD
Executive Assistant: Jillian Morgan
E-mail: jmorgan@cugh.org
Membership: membership@cugh.org
1608 Rhode Island Ave NW #241, Washington, DC 20036
Tel.: +1 202 9746363
Website: www.cugh.org; Twitter: @cughnews

14. Council on Linkages Between Academia and Public Health Practice (CLAPHP)

Background

The Council on Linkages is a collaborative of 20 national organizations focused on improving public health education and training, practice, and research within the United States. The Council on Linkages was established in 1992 to implement the recommendations of the Public Health Faculty/Agency Forum and works to further academic/practice collaboration to ensure a well-trained, competent workforce and the development and use of a strong evidence base for public health practice. Activities of the Council on Linkages include producing the Core Competencies for Public Health Professionals (Core Competencies), providing support for academic health department

(AHD) efforts, developing resources to enhance public health training, and exploring public health worker recruitment and retention. The Council on Linkages is funded by the U.S. Centers for Disease Control and Prevention. Staff support is provided by the Public Health Foundation.

Mission

To improve public health practice, education, and research by fostering, coordinating, and monitoring links among academia and the public health and health care community; developing and advancing innovative strategies to build and strengthen public health infrastructure; and creating a process for continuing public health education throughout one's career.

Values

- Teamwork and collaboration
- Focus on the future
- People and partners
- Creativity and innovation
- Results and creating value
- Public responsibility and citizenship

Recent Achievements

- *Academic Health Department Learning Community.* In 2011, the Council on Linkages established the AHD Learning Community, a national community that brings together public health practitioners, educators, and researchers to engage in collaborative learning, knowledge sharing, and resource development in support of AHD partnerships.
- *Core Competencies for Public Health Professionals.* Developed by the Council on Linkages, the Core Competencies are a consensus set of skills for the broad practice of public health and provide a foundation for public health workforce development. The Core Competencies are widely used by public health practice organizations, including state and local health departments, as well as academic institutions across the United States. Originally developed in 2001, the Core Competencies were most recently revised in June 2014.
- *Guide to Improving and Measuring the Impact of Training.* In May 2014, the Council on Linkages released a *Guide to Improving and Measuring the Impact of Training* to help support the ongoing training of public health professionals. Based on expert opinion and published literature, this online resource contains strategies and methods aimed at enhancing training activities, as well as references to literature on training and evaluation of training.
- *Public Health Workers Survey.* In 2010, the Council on Linkages conducted a survey to collect information about characteristics of public health workers and influences on their decisions to become and remain part of the public health workforce. This was the first large-scale effort to directly survey U.S. public health workers. Data were gathered from nearly 12,000 individuals and comprise the largest set of data on individual U.S. public health workers.

Priorities (2015 Onward)

The current version of the *Strategic Directions* runs through 2015 and can be found online at www.phf.org/programs/council/Pages/Council_Strategic_Directions.aspx

Newsletter/Key Publications

The Council on Linkages distributes a monthly newsletter, the *Council on Linkages Update*. To subscribe, visit visitor.r20.constantcontact.com/manage/optin?v=001Blh3vqF6Hksj8QL4CA-_sCbuEtO8QMnjqLpRvRp8fp5YLPHfBf8uP-WHesAE53mUOIiHrSq_lS63hZJw9UqnQSl-Q3RPiHslEEykxp59SNEo%3D

Other Information

Information about selected past accomplishments of the Council on Linkages is online at www.phf.org/programs/council/Pages/Council_on_Linkages_Accomplishments.aspx

Contact Information

www.phf.org/councilonlinkages

15. Euclid Consortium of Universities

Euclid University, with its headquarters currently in Gambia, is an intergovernmental treaty-based organization with 12 participating states with a university charter, established in 2008.

Vision

To become the international reference in delivering best-of-class higher education programs under treaty-mandate, with a focus on sustainable development and quality of life in the Global South.

Mission

To deliver best-of-class distance education and consulting services to our participating states' officials as well as to our general public students.

Values

- Academic excellence
- Critical thinking
- Inter-cultural and inter-religious dialogue

Achievements (in the Last Few Years)

Successful finalization of all institution processes, including UN treaty publication; Association of African Universities membership; accreditation with university headquarters' state (Gambia/Ministry of Higher Education); being featured in recent ACUNS (Academic Council on United Nations System) publication; successful launch of International Public Health programs in 2014.

Priorities (2015 Onward)

Focus on international public health program with emphasis on educating civil servants in and for the Global South.

Annual Conference(s)

No annual conferences related to public health as yet.

Newsletter/Key Publications

Papers and publications posted at www.euclid.int/publications

Other Information

Scholarships available for ECOWAS residents and officials of EUCLID participating states.

Contact information:

www.euclid.int and http://www.euclidconsortium.org/

16. European Association of Dental Public Health (EADPH)

EADPH was founded in 1996 as an international and independent science-based forum for professionals having a special interest in dental public health and community dentistry. EADPH is a member of the Oral Health Group of the World Federation of Public Health Associations. In 2011, it combined with the Association for Dental Education in Europe and the Council of European Chief Dental Officers to form the Platform for Better Oral Health in Europe. The Platform has a secretariat in Brussels and lobbies the European Commission and Parliament on oral health issues. The agenda for the next decade includes working with professionals from all areas of health care to address the common problems for health and oral health; in particular, chronic diseases, cancer, diabetes, cardiovascular diseases, respiratory diseases, and obesity, all of which have common risk factors with oral diseases.

EADPH organizes an annual meeting where exchange of information takes place between researchers, practitioners, and policy makers. Meetings consist of plenary sessions with invited keynote speakers and free contributions.

The Association has special interest groups in eight areas, including

- Periodontal
- Epidemiology
- Oral cancer
- Dental caries
- Gerontology

In collaboration with the British Society for the Study of Community Dentistry, the Association publishes the journal *Community Dental Health*.

Contact Information

For further details, visit www.eadph.org

17. European Public Health Alliance (EPHA)

Background

- *EPHA is a change agent*—Europe's leading NGO advocating for better health. EPHA is a dynamic, member-led, nonprofit association registered in Brussels.
- *EPHA* has 91 members from 29 countries of the European region. Our membership is composed of public health NGOs, patient and disease groups, and health professionals.
- *Our mission* is to bring together the public health community to provide thoughtful leadership and to facilitate change; to build public health capacity to deliver equitable solutions to European public health challenges; and to improve health and reduce health inequalities.
- *Our vision* is of a Europe with universal good health and well-being, where all have access to a sustainable and high quality health system.

What We Do

- We monitor the policy making process within the EU institutions.
- We promote greater awareness amongst European citizens and NGOs about policy developments.
- We train, mentor, and support NGOs and health actors to engage with the EU.
- We participate in policy debates and stakeholder dialogues to raise the profile of health in all policy areas.

Our Priorities Are

- To improve population health and increase healthy life years
- To increase equity and access in health and reduce health inequalities
- To support a health-promoting European institutional framework and policy
- To strengthen and increase effective public health capacity

Latest Achievements

2013: 800 advocacy meetings; 26 papers (position papers and briefings); and 9 working groups' meetings; issue leader on eHealth Stakeholder Group; publication of several joint statements and tender participation on health professionals; successful proposition of several amendments in clinical trials/medical devices legislation; contribution to the European Parliament Committee on Employment and Social Affairs (EP EMPL) Committee report; co-organizers of the European Citizens' Summit; numerous activities around Roma Health, fundamental rights schemes, and agricultural and environmental policy; key advocate on tobacco policy.

EPHA's Annual Conferences

EPHA Annual Conferences (ACs) set the tone of the conversation on public health at the EU level. See the reports of our 2013 and 2012 ACs.

EPHA Newsletter

EPHA issues an electronic monthly newsletter that is posted on our website and also sent out to the e-mail inboxes of more than 4,000 subscribers.

Contact Information

Javier Delgado, EPHA Communications Coordinator
E-mail: javier@epha.org
Tel.: +32 2 233 38 76

18. European Public Health Association (EUPHA)

EUPHA is an umbrella organization for public health associations and institutes in Europe. It was founded in 1992 by 15 members (12 countries). EUPHA now has 68 members from 40 countries. It is an international, multidisciplinary, scientific organization, bringing together around 14,000 public health experts for professional exchange and collaboration throughout Europe. We encourage a multidisciplinary approach to public health.

Our Vision

Our vision is of improved health and reduced health inequalities for all Europeans. We seek to support our members to increase the impact of public health in Europe, adding value to the efforts of regions and states, national and international organizations, and individual public health experts.

Our Mission

Our mission is to build capacity, knowledge, and policy in the field of public health, and to support practice and policy decisions through scientific evidence and producing and sharing knowledge with our members and partners in Europe.

Our Values

Sustainable advancements in public health can only be achieved through collaboration. EUPHA is dedicated to working in partnership with European and international intergovernmental and nongovernmental organizations as well as national institutes and organizations endorsing EUPHA's values and commitment to improve public health in Europe.

Achievements

European Journal of Public Health

EUPHA publishes the *European Journal of Public Health* (*EJPH*), a multidisciplinary journal in the field of public health, publishing contributions from social medicine, epidemiology, health services research, management, ethics and law, health economics, social sciences, and environmental health. *EJPH* is published bimonthly.

Theme-Specific Sections

EUPHA encourages the creation of sections for specific public health themes, which are international and open to all public health experts. The goal is to bring together researchers, policy makers, and practitioners working in the same field for knowledge sharing and capacity building, including, inter alia, child and adolescent public health, chronic diseases, food and nutrition, health promotion, public mental health, social security and health, and urban public health.

Projects

- Public Health Innovation and Research in Europe (PHIRE): A collaboration between seven partners, co-funded by the European Union and drawing on the expertise of members of EUPHA (completed in 2013)
- EUPHAnxt: A strategy to actively involve students and the young generation of early career researchers and practitioners committed to public health in the EUPHA network

Publications

Next to the regular publications like the electronic newsletter (www.eupha.org./news letters; monthly) and *EJPH* (bimonthly), EUPHA also produces a number of interesting tools to build capacity, knowledge, and policy in the field of European public health:

- EUPHActs: Two-page summaries on a specific public health issue
- EUPHA snapshots: Two-page summaries based on abstracts presented at the European public health conferences (2002–2013) on a specific public health issue
- EUPHA statements: Specific statements to influence policy making at the European level

Annual Conferences

The annual European Public Health conferences (www.eupha.org) are organized at the initiative of EUPHA. EPH conferences attract around 1,500 public health professionals from about 60 countries worldwide.

Contact Information

Website: www.eupha.org

19. Faculty of Public Health (FPH [UK])

Background

FPH is the standard setting body for specialists in public health in the United Kingdom. FPH was established as a registered charity in 1972 following a central recommendation of the Royal Commission on Medical Education (1965–1968). FPH is a joint faculty of the three Royal Colleges of Physicians of the United Kingdom (London, Edinburgh, and Glasgow) and also a member of the World Federation of Public Health Associations. Although an integral part of the three Royal Colleges, FPH is an independently constituted body with its own membership, governance structure, and financial arrangements.

FPH is the professional home for more than 3,300 professionals working in public health. Our members come from a diverse range of professional backgrounds (including clinical, academic, policy) and are employed in a variety of settings, usually working at a strategic or specialist level.

FPH is a strategic organization and, as such, works collaboratively, drawing on the specialist skills, knowledge, and experience of our members as well as building relationships with a wide range of external organizations.

For more than 40 years, FPH has been at the forefront of the development and transformation of the public health profession.

Mission

Our overarching mission is to promote and protect the health and well-being of everyone in society by playing a leading role in assuring an effective public health workforce, promoting public health knowledge, and advocating for the very best conditions for good health.

Vision

Better health for all.

Objectives

- To promote for the public benefit the advancement of knowledge in the field of public health
- To develop public health with a view to maintaining the highest possible standards of professional competence and practice
- To act as an authoritative body for the purpose of consultation and advocacy in matters of educational or public interest concerning public health

Achievements

See http://www.fph.org.uk/uploads/about_us_leaflet_2007.pdf

Strategy

FPH is currently reviewing its strategy; some details are available here: www.fph.org .uk/Strategy_Consultation_Exercise

Conferences

www.fph.org.uk/fph_annual_conference_2014
The 2015 conference will be held in Gateshead, Newcastle, June 22 to 24, 2015.

Newsletter

Public Health Today: www.fph.org.uk/Public_Health_Today

Contact Information

www.fph.org.uk

20. Foundation for Advancement of International Medical Education and Research (FAIMER®)

Background

FAIMER seeks to improve the health of communities by improving health professions education. FAIMER is a nonprofit foundation of the Educational Commission for Foreign Medical Graduates (ECFMG®) with headquarters in Philadelphia, Pennsylvania, in the United States.

Vision, Mission, Values, Achievements

By creating educational opportunities, conducting research, and providing data resources, FAIMER serves international communities of educators, researchers, regulators, and policy makers—each a potential change agent for better health care. Through worldwide activities, FAIMER combines its own expertise with that of local experts to create meaningful and sustained improvements in the systems that produce health care providers and deliver health care.

FAIMER offers a growing number of educational programs for those who educate physicians and other health care providers. These programs—which include the FAIMER Institute, six Regional Institutes, the International Fellowship in Medical Education (IFME) program, and the FAIMER Distance Learning program—provide health professions educators with opportunities to acquire skills and learn new methodologies in teaching and assessment, develop leadership and management skills, exchange educational expertise, and pursue advanced degrees in health professions education. Participants apply this knowledge to improve teaching and learning at their home institutions. As a result, these institutions are able to produce better health care practitioners.

FAIMER research endeavors are categorized into three broad domains:

- International migration of physicians
- U.S. physician workforce issues
- International medical education programs

By exploring issues that affect the quality of health care and the functioning of health care systems, FAIMER's research program informs health professions education and health workforce policy. The knowledge generated is used by researchers, educators, and policy makers to understand and address some of the challenges, both local and global, of providing quality health care.

In keeping with its goal of developing resources on medical education worldwide, FAIMER builds data resources on international medical education and international physicians. These resources—which include the *Directory of Organizations That Recognize/Accredit Medical Schools*, the *International Medical Education Directory* (*IMED*), International Opportunities in Medical Education, master's programs in health professions education, and the Postgraduate Medical Education Project—provide comparative data that aim to inform the work of medical educators, researchers, policy makers, and those responsible for the credentialing and licensing of physicians.

Priorities

In 2014, FAIMER and the World Federation for Medical Education (WFME) merged their respective directories—FAIMER's *IMED* and WFME's *Avicenna Directory*—to produce a single comprehensive resource on undergraduate medical education worldwide. The new resource, developed in collaboration with WHO and the University of Copenhagen, is known as the *World Directory of Medical Schools*. Continued expansion of FAIMER's educational program is expected, including the launch of a new regional institute for Spanish-speaking health professions educators from Latin America and the Caribbean in April 2014. Expansion of FAIMER's research program is also expected, including continued collaboration with other institutes and researchers.

Contact Information

Website: www.faimer.org
E-mail: inquiry@faimer.org

21. General Medical Council (GMC, [UK])

GMC is an independent organization that helps to protect patients and improve medical practice across the United Kingdom.

- We set the standards that are required of doctors practicing here.
- We decide which doctors are qualified to work in the United Kingdom and we oversee their education and training.
- We make sure that they continue to meet these standards throughout their careers.
- We take action when we believe a doctor may be putting the safety of patients at risk.

Every patient should receive a high standard of care. Our role is to help achieve that by working closely with doctors, their employers, and patients, thereby making sure that the trust patients have in their doctors is fully justified.

Our Recent Achievements

- We have introduced revalidation, a system of regular checks to make sure all doctors working in the United Kingdom are competent and keeping their knowledge and skills up to date. It is the most comprehensive system of its kind in the world and requires doctors to revalidate to maintain their license to practice. See www.gmc-uk.org/revalidation.
- We have revised and updated our core guidance, *Good medical practice*, and developed a range of tools and advice to help doctors to meet our standards in their day-to-day work. You can find all our guidance and interactive resources at www.gmc-uk.org/guidance.
- We have published a guide for patients on what they can expect from their doctor: http://www.gmc-uk.org/guidance/patients.asp?
- We have been involved in a major independent review of the way doctors are trained as specialists and general practitioners (GPs; www.shapeoftraining.co.uk), and we will be working with medical royal colleges and the UK governments who fund training to drive forward key reforms.
- We have launched the Medical Practitioners Tribunal Service to provide high quality, consistent, and impartial decisions to protect patients. See www.mpts-uk.org

Our Priorities

We will continue to transform the way we work, to engage more with doctors, patients, and partners in the health care system, and to identify and act on risks to patient safety before problems occur. Our goals are set out in our *Corporate strategy 2014–17* (http://www.gmc-uk.org/Corporate_strategy_2014_17.pdf_54828872.pdf?).

Find Out More About Our Work

Stay up-to-date with our work by registering to receive our e-bulletins:

- *GMC News* for doctors: e-mail ebulletin@gmc-uk.org
- *GMC Student News* for medical students: go to www.gmc-uk.org/studentnewssignup
- *Education Update* for people involved in medical education and training: e-mail education@gmc-uk.org
- Website: www.gmc-uk.org

Join our conversation on Twitter (twitter.com/gmcuk), Facebook (facebook.com/gmcuk), LinkedIn (linkd.in/gmcuk), and YouTube (youtube.com/gmcuktv).

22. Global Health Council (GHC)

GHC is the leading membership organization supporting and connecting advocates, implementers, and stakeholders around global health priorities worldwide. GHC convenes stakeholders around key global health priorities and actively engages key decision makers to influence health policy. As a membership organization of over 300 institutions and 4,500 individuals, GHC provides a platform for discussion, dialogue, and resource sharing, bringing together these diverse voices and facilitating their contribution to the global health policy arena.

Vision

We envision a world where health for all is ensured through equitable, inclusive, and sustainable investment, policies, and services.

Mission

To improve health globally through increased investment, robust policies, and the power of the collective voice.

Values

GHC provides a dynamic platform for the global health community's shared voice and common vision. Leadership reflects the constituency through an elected board of directors and an executive director whose profile and experience align with GHC's mandate and vision. GHC leadership is committed to a transparent business model that includes providing members with regular updates and opportunities to offer input to GHC governance. GHC will strive to provide members with the highest possible value of state-of-the-art services.

Achievements (to 2013)

- Global Health Week on the Hill with Congressional staff outlining government funding, partnerships, and a simulcast of the Global Burden of Disease Study results with Bill Gates
- Consortium of Universities for Global Health Annual Conference where the GHC sponsored a Forging Strong Relationships Between Faith and Secular Global Health Programs panel
- World Health Assembly 2013 where the GHC hosted a roundtable and reception
- GHC partnered in a Management Sciences for Health study tour at the Women Deliver Global Conference
- UN General Assembly Side Event: The Road Forward: What's Next for Global Health? This was the first collaborative effort by the GHC, Action for Global Health, and Global Health South on recommendations to address health changes, its partners, and post-2015 financing
- GHC Clinton Global Initiative (CGI) Breakfast discussion to create a shared voice for global health
- GHC hosted a booth and panel session, Engagement of Public Health Professionals in Global Health Advocacy, at the APHA 2013

Priorities

1. Raise visibility, influence policy, and expand investment for global health
   - Advocate for expanded funding levels
   - Promote evidence-based policies
   - Facilitate and encourage member engagement
   - Increase visibility and political support
2. Increase member effectiveness, sharing, and partnership across the global health community
   - Provide comprehensive and accessible platforms
   - Represent the full range of interests of the global health community
   - Promote GHC and nourish global health thought leadership, networking, and visibility
   - Encourage stronger partnership with and participation by the Global South
3. Achieve organizational and financial efficacy for sustained GHC impact
   - Develop and maintain a sustainable resourcing model
   - Create an effective, efficient member support model
   - Optimize member engagement
   - Grow and maintain member ownership of GHC
   - Ensure GHC's status as a state-of-the-art alliance

Contact Information

Global Health Council
1120 20th St. NW, Suite 500 N
Washington, DC 20036
USA

23. Global Health Workforce Alliance (GHWA)

Background

GHWA (The Alliance) was created in 2006 as a common platform for action to address the workforce crisis and is hosted by WHO at Geneva. The Alliance is a partnership of national governments, civil society, international agencies, finance institutions, researchers, educators, and professional associations dedicated to identifying, implementing, and advocating for solutions.

Vision

All people everywhere will have access to a skilled, motivated, and supported health worker, within a robust health system.

Mission

To advocate and catalyze global and country actions to resolve the human resources for health crisis; to support the achievement of the health-related Millennium Development Goals (MDGs), and health for all.

Global Forum Program on Human Resources for Health

The first Global Forum on Human Resources for Health (HRH) was held in Kampala, Uganda, from March 2 to 7, 2008; the second was convened by GHWA, the Prince Mahidol Award Conference, WHO, and the Japan International Cooperation Agency, supported by many other agencies, especially the Rockefeller Foundation, the China Medical Board, and the World Bank.

The third forum was one of the main global health events in 2013. It brought together over 1,800 participants; that included delegates from 89 countries, including 40 ministers, as well as a number of Alliance members, key partners, and experts from around the globe and Brazil. The theme was Human Resources for Health: Foundation for Universal Health Coverage and the post-2015 development agenda. These forum programs renewed the focus on HRH and accentuated a need to accelerate progress toward attaining the MDGs and achieving the universal health coverage (UHC) as well as identifying post-2015 health development priorities.

One of the main objectives of the 2013 forum was to elicit new tangible HRH commitments from governments, donors, development partners, private sector, civil society, and other key HRH stakeholders. Based on a template developed by WHO and GHWA, over 70 countries and GHWA partners announced their national and/or organizational commitments. These commitments proclaimed in the forum have stirred a new wave of enthusiasm to galvanize policy actions and strategic moves to address the prevailing HRH challenges and priorities by employing additional efforts and resources.

Convening and working with key stakeholders, the Alliance has succeeded in placing HRH issues high on the global health agenda, as well as promoting a multistakeholder approach in countries to address the HRH challenges by developing, financing, implementing, and monitoring evidence-based, country-specific HRH plans integrated within the national health policies and priorities.

Capitalizing on its core functions and operating largely through partners, the Alliance is lean and cost-effective, always striving to ensure that it can trigger a cascade effect for lasting change. The Alliance is a vital contributor to efforts in improving the health workforce and thus ensures universal health coverage.

Contact Information

www.who.int/workforcealliance/about/en

24. ICAP and the Nursing Educational Partnership Initiative (NEPI)

Background

Overview: ICAP is a global health leader situated at Columbia University. NEPI is among the ICAP portfolio of programs. NEPI was developed in response to the fact that nurses and midwives are the main providers of health care in the countries where ICAP works: Nurses provide upwards of 90% of health services and are people's point of access to the larger health care system. As the frontline defense against the leading causes of mortality, nurses often shoulder responsibility for the survival of communities. Yet, many countries face a nursing shortage. In 2011, there were only 103 nurses and midwives for every 100,000 people in Africa. This shortage of critical health workers contributes directly to poor health outcomes. ICAP has worked since 2004 with one central goal: to improve the health of families and communities. To date, ICAP has worked to address major public health challenges and the needs of local health systems in more than 3,300 sites across 21 countries.

Mission

ICAP's mission is to ensure the wellness of families and communities by strengthening health systems around the world.

Origins: ICAP has supported the professional development of nurses and midwives in sub-Saharan Africa since 2006. ICAP piloted the Nurse Mentorship Training Program (NMTP) in Eastern Cape Province, South Africa. It included a comprehensive curriculum to increase the knowledge, clinical skills, and system skills nurses needed to play a larger role in HIV care. The program created an effective, replicable model of nurse mentorship, which was subsequently adopted by ICAP programs in other countries. The success of the NMTP both inspired and established a strong foundation for ICAP's Global Nurse Capacity Building Program (GNCBP) within which the work of NEPI is achieved.

Objectives

The objectives of the GNCBP program are:

1. To improve the quantity, quality, and relevance of nurses and midwives to address essential population-based health care needs, including HIV and other life-threatening conditions
2. To identify, evaluate, and disseminate innovative human resources for health models and practices that are generalizable for national scale-up of nursing and midwifery education
3. To build local and regional nursing

The GNCBP consists of two subprojects, Nursing Education Partnership-Initiative (NEPI) and General Nursing (GN). Both projects aim to improve the quantity, quality, and relevance of nurse training. NEPI focuses on pre-service education and GN focuses on in-service training and ongoing professional development. GNCBP promotes cross country collaboration through organizations such as FUNDISA and ECSACON. National Nursing leaders such as chief nursing officers and nursing regulatory bodies are supported to promote the practice and regulation of the nursing profession.

Achievements

- 14,638 nurses enrolled in pre-service education programs with 6,232 nurses graduating from pre-service nursing education programs
- 16,372 students successfully meeting competencies and completing skills labs
- 2,391 nurses/midwives completing in-service training courses
- 434 new faculty produced through PhD and bachelor's/master's programs in nursing education
- Option B+ PMTCT on-line module developed and available online

Priorities (2015 Onward)

- Continued support for the development of clinical simulation laboratories, model wards, and education programs relevant to antiretroviral care and treatment
- Option B+ e-learning for nurses and midwives
- Pediatric ART e-learning for nurses and midwives

Annual Conference(s)

Annual NEPI Nursing Summit; participation in relevant regional and global nursing conferences such as ECSACON, ICN, CUGH, and ANAC.

Key Publications

- Middleton L, Howard AA, Dohrn J, et al. The Nursing Education Partnership Initiative (NEPI): Innovations in nursing and midwifery education. *Academic Medicine*. 2014;89:S24–S28.
- Option B+ e-learning. Accessed from https://elearning.icap.columbia.edu/accounts/login/?next=
- ICAP. *Nurses & midwives: The frontline against HIV/AIDS*. New York: ICAP; 2013.
- ICAP. *Campus to clinic mentoring guide for participants*. Accessed http://www.medbox.org/gynaecology-obstetrics/campus-to-clinic-manual-mentoring-guide-for-participants/preview?q=
- ICAP. *Campus to clinic mentoring guide for facilitators*. Accessed from http://files.icap.columbia.edu/files/uploads/South_Africa._Campus_to_Clinic._Facilitators_guide.pdf

Contact Information

Website: icap.columbia.edu

25. India Public Health Association (IPHA)

Following independence, primary health centers in India emerged on the basis of the recommendation of the Bhore committee (1946). With the expanding public health programs and nation building activities, people of the country were expected to better realize the dictum "Prevention is better than cure." With such a short history, modern public health as a science or service is still young in India, and the need for an All India Association of Public Health was not actually thought of until the All India Institute of Hygiene and Public Health was established at Calcutta. However, with the redesignation of medical services as health services and the establishment of the Ministry of Health Services and the Ministry of Health (now Ministry of Health and Family Welfare) at the central and state levels, the situation turned favorable for the establishment of IPHA as an all India body. It was inaugurated in 1956, the same year when the Society for Medical Officers of Health in England celebrated their first centenary and the American Public Health Association was running its 84th year and the Canadian Association its 46th year of their establishment.

Since its inception, the headquarters of the Association was located at the All India Institute of Hygiene and Public Health (AIIH&PH), Calcutta, with the concurrence and active support of the authorities of the Institute. The propriety and wisdom of such a selection are unquestionable; the Institute was the only unique center wherefrom the knowledge of public health in India emanated and where the best and the biggest library on public health and associated subjects, as well as a large array of foreign and Indian journals, were available. The Association was also fortunate to have the honorary services of all faculty members and staff including the director, professional and administrative, and other supporting staff, who normally volunteer to work for the Association and its cause. In fact, whatever achievements the Association could have claimed were undoubtedly due to the close cooperation and collaboration of the entire Institute and its staff. Another advantage was that AIIH&PH, the School of Tropical Medicine (of international fame), and the Calcutta Medical College were all situated close to each other. These institutes were equipped with big scientific libraries and staff with great experience, whose guidance and assistance were available, whenever asked for.

Mission

The mission is to protect and promote the health of the people of India by facilitating the exchange of information, experience, and research, and advocating for policies, programs, and practices that improve public health.

Vision

"Healthy people living in a healthy environment." IPHA, the leading professional association in public health in India, strives to protect and promote the health and well-being of all people and the environment in our county so that all people can enjoy the best health possible and can live, grow, and prosper in clean and safe communities.

Goals

The goals of the Association include (a) promotion and advancement of public health and allied sciences in India; (b) protection and promotion of health of the people of the country; and (c) promotion of cooperation and fellowship among the members of the Association.

Activities include the following:

- Hold an annual convention and periodic meetings or conferences of members of the Association and of the public health profession in general.
- Initiate, hold, direct, manage, take part in, and contribute to conferences, congresses, meetings, lectures, and demonstrations on any aspect of public health and social welfare for the purpose of advancing any of the objectives of the Association.
- Publish and circulate a scientific journal, which will be the official organ of the Association, specially adapted to the needs of the administrators, program managers, and research workers in the field of public health in India.
- Disseminate health knowledge and conduct educational campaigns among schools, colleges, cultural bodies, village organizations, and other people in cooperation with different public bodies working with the same objectives by holding health exhibitions, publishing or sponsoring popular health journals, and preparing and distributing literature, posters, and information about health and social welfare.
- Encourage research in public health and social work with grants-in-aid or with grants out of the funds of the Association; by establishment of scholarships, prizes, or rewards; and in such other manner as may from time to time be determined by the Association.

Contact Information

office@iphaonline.org (for all purposes except journal)

26. Institute of Medicine (IOM, U.S.)

Established in 1970, IOM (since July 1, 2015, renamed within the National Research Council [NRC]) is the health arm of the National Academy of Sciences (NAS), which was chartered as a private organization by the Congress and President Abraham Lincoln in 1863. Since July 1, 2015, the IOM has become the program unit of the National Academy of Medicine, part of the United States National Academies.

Vision

- IOM asks and answers the nation's most pressing questions about health and health care.
- IOM's aim is to help those in government and the private sector make informed health decisions by providing evidence upon which they can rely.
- Each year, more than 2,000 individuals, members, and nonmembers volunteer their time, knowledge, and expertise to advance the nation's health through the work of the IOM.

Mission

- IOM serves as adviser to the nation to improve health.
- IOM is an independent, nonprofit organization that works outside of government to provide unbiased and authoritative advice to decision makers and the public.
- The mission of IOM embraces the health of people everywhere.

Priorities (2015 Onward)

IOM's priorities are a blend of responding to questions from our sponsors per our 1863 charter from the U.S. Congress, with a specific focus on a few selected topics—such as value in health care and creating a culture of health rather than solely focusing on disease control—and increasing our impact on the nation's health.

Contact Information

http://nam.edu/about-the-nam

27. International Association of National Public Health Institutes (IANPHI)

IANPHI links and strengthens the national agencies responsible for public health. IANPHI improves the world's health by sharing the experience and expertise of its members to build robust public health systems.

IANPHI, funded by member dues, the Bill & Melinda Gates Foundation, and other partners, was chartered in 2006 and is coordinated by secretariats at Mexico's National Institute of Public Health (INSP), France's Institute for Public Health Surveillance (InVS), and Emory University's Global Health Institute. Its 90-plus members represent close to 90% of the world's population.

Organization

IANPHI's president is Pekka Puska, former director general of Finland's National Institute for Health and Welfare (THL). Its secretary general is Mauricio Hernandez Avila, director general of Mexico's National Institute of Public Health (INSP). IANPHI is governed by an 11-member executive board that includes the directors of the Public Health Agency of Canada; the National Institute for Medical Research of Tanzania; the National Institute for Health Development of Estonia; the National Centre for Disease Control of India; the Public Health Institute of Sudan; the National Institute of Health of Peru; the Ethiopia CDC; the Institute of Epidemiology, Disease Control and Research of Bangladesh; the Robert Koch Institute of Germany; and the National Institute of Health of Mozambique.

Priorities

IANPHI's priorities for 2015 to 2020 are to continue its work to improve capacity and linkages within and between its members through an annual meeting, benchmarking, IANPHI development tools, and investments in capacity-building initiatives.

Contact Information

www.ianphi.org

28. International Council of Nurses (ICN)

Strategic Plan

The ICN strategic plan presents a concise framework of ICN planned activities and action to be implemented to meet ICN objectives over the period. It is designed to advance the vision of our organization. Since its inception in 1899, ICN works to ensure quality nursing care for all, sound health policies globally, the advancement of nursing knowledge, and the presence worldwide of a respected nursing profession and a competent, motivated, and satisfied nursing workforce. The strategic plan, congruent with ICN's purpose, mission, goals, and core values, details the activities and action to be carried out over the period and across the three key domains—professional practice, regulation, and socioeconomic welfare—supported by transparent and outcome-focused governance.

Purpose

To represent nurses worldwide, and to be the voice of nursing internationally, thereby advancing the profession and influencing health policy.

Goals

- To bring nursing together worldwide
- To advance nurses and nursing worldwide
- To influence health policy

Core Values

- Visionary leadership: Keeping the nursing profession's contribution at the forefront of contemporary policy, health, and well-being
- Inclusiveness: Reaching out, to bring nurses and key stakeholders together to ensure informed and participatory decision making
- Innovativeness: Ensuring the organization is forward thinking, dynamic, and achievement focused
- Partnership: Working to place nurses and nursing as key contributors and equal partners in policy debate and systems design and delivery
- Transparency: Guaranteeing open and accountable decision making and action

Achieving Our Purpose

To achieve our purpose, ICN sets objectives and monitors progress against these through the use of key result indicators. Generally speaking, the following objectives have been agreed upon:

- To influence nursing, health, and social policy, as well as professional and socio-economic standards, worldwide
- To assist national nurses associations (NNAs) to improve the standards of nursing and the competence of nurses
- To promote the development of strong NNAs

- To represent nurses and nursing internationally
- To establish, receive, and manage funds and trusts that contribute to the advancement of nursing and of ICN. Each objective has been augmented by subobjectives that provide a more detailed framework for performance tracking.

Contact Information

International Council of Nurses
3, Place Jean Marteau
1201 Geneva
Switzerland
Tel.: +41 22 908 01 00
Fax: +41 22 908 01 01
E-mail: icn@icn.ch (general inquiries); webmaster@icn.ch (website inquiries)

29. International Federation of Dental Educators and Associations (IFDEA)

Background

IFDEA was originally established as an umbrella organization of dental education associations. It held a couple of international meetings culminating in 2000, 2001, and 2007 global congresses, bringing consensus to the challenges and solutions facing dental education at the global level. Today, IFDEA has matured into a virtual organization of dental educators and associations. Membership is free. IFDEA uses technology to help dental educators interact and share knowledge and educational material. In addition, IFDEA collaborates with the Academy for Academic Leadership (AAL) to provide faculty development opportunities worldwide.

Vision

- A *trusted source* for reliable dental education information
- A wellspring of *free dental education resources*
- A *thriving community* where dental educators from all parts of the globe can connect and share knowledge
- An *integral player* in the effort to improve health worldwide

Mission

- Establish a pool of international intellectual resources and expertise
- Create a global network of dental educators based on a hub and spoke arrangement
- Establish an efficient web-based communications system
- Create an accessible repository of information for dental educators
- Assist dental educators' ability to implement recent developments in educational methodologies, research, biomedical sciences, biotechnology, information technology, and clinical dentistry

Achievements

- First Global Congress in dental education in Prague, 2000
- Second Global Congress in dental education in Singapore, 2001
- Third Global Congress in dental education in Dublin, 2007
- Building a virtual organization with online only presence: website gets 2 million visits per month
- Developing opportunities for dental educator faculty development globally in combination with other professional meetings

Priorities

- Continue to develop and host resources for dental educators to improve oral health by improving oral health education
- Continue to offer faculty development opportunities on a global scale

Contact Information

www.ifdea.org

30. International Union for Health Promotion and Education (IUHPE)

Background

IUHPE is over half a century old and draws its strength from being a unique world-wide, independent, and professional association of individuals and organizations committed to improving the health and well-being of the people through education, community action, and the development of healthy public policy.

The *vision* of IUHPE is a world where all people achieve optimum health and well-being.

The *values* critical to the achievement of this vision include:

- Respect for the innate dignity of all people, for cultural identity, for cultural diversity, and for natural resources and the environment
- Inclusion and involvement of people in making the decisions that shape their lives and impact upon their health and well-being
- Equity in health, social, and economic outcomes for all people
- Accountability and transparency within governments, organizations, and communities
- Sustainability
- Social justice for all people and
- Compassion and empowerment

Mission

IUHPE's *mission* is to promote global health and well-being and to contribute to the achievement of equity in health between and within countries of the world. IUHPE fulfills its mission by building and operating an independent, global, professional network of people and institutions to encourage the free exchange of ideas, knowledge, know-how, experiences, and the development of relevant collaborative projects, both at global and regional levels. IUHPE aims to achieve the following goals.

Objectives, inter alia, include

- Increased investment in health promotion by governments, intergovernmental and nongovernmental organizations, academic institutions, and the private sector
- An increase in organizational, governmental, and inter-governmental policies and practices that result in greater equity in health between and within countries
- Improvements in policy and practice of governments at all levels, organizations, and sectors that influence the determinants of the health of populations

Regions

IUHPE can play an important and meaningful role in the world arena. The regional offices have a key role in achieving the overall global strategy through regionally focused priority actions and contributions to global programs and activities.

- Africa—AFRO
- Europe—EURO
- North America Regional Office—NARO
- Northern Part of the Western Pacific—NPWP
- Latin America—ORLA
- South East Asia—SEAR
- South West Pacific—SWP

Activities

- Advocacy
- Capacity-building, education, and training
- Communications and marketing
- Finance and internal control
- Partnership and institutional affairs
- Strategy and governance

Collaborating partners, inter alia, include U.S. Centers for Disease Control and Prevention, Atlanta, USA; Chair, Community Approaches and Health Inequalities, Montreal, Canada; European Commission, Brussels, Belgium; EuroHealthNet, Brussels, Belgium; European Observatory on Health Systems and Policies, Brussels, Belgium; Public Health Agency of Canada, Ottawa, Canada; WHO, Geneva, Switzerland.

Contact Information

International Union for Health Promotion and Education—IUHPE
42 boulevard de la Libération
92303 Saint-Denis Cedex
France
Tel: +33 (0)1 48 13 71 20
Fax: +33 (0)1 48 09 17

31. IntraHealth International (IHI)

Background

IHI is a global health nonprofit that champions the critical role of health workers in health and development. For over 30 years, in 100 countries, IntraHealth has empowered hundreds of thousands of health workers to better serve communities in need, fostering local solutions to health care challenges by improving health worker performance, strengthening health systems, harnessing technology, and leveraging partnerships. IntraHealth has led USAID's flagship global health workforce projects (Capacity*Plus* and the Capacity Project) as well as multiple country-level projects in HIV/AIDS; family planning/reproductive health; maternal, newborn, and child health; tuberculosis; and malaria. IntraHealth has offices in Chapel Hill, NC, Washington, DC, and 19 other countries worldwide. IntraHealth's work is supported and funded by the USAID, the U.S. Centers for Disease Control and Prevention (CDC), the UK Department for International Development (DfID), private foundations (Gates, Rockefeller, Hewlett, etc.), corporations, and individuals.

Vision

IHI believes in a world where all people have the best possible opportunity for health and well-being. We aspire to achieve this vision by being a global champion for health workers.

Mission

IntraHealth empowers health workers to better serve communities in need around the world. We foster local solutions to health care challenges by improving health worker performance, strengthening health systems, harnessing technology, and leveraging partnerships.

Values

- Excellence: We are committed to delivering outstanding performance and demonstrating results achieved.
- Openness: We seek and actively engage new and diverse voices, perspectives, and ways of working.
- Partnership: We work transparently and respectfully with a wide range of stakeholders, donors, and partners to achieve shared goals.
- Accountability: We adhere to high standards of integrity, honesty, transparency, and stewardship in all that we do.

Achievements

- In 2013, IntraHealth reached 178,000 health workers through its many programs. Those health workers provided care to an estimated 356 million people around the world.
- Our iHRIS open source health workforce information systems software has saved 19 countries over $177 million in proprietary software costs.

- We helped the Dominican Republic identify and remove over 4,000 "ghost workers" from the Ministry of Health payroll and save over $6 million in annual lost wages. These savings have been reinvested in the health sector in hiring more health workers, increasing the salaries of health workers, and eliminating users' fees.
- We assisted Uganda in adding 7,200 new members to its health workforce, boosting the percentage of positions filled from 58% to 70% nationwide.
- IntraHealth is developing innovative mHealth solutions, including mSakhi, a mobile phone app for community health workers in India that serves as a resource during client interactions, and mHero, a mobile phone software created in partnership with UNICEF to help Ebola-affected governments communicate systematically with their health workers via SMS.

Priorities

- By 2020, IntraHealth aims to be reaching 400,000 health workers annually.
- Our commitment as a global champion for health workers includes increasing the number of health workers who are *present* on the job where needed; *ready* with the necessary competencies and motivation; *connected* to information and networks; and *safe* from infection, violence, and conflict.

Annual Conference(s)

SwitchPoint (www.intrahealth.org/page/switchpoint-2015), IntraHealth's annual conference, draws innovators, implementers, and donors from around the world to address current and future challenges in global health. SwitchPoint is held in the beautiful rural town Saxapahaw (near Chapel Hill, North Carolina) in a converted garment dying factory, and is the perfect venue for developing creative solutions.

Newsletter

www.intrahealth.org/page/enewsletter

Blog and Social Media

Vital blog: www.intrahealth.org/blog; Twitter: twitter.com/IntraHealth; Facebook: facebook.com/IntraHealth

Contact Information

www.intrahealth.org, www.capacityplus.org, intrahealth@intrahealth.org
Tel.: +1 919 313 9100
Fax: +1 919 313 9108

32. Josiah Macy Jr. Foundation (JMJF)

Background

Kate Macy Ladd established the Josiah Macy Jr. Foundation in 1930 to honor the memory of her father, a well-known philanthropist who died young. Ladd intended the Foundation to devote itself to the promotion of health and the ministry of healing.

Over the decades, the founding mission has remained the same while the focus has shifted from medical research to health professions education. Today, the Josiah Macy Jr. Foundation is the only national foundation dedicated solely to improving the education of health professionals.

Until 1945, the Macy Foundation focused its grant-making efforts on medical research in such fields as traumatic shock and war-related psychiatric disorders, geriatrics and aging, arteriosclerosis, genetics and human development, and psychosomatic medicine. From the end of World War II through the mid-1960s, the Macy Foundation shifted its focus to support the efforts of medical schools to expand and strengthen their basic science faculties. During that time, the Macy Foundation also began supporting the emerging fields of basic reproductive biology, human reproduction, and family planning and fostered their incorporation into the biological, behavioral, and social science bases of academic obstetrics and gynecology.

Since the mid-1970s, the overwhelming majority of the Macy Foundation's grants have supported projects that broaden and improve medical and health professional education.

Values

The Foundation's guiding principle is that the core of health professional education is a strong social mission: To serve the public's needs and improve the health of the public.

Achievements

Over the last 6 years, the Foundation has placed a strong emphasis on the following:

- *Interprofessional education and teamwork:* There is strong evidence that health care delivered by well-functioning teams leads to better outcomes, but health professionals are still educated in silos. We need more planned and rigorous interprofessional education.
- *New curriculum content:* We do a very good job of teaching the biologic and physical sciences as the basis for the practice of medicine, but we have not done as well incorporating other content such as patient safety, quality improvement, and population health in our teaching. We need to broaden and integrate our curriculum across the educational continuum.
- *New models for clinical education:* The management of chronic diseases over time, primarily in outpatient or community-based settings, is the predominant work of health care professionals today, but clinical education is still largely focused on episodic care and is predominately hospital-based. We need new sites and longitudinal models for clinical education and training.
- *Education for the care of underserved populations:* A large number of people enter the health professions each year, but an insufficient number of health professionals choose to serve in rural and inner city areas and some of the most vulnerable people in society—racial and ethnic minorities, elderly people, low-income patients, and others—are not receiving the care they need. We need to provide training and incentives that support and promote care that meets the needs of these underserved populations.

- *Career development in health professions education:* In developing the next generation of national leaders in health professions education, creative faculty members devoted to educational reform must be nurtured. In addition, while we have made progress, we need to diversify the health professions if we are to achieve our goal of uniform excellence in health care.

To complement our grant-making, the Foundation has developed the first of its kind faculty development program. Through the Macy Faculty Scholars program, the Foundation aims to accelerate needed reforms in health professions education to accommodate the dramatic changes occurring in medical practice and health care delivery.

The Foundation selects up to five faculty leaders each year and provides salary support of up to $100,000 per year for 2 years to protect the faculty member's time to pursue an education innovation project at his or her institution.

The final complement to our grant-making is the Macy Conference program. Each year, the Foundation hosts an invitation-only conference on a topic related to the Macy priority areas. The goal of the conference is to come up with actionable recommendations that are disseminated to stakeholders. To view conference monographs, please visit our website and select the publications tab: macyfoundation.org/publications/c/foundation-publication

Contact Information

For more information on the Josiah Macy Jr. Foundation, contact: George E. Thibault, MD, President, at gthibault@macyfoundation.org

33. One Health Commission (OHC)

Background

The term 'One Health' refers to a very old concept that has been resurrected over the past decade in a return to interdisciplinary ways of approaching complex health issues by recognizing the interconnectedness of human, plant, animal, and environmental health. The One Health conversation encourages people to move beyond narrow, professional perspectives toward a more holistic, interactive view of health. The One Health Commission (OHC) was formed as a result of a pioneering partnership between the American Veterinary Medical Association (AVMA) and the American Medical Association (AMA). A task force, formed within that partnership, recommended creation of an organization that would actively promote One Health actions and provide a forum for interdisciplinary professional interactions. Thus, the Commission was charted as a 501c3 nonprofit, NGO (see Executive Report of the Task Force). It works to enhance collaborations among physicians; veterinarians; public health, plant, environmental, and other global health professionals and to increase public awareness of the interconnectedness of people, animals, and the environment. Governed by a board of directors comprised of representatives from organizations that financially sponsor its work, the Commission is also supported by individuals and corporate donations.

Vision

The Commission and its community of stakeholders envisions a day when interdisciplinary "team" approaches are the default standard for education, research, and health applications.

Mission

The Commission's charter is to "Educate and create networks to improve health outcomes and well-being of humans, animals and plants and to promote environmental resilience through a collaborative, global, One Health approach." Hence the slogan "Connect, Create, Educate."

Values

Transdisciplinary collaborations don't just spontaneously happen; they start with relationships, which don't just magically form; they can only occur when professionals have an opportunity to meet each other across disciplines. Within the OHC, like-minded professionals from different disciplines can find each other, relationships can form, and beneficial collaborations can emerge. By its very existence and leadership structure, the OHC provides an opportunity for like-minded professionals to find each other and connect across disciplines.

Achievements (in the Last Few Years)

- Summer 2013, the OHC partnered with the Global Alliance for Rabies Control (GARC) and Bat Conservation International (BCI) to develop two, free to download, *bat rabies educational posters* that are now circulating around the world (Adult Version; Child Version).
- Early in 2014, the Commission was able to assist in connecting many students who work for One Health at their respective academic institutions via a *Students for One Health* listserv. Once connected, they immediately formed a Students for One Health Facebook page and Future Leaders of One Health LinkedIn pages. There are plans for the OHC to become a parent organization for Student One Health Chapters in the United States and beyond and to hold a Student One Health Congress that includes students from human, animal, plant, and environmental domains.
- November 2014, hosted the *1st International Who's Who in One Health Webinar*. Over 1,000 attendees from 61 countries logged in. Over an 8-hour period in 30-minute time slots, prominent One Health leaders from around the world spoke about ongoing One Health activities in their regions from Brazil to Africa, Australia, and the United Kingdom.

Priorities (2015 Onward)

- Professional Continuing Education (CE/CME) Webinars on One Health issues targeted jointly toward *clinical* veterinary and human health practitioners
- Communications/Public Service Announcements: Creating a series of One Health Public Service radio announcements

- Sharing One Health Narratives/Case Studies: Identify and collect One Health narratives and scientific, evidence-based case studies from the One Health Community to post on the OHC website and circulate in newsletters to "teach by example"

Newsletter/Key Publications

See the inaugural *One Health Commission Newsletter* published online in July 2014.

Other Information

One Health requires passionate individuals to step forward, become involved, and help "lead" the many teams that can be formed to take significant actions that will eventually open the eyes of policy makers and funding agents so that more resources can be directed to needed One Health actions like creating cutting-edge diagnostics and strategies to "prevent'" the next Ebola or other zoonotic disease outbreak.

Contact Information

www.onehealthcommission.org

34. One Health Initiative Movement (OHIM)

Background

"One Health," formerly referred to as "One Medicine" during the 20th century, is a documented, efficacious underutilized health advancing concept known about for centuries. One Health activities and promotion were ignited during the early 21st century, arguably following the visionary liaison developed between AVMA and AMA in 2007; its premise of having a co-equal interdisciplinary/multidisciplinary approach helps synergistically enhance public health, clinical health (comparative medicine/surgery), and environmental health goals for society.

Numerous other reputable independent high profile and important national and international organizations, educational institutions, and many visionary/prominent health and scientific leaders henceforth became more proactive in the quest for "One Health" implementation.

The *One Health Initiative* Autonomous *pro bono Team* was established in April 2006 by Laura H. Kahn, MD, MPH, MPP, a physician author and research scholar at the Woodrow Wilson School of Public and International Affairs, Princeton University; and Bruce Kaplan, DVM, a retired private practice veterinarian practitioner, U.S. CDC epidemiologist, U.S. Department of Agriculture, Food Safety and Inspection Service (USDA-FSIS) public affairs professional, and Office of Public Health and Science (OPHS) staff member. They were joined in 2007 by physician virologist/vaccinologist Thomas P. Monath, MD, formerly with the CDC and U.S. Army Medical Research Institute of Infectious Diseases (USAMRIID). The OHI team was subsequently joined by epidemiologist/scientist/co-founder of ProMED-mail Jack Woodall, PhD (2009), formerly with CDC and WHO, and Lisa A. Conti,

DVM, MPH (2012), veterinarian, public health/environmental health authority and co-author/writer of the first One Health textbook, *Human-Animal Medicine: Clinical Approaches to Zoonoses, Toxicants, and Other Shared Health Risks*. The OHI team originated the OHI website in October 2008.

It works pro bono and receives no external funding while not requiring or accepting fees from any and all One Health supporters/advocates. To date (October 2014) the OHI Supporter list (www.onehealthinitiative.com/supporters.php) includes 897 Supporting Organizations and individuals worldwide (from 64 countries) and has a distinguished Honorary International Advisory Board (www.onehealthinitiative .com/advBoard.php).

Since its onset, the OHI team has endeavored to ecumenically work with and report about—on the OHI website—all reputable national and international One Health "silos" (organizations, educational institutions, individuals, etc.) co-equally and without discrimination. The OHI team recognizes that no one person, organization, nation, or governmental entity owns or solely represents the international One Health movement.

Mission and Goals

Recognizing that human health (including mental health via the human–animal bond phenomenon), animal health, and ecosystem health are inextricably linked, One Health seeks to promote, improve, and defend the health and well-being of all species by enhancing cooperation and collaboration between physicians, veterinarians, and other scientific health and environmental professionals and by promoting strengths in leadership and management to achieve these goals.

One Health is dedicated to improving the lives of all species—human and animal—through the integration of human medicine, veterinary medicine, and environmental science.

The OHI team's goals: To educate the international scientific community, political and governmental leaders, the news media, and the general public and about the One Health concept and to promote the One Health concept for global implementation.

Contact Information

OHI website contents manager: kkm@onehealthinitiative.com
Dr. Laura H. Kahn: lkahn@Princeton.edu
Dr. Bruce Kaplan: bkapdvm@verizon.net
Dr. Thomas P. Monath: tpmonath@gmail.com
Dr. Jack Woodall: Jackwoodall13@gmail.com
Dr. Lisa A. Conti: xc2001@gmail.com

35. Open Society Foundations (OSF)

Background

The Open Society Foundations began in 1979 when George Soros decided he had enough money. His great success as a hedge fund manager allowed him to pursue his ambition of establishing open societies in place of authoritarian forms of government.

"Open society is based on the recognition that our understanding of the world is inherently imperfect," Soros said. "What is imperfect can be improved." He started by supporting scholarships for Black students at the University of Cape Town in South Africa and for Eastern European dissidents to study abroad.

In its public health work, the Open Society Foundations emphasize the protection of the rights of marginalized people and their full participation in society. The Foundations focus on the health and rights of people who use drugs, sexual minorities, people living with HIV, people living with mental disabilities, sex workers, and Roma in Europe. Examples of its work include support for peer paralegal programs for sex workers, service-oriented collaborations between people who use drugs and police groups, hospice and palliative care provision in rural areas, reform of national policies that block access to essential pain medicines, and supported living for persons with disabilities within their home communities—among much more.

The staff of Open Society Foundations are active in more than 100 countries in every region of the world. The Foundations' expenditures in 2010 amounted to US$820 million.

Mission

- The Open Society Foundations work to build vibrant and tolerant societies whose governments are accountable and open to the participation of all people.
- We support marginalized populations, who often lack appropriate health care because of the stigma they face, to fight for and protect their fundamental rights, and to develop inclusive, responsive, and just societies in which health-related policies and practices reflect these values.
- We seek to strengthen the rule of law; respect for human rights, minorities, and a diversity of opinions; democratically elected governments; and a civil society that helps keep government power in check.
- We help to shape public policies that assure greater fairness in political, legal, and economic systems and safeguard fundamental rights.
- We implement initiatives to advance justice, education, and independent media.
- We build alliances across borders and continents on issues such as corruption and freedom of information.
- Working in every part of the world, the Open Society Foundations place a high priority on protecting and improving the lives of people in marginalized communities.

Values

- We believe in fundamental human rights, dignity, and the rule of law.
- We believe in a society where all people are free to participate fully in civic, economic, and cultural life.
- We believe in addressing inequalities that cut across multiple lines, including race, class, gender, sexual orientation, and citizenship.
- We believe in holding those in power accountable for their actions and in increasing the power of historically excluded groups.

- We believe in helping people and communities press for change on their own behalf.
- We believe in responding quickly and flexibly to the most critical threats to open society.
- We believe in taking on controversial issues and supporting bold, innovative solutions that address root causes and advance systemic change.
- We believe in encouraging critical debate and respecting diverse opinions.

Programs

- Documentary Photography Project: www.opensocietyfoundations .org/about/staff/programs/10317
- Early Childhood Program: www.opensocietyfoundations.org/about/staff/programs/10318
- Education Support Program: www.opensocietyfoundations.org/about/staff/programs/10320
- Eurasia Program: www.opensocietyfoundations.org/about/staff/programs/52159
- Fiscal Governance Program: www.opensocietyfoundations.org/about/staff/programs/50631
- Global Drug Policy Program: www.opensocietyfoundations.org/about/staff/programs/10321
- Human Rights Initiative: www.opensocietyfoundations.org/about/staff/programs/49735
- Independent Journalism: www.opensocietyfoundations.org/about/staff/programs/10329
- Information Program: www.opensocietyfoundations.org/about/staff/programs/10323
- International Higher Education Support Program: www.opensociety foundations.org/about/staff/programs/10324
- International Migration Initiative: www.opensocietyfoundations.org/about/staff/programs/10325
- Latin America Program: www.opensocietyfoundations.org/about/staff/programs/10327
- Making the Most of EU Funds for Roma: www.opensocietyfoundations.org/about/staff/programs/40943
- New Executives Fund: www.opensocietyfoundations.org/about/staff/programs/52724

36. Pan American Health Organization/WHO (PAHO/WHO)

The Pan American Sanitary Bureau (PASB), the oldest international health agency in the world, is the secretariat of the Pan American Health Organization (PAHO). The Bureau is committed to providing technical support and leadership to PAHO member states as they pursue their goal of "Health for All" and the values therein. Toward that end, the following values, vision, and mission guide the Bureau's work.

Vision

PASB will be the major catalyst for ensuring that all the peoples of the Americas enjoy optimal health and contribute to the well-being of their families and communities.

Mission

To lead strategic collaborative efforts among member states and other partners to promote equity in health, to combat disease, and to improve the quality of, and lengthen, the lives of the peoples of the Americas.

Values

- Equity: Striving for fairness and justice by eliminating differences that are unnecessary and avoidable
- Excellence: Achieving the highest quality in what we do
- Solidarity: Promoting shared interests and responsibilities and enabling collective efforts to achieve common goals
- Respect: Embracing the dignity and diversity of individuals, groups, and countries
- Integrity: Assuring transparent, ethical, and accountable performance

Achievements, inter alia, included

- Throughout 2012 to 2013, the Organization worked with member states to strengthen health systems based on a renewed primary health care strategy and with a view to advancing universal health coverage.
- PAHO's technical cooperation supported member states' efforts to reduce the burden of communicable diseases and to progress toward the elimination of those diseases considered eliminable.
- PAHO recognizes the central role of the family and community in promoting and protecting health as a social value and a human right and uses a life-course approach, addressing the specific needs of each population group. A central priority of this work was to accelerate reductions in maternal and neonatal mortality.

Strategic Plan 2014 to 2019

- Communicable diseases: Reducing the burden of communicable diseases, including HIV/AIDS, sexually transmitted infections, and viral hepatitis; tuberculosis; malaria and other vector-borne diseases; neglected, tropical, and zoonotic diseases; and vaccine-preventable diseases.
- Noncommunicable diseases and risk factors: Reducing the burden of noncommunicable diseases, including cardiovascular diseases, cancers, chronic lung diseases, diabetes, and mental health disorders, as well as disability, violence, and injuries, through health promotion and risk reduction, prevention, treatment, and monitoring of noncommunicable diseases and their risk factors.

- Determinants of health and promoting health throughout the life course: Promoting good health at key stages of life, taking into account the need to address the social determinants of health (societal conditions in which people are born, grow, live, work, and age), and implementing approaches based on gender equality, ethnicity, equity, and human rights.
- Health systems: Strengthening health systems based on primary care; focusing health governance and financing toward progressive realization of universal health coverage; organizing people-centered, integrated service delivery; promoting access to and rational use of health technologies; strengthening health information and research systems and the integration of evidence into health policies and health care; facilitating transfer of knowledge and technologies; and developing human resources for health.
- Preparedness, surveillance, and response: Reducing mortality, morbidity, and societal disruption resulting from epidemics, disasters, conflicts, and environmental and food-related emergencies by focusing on risk reduction, preparedness, response, and recovery activities that build resilience and use a multisectoral approach to contribute to health security.
- Corporate services/enabling functions: Fostering and implementing the organizational leadership and corporate services that are required to maintain the integrity and efficient functioning of the Organization, enabling it to deliver effectively on its mandates.

Contact Information

www.paho.org

37. People's Health Movement (PHM)

Background

PHM is a global network bringing together grassroots health activists, civil society organizations, and academic institutions from around the world, particularly from low- and middle-income countries. We currently have a presence in around 70 countries. The world is facing a global health crisis characterized by growing inequities within and among nations and millions of preventable deaths, especially among the poor. These are in large degree due to unfair economic structures that lock people into poverty and poor health. In 2000, concerned activists, academics, and health workers got together for the first People's Health Assembly. The People's Charter for Health (PCH), our founding document, was developed and PHM was born. The global Steering Committee (SC) is the principal decision making body of PHM. The main task of the SC is to provide strategic guidance to the movement, promoting the PCH, developing positions, and ensuring fluent two-way communications between PHM and the region/network/program they represent. Communication with country circles is an important function of regional representatives.

The People's Charter for Health

PCH is the framework within which PHM acts and offers strategic guidance to the movement. It is both a tool for advocacy and a framework for action. By endorsing the charter, one becomes part of PHM. The PCH endorses the Alma Ata Declaration, and affirms health as a social, economic, and political issue but, above all, a fundamental human right.

Vision

"Equity, ecologically-sustainable development and peace are at the heart of our vision of a better world—a world in which a healthy life for all is a reality; a world that respects, appreciates and celebrates all life and diversity; a world that enables the flowering of people's talents and abilities to enrich each other; a world in which people's voices guide the decisions that shape our lives . . . ."

Objectives, inter alia, include

- To promote "Health for All" through an equitable, participatory, and intersectoral movement and as a rights issue.
- To advocate for government and other health agencies to ensure universal access to quality health care, education, and social services according to people's needs and not their ability to pay.

Structure of PHM

PHM is a network of networks, organizations, and individuals with some centrally supported programs (for more information, refer below). As a movement, we do not follow rigid structures; broadly speaking, however, PHM is structured as follows:

Country Circles

At the country level, PHM manifests in the form of groups coming together nationally or locally. Country circles, sometimes called "local chapters," grow according to the country's need; they are most often loose networks that come together for joint action around specific issues, but can be formalized and legalized as an organization. There is no set way on how PHM organizes locally as this depends on the local context, chosen activities, and the circumstances of the people building PHM.

Regional PHM

Regionally, PHM aims to build coalitions and networks to encourage support, sharing, and learning. Regional collaboration also offers a platform for organizing and advocacy on regional and global health governance. It builds solidarity around issues specific to the region and a strong base for action (locally, regionally, and globally). The way each region coordinates itself is defined by the needs and context of the region. Centrally PHM aims to employ regional coordinators for each region. So far, only Africa and the Middle East regions have such a coordinator. Each PHM region is represented in the Global Steering Council.

Contact Information

Global Secretariat (Global Coordinators):
Cape Town (South Africa): Bridget Lloyd (blloyd@phmovement.org)
Delhi (India): Hani Serag (hserag@phmovement.org)
Cairo (Egypt): Amit Sengupta (asengupta@phmovement)

38. Public Health Association of Australia (PHAA)

Background

PHAA is recognized as the principal nongovernment organization for public health in Australia and works to promote the health and well-being of all Australians. The Association seeks better population health outcomes based on prevention, the social determinants of health, and equity principles. PHAA is a national organization comprising around 1,900 individual members and representing over 40 professional groups concerned with the promotion of health at a population level.

PHAA has branches in every state and territory and a wide range of special interest groups. The branches work with the national office in providing policy advice, in organizing seminars and public events, and in mentoring public health professionals. This work is based on the agreed policies of PHAA. Our special interest groups provide specific expertise, peer review, and professionalism in assisting the national organization to respond to issues and challenges as well as a close involvement in the development of policies. In addition to these groups, the *Australian and New Zealand Journal of Public Health* (*ANZJPH*) draws on individuals from within PHAA who provide editorial advice and review and edit the journal.

In recent years, PHAA has further developed its role in advocacy to achieve the best possible health outcomes for the community, both by working with all levels of government and agencies and by promoting key policies and advocacy goals through the media, public events, and other means.

Vision for a Healthy Population

PHAA has a vision for a healthy region, a healthy nation, healthy people: Living in a healthy society and a sustaining environment, improving and promoting health for all.

Mission

To be the leading public health advocacy group, and to drive better health outcomes through health equity and sound, population-based policy, and vigorous advocacy.

Priorities

Key roles of the organization include capacity building, advocacy, and the development of policy. Core to our work is an evidence base drawn from a wide range of members working in public health practice, research, administration, and related fields who volunteer their time to inform policy, support advocacy, and assist in capacity building within the sector. The aims of PHAA include a commitment to:

- Advance a caring, generous, and equitable Australian society with particular respect for Aboriginal and Torres Strait Islanders as the first peoples of the nation
- Promote and strengthen public health research, knowledge, training, and practice
- Promote a healthy and ecologically sustaining human society across Australia, including tackling global warming, environmental change, and a sustainable population
- Promote universally accessible people centered and health promoting primary health care and hospital services that are complemented by health and community workforce training and development
- Promote universal health literacy as part of comprehensive health care
- Support health promoting settings, including the home, as the norm
- Assist other countries in our region to protect the health of their populations, and to advocate for trade policies that enable them to do so
- Promote PHAA as a vibrant living model of its vision and aims

Contact Information

Units 2 & 3, 20 Napier Close
Deakin ACT 2600
PO Box 319
Curtin ACT 2605
Australia
Tel.: +61 2 6285 2373
Fax: +61 2 6282 5438
E-mail: phaa@phaa.net.au
Website: www.phaa.net.au

39. Public Health Association of South Africa (PHASA)

Background

PHASA was launched in 2004, and has just celebrated its tenth anniversary. It is an association of public health practitioners advocating equitable access to the basic conditions necessary for all South Africans to achieve health, including equitable access to effective health care.

PHASA works with national and international public health associations and related organizations to advocate on national and international issues that have an impact on the conditions for a healthy society.

Achievements

- Establishing special interest groups
- Launching a PHILA award that recognizes excellence in public health

- Capacity building at pre-conference workshops and mentoring of young public health professionals
- Growing the organization annually

Key Objectives

- To advocate for the conditions for a healthy society
- To build an effective organization
- To create a multidisciplinary environment of professional exchange and debate, study, and activity through meetings, conferences, and workshops for interested people
- To promote teaching and research in public health issues
- To support the publication of relevant materials
- To network with other public health organizations and related organizations
- To encourage and facilitate measures for disease prevention and health promotion

Priorities

- To increase membership
- To raise funds for the organization
- To strengthen and grow the advocacy role
- To launch regional/provincial organizations
- To expand the special interest groups
- To strengthen and grow student membership and JuPHASA (junior PHASA)

Website and Newsletter

To help achieve our association's goals, we have a dynamic website (www.phasa.org .za) and currently produce monthly newsletters for members and those accessing the website.

Contact Information
Website: http://www.phasa.org.za/

40. Public Health England (PHE)

Background

PHE was established on April 1, 2013, to bring together public health specialists from more than 70 organizations into a single public health service. PHE is an executive agency of the Department of Health. It fulfills the Secretary of State for Health's statutory duty to protect health and address inequalities, and to promote the health and well-being of the nation.

Values

PHE is committed to working with a range of stakeholders—national and local government, the NHS, industry, academia, the public, and the voluntary and community sector—to improve population health and reduce inequalities. PHE is an open organization, committed to carrying out its activities in a transparent manner.

Priorities 2014 to 2015

- Improving global health security and meeting responsibilities under the International Health Regulations, focusing on: antimicrobial resistance, mass gatherings, extreme events, climate change, bioterrorism, emergency response, new and emerging infections, cross-border threats, and migrant and travel health
- Responding to outbreaks and incidents of international concern, and supporting the public health response to humanitarian disasters
- Building public health capacity, particularly in low- and middle-income countries, through, for example, a program of staff secondments and global health initiatives
- Developing our focus on, and capacity for, engagement on international aspects of health and well-being, and noncommunicable diseases (NCD)
- Strengthening UK partnerships for global health activity

Achievements

PHE's achievements build on public health efforts across a number of areas and include:

- A new national focus on health and well-being; making the case for prevention and early intervention
- In knowledge and intelligence, a new data tool—Longer Lives—highlighting premature mortality across every local authority in England
- In campaigns, increased public engagement with core health and well-being messages: PHE's anti-smoking campaign, Stoptober, is estimated to have generated an additional 350,000 quit attempts (2012)
- In screening, introducing HPV testing into the cervical cancer screening program (including piloting its use as the primary test)
- Oversight and support of NHS Health Check, a world-leading risk awareness, risk assessment, and risk and disease management program involving 15 million people (aged 40–74)
- Leading the national agenda across a range of public health issues, including tackling childhood obesity, developing a national program on mental health, and improving sexual health and recovery rates from drug dependency
- Support for the public health role of local authorities through PHE's 15 centers, and through the provision of local information, intelligence, and commissioning toolkits

Annual Conferences
September

Newsletter

- PHE publishes a monthly newsletter (*PHE Bulletin* accessed at www.gov.uk/government/collections/phe-bulletin) providing public health news and information to local authorities, professionals, and stakeholders across the health and social care system.
- PHE sends out a weekly update from its chief executive, Duncan Selbie (accessed at www.gov.uk/government/collections/duncan-selbies-friday-messages).
- PHE publishes regular blogs on topical issues in public health (public health matters accessed at https://publichealthmatters.blog.gov.uk).

Contact Information

Public Information Access Office
Public Health England
Wellington House
133-155 Waterloo Road
London SE1 8UG
E-mail: enquiries@phe.gov.uk
Main switchboard: +44 020 7654 8000
Health Advice for Members of the Public: 0845 4647 (NHS Direct)

41. Public Health Foundation of India (PHFI)

Background

PHFI is a public–private initiative formed to redress the limited institutional capacity in India for strengthening training, research, and policy development in the area of public health. Structured as an independent foundation, PHFI adopts a broad, integrative approach to public health, tailoring its endeavors to Indian conditions and bearing relevance to countries facing similar challenges and concerns. PHFI was launched on March 28, 2006, by then prime minister of India, Dr. Manmohan Singh, at New Delhi. Under the governance structure adopted, the Foundation is governed by a fully empowered, independent, general body (comprising of all the members of the society) that has representatives from multiple constituencies—government, Indian and international academia and scientific community, civil society, and private sector.

Vision

Strengthen India's public health institutional and systems capability and provide knowledge to achieve better health outcomes for all.

Mission

- Developing the public health workforce and setting standards
- Advancing public health research and technology
- Strengthening knowledge application and evidence-informed public health practice and policy

Values

- Transparency
- Impact
- Informed
- Excellence
- Independence
- Inclusiveness

Achievements and Priorities

The PHFI network: Since its inception in 2006, the network of PHFI and its constituent units, including Indian Institutes of Public Health (IIPHs) and Centres of Excellence in priority public health themes, has developed significant scale and capability with focus on multidisciplinary teaching, research, and practice. This network has a multidisciplinary talent pool of 700 plus faculty and research and program staff with 90 full-time faculty (more than half with PhDs). Its experts include doctors, economists, engineers, sociologists, and others. The PHFI network has collaborations, both national and international, with over 50 academic and research organizations; several government, bilateral, and multilateral agencies; private sector; and foundations. PHFI is also building capacity and is a catalyst for transformational and enabling change through an integrated set of activities in education, training, research, technology, communications, and policy development.

Education and Training

Since the launch of academic and training programs in 2008, over 680 public health professionals have graduated from on campus programs, more than 17,000 participants have been trained through short-term programs, and more than 750 have been covered through distance learning programs.

Research and Technology

PHFI is recognized as a scientific and industrial research organization (SIRO) by the Government of India. PHFI has also been designated by WHO's Global Alliance for Health Systems and Policy Research as one of six Global Nodal Centers.

To date, research at PHFI has resulted in more than 1,200 publications with an average impact factor of over 5, in addition to over 400 conference papers and abstracts. Our division of affordable health technologies has developed *Swasthya Slate*, an electronic tablet-based solution for point-of-care diagnostics that is being considered and adopted in national health programs by state governments and has received interest from several international governments.

Health Systems, Policy, Advocacy, and Priorities

PHFI is advocating policy change in several areas including advancing the universal health coverage framework, establishing public health cadre in states, shaping tobacco control policy, enhancing capacity for allied health professionals, and initiatives in maternal and child health. PHFI also provides technical support to national programs such as the routine immunization program of the Ministry of Health and Family Welfare and the National HIV-AIDS Control Programme. Our priorities for the future include capacity building in the areas of health systems, policy and financing, women and child health, noncommunicable diseases, infectious diseases, public health nutrition, social determinants of health, and disability.

Contact Information

Offices
ISID Complex
4 Institutional Area
Vasant Kunj
New Delhi 110070, India
Tel.: +91 11 49566000
Fax: +91 11 49566063
E-mail: contact@phfi.org
Delhi NCR
Plot No. 47, Sector 44
Institutional Area Gurgaon 122002
Tel.: +91 0124 4781400
Fax: +91 0124-4781601
E-mail: contact@phfi.org

42. Towards Unity for Health (TUFH)

Background

The Network: Towards Unity for Health (The Network: TUFH) is an international non-profit organization that mobilizes individuals and institutions committed to improving global health through community-oriented education, service, and research. With its longstanding history of over 30 years, The Network: TUFH has played an important role in fostering community-oriented innovations, leading to curriculum reforms around the globe.

The Network: TUFH is a non-governmental organization (NGO) in official relation with the World Health Organization (WHO).

Vision

The Network: Towards Unity for Health is actively working together with its members toward a common goal: unity in health for all, based on equity, making primary health care accessible, with sufficient high quality health care providers, and education institutions that offer high quality training for its students, adapted to the needs of the community.

Mission

The Network: TUFH is defined through the strengths of its members consisting of professionals, practitioners, students, community leaders, and organizations from various disciplines in health. The global impact of The Network: TUFH can be observed through programs and collaborations on community health, women's health, inter-professional health education and practice, social accountability in health education and service, and the well-being of underserved populations.

Values

The core values of The Network: TUFH are equity, solidarity, diversity, sustainability, and innovation.

Achievements

Each year The Network: TUFH organizes an international conference that fosters a brotherly atmosphere, provides opportunities to identify new colleagues for collaborations with like-minded organizations, and strengthens existing links, while stimulating new ideas and refreshing approaches.

Priorities (2015 Onward)

From 2015 onward, The Network will focus on its contribution to universal health coverage and strengthening the social accountability of institutions for health professional education worldwide. The Network: TUFH wants to become an international umbrella organization, bringing people, institutions, and movements together that contribute to the mission.

Annual Conference

Conference 2015: www.the-networktufh.org/conferences
Overview Conferences: www.the-networktufh.org/conferences/our-history-and-future

Newsletter/Key Publications

The Biannual Network: TUFH Newsletter, which provides current news on member institutions, regional activities and future events, has a circulation of over 800 copies.
www.the-networktufh.org/resources/newsletter

The Network: TUFH publishes the peer-reviewed, MEDLINE indexed, unique journal, *Education for Health: Change in Learning and Practice* (EfH). It is an open access e-journal, the content of which reflects the mission and objectives of its parent organization, The Network: TUFH.
www.educationforhealth.net

Contact information

Website: www.the-networktufh.org
Contact: www.the-networktufh.org/about/office

43. United Nations Educational, Scientific and Cultural Organization (UNESCO)

Background

UNESCO was founded on November 16, 1945 (www.unesco.org/new/en/unesco/about-us) as a specialized agency of the UN after ratification by 20 countries (Australia, Brazil, Canada, China, Czechoslovakia, Denmark, Dominican Republic, Egypt, France, Greece, India, Lebanon, Mexico, New Zealand, Norway, Saudi

Arabia, South Africa, Turkey, United Kingdom, and United States). With headquarters in Paris, France, it contributes to peace and security across 195 member states and 8 associate members (http://en.unesco.org). Its main mission is achieved by "promoting international collaboration through education, science, and culture in order to further universal respect for justice, the rule of law, and human rights along with fundamental freedom proclaimed in the United Nations Charter." UNESCO pursues its objectives through five major programs: education (ED), natural sciences (SC), social and human sciences (SHS), culture (CLT), and communication and information (CI).

The secretariat consists of the director-general and the staff. The secretariat employs around 2,000 civil servants from some 170 countries. The staff is divided into professional and general service categories. More than 700 staff members work in UNESCO's 65 field offices around the world. The director-general draws up the program and budget, and the secretariat is responsible for implementing these programs in the respective five sectors. The General Conference is the supreme decision-making body and is held every 2 years. It decides policy of UNESCO activity, approves programs and budgets, and appoints the director-general.

Achievements (www.unesco.org/new/en/unesco/about-us/who-we-are/history/milestones)

In the past 70 years, it has contributed to key areas, including:

- Safeguarding and sharing our culture
- Safeguarding our planet
- Sharing knowledge
- Fighting for human rights
- Inspiring creativity, dialogue, and the community
- Promoting international standards
- Promoting gender equality
- Reaching the marginalized
- Fostering UNESCO communities

Significant steps toward defining the education agenda beyond 2015 (Education Sustainable Development [ESD]) has included the adoption of the draft Muscat Agreement by over 250 delegates at the Global Meeting on Education for All, held in Muscat, Oman, on May 12 to 14, 2014. The Agreement outlines an overarching goal—to "ensure equitable and inclusive quality education and lifelong learning for all by 2030"—and a set of seven global targets for education post-2015 with regard to: early childhood care and education, youth and adult literacy, skills for work, and skills for citizenship and sustainable development, teachers, and financing of education. The latter conference was followed by the World Conference on Education for Sustainable Development in Japan with over 1,000 attendees, co-organized by UNESCO and the Government of Japan, November 10 to 12, 2014, leading to a formal Declaration and, inter alia, the urgent need to ensure "adequate resources including funding for ESD," to be discussed further at the World Education Forum in the Republic of Korea, May 10 to 22, 2015.

UNESCO's Medium-Term Strategy for 2014 to 2021 (http://unesdoc.unesco.org /images/0018/001887/188700e.pdf)

Building on its central mission of focusing on peace, poverty, sustainable development, and intercultural dialogue through education, the sciences, culture, communication, and information, the strategy aspires to strengthen UNESCO's fieldwork, UN participation, and partnerships. Africa and gender equality remain the two global priorities of UNESCO's agenda for this decade and beyond, including an "Operational Strategy on Youth for 2014-2021." Ms. Irina Bokova, the present director-general and the first woman—as well as the first representative of Eastern Europe—in the top position of UNESCO, in her inaugural address in 2009 highlighted that "cultural diversity and inter-cultural dialogue contribute to the emergence of a new humanism that reconciles the global and the local, and teaches us anew how to build the world. [. . .] For me, humanism means aspiring to peace, democracy, justice and human rights. For me, humanism means aspiring to tolerance, knowledge and cultural diversity. It is rooted in ethics and in social and economic responsibility. It comes into its own by extending assistance to the most vulnerable. It is at the heart of the commitment to struggle to face our greatest common challenges, particularly respect for the environment."

44. World Bank (WB)

Background

The World Bank was established in 1944 as facilitator of post-war reconstruction and development, as the International Bank for Reconstruction and Development (IBRD). Since that time, the World Bank has expanded from a single institution to the present-day associated group of five development institutions: the IBRD, the International Development Association (IDA) for lowest income countries, the International Finance Corporation (IFC) for private sector investments, the Multilateral Guarantee Agency (MIGA), and the International Centre for the Settlement of Investment Disputes (ICSID). The five institutions are collectively known as the World Bank Group.

Organization

The World Bank Group is a cooperative, made up of some 188 member countries. These member countries, or shareholders, are represented by a board of governors, who are the ultimate policy makers at the World Bank. The board of governors is composed of member countries' ministers of finance or ministers of development. They meet once a year at the annual meetings of the boards of governors of the World Bank Group and the International Monetary Fund. The executive directors make up the boards of directors of the World Bank. They normally meet regularly to oversee the Bank's business, including approval of loans and guarantees, new policies, the administrative budget, country assistance strategies, and borrowing and financial decisions. The president of the World Bank Group, Jim Yong Kim, chairs meetings of the boards of directors and is responsible for overall management of the Bank.

Vision

The World Bank Group vision is to support low- and middle-income countries in achieving the goal of ending extreme poverty and boosting shared prosperity through inclusive and sustainable development.

Mission

The World Bank Group's mission is to provide financing, state-of-the-art analysis, and policy advice to help countries achieve the goal of ending extreme poverty and boosting shared prosperity. Health is one of the major components of this mission, and the World Bank Group assists countries to expand access to quality, affordable health care; protect people from falling into poverty due to illness; and promote investments in all sectors that reduce public health risks and form the foundation of healthy societies.

Achievements in the Last 3 Years

Between July 2011 and June 2013 (fiscal years 2011–2013), the World Bank Group financed on average US$2.5 billion per year to health, nutrition, and population sector projects. These projects contributed to a wide range of activities in all the regions across the globe, but focused on investments to accelerate the achievement of health-related MDGs, including reproductive health, maternal and child health, nutrition, HIV/AIDS, malaria, and tuberculosis. A significant share of the projects also supported health systems strengthening activities, including investments in management and information systems, human resources in health, and essential infrastructure and supplies.

Priorities

The World Bank Group is committed to helping countries achieve universal health coverage, and to this end, two overarching targets have been identified:

- For financial protection, by 2020, the World Bank Group proposes to reduce by half the number of people who are impoverished due to out-of-pocket health care expenses. By 2030, no one should fall into poverty because of out-of-pocket health care expenses. Achieving this target will require moving from 100 million people impoverished every year at present to 50 million by 2020, and then to zero by 2030.
- For service delivery, the World Bank Group proposes to double the proportion of poor people in developing countries who have access to essential health services, such as vaccination for children, access to skilled attendant at childbirth, and programs to address chronic conditions and injuries, from 40% today to 80% by 2030.

Better health outcomes depend on strong health systems and the right investments outside of the health sector, including education, social protection, transport and road safety, agriculture, and water and sanitation. The Bank is shaping the science of delivery in health across all sectors, building on decades of experience working with countries to improve services for poor people.

Contact Information

Akiko Maeda, Lead Health Specialist, Health, Nutrition, & Population
Human Development Network, The World Bank
Tel.: +1 202 473 3793 (work); +1 240 486 5707 (mobile)
E-mail: amaeda@worldbank.org
Website: www.worldbank.org/en/topic/health

45. World Federation for Medical Education (WFME)

Background

WFME was founded in 1972, on the initiative of a worldwide group of medical educators, supported by WHO and the World Medical Association (WMA). The primary members of WFME are the six Regional Associations for Medical Education, one for each of the six WHO regions. The governing body is the Executive Council, on which each Regional Association has one vote. Nonvoting members of the Executive Council include WHO, WMA, the International Federation of Medical Students' Associations (IFMSA), and the Educational Commission for Foreign Medical Graduates of the USA (ECFMG).

WFME is led by a president, appointed by the Executive Council, who is supported by a worldwide team of advisors.

Mission

The mission of WFME is to enhance the quality of medical education worldwide, and to promote the highest standards in medical education. This mission is met through the development of standards in medical education, by the promotion of accreditation of medical schools, with the development of databases on medical education, through projects on the future of medicine and medical education, and through other publications and partnerships.

WFME works in partnership with its six Regional Associations for Medical Education, with global professional and international organizations including WHO and WMA, with WFME's associate members, and with medical schools worldwide.

The purpose of WFME in promoting better medical education is to improve health care for all mankind.

WFME's activities cover all stages of medical education, from basic (undergraduate) medical education, through postgraduate medical education—including vocational training, specialist training, and research doctoral education—and continuing medical education and the continuing professional development of medical doctors.

Achievements in the 21st Century

- Creation of standards for medical education at all stages, in extensive use worldwide.
- Development (jointly with WHO) of policies and procedures for the accreditation of medical education.
- Foundation, in partnership, of the new *World Directory of Medical Schools*.

Current Activities
- Continuation of the above activities, including processes for the recognition of accreditation agencies.
- Being an authoritative source of information and advice on issues in the quality, management, and delivery of medical education worldwide. The obligation to provide this is primarily to WFME's major partners, particularly to WHO, and also to WMA, IFMSA, and ECFMG.

Contact Information

Full information on WFME, and contact details, can be found on the website: www .wfme.org

46. World Federation of Public Health Associations (WFPHA)

Background

In May 1967, during the 20th World Health Assembly, a group of delegates representing 32 national public health associations convened to discuss the concept of a nongovernmental civil society voice for public health. The World Federation of Public Health Associations (WFPHA) was established and incorporated that same month in Geneva (Switzerland), with 16 core ember associations. WFPHA is an international NGO composed of multidisciplinary national public health associations. It is the only worldwide professional society representing and serving the broad field of public health. WFPHA's mission is to promote and protect global public health. WFPHA is accredited as an NGO in official relations with WHO. It collaborates with WHO to advance the field of public health through the promotion of pro-health policies, strategies, and best practices around the world. The Federation also holds consultation status with the United Nations Economic and Social Council (ECOSOC).

Vision and Mission
- Goal 1: To develop and promote effective global policies to improve the health of populations
- Goal 2: To advance public health practice, education/training, and research
- Goal 3: To expand and strengthen internal and external partnerships
- Goal 4: To achieve and maintain an effective, efficient, and sustainable organization
- Goal 5: To support member associations in improving their infrastructure and organizational capacity

Values
- Right to health: We hold that health is a fundamental human right and a public good.
- Social justice: We advocate for equity and nondiscrimination and the elimination of health disparities.

- Diversity and inclusion: We promote a global public health perspective that includes diverse social and cultural backgrounds, ethnicity, race, gender, sexual orientation, and disability.
- Partnership: We use partnership as the basis for mutual learning and capacity building.
- Ethical conduct: We believe in the ethical practice of public health for individuals and populations.

Achievements (Examples)

- Transparent and enabling governance structure
- External and internal visibility and expanding relationships
- Organized regular communication
- Triennial conferences: opportunity for global public health community to come together

Priorities

- Advocate for effective global policies to improve the health of populations
- Advance public health practice, education, training, and research
- Expand and strengthen partnerships
- Promote and support the advancement of strong member associations
- Build an effective, responsive, and sustainable WFPHA

Annual Conference(s)

www.wfpha.org/world-congress-on-public-health.html
WFPHA conducts two main types of events: an annual meeting and an International Congress on Public Health.

Newsletter

WFPHA publishes a bimonthly newsletter (www.wfpha.org/wfpha-newsletter.html) and WFPHA Annual Report to inform on the activities of the Federation, its member associations, and international organizations. Occasional special studies, reports, and conference proceedings are published that address key issues in international health. WFPHA members exchange journals, newsletters, and other association publications. Moreover, the *Journal of Public Health Policy* informs policy in other communities, countries, or regions to provide a platform of debates about public health policy globally.

Contact Information

www.wfpha.org and www.wfpha.org/contact-us.html

47. World Health Organization (WHO)

Background

When diplomats met to form the United Nations in 1945, one of the things they discussed was setting up a global health organization. WHO's Constitution came into force on April 7, 1948—a date we now celebrate every year as World Health Day. The World Health Assembly is the supreme decision-making body for WHO. It generally meets in Geneva in May each year, and is attended by delegations from all 194 member states. Its main function is to determine the policies of the Organization. The secretariat of WHO is staffed by some 8,000 health and other experts and support staff on fixed-term appointments in 150 WHO offices in countries, territories and areas, six regional offices (Africa, Americas, Eastern Mediterranean, Europe, Southeast Asia, Western Pacific), and at the headquarters in Geneva, Switzerland The Organization is headed by the director-general, who is appointed by the health assembly on the nomination of the executive board. In addition to medical doctors, public health specialists, scientists, and epidemiologists, WHO staff include people trained to manage administrative, financial, and information systems, as well as experts in the fields of health statistics, economics, and emergency relief.

Vision, Mission, Values (Constitution of WHO)

THE STATES Parties to this Constitution declare, in conformity with Charter of the United Nations, that the following principles are basic to the happiness, harmonious relations, and security of all peoples:

- Health is a state of complete physical, mental, and social well-being and not merely the absence of disease or infirmity.
- The enjoyment of the highest attainable standard of health is one of the fundamental rights of every human being without distinction of race, religion, political belief, or economic or social condition.
- The health of all peoples is fundamental to the attainment of peace and security and is dependent upon the fullest cooperation of individuals and states.
- The achievement of any state in the promotion and protection of health is of value to all.
- Unequal development in different countries in the promotion of health and control of disease, especially communicable disease, is a common danger.
- Healthy development of the child is of basic importance; the ability to live harmoniously in a changing total environment is essential to such development.
- The extension to all peoples of the benefits of medical, psychological, and related knowledge is essential to the fullest attainment of health.
- Informed opinion and active cooperation on the part of the public are of the utmost importance in the improvement of the health of the people.
- Governments have a responsibility for the health of their peoples, which can be fulfilled only by the provision of adequate health and social measures.

Leadership Priorities and Strategies (2014 to 2019)

- *Universal health coverage:* respond to demand from countries seeking practical advice on how to take universal health coverage forward

- *The International Health Regulations* (2005): global defense against shocks coming from the microbial world
- *Increasing access to medical products:* improve access to safe, quality, affordable, and effective medicines
- *Social, economic, and environmental determinants:* work with other sectors to act on what causes disease and ill health
- *Noncommunicable diseases:* coordinate a coherent, multisectoral response at global, regional, and local levels
- *Health-related MDGs:* integrate many aspects of our work, particularly building robust health systems and effective health institutions for sustainable and equitable health outcomes

Contact Information

For General Information:
WHO website: www.who.int/en/
World Health Organization
Avenue Appia 20
1211 Geneva 27
Switzerland
Tel.: + 41 22 791 21 11
Fax: + 41 22 791 31 11

48. World Health Professions Alliance (WHPA)

Background

Founded in 1999, WHPA speaks for more than 26 million health professionals in 130 countries. The Alliance works to improve global health and the quality of patient care and facilitates collaboration among the health professions and major stakeholders.

WHPA brings together the International Council of Nurses (1999), International Pharmaceutical Federation (1999), World Confederation for Physical Therapy (2010), World Dental Federation (2005), and World Medical Association (1999).

Each member of WHPA comes to the Alliance with a long history of representation, policy development, and advocacy on behalf of its members. Coming together does not diminish their role as independent organizations but provides opportunities to build on individual strength through a collective voice. Benefits of the Alliance include:

- Increased leverage
- Shared/common goals
- Increased networking and information sharing opportunities
- Benefits for patients and communities
- Improved health of the patient and communities
- Enhanced service to society = health + well-being
- Advocate for and advance the professions

Vision

WHPA improves public health and health of people by mobilizing (enhancing and exploiting) the common interests of its global member organizations.

Mission

WHPA exists to create value for member organizations, and through these organizations, for patients. WHPA creates value through:

Policy and advocacy

- Amplifying the policy/advocacy messages of member organizations
- Facilitating coherence between the policy/advocacy messages of member organizations

Information exchange and learning

- Sharing existing information about emerging trends and issues in health among the partners (professional associations)
- Sharing lessons learnt and best practice in association management and advocacy
- Enhancing the quality of individual members' policy work by providing perspectives from across the health professions

Contact Information

WHPA Secretariat
c/o World Medical Association
BP 63
01210 Ferney Voltaire, France
Tel.: +33 450 40 7575
Fax: +33 450 40 5937
Website: www.whpa.org
E-mail: whpa@wma.net

49. World Health Summit (WHS)

Background

Following the inaugural WHS, organized in 2009 on the occasion of the 300th anniversary of the Charité—Universitätsmedizin Berlin, it is being held annually and became the pre-eminent international forum for global health. Underpinned by the M8 Alliance of Academic Health Centers, Universities, and National Academies, WHS is organized in collaboration with the National Academies of Sciences of more than 67 countries and their InterAcademy Medical Panel (IAMP).

WHS's mission is to bring together representatives from academia, politics, the private sector, and civil society to address the most pressing issues facing medicine and health care over the next decade and beyond.

Traditionally, WHS enjoys the high patronage of the chancellor of the Federal Republic of Germany and the president of the French Republic. In 2013, José Manuel Barroso, president of the European Commission, shared the high patronage.

Goals

- Maintain a unique, international, multi-sectoral health forum with a sustaining dialogue
- Create networks and foster collaborations as a catalyst for innovation
- Guide and support positive action by policy and decision makers
- Promote thought leadership in scientific and health agendas

Outcomes

Outcomes of each WHS include statements and recommendations of the National Academies and the M8 Alliance to governments and international organizations. These are accompanied by a heightened public awareness for global health issues and a growing network of experts from all over the world and from all involved sectors.

Meetings

WHS is being held annually in Berlin, Germany, in October. Since 2013, WHS Regional Meetings put special emphasis on health challenges in specific regions. The first WHS Regional Meeting was held from April 8 to 10, 2013, in Singapore, the second one from April 6 to 8, 2014, in São Paulo, Brazil. The WHS Regional Meeting Asia is to be held from April 13 to 14, 2015, in Kyoto, Japan.

More information about WHS is available online (www.worldhealthsummit. org) and via the newsletter (www.worldhealthsummit.org/about-whs/newsletter .html).

Contact Information

World Health Summit
c/o Charité—Universitätsmedizin Berlin
Charitéplatz 1
10117 Berlin
Germany
Tel.: +49 30 450 57 2102
Fax: +49 30 450 51 7911
E-mail: secretariat@worldhealthsummit.org

50. World Organization of Family Doctors (WONCA)

Background

WONCA is a global not-for-profit professional organization representing family physicians and general practitioners from all regions of the world. WONCA's mission is to improve the quality of life of the peoples of the world through high standards of care in general practice/family medicine by:

- Promoting personal, comprehensive, and continuing care for the individual and the family in the context of the community and society

- Promoting equity through the equitable treatment, inclusion, and meaningful advancement of all groups of people, particularly women and girls, in the context of all health care and other societal initiatives
- Encouraging and supporting the development of academic organizations of general practitioners/family physicians
- Providing a forum for exchange of knowledge and information between member organizations and between general practitioners/family physicians
- Representing the policies and the educational, research, and service provision activities of general practitioners/family physicians to other world organizations and forums concerned with health and medical care

WONCA is an organization in official collaborative relations with WHO, representing family doctors and family medicine. WONCA was founded in 1972 and now has 118 member organizations representing some 500,000 family doctors in over 130 countries and territories around the world. WONCA has seven regions—Africa, Asia Pacific, Eastern Mediterranean, Europe, Iberoamericana-CIMF, North America, and South Asia—each with a regional president and regional council.

WONCA Structure

WONCA is governed by a World Council that meets once every 3 years just before the world conference. The Council comprises the representatives of member organizations and the officers of WONCA. WONCA's Council appoints a number of committees every 3 years.

Working Parties, Special Interest Groups, and Young Doctors Movements

WONCA supports a number of working parties, special interest groups, and young doctors movements. These bodies work to progress specific areas of interest to WONCA and its members around the globe. The groups involve hundreds of family doctors in their activities. Over the years, they have carried out groundbreaking studies and research, and have produced many important publications. There are currently 11 working parties, including Education, Research, Quality Care, and Classification, and several special interest groups. Young doctors movements include the Vasco da Gama Group in Europe, Rajakumar Group in Asia Pacific, Spice Route Group in South Asia, Waynakay Group in Iberoamericana, AfriWON in Africa, and Al Razi in Eastern Mediterranean.

Contact Information

WONCA Secretariat: CEO Dr. Garth Manning
12A-05 Chartered Square Building
152 North Sathon Road
Silom, Bangrak
Bangkok 10500
Thailand
E-mail: manager@wonca.net
Tel.: +66 2 637 9010
Fax: +66 2 637 901

APPENDIX A2: PROFILES OF LEADING SCHOOLS/INSTITUTES OF PUBLIC HEALTH

1. Addis Ababa University, College of Health Sciences, School of Public Health (AAUSPH), Doha, Ethiopia
2. All India Institute of Hygiene & Public Health (AIIH&PH), New Delhi, India
3. Asian Institute of Public Health (AIPH), Bhubaneswar, India
4. BRAC Institute of Global Health (BIGH), Mohakhali, Dhaka, Bangladesh
5. Emory Global Health Institute (EGHI), Atlanta, Georgia, United States
6. Harvard University School of Public Health (HSPH), Boston, Massachusetts, United States
7. Johns Hopkins University Bloomberg School of Public Health (JHUBSPH), Baltimore, Maryland, United States
8. London School of Hygiene & Tropical Medicine (LSHTM), London, United Kingdom
9. CAPHRI School for Public Health and Primary Care, Maastricht University, Maastricht, The Netherlands
10. Melbourne University School of Population and Global Health (MUSPGH), Melbourne, Australia
11. National Institute for Health and Welfare (THL), Helsinki, Finland
12. Peking University School of Public Health (PUSPH), Peking, China
13. University of São Paulo School of Public Health (SPSPH), São Paulo, Brazil
14. University of North Carolina Gillings School of Global Public Health (UNCGSPH), Chapel Hill, North Carolina, United States
15. Dalla Lana School of Public Health (DLSPH), University of Toronto, Toronto, Ontario, Canada

1. Addis Ababa University, College of Health Sciences School of Public Health (AAUSPH; Doha, Ethiopia)

Background

The School of Public Health (SPH) was conceived as the Department of Community Health (DCH) in 1964 as part of the then Faculty of Medicine of Addis Ababa University (AAU). The Department expanded and pioneered to start the first graduate training in public health (MPH) in Ethiopia in 1984 and its doctoral program (PhD) in 2003. The Department was transformed into the SPH in 2007 and formally recognized in February 2010. Following the restructuring in AAU, the School was reorganized into two departments: the Department of Preventive Medicine and the Department of Reproductive Health and Health Services Management.

Programs

The School runs different programs:

- MPH with specialty tracks (epidemiology, health management, environmental health, reproductive health, and general MPH)
- The Ethiopian Field Epidemiology Training Program (EFETP)

- MSc in health informatics program, which is jointly run by the School of Information Science and SPH of AAU
- Master's in hospital and health care
- PhD in public health

The School also provides teaching services for undergraduate medical students composed of course work and a 6-week rural community health training program.

Vision

SPH aspires to become a center of excellence for public health education, training, research, community services, and advancing knowledge in public health that will contribute to the improvement of the health of individuals and populations, and to the attainment of equitable socioeconomic development in Ethiopia, East Africa, and beyond.

Mission

SPH is dedicated to the training of health and allied professionals in public health; to the discovery, application, and dissemination of new knowledge; and to the promotion of health and prevention of disease in communities and populations in collaboration with governmental, nongovernmental, and international agencies in policy development, planning, implementation, and evaluation of public health programs.

Capacity

SPH has 39 full-time academic staff, 14 of them acquired PhDs. There are 4 full professors, 8 associate professors, 12 assistant professors, and 15 lecturers. SPH enrolls over 150 master's and 8 to 10 PhD students annually. SPH and the Ethiopian Public Health Association jointly own and run *The Ethiopian Journal of Health Development*, which is one of the oldest scientific journals in Ethiopia; it is consistently published three times a year. SPH runs the *Butajira Rural Health Program (BRHP)*, which is a field laboratory maintained since 1986. The site is located about 130 kilometers southwest of Addis Ababa. BRHP performs a continuous registration of vital and migratory events such as birth, death, marriage, migration, and internal mobility at a household level in a population of more than 60,000. Over 20 PhD dissertations, 50 MPH/MSc theses, and more than 100 articles in peer-reviewed journals from BRHP are published.

Collaborations

The School collaborates with many national and international partners. The School has established partnerships with overseas universities such as the Johns Hopkins Bloomberg School of Public Health (USA), University of Bergen (Norway), Umeå International School of Public Health (Sweden), University of Southern California, and many others. At the national level, it collaborates with the Ministry of Health, Ethiopian Public Health Association, and many other organizations. Areas of collaboration include joint research and evaluation, in-service training and capacity building, and graduate training.

Contact Information

School of Public Health
P.O. Box: 9086, Addis Ababa, Ethiopia
Tel: 251-115-157701
Fax: 251-115-157701
Email: jemal.haidar@aau.edu.et

2. All India Institute of Hygiene & Public Health (AIIH&PH; New Delhi, India)

Background

AIIH&PH was established in Calcutta on December 30, 1932. This is the only post-graduate institute of its kind in India, devoted to teaching and research in various disciplines in the health and related sciences and is the oldest school of public health in the Southeast Asia region. The Institute was started with a generous assistance from the Rockefeller Foundation. The administrative control of AIIH&PH rests with the director general of health services, New Delhi, under the Ministry of Health and Family Welfare, Government of India.

Objectives
- To develop health manpower by providing postgraduate (training) facilities of the highest order
- To conduct research directed toward the solution of various problems of health and diseases in the community
- To undertake operational research to develop methods for optimum utilization of health resources and application of the findings for protection and promotion of health care services

Organizational Aspects

The director is the head of the Institute and looks after all administrative management of the organization. Dean of the Institute looks after the academic (examinations and research) and sports (training) activities of the Institute. Technical assistance to the dean in academic matters is provided by the Faculty Council. Administrative assistance is provided by an additional director and an administrative officer, who are well supported by four office superintendents, SAS accountant, and ministerial staff.

The Institute is well equipped and has well qualified and experienced teaching faculty on its full-time staff. There are 12 academic departments and two field practice units, each controlled by a professor and head of the department/officer-in-charge. All the departments provide good facilities for research in various health and allied sciences.

- Biochemistry and nutrition
- Epidemiology
- Health promotion and education
- Maternal and child health
- Microbiology

- Occupational health
- Public health administration
- Public health nursing
- Environmental sanitation and sanitary engineering
- Preventive and social medicine
- Statistics
- Behavioral sciences

The Institute has two field practice units, controlled by the officer-in-charge of administration: Rural Health Unit and Training Centre, Singur; Urban Health Centre, Chetla. These centers are the field practice areas and the population laboratories, and form special features of the Institute. These centers provide an excellent opportunity for field training, research, and learning in all aspects of community health care in a true setting, both urban and rural

Contact Information

Further details are available at www.aiihph.gov.in

3. Asian Institute of Public Health (AIPH; Bhubaneswar, India)

Background

AIPH is the first of its kind institution for public health education, research, and training located in Bhubaneswar in the state of Odisha in India. Although rich in minerals, water resources, forests, and a long seacoast, Odisha continues to be one of the poorest states in India. The state faces serious health problems with large infant and maternal mortality rates. Prevalence of undernutrition, cholera, malaria, filariasis, dengue, chikungunya, and other similar diseases are widespread in the state. Traditionally an agricultural state with farmers of small holdings, Odisha has seen rapid growth in mining and mineral-based industries in the recent past, leading to a rapid upsurge of environmental pollution and serious health impacts.

Mission

The mandate of the institution is to establish an excellent platform for public health education and research with continuous efforts toward creating solutions to local health problems while learning the lessons from innovations across the globe. AIPH emerged from the needs felt and the enormous insights gained by the physicians and public health researchers working in India over the last decade.

Vision

To provide a platform of synergy and learning where innovation and intellectual excellence transform the health of mankind.

Values

AIPH has emerged from community-based activities and research to improve neonatal and child health in the state and country. Although several new educational programs have been introduced during the last 4 years, AIPH's interest and commitment still lies in the community and population health.

Achievements (in the Last Few Years)

Starting with investigations on causes of neonatal morbidity and mortality, population-based surveillance of neonatal infection along with sophisticated laboratory research, and birth asphyxia, the AIPH team has implemented many other projects in childhood nutrition, malaria, health systems strengthening, and organized health promotion activities using varied social media.

Priorities

- Waiting for passing of state approval for establishment of a state "public health university" (first of its kind in India). High-level governmental approvals already in place
- Launching of PhD program in public health in collaboration with Ravenshaw
- Construction of the teaching and the administrative blocks of the university in the newly allotted land by the government
- Opening of master's courses in epidemiology and BSc courses in "public health," which are newly introduced by the Government of India
- New research projects on nutrition, gender equity, water, and sanitation

Annual Conference(s)

AIPH conducts local, state-wide, regional, and national conferences regularly every year on topics related to public health, inviting eminent persons in the field.

Newsletter

www.masterstudies.co.uk/universities/India/Asian-Institute-of-Public-Health/

Contact Information

Asian Institute of Public Health
1037, Sriram Nagar, Samantarapur, Bhubaneswar 751002
Tel.: +91 674 6574656 or 674 6005040
E-mail: contact@aiph.ac.in
Website: www.aiph.ac.in

4. BRAC Institute of Global Health (BIGH; Bangladesh)

Background

BIGH at BRAC University was established as an autonomous institute in 2013, incorporating the James P. Grant School of Public Health (JPGSPH) and the Department of Midwifery. (Dr. Sadia Chowdhury is the executive director of BIGH and is overall in charge of the School and the Department of Midwifery. Dr. Sabina Faiz Rashid is dean of the School of Public Health, BRAC University.)

JPGSPH was founded in 2004 as a collaborative effort between BRAC University, BRAC, and icddr,b (the International Center for Diarrhoeal Disease Research, Bangladesh—an international health research institution located in Dhaka). The School was named after a former executive director of UNICEF, the late James P. Grant, whose energy and vision was a major force behind the child survival and development revolution. In January 2005, JPGSPH initiated its flagship Masters of Public Health (MPH) program with the aim of developing public health leaders. Grant's legacy is one that inspires the School's mission in the 21st century—to harness knowledge and know-how in the pursuit of health equity.

Since its launch in 2004 and the commencement of its first MPH program in 2005, over 326 students from 26 different corners of the globe, such as South Asia, Southeast Asia, Africa, Australia, North and South America, and Europe, have participated and are now in governments, national and international NGOs, donor programs, and UN agencies in their respective countries. Another reason for which the JPGSPH MPH is well known now for is its international faculty. At present, the School has over 20 international faculty members.

WHO in its December 2007 *Bulletin* (www.who.int/bulletin/volumes/85/12 /07-011207.pdf), recognized the School as one of the six best in the world in promoting and practicing innovative higher public health education.

Vision

The new vision of the School is to harness "Knowledge and know-how for health equity."

Core Principles

The School's core principles that underlie all of its activities are to:

- Be community oriented, providing experiential learning centered around the public health problems of Bangladesh and other developing countries
- Promote critical, innovative thinking that is rooted in best practice and rigorous research
- Use a multidisciplinary, intersectoral approach to learning and problem solving
- Inculcate the values and ethos of its founders and partner institutions—equity, fairness, and concern for the poor, women, and the disadvantaged
- Build capacity and prepare individuals to become public health leaders, practitioners, critical thinkers, researchers, advocates, and stewards of public health and policy at local, national, and international levels

Knowledge and Know-How for Health Equity

Encouraged by this vision, JPGSPH intervenes through its education program, research program, and leadership and advocacy.

Recent Achievements and Initiatives

Recent achievements and initiatives by JPGSPH at BIGH include Next Generation of Public Health Experts (NGPHE), Reaching Out and Linking In: Health Systems and Close-to-Community Services (REACHOUT), Bangladesh Health Watch, 4-year Nuffic grant.

Contact Information

For additional information, please contact:

JPGSPH@bracu.ac.bd
James P. Grant School of Public Health
5th Floor (Level G), icddr,b Building
68 Shahud Tajuddin, Ahmed Sarani,
Mohakhali, Dhaka-1212
Bangladesh

Tel: 8802 -8825131, 8825141 ext. 6053
Fax: +88028831682
Web: http://sph.bracu.ac.bd

5. Emory Global Health Institute (EGHI; Atlanta, Georgia, United States)

Background

EGHI is a global health organization that works across all of Emory University's schools and departments. Its vision is to be a catalyst for advancing global health through collaborative, innovative, and impactful discovery, scholarship, and service. Its mission is to advance Emory University's efforts to improve health around the world by recruiting outstanding faculty, initiating and facilitating multidisciplinary global health research programs and policies, and creating innovative new ways to attract and train the next generation of global health leaders.

Achievements

Founded in 2006 by Dr. Jeffrey P. Koplan and currently led by Dr. Robert F. Breiman, EGHI has assisted Emory University in establishing a robust global health academic infrastructure and reputation. Specific accomplishments since its founding include:

- Advanced global health research at Emory
- Increased Emory University's global health capacity
- Expanded global health teaching
- Increased global health scholarship
- Responded to student demands
- Expanded organizational reach
- Expanded national and international reach
- Increased Emory's global health visibility

Programs

EGHI has supported a variety of faculty and student programs dealing with numerous critical global health issues around the world. EGHI annually hosts a Global Health

Scholars Symposium to highlight Emory students' Field Scholars Award projects and a Global Health Student Photography Contest for Emory students. EGHI also hosts two global health case competitions each year; one competition is an intramural competition that includes Emory students only, whereas the other is an international competition that includes multidisciplinary student teams from universities around the world.

Priorities

EGHI's future priorities are to continue these existing activities as well as to strengthen existing and foster new partnerships locally, nationally, and internationally to address critical global health issues around the world.

Contact Information

Rebecca Baggett, MPH
Communications and Program Manager
Emory Global Health Institute
Tel.: +1 404 727 1427
Visit the Emory Global Health Institute website to learn more about its leadership, programs, and activities (www.globalhealth.emory.edu).

6. Harvard University School of Public Health (HSPH; Boston, Massachusetts, United States)

Background

HSPH began in 1913 as the Harvard-MIT School of Health Officers, the first professional public health training program in the United States. Many of the innovations that have helped double life expectancy in the United States and improved health globally in the past century have their origins in HSPH's teaching and research programs. These include discoveries that made it possible to:

- Develop the polio vaccine
- Protect the blood supply from HIV/AIDS
- Determine the difference between good and bad fats in one's diet
- Recognize the dangers of second-hand tobacco smoke
- Develop clean air regulations to protect people from heart and lung diseases

Mission and Vision

- Provides the highest level of education to public health scientists, practitioners, and leaders
- Fosters research discoveries leading to improved health for all
- Strengthens health capacities and services for communities around the globe
- Informs policy debate, disseminates health information, and increases awareness of health as a public good

Values

- Health is a fundamental right of every human being.
- Children, the elderly, the poor, and the underserved must be protected.

- Education and research must transcend local and national boundaries to improve health globally.
- Knowledge can promote healthy populations and empower individuals to make sound decisions.

Achievements (in the Last 3 Years)
- Safer surgery and childbirth
- Measuring effects of Medicaid coverage
- Health reform
- Training humanitarian leaders
- Turning the tide on the AIDS epidemic

Priorities

To improve health globally, HSPH is seeking new ways to address:

- Failing health systems
- Old and new pandemics ranging from AIDS and tuberculosis to obesity and heart disease
- Harmful physical and social environments ranging from air and water pollution to domestic violence and mental health issues
- Poverty and humanitarian crises that impact health, including both war and natural disasters

Our priorities are:

- Research to discover new solutions
- Education of current and future public health leaders to better tackle these threats
- Informing public policy to improve health systems worldwide

Newsletter

Harvard Public Health Magazine (print): www.hsph.harvard.edu/news/magazine
Nutrition Source Newsletter; HSPH Update (e-mail newsletters): harvard.qualtrics.com/SE/?SID=SV_2bZDgkpV4MaysPH

Contact Information

Website: www.hsph.harvard.edu
Twitter: @HarvardHSPH
Facebook: HarvardPublicHealth

7. Johns Hopkins University Bloomberg School of Public Health (JHUBSPH; Baltimore, Maryland, United States)

Background

In 1915, the seminal Welch-Rose Report established the need to train public health workers as a separate profession from medicine. The following year, the Johns Hopkins School of Hygiene and Public Health was founded as the world's first independent graduate school of public health by William H. Welch with grant support from the Rockefeller Foundation. In 2001, the School was renamed the Bloomberg School of

Public Health (BSPH) to honor Michael Bloomberg's financial support and commitment to the school and to public health. It is the oldest continuously operating school of public health in the world and the largest school of public health in terms of student enrollment (2,164 in AY2013), number of faculty (619 full-time and 785 part-time), and research funding ($360 million for sponsored projects in the total FY2013 budget of $529 million). The School exemplifies the goal of global engagement with research initiatives in more than 90 countries and students enrolled from more than 87 countries. BSPH offers nine degrees with more than 100 concentrations, tracks, and certificates, and is a pioneer in online graduate education. The school has been ranked the number one school of public health by *U.S. News & World Report* since 1994. Some notable achievements by the school's faculty can be found at www.jhsph.edu/about/history

Vision

Protecting Health, Saving Lives—Millions at a Time

Mission

The *mission* statement reflects the School's commitment to its three core enterprises: education, research, and public health practice. "The Johns Hopkins Bloomberg School of Public Health is dedicated to the improvement of health through discovery, dissemination, and translation of knowledge and the education of a diverse global community of research scientists and public health professionals."

Values

- Excellence, integrity, equity, diversity, and civility in all of our activities and initiatives
- Scholarship, critical thinking, innovation, and scientific rigor
- Discovery, dissemination, and translation of knowledge into sustainable, evidence-based public health programs and policies
- Collaboration and capacity building with communities and public health practitioners locally, nationally, and globally
- Education of current and future public health leaders who will embrace these values in their research and practice, adhering to the tenets of the International Declaration of Health Rights

---

School Goals
Education: Academic Programs and Instruction

- Prepare leaders in public health science and practice to address current and future public health challenges
- Promote, value, and achieve excellence in teaching and learning

Research, Practice, and Service

- Advance and translate research leading to the discovery of knowledge to improve population health throughout the world
- Advance the evidence base for the practice of public health and strengthen local, national, and global partnerships with public health practitioners

---

Faculty and Students

- Recruit and retain diverse, outstanding faculty and students
- Empower faculty and students to achieve excellence in public health scholarship and practice

The School and Its Environment

- Sustain a thriving academic community and environment that embraces diversity in expertise and interests
- Enhance and enrich our unique ties and obligations to the Baltimore community
- Raise awareness of public health in the global community

Contact Information

Professor Laura L. Morlock, Associate Dean for Education

E-mail: lmorloc1@jhu.edu

8. London School of Hygiene & Tropical Medicine (LSHTM; London, United Kingdom)

Background

The School opened in 1899 at London's Royal Albert Dock, under the directorship of Sir Patrick Manson. It was established to train doctors for government service overseas and conduct research into infectious diseases. In 1924, the School received its Royal Charter as part of the University of London, and moved into its art-deco Keppel Street building in 1929. The School has continued to expand and develop, pioneering research into all aspects of tropical medicine and, increasingly, public health. For example, Sir Austin Bradford Hill and colleagues developed the modern randomized controlled trial, and with Sir Richard Doll showed the links between smoking and lung cancer. Professor Jerry Morris, known as the "inventor of exercise," worked at the School for over 50 years. Since 2007, the Keppel Street buildings were extensively modernized, and in 2009, we opened new buildings in Tavistock Place. For a full history, see the timeline on our website (timeline.lshtm.ac.uk).

Vision

Our vision is to be a world-leading school of public and global health, working closely with partners in the United Kingdom and worldwide to address contemporary and future critical health challenges.

Mission

Our mission is to improve health and health equity in the United Kingdom and worldwide; working in partnership to achieve excellence in public and global health research, education, and translation of knowledge into policy and practice.

Values

The School seeks to foster and sustain a creative and supportive working environment based upon an ethos of respect and rigorous scientific enquiry. We are committed to:

- Excellence and creativity
- Maximizing synergies between research, education, and knowledge translation and innovation
- Sharing expertise to strengthen capacity globally
- Partnerships based on mutual respect and openness
- Equity and diversity
- Financial and environmental sustainability

Achievements, inter alia, include

- In 2009, the School became the first academic institution in the world to be awarded the Gates Award for Global Health by the Bill & Melinda Gates Foundation.
- In 2010, we were awarded 2 out of 10 national multi-million pound Policy Research Units funded by the UK Department of Health, based on our new Faculty of Public Health and Policy campus at Tavistock Place.

Priority Strategic Plans: From our *Strategy 2012-17* (www.lshtm.ac.uk/aboutus/introducing/mission/index.html).

Research, inter alia, includes

- Sustain areas of established expertise in which the School has an international reputation
- Focus investment on areas critical to the School's mission, which involve cross-institutional working across traditional boundaries in research interest groups, School centers, and partnerships

Education, inter alia, includes

- To meet changing student needs and market supply and demand, develop new programs in Global Mental Health and One Health

Knowledge Translation and Innovation, inter alia, includes

- Implement a plan for responsible partnerships with industry, business development, consultancy, and contract research activities, including strengthening relevant School leadership, legal advice, and management systems in this area

Annual Conference

Staff symposium in September, but many events and conferences throughout the year: www.lshtm.ac.uk/newsevents

Newsletter

Chariot (monthly): Read and sign up at www.lshtm.ac.uk/newsevents/chariotnews-letter/index.html

Contact Information

Patrick Wilson
Head of Communications
London School of Hygiene & Tropical Medicine
Keppel Street, London WC1E 7HT
Tel: +44 20 7927 2704; 07951 797975 (mobile)
Website: www.lshtm.ac.uk

9. CAPHRI School for Public Health and Primary Care
(Maastricht University, The Netherlands)

Background

CAPHRI is the largest of six Maastricht Graduate Schools. Maastricht is well known for its expertise in the prevention of diseases, diagnostic and prognostic research in primary care and public health, the promotion of healthy behavior, and the redesign of health care services. CAPHRI plays a pivotal role in the Maastricht UMC+, as it finds itself at the forefront of scientific, innovative, applied, ethical, and policy-related research in public health and primary care. CAPHRI coordinates research, PhD training, and master's education.

Vision

Health care is an exceptionally broad concept in our society. It takes place in hospitals, health care organizations, and primary care, but also in the workplace, at home, and in society at large. When described in a model, health care can be imagined as a chain. This chain takes us from prevention of illness, through diagnosis and care, to cure and maintenance of good health. Each stage is linked to the next. CAPHRI focuses its research on each of the stages in the chain of care, but, more specifically, looks at the synergies between the stages and at integrated care pathways.

Mission

CAPHRI provides high quality multidisciplinary research and teaching aimed at the improvement of the individual's quality of life and population's health through innovation in public health and health care.

Values

CAPHRI values a strong combination of research quality and societal relevance.

Achievements

Three years ago, an official international external review committee awarded CAPHRI with an overall score of "excellent," which is the highest score possible. Furthermore, in 2011 CAPHRI received a prestigious block grant of €800,000 from the Netherlands Organisation for Scientific Research (NWO), aimed at Graduate Schools that provide an excellent training and research environment for very talented young researchers.

In 2013, the Researchschool CaRe, of which CAPHRI is the founding participant and coordinator, was re-accredited as a research school.

Priorities

- Maintain and even further increase CAPHRI's excellent scientific performance
- Continue to strengthen the interaction between research and education
- Develop a strong triangular interaction between research, education, and patient-centered care
- Invest in CAPHRI's talent system ("breeding ground policy")
- Try to influence policies and practice of (prestigious) funding organizations, such as NWO, KNAW, EU, and the industry to ensure that public health and primary care is on the agenda
- Continue to invest heavily in linkages with key organizations, memberships in advisory committees, and contacts with international organizations
- Invest in an effective PR and communication strategy, of which the key components will be careful targeting and clear messages, supported by sound evidence
- Maintain an efficient CAPHRI management office

Annual CAPHRI Conferences

- Annual CAPHRI research meeting: www.caphri.nl/en/about-caphri/annual-caphri-research-meeting-2012.aspx
- Special annual meetings aimed at PhD students
  - annual fall meeting, annual spring meeting aimed at all PhD students
  - annual meeting for new CAPHRI PhD students (first year students)

Newsletters

The CAPHRI newsletter is mailed every 2 weeks to all CAPHRI staff, PhD students, and external contacts. A special CAPHRI "PhD-Infomail" is sent to all CAPHRI PhD-students, approximately once a month.

Contact Information

www.caphri.nl/en/about-caphri/contact-information.aspx

10. Melbourne University School of Population and Global Health (MUSPGH; Melbourne, Australia)

Background

From origins in the Melbourne Medical School going back to the 1980s, the Melbourne School of Population and Global Health was established in 2001. It has expertise in public health sciences of epidemiology, biostatistics, and economics as well as in sociology, anthropology, ethics, and health humanities, and in newer disciplines such as informatics, mathematical modeling, and molecular and genetic epidemiology. The School is composed of four centers, one institute, and two partnership units: Centre for Health Equity, Centre for Health Policy, Centre for Epidemiology and Biostatistics, Centre for Mental Health, Nossal Institute for Global Health, and the Global Burden of Disease Group and Vaccine and Immunisation Research Group.

Vision, Mission, Values

The Melbourne School aims to strengthen the understanding, capacity, and services of society to meet population health needs locally and globally, especially through disease and injury prevention, and to improve the quality, efficiency, and equity of health care everywhere. The framework for research, teaching and learning, and engagement (the University's "Triple Helix") is built on a deep appreciation of the genetic, environmental, and socioeconomic determinants of health. Major research strengths are in many areas, but especially in cancer genetic epidemiology and screening, health inequalities, mental health, vaccinology and mathematical modeling, indigenous health, alcohol social policy, health policy and economics, noncommunicable diseases, and in global health systems and inclusive development.

The School commits to provide a high quality educational experience, an exciting range of professional education, research training, and employment opportunities, and a strong graduate network. Its degrees include master of public health, master of epidemiology, master of science (epidemiology), master of biostatistics, and a new master of ageing and diploma in tropical medicine and hygiene. Forty percent of our students are international, representing 40 nationalities. We have over 130 doctoral students. Students enroll at different ages and career stages and are supported by a strong and highly active Melbourne Population Health Student Association.

Recent Major Achievements

- World's first randomized controlled trial of chlamydia screening in primary care
- With IHME, the Global Burden of Disease 2010 Study with significant impact on health policy/priority debates worldwide
- Publication of three separate global analyses on MDG 4, 5, and 6
- First systematic national and global assessment of tobacco prevalence and consumption, 1990 to 2012
- Systematic analysis of the changing risks of smoking over the past 50 years using large cohort studies in the United States and the United Kingdom
- Discovered that obesity has different effects on risk of the main molecular subtypes of colorectal cancer, thus explaining some of the heterogeneity that has plagued studies of colorectal cancer
- The direct translation of Alcohol Management Plans research to federal policy to support indigenous health
- The reduction of trachoma in Aboriginal children from 14% to 4% in 4 years
- Mental Health First Aid training received by over 1% of Australians
- Economic research showing that achievable reductions in the price of publically funded statins would save an estimated billion dollars over 4 years

- Research on suicide hotspots influenced the installation of barriers at several Australian and international sites
- Derived the genetic risks of bowel cancer now used worldwide to guide treatment and prevention
- Leadership of NIH-funded Colon Cancer Family Registry enabling breakthroughs in the etiology, prevention, and treatment of colon cancer
- Research, policy development, and advocacy to assist implementation of world's first plain packaging laws for cigarettes

Priorities

Priority strategies will focus on:

- Data science and disease modeling
- Screening and early detection of disease in populations
- Disparities and disadvantage
- Mental health and well-being
- Prevention and management of chronic disease

Annual Conference(s)

Nossal Oration and FORUM

Head of School

Professor Terry Nolan, AO, BMedSc, MBBS, PhD, FRACP, FAFPHM

Annual Reports

http://mspgh.unimelb.edu.au/about/annual_reports

Contact Information

http://mspgh.unimelb.edu.au

11. National Institute for Health and Welfare (THL; Helsinki, Finland)

Background

THL is a research and development institute under the Finnish Ministry of Social Affairs and Health. THL started its work in 2009, following the merger of the National Public Health Institute (KTL) and the National Research and Development Centre for Welfare and Health (STAKES). The purpose of THL is to promote health and welfare, to prevent diseases and social problems, and to develop social welfare and health care sectors. Also, in its capacity as the statutory statistical authority for health and welfare, THL maintains and promotes the use of a strong knowledge base within the field. THL is a community of more than a thousand experts, whose work in the health and welfare research fields and in the social welfare and health care sectors is carried out across Finland. THL has headquarters in Helsinki and bases in other Finnish cities.

Our Vision

A just and sustainable society for all where people in Finland live a good and healthy life.

Our Mission

THL is an effective expert agency, committed to protecting and promoting health and welfare in Finland.

Our Values

Effectiveness, partnership, responsibility, and independence

Achievements (in the Last Few Years)

- Extensive population studies (Health 2011 Survey, National FINRISK 2012 study, and Migrant Health and Wellbeing study, Regional Health and Welfare survey 2012-2014), which give a comprehensive overview of the state of welfare and public health in Finland
- Support to several legislative and reform projects (including the restructuring of the service delivery system in social welfare and health care, the act on care services for older people, and reform of the alcohol legislation) and assessment of different policy options and production of an overview of the state of policy impact assessment in the area of social welfare and health care
- Around 1,000 articles published annually in international and Finnish scientific journals and trade magazines. Internationally THL is one of the most cited Finnish research agencies, with a substantial number of articles in peer-reviewed scientific journals ranked in the top quarter in terms of influence
- Establishment of THL Biobank in 2014, which further strengthens the data resources for population health studies

Priorities (2015 Onward)

- Sustainability of welfare state in the context of demographic change
- Reduced health and welfare inequalities
- Prevention of the main national diseases
- Capacity to prevent global and national threats to health and welfare
- Safe living environment
- Support the restructuring and development of social welfare and health care services

Annual Conferences

www.thl.fi/fi/web/thlfi-en/search-results?q=conferences&qisite=&qesite=

Newsletters

www.thl.fi/en/web/thlfi-en/whats-new/newsletters

Contact Information

www.thl.fi/en/web/thlfi-en/about-us/contact-us

12. Peking University School of Public Health (PUSPH; Peking, China)

Background

Peking University School of Public Health (PKU-SPH) can be traced to 1931 when a division of public health was set up in Peking University. The Department of Public Health within the School of Medicine, Peking University, was established in 1950. In 1952, following the national restructuring of higher education institutions, the medical school was separated from Peking University and promoted to Beijing Medical College. The office was consequently elevated to a department 4 years later and then a school in June 1985. In 2000, Beijing Medical College reemerged with Peking University and has since been known as Peking University Health Science Center, of which the School of Public Health constitutes an important part.

Vision

The vision of PKU-SPH is to improve the health of Chinese people through education, research, and social services. Over the past 60 years, the school has grown from an office of fewer than 10 staff members to a leading public health school in China that hosts 167 faculty members and staff, as well as 960 students (103 doctoral candidates, 254 master's degree candidates, 201 MPH candidates, and 402 undergraduates).

Organization

The school consists of eight departments (Department of Epidemiology and Biostatistics; Department of Occupational and Environmental Health Sciences; Department of Nutrition and Food Hygiene; Department of Child, Adolescent and Women's Health; Department of Toxicology; Department of Health Policy and Management; Department of Social Medicine and Health Education; and Department of Global Health), one central laboratory, two research institutes (Institute of Child and Adolescent Health and Institute of Reproductive Health, PKU), five joint research centers (Center for Evidence-Based Medicine, Center for AIDS Prevention Studies, Nutritional and Functional Food Assessment Center, Health Emergency Management Center of PKU, and Research Center of Ageing Health Services), and two educational centers (Teaching Center for Preventive Medicine Experiments and Center for Educational Services). Besides, the school has one national key discipline (epidemiology and biostatistics), one national key fostering discipline (child, adolescent, and women's health), one municipal key discipline (child, adolescent, and women's health), and three provincial key laboratories.

Programs

The school offers a bachelor's degree in preventive medicine, as well as master's and doctor's degrees in epidemiology and biostatistics; occupational and environmental health sciences; nutrition and food hygiene; child, adolescent, and women's health; toxicology; and social medicine and health management. It also offers postdoctoral fellowships in all public health and preventive medicine related disciplines. In 2001, the school's pilot project of 7-year bachelor's to master's degree program was approved by the Ministry of Education (MOE). In this combined program, students go into secondary disciplines in their sixth year. In addition, the school established nine practice bases in Beijing, Qingdao, and Shenzhen, which have provided hands-on training to students from the combined program for seven consecutive years. In 2003, the school launched the MPH program. In 2009, as part of the MOE pilot project for master's program reform, the school expanded the MPH program to a full-time program.

Research

Sponsored by National Key Projects, National Natural Science Foundation, Ministerial Foundation, and International Research Foundation, the school has launched more than 200 research projects and won over 50 awards for its scientific achievements, representing the A team in public health research and education that China has to offer.

Collaboration

The school also maintains strong collaboration with many prestigious international organizations including the WHO, the United Nations Infants and Children Fund, the U.S. CDC, and the China Medical Board, as well as world-class universities including Harvard University, Duke University, Johns Hopkins University, University of North Carolina, University of Michigan, London School of Hygiene and Tropical Medicine, University of Sydney, Monash University, Seoul National University, and University of Tokyo.

Contact Information

Peking School of Public Health
Tel.: +86 010 82801620
Fax: +86 010 82801518
E-mail: sphadmin@126.com

13. University of São Paulo School of Public Health (SPSPH; São Paulo, Brazil)

Background

The origin of SPSPH is linked to the Hygiene Laboratory's creation in 1918 by agreement between the São Paulo State Government and The Rockefeller Foundation, as part of the School of Medicine. Four years later, the Laboratory emancipated from the School of Medicine and became the Institute of Hygiene. With the creation of the University of São Paulo, in 1934, by the State Government, the Institute of Hygiene became the School of Public Health of the University of São Paulo. The nutrition undergraduate course of the School started in 1939, as a pioneer in Brazil.

Since its origin, the School has contributed significantly to actions of control and prevention of diseases. Its scope is the production and dissemination of public health and nutrition sciences.

The faculty comprises 97 professors with different academic backgrounds, distributed among five departments: nutrition, epidemiology, environmental health, public health practice, and maternal and child health. They work with outstanding graduate students and laboratory technicians in integrated research.

Mission

To produce and disseminate knowledge and educate students in public health and nutrition, by means of research, education, and extension, contributing toward improving the population's health conditions and formulating public policies.

Vision

To educate students to become nutritionists, sanitarians, masters, and doctors with high scientific abilities, beyond humanitarian and ethical points of view. Contribute highly to public health scientific literature through excellence in research and publications.

Values

- Excellence
- Transformative vision
- Interdisciplinarity
- Participation
- Environmental awareness
- Innovation

Achievements (in the Last Few Years)

- Creation of undergraduate course in public health, in 2012
- Renewal of nutrition undergraduate courses, in 2012
- Creation of professional master's course in environment, health, and sustainability, in 2013
- Creation of PhD program in global health and sustainability, in 2013
- Program in public health formed 23% of all PhDs (134 PhD dissertations) and 10% of master's (192 master's theses) in the area of public health, of Brazil, in the years 2007 to 2009
- Contribution to academic development of other Brazilian regions by offering master's and PhD courses in the states of Acre, Ceará
- Yearly summer program with over 800 students from Brazil and Latin America

Priorities

- To increase internalization
- To display social commitment
- To promote excellence in teaching, research, and extension activities
- To improve and modernize infrastructure
- To promote environmental sustainability

Annual Conference

Annual Research Week–first week of November

Newsletter

www.fsp.usp.br/site/noticias

Contact Information

www.fsp.usp.br/site/faleconosco

crint@fsp.usp.br

14. University of North Carolina Gillings School of Global Public Health (UNC-GSPH; Chapel Hill, North Carolina, United States)

Background

In 1936, a public health department was created within the UNC School of Medicine. In 1940, the UNC Board of Trustees approved public health as a separate school within the university; the School awarded its first degrees in 1940. Since its founding, the School has been involved in both global and local public health through teaching, research, practice, and service. Faculty, staff, and students work in all 100 NC counties, throughout the United States, and in 55 countries around the world.

Today, the School is ranked the top *public* school of public health (#2 overall) in the United States by *U.S. News and World Report* (2011, 2012).

Mission

The mission of UNC-GSPH is to improve public health, promote individual well-being, and eliminate health disparities across North Carolina and around the world.

Values

Values articulated and embraced by UNC-GSPH faculty, staff, and students—in their own words—include, inter alia, the following:

- We are committed to diversity in our faculty, staff, and students.
- We believe that public health is accountable and responsible to communities and should work collaboratively with them.
- We believe that all people should be treated with dignity and respect.
- We are committed to high standards of excellence, professional ethics, and personal integrity in all that we do.

MPH Training Programs include

- Discipline-specific MPH programs
- Generalist MPH programs

The UNC-GSPH will launch a new global, online MPH in fall 2015, with concentrations in three critically important public health areas: water, population science, and implementation science.

Recent Achievements

Recent research by Gillings School faculty, staff, and students crosses a wide span of public health issues (sph.unc.edu/comm/sph-news). Several examples of high-impact work by Gillings School faculty include:

- Solving potable water access and sanitation problems
- Reducing HIV worldwide: preventing interpersonal violence program
- Harnessing the power of genomics: discovering the biological mechanisms for the obesity/cancer link

Priority Strategic Plans

Cross-cutting strategic priority research and practice areas for UNC-GSPH include:

- Ending the obesity epidemic
- Improving global health
- Eliminating health disparities
- Providing safe water in North Carolina and around the world
- Defeating cancer
- Accelerating our impact through research on implementation science

Contact Information

Barbara K. Rimer, DrPH
Dean and Alumni Distinguished Professor
170 Rosenau Hall, CB#7400
UNC Gillings School of Global Public Health
UNC-Chapel Hill
Chapel Hill, NC 27599-7400
E-mail: brimer@unc.edu

15. Dalla Lana School of Public Health (DLSPH; University of Toronto)

Background

DLSPH's predecessor, the University of Toronto School of Hygiene, was established in the 1920s and was a world leader in sanitation science, nutrition, and vaccine development. In 2008, the School was renamed the Dalla Lana School of Public Health, endowed by the Dalla Lana family.

Today, the School is home to more than 300 outstanding faculty members, $30 million in annual research, 450 students, and numerous partnerships with institutions throughout Toronto and internationally; it is one of the largest public health schools in the world.

Vision

We will lead in public health research, education, and service for a healthier Canada and a healthier world.

Achievements

1. *Trailblazing HIV-AIDS research.* The School's HIV Studies Unit (www.dlsph. utoronto.ca/discipline/social-and-behavioural-health-sciences) was one of the first to examine social and behavioral aspects of HIV transmission, disease impact, and treatment services.

2. *Identifying 12 million missing girls in India.* Researchers revealed a growing imbalance between the numbers of girls and boys in India is a result of selective abortion of female fetuses.
3. *Preparing for global pandemics.* The School played a vital role in overcoming the 2003 SARS crisis by building a flu surveillance algorithm and an ethical framework for pandemic planning.
4. *Delivering safer health care by measuring hospital performance.* In 2005, experts developed the first and largest standardized hospital evaluation metric.
5. *Embarking on one of the largest chronic disease studies.* The School is leading the Ontario Health Study, one of the largest population studies to examine risk factors and chronic diseases.
6. *Closing the gap between the health of indigenous and nonindigenous people.* In June 2014, the School received a $10 million donation to create an Institute for Indigenous Health that will generate community-based research and new scholars that are critical to improving indigenous health in Canada and around the world.

Strategic Priorities

1. *Healthy Cities and Communities.* The School is researching inner-city health, HIV/AIDS, community development, urban air and water pollution, nutrition, health care delivery in urban settings, healthy work environments, aboriginal health, and the built environment.
2. *Global Health: Equity and Innovation.* The School is addressing massive global health inequalities within and across countries by exploring transnational health issues, determinants, and solutions using a multidisciplinary approach to research and education.
3. *Clinical Public Health.* The School is building bridges between primary care and public health and positioning the School as a global leader in education, research, and service related to population health, disease prevention, and health policy
4. *Big Data for Health.* By connecting genomics and exposomics scientists to large population databases that encompass health outcomes across the whole population and life span, the School is harnessing the power of major cohort studies and opening new avenues for discovery and innovation in disease causation, prevention, and treatment.

Contact Information

Nicole Bodnar, Director of Communications
Dalla Lana School of Public Health
Tel: +1 416 946 7521
E-mail: Nicole.bodnar@utoronto.ca
Website: www.dlsph.utoronto.ca
eBulletin: www.dlsph.utoronto.ca/NODE/1742
Facebook: www.facebook.com/DallaLanaSchoolOfPublicHealth

APPENDIX A3: COMMON THEMES AND PRIORITIES EMERGING FROM THE PROFILES

Recurring themes or features from the profiles of leading health/health-related organizations are shown in Boxes A and B.

BOX A

Recurring Themes From the Profiles of Leading Health/Health-Related Organizations

- Ensuring all people achieve optimum health and well-being
- Improving the quality of life and addressing major public health challenges through the delivery of education, research, and population health services
- Promoting international collaboration and working with professionals from all areas of health care to address the common problems for health
- Developing skilled, motivated, and supported health workers within robust health systems and fostering a multidisciplinary approach to public health education, research, and practice
- Building global networks and platforms for discussion, dialogue, and resource sharing involving grassroots health activists, civil society organizations, and academic institutions, particularly from low- and middle-income countries
- Emphasizing values such as equity, solidarity, diversity, sustainability
- Promoting mutually beneficial partnerships

BOX B

Recurring Themes From the Profiles of Leading Schools/Institutes of Public Health

- Advancing roles as national and global centers of excellence for public health education, training, research, community services, and advancing knowledge in public health
- Striving toward a "just and sustainable society," eliminating inequalities and promoting disease prevention and capacity building

All profiles demonstrate clear and valuable strategies in helping to achieve the highest possible level of health and well-being of people across the globe. Box C summarizes several possibilities for strengthening organizational strategies and meeting future aspirations.

BOX C

Strengthening Organizational Strategies and Meeting Future Aspirations

- Recognizing the interconnectedness of human, plant, animal, and environmental health and well-being through *One World, One Health* initiatives
- Raising awareness of and engaging directly with the UN Sustainable Development Goals (2016–2030), in particular supporting goals relating to "ending extreme poverty, boosting shared prosperity through inclusive and sustainable development and working toward happiness, harmonious relations, and security of all peoples"
- Focusing on prevention, early detection of disease, and the promotion of healthy lifestyles

Appendix B

Think Tank on Global Health, Governance, and Education

Note: Numbers within parentheses in Column 4 relate to nations represented in think tank

NAME	AFFILIATION	E-MAIL	COUNTRY
1. Dr. Richard **ADANO**	Dean, School of Public Health		**Ghana, Sub-Saharan Africa (1)**
2. Dr. Muhammad Mahmood **AFZAL**	Global Health Workforce Alliance (GHWA), World Health Organization (WHO)	afzalm@who.int	**Switzerland (2), Pakistan (3)**
3. Dr. Muhammad Wasif **ALAM**	Director, Public Health and Safety Department, Dubai Health Authority - Headquarters	MAlam@dha.gov.ae wasifsuper@juno.com	**Dubai, United Arab Emirates (4)**
4. Prof. John **ASTON**	President, UK Faculty of Public Health	president@fph.org.uk karengoodwin@fph.org.uk	**United Kingdom (5)**
5. Dr. Blaise **BIKANDOU**	Freelance Consultant in Global International Health	bikandob@gmail.com bikandob@yahoo.com	**France (6)**
6. Dr. Francisco **BECERRA**	Assistant Director, Pan American Health Organization	becerraf@paho.org	**Mexico (7)**
7. Dr. Georges **BENJAMIN**	Executive Director, American Public Health Association	georges.benjamin@apha.org	**United States (8)**
8. Prof. Vesna **BJEGOVIC-MIKANOVIC**	Vice Dean of the Faculty of Medicine, University of Belgrade; President of the Association of Schools of Public Health in the European Region (ASPHER)	bjegov@gmail.com	**Republic of Serbia (9)**
9. Prof. Bettina **BORISH**	Director of the Geneva Office, World Federation of Public Health Associations	bettina.borisch@unige.ch	**Switzerland (10)**

(continued)

NAME	AFFILIATION	E-MAIL	COUNTRY
10. Prof. Peter **BROOKS**	Professorial Fellow, University of Melbourne; previously director, Australian Health Workforce Institute	brooksp@unimelb.edu.au	**Australia (11)**
11. Prof. Peter **CHANG**	Coordinator, Asian Health Literacy Study (AHLS); Research Partner, EU FP7 Diabetes Literacy - Self Management and Education [2013-2015]; Physician Senior Advisor, National Taipei Hospital, Ministry of Health & Welfare	peter.chang3@gmail.com	**Taiwan (12)**
12. Dr. Katarzyna **CZABANOWSKA**	Professor in Department of International Health, Faculty of Health, Medicine and Life Sciences, CAPHRI School of Public Health and Primary Care, Maastricht University and Coordinator of Leadership for European Public Health Professionals Curriculum Module	kasia.czabanowska@ maastrichtuniversity.nl	**The Netherlands (13), Poland (14)**
13. Dr. Manuel **DAYRIT**	Dean of Ateneo School of Medicine and Public Health, Philippines; formerly Minister of Health, Philippines; and Director Human Resources for Health, WHO	manuel_m_dayrit@yahoo. com mdayrit@asmph .ateneo.edu	**The Philippines (15)**
14. Dr. Madhumita **DOBE**	Director-Professor (Public Health); Head, Department of Health Promotion & Education, All India Institute of Hygiene and Public Health (AIIH&PH)	madhumitadobe@gmail.com	**India (16)**
15. Dr. Eliudi **ELIAKIMU**	Acting Assistant Director, Health Services Inspectorate and Quality Assurance Section, Ministry of Health and Social Welfare	eliakimueliudi@yahoo.co.uk eliakimueliudi@gmail.com	**Tanzania Mainland (17)**
16. Prof. N. K. **GANGULY**	Former Director General, Indian Council of Medical Research (ICMR), Coordinator and Chair, Policy Center for Biomedical Research (PCBR), Translational Health Science and Technology Institute (THSTI)	nkganguly@nii.ac.in	**India**

(*continued*)

NAME	AFFILIATION	E-MAIL	COUNTRY
17. Prof. Tomiko **HOKAMA**	Emeritus Professor; Executive Vice President, University of the Ryukyus; Former President of Asia Pacific Academic Consortium for Public Health (APACPH)	b987390@med.u-ryukyu.ac.jp	**Japan (18)**
18. Dr. Howard **HU**	Dean, Dalla Lana School of Public Health, University of Toronto; Interim Director, Institute for Global Health Equity & Innovation; Professor of Environmental Health, Epidemiology and Global Health; Professor of Medicine	Howard.Hu@utoronto.ca	**Canada (19)**
19. Prof. Ehi **IGUMBOR**	Extraordinary Associate Professor of Public Health, School of Public Health, University of the Western Cape, Bellville, Cape Town, South Africa; member of the Executive Committee of the Public Health Association of South Africa (PHASA)	ehi.igumbor@gmail.com	**South Africa (20)**
20. Dr. Martin **MCNAMARA**	Dean of Nursing and Head, UCD School of Nursing; Midwifery and Health Systems, University College Dublin (UCD) College of Health Sciences	martin.mcnamara@ucd.ie	**Ireland (21)**
21. Prof. Getnet **MITIKE**	Professor of Public Health, Addis Ababa University, College of Health Sciences, School of Public Health	getnetmk@gmail.com	**Ethiopia (22)**
22. Dr. John **NORCINI**	President and CEO of Foundation for Advancement of International Medical Education and Research (FAIMER)	JNorcini@Faimer.Org	**United States**
23. Prof. Ulrich **LAASER**	Section of International Public Health (S-IPH), Faculty of Health Sciences, University of Bielefeld; past president of the World Federation of Public Health Associations (WFPHA); German Association for Health Sciences and Public Health (DVGPH)	ulrich.laaser@uni-bielefeld.de	**Germany (23)**

(continued)

NAME	AFFILIATION	E-MAIL	COUNTRY
24. Dr. George **LUEDDEKE**	GRL Consulting–in Higher and Medical Education, Southampton	glueddeke@aol.com	**United Kingdom**
25. Prof. Geoff **MCCOLL**	Dean of Medical Education and Training, University of Melbourne; Director of the *Medical Journal of Australia*	gjmccoll@unimelb.edu.au	**Australia**
26. Dr. Gorik **OOMS**	Commissioner, *The Lancet*–University of Oslo Commission on Global Governance for Health, Researcher, Institute of Tropical Medicine, former executive director, Médecins Sans Frontières	gooms@itg.be	**Belgium (24)**
27. Mr. Robert **OTOK**	Director, Association of Schools of Public Health in the European Region (ASPHER)	robert.otok@aspher.org	**Belgium**
28. Prof. Meng **QINGYUE**	Professor in Health Economics and Policy, Dean of Peking University School of Public Health; Executive Director of Peking University China Center for Health Development Studies	qmeng@bjmu.edu.cn	**China (26)**
29. Prof. K Srinath **REDDY**	President, Public Health Foundation of India; President, World Heart Federation; the First Bernard Lown Visiting Professor of Cardiovascular Health at the Harvard School of Public Health; former Professor and Head, Department of Cardiology at the All India Institute of Medical Sciences	ksrinath.reddy@phfi.org ruchira.sharma@phfi.org	**India**
30. Prof. Helena **RIBEIRO**	Dean of the School of Public Health at the University of São Paulo	lena@usp.br	**Brazil (25)**
31. Dr. Barbara **RIMER**	Dean and Alumni Distinguished Professor UNC Gillings School of Global Public Health	brimer@unc.edu	**United States**

(continued)

NAME	AFFILIATION	E-MAIL	COUNTRY
32. Prof. Flavia **SENKUBUGE**	University of Pretoria; Vice-President of the African Federation of Public Health Associations; member of WFPHA	Flavia.Senkubuge@up.ac.za	**South Africa**
33. Dr. Henry **SONDHEIMER**	Senior Director, Medical Education Projects, Association of American Medical Colleges (AAMC)	hsondheimer@aamc.org	**United States**
34. Dr. Christine **SOW**	Executive Director, Global Health Council (GHC)	cksow@earthlink.net	**United States**
35. Prof. Charles **SURJADI**	Chief Technical Advisor, Indonesian Epidemiology Network; Atmajaya Faculty of Medicine, Djakarta	kotasehat@hotmail.com	**Indonesia (27)**

Appendix C

Global Partnerships for Transformative Education Initiatives

INTRODUCTION AND ACKNOWLEDGMENTS

Along with the Global Health Workforce Alliance (GHWA) aim to "scale up" education and training of health professionals, spearheaded by Dr. James Campbell, executive director of the GHWA, and Dr. Erica Wheeler, technical officer with the World Health Organization (WHO), discussed in Section 8.10, several other major global education partnership projects merit special mention. The overall purpose of these partnerships is to support health professional education and training with a view to cultivating, sharing, and implementing new ideas.

- *The Medical Education Partnership Initiative (MEPI)*

MEPI is a coordinated effort funded by the Office of the U.S. Global AIDS Coordinator (OGAC) and by the National Institutes of Health (NIH) and administered by the NIH's Fogarty International Center and the Health Resources and Services Administration (HRSA).

The initiative supports medical education and research in sub-Saharan African institutions with a view to increasing "the quantity, quality and retention of graduates with specific skills addressing the health needs of their national populations." MEPI "is based on the idea of "Transformative Medical Education," essentially "premised on the understanding that a nation's healthcare workers (HCWs), their education, the health system, and the health of the population are interrelated." MEPI investments in education emphasize three themes:

1. Increasing the numbers of HCWs trained
2. Retaining HCWs over time and in areas where they are most needed
3. Supporting regionally relevant research

Taking a holistic approach, "Transformative Education means making education and training relevant to the needs of the population, strengthening educational infrastructure, training and retaining faculty, investing in innovative educational strategies and technologies, and improving quality assurance mechanisms."

Reflecting Professor Fonn's advocacy for partnerships and networking in Section 9.4, "MEPI envisions strong links among MEPI institutions and between the institutions and their respective ministries of health and education," thereby "promoting collaborative planning, the retention of graduates, and the sustainability of innovations in education and research." The project coordinators "require clear, measurable outcomes for all interventions" as "the success of MEPI programs will be judged on outcomes achieved with an emphasis on their impact on population health."

More specifically, MEPI aims to advance the goal of the U.S. President's Emergency Plan for AIDS Relief (PEPFAR): "increasing the number of new healthcare workers by 140,000; strengthen in-country medical education systems; and build clinical and research capacity in Africa as part of a retention strategy for faculty of medical schools and clinical professors."

For further information, see www.mepinetwork.org

- *Global Forum on Innovation in Health Professional Education*

Another key initiative is "The Global Forum," "an ongoing, convening activity of the Institute of Medicine (IOM) that brings together stakeholders from multiple nations and professions to network, discuss and illuminate issues within health professional education. Currently, there are over 60 appointed members to the Forum who are academic experts and health professionals representing 18 different disciplines from 9 countries. Of these members, 46 are sponsors."

Since its inception in 2012, the Global Forum has used its guiding principles to direct much of the work of the forum. These principles emphasize engaging students, being patient- and person-centered, and creating an environment of learning with and from partners outside of the United States. Members of the forum gather twice a year to attend forum-sponsored events that consider these principles during the agenda planning process. Topics for these activities are selected and developed by the forum members themselves at separate meetings of the forum. Discussion topics have included:

- Assessing Health Professional Education—Workshop Summary (2014)
- Workshop on Empowering Women and Strengthening Health Systems and Services Through Investing in Nursing and Midwifery Enterprise: Lessons From Lower Income Countries (2014)
- Interprofessional Education for Collaboration: Learning How to Improve Health From Interprofessional Models Across the Continuum of Education to Practice—Workshop Summary (2013)

For further information, see www.iom.edu/Activities/Global/InnovationHealth ProfEducation.aspx

- **The Training for Health Equity Network (THEnet)**

Finally, the THEnet is a global movement of schools committed to transforming health professional education to improve health equity. They were brought together initially through a project at the Global Health Education Consortium that sought out innovators in addressing global health–workforce challenges.

Realizing they shared common principles and goals, these previously isolated innovators then joined forces in December 2008. The aim was to work together to increase the impact of academic institutions on health and the development of equitable health systems. Located in underserved and rural regions of Africa, Asia, Europe, the Americas, and Australia, they are pioneering innovative approaches to increase access and quality of care in disadvantaged communities.

THEnet is a learning community where institutions and individuals committed to eliminating inequity and injustice in health services and outcomes can learn globally and get support to reinvent locally. They conduct joint research to help build evidence to support effective and credible change toward greater impact and accountability of academic institutions. They also provide peer support and partner with like-minded groups to develop tools to help schools strengthen their efforts and evaluate their impact.

Member schools are committed to measuring success by how well they meet those needs. They also aim to become more vocal actors in health and development policy debates, making the case for "better health for all."

For further information, see thenetcommunity.org

Index